1991 *89*

NISSAN STANZA 1982-92 REPAIR MANUAL

NISSAN 240 SX

Covers all U.S. and Canadian models of Nissan Stanza, 200SX and 240SX

by **Tony Tortorici,** A.S.E., S.A.E.

CHILTON *Automotive Books*

PUBLISHED BY **HAYNES NORTH AMERICA, Inc.**

Manufactured in USA
© 1992 Haynes North America, Inc.
ISBN 0-8019-8262-6
Library of Congress Catalog Card No. 91-058873
12 13 14 15 16 9876543210

Haynes Publishing Group
Sparkford Nr Yeovil
Somerset BA22 7JJ England

Haynes North America, Inc
861 Lawrence Drive
Newbury Park
California 91320 USA

ABCDE
FGHIJ
KLMNO
PQR   2

2F1

Contents

Contents

SAFETY NOTICE

Proper service and repair procedures are vital to the safe, reliable operation of all motor vehicles, as well as the personal safety of those performing repairs. This manual outlines procedures for servicing and repairing vehicles using safe, effective methods. The procedures contain many NOTES, CAUTIONS and WARNINGS which should be followed, along with standard procedures to eliminate the possibility of personal injury or improper service which could damage the vehicle or compromise its safety.

It is important to note that repair procedures and techniques, tools and parts for servicing motor vehicles, as well as the skill and experience of the individual performing the work vary widely. It is not possible to anticipate all of the conceivable ways or conditions under which vehicles may be serviced, or to provide cautions as to all possible hazards that may result. Standard and accepted safety precautions and equipment should be used when handling toxic or flammable fluids, and safety goggles or other protection should be used during cutting, grinding, chiseling, prying, or any other process that can cause material removal or projectiles.

Some procedures require the use of tools specially designed for a specific purpose. Before substituting another tool or procedure, you must be completely satisfied that neither your personal safety, nor the performance of the vehicle will be endangered.

Although information in this manual is based on industry sources and is complete as possible at the time of publication, the possibility exists that some car manufacturers made later changes which could not be included here. While striving for total accuracy, the authors or publishers cannot assume responsibility for any errors, changes or omissions that may occur in the compilation of this data.

PART NUMBERS

Part numbers listed in this reference are not recommendations by Haynes North America, Inc. for any product brand name. They are references that can be used with interchange manuals and aftermarket supplier catalogs to locate each brand supplier's discrete part number.

SPECIAL TOOLS

Special tools are recommended by the vehicle manufacturer to perform their specific job. Use has been kept to a minimum, but where absolutely necessary, they are referred to in the text by the part number of the tool manufacturer. These tools can be purchased, under the appropriate part number, from your local dealer or regional distributor, or an equivalent tool can be purchased locally from a tool supplier or parts outlet. Before substituting any tool for the one recommended, read the SAFETY NOTICE at the top of this page.

ACKNOWLEDGMENTS

The publisher expresses appreciation to Nissan Motor Company, Ltd. for their generous assistance.

1

GENERAL INFORMATION AND MAINTENANCE

HOW TO USE THIS BOOK

This Chilton's Total Car Care manual is intended to help you learn more about the inner workings of your 1982–92 Nissan Stanza/200SX or 240SX while saving you money on its upkeep and operation.

The beginning of the book will likely be referred to the most, since that is where you will find information for maintenance and tune-up. The other sections deal with the more complex systems of your vehicle. Systems (from engine through brakes) are covered to the extent that the average do-it-yourselfer can attempt. This book will not explain such things as rebuilding a differential because the expertise required and the special tools necessary make this uneconomical. It will, however, give you detailed instructions to help you change your own brake pads and shoes, replace spark plugs, and perform many more jobs that can save you money and help avoid expensive problems.

A secondary purpose of this book is a reference for owners who want to understand their vehicle and/or their mechanics better.

Where to Begin

Before removing any bolts, read through the entire procedure. This will give you the overall view of what tools and supplies will be required. There is nothing more frustrating than having to walk to the bus stop on Monday morning because you were short one bolt on Sunday afternoon. So read ahead and plan ahead. Each operation should be approached logically and all procedures thoroughly understood before attempting any work.

All sections contain adjustments, maintenance, removal and installation procedures, and in some cases, repair or overhaul procedures. When repair is not considered practical, we tell you how to remove the part and then how to install the new or rebuilt replacement. In this way, you at least save labor costs. "Backyard" repair of some components is just not practical.

Avoiding Trouble

Many procedures in this book require you to "label and disconnect . . . " a group of lines, hoses or wires. Don't be lulled into thinking you can remember where everything goes—you won't. If you hook up vacuum or fuel lines incorrectly, the vehicle may run poorly, if at all. If you hook up electrical wiring incorrectly, you may instantly learn a very expensive lesson.

You don't need to know the official or engineering name for each hose or line. A piece of masking tape on the hose and a piece on its fitting will allow you to assign your own label such as the letter A or a short name. As long as you remember your own code, the lines can be reconnected by matching similar letters or names. Do remember that tape will dissolve in gasoline or other fluids; if a component is to be washed or cleaned, use another method of identification. A permanent felt-tipped marker or a metal scribe can be very handy for marking metal parts. Remove any tape or paper labels after assembly.

Maintenance or Repair?

It's necessary to mention the difference between maintenance and repair. Maintenance includes routine inspections, adjustments, and replacement of parts which show signs of normal wear. Maintenance compensates for wear or deterioration. Repair implies that something has broken or is not working. A need for repair is often caused by lack of maintenance. Example: draining and refilling the automatic transmission fluid is maintenance recommended by the manufacturer at specific mileage intervals. Failure to do this can shorten the life of the transmission/transaxle, requiring very expensive repairs. While no maintenance program can prevent items from breaking or wearing out, a general rule can be stated: MAINTENANCE IS CHEAPER THAN REPAIR.

Two basic mechanic's rules should be mentioned here. First, whenever the left side of the vehicle or engine is referred to, it is meant to specify the driver's side. Conversely, the right side of the vehicle means the passenger's side. Second, screws and bolts are removed by turning counterclockwise, and tightened by turning clockwise unless specifically noted.

Safety is always the most important rule. Constantly be aware of the dangers involved in working on an automobile and take the proper precautions. See the information in this section regarding SERVICING YOUR VEHICLE SAFELY and the SAFETY NOTICE on the acknowledgment page.

Avoiding the Most Common Mistakes

Pay attention to the instructions provided. There are 3 common mistakes in mechanical work:

1. Incorrect order of assembly, disassembly or adjustment. When taking something apart or putting it together, performing steps in the wrong order usually just costs you extra time; however, it CAN break something. Read the entire procedure before beginning disassembly. Perform everything in the order in which the instructions say you should, even if you can't immediately see a reason for it. When you're taking apart something that is very intricate, you might want to draw a picture of how it looks when assembled at one point in order to make sure you get everything back in its proper position. We will supply exploded views whenever possible. When making adjustments, perform them in the proper order. One adjustment possibly will affect another.

2. Overtorquing (or undertorquing). While it is more common for overtorquing to cause damage, undertorquing may allow a fastener to vibrate loose causing serious damage. Especially when dealing with aluminum parts, pay attention to torque specifications and utilize a torque wrench in assembly. If a torque figure is not available, remember that if you are using the right tool to perform the job, you will probably not have to strain yourself to get a fastener tight enough. The pitch of most threads is so slight that the tension you put on the wrench will be multiplied many times in actual force on what you are tightening. A good example of how critical torque is can be seen in the case of spark plug installation, especially where you are putting the plug into an aluminum cylinder head. Too little torque can fail to crush the gasket, causing leakage of combustion gases and consequent overheating of the plug and engine parts. Too much torque can damage the threads or distort the plug, changing the spark gap.

There are many commercial products available for ensuring that fasteners won't come loose, even if they are not torqued just right (a very common brand is Loctite®). If you're worried about getting something together tight enough to hold, but loose enough to avoid mechanical damage during assembly, one of these products might offer substantial insurance. Before choosing a threadlocking compound, read the label on the package and make sure the product is compatible with the materials, fluids, etc. involved.

3. Crossthreading. This occurs when a part such as a bolt is screwed into a nut or casting at the wrong angle and forced. Crossthreading is more likely to occur if access is difficult. It helps to clean and lubricate fasteners, then to start threading the bolt, spark plug, etc. with your fingers. If you encounter resistance, unscrew the part and start over again at a different angle until it can be inserted and turned several times without much effort. Keep in mind that many parts, especially spark plugs, have tapered threads, so that gentle turning will automatically bring the part you're threading to the proper angle. Don't put a wrench on the part until it's been tightened a couple of turns by hand. If you suddenly encounter resistance, and the part has not seated fully, don't force it. Pull it back out to make sure it's clean and threading properly.

Be sure to take your time and be patient, and always plan ahead. Allow yourself ample time to perform repairs and maintenance. You may find maintaining your car a satisfying and enjoyable experience.

TOOLS AND EQUIPMENT

▶ **See Figures 1 thru 15**

Naturally, without the proper tools and equipment it is impossible to properly service your vehicle. It would also be virtually impossible to catalog every tool that you would need to perform all of the operations in this book. Of course, it would be unwise for the amateur to rush out and buy an expensive set of tools on the theory that he/she may need one or more of them at some time.

The best approach is to proceed slowly, gathering a good quality set of those tools that are used most frequently. Don't be misled by the low cost of bargain tools. It is far better to spend a little more for better quality. Forged wrenches, 6 or 12-point sockets and fine tooth ratchets are by far preferable to their less expensive counterparts. As any good mechanic can tell you, there are few worse experiences than trying to work on a vehicle with bad tools. Your monetary savings will be far outweighed by frustration and mangled knuckles.

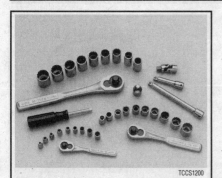

Fig. 1 All but the most basic procedures will require an assortment of ratchets and sockets

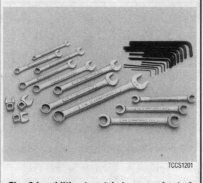

Fig. 2 In addition to ratchets, a good set of wrenches and hex keys will be necessary

Fig. 3 A hydraulic floor jack and a set of jackstands are essential for lifting and supporting the vehicle

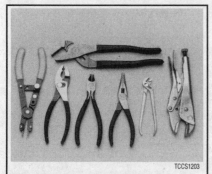

Fig. 4 An assortment of pliers, grippers and cutters will be handy for old rusted parts and stripped bolt heads

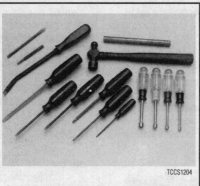

Fig. 5 Various drivers, chisels and prybars are great tools to have in your toolbox

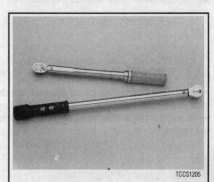

Fig. 6 Many repairs will require the use of a torque wrench to assure the components are properly fastened

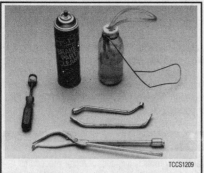

Fig. 7 Although not always necessary, using specialized brake tools will save time

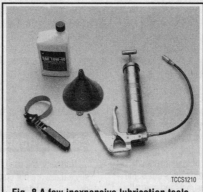

Fig. 8 A few inexpensive lubrication tools will make maintenance easier

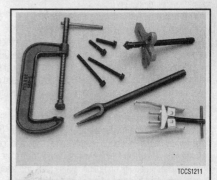

Fig. 9 Various pullers, clamps and separator tools are needed for many larger, more complicated repairs

Fig. 10 A variety of tools and gauges should be used for spark plug gapping and installation

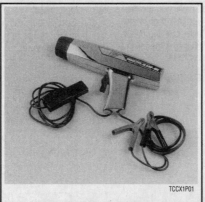

Fig. 11 Inductive type timing light

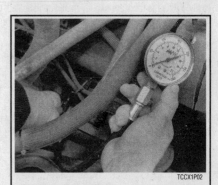

Fig. 12 A screw-in type compression gauge is recommended for compression testing

TCCX1P03

Fig. 13 A vacuum/pressure tester is necessary for many testing procedures

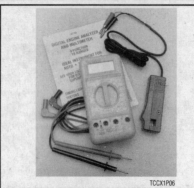

TCCX1P06

Fig. 14 Most modern automotive multimeters incorporate many helpful features

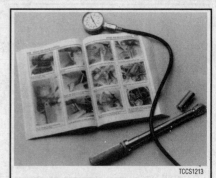

TCCS1213

Fig. 15 Proper information is vital, so always have a Chilton Total Car Care manual handy

Begin accumulating those tools that are used most frequently: those associated with routine maintenance and tune-up. In addition to the normal assortment of screwdrivers and pliers, you should have the following tools:
- Wrenches/sockets and combination open end/box end wrenches in sizes 3mm–19mm $^{13}/_{16}$ in. or $^{5}/_{8}$ in. spark plug socket (depending on plug type).

➡**If possible, buy various length socket drive extensions. Universal-joint and wobble extensions can be extremely useful, but be careful when using them, as they can change the amount of torque applied to the socket.**

- Jackstands for support.
- Oil filter wrench.
- Spout or funnel for pouring fluids.
- Grease gun for chassis lubrication (unless your vehicle is not equipped with any grease fittings—for details, please refer to information on Fluids and Lubricants, later in this section).
- Hydrometer for checking the battery (unless equipped with a sealed, maintenance-free battery).
- A container for draining oil and other fluids.
- Rags for wiping up the inevitable mess.

In addition to the above items there are several others that are not absolutely necessary, but handy to have around. These include Oil Dry® (or an equivalent oil absorbent gravel—such as cat litter) and the usual supply of lubricants, antifreeze and fluids, although these can be purchased as needed. This is a basic list for routine maintenance, but only your personal needs and desire can accurately determine your list of tools.

After performing a few projects on the vehicle, you'll be amazed at the other tools and non-tools on your workbench. Some useful household items are: a large turkey baster or siphon, empty coffee cans and ice trays (to store parts), ball of twine, electrical tape for wiring, small rolls of colored tape for tagging lines or hoses, markers and pens, a note pad, golf tees (for plugging vacuum lines), metal coat hangers or a roll of mechanic's wire (to hold things out of the way), dental pick or similar long, pointed probe, a strong magnet, and a small mirror (to see into recesses and under manifolds).

A more advanced set of tools, suitable for tune-up work, can be drawn up easily. While the tools are slightly more sophisticated, they need not be outrageously expensive. There are several inexpensive tach/dwell meters on the market that are every bit as good for the average mechanic as a professional model. Just be sure that it goes to a least 1200–1500 rpm on the tach scale and that it works on 4, 6 and 8-cylinder engines. The key to these purchases is to make

them with an eye towards adaptability and wide range. A basic list of tune-up tools could include:
- Tach/dwell meter.
- Spark plug wrench and gapping tool.
- Feeler gauges for valve adjustment.
- Timing light.

The choice of a timing light should be made carefully. A light which works on the DC current supplied by the vehicle's battery is the best choice; it should have a xenon tube for brightness. On any vehicle with an electronic ignition system, a timing light with an inductive pickup that clamps around the No. 1 spark plug cable is preferred.

In addition to these basic tools, there are several other tools and gauges you may find useful. These include:
- Compression gauge. The screw-in type is slower to use, but eliminates the possibility of a faulty reading due to escaping pressure.
- Manifold vacuum gauge.
- 12V test light.
- A combination volt/ohmmeter
- Induction Ammeter. This is used for determining whether or not there is current in a wire. These are handy for use if a wire is broken somewhere in a wiring harness.

As a final note, you will probably find a torque wrench necessary for all but the most basic work. The beam type models are perfectly adequate, although the newer click types (breakaway) are easier to use. The click type torque wrenches tend to be more expensive. Also keep in mind that all types of torque wrenches should be periodically checked and/or recalibrated. You will have to decide for yourself which better fits your pocketbook, and purpose.

Special Tools

Normally, the use of special factory tools is avoided for repair procedures, since these are not readily available for the do-it-yourself mechanic. When it is possible to perform the job with more commonly available tools, it will be pointed out, but occasionally, a special tool was designed to perform a specific function and should be used. Before substituting another tool, you should be convinced that neither your safety nor the performance of the vehicle will be compromised.

Special tools can usually be purchased from an automotive parts store or from your dealer. In some cases special tools may be available directly from the tool manufacturer.

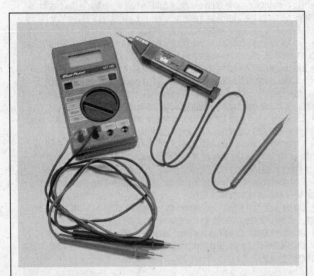

Digital multimeters come in a variety of styles and are a "must-have" for any serious home mechanic. Digital multimeters measure voltage (volts), resistance (ohms) and sometimes current (amperes). These versatile tools are used for checking all types of electrical or electronic components

Modern vehicles equipped with computer-controlled fuel, emission and ignition systems require modern electronic tools to diagnose problems. Many of these tools are designed solely for the professional mechanic and are too costly and difficult to use for the average do-it-yourselfer. However, various automotive aftermarket companies have introduced products that address the needs of the average home mechanic, providing sophisticated information at affordable cost. Consult your local auto parts store to determine what is available for your vehicle.

Trouble code tools allow the home mechanic to extract the "fault code" number from an on-board computer that has sensed a problem (usually indicated by a Check Engine light). Armed with this code, the home mechanic can focus attention on a suspect system or component

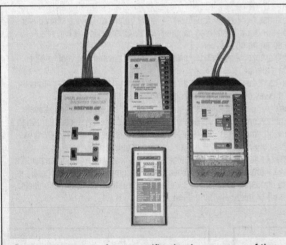

Sensor testers perform specific checks on many of the sensors and actuators used on today's computer-controlled vehicles. These testers can check sensors both on or off the vehicle, as well as test the accompanying electrical circuits

Hand-held scanners represent the most sophisticated of all do-it-yourself diagnostic tools. These tools do more than just access computer codes like the code readers above; they provide the user with an actual interface into the vehicle's computer. Comprehensive data on specific makes and models will come with the tool, either built-in or as a separate cartridge

SERVICING YOUR VEHICLE SAFELY

▶ See Figures 16, 17, 18 and 19

It is virtually impossible to anticipate all of the hazards involved with automotive maintenance and service, but care and common sense will prevent most accidents.

The rules of safety for mechanics range from "don't smoke around gasoline," to "use the proper tool(s) for the job." The trick to avoiding injuries is to develop safe work habits and to take every possible precaution.

Do's

- Do keep a fire extinguisher and first aid kit handy.
- Do wear safety glasses or goggles when cutting, drilling, grinding or prying, even if you have 20–20 vision. If you wear glasses for the sake of vision, wear safety goggles over your regular glasses.
- Do shield your eyes whenever you work around the battery. Batteries contain sulfuric acid. In case of contact with the eyes or skin, flush the area with water or a mixture of water and baking soda, then seek immediate medical attention.
- Do use safety stands (jackstands) for any undervehicle service. Jacks are for raising vehicles; jackstands are for making sure the vehicle stays raised until you want it to come down. Whenever the vehicle is raised, block the wheels remaining on the ground and set the parking brake.
- Do use adequate ventilation when working with any chemicals or hazardous materials. Like carbon monoxide, the asbestos dust resulting from some brake lining wear can be hazardous in sufficient quantities.

- Do disconnect the negative battery cable when working on the electrical system. The secondary ignition system contains EXTREMELY HIGH VOLTAGE. In some cases it can even exceed 50,000 volts.
- Do follow manufacturer's directions whenever working with potentially hazardous materials. Most chemicals and fluids are poisonous if taken internally.
- Do properly maintain your tools. Loose hammerheads, mushroomed punches and chisels, frayed or poorly grounded electrical cords, excessively worn screwdrivers, spread wrenches (open end), cracked sockets, slipping ratchets, or faulty droplight sockets can cause accidents.
- Likewise, keep your tools clean; a greasy wrench can slip off a bolt head, ruining the bolt and often harming your knuckles in the process.
- Do use the proper size and type of tool for the job at hand. Do select a wrench or socket that fits the nut or bolt. The wrench or socket should sit straight, not cocked.
- Do, when possible, pull on a wrench handle rather than push on it, and adjust your stance to prevent a fall.
- Do be sure that adjustable wrenches are tightly closed on the nut or bolt and pulled so that the force is on the side of the fixed jaw.
- Do strike squarely with a hammer; avoid glancing blows.
- Do set the parking brake and block the drive wheels if the work requires a running engine.

Don'ts

- Don't run the engine in a garage or anywhere else without proper ventilation—EVER! Carbon monoxide is poisonous; it takes a long time to leave the human body and you can build up a deadly supply of it in your system by simply breathing in a little every day. You may not realize you are slowly poisoning yourself. Always use power vents, windows, fans and/or open the garage door.
- Don't work around moving parts while wearing loose clothing. Short sleeves are much safer than long, loose sleeves. Hard-toed shoes with neoprene soles protect your toes and give a better grip on slippery surfaces. Jewelry such as watches, fancy belt buckles, beads or body adornment of any kind is not safe working around a vehicle. Long hair should be tied back under a hat or cap.
- Don't use pockets for toolboxes. A fall or bump can drive a screwdriver deep into your body. Even a rag hanging from your back pocket can wrap around a spinning shaft or fan.
- Don't smoke when working around gasoline, cleaning solvent or other flammable material.
- Don't smoke when working around the battery. When the battery is being charged, it gives off explosive hydrogen gas.
- Don't use gasoline to wash your hands; there are excellent soaps available. Gasoline contains dangerous additives which can enter the body through a cut or through your pores. Gasoline also removes all the natural oils from the skin so that bone dry hands will suck up oil and grease.
- Don't service the air conditioning system unless you are equipped with the necessary tools and training. When liquid or compressed gas refrigerant is released to atmospheric pressure it will absorb heat from whatever it contacts. This will chill or freeze anything it touches.

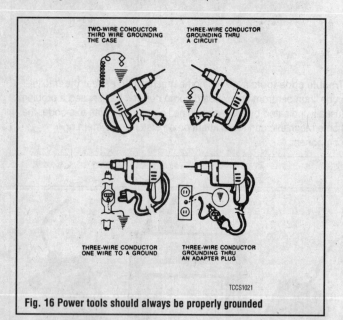

TCCS1021

Fig. 16 Power tools should always be properly grounded

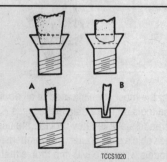

TCCS1020

Fig. 17 Screwdrivers should be kept in good condition to prevent injury or damage which could result if the blade slips from the screw

TCCS1022

Fig. 18 Using the correct size wrench will help prevent the possibility of rounding off a nut

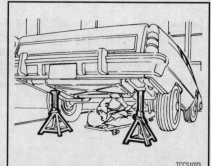

TCCS1023

Fig. 19 NEVER work under a vehicle unless it is supported using safety stands (jackstands)

• Don't use screwdrivers for anything other than driving screws! A screwdriver used as an prying tool can snap when you least expect it, causing injuries. At the very least, you'll ruin a good screwdriver.

• Don't use an emergency jack (that little ratchet, scissors, or pantograph jack supplied with the vehicle) for anything other than changing a flat! These jacks are only intended for emergency use out on the road; they are NOT designed as a maintenance tool. If you are serious about maintaining your vehicle yourself, invest in a hydraulic floor jack of at least a 1½ ton capacity, and at least two sturdy jackstands.

FASTENERS, MEASUREMENTS AND CONVERSIONS

Bolts, Nuts and Other Threaded Retainers

▶ See Figures 20, 21, 22 and 23

Although there are a great variety of fasteners found in the modern car or truck, the most commonly used retainer is the threaded fastener (nuts, bolts, screws, studs, etc.). Most threaded retainers may be reused, provided that they are not damaged in use or during the repair. Some retainers (such as stretch bolts or torque prevailing nuts) are designed to deform when tightened or in use and should not be reinstalled.

Whenever possible, we will note any special retainers which should be replaced during a procedure. But you should always inspect the condition of a retainer when it is removed and replace any that show signs of damage. Check all threads for rust or corrosion which can increase the torque necessary to achieve the desired clamp load for which that fastener was originally selected. Additionally, be sure that the driver surface of the fastener has not been compromised by rounding or other damage. In some cases a driver surface may become only partially rounded, allowing the driver to catch in only one direction. In many of these occurrences, a fastener may be installed and tightened, but the driver would not be able to grip and loosen the fastener again. (This could lead to frustration down the line should that component ever need to be disassembled again).

If you must replace a fastener, whether due to design or damage, you must ALWAYS be sure to use the proper replacement. In all cases, a retainer of the

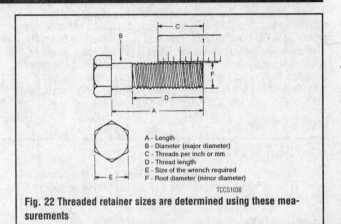

A - Length
B - Diameter (major diameter)
C - Threads per inch or mm
D - Thread length
E - Size of the wrench required
F - Root diameter (minor diameter)

TCCS1038

Fig. 22 Threaded retainer sizes are determined using these measurements

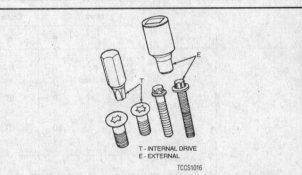

T - INTERNAL DRIVE
E - EXTERNAL

TCCS1016

Fig. 23 Special fasteners such as these Torx® head bolts are used by manufacturers to discourage people from working on vehicles without the proper tools

same design, material and strength should be used. Markings on the heads of most bolts will help determine the proper strength of the fastener. The same material, thread and pitch must be selected to assure proper installation and safe operation of the vehicle afterwards.

Thread gauges are available to help measure a bolt or stud's thread. Most automotive and hardware stores keep gauges available to help you select the proper size. In a pinch, you can use another nut or bolt for a thread gauge. If the bolt you are replacing is not too badly damaged, you can select a match by finding another bolt which will thread in its place. If you find a nut which threads properly onto the damaged bolt, then use that nut to help select the replacement bolt. If however, the bolt you are replacing is so badly damaged (broken or drilled out) that its threads cannot be used as a gauge, you might start by looking for another bolt (from the same assembly or a similar location on your vehicle) which will thread into the damaged bolt's mounting. If so, the other bolt can be used to select a nut; the nut can then be used to select the replacement bolt.

In all cases, be absolutely sure you have selected the proper replacement. Don't be shy, you can always ask the store clerk for help.

✳ WARNING

Be aware that when you find a bolt with damaged threads, you may also find the nut or drilled hole it was threaded into has also been damaged. If this is the case, you may have to drill and tap the hole, replace the nut or otherwise repair the threads. NEVER try to force a replacement bolt to fit into the damaged threads.

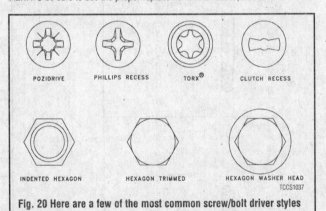

POZIDRIVE   PHILLIPS RECESS   TORX®   CLUTCH RECESS

INDENTED HEXAGON   HEXAGON TRIMMED   HEXAGON WASHER HEAD

TCCS1037

Fig. 20 Here are a few of the most common screw/bolt driver styles

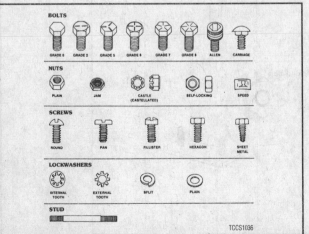

BOLTS

GRADE 0   GRADE 2   GRADE 5   GRADE 6   GRADE 7   GRADE 8   ALLEN   CARRIAGE

NUTS

PLAIN   JAM   CASTLE (CASTELLATED)   SELF-LOCKING   SPEED

SCREWS

ROUND   PAN   FILLISTER   HEXAGON   SHEET METAL

LOCKWASHERS

INTERNAL TOOTH   EXTERNAL TOOTH   SPLIT   PLAIN

STUD

TCCS1036

Fig. 21 There are many different types of threaded retainers found on vehicles

Torque

Torque is defined as the measurement of resistance to turning or rotating. It tends to twist a body about an axis of rotation. A common example of this would be tightening a threaded retainer such as a nut, bolt or screw. Measuring torque is one of the most common ways to help assure that a threaded retainer has been properly fastened.

When tightening a threaded fastener, torque is applied in three distinct areas, the head, the bearing surface and the clamp load. About 50 percent of the measured torque is used in overcoming bearing friction. This is the friction between the bearing surface of the bolt head, screw head or nut face and the base material or washer (the surface on which the fastener is rotating). Approximately 40 percent of the applied torque is used in overcoming thread friction. This leaves only about 10 percent of the applied torque to develop a useful clamp load (the force which holds a joint together). This means that friction can account for as much as 90 percent of the applied torque on a fastener.

TORQUE WRENCHES

▶ **See Figures 24, 25 and 26**

In most applications, a torque wrench can be used to assure proper installation of a fastener. Torque wrenches come in various designs and most automotive supply stores will carry a variety to suit your needs. A torque wrench should be used any time we supply a specific torque value for a fastener. A torque wrench can also be used if you are following the general guidelines in the accompanying charts. Keep in mind that because there is no worldwide standardization of fasteners, the charts are a general guideline and should be used with caution. Again, the general rule of "if you are using the right tool for the job, you should not have to strain to tighten a fastener" applies here.

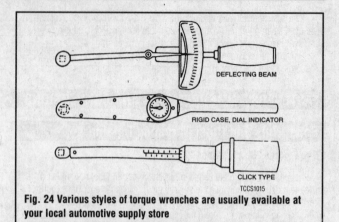

Fig. 24 Various styles of torque wrenches are usually available at your local automotive supply store

	Mark	Class		Mark	Class
Hexagon head bolt	Bolt head No. 4 → 4 5 — 6 — 7 — 8 — 9 — 10 — 11 —	4T 5T 6T 7T 8T 9T 10T 11T	Stud bolt	No mark	4T
	No mark	4T			
Hexagon flange bolt w/ washer hexagon bolt	No mark	4T		Grooved	6T
Hexagon head bolt	Two protruding lines	5T			
Hexagon flange bolt w/ washer hexagon bolt	Two protruding lines	6T	Welded bolt		4T
Hexagon head bolt	Three protruding lines	7T			
Hexagon head bolt	Four protruding lines	8T			

Fig. 25 Determining bolt strength of metric fasteners—NOTE: this is a typical bolt marking system, but there is not a worldwide standard

Class	Diameter mm	Pitch mm	Specified torque					
			Hexagon head bolt			Hexagon flange bolt		
			N·m	kgf·cm	ft·lbf	N·m	kgf·cm	ft·lbf
4T	6	1	5	55	48 in.·lbf	6	60	52 in.·lbf
	8	1.25	12.5	130	9	14	145	10
	10	1.25	26	260	19	29	290	21
	12	1.25	47	480	35	53	540	39
	14	1.5	74	760	55	84	850	61
	16	1.5	115	1,150	83	–	–	–
5T	6	1	6.5	65	56 in.·lbf	7.5	75	65 in.·lbf
	8	1.25	15.5	160	12	17.5	175	13
	10	1.25	32	330	24	36	360	26
	12	1.25	59	600	43	65	670	48
	14	1.5	91	930	67	100	1,050	76
	16	1.5	140	1,400	101	–	–	–
6T	6	1	8	80	69 in.·lbf	9	90	78 in.·lbf
	8	1.25	19	195	14	21	210	15
	10	1.25	39	400	29	44	440	32
	12	1.25	71	730	53	80	810	59
	14	1.5	110	1,100	80	125	1,250	90
	16	1.5	170	1,750	127	–	–	–
7T	6	1	10.5	110	8	12	120	9
	8	1.25	25	260	19	28	290	21
	10	1.25	52	530	38	58	590	43
	12	1.25	95	970	70	105	1,050	76
	14	1.5	145	1,500	108	165	1,700	123
	16	1.5	230	2,300	166	–	–	–
8T	8	1.25	29	300	22	33	330	24
	10	1.25	61	620	45	68	690	50
	12	1.25	110	1,100	80	120	1,250	90
9T	8	1.25	34	340	25	37	380	27
	10	1.25	70	710	51	78	790	57
	12	1.25	125	1,300	94	140	1,450	105
10T	8	1.25	38	390	28	42	430	31
	10	1.25	78	800	58	88	890	64
	12	1.25	140	1,450	105	155	1,600	116
11T	8	1.25	42	430	31	47	480	35
	10	1.25	87	890	64	97	990	72
	12	1.25	155	1,600	116	175	1,800	130

TCCS1241

Fig. 26 Typical bolt torques for metric fasteners—WARNING: use only as a guide

Beam Type

▶ **See Figure 27**

The beam type torque wrench is one of the most popular types. It consists of a pointer attached to the head that runs the length of the flexible beam (shaft) to a scale located near the handle. As the wrench is pulled, the beam bends and the pointer indicates the torque using the scale.

Click (Breakaway) Type

▶ **See Figure 28**

Another popular design of torque wrench is the click type. To use the click type wrench you pre-adjust it to a torque setting. Once the torque is reached, the wrench has a reflex signaling feature that causes a momentary breakaway of the torque wrench body, sending an impulse to the operator's hand.

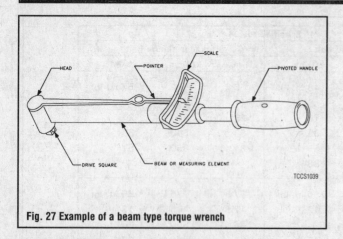

Fig. 27 Example of a beam type torque wrench

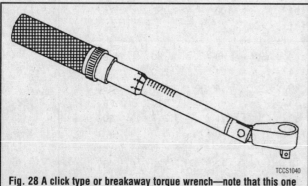

Fig. 28 A click type or breakaway torque wrench—note that this one has a pivoting head

Pivot Head Type

▶ **See Figures 28 and 29**

Some torque wrenches (usually of the click type) may be equipped with a pivot head which can allow it to be used in areas of limited access. BUT, it must be used properly. To hold a pivot head wrench, grasp the handle lightly, and as you pull on the handle, it should be floated on the pivot point. If the handle comes in contact with the yoke extension during the process of pulling, there is a very good chance the torque readings will be inaccurate because this could alter the wrench loading point. The design of the handle is usually such as to make it inconvenient to deliberately misuse the wrench.

➡**It should be mentioned that the use of any U-joint, wobble or extension will have an effect on the torque readings, no matter what type of wrench you are using. For the most accurate readings, install the socket directly on the wrench driver. If necessary, straight extensions (which hold a socket directly under the wrench driver) will have the least effect on the torque reading. Avoid any extension that alters the length of the**

wrench from the handle to the head/driving point (such as a crow's foot). U-joint or wobble extensions can greatly affect the readings; avoid their use at all times.

Rigid Case (Direct Reading)

▶ **See Figure 30**

A rigid case or direct reading torque wrench is equipped with a dial indicator to show torque values. One advantage of these wrenches is that they can be held at any position on the wrench without affecting accuracy. These wrenches are often preferred because they tend to be compact, easy to read and have a great degree of accuracy.

TORQUE ANGLE METERS

▶ **See Figure 31**

Because the frictional characteristics of each fastener or threaded hole will vary, clamp loads which are based strictly on torque will vary as well. In most applications, this variance is not significant enough to cause worry. But, in certain applications, a manufacturer's engineers may determine that more precise clamp loads are necessary (such is the case with many aluminum cylinder heads). In these cases, a torque angle method of installation would be specified. When installing fasteners which are torque angle tightened, a predetermined seating torque and standard torque wrench are usually used first to remove any compliance from the joint. The fastener is then tightened the specified additional portion of a turn measured in degrees. A torque angle gauge (mechanical protractor) is used for these applications.

Standard and Metric Measurements

▶ **See Figure 32**

Throughout this manual, specifications are given to help you determine the condition of various components on your vehicle, or to assist you in their installation. Some of the most common measurements include length (in. or cm/mm), torque (ft. lbs., inch lbs. or Nm) and pressure (psi, in. Hg, kPa or mm Hg). In most cases, we strive to provide the proper measurement as determined by the manufacturer's engineers.

Though, in some cases, that value may not be conveniently measured with what is available in your toolbox. Luckily, many of the measuring devices which are available today will have two scales so the Standard or Metric measurements may easily be taken. If any of the various measuring tools which are available to you do not contain the same scale as listed in the specifications, use the accompanying conversion factors to determine the proper value.

The conversion factor chart is used by taking the given specification and multiplying it by the necessary conversion factor. For instance, looking at the first line, if you have a measurement in inches such as "free-play should be 2 in." but your ruler reads only in millimeters, multiply 2 in. by the conversion factor of 25.4 to get the metric equivalent of 50.8mm. Likewise, if the specification was given only in a Metric measurement, for example in Newton Meters (Nm), then look at the center column first. If the measurement is 100 Nm, multiply it by the conversion factor of 0.738 to get 73.8 ft. lbs.

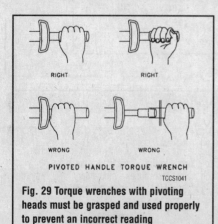

Fig. 29 Torque wrenches with pivoting heads must be grasped and used properly to prevent an incorrect reading

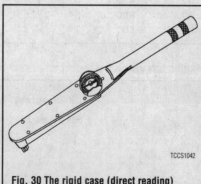

Fig. 30 The rigid case (direct reading) torque wrench uses a dial indicator to show torque

Fig. 31 Some specifications require the use of a torque angle meter (mechanical protractor)

CONVERSION FACTORS

LENGTH–DISTANCE

Inches (in.)	x 25.4	= Millimeters (mm)	x .0394	= Inches
Feet (ft.)	x .305	= Meters (m)	x 3.281	= Feet
Miles	x 1.609	= Kilometers (km)	x .0621	= Miles

VOLUME

Cubic Inches (in3)	x 16.387	= Cubic Centimeters	x .061	= in3
IMP Pints (IMP pt.)	x .568	= Liters (L)	x 1.76	= IMP pt.
IMP Quarts (IMP qt.)	x 1.137	= Liters (L)	x .88	= IMP qt.
IMP Gallons (IMP gal.)	x 4.546	= Liters (L)	x .22	= IMP gal.
IMP Quarts (IMP qt.)	x 1.201	= US Quarts (US qt.)	x .833	= IMP qt.
IMP Gallons (IMP gal.)	x 1.201	= US Gallons (US gal.)	x .833	= IMP gal.
Fl. Ounces	x 29.573	= Milliliters	x .034	= Ounces
US Pints (US pt.)	x .473	= Liters (L)	x 2.113	= Pints
US Quarts (US qt.)	x .946	= Liters (L)	x 1.057	= Quarts
US Gallons (US gal.)	x 3.785	= Liters (L)	x .264	= Gallons

MASS–WEIGHT

Ounces (oz.)	x 28.35	= Grams (g)	x .035	= Ounces
Pounds (lb.)	x .454	= Kilograms (kg)	x 2.205	= Pounds

PRESSURE

Pounds Per Sq. In. (psi)	x 6.895	= Kilopascals (kPa)	x .145	= psi
Inches of Mercury (Hg)	x .4912	= psi	x 2.036	= Hg
Inches of Mercury (Hg)	x 3.377	= Kilopascals (kPa)	x .2961	= Hg
Inches of Water (H_2O)	x .07355	= Inches of Mercury	x 13.783	= H_2O
Inches of Water (H_2O)	x .03613	= psi	x 27.684	= H_2O
Inches of Water (H_2O)	x .248	= Kilopascals (kPa)	x 4.026	= H_2O

TORQUE

Pounds–Force Inches (in–lb)	x .113	= Newton Meters (N·m)	x 8.85	= in–lb
Pounds–Force Feet (ft–lb)	x 1.356	= Newton Meters (N·m)	x .738	= ft–lb

VELOCITY

Miles Per Hour (MPH)	x 1.609	= Kilometers Per Hour (KPH)	x .621	= MPH

POWER

Horsepower (Hp)	x .745	= Kilowatts	x 1.34	= Horsepower

FUEL CONSUMPTION*

Miles Per Gallon IMP (MPG)	x .354	= Kilometers Per Liter (Km/L)
Kilometers Per Liter (Km/L)	x 2.352	= IMP MPG
Miles Per Gallon US (MPG)	x .425	= Kilometers Per Liter (Km/L)
Kilometers Per Liter (Km/L)	x 2.352	= US MPG

*It is common to covert from miles per gallon (mpg) to liters/100 kilometers (1/100 km), where mpg (IMP) x 1/100 km = 282 and mpg (US) x 1/100 km = 235.

TEMPERATURE

Degree Fahrenheit (°F)	= (°C x 1.8) + 32
Degree Celsius (°C)	= (°F – 32) x .56

TCCS1044

Fig. 32 Standard and metric conversion factors chart

SERIAL NUMBER IDENTIFICATION

Chassis

The chassis number is on the firewall under the hood on all models. All vehicles also have the chassis number (also known as the Vehicle Identification Number) on a plate attached to the top of the instrument panel on the driver's side, visible through the windshield. The chassis serial number is preceded by the model designation. All models have an Emission Control information label on the firewall or on the underside of the hood. Refer to the illustrations.

Vehicle Identification Plate

The vehicle identification plate is attached to the right-side of the firewall. This plate gives the vehicle type, identification number, model, body color code, trim color code, engine model and displacement, transmission/transaxle model and axle model. Refer to the illustrations.

Engine

▶ **See Figures 33 thru 38**

200SX AND 240SX

On the 1982–83 200SX engine (Z20, Z22 engines) serial numbers are stamped on the left side top edge of the cylinder block when viewed from the driver's seat. The 1984–88 200SX models (CA20, CA18ET engines) engine serial numbers are stamped on the left side rear edge of the block, next to the bell-housing when viewed from the driver's seat.

On the 1989–90 240SX engine (KA24E engine) serial number is stamped on the left side top edge of the cylinder block when viewed from the driver's seat between No. 2 and No. 3 cylinders.

On the 1990–92 240SX engine (KA24DE engine) serial number is stamped on the left side top edge of the cylinder block (near bell-housing) when viewed from the driver's seat.

STANZA

The CA20, CA20S and CA20E engine serial number is stamped on the right side top edge of the cylinder block when view from outside the car looking into the engine compartment on Stanza 1982–89 models.

On the 1990–92 Stanza (KA24E engine) engine serial number is stamped on top edge of the cylinder block between No. 2 and No. 3 cylinders when view from outside the car looking into the engine compartment.

Transaxle

▶ **See Figures 39, 40, 41 and 42**

All applications the transaxle number is stamped on the upper area of the transaxle see illustrations or attached to the clutch withdrawal lever (only some manual applications).

Fig. 33 1982–83 200SX Z-series engine serial number location

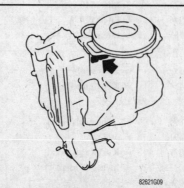

Fig. 34 1984–88 200SX CA20E and CA18ET engine serial number location

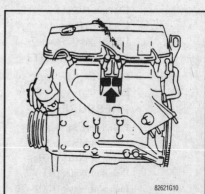

Fig. 35 1989–90 240SX KA24E engine serial number location

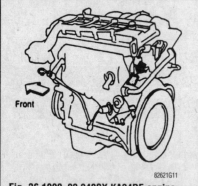

Fig. 36 1990–92 240SX KA24DE engine serial number location

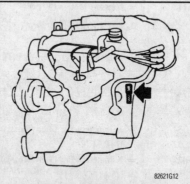

Fig. 37 1982–89 Stanza CA20 series engine serial number location

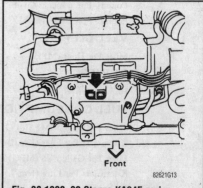

Fig. 38 1990–92 Stanza KA24E series engine serial number location

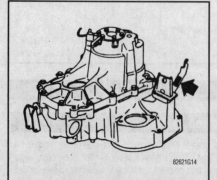

Fig. 39 1985 Stanza manual transaxle serial number location

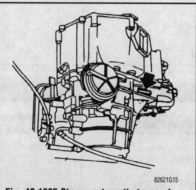

Fig. 40 1985 Stanza automatic transaxle serial number location

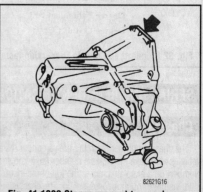

Fig. 41 1992 Stanza manual transaxle serial number location

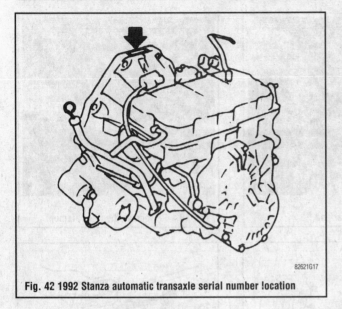

Fig. 42 1992 Stanza automatic transaxle serial number location

Transmission

♦ See Figures 43, 44, 45 and 46

The transmission serial number is stamped on the front upper face of the transmission case on manual transmissions, or on the lower right side of the case on automatic transmissions except for the 240SX model (automatic transmission) which is on the right side but in the tailshaft area.

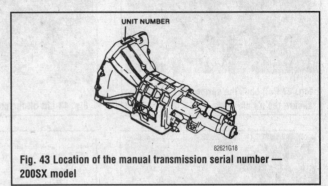

Fig. 43 Location of the manual transmission serial number — 200SX model

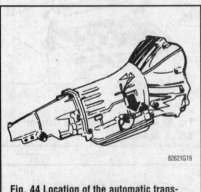

Fig. 44 Location of the automatic transmission serial number — 200SX model

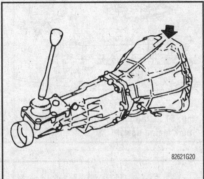

Fig. 45 240SX manual transmission serial number location

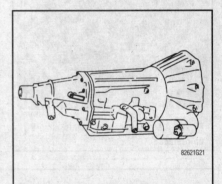

Fig. 46 240SX automatic transmission serial number location

ROUTINE MAINTENANCE

Routine maintenance is the self-explanatory term used to describe the sort of periodic work necessary to keep a car in safe and reliable working order. A regular program aimed at monitoring essential systems ensure that the car's components are functioning correctly (and will continue to do so until the next inspection, one hopes), and can prevent small problems from developing into major headaches. Routine maintenance also pays off big dividends in keeping major repair costs at a minimum, extending the life of the car, and enhancing resale value, should you ever desire to part with your Datsun/Nissan.

A very definite maintenance schedule is provided by Datsun/Nissan, and must be followed, not only to keep the new car warranty in effect, but also to keep the car working properly. The "Maintenance Interval Chart" in this section outlines the routine maintenance which must be performed according to intervals based on either accumulated mileage or time. Your car also came with a maintenance schedule provided by Datsun/Nissan. Adherence to these schedules will result in a longer life for your car, and will, over the long run, save you money and time.

The checks and adjustments in the following sections generally require only a few minutes of attention every few weeks. The services to be performed can be easily accomplished in a morning. The most important part of any maintenance program is regularity. The few minutes or occasional morning spent on these seemingly trivial tasks will forestall or eliminate major problems later.

Air Cleaner

♦ See Figures 47 thru 53

➥The air cleaner assembly also functions as a flame arrester if the engine should backfire. It should be installed at all times when operating the vehicle.

An air cleaner and element is used to keep airborne dirt and dust out of the air flowing through the engine. Proper maintenance is vital, as a clogged element will undesirably enrich the fuel mixture, restrict air flow and power, and allow excessive contamination of the oil with abrasives.

All models covered in this book are equipped with a disposable, paper cartridge air cleaner element. The filter should be checked at every tune-up (sooner if the car is operated in a dusty area). Loose dust can sometimes be removed by striking the filter against a hard surface several times or by blowing through it with compressed air. The filter should be replaced every 30,000 miles or every 24 months.

To remove the filter, unscrew the wing nut(s), lift off the housing cover and remove the filter element. There are thumb latches which will also have to be released before removing the housing cover. Before installing the original or the replacement filter, wipe out the inside of the housing with a clean rag or paper towel. Install the paper air cleaner filter, seat the top cover on the bottom housing and tighten the wing nut(s). Clip on the thumb latches if so equipped.

Fig. 47 Pull back the spring clips which secure the air cleaner cover

Fig. 48 Lift off the cover and . . .

Fig. 49 . . . remove the filter element

Fig. 50 A dirty filter, such as this, should be replaced

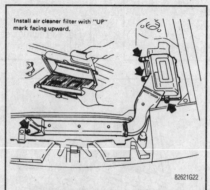

Fig. 51 Install the air filter with "UP" mark facing upward

Fig. 52 Replacing the air filter element Stanza model

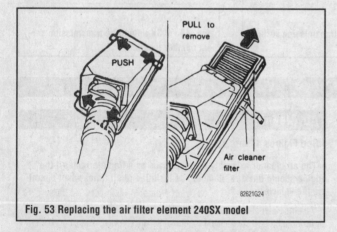

Fig. 53 Replacing the air filter element 240SX model

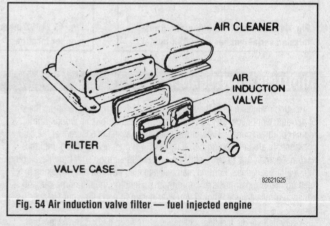

Fig. 54 Air induction valve filter — fuel injected engine

➡ All models utilize a flat, cartridge type air cleaner element. Although removal and installation procedures for these models are the same as for those with round air cleaners, make sure that the word UP is facing up when you install the air filter element.

Air Induction Valve Filter

♦ See Figures 54 and 55

Certain later models use an air induction valve filter. It is located in the side of the air cleaner housing and is easily replaced. Unscrew the mounting screws and remove the valve filter case. Pull the air induction valve out and remove the filter that lies underneath it. Install the new filter and then the valve. Pay particular attention to which way the valve is facing so that the exhaust gases will not flow backward through the system. Install the valve case. Replacement intervals are every 30,000 miles or 24 months.

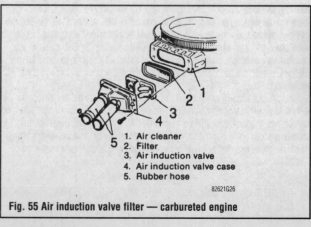

1. Air cleaner
2. Filter
3. Air induction valve
4. Air induction valve case
5. Rubber hose

Fig. 55 Air induction valve filter — carbureted engine

Fuel Filter

▶ See Figures 56 thru 67

FUEL PRESSURE RELEASE PROCEDURE

The fuel pressure must be released on fuel injected models before removing the fuel filter. To relieve the fuel pressure remove the gas cap then remove/disconnect the fuel pump fuse, fuel pump relay or electrical fuel pump connection to disable the electrical fuel pump.

Start the engine and run, after the engine stalls crank the engine a couple times to release pressure. Turn ignition switch OFF and install/connect fuse, relay or electrical connection to fuel pump.

On some late models the "Check Engine Light" will stay on after installation is completed. The memory code in the control unit must be erased. To erase the code disconnect the battery cable for 1 minute then reconnect after installation of fuel filter. Refer to Sections 4 and 5 for more information.

REMOVAL & INSTALLATION

Datsun/Nissan recommended if the vehicle is operated under extremely adverse weather conditions or in areas of extreme high or low ambient temperatures the fuel filter may become clogged. Is so, replace the fuel filter immediately. The fuel filter and fuel lines should be inspected 30,000 mile or 24 months. Check fuel lines and fuel tank assembly for proper attachment to the vehicle. Check fuel lines and filter for leaks, cracks, damage or loose connections.

The fuel filter on all models is a disposable or replaceable unit if necessary. Most models the fuel filter is located in the engine compartment (refer to the illustrations) on the right inner fender well. On the Stanza wagon, the fuel filter is found inline, outside the vehicle under the floor, near the fuel pump assembly.

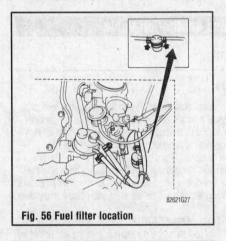

Fig. 56 Fuel filter location

Fig. 57 Loosen the fuel filter's hose clamps before detaching the hoses

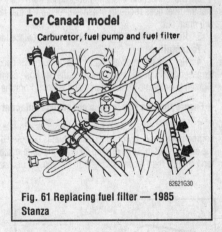

Fig. 58 The fuel filter is held by a metal clip

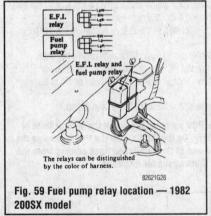

Fig. 59 Fuel pump relay location — 1982 200SX model

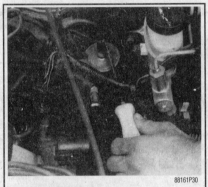

Fig. 60 The fuel pump harness connector is in the tool box on the rear right-hand side on the 1984 and later 200SX models

Fig. 61 Replacing fuel filter — 1985 Stanza

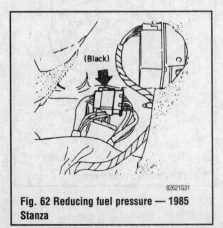

Fig. 62 Reducing fuel pressure — 1985 Stanza

Fig. 63 Removing the fuel pump fuse — 1987 Stanza

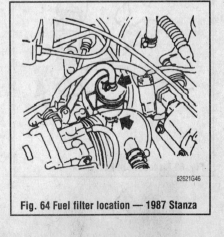

Fig. 64 Fuel filter location — 1987 Stanza

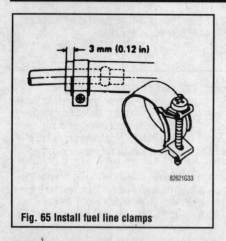

3 mm (0.12 in)

82621G33

Fig. 65 Install fuel line clamps

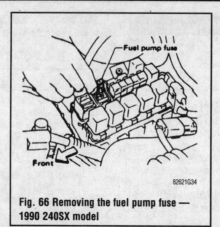

Fuel pump fuse

Front

82621G34

Fig. 66 Removing the fuel pump fuse — 1990 240SX model

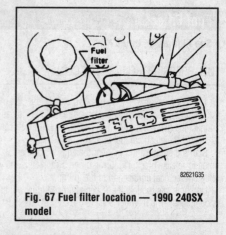

Fuel filter

82621G35

Fig. 67 Fuel filter location — 1990 240SX model

➡ A DIRTY FUEL FILTER WILL STARVE THE ENGINE AND CAUSE POOR RUNNING!

❋❋ CAUTION

If equipped with an Electronic Fuel Injected (EFI) engine, refer to the "Fuel Pressure Release Procedure" in this section and release the fuel pressure before removing filter. OBSERVE ALL NECESSARY SAFETY PRECAUTIONS. READ THE COMPLETE SERVICE PROCEDURE BEFORE STARTING THIS REPAIR.

1. Release the fuel pressure. Disconnect the negative battery cable. Locate fuel filter on right-side of the engine compartment and place a container under the filter to catch the excess fuel.

➡ **On the Stanza wagon, the fuel filter is found inline, under the floor, near the fuel pump.**

2. Disconnect the inlet and outlet hoses from the fuel filter. Make certain that the inlet hose (bottom) doesn't fall below the fuel tank level or the gasoline will drain out.
3. Remove the fuel filter from its clip and replace the assembly.
To install:
4. Replace the inlet and outlet gas hose lines if necessary. Install the fuel filter assembly in place, always replace the gas hose clamps on EFI models. Tighten hose clamp so that clamp end is 3mm from the hose end.

➡ **Ensure that the screw does not contact adjacent parts.**

5. Start the engine and check for fuel leaks. On late models the "Check Engine Light" will stay on after installation is completed. The memory code in the control unit must be erased. To erase the code disconnect the battery cable for 1 minute then reconnect. Refer to Section 4 if necessary.

Positive Crankcase Ventilation Valve

REMOVAL & INSTALLATION

▶ **See Figures 68 thru 76**

The PCV valve feeds crankcase blow-by gases into the intake manifold to be burned with the normal air/fuel mixture. The PCV valve, hose and connections should be inspected every 30,000 miles or 24 months. Make sure that all PCV connections are tight. Check that the connecting hoses are clear and not clogged. Replace any brittle or broken hoses.

To check the valve's operation, remove the valve's ventilation hose with the engine idling. If the valve is working, a hissing noise will be heard as air passes through the valve, and a strong vacuum will be felt when you place a finger over the valve opening.

On all Stanza models with a carburetor CA20 and CA20S engines a PCV filter is used. To replace this filter just remove the wing nut from the air cleaner lid and remove lid, gently lift out the filter which is mounted on the side of the air cleaner. This filter is usually about 4 in. (102mm) long.

To replace the valve, which is located in the side or bottom of the intake manifold:

1. Squeeze the hose retaining clamp with pliers and remove the hose.
2. Using a wrench, unscrew the PCV valve and remove the valve.
3. Disconnect the ventilation hose and flush with solvent or clean as necessary.
4. Install the new PCV valve and replace the hoses and clamp.

➡ **On the 240SX model the PCV valve is located on the side or front of the intake collector assembly. On the 200SX with the VG30E engine the PCV valve is located in the end of the ventilation hose coming from the rocker cover. Refer to the illustrations for locations.**

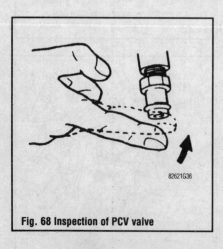

82621G36

Fig. 68 Inspection of PCV valve

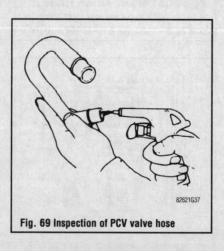

82621G37

Fig. 69 Inspection of PCV valve hose

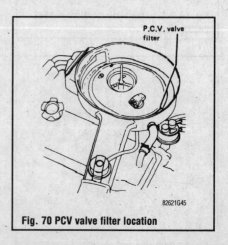

P.C.V. valve filter

82621G45

Fig. 70 PCV valve filter location

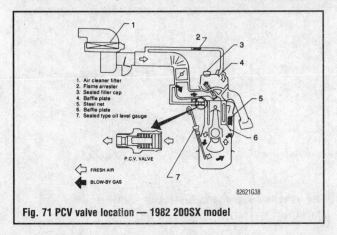

Fig. 71 PCV valve location — 1982 200SX model

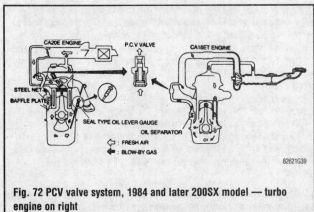

Fig. 72 PCV valve system, 1984 and later 200SX model — turbo engine on right

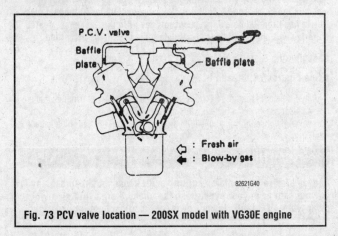

Fig. 73 PCV valve location — 200SX model with VG30E engine

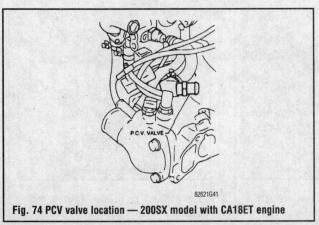

Fig. 74 PCV valve location — 200SX model with CA18ET engine

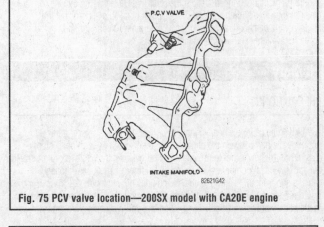

Fig. 75 PCV valve location—200SX model with CA20E engine

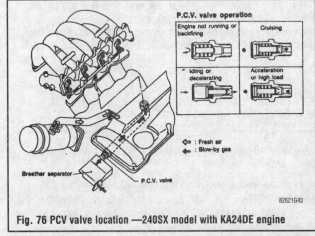

Fig. 76 PCV valve location —240SX model with KA24DE engine

Evaporative Emission Control System

SERVICING

▶ **See Figure 77**

The Emission Control System (canister and hoses) should be inspected every 30,000 miles or 24 months to inspect system make sure that all vapor hose connections are tight. Check that vapor hoses are not cracked. Replace any brittle or broken vapor hoses. No further service should be necessary.

A carbon filled canister stores fuel vapors until the engine is started and the vapors are drawn into the combustion chambers and burned. To check the operation (if necessary) of the carbon canister purge control valve, disconnect the rubber hose between the canister control valve and the T-fitting, at the T-fitting. Apply vacuum to the hose leading to the control valve. The vacuum condition

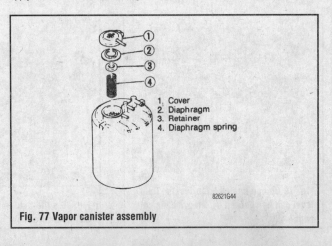

Fig. 77 Vapor canister assembly

should be maintained indefinitely. If the control valve leaks, remove the top cover of the valve and check for a dislocated or cracked diaphragm. If the diaphragm is damaged, a repair kit containing a new diaphragm, retainer and spring is available and should be installed.

Battery

PRECAUTIONS

Always use caution when working on or near the battery. Never allow a tool to bridge the gap between the negative and positive battery terminals. Also, be careful not to allow a tool to provide a ground between the positive cable/terminal and any metal component on the vehicle. Either of these conditions will cause a short circuit, leading to sparks and possible personal injury.

Do not smoke or all open flames/sparks near a battery; the gases contained in the battery are very explosive and, if ignited, could cause severe injury or death.

All batteries, regardless of type, should be carefully secured by a battery hold-down device. If not, the terminals or casing may crack from stress during vehicle operation. A battery which is not secured may allow acid to leak, making it discharge faster. The acid can also eat away at components under the hood.

Always inspect the battery case for cracks, leakage and corrosion. A white corrosive substance on the battery case or on nearby components would indicate a leaking or cracked battery. If the battery is cracked, it should be replaced immediately.

GENERAL MAINTENANCE

Always keep the battery cables and terminals free of corrosion. Check and clean these components about once a year.

Keep the top of the battery clean, as a film of dirt can help discharge a battery that is not used for long periods. A solution of baking soda and water may be used for cleaning, but be careful to flush this off with clear water. DO NOT let any of the solution into the filler holes. Baking soda neutralizes battery acid and will de-activate a battery cell.

Batteries in vehicles which are not operated on a regular basis can fall victim to parasitic loads (small current drains which are constantly drawing current from the battery). Normal parasitic loads may drain a battery on a vehicle that is in storage and not used for 6–8 weeks. Vehicles that have additional accessories such as a phone or an alarm system may discharge a battery sooner. If the vehicle is to be stored for longer periods in a secure area and the alarm system is not necessary, the negative battery cable should be disconnected to protect the battery.

Remember that constantly deep cycling a battery (completely discharging and recharging it) will shorten battery life.

BATTERY FLUID

♦ See Figure 78

Check the battery electrolyte level at least once a month, or more often in hot weather or during periods of extended vehicle operation. On non-sealed batter-

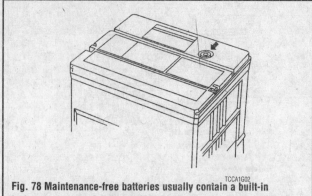
Fig. 78 Maintenance-free batteries usually contain a built-in hydrometer to check fluid level

ies, the level can be checked either through the case (if translucent) or by removing the cell caps. The electrolyte level in each cell should be kept filled to the split ring inside each cell, or the line marked on the outside of the case.

If the level is low, add only distilled water through the opening until the level is correct. Each cell must be checked and filled individually. Distilled water should be used, because the chemicals and minerals found in most drinking water are harmful to the battery and could significantly shorten its life.

If water is added in freezing weather, the vehicle should be driven several miles to allow the water to mix with the electrolyte. Otherwise, the battery could freeze.

Although some maintenance-free batteries have removable cell caps, the electrolyte condition and level on all sealed maintenance-free batteries must be checked using the built-in hydrometer "eye." The exact type of eye will vary. But, most battery manufacturers, apply a sticker to the battery itself explaining the readings.

➡ Although the readings from built-in hydrometers will vary, a green eye usually indicates a properly charged battery with sufficient fluid level. A dark eye is normally an indicator of a battery with sufficient fluid, but which is low in charge. A light or yellow eye usually indicates that electrolyte has dropped below the necessary level. In this last case, sealed batteries with an insufficient electrolyte must usually be discarded.

Checking the Specific Gravity

♦ See Figures 79, 80 and 81

A hydrometer is required to check the specific gravity on all batteries that are not maintenance-free. On batteries that are maintenance-free, the specific gravity is checked by observing the built-in hydrometer "eye" on the top of the battery case.

✴✴ CAUTION

Battery electrolyte contains sulfuric acid. If you should splash any on your skin or in your eyes, flush the affected area with plenty of clear water. If it lands in your eyes, get medical help immediately.

Fig. 79 On non-sealed batteries, the fluid level can be checked by removing the cell caps

Fig. 80 If the fluid level is low, add only distilled water until the level is correct

Fig. 81 Check the specific gravity of the battery's electrolyte with a hydrometer

The fluid (sulfuric acid solution) contained in the battery cells will tell you many things about the condition of the battery. Because the cell plates must be kept submerged below the fluid level in order to operate, the fluid level is extremely important. And, because the specific gravity of the acid is an indication of electrical charge, testing the fluid can be an aid in determining if the battery must be replaced. A battery in a vehicle with a properly operating charging system should require little maintenance, but careful, periodic inspection should reveal problems before they leave you stranded.

At least once a year, check the specific gravity of the battery. It should be between 1.20 and 1.26 on the gravity scale. Most auto stores carry a variety of inexpensive battery hydrometers. These can be used on any non-sealed battery to test the specific gravity in each cell.

The battery testing hydrometer has a squeeze bulb at one end and a nozzle at the other. Battery electrolyte is sucked into the hydrometer until the float is lifted from its seat. The specific gravity is then read by noting the position of the float. If gravity is low in one or more cells, the battery should be slowly charged and checked again to see if the gravity has come up. Generally, if after charging, the specific gravity between any two cells varies more than 50 points (0.50), the battery should be replaced, as it can no longer produce sufficient voltage to guarantee proper operation.

CABLES

▶ See Figures 82, 83, 84 and 85

Once a year (or as necessary), the battery terminals and the cable clamps should be cleaned. Loosen the clamps and remove the cables, negative cable first. On top post batteries, the use of a puller specially made for this purpose is recommended. These are inexpensive and available in most parts stores. Side terminal battery cables are secured with a small bolt.

Clean the cable clamps and the battery terminal with a wire brush, until all corrosion, grease, etc., is removed and the metal is shiny. It is especially important to clean the inside of the clamp thoroughly (an old knife is useful here), since a small deposit of oxidation there will prevent a sound connection and inhibit starting or charging. Special tools are available for cleaning these parts, one type for conventional top post batteries and another type for side terminal batteries. It is also a good idea to apply some dielectric grease to the terminal, as this will aid in the prevention of corrosion.

After the clamps and terminals are clean, reinstall the cables, negative cable last; DO NOT hammer the clamps onto battery posts. Tighten the clamps securely, but do not distort them. Give the clamps and terminals a thin external coating of grease after installation, to retard corrosion.

Check the cables at the same time that the terminals are cleaned. If the cable insulation is cracked or broken, or if the ends are frayed, the cable should be replaced with a new cable of the same length and gauge.

CHARGING

✳✳ CAUTION

The chemical reaction which takes place in all batteries generates explosive hydrogen gas. A spark can cause the battery to explode and splash acid. To avoid personal injury, be sure there is proper ventilation and take appropriate fire safety precautions when working with or near a battery.

A battery should be charged at a slow rate to keep the plates inside from getting too hot. However, if some maintenance-free batteries are allowed to discharge until they are almost "dead," they may have to be charged at a high rate to bring them back to "life." Always follow the charger manufacturer's instructions on charging the battery.

REPLACEMENT

When it becomes necessary to replace the battery, select one with an amperage rating equal to or greater than the battery originally installed. Deterioration and just plain aging of the battery cables, starter motor, and associated wires makes the battery's job harder in successive years. This makes it prudent to install a new battery with a greater capacity than the old.

Belts

INSPECTION

▶ See Figures 86, 87, 88, 89 and 90

Inspect the belts for signs of glazing or cracking. A glazed belt will be perfectly smooth from slippage, while a good belt will have a slight texture of fabric visible. Cracks will usually start at the inner edge of the belt and run outward. All worn or damaged drive belts should be replaced immediately. It is best to replace all drive belts at one time, as a preventive maintenance measure, during this service operation.

TCCS1207

Fig. 82 The underside of this special battery tool has a wire brush to clean post terminals

TCCS1208

Fig. 83 Place the tool over the battery posts and twist to clean until the metal is shiny

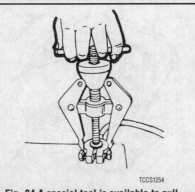

TCCS1254

Fig. 84 A special tool is available to pull the clamp from the post

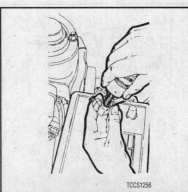

TCCS1256

Fig. 85 The cable ends should be cleaned as well

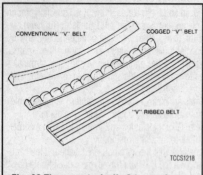

Fig. 86 There are typically 3 types of accessory drive belts found on vehicles today

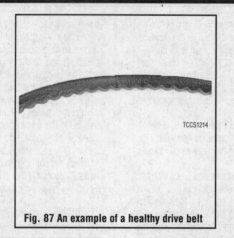

Fig. 87 An example of a healthy drive belt

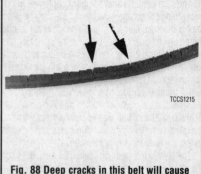

Fig. 88 Deep cracks in this belt will cause flex, building up heat that will eventually lead to belt failure

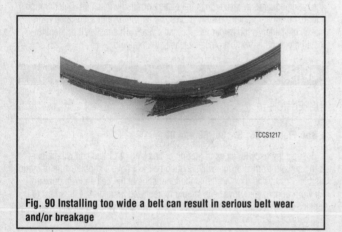

Fig. 89 The cover of this belt is worn, exposing the critical reinforcing cords to excessive wear

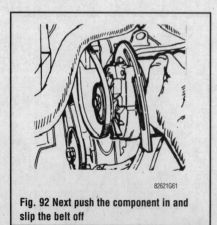

Fig. 90 Installing too wide a belt can result in serious belt wear and/or breakage

REMOVAL & INSTALLATION

▶ **See Figures 91 thru 98**

The replacement of the inner belt on multi-belted engines may require the removal of the outer belts. To replace a drive belt loosen the pivot and mounting bolts of the component which the belt is driving, then, using a wooden lever or equivalent pry the component inward to relieve the tension on the drive belt, always be careful where you locate the pry bar not to damage the component. Slip the belt off the component pulley, match up the new belt with the old belt for length and width, these measurement must be the same or problems will occur when you go to adjust the new belt. After new belt is installed correctly adjust the tension of the new belt.

➡ **When replacing more than one belt it is a good idea, to make note or mark what belt goes around what pulley. This will make installation fast and easy.**

Fig. 91 To adjust the belt tension or replace the belts, first loosen the component's mounting and adjusting bolts slightly

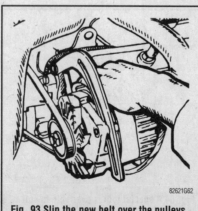

Fig. 92 Next push the component in and slip the belt off

Fig. 93 Slip the new belt over the pulleys

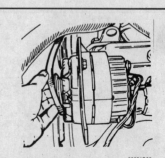

Fig. 94 Pull outward on the component while you tighten the mounting and adjusting bolts. Make sure the belt has the proper adjustment

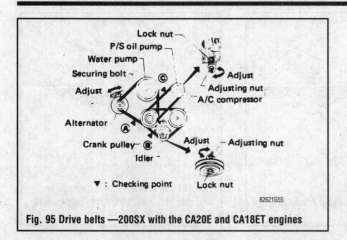

Fig. 95 Drive belts —200SX with the CA20E and CA18ET engines

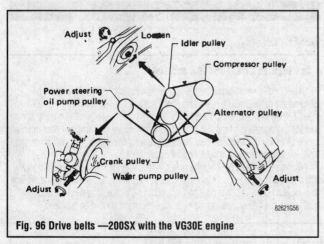

Fig. 96 Drive belts —200SX with the VG30E engine

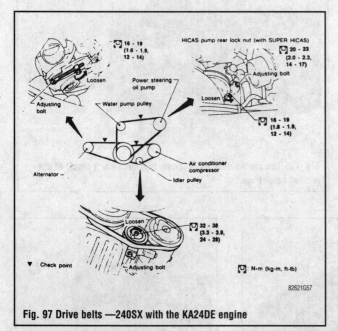

Fig. 97 Drive belts —240SX with the KA24DE engine

On air conditioning compressor and power steering pump belt replacements loosen the lock bolt for the adjusting bolt on idler pulley or power steering pump and then loosen the adjusting bolt. Pry pulley or pump inward to relieve the tension on the drive belt, always be careful where you locate the pry bar not to damage the component or pulley.

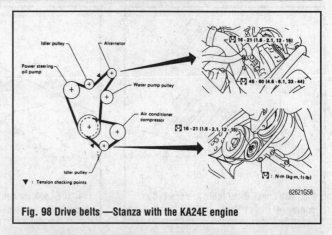

Fig. 98 Drive belts —Stanza with the KA24E engine

Timing Belts

SERVICING

▶ **See Figures 99 thru 104**

The CA and VG series engines utilizes a timing belt to drive the camshaft from the crankshaft's turning motion and to maintain proper valve timing. Some manufacturers schedule periodic timing belt replacement to assure optimum engine performance, to make sure the motorist is never stranded should the belt break (as the engine will stop instantly) and for some (manufacturers with interference motors) to prevent the possibility of severe internal engine damage should the belt break.

Fig. 99 Do not bend, twist or turn the timing belt inside out. Never allow oil, water or steam to contact the belt

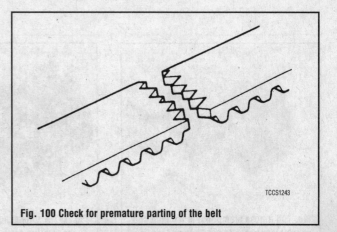

Fig. 100 Check for premature parting of the belt

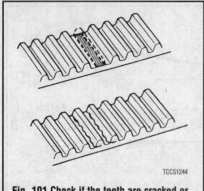

Fig. 101 Check if the teeth are cracked or damaged

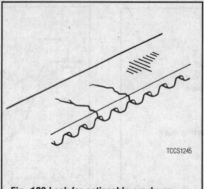

Fig. 102 Look for noticeable cracks or wear on the belt face

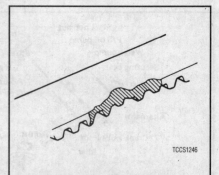

Fig. 103 You may only have damage on one side of the belt; if so, the guide could be the culprit

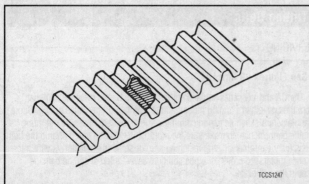

Fig. 104 Foreign material can get in-between the teeth and cause damage

Although theses engines are not listed as an interference motors (it is not listed by the manufacturer as a motor whose valves might contact the pistons if the camshaft was rotated separately from the crankshaft) the first 2 reasons for periodic replacement still apply. Nissan does not publish a replacement interval for these motors, but most belt manufacturers recommend intervals anywhere from 45,000 miles (72,500 km) to 90,000 miles (145,000 km). You will have to decide for yourself if the peace of mind offered by a new belt is worth it on higher mileage engines.

Whether or not you decide to replace it, you would be wise to check it periodically to make sure it has not become damaged or worn. Generally speaking, a severely worn belt may cause engine performance to drop dramatically, but a damaged belt (which could give out suddenly) may not give as much warning. In general, any time the engine timing cover(s) is (are) removed you should inspect the belt for premature parting, severe cracks or missing teeth.

Hoses

INSPECTION

▶ See Figures 105, 106, 107 and 108

Upper and lower radiator hoses, along with the heater hoses, should be checked for deterioration, leaks and loose hose clamps at least every 15,000 miles (22,000 km). It is also wise to check the hoses periodically in early spring and at the beginning of the fall or winter when you are performing other maintenance. A quick visual inspection could discover a weakened hose which might have left you stranded if it had remained unrepaired.

Whenever you are checking the hoses, make sure the engine and cooling system are cold. Visually inspect for cracking, rotting or collapsed hoses, and replace as necessary. Run your hand along the length of the hose. If a weak or swollen spot is noted when squeezing the hose wall, the hose should be replaced.

Fig. 105 The cracks developing along this hose are a result of age-related hardening

Fig. 106 A hose clamp that is too tight can cause older hoses to separate and tear on either side of the clamp

Fig. 107 A soft spongy hose (identifiable by the swollen section) will eventually burst and should be replaced

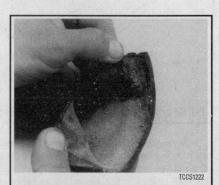

Fig. 108 Hoses are likely to deteriorate from the inside if the cooling system is not periodically flushed

REMOVAL & INSTALLATION

▶ **See Figure 109**

1. Remove the radiator pressure cap.

☆☆ CAUTION

Never remove the pressure cap while the engine is running, or personal injury from scalding hot coolant or steam may result. If possible, wait until the engine has cooled to remove the pressure cap. If this is not possible, wrap a thick cloth around the pressure cap and turn it slowly to the stop. Step back while the pressure is released from the cooling system. When you are sure all the pressure has been released, use the cloth to turn and remove the cap.

2. Position a clean container under the radiator and/or engine draincock or plug, then open the drain and allow the cooling system to drain to an appropriate level. For some upper hoses, only a little coolant must be drained. To remove hoses positioned lower on the engine, such as a lower radiator hose, the entire cooling system must be emptied.

☆☆ CAUTION

When draining coolant, keep in mind that cats and dogs are attracted by ethylene glycol antifreeze, and are quite likely to drink any that is left in an uncovered container or in puddles on the ground. This will prove fatal in sufficient quantity. Always drain coolant into a sealable container.

3. Loosen the hose clamps at each end of the hose requiring replacement. Clamps are usually either of the spring tension type (which require pliers to squeeze the tabs and loosen) or of the screw tension type (which require screw or hex drivers to loosen). Pull the clamps back on the hose away from the connection.

4. Twist, pull and slide the hose off the fitting, taking care not to damage the neck of the component from which the hose is being removed.

➡ **If the hose is stuck at the connection, do not try to insert a screwdriver or other sharp tool under the hose end in an effort to free it, as the connection and/or hose may become damaged. Heater connections especially may be easily damaged by such a procedure. If the hose is to be replaced, use a single-edged razor blade to make a slice along the portion of the hose which is stuck on the connection, perpendicular to the end of the hose. Do not cut too deep so as to prevent damaging the connection. The hose can then be peeled from the connection and discarded.**

5. Clean both hose mounting connections. Inspect the condition of the hose clamps and replace them, if necessary.

To install:

6. Dip the ends of the new hose into clean engine coolant to ease installation.

7. Slide the clamps over the replacement hose, then slide the hose ends over the connections into position.

8. Position and secure the clamps at least ¼ in. (6.35mm) from the ends of the hose. Make sure they are located beyond the raised bead of the connector.

9. Close the radiator or engine drains and properly refill the cooling system with the clean drained engine coolant or a suitable mixture of coolant and water.

10. If available, install a pressure tester and check for leaks. If a pressure tester is not available, run the engine until normal operating temperature is reached (allowing the system to naturally pressurize), then check for leaks.

☆☆ CAUTION

If you are checking for leaks with the system at normal operating temperature, BE EXTREMELY CAREFUL not to touch any moving or hot engine parts. Once temperature has been reached, shut the engine OFF, and check for leaks around the hose fittings and connections which were removed earlier.

CV-Boots

INSPECTION

▶ **See Figures 110 and 111**

The CV (Constant Velocity) boots should be checked for damage each time the oil is changed and any other time the vehicle is raised for service. These boots keep water, grime, dirt and other damaging matter from entering the CV-joints. Any of these could cause early CV-joint failure which can be expensive to repair. Heavy grease thrown around the inside of the front wheel(s) and on the brake caliper/drum can be an indication of a torn boot. Thoroughly check the boots for missing clamps and tears. If the boot is damaged, it should be replaced immediately. Please refer to Section 7 for procedures.

Air Conditioning System

SYSTEM SERVICE & REPAIR

➡ **It is recommended that the A/C system be serviced by an EPA Section 609 certified automotive technician utilizing a refrigerant recovery/recycling machine.**

The do-it-yourselfer should not service his/her own vehicle's A/C system for many reasons, including legal concerns, personal injury, environmental damage and cost.

According to the U.S. Clean Air Act, it is a federal crime to service or repair (involving the refrigerant) a Motor Vehicle Air Conditioning (MVAC) system for money without being EPA certified. It is also illegal to vent R-12 and R-134a refrigerants into the atmosphere. State and/or local laws may be more strict than the federal regulations, so be sure to check with your state and/or local authorities for further information.

➡ **Federal law dictates that a fine of up to $25,000 may be levied on people convicted of venting refrigerant into the atmosphere.**

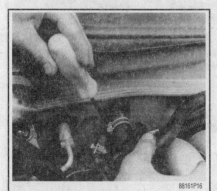

88161P16

Fig. 109 Unfasten the hose clamp before removing the hose

TCCS1011

Fig. 110 CV-boots must be inspected periodically for damage

TCCS1010

Fig. 111 A torn boot should be replaced immediately

When servicing an A/C system you run the risk of handling or coming in contact with refrigerant, which may result in skin or eye irritation or frostbite. Although low in toxicity (due to chemical stability), inhalation of concentrated refrigerant fumes is dangerous and can result in death; cases of fatal cardiac arrhythmia have been reported in people accidentally subjected to high levels of refrigerant. Some early symptoms include loss of concentration and drowsiness.

➡**Generally, the limit for exposure is lower for R-134a than it is for R-12. Exceptional care must be practiced when handling R-134a.**

Also, some refrigerants can decompose at high temperatures (near gas heaters or open flame), which may result in hydrofluoric acid, hydrochloric acid and phosgene (a fatal nerve gas).

It is usually more economically feasible to have a certified MVAC automotive technician perform A/C system service on your vehicle.

R-12 Refrigerant Conversion

If your vehicle still uses R-12 refrigerant, one way to save A/C system costs down the road is to investigate the possibility of having your system converted to R-134a. The older R-12 systems can be easily converted to R-134a refrigerant by a certified automotive technician by installing a few new components and changing the system oil.

The cost of R-12 is steadily rising and will continue to increase, because it is no longer imported or manufactured in the United States. Therefore, it is often possible to have an R-12 system converted to R-134a and recharged for less than it would cost to just charge the system with R-12.

If you are interested in having your system converted, contact local automotive service stations for more details and information.

PREVENTIVE MAINTENANCE

Although the A/C system should not be serviced by the do-it-yourselfer, preventive maintenance should be practiced to help maintain the efficiency of the vehicle's A/C system. Be sure to perform the following:

• The easiest and most important preventive maintenance for your A/C system is to be sure that it is used on a regular basis. Running the system for five minutes each month (no matter what the season) will help ensure that the seals and all internal components remain lubricated.

➡**Some vehicles automatically operate the A/C system compressor whenever the windshield defroster is activated. Therefore, the A/C system would not need to be operated each month if the defroster was used.**

• In order to prevent heater core freeze-up during A/C operation, it is necessary to maintain proper antifreeze protection. Be sure to properly maintain the engine cooling system.

• Any obstruction of or damage to the condenser configuration will restrict air flow which is essential to its efficient operation. Keep this unit clean and in proper physical shape.

➡**Bug screens which are mounted in front of the condenser (unless they are original equipment) are regarded as obstructions.**

• The condensation drain tube expels any water which accumulates on the bottom of the evaporator housing into the engine compartment. If this tube is obstructed, the air conditioning performance can be restricted and condensation buildup can spill over onto the vehicle's floor.

SYSTEM INSPECTION

Although the A/C system should not be serviced by the do-it-yourselfer, system inspections should be performed to help maintain the efficiency of the vehicle's A/C system. Be sure to perform the following:

The easiest and often most important check for the air conditioning system consists of a visual inspection of the system components. Visually inspect the system for refrigerant leaks, damaged compressor clutch, abnormal compressor drive belt tension and/or condition, plugged evaporator drain tube, blocked condenser fins, disconnected or broken wires, blown fuses, corroded connections and poor insulation.

A refrigerant leak will usually appear as an oily residue at the leakage point in the system. The oily residue soon picks up dust or dirt particles from the surrounding air and appears greasy. Through time, this will build up and appear to be a heavy dirt impregnated grease.

For a thorough visual and operational inspection, check the following:

• Check the surface of the radiator and condenser for dirt, leaves or other material which might block air flow.

• Check for kinks in hoses and lines. Check the system for leaks.

• Make sure the drive belt is properly tensioned. During operation, make sure the belt is free of noise or slippage.

• Make sure the blower motor operates at all appropriate positions, then check for distribution of the air from all outlets.

➡**Remember that in high humidity, air discharged from the vents may not feel as cold as expected, even if the system is working properly. This is because moisture in humid air retains heat more effectively than dry air, thereby making humid air more difficult to cool.**

Windshield Wipers

ELEMENT (REFILL) CARE & REPLACEMENT

▶ **See Figures 112 thru 121**

For maximum effectiveness and longest element life, the windshield and wiper blades should be kept clean. Dirt, tree sap, road tar and so on will cause streaking, smearing and blade deterioration if left on the glass. It is advisable to wash the windshield carefully with a commercial glass cleaner at least once a month. Wipe off the rubber blades with the wet rag afterwards. Do not attempt to move wipers across the windshield by hand; damage to the motor and drive mechanism will result.

To inspect and/or replace the wiper blade elements, place the wiper switch in the **LOW** speed position and the ignition switch in the **ACC** position. When the wiper blades are approximately vertical on the windshield, turn the ignition switch to **OFF**.

Examine the wiper blade elements. If they are found to be cracked, broken or torn, they should be replaced immediately. Replacement intervals will vary with usage, although ozone deterioration usually limits element life to about one year. If the wiper pattern is smeared or streaked, or if the blade chatters across the glass, the elements should be replaced. It is easiest and most sensible to replace the elements in pairs.

If your vehicle is equipped with aftermarket blades, there are several different types of refills and your vehicle might have any kind. Aftermarket blades and arms rarely use the exact same type blade or refill as the original equipment. Here are some typical aftermarket blades; not all may be available for your vehicle:

The Anco® type uses a release button that is pushed down to allow the refill to slide out of the yoke jaws. The new refill slides back into the frame and locks in place.

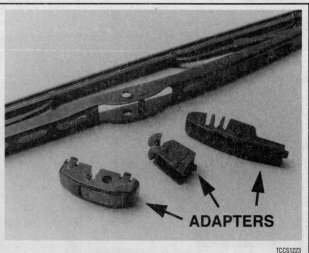

TCCS1223

Fig. 112 Bosch® wiper blade and fit kit

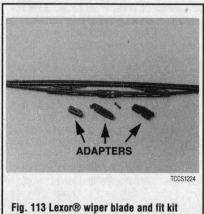

Fig. 113 Lexor® wiper blade and fit kit

Fig. 114 Pylon® wiper blade and adapter

Fig. 115 Trico® wiper blade and fit kit

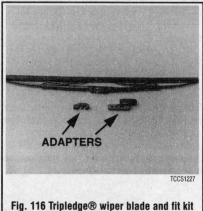

Fig. 116 Tripledge® wiper blade and fit kit

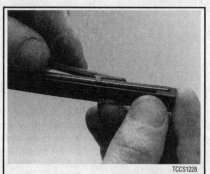

Fig. 117 To remove and install a Lexor® wiper blade refill, slip out the old insert and slide in a new one

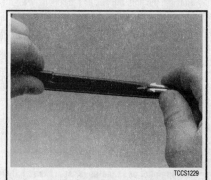

Fig. 118 On Pylon® inserts, the clip at the end has to be removed prior to sliding the insert off

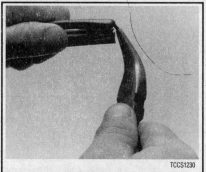

Fig. 119 On Trico® wiper blades, the tab at the end of the blade must be turned up . . .

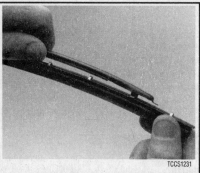

Fig. 120 . . . then the insert can be removed. After installing the replacement insert, bend the tab back

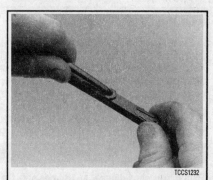

Fig. 121 The Tripledge® wiper blade insert is removed and installed using a securing clip

Some Trico® refills are removed by locating where the metal backing strip or the refill is wider. Insert a small screwdriver blade between the frame and metal backing strip. Press down to release the refill from the retaining tab.

Other types of Trico® refills have two metal tabs which are unlocked by squeezing them together. The rubber filler can then be withdrawn from the frame jaws. A new refill is installed by inserting the refill into the front frame jaws and sliding it rearward to engage the remaining frame jaws. There are usually four jaws; be certain when installing that the refill is engaged in all of them. At the end of its travel, the tabs will lock into place on the front jaws of the wiper blade frame.

Another type of refill is made from polycarbonate. The refill has a simple locking device at one end which flexes downward out of the groove into which the jaws of the holder fit, allowing easy release. By sliding the new refill through all the jaws and pushing through the slight resistance when it reaches the end of its travel, the refill will lock into position.

To replace the Tridon® refill, it is necessary to remove the wiper blade. This refill has a plastic backing strip with a notch about 1 in. (25mm) from the end.

Hold the blade (frame) on a hard surface so that the frame is tightly bowed. Grip the tip of the backing strip and pull up while twisting counterclockwise. The backing strip will snap out of the retaining tab. Do this for the remaining tabs until the refill is free of the blade. The length of these refills is molded into the end and they should be replaced with identical types.

Regardless of the type of refill used, be sure to follow the part manufacturer's instructions closely. Make sure that all of the frame jaws are engaged as the refill is pushed into place and locked. If the metal blade holder and frame are allowed to touch the glass during wiper operation, the glass will be scratched.

Tires and Wheels

Common sense and good driving habits will afford maximum tire life. Make sure that you don't overload the vehicle or run with incorrect pressure in the tires. Either of these will increase tread wear. Fast starts, sudden stops and sharp cornering are hard on tires and will shorten their useful life span.

➡For optimum tire life, keep the tires properly inflated, rotate them often and have the wheel alignment checked periodically.

Inspect your tires frequently. Be especially careful to watch for bubbles in the tread or sidewall, deep cuts or underinflation. Replace any tires with bubbles in the sidewall. If cuts are so deep that they penetrate to the cords, discard the tire. Any cut in the sidewall of a radial tire renders it unsafe. Also look for uneven tread wear patterns that may indicate the front end is out of alignment or that the tires are out of balance.

TIRE ROTATION

▶ See Figure 122

Tires must be rotated periodically to equalize wear patterns that vary with a tire's position on the vehicle. Tires will also wear in an uneven way as the front steering/suspension system wears to the point where the alignment should be reset.

Rotating the tires will ensure maximum life for the tires as a set, so you will not have to discard a tire early due to wear on only part of the tread. Regular rotation is required to equalize wear.

When rotating "unidirectional tires," make sure that they always roll in the same direction. This means that a tire used on the left side of the vehicle must not be switched to the right side and vice-versa. Such tires should only be rotated front-to-rear or rear-to-front, while always remaining on the same side of the vehicle. These tires are marked on the sidewall as to the direction of rotation; observe the marks when reinstalling the tire(s).

Some styled or "mag" wheels may have different offsets front to rear. In these cases, the rear wheels must not be used up front and vice-versa. Furthermore, if these wheels are equipped with unidirectional tires, they cannot be rotated unless the tire is remounted for the proper direction of rotation.

➡The compact or space-saver spare is strictly for emergency use. It must never be included in the tire rotation or placed on the vehicle for everyday use.

TIRE DESIGN

▶ See Figure 123

For maximum satisfaction, tires should be used in sets of four. Mixing of different brands or types (radial, bias-belted, fiberglass belted) should be avoided. In most cases, the vehicle manufacturer has designated a type of tire on which the vehicle will perform best. Your first choice when replacing tires should be to use the same type of tire that the manufacturer recommends.

When radial tires are used, tire sizes and wheel diameters should be selected to maintain ground clearance and tire load capacity equivalent to the original specified tire. Radial tires should always be used in sets of four.

✳✳ CAUTION

Radial tires should never be used on only the front axle.

When selecting tires, pay attention to the original size as marked on the tire. Most tires are described using an industry size code sometimes referred to as P-Metric. This allows the exact identification of the tire specifications, regardless of the manufacturer. If selecting a different tire size or brand, remember to check the installed tire for any sign of interference with the body or suspension while the vehicle is stopping, turning sharply or heavily loaded.

Snow Tires

Good radial tires can produce a big advantage in slippery weather, but in snow, a street radial tire does not have sufficient tread to provide traction and control. The small grooves of a street tire quickly pack with snow and the tire behaves like a billiard ball on a marble floor. The more open, chunky tread of a snow tire will self-clean as the tire turns, providing much better grip on snowy surfaces.

To satisfy municipalities requiring snow tires during weather emergencies, most snow tires carry either an M + S designation after the tire size stamped on the sidewall, or the designation "all-season." In general, no change in tire size is necessary when buying snow tires.

Most manufacturers strongly recommend the use of 4 snow tires on their vehicles for reasons of stability. If snow tires are fitted only to the drive wheels, the opposite end of the vehicle may become very unstable when braking or turning on slippery surfaces. This instability can lead to unpleasant endings if the driver can't counteract the slide in time.

Note that snow tires, whether 2 or 4, will affect vehicle handling in all non-snow situations. The stiffer, heavier snow tires will noticeably change the turning and braking characteristics of the vehicle. Once the snow tires are installed, you must re-learn the behavior of the vehicle and drive accordingly.

➡Consider buying extra wheels on which to mount the snow tires. Once done, the "snow wheels" can be installed and removed as needed. This eliminates the potential damage to tires or wheels from seasonal removal and installation. Even if your vehicle has styled wheels, see if inexpensive steel wheels are available. Although the look of the vehicle will change, the expensive wheels will be protected from salt, curb hits and pothole damage.

TIRE STORAGE

If they are mounted on wheels, store the tires at proper inflation pressure. All tires should be kept in a cool, dry place. If they are stored in the garage or basement, do not let them stand on a concrete floor; set them on strips of wood, a mat or a large stack of newspaper. Keeping them away from direct moisture is of paramount importance. Tires should not be stored upright, but in a flat position.

INFLATION & INSPECTION

▶ See Figures 124 thru 129

The importance of proper tire inflation cannot be overemphasized. A tire employs air as part of its structure. It is designed around the supporting strength of the air at a specified pressure. For this reason, improper inflation drastically reduces the tire's ability to perform as intended. A tire will lose some air in day-to-day use; having to add a few pounds of air periodically is not necessarily a sign of a leaking tire.

Two items should be a permanent fixture in every glove compartment: an

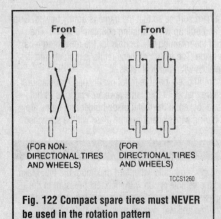

(FOR NON-DIRECTIONAL TIRES AND WHEELS)

(FOR DIRECTIONAL TIRES AND WHEELS)

TCCS1260

Fig. 122 Compact spare tires must NEVER be used in the rotation pattern

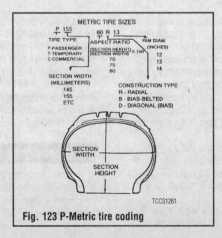

METRIC TIRE SIZES

TCCS1261

Fig. 123 P-Metric tire coding

TCCS1095

Fig. 124 Tires with deep cuts, or cuts which bulge, should be replaced immediately

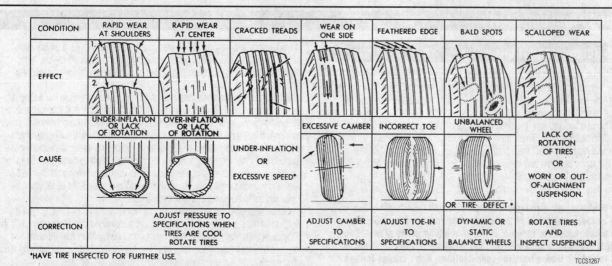

CONDITION	RAPID WEAR AT SHOULDERS	RAPID WEAR AT CENTER	CRACKED TREADS	WEAR ON ONE SIDE	FEATHERED EDGE	BALD SPOTS	SCALLOPED WEAR
EFFECT							
CAUSE	UNDER-INFLATION OR LACK OF ROTATION	OVER-INFLATION OR LACK OF ROTATION	UNDER-INFLATION OR EXCESSIVE SPEED*	EXCESSIVE CAMBER	INCORRECT TOE	UNBALANCED WHEEL OR TIRE DEFECT*	LACK OF ROTATION OF TIRES OR WORN OR OUT-OF-ALIGNMENT SUSPENSION.
CORRECTION	ADJUST PRESSURE TO SPECIFICATIONS WHEN TIRES ARE COOL ROTATE TIRES			ADJUST CAMBER TO SPECIFICATIONS	ADJUST TOE-IN TO SPECIFICATIONS	DYNAMIC OR STATIC BALANCE WHEELS	ROTATE TIRES AND INSPECT SUSPENSION

*HAVE TIRE INSPECTED FOR FURTHER USE.

TCCS1267

Fig. 125 Common tire wear patterns and causes

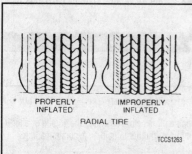

PROPERLY INFLATED   IMPROPERLY INFLATED
RADIAL TIRE

TCCS1263

Fig. 126 Radial tires have a characteristic sidewall bulge; don't try to measure pressure by looking at the tire. Use a quality air pressure gauge

TCCS1265

Fig. 127 Tread wear indicators will appear when the tire is worn

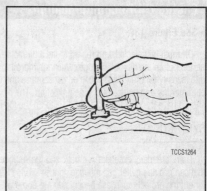

TCCS1264

Fig. 128 Accurate tread depth indicators are inexpensive and handy

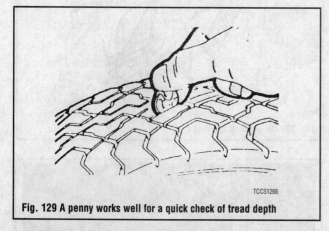

TCCS1266

Fig. 129 A penny works well for a quick check of tread depth

accurate tire pressure gauge and a tread depth gauge. Check the tire pressure (including the spare) regularly with a pocket type gauge. Too often, the gauge on the end of the air hose at your corner garage is not accurate because it suffers too much abuse. Always check tire pressure when the tires are cold, as pressure increases with temperature. If you must move the vehicle to check the tire inflation, do not drive more than a mile before checking. A cold tire is generally one that has not been driven for more than three hours.

A plate or sticker is normally provided somewhere in the vehicle (door post, hood, tailgate or trunk lid) which shows the proper pressure for the tires. Never counteract excessive pressure build-up by bleeding off air pressure (letting some air out). This will cause the tire to run hotter and wear quicker.

✳✳ CAUTION

Never exceed the maximum tire pressure embossed on the tire! This is the pressure to be used when the tire is at maximum loading, but it is rarely the correct pressure for everyday driving. Consult the owner's manual or the tire pressure sticker for the correct tire pressure.

Once you've maintained the correct tire pressures for several weeks, you'll be familiar with the vehicle's braking and handling personality. Slight adjustments in tire pressures can fine-tune these characteristics, but never change the cold pressure specification by more than 2 psi. A slightly softer tire pressure will give a softer ride but also yield lower fuel mileage. A slightly harder tire will give crisper dry road handling but can cause skidding on wet surfaces. Unless you're fully attuned to the vehicle, stick to the recommended inflation pressures.

All automotive tires have built-in tread wear indicator bars that show up as ½ in. (13mm) wide smooth bands across the tire when 1/16 in. (1.5mm) of tread remains. The appearance of tread wear indicators means that the tires should be replaced. In fact, many states have laws prohibiting the use of tires with less than this amount of tread.

You can check your own tread depth with an inexpensive gauge or by using a Lincoln head penny. Slip the Lincoln penny (with Lincoln's head upside-down) into several tread grooves. If you can see the top of Lincoln's head in 2 adjacent grooves, the tire has less than 1/16 in. (1.5mm) tread left and should be replaced. You can measure snow tires in the same manner by using the "tails" side of the Lincoln penny. If you can see the top of the Lincoln memorial, it's time to replace the snow tire(s).

FLUIDS AND LUBRICANTS

Fuel Recommendations

All engines covered in this book have been designed to run on unleaded fuel. The minimum octane requirement is 91 RON (Research Octane Number) or 87 AKI (Anti-Knock Index); all unleaded fuels sold in the U.S. are required to meet this minimum octane rating.

The use of a fuel too low in octane (a measurement of anti-knock quality) will result in spark knock. Since many factors such as altitude, terrain, air temperature and humidity affect the operating efficiency, knocking may result even though the recommended fuel is being used. If persistent knocking occurs, it may be necessary to switch to a higher grade of fuel. Continuous or heavy knocking may result in engine damage.

➡️**Your engine's fuel requirement can change with time, mainly due to carbon buildup, which will in turn change the compression ratio. If your engine pings, knocks or runs on, switch to a higher grade of fuel. Sometimes just changing brands will cure the problem. If it becomes necessary to retard the timing from the specifications, don't change it more than a few degrees. Retarded timing will reduce power output and fuel mileage, in addition to increasing the engine temperature.**

Engine Oil Recommendations

▶ **See Figure 130**

Oil must be selected with regard to the anticipated temperatures during the period before the next oil change. When buying oil for your vehicle select the oil viscosity for the lowest expected temperature and you will be assured of easy cold starting and sufficient engine protection. The oil you pour into your engine should have the designation "SG" marked on the top of its container.

SYNTHETIC OIL

There are many excellent synthetic and fuel-efficient oils currently available that can provide better gas mileage, longer service life, and in some cases better engine protection. These benefits do not come without a few hitches, however ® the main one being the price of synthetic oils, which is 3 or 4 times the price per quart of conventional oil.

Synthetic oil is not for every car and every type of driving, so you should consider your engine's condition and your type of driving. Also, check your car's warranty guidelines at the dealership that you purchased the car from, regarding the use of synthetic oils and your powertrain and or extended warranty.

Both brand new engines and older, high mileage engines are the wrong candidates for synthetic oil. The synthetic oils are so slippery that they can prevent the proper break-in of new engines; most manufacturers recommend that you wait until the engine is properly broken in (5,000 miles) until using synthetic oil. Older engines with wear have a different problem with synthetics: they use (consume during operation) more oil as they age. Slippery synthetic oils get past these worn parts easily. If your engine is using conventional oil, it will use synthetics much faster. Also, if your car is leaking oil past old seals you'll have a much greater leak problem with synthetics.

Cars used under harder circumstances, such as stop-and-go, city type driving, short trips, or extended idling, should be serviced more frequently. For the engines in these cars, the much greater cost of synthetic or fuel-efficient oils may not be worth the investment. Internal wear increases much quicker on these cars, causing greater oil consumption and leakage.

➡️**The mixing of conventional and synthetic oils is not recommended. If you are using synthetic oil, it might be wise to carry 2 or 3 quarts with you no matter where you drive, as not all service stations carry this type of lubricant.**

Engine

OIL LEVEL CHECK

▶ **See Figure 131**

The best time to check the engine oil is before operating the engine or after it has been sitting for at least 10 minutes in order to gain an accurate reading.

REFILL OIL TO "H" LEVEL.
DO NOT OVERFILL.

82621G72

Fig. 131 Oil dipstick markings

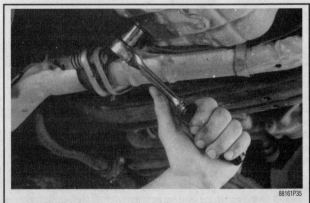

88161P35

Fig. 132 Use the correct size wrench to loosen the drain plug

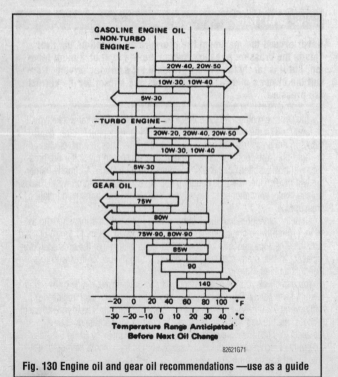

GASOLINE ENGINE OIL
—NON-TURBO
ENGINE—

20W-40, 20W-50
10W-30, 10W-40
5W-30

—TURBO ENGINE—

20W-20, 20W-40, 20W-50
10W-30, 10W-40
5W-30

GEAR OIL

75W
80W
75W-90, 80W-90
85W
90
140

-20   0   20   40   60   80 100 °F
-30 -20 -10 0 10 20 30 40 °C
Temperature Range Anticipated
Before Next Oil Change

82621G71

Fig. 130 Engine oil and gear oil recommendations —use as a guide

This will allow the oil to drain back in the crankcase. To check the engine oil level, make sure that the vehicle is resting on a level surface, remove the oil dipstick, wipe it clean and reinsert the stick firmly for an accurate reading. The oil dipstick has two marks to indicate high and low oil level. If the oil is at or below the "low level" mark on the dipstick, oil should be added as necessary. The oil level should be maintained in the safety margin, neither going above the "high level" mark or below the "low level" mark.

➡**It is normal to add some oil between oil maintenance intervals or during break-in period, depending on the operating conditions.**

OIL AND FILTER CHANGE

▶ **See Figures 132 thru 140**

The Datsun/Nissan factory maintenance intervals (every 7,500 miles or 6 months up till 1989 models and every 3,750 miles or 3 months for 1990–92 models) specify changing the oil filter at every second oil change after the initial service. We recommend replacing the oil filter with every oil change. For the small price of an oil filter, it's cheap insurance to replace the filter at every oil change. One of the larger filter manufacturers points out in its advertisements that not changing the filter leaves about 1 quart of dirty oil in the engine. This claim is true and should be kept in mind when changing your oil.

➡**On turbocharged engines factory maintenance intervals are every 5,000 miles or 6 months.**

1. Run the engine until it reaches normal operating temperature.
2. Jack up the front of the car and support it on safety stands if necessary to gain access to the filter.
3. Slide a drain pan of at least 6 quarts capacity under the oil pan.

✳✳ CAUTION

The EPA warns that prolonged contact with used engine oil may cause a number of skin disorders, including cancer! You should make every effort to minimize your exposure to used engine oil.

Protective gloves should be worn when changing the oil. Wash your hands and any other exposed skin areas as soon as possible after exposure to used engine oil. Soap and water, or waterless hand cleaner should be used.

4. Loosen the drain plug. Turn the plug out by hand. By keeping an inward pressure on the plug as you unscrew it, oil won't escape past the threads and you can remove it without being burned by hot oil.
5. Allow the oil to drain completely and then install the drain plug. Don't overtighten the plug or you'll be buying a new pan or a trick replacement plug for damaged threads.
6. Using a strap wrench, remove the oil filter. Keep in mind that it's holding about one quart of dirty, hot oil.
7. Empty the old filter into the drain pan and dispose of the filter and old oil.

➡**One ecologically desirable solution to the used oil disposal problem is to find a cooperative gas station owner who will allow you to dump your used oil into his tank or take the oil to a reclamation center (often at garages and gas stations).**

8. Using a clean rag, wipe off the filter adapter on the engine block. Be sure that the rag doesn't leave any lint which could clog an oil passage.
9. Coat the rubber gasket on the filter with fresh oil. Spin it onto the engine by hand; when the gasket touches the adapter surface give it another ⅔ turn. Refer to the illustration. No more or you'll squash the gasket and it will leak.
10. Refill the engine with the correct amount of fresh oil. See the Capacities chart.
11. Crank the engine over several times and then start it. If the oil pressure indicator light doesn't go out or the pressure gauge shows zero, shut the engine down and find out what's wrong.
12. If the oil pressure is OK and there are no leaks, shut the engine off and lower the car. Check oil level.

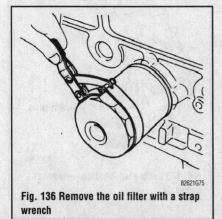
Fig. 133 Remove the plug, allowing the oil to drain into a suitable container

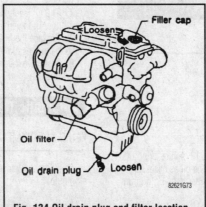
Fig. 134 Oil drain plug and filter location

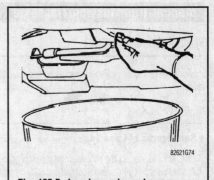
Fig. 135 By keeping an inward pressure on the plug as you unscrew it, oil won't escape past the threads

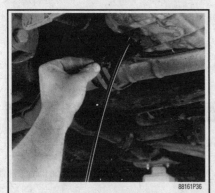
Fig. 136 Remove the oil filter with a strap wrench

Fig. 137 Coat the new oil filter gasket with clean oil

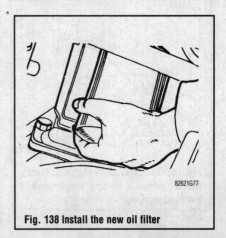
Fig. 138 Install the new oil filter

Fig. 139 Add oil through the capped opening in the camshaft (valve) cover

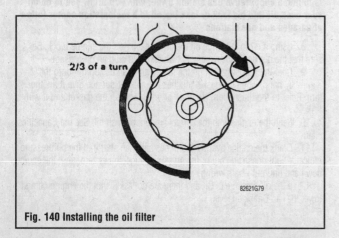

Fig. 140 Installing the oil filter

Manual Transmission/Transaxle

FLUID RECOMMENDATION

For manual transmission/transaxles be sure to use fluid with an API GL-4 rating.

LEVEL CHECK

▶ See Figures 141 and 142

You should inspect the manual transmission gear oil at 12 months or 15,000 miles at this point you should correct the level or replace the oil as necessary. The lubricant level should be even with the bottom of the filler hole. Hold in on the filler plug when unscrewing it. When you are sure

that all of the threads of the plug are free of the transaxle case, move the plug away from the case slightly. If lubricant begins to flow out of the transmission, then you know it is full. If not, add the correct gear oil as necessary

Inspect the manual transaxle gear oil at 12 months or 15,000 miles at this point you should also correct the level. To check the oil level in the manual transaxle you have to remove the filler plug to determine the fluid level. The lubricant level should be even with the bottom of the filler hole.

DRAIN AND REFILL

▶ See Figure 143

➡ It is recommended that the manual transmission/transaxle fluid be changed every 30,000 miles or 24 months if the vehicle is used in severe service, towing a trailer and or using a camper or a car-top carrier.

1. Run the engine until it reaches normal operating temperature then turn key to the **OFF** position.
2. Jack up the front of the car and support it on safety stands level, if necessary to gain access.
3. Remove the filler plug from the left-side of the transmission/transaxle to provide a vent.
4. The drain plug is located on the bottom of the transmission/transaxle case. Place a pan under the drain plug and remove it.

❊❊ CAUTION

The oil will be HOT! Push up against the threads as you unscrew the plug to prevent leakage.

5. Allow the oil to drain completely. Clean off the plug and replace it. DO NOT OVERTIGHTEN PLUG.
6. Fill the transmission/transaxle with gear oil through the filler plug hole. Use API service GL-4 gear oil of the proper viscosity. This oil usually comes in a squeeze bottle with a long nozzle. If yours isn't, use a plastic squeeze bottle (the type used in the kitchen). Refer to the "Capacities" chart for the amount of oil needed.
7. The oil level should come up to the edge of the filler hole. You can stick your finger in to verify this. Watch out for sharp threads.
8. Replace the filler plug. Lower the vehicle, dispose of the old oil in the same manner as old engine oil.
9. Test drive the vehicle, stop and check for leaks. Automatic Transmission/Transaxle

Automatic Transmission/Transaxle

FLUID RECOMMENDATIONS

All automatic transmission/transaxle, use Dexron® ATF (automatic transmission fluid)

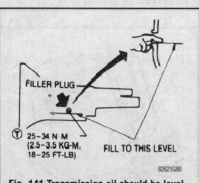

Fig. 141 Transmission oil should be level with the bottom of the filler plug on manual transmissions

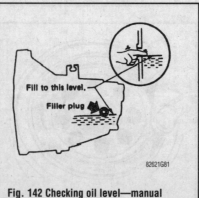

Fig. 142 Checking oil level—manual transaxle

Fig. 143 Drain plug location — manual transaxle

LEVEL CHECK

▶ **See Figures 144, 145 and 146**

The fluid level in the automatic transmission/transaxle should be checked every 6 months or 7,500 miles whichever comes first. The transmission/transaxle has a dipstick for fluid level checks.

1. Drive the car until it is at normal operating temperature. The level should not be checked immediately after the car has been driven for a long time at high speed, or in city traffic in hot weather. In those cases, the transaxle should be given a half hour to cool down.

2. Stop the car, apply the parking brake, then shift slowly through all gear positions, ending in Park. Let the engine idle for about five minutes with the transmission/transaxle in Park. The car should be on a level surface.

3. With the engine still running, remove the dipstick, wipe it clean, then reinsert it, pushing it fully home.

4. Pull the dipstick again and, holding it horizontally, read the fluid level.

5. Cautiously feel the end of the dipstick to determine the temperature. Note that on Datsuns/Nissans there is a scale, on each side, HOT on one, COLD on the other. If the fluid level is not in the correct area, more will have to be added.

6. Fluid is added through the dipstick tube. You will probably need the aid of a spout or a long necked funnel. Be sure that whatever you pour through is perfectly clean and dry. Use an automatic transmission fluid marked DEXRON®. Add fluid slowly, and in small amounts, checking the level frequently between additions. Do not overfill, which will cause foaming, fluid loss, slippage, and possible transmission damage. It takes only one pint to raise the level from L to H when the transaxle is hot.

DRAIN AND REFILL

▶ **See Figures 147, 148 and 149**

➡**It is recommended that the automatic transmission/transaxle fluid be changed every 30,000 miles or 24 months if the vehicle is used in severe service, towing a trailer and or using a camper or a car-top carrier.**

Transmission

1. There is no drain plug. The fluid pan must be removed. Partially remove the pan screws until the pan can be pulled down at one corner. Place a container under the transmission, lower a rear corner of the pan, and allow the fluid to drain.

➡**If the drained fluid is discolored (brown or black), thick, or smells burnt, serious transmission problems due to overheating should be suspected. Your car's transmission should be inspected by a transmission specialist to determine the cause.**

2. After draining, remove the pan screws completely, and remove the pan and gasket.

3. Clean the pan thoroughly and allow it to air dry. If you wipe it out with a rag you risk leaving bits of lint in the pan which will clog the tiny hydraulic passages in the transmission.

➡**It is very important to clean the old gasket from the oil pan, to prevent leaks upon installation, a razor blade does a excellent job at this.**

4. Install the pan using a new gasket. If you decide to use sealer on the gasket apply it only in a very thin bead running to the outside of the pan screw holes. Tighten the pan screws evenly in rotation from the center outwards, to 36–60 inch lbs.

5. It is a good idea to measure the amount of fluid drained to determine how much fresh fluid to add. This is because some part of the transmission, such as the torque converter, will not drain completely, and using the dry refill amount specified in the Capacities chart may lead to overfilling. Fluid is added through the dipstick tube. Make sure that the funnel, hose, or whatever you are using is completely clean and dry before pouring transmission fluid through it. Use DEXRON® automatic transmission fluid.

6. Replace the dipstick after filling. Start the engine and allow it to idle. Do NOT race the engine. Check the installation of the new pan gasket for leaks.

7. After the engine has idled for a few minutes, shift the transmission slowly through the gears, then return the lever to Park. With the engine idling, check

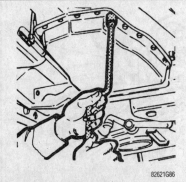

Fig. 144 Remove the automatic transmission dipstick with the engine warm and idling in Park

Fig. 145 Add automatic transmission fluid through the transmission dipstick tube — use a funnel

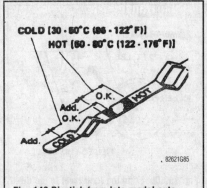

Fig. 146 Dipstick from late model automatic transaxle

Fig. 147 Remove the pan to drain the automatic transmission

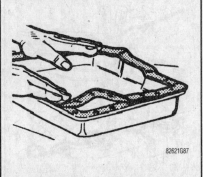

Fig. 148 Install a pan gasket — automatic transmission

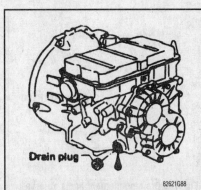

Fig. 149 Drain plug location—automatic transaxle

the fluid level on the dipstick. It should be between the **H** and **L** marks. If below **L**, add sufficient fluid to raise the level to between the marks.

8. Drive the car until it is at operating temperature. The fluid should be at the **H** mark. If not, add sufficient fluid until this is the case. Be careful not to overfill. Overfilling causes slippage, overheating, and seal damage.

Transaxle

To change the transaxle fluid on early models the transaxle fluid oil pan must be removed and the gasket must be replaced. This procedure is similar to the transmission procedure with the exception of the oil pan location.

On late models there is a drain plug located on the side of the transaxle case. Remove the drain plug and allow the fluid to drain then refill with new fluid, start engine and correct the fluid level as necessary. Before attempting this service read the complete section above on "DRAIN AND REFILL" procedure.

Rear Drive Axle

FLUID RECOMMENDATIONS

Use only standard GL-5 hypoid type gear oil: SAE 80W or SAE 80W/90.

LEVEL CHECK

▶ **See Figures 150 and 151**

The oil in the differential should be checked at least every 15,000 miles or 12 months.

1. With the car on a level surface, remove the filler plug from the back side of the differential.
2. If the oil begins to trickle out of the hole, there is enough. Otherwise, carefully insert your finger (watch out for sharp threads) into the hole and check that the oil is up to the bottom edge of the filler hole.
3. If not, add oil through the hole until the level is at the edge of the hole. Most gear oils come in a plastic squeeze bottle with a nozzle; making additions

is simple. You can also use a common kitchen baster. Use only the specified fluid.

4. Replace the plug and check for leaks.

DRAIN AND REFILL

▶ **See Figures 152 and 153**

➡ **It is recommended that the rear drive axle fluid be changed every 30,000 miles or 24 months if the vehicle is used in severe service, towing a trailer and or using a camper or a car-top carrier.**

1. Park the car on a level surface. Place a pan of at least two quarts capacity underneath the drain plug. The drain plug is located on the center rear of the differential carrier, just below the filler plug on some models, on others it can be found at the bottom of the carrier. Remove the drain plug.
2. Allow the lubricant to drain completely.
3. Refill the differential housing with API GL-5 gear oil of the proper viscosity. The correct level is to the edge of the filler hole.
4. Install the filler plug. Tighten to 29–43 ft. lbs.

Cooling System

FLUID RECOMMENDATION

▶ **See Figures 154 and 155**

The cooling fluid or antifreeze, should be changed every 30,000 miles or 24 months on all vehicles except the 1991–92 240SX with KA24DE engine on these vehicles change at 60,000 miles or 48 months then every 30,000 miles or 24 months. When replacing the fluid, use a mixture of 50% water and 50% ethylene glycol antifreeze.

Check the freezing protection rating at least once a year, preferably just before the winter sets in. This can be done with an antifreeze tester (most service stations will have one on hand and will probably check it for you, if not,

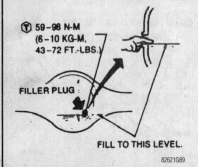

Fig. 150 Checking the fluid level in the differential on models with a solid rear axle assembly

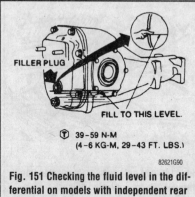

Fig. 151 Checking the fluid level in the differential on models with independent rear suspension

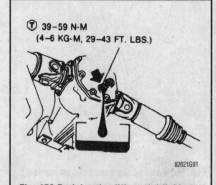

Fig. 152 Draining the differential fluid on models with independent rear suspension

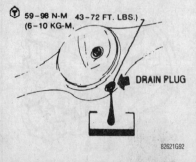

Fig. 153 Draining the fluid in the differential on models with a solid rear axle assembly

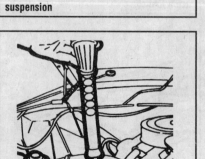

Fig. 154 Coolant protection can be checked with float type tester

Fig. 155 The cooling system should be pressure tested at least once a year

they are available at an auto parts store). Maintain a protection rating of at least 20°F (29°C) to prevent engine damage as a result of freezing and to assure the proper engine operating temperature.

It is also a good idea to have the cooling system check for leaks. A pressure test gauge is available to perform such a task. Checking and repairing a coolant leak in the early stages while save time and money.

LEVEL CHECK

◆ **See Figures 156, 157, 158, 159 and 160**

Check the coolant level every 3,000 miles or once a month. In hot weather operation, it may be a good idea to check the level once a week. Check for loose connections and signs of deterioration of the coolant hoses. Maintain the coolant level ¾–1¼ in. (19–32mm) below the level of the filler neck when the engine is cold.

Check the coolant level in the coolant recovery bottle when the engine is cold, the level should be up to the MAX mark. If the bottle is empty, check the level in the radiator and refill as necessary, then fill the bottle up to the MAX level.

❋❋ CAUTION

Never remove the radiator cap when the vehicle is hot or overheated. Wait until it has cooled. Place a thick cloth over the radiator cap to shield yourself from the heat and turn the radiator cap, SLIGHTLY, until the sound of escaping pressure can be heard. DO NOT turn any more; allow the pressure to release gradually. When no more pressure can be heard escaping, remove the cap with the heavy cloth, CAUTIOUSLY.

➡**Never add cold water to an overheated engine while the engine is not running.**

After filling the radiator, run the engine until it reaches normal operating temperature, to make sure that the thermostat has opened and all the air is bled from the system.

DRAIN AND REFILL

◆ **See Figures 161 thru 167**

➡**Refer to the correct procedure for your year and model. Read the complete service procedure before starting this repair. Bleed the cooling system as outlined if necessary.**

To drain the cooling system, allow the engine to cool down **BEFORE ATTEMPTING TO REMOVE THE RADIATOR CAP**. Then turn the cap until it hisses. Wait until all pressure is off the cap before removing it completely.

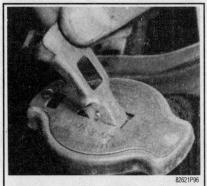

Fig. 156 If the engine is HOT, cover the radiator cap with a rag

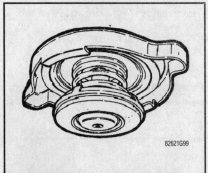

Fig. 157 Some type radiator caps have pressure release levers

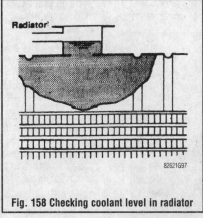

Fig. 158 Checking coolant level in radiator

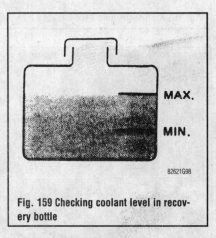

Fig. 159 Checking coolant level in recovery bottle

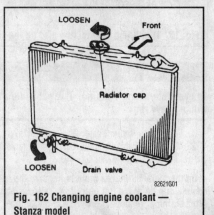

Fig. 160 Always check the gasket in the radiator cap when checking the radiator's coolant level

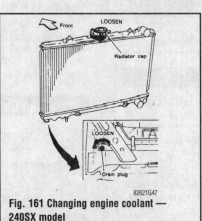

Fig. 161 Changing engine coolant — 240SX model

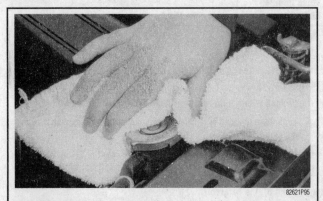

Fig. 162 Changing engine coolant — Stanza model

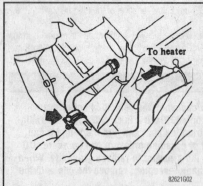

Fig. 163 Removing the inlet hose from the connector pipe 1982–86 Stanza

Fig. 164 Using the 3-way valve to bleed the cooling system 1982–86 Stanza

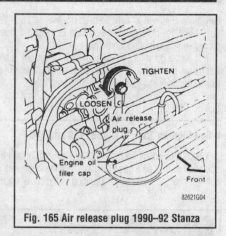

Fig. 165 Air release plug 1990–92 Stanza

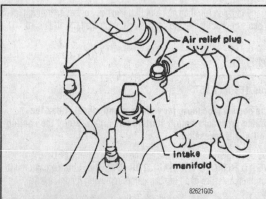

Fig. 166 Air release plug 240SX model

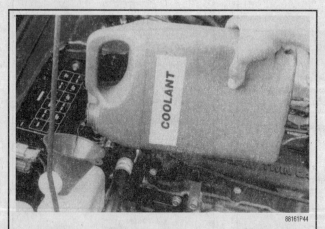

Fig. 167 After filling the radiator, also fill the coolant reservoir

✳✳ CAUTION

To avoid burns and scalding, always handle a warm radiator cap with a heavy rag.

1. At the dash, set the heater TEMP control lever to the fully HOT position.
2. With the radiator cap removed, drain the radiator by loosening the petcock at the bottom of the radiator.

➡️**On the 1982–86 Stanza models, remove the heater inlet hose from the connector pipe at the left rear of the cylinder block to drain completely. After draining, reconnect the hose to the pipe.**

3. Close the petcock (be careful not to damage the petcock when closing), then refill the system with a 50/50 mix of ethylene glycol antifreeze; fill the system to ¾–1¼ in. (1932mm) from the bottom of the filler neck. Reinstall the radiator cap.

➡️**If equipped with a fluid reservoir tank, fill it up to the MAX level.**

4. If you have replaced or repaired any cooling system component the cooling system must be bled as outlined:

➡️**On 1982–86 Stanza models insert a 3mm pin into the 3-way valve, located at the firewall, and push it in as far as it will go. While pushing in on the pin, fill the radiator up to the filler opening. Replace the radiator cap and fill the reservoir.**

➡️**On all year 200SX and 1987–89 Stanza models slowly pour coolant through the filler neck to release air in the system.**

➡️**On all year 240SX and 1990–92 Stanza models slowly pour coolant through the filler neck to release air in the system with the air relief bolt or plug loosen.**

5. Operate the engine to normal operating temperature. Check the system for signs of leaks and for the correct level.

FLUSHING AND CLEANING THE SYSTEM

To flush the system you must first, drain the cooling system but do not close the petcock valve on the bottom of the radiator. You can insert a garden hose, in the filler neck, turn the water pressure on moderately then start the engine. After about 5 minutes or less the water coming out of the bottom of the radiator should be clear. Shut off the engine and water supply, allow the radiator to drain then refill and bleed the system as necessary.

➡️**DO NOT allow the engine to overheat. The supply of water going in the top must be equal in amount to the water draining from the bottom, this way the radiator will always be full when the engine us running.**

Usually flushing the radiator using water is all that is necessary to maintain the proper condition in the cooling system.

Radiator flush is the only cleaning agent that can be used to clean the internal portion of the radiator. Radiator flush can be purchased at any auto supply store. Follow the directions on the label.

Brake and Clutch Master Cylinder

FLUID RECOMMENDATION

▸ **See Figure 168**

When adding or changing the fluid in the systems, use a quality brake fluid of the DOT 3 specifications.

➡️**Never reuse old brake fluid.**

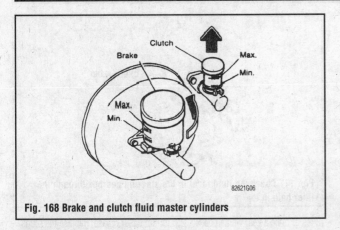

Fig. 168 Brake and clutch fluid master cylinders

LEVEL CHECK

▶ **See Figures 169, 170 and 171**

The brake and clutch master cylinders are located under the hood, in the left rear section of the engine compartment. They are made of translucent plastic so that the levels may be checked (check fluid level periodically) without removing the tops. The fluid level in both reservoirs must be checked at least every 15,000 miles or 12 months. The fluid level should be maintained at the upper most mark on the side of the reservoir. Any sudden decrease in the level indicates a possible leak in the system and should be checked out immediately.

➡**Some models may have two reservoirs for the brake master cylinder, while other models (those with an automatic transmission/transaxle) will not have a clutch master cylinder at all.**

When making additions of brake fluid, use only fresh, uncontaminated brake fluid meeting or exceeding DOT 3 standards. Be careful not to spill any brake fluid on painted surfaces, as it eats the paint. Do not allow the brake fluid container or the master cylinder reservoir to remain open any longer than necessary. Brake fluid absorbs moisture from the air, reducing its effectiveness and causing corrosion in the lines.

Power Steering System

FLUID RECOMMENDATION

When adding or changing the power steering fluid, use Dexron® ATF (Automatic Transmission Fluid).

LEVEL CHECK

▶ **See Figures 172, 173, 174, 175 and 176**

The power steering hydraulic fluid level is checked with a dipstick inserted into the pump reservoir. The level can be checked (check fluid level periodically) with the fluid either warm or cold. The car should be parked on a level surface. Check the fluid level every 12 months or 15,000 miles, whichever comes first.

1. With the engine OFF, unscrew the dipstick and check the level. If the engine is warm, the level should be within the proper range on the HOT scale. If the engine is cold, the level should be within the proper range on the COLD scale (see illustrations).

2. If the level is low, add DEXRON® ATF until correct. Be careful not to overfill, which will cause fluid loss and seal damage.

Fig. 169 Unscrew the cap from the top of the brake master cylinder

Fig. 170 A filter helps keep contaminants from entering the brake hydraulic system

Fig. 171 Add only clean brake fluid from a sealed container

Fig. 172 Unscrew the cap, which has a built-in dipstick

Fig. 173 Slowly add the power steering fluid; be careful not to overfill

Fig. 174 Instead of a dipstick, some reservoirs have level markings on the side

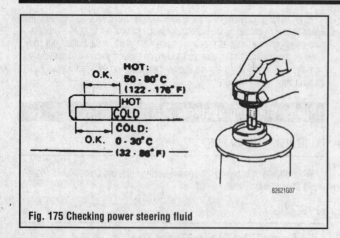

Fig. 175 Checking power steering fluid

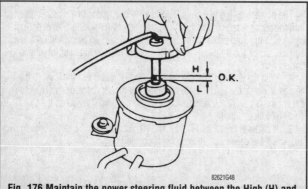

Fig. 176 Maintain the power steering fluid between the High (H) and Low (L) marks

Steering Gear Box—Except Rack and Pinion Type

FLUID RECOMMENDATIONS

When fill the steering gear box use only standard GL-4 hypoid type gear oil, SAE 80W or SAE 80W/90.

LEVEL CHECK

▶ See Figure 177

Check the level of the lubricant in the steering gear every 15,000 miles or 12 months. If the level is low, check for leakage. Any oily film is not considered a leak; solid grease must be present. The lubricant is added and checked through the filler plug hole in the top of the steering gearbox.

Chassis Greasing

The manufacturer doesn't install lubrication fittings in lube points on the steering linkage or suspension. On some replacement part applications you can buy metric threaded fittings to grease these points or use a pointed, rubber tip end on your grease gun. Lubricate all joints equipped with a plug, every 15,000

TRAILER TOWING

General Recommendations

Your vehicle was primarily designed to carry passengers and cargo. It is important to remember that towing a trailer will place additional loads on your vehicles engine, drive train, steering, braking and other systems. However, if you decide to tow a trailer, using the prior equipment is a must.

Local laws may require specific equipment such as trailer brakes or fender mounted mirrors. Check your local laws.

Fig. 177 Check the fluid level in the steering gearbox through the filler hole in top

miles or once a year with NLGI No. 2 (Lithium base) grease. Replace the plugs after lubrication.

Body Lubrication

Lubricate all locks and hinges with multipurpose grease every 15,000 miles or 12 months.

Wheel Bearings

REMOVAL, PACKING AND INSTALLATION

Rear Wheel Drive Vehicles

200SX AND 240SX MODELS

Clean, inspect and repack wheel front wheel bearings every 30,000 miles or 24 months on 1982–88 200SX rear wheel drive models. The 1989–92 240SX rear wheel drive models uses a one-piece style front wheel bearing assembly no maintenance is required.

In order to clean and repack the front wheel bearings on the 200SX rear wheel drive models the wheel bearings must be removed from the wheel hub. You should also check that the wheel bearings operate smoothly and their is no excess amount of play (looseness) in the bearing assembly before removing the wheel bearing. To remove, install and adjust the wheel bearings and for all other service procedures for "Front Wheel Bearings" rear wheel drive vehicles refer to Section 8 in this manual.

Front Wheel Drive Vehicles

STANZA MODELS

On front wheel drive vehicles the front wheel bearings are different than on rear wheel drive vehicles and (front hub must be removed — bearing assembly pressed in and out) no normal maintenance is required. For service procedures (removal and installation) for "Front Wheel Bearings" front wheel drive vehicles refer to Section 8 in this manual.

The rear wheel bearings on front wheel drive vehicles are similar to the front bearings on rear wheel drive vehicles. In order to clean and repack the rear wheel bearings on the Stanza front wheel drive models the wheel bearings must be removed from the wheel hub. Clean, inspect and repack wheel rear wheel bearings every 60,000 miles or 48 months. To remove, install and adjust the rear wheel bearings and for all other service procedures for "Rear Wheel Bearings" front wheel drive vehicles refer to Section 8 in this manual.

Trailer Weight

The weight of the trailer is the most important factor. A good weight-to-horsepower ratio is about 35:1, 35 lbs. of Gross Combined Weight (GCW) for every horsepower your engine develops. Multiply the engine's rated horsepower by 35 and subtract the weight of the vehicle passengers and luggage. The number remaining is the approximate ideal maximum weight you should tow, although a numerically higher axle ratio can help compensate for heavier weight.

Hitch (Tongue) Weight

▶ **See Figure 178**

Calculate the hitch weight in order to select a proper hitch. The weight of the hitch is usually 9–11% of the trailer gross weight and should be measured with the trailer loaded. Hitches fall into various categories: those that mount on the frame and rear bumper, the bolt-on type, or the weld-on distribution type used for larger trailers. Axle mounted or clamp-on bumper hitches should never be used.

Check the gross weight rating of your trailer. Tongue weight is usually figured as 10% of gross trailer weight. Therefore, a trailer with a maximum gross weight of 2000 lbs. will have a maximum tongue weight of 200 lbs. Class I trailers fall into this category. Class II trailers are those with a gross weight rating of 2000–3000 lbs., while Class III trailers fall into the 3500–6000 lbs. category. Class IV trailers are those over 6000 lbs. and are for use with fifth wheel trucks, only.

When you've determined the hitch that you'll need, follow the manufacturer's installation instructions, exactly, especially when it comes to fastener torques. The hitch will subjected to a lot of stress and good hitches come with hardened bolts. Never substitute an inferior bolt for a hardened bolt.

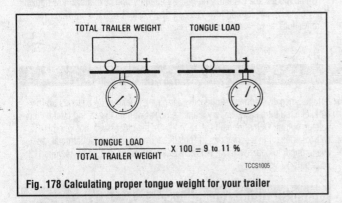

$$\frac{\text{TONGUE LOAD}}{\text{TOTAL TRAILER WEIGHT}} \times 100 = 9 \text{ to } 11 \%$$

TCCS1005

Fig. 178 Calculating proper tongue weight for your trailer

Engine

One of the most common, if not THE most common, problems associated with trailer towing is engine overheating. If you have a cooling system without an expansion tank, you'll definitely need to get an aftermarket expansion tank kit, preferably one with at least a 2 quart capacity. These kits are easily installed on the radiator's overflow hose, and come with a pressure cap designed for expansion tanks.

Aftermarket engine oil coolers are helpful for prolonging engine oil life and reducing overall engine temperatures. Both of these factors increase engine life. While not absolutely necessary in towing Class I and some Class II trailers, they are recommended for heavier Class II and all Class III towing. Engine oil cooler systems usually consist of an adapter, screwed on in place of the oil filter, a remote filter mounting and a multi-tube, finned heat exchanger, which is mounted in front of the radiator or air conditioning condenser.

Transmission/Transaxle

An automatic transmission/transaxle is usually recommended for trailer towing. Modern automatics have proven reliable and, of course, easy to operate, in trailer towing. The increased load of a trailer, however, causes an increase in the temperature of the automatic transmission/transaxle fluid. Heat is the worst enemy of an automatic transmission. As the temperature of the fluid increases, the life of the fluid decreases.

It is essential, therefore, that you install an automatic transmission/transaxle cooler. The cooler, which consists of a multi-tube, finned heat exchanger, is usually installed in front of the radiator or air conditioning compressor, and hooked in-line with the transmission/transaxle cooler tank inlet line. Follow the cooler manufacturer's installation instructions.

Select a cooler of at least adequate capacity, based upon the combined gross weights of the vehicle and trailer.

Cooler manufacturers recommend that you use an aftermarket cooler in addition to, and not instead of, the present cooling tank in your radiator. If you do want to use it in place of the radiator cooling tank, get a cooler at least two sizes larger than normally necessary.

➡**A transmission/transaxle cooler can, sometimes, cause slow or harsh shifting in the transmission/transaxle during cold weather, until the fluid has a chance to come up to normal operating temperature. Some coolers can be purchased with or retrofitted with a temperature bypass valve which will allow fluid flow through the cooler only when the fluid has reached above a certain operating temperature.**

Handling A Trailer

Towing a trailer with ease and safety requires a certain amount of experience. It's a good idea to learn the feel of a trailer by practicing turning, stopping and backing in an open area such as an empty parking lot.

TOWING THE VEHICLE

▶ **See Figures 179, 180, 181 and 182**

On rear wheel drive vehicles the car can be flat-towed safely (with the transmission in Neutral and the ignition key **OFF** — see the following note) from the front at speeds of 30 mph or less (no more than 40 miles distance). The car must either be towed with the rear drive wheels off the ground or the driveshaft disconnected if: towing speeds are to be over 30 mph, or towing distance is over 40 miles, or transmission or rear axle problems exist.

➡**When towing rear wheel drive vehicle with the front wheels on the ground secure the steering wheel in a straight-ahead position with a**

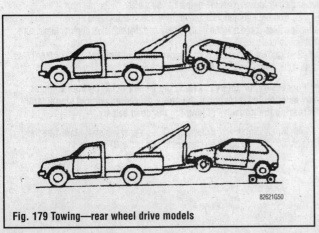

82621G50

Fig. 179 Towing—rear wheel drive models

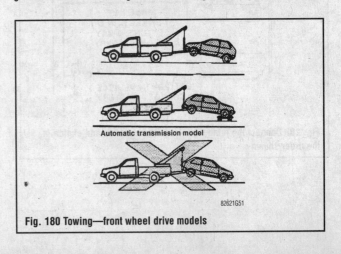

Automatic transmission model

82621G51

Fig. 180 Towing—front wheel drive models

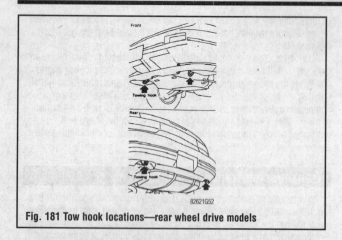

Fig. 181 Tow hook locations—rear wheel drive models

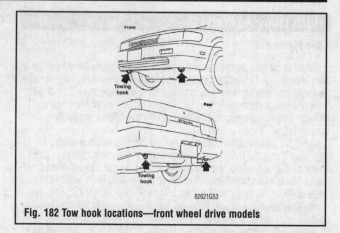

Fig. 182 Tow hook locations—front wheel drive models

rope or similar device. Never place the ignition key in the LOCK position. This will result in damage to the steering lock mechanism.

When towing from the front of the vehicle, make sure that the transmission, axles, steering system and power train are in working condition. If any unit is damaged, a dolly under the rear wheels must be used.

On front wheel drive vehicles never tow with rear wheels raised (with front drive wheels on the ground) as this may cause serious and expensive damage

to the transaxle. On front wheel drive models Datsun/Nissan recommends that the vehicle be towed with the driving (front) wheels off the ground using proper equipment. Refer to the illustrations.

On all models there are towing hooks under the vehicle to attach tow hooks. If any question concerning towing are in doubt, check with the "Towing Procedure Manual" at your local Datsun/Nissan dealer.

JUMP STARTING A DEAD BATTERY

♦ See Figure 183

Whenever a vehicle is jump started, precautions must be followed in order to prevent the possibility of personal injury. Remember that batteries contain a small amount of explosive hydrogen gas which is a by-product of battery charging. Sparks should always be avoided when working around batteries, especially when attaching jumper cables. To minimize the possibility of accidental sparks, follow the procedure carefully.

✳✳ CAUTION

NEVER hook the batteries up in a series circuit or the entire electrical system will go up in smoke, including the starter!

Vehicles equipped with a diesel engine may utilize two 12 volt batteries. If so, the batteries are connected in a parallel circuit (positive terminal to positive

terminal, negative terminal to negative terminal). Hooking the batteries up in parallel circuit increases battery cranking power without increasing total battery voltage output. Output remains at 12 volts. On the other hand, hooking two 12 volt batteries up in a series circuit (positive terminal to negative terminal, positive terminal to negative terminal) increases total battery output to 24 volts (12 volts plus 12 volts).

Jump Starting Precautions

- Be sure that both batteries are of the same voltage. Vehicles covered by this manual and most vehicles on the road today utilize a 12 volt charging system.
- Be sure that both batteries are of the same polarity (have the same terminal, in most cases NEGATIVE grounded).
- Be sure that the vehicles are not touching or a short could occur.
- On serviceable batteries, be sure the vent cap holes are not obstructed.
- Do not smoke or allow sparks anywhere near the batteries.
- In cold weather, make sure the battery electrolyte is not frozen. This can occur more readily in a battery that has been in a state of discharge.
- Do not allow electrolyte to contact your skin or clothing.

Jump Starting Procedure

1. Make sure that the voltages of the 2 batteries are the same. Most batteries and charging systems are of the 12 volt variety.
2. Pull the jumping vehicle (with the good battery) into a position so the jumper cables can reach the dead battery and that vehicle's engine. Make sure that the vehicles do NOT touch.
3. Place the transmissions of both vehicles in **Neutral** (MT) or **P** (AT), as applicable, then firmly set their parking brakes.

➡️If necessary for safety reasons, the hazard lights on both vehicles may be operated throughout the entire procedure without significantly increasing the difficulty of jumping the dead battery.

4. Turn all lights and accessories OFF on both vehicles. Make sure the ignition switches on both vehicles are turned to the **OFF** position.

```
MAKE CONNECTIONS IN NUMERICAL ORDER

①  FIRST JUMPER CABLE

DO NOT ALLOW
VEHICLES TO TOUCH
                              DISCHARGED
                              BATTERY

          ④        SECOND JUMPER CABLE

                    MAKE LAST
                    CONNECTION ON
                    ENGINE, AWAY
                    FROM BATTERY

                    ③

                    BATTERY IN VEHICLE
                    WITH CHARGED BATTERY
                              ②
                                    TCCS1080
```

Fig. 183 Connect the jumper cables to the batteries and engine in the order shown

5. Cover the battery cell caps with a rag, but do not cover the terminals.

6. Make sure the terminals on both batteries are clean and free of corrosion or proper electrical connection will be impeded. If necessary, clean the battery terminals before proceeding.

7. Identify the positive (+) and negative (-) terminals on both batteries.

8. Connect the first jumper cable to the positive (+) terminal of the dead battery, then connect the other end of that cable to the positive (+) terminal of the booster (good) battery.

9. Connect one end of the other jumper cable to the negative (-) terminal on the booster battery and the final cable clamp to an engine bolt head, alternator bracket or other solid, metallic point on the engine with the dead battery. Try to pick a ground on the engine that is positioned away from the battery in order to minimize the possibility of the 2 clamps touching should one loosen during the procedure. DO NOT connect this clamp to the negative (-) terminal of the bad battery.

✳✳ CAUTION

Be very careful to keep the jumper cables away from moving parts (cooling fan, belts, etc.) on both engines.

10. Check to make sure that the cables are routed away from any moving parts, then start the donor vehicle's engine. Run the engine at moderate speed for several minutes to allow the dead battery a chance to receive some initial charge.

11. With the donor vehicle's engine still running slightly above idle, try to start the vehicle with the dead battery. Crank the engine for no more than 10 seconds at a time and let the starter cool for at least 20 seconds between tries. If the vehicle does not start in 3 tries, it is likely that something else is also wrong or that the battery needs additional time to charge.

12. Once the vehicle is started, allow it to run at idle for a few seconds to make sure that it is operating properly.

13. Turn ON the headlights, heater blower and, if equipped, the rear defroster of both vehicles in order to reduce the severity of voltage spikes and subsequent risk of damage to the vehicles' electrical systems when the cables are disconnected. This step is especially important to any vehicle equipped with computer control modules.

14. Carefully disconnect the cables in the reverse order of connection. Start with the negative cable that is attached to the engine ground, then the negative cable on the donor battery. Disconnect the positive cable from the donor battery and finally, disconnect the positive cable from the formerly dead battery. Be careful when disconnecting the cables from the positive terminals not to allow the alligator clips to touch any metal on either vehicle or a short and sparks will occur.

JACKING

▶ **See Figures 184 and 185**

Never use the tire changing jack (the little jack supplied with the car) for anything other than changing a flat out on the road. These jacks are simply not safe enough for any type of vehicle service except tire changing!

The service operations in this manual often require that one end or the other,

or both, of the car be raised and safely supported. For this reason a hydraulic floor jack of at least 1½ ton capacity is as necessary as a spark plug socket to you, the do-it-yourself owner/mechanic. The cost of these jacks (invest in a good quality unit) is actually quite reasonable considering how they pay for themselves again and again over the years.

Along with a hydraulic floor jack should be at least two sturdy jackstands. These are a necessity if you intend to work underneath the car. Never work under the car when it is only supported by a jack!

Drive-on ramps are an alternative method of raising the front end of the car. They are commercially available or can be fabricated from heavy lumber or steel. Be sure to always block the wheels when using ramps.

✳✳ CAUTION

NEVER use concrete cinder blocks to support the car. They are likely to break if the load is not evenly distributed. They should never be trusted when you are underneath the car!

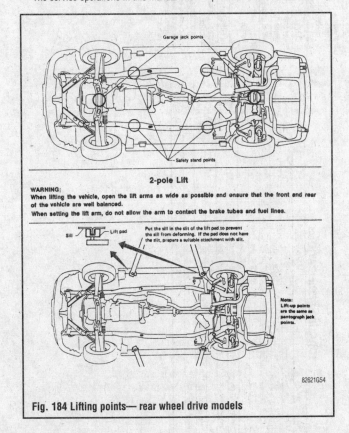

Fig. 184 Lifting points — rear wheel drive models

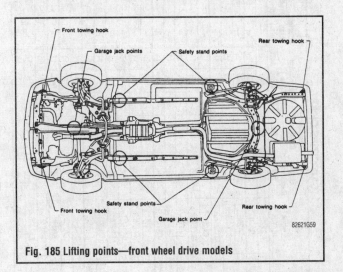

Fig. 185 Lifting points—front wheel drive models

MAINTENANCE INTERVALS CHART

Intervals are for number of months or thousands of miles, whichever comes first.

NOTE: Heavy-duty operation (trailer towing, prolonged idling, severe stop and start driving) should be accompanied by a 50% increase in maintenance. Cut the intervals in half for these conditions. Refer to text.

Maintenance	Service Interval
Air Cleaner (Replace)	30,000 miles or 24 months
Air Induction Valve Filter (Replace) ①	30,000 miles or 24 months
PCV Valve (Inspect)	30,000 miles or 24 months
Evaporative Emissions System	30,000 miles or 24 months
Check Fuel/Vapor Lines	
Carbon Canister	
Battery	
Fluid Level (Check)	Once a Month
Specific Gravity (Check)	Once a Year
Cables and Clamps (Check)	Once a Year
Belt Tension (Inspect)	15,000 miles or 12 months
Hoses (Check)	15,000 miles or 12 months
Radiator Coolant	
Check	Weekly
Change	24 months or 30,000 miles
Engine Oil and Filter	
Check Oil Level	Weekly
Change	6 months or 7,500 miles (3,750 miles or 3 months 1990-92)
	6 months or 5,000 miles (Turbocharged Engine)
Manual Transmission/Transaxle	
Check	12 months or 15,000 miles
Change	24 months or 30,000 miles (Heavy Duty Operation)
Automatic Transmission/Transaxle	
Check	6 months or 7,500 miles
Change	30,000 miles or 24 months (Heavy Duty Operation)
Brake and Clutch Fluid	
Check	15,000 miles or 12 months
Rear Axle	
Check	12 months or 15,000 miles
Change	30,000 miles Heavy Duty Operation
Steering Gear	
Check	15,000 miles or 12 months
Power Steering Fluid	
Check	12 months or 15,000 miles
Power Steering Lines and Hoses	12 months or 15,000 miles
Tires	
Rotate	7,500 miles or 6 months
	15,000 miles or 12 months
Fuel Filter (Inspect)	30,000 miles or 24 months ②
Chassis Lubrication	
Lubricate	12 months or 15,000 miles
Inspect seals	

① On models so equipped
② Change the filter as soon as there is any indication of clogging by abnormal dirt in the fuel

82621C02

CAPACITIES CHART

Year	Model	Engine ID/VIN	Engine Displacement liter	Engine Crankcase with Filter	Transmission (pts.) 4-Spd	Transmission (pts.) 5-Spd	Transmission (pts.) Auto.	Transfer case (pts.)	Drive Axle Front (pts.)	Drive Axle Rear (pts.)	Fuel Tank (gal.)	Cooling System (qts.)
1982-83	200SX	222E	2.2L	4.5	4¼	—	12	—	—	2⅛	14①	10⅛
	Stanza	CA20	2.0L	4.0	5¾	—	—	—	—	—	14¼	7¾
1984-85	200SX	CA20E	2.0L	4.0	4½	—	15	—	—	2½	14	9⅛
	200SX	CA18ET (Turbo)	1.8L	4.0	4½	—	15	—	—	2½	14	9⅛
	Stanza	CA20, CA20E	2.0L	4.0	5¾	—	14	—	—	—	14¼	7½
1986	200SX	CA20E	2.0L	4.0	4½	—	15	—	—	2½	14	9⅛
	200SX	CA18ET (Turbo)	1.8L	4.0	4½	—	15	—	—	2½	14	9⅛
	Stanza	CA20E	2.0L	4.0	5¾	—	14	—	—	—	14¼	7½
	Stanza Wagon (2WD)	CA20E	2.0L	4.0	—	10	14	—	—	—	15⅞	7⅛
	Stanza Wagon (4WD)	CA20E	2.0L	4.0	—	10	14	3	2½	—	15⅞	7⅛
1987-88	200SX	VG30E	3.0L	4.5	4¼	—	15	—	—	2½	14	9⅝
	200SX	CA20E	2.0L	4.0	4¼	—	15	—	—	2½	14	9⅛
	200SX	CA18ET	1.8L	4.0	4¼	—	15	—	—	2½	14	9⅛
	Stanza	CA20E	2.0L	4.0	—	10	14	—	—	—	15⅞	7¾
	Stanza Wagon (2WD)	CA20E	2.0L	4.0	—	10	14	—	—	—	15⅞	7⅛
	Stanza Wagon (4WD)	CA20E	2.0L	4.0	—	10	14	3	2⅛	—	13¼	7⅛
1989	240SX	KA24E	2.4L	4.0	5⅛	—	17	—	—	2¾	15⅞	7⅛
	Stanza	CA20E	2.0L	4.0	—	10	14	—	—	—	15⅞	7¾
1990	240SX	KA24E	2.4L	4.0	5⅛	—	17	—	—	4	15⅞	7⅛
	Stanza	KA24E	2.4L	4.0	—	10	15	—	—	—	16⅞	7⅞
1991-92	240SX	KA24DE	2.4L	4.0	5⅛	—	17	—	—	4	15⅞	7⅛
	Stanza	KA24E	2.4L	4.0	—	10	15	—	—	—	16⅞	7⅞

① 1982 200SX Hatchback 15⅞ gal.

82621C01

TORQUE SPECIFICATIONS

Component	U.S.	Metric
Fuel line clamps:	1 ft. lb.	1.5 Nm
Engine oil drain plug:	22-29 ft. lbs	29-39Nm
Spark plug:	14-22 ft. lbs.	20-29 Nm
Wheel Lug nuts:	58-72 ft. lbs.	78-98 Nm
Alternator adjusting bolt:	10-12 ft. lbs	14-17 Nm
Manual transmission drain and fill plugs:	18-25 ft. lbs	25-34 Nm
Differential carrier drain and fill plugs:	29-43 ft. lbs.	39-59 Nm
Transfer drain and fill plug	14-22 ft. lbs.	20-29 Nm
Manual transaxle drain and fill plugs:	11-14 ft. lbs.	15-20 Nm
Automatic transaxle drain and fill plugs:	11-14 ft. lbs.	15-20 Nm
Engine block drain plug:	25-33 ft. lbs.	34-44 Nm

82621C03

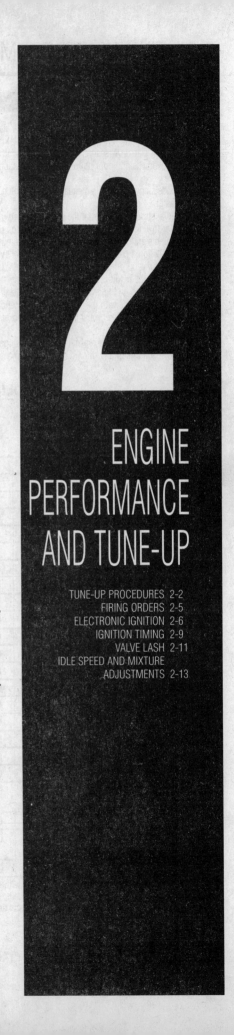

2

ENGINE PERFORMANCE AND TUNE-UP

TUNE-UP PROCEDURES

In order to extract the full measure of performance and economy from your engine it is essential that it is properly tuned at regular intervals. A regular tune-up will keep your Datsun/Nissan engine running smoothly and will prevent the annoying breakdowns and poor performance often associated with an unmaintained engine.

On all models covered in this manual, the spark plug replacement interval is 30,000 miles or 24 months.

This interval should be halved if the car is operated under severe conditions such as trailer towing, prolonged idling, start-and-stop driving, or if starting or running problems are noticed. It is assumed that the routine maintenance described in Section 1 has been kept up, as this will have a decided effect on the results of a tune-up. All of the applicable steps of a tune-up should be followed in order, as the result is a cumulative one.

If the specifications on the underhood tune-up sticker in the engine compartment of your car disagree with the "Tune-Up Specifications Chart" in this section, the figures on the sticker must be used. The sticker often reflects changes made during the production run.

A tune-up should consist of replacing the spark plugs and checking spark plug wires, distributor cap and rotor. If necessary replace the air filter, gas and all other emission filters. All vacuum lines and hoses should also be checked and all necessary engine adjustments should also be made at this time. It might be noted that the tune-up is a good time to take a look around the engine compartment for problems in the making, such as oil and fuel leaks, deteriorating radiator or heater hoses, loose and/or frayed fan belts and etc.

Spark Plugs

▶ See Figure 1

A typical spark plug consists of a metal shell surrounding a ceramic insulator. A metal electrode extends downward through the center of the insulator and protrudes a small distance. Located at the end of the plug and attached to the side of the outer metal shell is the side electrode. The side electrode bends in at a 90° angle so that its tip is just past and parallel to the tip of the center electrode. The distance between these two electrodes (measured in thousandths of an inch or hundredths of a millimeter) is called the spark plug gap.

The spark plug does not produce a spark, but instead provides a gap across

GASOLINE ENGINE TUNE-UP SPECIFICATIONS

Year	Engine ID/VIN	Engine Displacement liter	Spark Plugs Gap (in.)	Ignition Timing (deg.) MT	Ignition Timing (deg.) AT	Fuel Pump (psi)	Idle Speed (rpm) MT	Idle Speed (rpm) AT	Valve Clearance (in.) In.	Valve Clearance (in.) Ex.
1982	222E	2.2L	0.031–0.035	8B	8B	37	750	700	0.012	0.012
	CA20	2.0L	0.039–0.043	0	0	3.8	650	—	0.012	0.012
1983	222E	2.2L	0.031–0.035	8B	8B	37	750	700	0.012	0.012
	CA20	2.0L	0.039–0.043	0	0	3.8	650	650	0.012	0.012
1984	CA20E	2.0L	0.039–0.043	0	0	37	750	700	0.012	0.012
	CA18ET	1.8L	0.039–0.043	15B	15B	37	750	700	0.012	0.012
1985	CA20E	2.0L	0.039–0.043	4B	0	37	750	700	0.012	0.012
	CA18ET	1.8L	0.039–0.043	15B	—	37	750	—	0.012	0.012
1986	CA20E	2.0L	0.039–0.043	4B	0①	37	750	700	0.012	0.012
	CA18ET	1.8L	0.039–0.043	15B	—	37	750	—	0.012	0.012
1987	CA20E	2.0L	0.039–0.043	15B	15B	37	750	700	NA②	NA②
	CA18ET	1.8L	0.039–0.043	15B	—	37	750	—	0.012	0.012
	VG30E	3.0L	0.039–0.043	20B	20B	37	700	700	NA	NA
1988	CA20E	2.0L	0.039–0.043	15B	15B	37	750	750	NA②	NA②
	CA18ET	1.8L	0.039–0.043	15B	—	37	750	—	0.012	0.012
	VG30E	3.0L	0.039–0.043	20B	20B	37	700	700	NA	NA
1989	KA24E	2.4L	0.039–0.043	15B	15B	37	750	750	NA	NA
	CA20E	2.0L	0.039–0.043	15B	15B	37	750	700	NA	NA
1990	KA24E	2.4L	0.039–0.043	15B	15B	37	750	750	NA	NA
1991	KA24DE	2.4L	0.039–0.043	20B	20B	37	700	700	0.012–0.015	0.013–0.016
	KA24E	2.4L	0.039–0.043	15B	15B	37	750	750	NA	NA
1992	KA24DE	2.4L	0.039–0.043	20B	20B	37	700	700	0.012–0.015	0.013–0.016
	KA24E	2.4L	0.039–0.043	15B	15B	37	750	750	NA	NA

NOTE: The lowest cylinder pressure should be within 75% of the highest cylinder pressure reading. For example, if the highest cylinder is 134 psi, the lowest should be 101. Engine should be at normal operating temperature with throttle valve in the wide open position.
The underhood specifications sticker often refects tune-up specification changes in production. Sticker figures must be used if they disagree with those in this chart.
NA—Non adjustable
① 4B—1986 2WD and 4WD Wagons
② Valve clearnace intake and exhaust 0.012—
   1987 Stanza Wagon only

82622C01

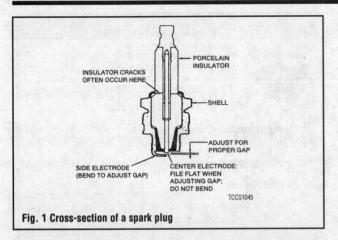

Fig. 1 Cross-section of a spark plug

which the current can arc. The coil produces anywhere from 20,000 to 50,000 volts (depending on the type and application) which travels through the wires to the spark plugs. The current passes along the center electrode and jumps the gap to the side electrode, and in doing so, ignites the air/fuel mixture in the combustion chamber.

SPARK PLUG HEAT RANGE

▶ **See Figure 2**

Spark plug heat range is the ability of the plug to dissipate heat. The longer the insulator (or the farther it extends into the engine), the hotter the plug will operate; the shorter the insulator (the closer the electrode is to the block's cooling passages) the cooler it will operate. A plug that absorbs little heat and remains too cool will quickly accumulate deposits of oil and carbon since it is not hot enough to burn them off. This leads to plug fouling and consequently to misfiring. A plug that absorbs too much heat will have no deposits but, due to the excessive heat, the electrodes will burn away quickly and might possibly lead to preignition or other ignition problems. Preignition takes place when plug tips get so hot that they glow sufficiently to ignite the air/fuel mixture before the actual spark occurs. This early ignition will usually cause a pinging during low speeds and heavy loads.

The general rule of thumb for choosing the correct heat range when picking a spark plug is: if most of your driving is long distance, high speed travel, use a colder plug; if most of your driving is stop and go, use a hotter plug. Original equipment plugs are generally a good compromise between the 2 styles and most people never have the need to change their plugs from the factory-recommended heat range.

REMOVAL & INSTALLATION

A set of spark plugs usually requires replacement after about 20,000–30,000 miles (32,000–48,000 km), depending on your style of driving. In normal operation plug gap increases about 0.001 in. (0.025mm) for every 2500 miles (4000 km). As the gap increases, the plug's voltage requirement also increases. It requires a greater voltage to jump the wider gap and about two to three times as much voltage to fire the plug at high speeds than at idle. The improved air/fuel ratio control of modern fuel injection combined with the higher voltage output of modern ignition systems will often allow an engine to run significantly longer on a set of standard spark plugs, but keep in mind that efficiency will drop as the gap widens (along with fuel economy and power).

When you're removing spark plugs, work on one at a time. Don't start by removing the plug wires all at once, because, unless you number them, they may become mixed up. Take a minute before you begin and number the wires with tape.

1. Disconnect the negative battery cable, and if the vehicle has been run recently, allow the engine to thoroughly cool.

2. Carefully twist the spark plug wire boot to loosen it, then pull upward and remove the boot from the plug. Be sure to pull on the boot and not on the wire, otherwise the connector located inside the boot may become separated.

3. Using compressed air, blow any water or debris from the spark plug well to assure that no harmful contaminants are allowed to enter the combustion chamber when the spark plug is removed. If compressed air is not available, use a rag or a brush to clean the area.

➡**Remove the spark plugs when the engine is cold, if possible, to prevent damage to the threads. If removal of the plugs is difficult, apply a few drops of penetrating oil or silicone spray to the area around the base of the plug, and allow it a few minutes to work.**

4. Using a spark plug socket that is equipped with a rubber insert to properly hold the plug, turn the spark plug counterclockwise to loosen and remove the spark plug from the bore.

✳✳ WARNING

Be sure not to use a flexible extension on the socket. Use of a flexible extension may allow a shear force to be applied to the plug. A shear force could break the plug off in the cylinder head, leading to costly and frustrating repairs.

To install:

5. Inspect the spark plug boot for tears or damage. If a damaged boot is found, the spark plug wire must be replaced.

6. Using a wire feeler gauge, check and adjust the spark plug gap. When using a gauge, the proper size should pass between the electrodes with a slight drag. The next larger size should not be able to pass while the next smaller size should pass freely.

7. Carefully thread the plug into the bore by hand. If resistance is felt before the plug is almost completely threaded, back the plug out and begin threading again. In small, hard to reach areas, an old spark plug wire and boot could be used as a threading tool. The boot will hold the plug while you twist the end of the wire and the wire is supple enough to twist before it would allow the plug to crossthread.

✳✳ WARNING

Do not use the spark plug socket to thread the plugs. Always carefully thread the plug by hand or using an old plug wire to prevent the possibility of crossthreading and damaging the cylinder head bore.

8. Carefully tighten the spark plug. If the plug you are installing is equipped with a crush washer, seat the plug, then tighten about ¼ turn to crush the washer. If you are installing a tapered seat plug, tighten the plug to specifications provided by the vehicle or plug manufacturer.

9. Apply a small amount of silicone dielectric compound to the end of the spark plug lead or inside the spark plug boot to prevent sticking, then install the boot to the spark plug and push until it clicks into place. The click may be felt or heard, then gently pull back on the boot to assure proper contact.

INSPECTION & GAPPING

▶ **See Figures 3, 4, 5, 6 and 7**

Check the plugs for deposits and wear. If they are not going to be replaced, clean the plugs thoroughly. Remember that any kind of deposit will decrease

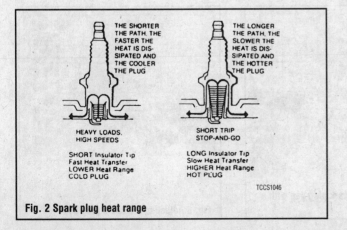

Fig. 2 Spark plug heat range

A normally worn spark plug should have light tan or gray deposits on the firing tip.

A carbon fouled plug, identified by soft, sooty, black deposits, may indicate an improperly tuned vehicle. Check the air cleaner, ignition components and engine control system.

This spark plug has been **left in the engine too long,** as evidenced by the extreme gap- Plugs with such an extreme gap can cause misfiring and stumbling accompanied by a noticeable lack of power.

An oil fouled spark plug indicates an engine with worn poston rings and/or bad valve seals allowing excessive oil to enter the chamber.

A physically damaged spark plug may be evidence of severe detonation in that cylinder. Watch that cylinder carefully between services, as a continued detonation will not only damage the plug, but could also damage the engine.

A bridged or almost bridged spark plug, identified by a build-up between the electrodes caused by excessive carbon or oil build-up on the plug.

TCCA1P40

Fig. 3 Inspect the spark plugs to determine engine running conditions

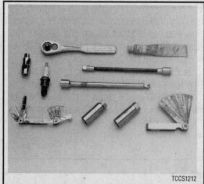

TCCS1212

Fig. 4 A variety of tools and gauges are needed for spark plug service

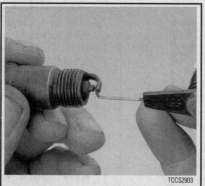

TCCS2903

Fig. 5 Checking the spark plug gap with a feeler gauge

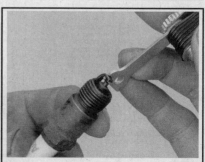

TCCS2904

Fig. 6 Adjusting the spark plug gap

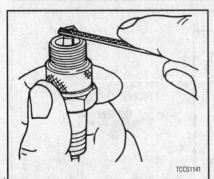

Fig. 7 If the standard plug is in good condition, the electrode may be filed flat—WARNING: do not file platinum plugs

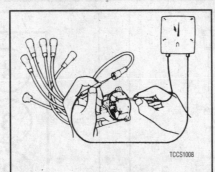

Fig. 8 Checking plug wire resistance through the distributor cap with an ohmmeter

Fig. 9 Checking individual plug wire resistance with a digital ohmmeter

the efficiency of the plug. Plugs can be cleaned on a spark plug cleaning machine, which can sometimes be found in service stations, or you can do an acceptable job of cleaning with a stiff brush. If the plugs are cleaned, the electrodes must be filed flat. Use an ignition points file, not an emery board or the like, which will leave deposits. The electrodes must be filed perfectly flat with sharp edges; rounded edges reduce the spark plug voltage by as much as 50%.

Check spark plug gap before installation. The ground electrode (the L-shaped one connected to the body of the plug) must be parallel to the center electrode and the specified size wire gauge (please refer to the Tune-Up Specifications chart for details) must pass between the electrodes with a slight drag.

➡**NEVER adjust the gap on a used platinum type spark plug.**

Always check the gap on new plugs as they are not always set correctly at the factory. Do not use a flat feeler gauge when measuring the gap on a used plug, because the reading may be inaccurate. A round-wire type gapping tool is the best way to check the gap. The correct gauge should pass through the electrode gap with a slight drag. If you're in doubt, try one size smaller and one larger. The smaller gauge should go through easily, while the larger one shouldn't go through at all. Wire gapping tools usually have a bending tool attached. Use that to adjust the side electrode until the proper distance is obtained. Absolutely never attempt to bend the center electrode. Also, be careful not to bend the side electrode too far or too often as it may weaken and break off within the engine, requiring removal of the cylinder head to retrieve it.

Spark Plug Wires

TESTING AND REPLACEMENT

⬧ **See Figures 8 and 9**

On every tune-up or 30 months/24,000 miles inspect the spark plug wires for burns, cuts, or breaks in the insulation. Check the boots and the nipples on the distributor cap. Replace any damaged wiring.

Every 45,000 miles (3 years) or so, the resistance of the wires should be checked with an ohmmeter. Wires with excessive resistance will cause misfiring, and may make the engine difficult to start in damp weather. Generally, the useful life of the cables is 45,000–60,000 miles.

To check resistance, remove the distributor cap, leaving the wires in place. Connect one lead of an ohmmeter to an electrode within the cap. Connect the other lead to the corresponding spark plug terminal (remove it from the spark plug for this test). Replace any wire which shows a resistance over 30,000Ω. Resistance should not be over 25,000Ω, and 30,000Ω must be considered the outer limit of acceptability. Also measure the resistance of the wires while shaking them to check for intermittent breaks. Refer to the illustration.

It should be remembered that resistance is also a function of length; the longer the wire, the greater the resistance. Thus, if the wires on your car are longer than the factory originals, resistance will be higher, quite possibly outside these limits.

When installing new wires, replace them one at a time to avoid mixups. Start by replacing the longest one first. Install the boot firmly over the spark plug. Route the wire over the same path as the original. Insert the nipple firmly onto the tower on the distributor cap, then install the cap cover and latches to secure the wires.

FIRING ORDERS

⬧ **See Figures 10, 11, 12, 13 and 14**

➡**To avoid confusion, remove and tag the wires one at a time, for replacement.**

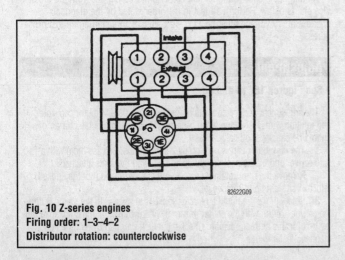

Fig. 10 Z-series engines
Firing order: 1–3–4–2
Distributor rotation: counterclockwise

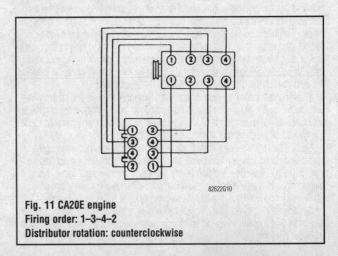

Fig. 11 CA20E engine
Firing order: 1–3–4–2
Distributor rotation: counterclockwise

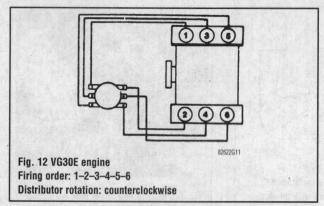

Fig. 12 VG30E engine
Firing order: 1–2–3–4–5–6
Distributor rotation: counterclockwise

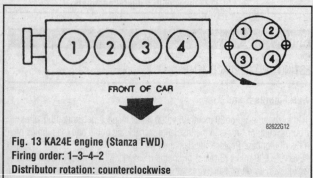

Fig. 13 KA24E engine (Stanza FWD)
Firing order: 1–3–4–2
Distributor rotation: counterclockwise

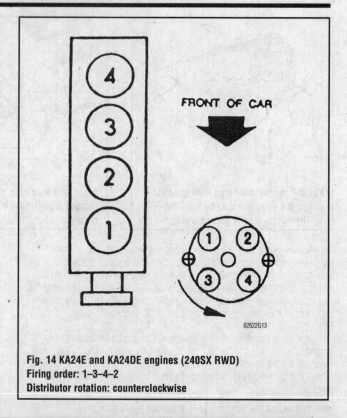

Fig. 14 KA24E and KA24DE engines (240SX RWD)
Firing order: 1–3–4–2
Distributor rotation: counterclockwise

ELECTRONIC IGNITION

Description and Operation

In 1975, in order to comply with California's tougher emission laws, Datsun/Nissan introduced electronic ignition systems for all models sold in that state. Since that time, the Datsun/Nissan electronic ignition system has undergone a metamorphosis from a standard transistorized circuit to an Integrated Circuit system (IC), and later to the special dual spark plug system used with some models.

The electronic ignition system differs from the conventional breaker points system in form only. Its function is exactly the same: to supply a spark to the spark plugs at precisely the right moment to ignite the compressed gas in the cylinders and create mechanical movement.

➡**On some late model vehicles a crankangle sensor mounted in the distributor is the basic component of the entire E.C.C.S. (Electronic Concentrated Control System). There are no adjustments necessary.**

Located in the distributor, in addition to the normal rotor cap, is a spoked rotor (reluctor) which fits on the distributor shaft where the breaker points cam is found on non-electronic ignitions. The rotor (reluctor) revolves with the top rotor cap and, as it passes a pickup coil or stator inside the distributor body, breaks a high flux phase which occurs while the space between the reluctor spokes passes the pickup coil or stator. This allows current to flow to the pickup coil or IC ignition unit. Primary ignition current is then cut off by the electronic ignition unit, allowing the magnetic field in the ignition coil to collapse, creating the spark which the distributor passes on to the spark plug.

The dual spark plug ignition system uses two ignition coils and each cylinder has two spark plugs which fire simultaneously. In this manner the engine is able to consume large quantities of recirculated exhaust gas which would cause a single spark plug cylinder to misfire and idle roughly.

Some later models use a crankangle sensor. This sensor monitors engine speed and piston position and sends to the computer signals on which the controls of the fuel injection, ignition timing and other functions are based. No maintenance is required but inspect and replace, if necessary, the spark plug wires, rotor head and the distributor cap every 30,000 miles or 24 months.

Service on electronic ignition systems consist of inspection of the distributor cap, rotor and ignition wires replacing them when necessary. Check the ignition wires for cracking of exterior insulation and for proper fit on the distributor cap

and spark plugs. These parts can be expected to last for at least 40,000 miles but you should inspect these parts every 2 years or 30,000 miles. In addition, the reluctor air gap should be checked periodically if the system has no crankangle sensor.

➡**All models without a crankangle sensor type ignition system use IC ignition unit and no pickup coil. Measure the air gap between the reluctor and stator assembly. If not within specifications (0.300.50mm), loosen stator retaining screws and adjust. Refer to the necessary service procedure.**

Diagnosis and Testing

IC IGNITION TYPE SYSTEM

▸ **See Figures 15, 16 and 17**

All diagnosis and testing should be perform in order according to the service charts below. Perform all test in the order stated by the diagnosis charts. Battery voltage must be 11.5–12.5 volts before starting all test procedures.

Adjustment

▸ **See Figures 18, 19 and 20**

The adjustment service consists of inspection of the distributor cap, rotor, and ignition wires, replacing when necessary. In addition, the reluctor air gap should be check periodically.

1. The distributor cap is held on by 2 spring clips. Release them with a screwdriver and lift the cap straight up and off, with the wires attached.

2. Remove the rotor retaining screw. Pull the rotor head (not the spoked reluctor) straight up to remove it.

3. Rotate the engine until a reluctor spoke is aligned with the stator. Bump the engine around with the starter or turn it with a wrench on the crankshaft pulley bolt for this correct position. Check the reluctor air gap by using a non-magnetic feeler gauge.

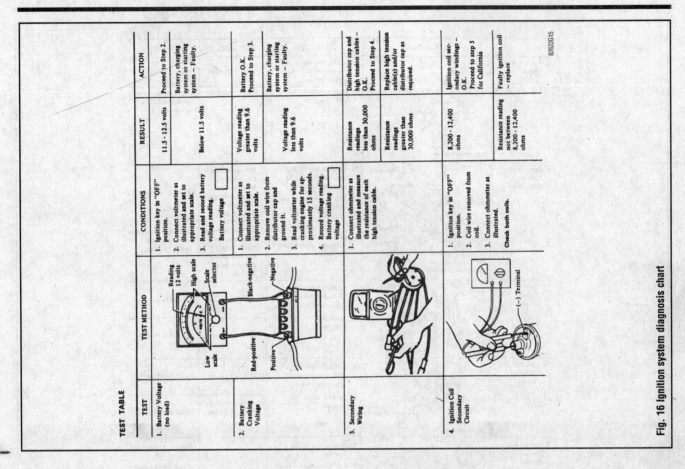

TEST TABLE

TEST	TEST METHOD	CONDITIONS	RESULT	ACTION
1. Battery Voltage (no load)	*Reading 12 volts; High scale; Low scale; Scale selector; Red-positive; Black-negative; Positive; Negative*	1. Ignition key in "OFF" position. 2. Connect voltmeter as illustrated and set to appropriate scale. 3. Read and record battery voltage reading. Battery voltage	11.5 - 12.5 volts	Proceed to Step 2.
			Below 11.5 volts	Battery, charging system or starting system – Faulty.
2. Battery Cranking Voltage		1. Connect voltmeter as illustrated and set to appropriate scale. 2. Remove coil wire from distributor cap and ground it. 3. Read voltmeter while cranking engine for approximately 15 seconds. 4. Record voltage reading. Battery cranking voltage	Voltage reading greater than 9.6 volts	Battery O.K. Proceed to Step 3.
			Voltage reading less than 9.6 volts	Battery, charging system or starting system – Faulty.
3. Secondary Wiring		1. Connect ohmmeter as illustrated and measure the resistance of each high tension cable.	Resistance readings less than 30,000 ohms	Distributor cap and high tension cables – O.K. Proceed to Step 4.
			Resistance readings greater than 30,000 ohms	Replace high tension cable(s) and/or distributor cap as required.
4. Ignition Coil Secondary Circuit	*(–) Terminal*	1. Ignition key in "OFF" position. 2. Coil wire removed from coil. 3. Connect ohmmeter as illustrated. Check both coils.	8,200 - 12,400 ohms	Ignition coil secondary windings – O.K. Proceed to step 5 for California
			Resistance reading not between 8,200 - 12,400 ohms	Faulty ignition coil – replace

Fig. 16 Ignition system diagnosis chart

82622615

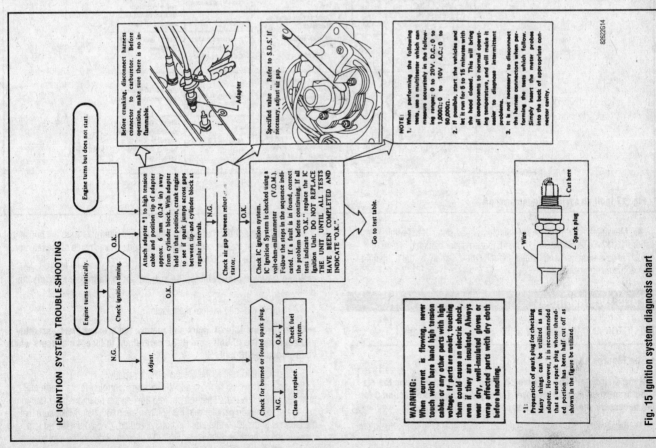

IC IGNITION SYSTEM TROUBLE-SHOOTING

Engine turns but does not start.

Engine turns erratically.

Check ignition timing. → O.K. →

N.G. → Adjust.

Check for burned or fouled spark plug. → O.K. → Check fuel system.

N.G. → Clean or replace.

Attach adapter *1 to high tension cable and position tip of adapter approx. 6 mm (0.24 in) away from cylinder block. With adapter held in that position, crank engine to see if spark jumps across gaps between tip and cylinder block at regular intervals.

Before cranking, disconnect harness connector to carburetor. Before operation, make sure there is no inflammable.

Adapter

N.G. → Check air gap between reluctor and stator. → O.K. →

Specified value .... Refer to S.D.S. If necessary, adjust air gap.

O.K. → Check IC ignition system.

Check IC Ignition system is checked using a volt-ohm-milliammeter (V.O.M.). Follow the steps in the sequence indicated. If a fault is found, correct the problem before continuing. If all tests indicate "O.K." replace the IC Ignition Unit. DO NOT REPLACE THE UNIT UNTIL ALL TESTS HAVE BEEN COMPLETED AND INDICATE "O.K."

Go to test table.

NOTE:
1. When performing the following tests, use a multitester which can measure accurately in the following ranges: 0 to 20V. D.C.:0 to 1,000Ω:0 to 10V A.C.:0 to 50,000Ω.
2. If possible, start the vehicles and let it run for 5 to 15 minutes with the hood closed. This will bring all components to normal operating temperature, and will make it easier to diagnose intermittent problem.
3. It is not necessary to disconnect the harness connectors when performing the tests which follow. Simply insert the meter probes into the back of appropriate connector cavity.

WARNING:
When current is flowing, never touch with bare hand high tension cables or any other parts with high voltage. If parts are moist, touching them could cause an electric shock, even if they are insulated gloves or wear dry, well-insulated gloves or wrap affected parts with dry cloth before handling.

Wire; Cut here; Spark plug

*1: Preparation of spark plug for checking Many things can be utilized as an adapter. However, it is recommended that a used spark plug whose threaded portion has been half cut off as shown in the figure be utilized.

Fig. 15 Ignition system diagnosis chart

82622614

TEST	TEST METHOD	CONDITIONS	RESULT	ACTION
5. Power Supply Circuit	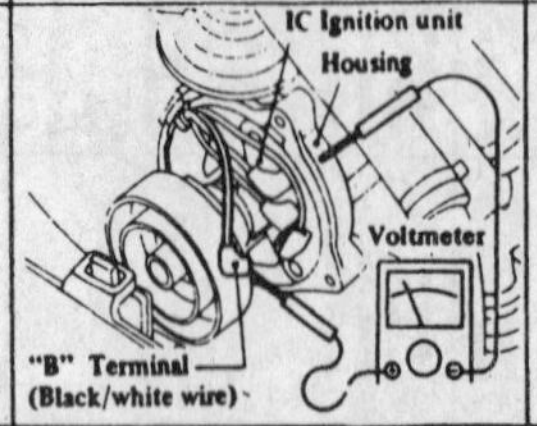 IC Ignition unit / Housing / Voltmeter / "B" Terminal (Black/white wire)	1. Connect voltmeter as illustrated and set to appropriate scale. 2. Turn ignition key to "ON" position.	11.5 - 12.5 volts	Proceed to Step 6.
			Below 11.5 volts	Check wiring from ignition switch to IC unit.
6. Power Supply Circuit (Cranking)	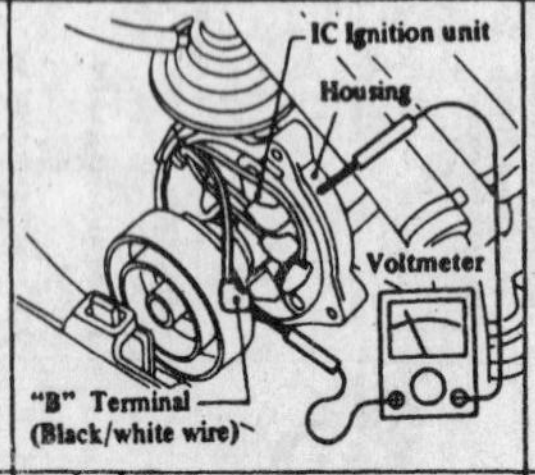 IC Ignition unit / Housing / Voltmeter / "B" Terminal (Black/white wire)	1. Connect voltmeter as illustrated and set to appropriate scale. 2. Pull out coil wire from distributor cap and ground it. 3. Turn key to "START" position and observe voltmeter while engine is cranking.	Voltage reading is less than 1 volt below battery cranking voltage and is greater than 8.6 volts.	Proceed to Step 7-A.
			Voltage reading is more than 1 volt below battery cranking voltage and/or is below 8.6 volts.	Check ignition switch and wiring from switch to IC unit.
7-A. Ignition Primary Circuit	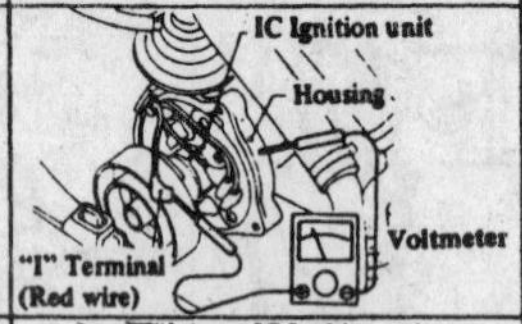 IC Ignition unit / Housing / Voltmeter / "I" Terminal (Red wire)	1. Connect voltmeter as illustrated and set to appropriate scale. 2. Ignition key in "ON" position.	11.5 - 12.5 volts	Proceed to Step 7-B.
			Below 11.5 volts	Proceed to Step 8.
7-B. Ignition Primary Circuit	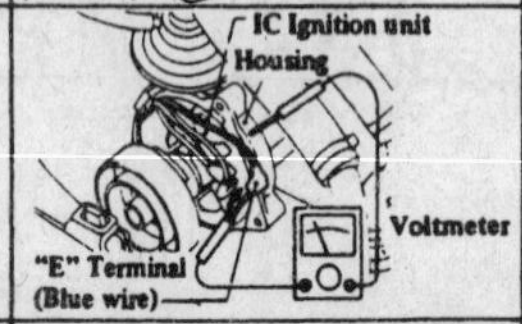 IC Ignition unit / Housing / Voltmeter / "E" Terminal (Blue wire)	1. Connect voltmeter as illustrated and set to appropriate scale. 2. Ignition key in "ON" position.	11.5 - 12.5 volts	Proceed to Step 9.
			Below 11.5 volts	Proceed to Step 8.
8. Ignition Coil Primary Circuit	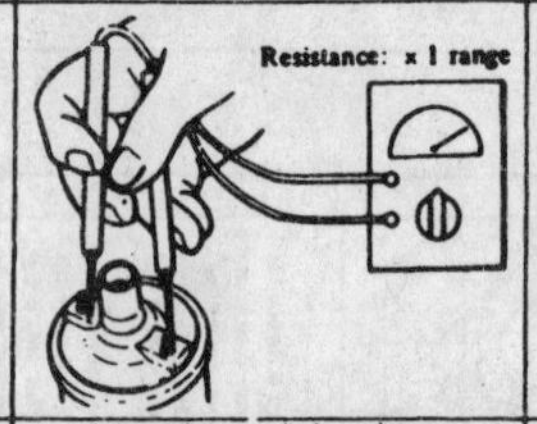 Resistance: × 1 range	1. Ignition key in "OFF" position. 2. Coil wire removed from coil. 3. Connect ohmmeter as illustrated. Check both coils.	0.84 - 1.02 ohms	Ignition coil primary winding O.K. Check ignition switch and wiring from ignition switch to coil and IC unit.
			Resistance reading not between 0.84 - 1.02 ohms	Faulty ignition coil – replace.
9. I.C. Unit Ground Circuit	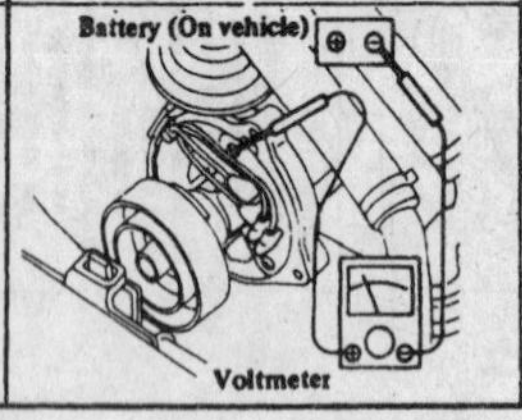 Battery (On vehicle) / Voltmeter	1. Connect voltmeter as illustrated and set to appropriate scale. 2. Pull out coil wire from distributor cap and ground it. 3. Turn key to "START" position and observe voltmeter while engine is cranking.	0.5 volts or less	Replace IC ignition unit assembly.
			More than 0.5 volts	Check distributor ground, wiring from chassis ground to battery including battery cable connections.

82622G16

Fig. 17 Ignition system diagnosis chart

4. Measure the air gap between the reluctor and stator. If not within specifications 0.012–0.020 in. (0.30–0.50mm), loosen stator retaining screws and adjust. Always properly center stator and reluctor assembly before tightening after adjustment procedure.

Parts Replacement

RELUCTOR AND IC IGNITION UNIT

♦ See Figures 18 thru 23

➥If the distributor assembly must be remove from the engine the distributor must be marked for correct installation. Refer to Section 3 for the necessary service procedures before starting this repair.

1. Remove the distributor cap and rotor. The rotor is held to the distributor shaft by a retaining screw, which must be removed.

2. Remove the wiring harness and the vacuum controller from the housing.
3. Using 2 flat bladed screwdrivers, place one on each side of the reluctor and pry it from the distributor shaft.

➥When removing the reluctor, be careful not to damage or distort the teeth.

4. Remove the roll pin from the reluctor.

➥To remove the IC unit, mark and remove the breaker plate assembly and separate the IC unit from it. Be careful not to lose the spacers when you remove the IC unit.

5. Install the IC unit to the breaker plate assembly.
6. Install the wiring harness and the vacuum controller to the distributor housing. When you install the roll pin into the reluctor position the cutout direction of the roll pin in parallel with the notch in the rotor shaft. Make sure that the harness to the IC ignition unit is tightly secured, then adjust the air gap between the reluctor and the stator to 0.30–0.50mm. Refer to the exploded views of the distributor in this manual.

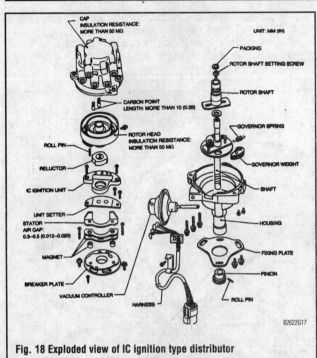

Fig. 18 Exploded view of IC ignition type distributor

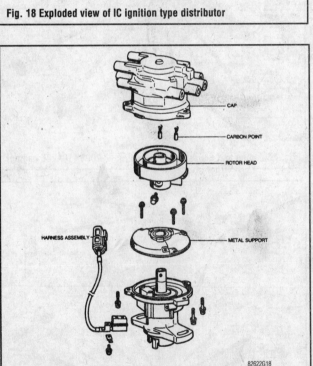

Fig. 19 Exploded view of crank angle sensor type distributor

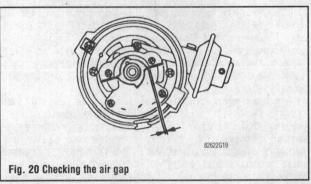

Fig. 20 Checking the air gap

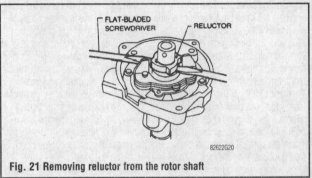

Fig. 21 Removing reluctor from the rotor shaft

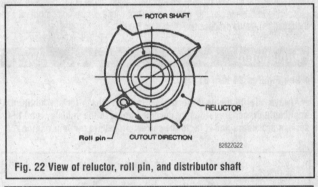

Fig. 22 View of reluctor, roll pin, and distributor shaft

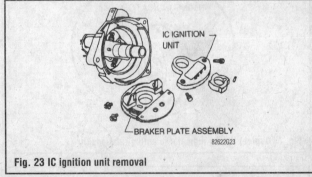

Fig. 23 IC ignition unit removal

IGNITION TIMING

Ignition timing is the measurement in degrees of crankshaft rotation, of the point at which the spark plugs fire in each of the cylinders. It is measured in degrees before or after Top Dead Center (TDC) of the compression stroke.

Because it takes a fraction of a second for the spark plug to ignite the mixture in the cylinder, the spark plug must fire a little before the piston reaches TDC. Otherwise, the mixture will not be completely ignited as the piston passes TDC and the full power of the explosion will not be used by the engine.

The timing measurement is given in degrees of crankshaft rotation before the piston reaches TDC (BTDC). If the setting for the ignition timing is 5° BTDC, the spark plug must fire 5° before each piston reaches TDC. This only holds true, however, when the engine is at idle speed.

As the engine speed increases, the pistons go faster. The spark plugs have to ignite the fuel even sooner if it is to be completely ignited when the piston reaches TDC. To do this, the distributor has two means to advance the timing of the spark as the engine speed increases: a set of centrifugal weights within the distributor, and a vacuum diaphragm, mounted on the side of the distributor.

➡ Late model 200SX (all turbo versions and 3.0L engine), 240SX and late model Stanza a crankangle sensor in the distributor is used. This sensor controls ignition timing and has other engine control functions. There is no vacuum or centrifugal advance all timing settings are controlled by the E.C.U.

If the ignition is set too far advanced (BTDC), the ignition and expansion of the fuel in the cylinder will occur too soon and tend to force the piston down while it is still traveling up. This causes engine ping. If the ignition spark is set too far retarded, after TDC (ATDC), the piston will have already passed TDC and started on its way down when the fuel is ignited. This will cause the piston to be forced down for only a portion of its travel. This will result in poor engine performance and lack of power.

Timing marks consist of a notch on the rim of the crankshaft pulley and a scale of degrees attached to the front of the engine. The notch corresponds to the position of the piston in the number 1 cylinder. A stroboscopic (dynamic) timing light is used, which is hooked into the circuit of the No. 1 cylinder spark plug. Every time the spark plug fires, the timing light flashes. By aiming the timing light at the timing marks, the exact position of the piston within the cylinder can be read, since the stroboscopic flash makes the mark on the pulley appear to be standing still. Proper timing is indicated when the notch is aligned with the correct number on the scale.

There are three basic types of timing light available. The first is a simple neon bulb with two wire connections (one for the spark plug and one for the plug wire, connecting the light in series). This type of light is quite dim, and must be held closely to the marks to be seen, but it is inexpensive. The second type of light operates from the car battery. Two alligator clips connect to the battery terminals, while a third wire connects to the spark plug with an adapter. This type of light is more expensive, but the xenon bulb provides a nice bright flash which can even be seen in sunlight. The third type replaces the battery source with 110 volt house current. Some timing lights have other functions built into them, such as dwell meters, tachometers, or remote starting switches. These are convenient, in that they reduce the tangle of wires under the hood, but may duplicate the functions of tools you already have.

You should use a timing light with an inductive pickup. This pickup simply clamps onto the No. 1 plug wire, eliminating the adapter. It is not prone to crossfiring or false triggering, which may occur with a conventional light, due to the greater voltages produced by electronic ignition.

Adjustment

▶ See Figures 24 thru 31

➡Always refer to the underhood specifications sticker for any additional applicable procedures. Identify the type engine in the vehicle, read the service procedure and refer to the correct procedure for your engine.

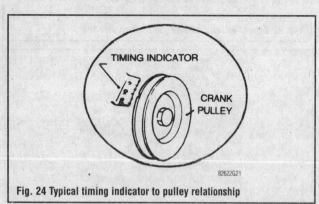

Fig. 24 Typical timing indicator to pulley relationship

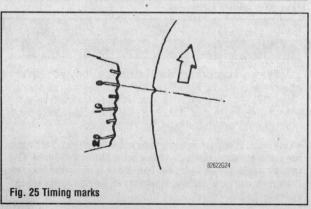

Fig. 25 Timing marks

1. Locate the timing marks on the crankshaft pulley and the front of the engine.
2. Clean off the timing marks, so that you can see them.
3. Use chalk or white paint to color the mark on the crankshaft pulley and the mark on the scale which will indicate the correct timing when aligned with the notch on the crankshaft pulley.

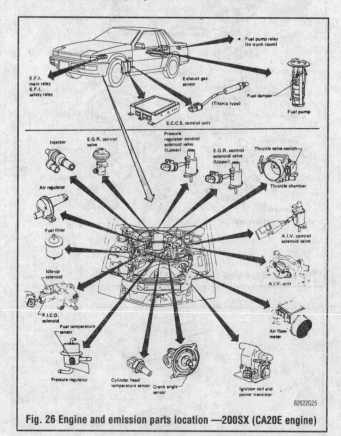

Fig. 26 Engine and emission parts location —200SX (CA20E engine)

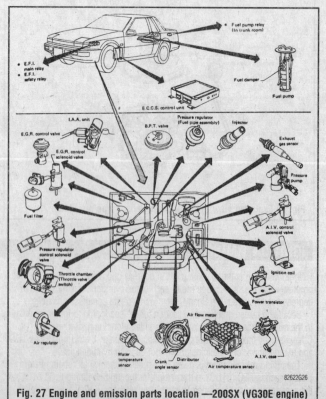

Fig. 27 Engine and emission parts location —200SX (VG30E engine)

4. Attach a tachometer to the engine.

5. Attach a timing light to the engine, according to the manufacturer's instructions. If the timing light has three wires, one, usually green or blue, is attached to the No. 1 spark plug with an adapter. The other wires are connected to the battery. The red wire goes to the positive side of the battery and the black wire is connected to the negative terminal of the battery.

6. Check that all of the wires clear the fan, pulleys, and belts, and then start the engine. Allow the engine to reach normal operating temperature.

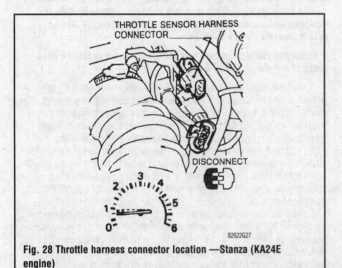

Fig. 28 Throttle harness connector location —Stanza (KA24E engine)

➡ **On 200SX models with the Z22E and CA20E and CA18ET engines and Stanza with the CA20E engine and with a distributor advance vacuum hose stop engine—disconnect distributor advance vacuum hose (if so equipped) from the distributor and plug hose.**

7. Check or adjust the idle speed (using correct procedure) to the correct setting. See the Idle Speed service procedures in this section.

8. Aim the timing light at the timing marks. If the marks which you put on the pulley and the engine are aligned when the light flashes, the timing is correct. Turn off the engine and remove the tachometer and the timing light. If the marks are not in alignment, proceed with the following steps.

➡ **On 200SX and Stanza models with a CA20E engine and no distributor advance vacuum hose stop engine—disconnect auxiliary air control (A.A.C.) valve harness connector which is part of idle air adjusting unit (I.A.A.) unit and throttle valve switch then follow Step 9.**

➡ **On 200SX models with a VG30E engine stop engine—disconnect idle up solenoid harness connector then follow Step 9.**

➡ **On 240SX and Stanza with KA24E and KA24DE engines stop engine— disconnect throttle sensor harness connector then follow step 9.**

9. Loosen the distributor lock-bolt just enough so that the distributor can be turned with a little effort.

10. Start the engine. Keep the wires of the timing light clear of the fan.

11. With the timing light aimed at the pulley and the marks on the engine, turn the distributor in the direction of rotor rotation to retard the spark, and in the opposite direction of rotor rotation to advance the spark. Align the marks on the pulley and the engine with the flashes of the timing light.

12. Tighten the distributor lock-bolt and recheck the timing. Reconnect all lines or electrical connections. Roadtest the vehicle for proper operation.

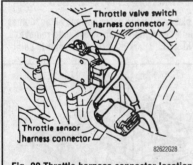

Fig. 29 Throttle harness connector location —240SX (KA24E and KA24DE engines)

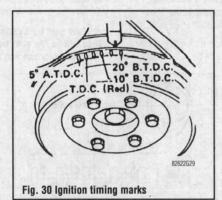

Fig. 30 Ignition timing marks

Fig. 31 Loosen the distributor lock-bolt and turn the distributor slightly to adjust timing

VALVE LASH

THE MAINTENANCE INTERVALS FOR VALVE ADJUSTMENT IS EVERY 15,000 MILES OR 12 MONTHS.

Valve adjustment determines how far the valves enter the cylinder and how long they stay open and closed.

If the valve clearance is too large, part of the lift of the camshaft will be used in removing the excessive clearance. Consequently, the valve will not be opening for as long as it should. This condition has two effects: the valve train components will emit a tapping sound as they take up the excessive clearance and the engine will perform poorly because the valves don't open fully and allow the proper amount of gases to flow into and out of the engine.

If the valve clearance is too small, the intake valves and the exhaust valves will open too far and they will not fully seat on the cylinder head when they close. When a valve seats itself on the cylinder head, it does two things: it seals the combustion chamber so that one of the gases in the cylinder escape and it cools itself by transferring some of the heat it absorbs from the combustion in the cylinder to the cylinder head and to the engine's cooling system. If the valve clearance is too small, the engine will run poorly because of the gases escaping from the combustion chamber. The valves will also become overheated and will warp, since they cannot transfer heat unless they are touching the valve seat in the cylinder head.

➡ **While all valve adjustments must be made as accurately as possible, it is better to have the valve adjustment slightly loose than slightly tight, as a burned valve may result from overly tight adjustments. Read the complete service procedure then refer to the correct model and year for your vehicle.**

Adjustment

1982–83 200SX TWIN PLUG ENGINES — Z SERIES ENGINE

◆ **See Figures 32, 33, 34 and 35**

1. The valves must be adjusted with the engine WARM, so start the car and run the engine until the needle on the temperature gauge reaches the middle of the gauge. After the engine is warm, shut it off.

2. Purchase either a new gasket or some silicone gasket sealer before removing the camshaft cover. Counting on the old gasket to be in good shape is a losing proposition. Always use new gaskets. Note the location of any wires and hoses which may interfere with cam cover removal, disconnect them and move them to one side. Remove the bolts holding the cover

in place and remove the cover. Remember, the engine will be hot, so be careful.

3. Place a wrench on the crankshaft pulley bolt and turn the engine over until the first cam lobe behind the camshaft timing chain sprocket is pointing straight down.

➡If you decide to turn the engine by bumping it with the starter, be sure to disconnect the high tension wire from the coil(s) to prevent the engine from accidentally starting and spewing oil all over the engine compartment. Never attempt to turn the engine by using a wrench on the camshaft sprocket bolt. There is a one to two turning ratio between the camshaft and the crankshaft which will put a tremendous strain on the timing chain.

4. See the illustration for primary adjustment and check the clearance of valves (1), (4), (6), and (7) using a flat bladed feeler gauge. The feeler gauge should pass between the valve stem end and the rocker arm screw with a very slight drag. Insert the feeler gauge straight, not at an angle.

5. If the clearance is not within specified value (0.012 in.) 0.30mm, loosen the rocker arm lock nut and turn the rocker arm screw to obtain the proper clearance. After correct clearance is obtained, tighten the lock nut.

6. Turn the engine over so that the first cam lobe behind the camshaft timing chain sprocket is pointing straight up and check the clearance of the valves marked (2), (3), (5), and (8) in the secondary adjustment illustration. They, too, should be adjusted to specifications as in Step 5.

7. Install the cam cover gasket, the cam cover and any wires and hoses which were removed.

1984–88 200SX WITH THE CA20E, CA18ET AND VG30E ENGINES

▶ **See Figures 36 and 37**

➡Starting in mid year 1986–88 the CA20E engine in the 200SX model valves are non-adjustable. On V6 equipped 200SX models the valves are also non-adjustable. Refer to Valve Clearance column in the Tune-Up Specifications Chart.

Valve adjustment should be made while engine is warm but no running. Follow the procedure above for 1982–83 models, with the following exceptions: on

Step 4, check and adjust the clearance valves 1, 2, 4 and 6 as shown in the accompanying illustration. This is with No. 1 cylinder at TDC on compression. On Step 6, check and adjust the clearance on valves 3, 5, 7 and 8 with the No. 4 cylinder at TDC on compression.

1982–92 STANZA WITH THE CA20, CA20E AND KA24E ENGINES

▶ **See Figures 38 and 39**

➡On Stanza models from 1987–92 (except 1986–88 station wagons) no routine valve adjustment is necessary or possible these models are equipped with hydraulic lash adjusters, which continually take up excess clearance in the valve train.

➡Datsun/Nissan recommends that valve adjustment should be done every 12 months or 15,000 miles.

1. Run the engine until it reaches normal operating temperature. Oil temperature, not water temperature, is critical to valve adjustment. With this in mind, make sure the engine is fully warmed up since this is the only way to make sure the parts have reached their full expansion. Generally speaking, this takes around 15 minutes. After the engine has reached normal operating temperature, shut it off.

2. Purchase a new valve cover gasket before removing the valve cover. The new silicone gasket sealers are just as good or better if you can't find a gasket.

3. Note the location of any hoses or wires which may interfere with valve cover removal, disconnect and move them aside. Remove the bolts which hold the valve cover in place.

4. After the valve cover has been removed, the next step is to get the number one piston at TDC on the compression stroke. There are at least two ways to do this: Bump the engine over with the starter or turn it over by using a wrench on the front crankshaft pulley bolt. The easiest way to find TDC is to turn the engine over slowly with a wrench (after first removing No. 1 plug) until the piston is at the top of its stroke and the TDC timing mark on the crankshaft pulley is in alignment with the timing mark pointer. At this point, the valves for No. 1 cylinder should be closed.

➡Make sure both valves are closed with the valve springs up as high as they will go. An easy way to find the compression stroke is to remove the distributor cap and observe which spark plug lead the rotor is point-

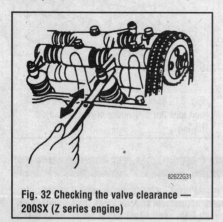

Fig. 32 Checking the valve clearance — 200SX (Z series engine)

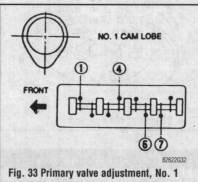

Fig. 33 Primary valve adjustment, No. 1 cam lobe pointing down —200SX (Z series engine)

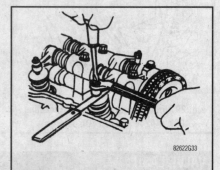

Fig. 34 Loosen the lock-nut and turn the adjusting screw to adjust the valve clearance

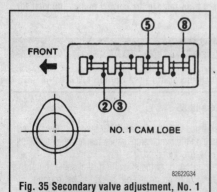

Fig. 35 Secondary valve adjustment, No. 1 cam lobe pointing up —200SX (Z series engine)

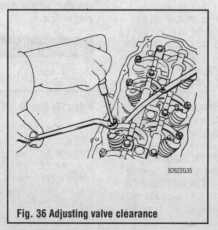

Fig. 36 Adjusting valve clearance

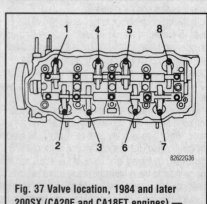

Fig. 37 Valve location, 1984 and later 200SX (CA20E and CA18ET engines) — See text for procedure

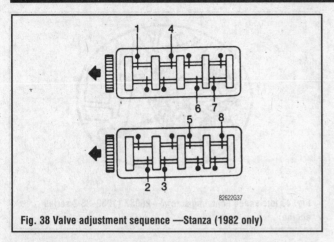

Fig. 38 Valve adjustment sequence —Stanza (1982 only)

ing to. **If the rotor points to No. 1 spark plug lead, No. 1 cylinder is on its compression stroke. When the rotor points to the No. 2 spark plug lead, No. 2 cylinder is on its compression stroke.**

5. Set the No. 1 piston at TDC of the compression stroke, then check and/or adjust the valve clearance on Stanza (1982 model only) Nos. 1, 4, 6 and 7; on the Stanza (1983–86 and 1986–88 Stanza wagon), Nos. 1, 2, 4 and 6.

6. To adjust the clearance, loosen the lock-nut with a wrench and turn the adjuster with a screwdriver while holding the lock-nut. The correct size feeler gauge (0.012 in.) 0.30mm should pass with a slight drag between the rocker arm and the valve stem.

7. Turn the crankshaft one full revolution to position the No. 4 piston at TDC of the compression stroke. Check and/or adjust the valves (counting from the front to the rear) on the Stanza (1982 model only), Nos. 2, 3, 5 and 8; on the Stanza (1983–86 and 1986–88 Stanza wagon), Nos. 3, 5, 7 and 8.

8. Replace the valve cover and torque the bolts on the valve cover down evenly. Check oil level.

1989–92 240SX WITH THE KA24E AND KA24DE ENGINES

▸ **See Figures 40 and 41**

➡On the 240SX KA24E engine no routine valve adjustment is necessary or possible these models are equipped with hydraulic lash adjusters, which continually take up excess clearance in the valve train.

➡Datsun/Nissan recommends that valve adjustment on the KA24DE engine should only be done if valve noise increases.

KA24DE Engine

1. Run the engine until it reaches normal operating temperature and shut if off.

2. Remove the rocker cover and all spark plugs.

3. Set No. 1 cylinder at TDC on compression stroke. Align pointer with TDC mark on crankshaft pulley. Check that the valve lifters on No. 1 cylinder are loose and valve lifters on No. 4 are tight. If not turn crankshaft one revolution 360° and align as above.

4. Refer to the illustration. Check both No. 1 intake and both No. 1 exhaust valves, both No. 2 intake valves and both No. 3 exhaust valves. Using a feeler gauge, measure the clearance between valve lifter and camshaft. Record any valve clearance measurements which are out of specification. Intake Valve clearance (hot) is 0.012–0.015 in. (0.30–0.38mm) and exhaust valve clearance (hot) is 0.013–0.016 in. (0.33–0.40mm).

5. Turn crankshaft one revolution 360° and align mark on crankshaft pulley with pointer. Refer to the illustration. Check both No. 2 exhaust valves, both No. 3 intake valves, both No. 4 intake valves and both No. 4 exhaust valves. Using a feeler gauge, measure the clearance between valve lifter and camshaft. Record any valve clearance measurements which are out of specification. Intake valve clearance (hot) is 0.012–0.015 in. (0.30–0.38mm) and exhaust valve clearance (hot) is 0.013–0.016 in. (0.33–0.40mm).

6. If all valve clearances are within specification, install all related parts as necessary.

7. If adjustment is necessary, adjust valve clearance while engine is cold by removing adjusting shim. Determine replacement adjusting shim size using formula. Using a micrometer determine thickness of removed shim. Calculate thickness of new adjusting shim so valve clearance comes within specified values. R = thickness of removed shim, N = thickness of new shim, M = measured valve clearance.
- INTAKE: $N = R + M$
- EXHAUST: $N = R + M$

8. Shims are available in 37 sizes (thickness is stamped on the shim—this side is always installed down), select new shims with thickness as close as possible to calculated value.

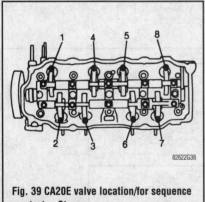

Fig. 39 CA20E valve location/for sequence see text —Stanza

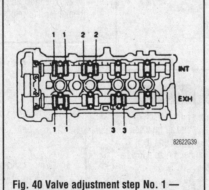

Fig. 40 Valve adjustment step No. 1 — KA24DE engine

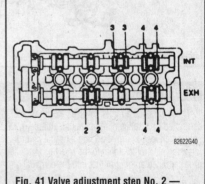

Fig. 41 Valve adjustment step No. 2 — KA24DE engine

IDLE SPEED AND MIXTURE ADJUSTMENTS

This section contains only tune-up adjustment procedures for carburetors. Descriptions, adjustments, and overhaul procedures for fuel systems can be found in Section 5.

Carbureted Engines

When the engine is running, the air/fuel mixture from the carburetor is being drawn into the engine by a partial vacuum which is created by the movement of the pistons downward on the intake stroke. The amount of air/fuel mixture that enters into the engine is controlled by the throttle plate(s) in the bottom of the carburetor. When the engine is not running the throttle plate(s) is closed, completely blocking off the bottom of the carburetor from the inside of the engine. The throttle plates are connected by the throttle linkage to the accelerator pedal in the passenger compartment of the vehicle. When you depress the pedal, you open the throttle plates in the carburetor to admit more air/fuel mixture to the engine.

When the engine is not running, the throttle plates are closed. When the engine is idling, it is necessary to have the throttle plates open slightly. To prevent having to hold your foot on the pedal when the engine is idling, an idle speed adjusting screw was added to the carburetor linkage.

The idle adjusting screw contacts a lever (throttle lever) on the outside of the carburetor. When the screw is turned, it either opens or closes the throttle plates of the carburetor, raising or lowering the idle speed of the engine. This screw is called the curb idle adjusting screw.

ADJUSTMENT PROCEDURE

1982–83 Stanza 49 States Models 1984–85 Stanza Canadian Models

▶ **See Figure 42**

➡**Always refer to the underhood specifications sticker for any additional applicable procedures.**

1. Connect a tachometer to the engine according the manufacturer's instructions.
2. Start the engine and run it until it reaches normal operating temperatures.
3. Operate it at 2,000 rpm for 2 minutes under no load, then idle for 1 minute.

➡**If the cooling fan is operating, wait until it stops.**

4. If equipped with a manual transaxle, place the shift selector in **NEUTRAL**; if equipped with an automatic transaxle, place the shift selector in **DRIVE**.
5. If the idle speed is not correct, adjust the throttle adjusting screw at the carburetor.
6. When the idle speed is correct, stop the engine and disconnect the tachometer.

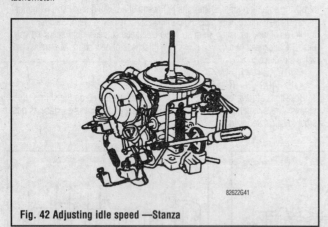

Fig. 42 Adjusting idle speed —Stanza

Electronic Fuel Injection (EFI)

These cars use a rather complex electronic fuel injection system which is controlled by a series of temperature, altitude (for California) and air flow sensors which feed information into a central control unit. The control unit then relays an electronic signal to the injector nozzle at each cylinder, which allows a predetermined amount of fuel into the combustion chamber.

ADJUSTMENT PROCEDURE

➡**Note: 1990 and later models have no idle speed adjustments.**

1982–83 200SX (Z Series Engine)

▶ **See Figure 43**

➡**Always refer to the underhood specifications sticker for any additional applicable procedures.**

1. Start the engine and run it until the water temperature indicator points to the middle of the temperature gauge. It might be quicker to take a short spin down the road and back.

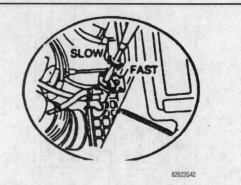

Fig. 43 Idle speed adjusting screw —200SX (1982–83 Z series engine)

2. Open the engine hood. Run the engine at about 2,000 rpm for a few minutes with the transmission in Neutral and all accessories off. If you have not already done so, check the ignition timing and make sure it is correct. Hook up a tachometer as per the manufacturer's instructions. For automatic transmission, set the parking brake, block the wheels and set the shift selector in the Drive position.
3. Run the engine at idle speed and disconnect the hose from the air induction pipe, then plug the pipe. Allow the engine to run for about a minute at idle speed.
4. Check the idle against the specifications given earlier in this section. Adjust the idle speed by turning the idle speed adjusting screw, located near the air cleaner. Turn the screw clockwise for slower idle speed and counterclockwise for faster idle speed.
5. Connect the hose and disconnect the tachometer. If idle speed increases, adjust it with the idle speed adjusting screw.

1984–86 $z\backslash x$ 200SX (CA20E and CA18ET Engines); 1984–86 Stanza with the CA20E Engine

▶ **See Figures 44 and 45**

➡**Always refer to the underhood specifications sticker for any additional applicable procedures.**

1. Start the engine and warm the engine so it reaches normal operating temperature. The water temperature indicator should be in the middle of the gauge.
2. Then race the engine to 2,000–3,000 rpm a few times under no load and then allow it to return to the idle speed.

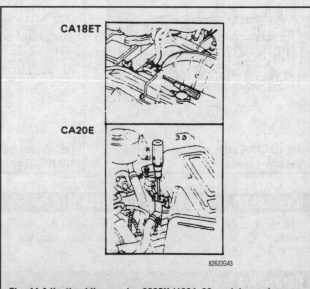

Fig. 44 Adjusting idle speed —200SX (1984–86 model years)

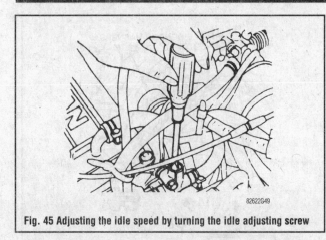

Fig. 45 Adjusting the idle speed by turning the idle adjusting screw

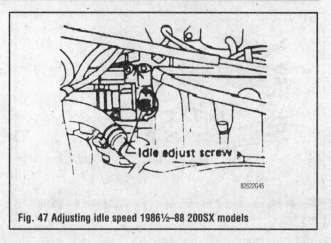

Fig. 47 Adjusting idle speed 1986½–88 200SX models

3. Connect a tachometer according to the instrument manufacturer's directions.

4. Check the idle speed on the manual transmission model in Neutral and on the automatic transmission model check in Drive.

➡️ **For automatic transmission, set the parking brake, block the wheels and set the shift selector in the Drive position.**

5. Adjust the idle speed to the figure shown in the Tune-Up Specifications Chart by turning the idle speed adjusting screw shown in the appropriate illustration.

6. Stop the engine. Remove the tachometer and road test for proper operation.

1986½–88 200SX with the CA20E Engine (Except VG30E Engine) and 1987–89 Stanza with the CA20E Engine

♦ **See Figures 46, 47 and 48**

➡️ **Always refer to the underhood specifications sticker for any additional applicable procedures.**

1. Before adjusting the idle speed on the engine you must visually check the following items first: air cleaner for being clogged, hoses and ducts for leaks, EGR valve for proper operation, all electrical connectors, gaskets and the throttle valve and throttle valve switch.

2. Start the engine and warm the engine so it reaches normal operating temperature. The water temperature indicator should be in the middle of the gauge.

3. Then race the engine to 2,000–3,000 rpm a few times under no load and then allow it to return to the idle speed.

4. Connect a tachometer according to the instrument manufacturer's directions.

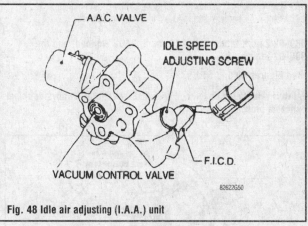

Fig. 48 Idle air adjusting (I.A.A.) unit

5. Check the idle speed on the manual transmission model in Neutral and on the automatic transmission model check in Drive.

➡️ **For automatic transmission, set the parking brake, block the wheels and set the shift selector in the Drive position.**

6. If the idle speed has to be adjusted you must disconnect the A.A.C. valve harness connector (Auxiliary Air Control) and the throttle valve switch harness connector.

7. Adjust the idle speed to the figure shown in the Tune-Up Specifications Chart by turning the idle speed adjusting screw shown in the appropriate illustration.

8. Stop the engine. Connect the A.A.C. valve harness connector (Auxiliary Air Control) and the throttle valve switch harness connector.

9. Remove the tachometer and road test for proper operation.

1987–88 200SX (VG30E Engine)

♦ **See Figure 49**

➡️ **Always refer to the underhood specifications sticker for any additional applicable procedures.**

1. Turn off the: headlights, heater blower, air conditioning, and rear window defogger. If the car has power steering, make sure the wheel is in the straight ahead position. The ignition timing must be correct to get an effective idle speed adjustment. Adjust the timing if do not know it to be correct. Connect a tachometer (a special adapter harness may be needed) according to the instrument manufacturer's directions.

2. Start engine and warm up until water temperature indicator points to the middle of the gauge.

3. Run engine at about 2,000 rpm for about 2 minutes under no load.

4. Disconnect idle up solenoid harness connector and then race engine 2 or 3 times under no load, then run engine at idle speed.

5. Apply the parking brake securely and then put the transmission into Drive, if the car has an automatic. Adjust the idle speed to the figure shown in the Tune-Up Specifications Chart by turning the idle speed adjusting screw shown in the appropriate illustration.

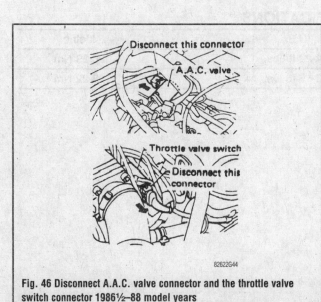

Fig. 46 Disconnect A.A.C. valve connector and the throttle valve switch connector 1986½–88 model years

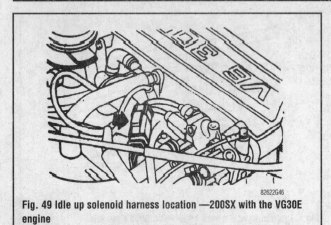

Fig. 49 Idle up solenoid harness location —200SX with the VG30E engine

6. Stop engine and connect idle up solenoid harness connector.
7. Remove tachometer and road test for proper operation.

1989–92 240SX Models (KA24E and KA24DE Engines) and the 1990–92 Stanza

▶ See Figures 50 and 51

➡Always refer to the underhood specifications sticker for any additional applicable procedures.

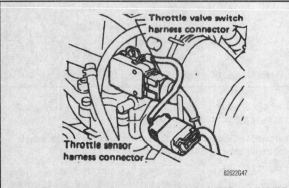

Fig. 50 Throttle harness connector location on KA24E and KA24DE engines

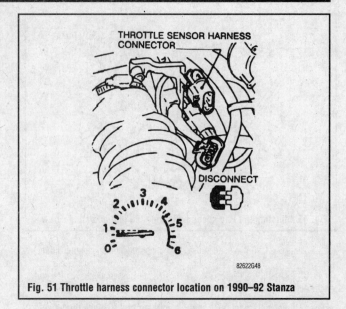

Fig. 51 Throttle harness connector location on 1990–92 Stanza

1. Before adjusting the idle speed on the engine you must visually check the following items first: air cleaner for being clogged, hoses and ducts for leaks, EGR valve for proper operation, all electrical connectors, gaskets and the throttle valve and throttle valve switch operation.
2. Start the engine and warm the engine so it reaches normal operating temperature. The water temperature indicator should be in the middle of the gauge.
3. Then race the engine to 2,000–3,000 rpm a few times under no load and then allow it to return to the idle speed.
4. Connect a tachometer according to the instrument manufacturer's directions.
5. Check the idle speed in the Neutral position for both manual and automatic transmission models.
6. If the idle speed has to be adjusted you must disconnect the throttle sensor harness connector.
7. Adjust the idle speed to the figure shown in the Tune-Up Specifications Chart by turning the idle speed adjusting screw.
8. Stop the engine. Connect the throttle sensor harness connector.
9. Remove the tachometer and road test for proper operation.

TORQUE SPECIFICATIONS

Component	U.S.	Metric
Spark plugs:	14-22 ft. lbs.	20-29 Nm
Throttle chamber retaining screws:	13-16 ft. lbs.	18-22 Nm

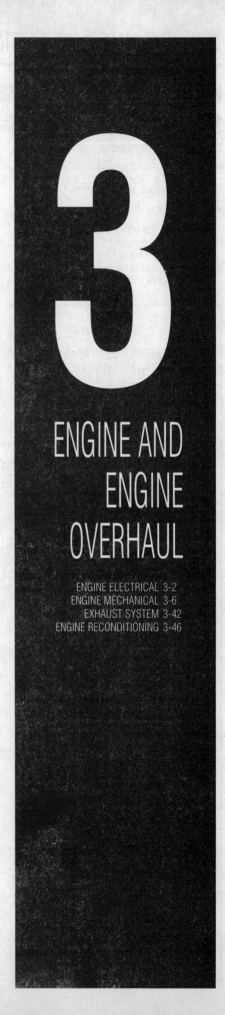

3

ENGINE AND ENGINE OVERHAUL

ENGINE ELECTRICAL

Ignition Coil

TESTING

200SX (1982–83 Z series engine)

♦ **See Figures 1, 2, 3, 4 and 5**

1. Make a check of the power supply circuit. Turn the ignition OFF. Disconnect the connector from the top of the IC unit. Turn the ignition ON. Measure the voltage at each terminal of the connector in turn by touch the probe of the positive lead of the voltmeter to one of the terminals, and touching the probe of the negative lead of the voltmeter to a ground, such as the engine. In each case,

battery voltage (12 volts) should be indicated. If not, check all wiring, the ignition switch, and all connectors for breaks, corrosion, discontinuity, etc., and repair as necessary.

2. Check the primary windings of the ignition coil. Turn the ignition OFF. Disconnect the harness connector from the negative coil terminal. Use an ohmmeter to measure the resistance between the positive and negative coil terminals. If resistance is 1.04–1.27Ω the coil is OK. Replace coil(s) if far from this specification range.

3. Turn the ignition switch to the OFF position.

4. Disable the electronic fuel injection so engine will not start (disconnect the EFI injection fusible link).

5. Disconnect the high tension cable from the distributor. Hold the cable with insulated pliers to avoid getting shocked. Position the wire about a ¼ in. (6mm) from the engine block and have an assistant turn over the engine using the starter. A good spark should jump from the cable to the engine block or ground.

➡ **The 1984–88 200SX, 1989–92 240SX and Stanza vehicles use a highly complex computerized ignition system. For complete testing, flow charts and engine code diagnostic procedures—See Sections 2 and 4.**

Stanza

PRIMARY RESISTANCE CHECK

Testing with a ohmmeter, the reading should be 0.84–1.02Ω for the Stanza models from 1982–86. On the Stanza models from 1987 and later a "Mold type" coil is used, first remove the coil wire then connect the leads of an ohmmeter to the positive (+) and negative (–) terminals.

➡ **Terminals at the bottom of the coil assembly the reading should 0.8–1.0Ω for this type coil. If the reading is more than specified, replace the ignition coil assembly.**

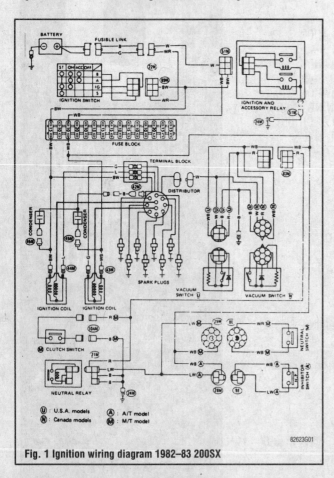

Fig. 1 Ignition wiring diagram 1982–83 200SX

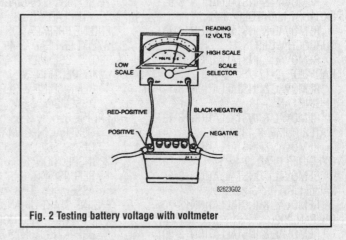

Fig. 2 Testing battery voltage with voltmeter

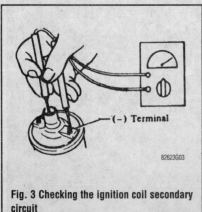

Fig. 3 Checking the ignition coil secondary circuit

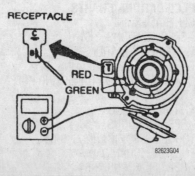

Fig. 4 Testing the power supply circuit — 1983 200SX

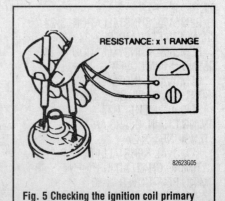

Fig. 5 Checking the ignition coil primary circuit

SECONDARY RESISTANCE CHECK

Turn the ignition key OFF, then remove the high tension and a primary coil wire from the coil using an ohmmeter, set it on the X1000 scale. Touch one lead to a primary terminal and the other lead to the center terminal. The resistance should be 8,200–12,400Ω; if not, replace the ignition coil.

➡On some later model vehicles, a power transistor is used with the ignition coil. The ignition signal from the ECU is amplified by the power transistor, which turns the ignition coil primary circuit on and off, inducing the proper high voltage in the secondary circuit. On these models the ignition coil is a small molded type.

REMOVAL & INSTALLATION

On all models, the coil assembly is either mounted to the wall of the engine compartment or the engine. To remove disconnect and mark all electrical connections—remove the coil assembly, then transfer coil mounting bracket if so equipped to the new coil. When installing the new coil make sure that the coil wire and all other electrical connections are properly installed.

Ignition Module

REMOVAL & INSTALLATION

▶ **See Figures 6 and 7**

➡Refer to Section 2 for additional service information and illustrations.

➡Later vehicle models do not use an "Ignition Module" in the distributor assembly.

1. Remove the distributor cap and pull the rotor from the distributor shaft.

➡The rotor on most vehicles is held to the distributor shaft by a retaining screw, which must be removed.

2. Remove the wiring harness and the vacuum controller from the housing.
3. Using 2 flat bladed screwdrivers, place one on each side of the reluctor and pry it from the distributor shaft.

➡When removing the reluctor, be careful not to damage or distort the teeth.

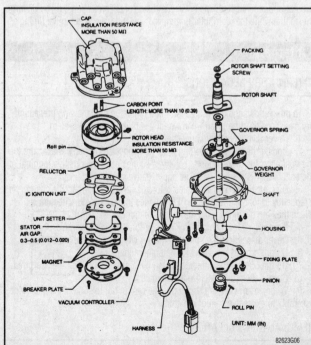

Fig. 6 Distributor assembly — 1984 and later 200SX, Stanza CA20E engines

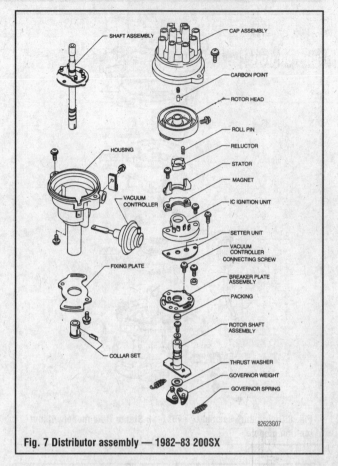

Fig. 7 Distributor assembly — 1982–83 200SX

4. Remove the roll pin from the reluctor.
5. Mark and remove the breaker plate assembly and separate the IC unit from it. Be careful not to loose the spacers when you remove the IC unit.
6. To install, reverse the removal procedures. When you install the roll pin into the reluctor position the cutout direction of the roll pin in parallel with the notch in the reluctor. Make sure that the harness to the IC ignition unit is tightly secured, then adjust the air gap between the reluctor and the stator.

Distributor

REMOVAL & INSTALLATION

▶ **See Figures 8 and 9**

1. Unfasten the retaining clips and lift the distributor cap straight up. It will be easier to install the distributor if the spark plug wires are not disconnected from the cap. If the wires must be removed from the cap remove the wires one at a time, mark or tag their positions to aid in installation.
2. Disconnect the distributor wiring harness and or the electrical connection if so equipped.

➡On late model Datsun/Nissan a crankangle sensor is the basic component of the distributor. No vacuum lines are used, just one electrical connection.

3. Disconnect the vacuum lines if so equipped.
4. Note the position of the rotor in relation to the base. Scribe a mark on the base of the distributor and on the engine block to facilitate reinstallation. Align the marks with the direction the metal tip of the rotor is pointing. (note the position of distributor base to engine block and distributor rotor to distributor assembly).
5. Remove the bolt(s) which holds the distributor to the engine.
6. Carefully lift the distributor assembly from the engine—DO NOT CRANK OR MOVE THE ENGINE AT THIS POINT OR INITIAL TIMING WILL HAVE TO BE SET!

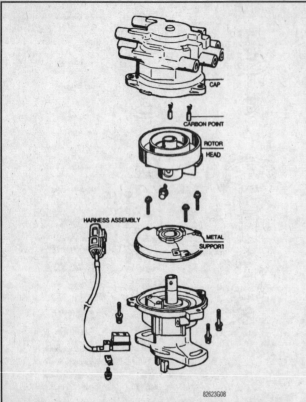

Fig. 8 Distributor assembly — 1987–88 Stanza (late model without ignition module)

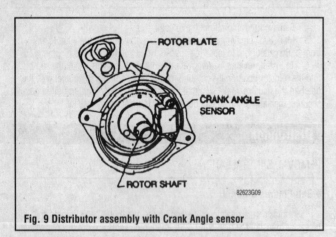

Fig. 9 Distributor assembly with Crank Angle sensor

To install:

7. Insert the distributor shaft and assembly into the engine. Line up the mark on the distributor and the one on the engine with the metal tip of the rotor. Make sure that the vacuum advance diaphragm if so equipped is pointed in the same direction as it was pointed originally. This will be done automatically if the marks on the engine and the distributor are lined up with the rotor.

8. Install the distributor hold-down bolt and clamp. Leave the screw loose enough so that you can move the distributor with heavy hand pressure.

9. Connect the primary wire to the coil and or the electrical connections. Install the distributor cap on the distributor housing. Secure the distributor cap with the spring clips.

10. Install the spark plug wires if removed. Make sure that the wires are pressed all the way into the top of the distributor cap and firmly onto the spark plug. Make sure the correct firing order is maintained.

11. Adjust the ignition timing as necessary.

➡️**If the crankshaft has been turned or the engine disturbed in any manner (i.e., disassembled and rebuilt) while the distributor was removed,**

or if the marks were not drawn, it will be necessary to initially time the engine. Follow the procedure given below.

INSTALLATION—CRANKSHAFT OR CAMSHAFT ROTATED

1. It is necessary to place the No. 1 cylinder in the firing position to correctly install the distributor. To locate this position, the ignition timing marks on the crankshaft front pulley are used.

2. Remove the No. 1 cylinder spark plug. Turn the crankshaft until the piston in the No. 1 cylinder is UP on the compression stroke. This can be determined by placing your thumb over the spark plug hole and feeling the air being forced out of the cylinder. Stop turning the crankshaft when the timing marks that are used to time the engine are aligned on the front timing cover assembly.

3. Oil the distributor housing lightly where the distributor bears on the cylinder block.

4. Install the distributor so that the rotor, which is mounted on the shaft, points toward the No. 1 spark plug terminal tower position when the cap is installed. Of course you won't be able to see the direction in which the rotor is pointing if the cap is on the distributor. Lay the cap on the top of the distributor and make a mark on the side of the distributor housing just below the No. 1 spark plug terminal. Make sure that the rotor points toward that mark when you install the distributor.

5. When the distributor shaft has reached the bottom of the hole, move the rotor back and forth slightly until the driving lug on the end of the shaft enters the slots cut in the end of the oil pump shaft and the distributor assembly slides down into place.

6. When the distributor is correctly installed, the reluctor teeth should be aligned with the stator assembly. This can be accomplished by rotating the distributor body after it has been installed in the engine. Once again, line up the marks that you made before the distributor was removed.

7. Install the distributor hold-down bolt.

8. Install the spark plug into the No. 1 spark plug hole and continue from Step 3 of the preceding distributor installation procedure.

If your engine has a distributor with a crankangle sensor set up read the above section and then you will be able to remove and install the distributor assembly.

Basically, you have to remove the distributor cap, mark or tag all the spark plug wires and the electrical connections then remove them. Next, mark the position of the base of the distributor with relation to the engine mounting location and the rotor position as opposed to the base of the distributor assembly.

When installing the distributor, line up your marks and gently install the distributor and reconnect all spark wires and electrical connections. If you disturb the engine while the distributor is removed you will have to set initial timing.

Alternator

ALTERNATOR PRECAUTIONS

To prevent damage to the alternator and regulator, the following precautionary measures must be taken when working with the electrical system.

1. Never reverse battery connections.

2. Booster batteries for starting must be connected properly. Make sure that the positive cable of the booster battery is connected to the positive terminal of the battery that is getting the boost and negative cable to ground.

3. Disconnect the battery cables before using a fast charger; the charger has a tendency to force current through the diodes in the opposite direction for which they are designed. This burns out the diodes.

4. Never use a fast charger as a booster for starting the vehicle.

5. Never disconnect the voltage regulator while the engine is running.

6. Do not ground the alternator output terminal.

7. Do not operate the alternator on an open circuit with the field energized.

8. Do not attempt to polarize an alternator.

9. When steam cleaning the engine, be careful not to subject the alternator assembly to excessive heat or moisture.

REMOVAL & INSTALLATION

1. Disconnect the negative battery terminal.

2. Disconnect the two lead wires and connector from the alternator.

3. Loosen the drive belt adjusting bolt and remove the belt.

4. Unscrew the alternator attaching bolts and remove the alternator from the vehicle.

To install:

5. Mount the alternator to the engine and partially tighten the attaching bolts.

6. Reconnect the lead wires and connector to the alternator.

7. Install the alternator drive belt.

8. Adjust the alternator belt correctly and completely tighten the mounting bolts.

➡**The correct belt tension is about ¼–½ in. (613mm) play on the longest span of the drive belt. The alternator belt tension is quite critical. A belt that is too tight may cause alternator bearing failure; one that is too loose will cause a gradual battery discharge.**

9. Connnect the battery cable. Start the engine and check for proper operation.

TESTING

Voltage Test

1. Make sure the engine is **OFF**, and turn the headlights on for 15–20 seconds to remove any surface charge from the battery.

2. Using a DVOM set to volts DC, probe across the battery terminals.

3. Measure the battery voltage.

4. Write down the voltage reading and proceed to the next test.

No-Load Test

1. Connect a tachometer to the engine.

❊❊ CAUTION

Ensure that the transmission is in PARK and the emergency brake is set. Blocking a wheel is optional and an added safety measure.

2. Turn off all electrical loads (radio, blower motor, wipers, etc.)

3. Start the engine and increase engine speed to approximately 1500 rpm.

4. Measure the voltage reading at the battery with the engine holding a steady 1500 rpm. Voltage should have raised at least 0.5 volts, but no more than 2.5 volts.

5. If the voltage does not go up more than 0.5 volts, the alternator is not charging. If the voltage goes up more than 2.5 volts, the alternator is overcharging.

➡**Usually under and overcharging is caused by a defective alternator, or its related parts (regulator), and replacement will fix the problem; however, faulty wiring and other problems can cause the charging system to malfunction. Further testing, which is not covered by this book, will reveal the exact component failure. Many automotive parts stores have alternator bench testers available for use by customers. An alternator bench test is the most definitive way to determine the condition of your alternator.**

6. If the voltage is within specifications, proceed to the next test.

Load Test

1. With the engine running, turn on the blower motor and the high beams (or other electrical accessories to place a load on the charging system).

2. Increase and hold engine speed to 2000 rpm.

3. Measure the voltage reading at the battery.

4. The voltage should increase at least 0.5 volts from the voltage test. If the voltage does not meet specifications, the charging system is malfunctioning.

➡**Usually under and overcharging is caused by a defective alternator, or its related parts (regulator), and replacement will fix the problem; however, faulty wiring and other problems can cause the charging system to malfunction. Further testing, which is not covered by this book, will reveal the exact component failure. Many automotive parts stores have alternator bench testers available for use by customers. An alternator bench test is the most definitive way to determine the condition of your alternator.**

Regulator

REMOVAL & INSTALLATION

All models are equipped with integral regulator assembly. Since the regulator is a internal part of the alternator no adjustments are possible or necessary. For removal and installation of voltage regulator refer to "Alternator Overhaul" service procedures.

Starter

Datsun/Nissan began using a reduction gear starter in the Canadian versions 200SX model. They were also available as an option on later models. The differences between the gear reduction and conventional starters are: the gear reduction starter has a set of ratio reduction gears while the conventional starter does not; the brushes on the gear reduction starter are located on a plate behind the starter drive housing, while the conventional starter's brushes are located in its rear cover. The extra gears on the gear reduction starter make the starter pinion gear turn at about half the speed of the starter, giving the starter twice the turning power of a conventional starter.

TESTING

Voltage Drop Test

➡**The battery must be in good condition and fully charged prior to performing this test.**

1. Disable the ignition system by unplugging the coil pack. Verify that the vehicle will not start.

2. Connect a voltmeter between the positive terminal of the battery and the starter **B+** circuit.

3. Turn the ignition key to the **START** position and note the voltage on the meter.

4. If voltage reads 0.5 volts or more, there is high resistance in the starter cables or the cable ground, repair as necessary. If the voltage reading is OK, proceed to the next step.

5. Connect a voltmeter between the positive terminal of the battery and the starter **M** circuit.

6. Turn the ignition key to the **START** position and note the voltage on the meter.

7. If voltage reads 0.5 volts or more, there is high resistance in the starter. Repair or replace the starter as necessary.

➡**Many automotive parts stores have starter bench testers available for use by customers. A starter bench test is the most definitive way to determine the condition of your starter.**

REMOVAL & INSTALLATION

1. Disconnect the negative battery cable from the battery.

2. Disconnect the starter wiring at the starter, taking note of the positions for correct installation.

3. Remove the bolts attaching the starter to the engine and remove the starter from the vehicle.

To install:

4. Install the starter to the engine.

5. Tighten the attaching bolts EVENLY. Be careful not overtorque the mounting bolts as this will crack the nose of the starter case assembly.

6. Install the starter wiring in the correct location.

7. Connect the negative battery cable.

8. Start the engine a few times to make sure of proper operation.

SOLENOID REPLACEMENT

➡**The starter solenoid is also know as the magnetic switch assembly.**

1. Remove the starter from the engine as outlined above.

2. Place the starter in a vise or equivalent to hold the starter in place while you are working on the solenoid. DO NOT tighten the vise to tight around the case of the starter. The case will crack if you tighten the vise too much.

3. Loosen the lock-nut and remove the connection from the starter motor going to the **M** terminal of the solenoid or bottom terminal of the solenoid.
4. Remove the securing screws and remove the solenoid.
5. Install the solenoid to the starter and tighten the securing screws.
6. Install the connection and lock-nut at bottom terminal of the starter.

Sending Units and Sensors

REMOVAL & INSTALLATION

Coolant Temperature Sensor

1. Disconnect the negative battery cable.
2. Drain the cooling system until coolant level is below coolant sensor.

ENGINE MECHANICAL

Engine

REMOVAL & INSTALLATION

200SX and 240SX (Rear Wheel Drive Models)

♦ See Figures 10, 11, 12 and 13

The following procedure can be used on all years and models. Slight variations may occur due to extra connections, etc., but the basic procedure should cover all years and models. The engine and transmission are removed together as assembly and then separated when out of the car. Always observe the following cautions:

• Make sure the vehicle is on a flat and level surface and that wheels are tightly chocked. Use the chocks on both sides of the rear wheels on front wheel drive cars.
• Allow the exhaust system to cool completely before starting work to prevent burns and possible fire as fuel lines are disconnected.
• Release fuel pressure from the fuel system before attempting to disconnect any fuel lines.
• When lifting the engine out, guide it carefully to avoid hitting parts such as the master cylinder.
• Mount the engine securely and then release the tension of lifting chains to avoid injury as you work on the engine.
1. Mark the location of the hinges on the hood. Unbolt and remove the hood.
2. Disconnect the battery cables. Remove the battery.
3. Drain the coolant and automatic transmission fluid.
4. Remove the radiator and radiator shroud after disconnecting the automatic transmission coolant tubes.
5. Remove the air cleaner.
6. Remove the fan and pulley.
7. Disconnect:
   a. water temperature gauge wire;
   b. oil pressure sending unit wire;
   c. ignition distributor primary wire;
   d. starter motor connections;
   e. fuel hose;

✱✱ CAUTION

On all fuel injected models, the fuel pressure must be released before the fuel lines can be disconnected. See the pressure releasing procedure under Gasoline Engine Fuel Filter in Section 1.

   f. alternator leads;
   g. heater hoses;
   h. throttle and choke connections;
   i. engine ground cable;
   j. thermal transmitter wire;
   k. wire to fuel cut-off solenoid;
   l. vacuum cut solenoid wire.

➡**A good rule of thumb when disconnecting the rather complex engine wiring of today's cars is to put a piece of masking tape on the wire and on**

3. Disconnect electrical connector from the sensor.
4. Remove the sensor from the engine. On some applications, the coolant sensor threads into the thermostat housing.
5. Installation is the reverse of the removal procedure. Fill and bleed cooling system.

Oil Pressure Switch

1. Disconnect the negative battery cable.
2. Disconnect electrical connector from the oil pressure switch.
3. Remove the oil pressure switch from the engine.
4. Installation is the reverse of the removal procedure. Check oil level.

the connection you removed the wire from, then mark both pieces of tape 1, 2, 3, etc. When replacing wiring, simply match the pieces of tape.

✱✱ CAUTION

On models with air conditioning, it is necessary to remove the compressor and the condenser from their mounts. DO NOT ATTEMPT TO UNFASTEN ANY OF THE AIR CONDITIONER HOSES. See Section 1 for additional warnings.

8. Disconnect the power brake booster hose from the engine.
9. Remove the clutch operating cylinder and return spring.
10. Disconnect the speedometer cable from the transmission. Disconnect the backup light switch and any other wiring or attachments to the transmission. On manual transmission models, remove the boot, withdraw the lock pin, and remove the lever from inside the car.
11. Detach the exhaust pipe from the exhaust manifold. Remove the front section of the exhaust system. Be careful not to break the retaining bolts to manifold. If the bolts or studs break in the manifold remove the manifold and drill and tap the hole.
12. Mark the relationship of the driveshaft flanges and remove the driveshaft.
13. Place a jack under the transmission. Remove the rear crossmember.
14. Attach a hoist to the lifting hooks on the engine (at either end of the cylinder head). Support the engine.

➡**On 1984 and later 200SX models, do not loosen the front engine mounting insulator cover securing nuts. When the cover is removed, the damper oil will flow out and the mounting insulator will not function.**

15. Unbolt the front engine mounts. Tilt the engine by lowering the jack under the transmission and raising the hoist. Remove the engine/transmission assembly from the vehicle.
   To install:
16. With the engine/transmission assembly mounted safely on the engine hoist slowly lower the engine/transmission assembly into place.

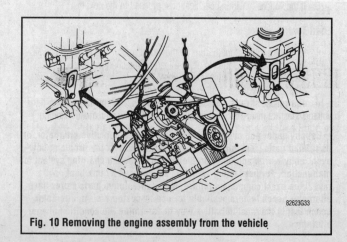

Fig. 10 Removing the engine assembly from the vehicle

Fig. 11 Gearshift lever removal

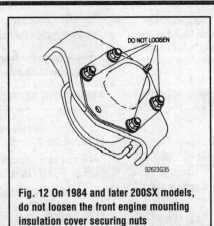

Fig. 12 On 1984 and later 200SX models, do not loosen the front engine mounting insulation cover securing nuts

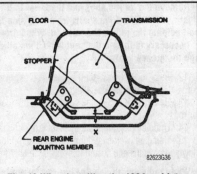

Fig. 13 When installing the 1984 and later 200SX engine, adjust the rear mounting stopper clearance (X) to 13mm

➡ **When installing the CA20E and CA18ET engines into 1984 and later 200SXs, the rear engine mounting bracket must be adjusted. Using the accompanying illustration as a guide, adjust the rear mounting stopper clearance (X in the illustration) to 13mm.**

17. Support the transmission with a jack or equivalent until the crossmember is installed.

18. Tighten the front engine mounts. It may be necessary to lower or raise the engine hoist to correctly position the engine assembly to line up with the mount holes. Remove the engine hoist.

19. Install the crossmember then remove the jack or equivalent supporting the transmission.

20. Install the driveshaft in the correct marked position.

21. Reconnect the front exhaust system to the exhaust manifold. Be careful not to tighten retaining bolts to manifold to tight. If the bolts or studs break in the manifold remove the manifold and drill and tap the hole.

22. Reconnect all wiring at the transmission and the speedometer cable.

23. On manual transmission models, install the lever, lock pin and shift boot.

24. Install the clutch cylinder and return spring. Reconnect the power brake hose to the engine if so equipped.

25. Install all wiring, brackets, vacuum hoses and water hoses to the engine. Make sure all connections are tight and in the correct location. It is always a good idea to replace all the old water hoses, drive belts, clamps, spark plugs oil and oil filter when installing the engine.

26. Install the fan and fan pulley.

27. Install the radiator shroud than the radiator reconnect the transmission lines if so equipped.

28. Refill the radiator and all other fluid levels.

29. Install the air cleaner, battery and reconnect the battery cables.

30. Install the hood in the same location as you removed it from.

31. Check all fluids, start engine, let it warm up and check for leaks.

32. Road test vehicle after you are sure there are no leaks. Check vehicle for proper operation. Recheck all fluid levels.

Stanza and Stanza Wagon (Front Wheel Drive Models)

▸ See Figure 14

The following procedure can be used on all years and models. Slight variations may occur due to extra connections, etc., but the basic procedure should cover all years and models. Refer to all " Engine Mounting" illustrations.

※※ CAUTION

On EFI equipped models, release the fuel pressure in the system before disconnecting the fuel lines. Situate the vehicle on as flat and solid a surface as possible. Place chocks or equivalent at front and rear of rear wheels to stop vehicle from rolling.

➡ **The engine and transaxle must be removed as a single unit. The engine and transaxle is removed from the top of the vehicle. If equipped with 4WD remove the engine, transaxle and transfer case as an assembly.**

1. Mark the location of the hinges on the hood. Remove the hood by holding at both sides and unscrewing bolts. This requires 2 people.

2. Disconnect the battery cables and remove the battery.

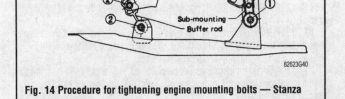

Fig. 14 Procedure for tightening engine mounting bolts — Stanza

3. Drain the coolant from the radiator, then remove the radiator and the heater hoses.

4. Remove the air cleaner-to-rocker cover hose and the air cleaner cover, then place a clean rag in the carburetor or throttle body opening to keep out the dirt or any foreign object.

➡ **Disconnect and label all the necessary vacuum hoses and electrical connectors, for reinstallation purposes. A good rule of thumb when disconnecting the rather complex engine wiring of today's cars is to put a piece of masking tape on the wire and on the connection you removed the wire from, then mark both pieces of tape 1, 2, 3, etc. When replacing wiring, simply match the pieces of tape.**

5. If equipped, disconnect the air pump cleaner and remove the carbon canister.

6. Remove the auxiliary fan, the washer tank and the radiator grille if necessary. Remove the radiator together with the fan motor assembly as a unit.

7. Remove the clutch control wire or cable from the transaxle. Remove the right and the left buffer rods but do not alter the length of these rods. Disconnect the speedometer cable from the transaxle and plug the hole with a clean rag.

➡ **Remove the EGR vacuum control valve with the bracket from the body.**

8. If equipped with air conditioning, loosen the idler pulley nut and the adjusting bolt, then remove the compressor belt. Remove the compressor to one side and suspend on a wire. Remove the condenser and the receiver drier and place them on the right fender.

➡ **If equipped with AC, DO NOT ATTEMPT TO UNFASTEN ANY OF THE REFRIGERANT HOSES. See Section 1 for additional warnings and service procedures. If equipped with power steering, loosen the idler pulley nut and adjusting bolt, then remove the drive belt and the power steering pulley.**

9. If equipped with a manual transaxle, disconnect the transaxle shifting rods by removing the securing bolts. If equipped with an automatic transaxle, disconnect the mounting bracket and the control wire from the transaxle.

➡ **On 4WD drive applications matchmark and remove the driveshaft from the transfer assembly.**

10. Attach the engine sling at each end of the engine block. Connect a chain or cable to the engine slingers.

11. Unbolt the exhaust pipe from the exhaust manifold. There are 3 bolts which attach the pipe to the manifold and bolts which attach the pipe support to the engine.

➡️**Remove the tie rod ends and the lower ball joints. Disconnect the right and left side drive shafts from their side flanges and remove the bolt holding the radius link support. When drawing out the halfshafts, it is necessary to loosen the strut head bolts also be careful not to damage the grease seals.**

12. Refer to Section 7, for the axle shaft, removal and installation procedures, then remove the axle shafts.

13. Remove the radius link support bolt, then lower the transaxle shift selector rods.

14. Unbolt the engine from the engine and the transaxle mounts.

15. Using an overhead lifting device, attach it to the engine lifting sling and slowly remove the engine and transaxle assembly from the vehicle.

➡️**When removing the engine, be careful not to knock it against the adjacent parts.**

16. Separate the engine from the transaxle if necessary. Install all the necessary parts on the engine before lowering it into the vehicle, such as, spark plugs, water pump etc.

To install:

17. Lower the engine and transaxle as an assembly into the car and onto the frame, make sure to keep it as level as possible.

18. Check the clearance between the frame and clutch housing and make sure that the engine mount bolts are seated in the groove of the mounting bracket.

19. Install the motor mounts, remove the engine sling and install the buffer rods, tighten the engine mount bolts first, then apply a load to the mounting insulators before tightening the buffer rod and sub-mounting bolts.

20. If the buffer rod length has not been altered, they should still be correct. Shims are placed under the engine mounts, be sure to replace the exact ones in the correct places.

21. Install the transaxle shift selector rods or cable and attaching parts.

22. Install the axle shafts and the attaching parts.

➡️**On 4WD drive applications install the driveshaft to the transfer assembly.**

23. Install the exhaust pipe to the manifold, it is a good idea to replace the gasket for the exhaust pipe at this time.

24. Install clutch cable if so equipped and speedometer cable.

25. Install the condenser, receiver drier, air conditioning compressor, power steering pump and all drive belts.

26. Install the radiator with fan motor attached as assembly, radiator grille as necessary, washer tank and the auxiliary fan.

27. Install air pump cleaner, if so equipped and the carbon canister.

28. Install all other attaching parts such as brackets etc. and the air cleaner that were removed and connect all the vacuum hoses and the electrical connectors.

29. Connect the radiator and heater hoses and refill the system with the correct amount of antifreeze.

30. Install the battery and reconnect the battery cables.

31. Install the hood in the same location as you removed it from.

32. Fill and check all fluids, start engine, let it warm up and check for leaks.

33. Road test vehicle after you are sure there are no leaks. Check vehicle for proper operation. Recheck all fluid levels.

Rocker Arm Cover

REMOVAL & INSTALLATION

1. Disconnect the negative battery cable. Remove or disconnect any electrical lines, hoses or tubes which may interfere with the removal procedures.

➡️**It may be necessary to remove the air cleaner (carburetor models) or the air duct (EFI and turbo models).**

2. Remove the rocker arm cover-to-cylinder head mounting screws , then lift the cover from the cylinder head.

3. Using a scraper or equivalent, clean the gasket mounting surfaces.

4. To install, use a NEW gasket and/or RTV sealant, then position the rocker arm cover in place. Torque the cover bolts-to-cylinder head EVENLY (working from the center to the end of the cover) to 5–8 ft. lbs. on Z series engine, 2–4 ft. lbs. on C and V series engines and 5–7 ft. lbs. on K series engines.

➡️**When using RTV sealant apply a even bead and make sure the surface that you are working on is very clean before applying sealer.**

Rocker Arm Shaft

REMOVAL & INSTALLATION

Rocker Arm Shaft removal, installation and overhaul procedures are included in the Camshaft Removal and Installation service procedures in this section, perform only the necessary service steps.

Thermostat

REMOVAL & INSTALLATION

◆ **See Figures 15, 16, 17 and 18**

➡️**On 200SX V6 engine it may be necessary to remove radiator shroud, coolant fan assembly and water suction pipe retaining bolts to gain access to the thermostat housing.**

1. Drain the engine coolant into a clean container so that the level is below the thermostat housing.

2. Disconnect the upper radiator hose at the water outlet.

3. Loosen the two securing nuts and remove the water outlet, gasket, and the thermostat from the thermostat housing.

To install:

4. Install the thermostat to the engine, using a new gasket with sealer and with the thermostat spring toward the inside of the engine.

5. Reconnect the upper radiator hose.

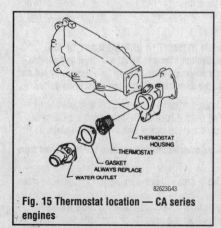

Fig. 15 Thermostat location — CA series engines

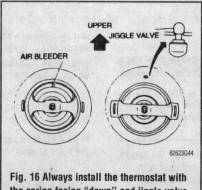

Fig. 16 Always install the thermostat with the spring facing "down" and jiggle valve facing "up"

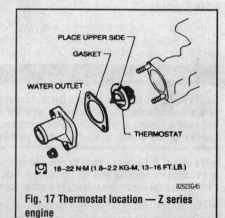

Fig. 17 Thermostat location — Z series engine

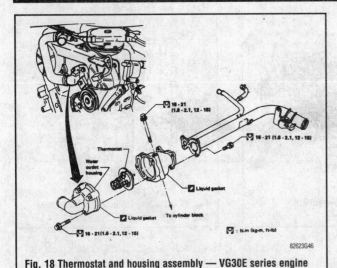

Fig. 18 Thermostat and housing assembly — VG30E series engine

6. Refill and bleed the cooling system. Refer to Section 1 for Drain And Refill procedures and illustrations if necessary. Make sure to let the engine reach normal operating temperature then check coolant for the correct level.

COOLING SYSTEM BLEEDING

♦ **See Figures 19 and 20**

1. Remove the radiator cap.
2. Fill the radiator and reservoir tank with the proper type of coolant. If equipped with an air relief plug, remove the plug and add coolant until it spills out the air relief opening. Install the plug.
3. Install and tighten the radiator cap.
4. Start the engine and allow the coolant to come up to operating temperature. If equipped allow the electric cooling fan to come on at least once. Run the heater at full force and with the temperature lever in the HOT position. Be sure the heater control valve is functioning.
5. Shut the engine off and recheck the coolant level, refill as necessary.

Intake Manifold

REMOVAL & INSTALLATION

1982–83 200SX (Z Series Engine)

➡**Always release the fuel pressure on fuel injected engines before removing any fuel system component.**

1. Drain the coolant and disconnect the battery cable.
2. Remove the air cleaner hoses.
3. Remove the radiator hoses from the manifold.

4. Remove the throttle cable and disconnect the fuel pipe and the return fuel line on fuel injection engines. Plug the fuel pipe to prevent spilling fuel.

➡**When unplugging wires and hoses, mark each hose and its connection with a piece of masking tape, then match code the two pieces of tape with the numbers 1, 2, 3, etc. When assembling, simply match the pieces of tape.**

5. Remove all remaining wires, tubes and the EGR. and PCV lines from the rear of the intake manifold. Remove the manifold supports.
6. Unbolt and remove the intake manifold. Remove the manifold with injectors, EGR. valve, fuel assembly, etc., still attached.

To install:

7. Clean the gasket mounting surfaces then install the intake manifold on the engine. Always use a new intake manifold gasket. Tighten the intake manifold bolts EVENLY in 23 stages (working from the center to the ends) to specifications.
8. Connect all electrical connections, tubes and the EGR. and PCV lines to the rear of the intake manifold. Install the manifold supports.
9. Install the throttle cable and reconnect the fuel pipe and the return fuel lines.
10. Install the radiator hoses to the intake manifold.
11. Install the air cleaner hoses.
12. Refill the coolant level and connect the battery cable. Start the engine and check for leaks.

1984–88 200SX (CA Series Engine) and Stanza (CA20E Engine)

1. Disconnnect the negative battery cable and drain the cooling system.
2. Remove the air cleaner hoses.
3. Remove the radiator hoses from the manifold.
4. Relieve the fuel pressure. Remove the throttle cable and disconnect the fuel pipe and the fuel return line. Plug the fuel pipe to prevent spilling fuel.
5. Remove all remaining wires, tubes and the EGR and PCV tubes from the rear of the intake manifold. Remove the manifold supports.
6. Unbolt and remove the intake manifold. Remove the manifold with the fuel injectors/injection body, EGR valve, fuel pipes and associated running gear still attached.
7. Remove the intake manifold gasket and clean the gasket surfaces.

To install:

8. Install the intake manifold with a new gasket. Tighten the intake manifold bolts EVENLY in 23 stages (working from the center to the ends) to specifications (14–19 ft. lbs.)
9. Install the intake manifold supports. Connect the fuel pipe, fuel return line and the throttle cable. Reconnect all necessary lines, hoses and or electrical connections.
10. Connect the radiator hoses to the intake manifold. Connect the air cleaner hoses.
11. Fill the cooling system and connect the negative battery cable. Roadtest the vehicle for proper operation.

200SX (VG30E Engine)

♦ **See Figures 21, 22, 23 and 24**

➡**When removing and installing the collector assembly and intake manifold follow the sequence patterns—refer to the illustrations.**

Fig. 19 Air relief plug — Stanza KA24E engine

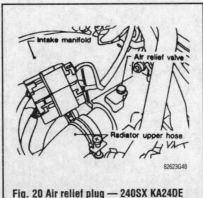

Fig. 20 Air relief plug — 240SX KA24DE engine

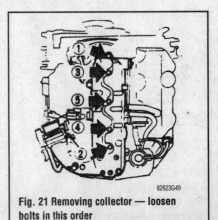

Fig. 21 Removing collector — loosen bolts in this order

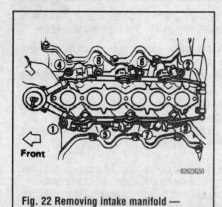

Fig. 22 Removing intake manifold —
loosen bolts in this order

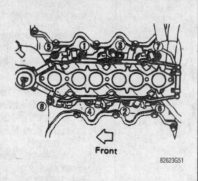

Fig. 23 Installing intake manifold —
tighten bolts in this order

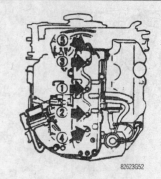

Fig. 24 Installing collector to intake manifold — tighten bolts in this order

1. Relieve the fuel system pressure, disconnect the negative battery cable and drain the cooling system.

2. Disconnect the valve cover-to-throttle chamber hose at the valve cover.

3. Disconnect the heater housing-to-water inlet tube at the water inlet.

4. Remove the bolt holding the water and fuel tubes to the head.

5. Remove the heater housing-to-thermostat housing tube.

6. Remove the intake collector cover and then remove the collector itself.

7. Disconnect the fuel line and remove the intake manifold bolts. Remove the intake manifold assembly, with the fuel tube assembly still attached, from the vehicle.

To install:

8. Install the intake manifold with a new gasket. Tighten the intake manifold bolts in 23 stages in the proper sequence to specifications.

9. Connect the fuel line.

10. Install the intake manifold collector with a new gasket. Install the collector cover assembly.

11. Connect the heater-to-thermostat housing tube.

12. Attach the water and fuel tubes to the cylinder head with the mounting bolt.

13. Connect the valve cover-to-throttle chamber hose.

14. Fill the cooling system to the proper level and connect the negative battery cable.

15. Road test the vehicle for proper operation. Make all the necessary engine adjustments.

240SX (KA24E and KA24DE Engines) and Stanza (KA24E Engine)

♦ **See Figures 25, 26, 27 and 28**

1. Relieve the fuel system pressure, disconnect the negative battery cable and drain the cooling system.

2. Remove the air duct between the air flow meter and the throttle body.

3. Disconnect the throttle cable.

4. Disconnect the fuel supply and return lines from the fuel injector assembly. Plug the lines to prevent leakage.

5. Disconnect and tag the electrical connectors and the vacuum hoses to the throttle body and intake manifold/collector assembly.

6. Remove the spark plug wires.

7. Disconnect the EGR valve tube from the exhaust manifold.

8. Remove the intake manifold mounting brackets.

9. Unbolt the intake manifold collector/throttle body from the intake manifold or just remove the mounting bolts and separate the intake manifold from the cylinder head with the collector attached.

10. Using a putty knife or equivalent, clean the gasket mounting surfaces. Check the intake manifold for cracks and warpage.

To install:

11. Install the intake manifold and gasket on the engine. Tighten the mounting bolts 1215 ft. lbs. from the center working to the end, in 23 stages. If the collector was separated from the intake manifold, torque the collector bolts to 1215 ft. lbs. from the center working to the end.

12. Install intake manifold mounting brackets.

13. Connect the EGR valve tube to the exhaust manifold.

14. Install the spark plug wires.

15. Connect the electrical connectors and the vacuum hoses to the throttle body and intake manifold/collector assembly.

16. Connect the fuel line(s) to the fuel injector assembly.

17. Connect the throttle cable.

18. Connect the air duct between the air flow meter and the throttle body.

19. Fill the cooling system to the proper level and connect the negative battery cable.

20. Make all the necessary engine adjustments. Road test the vehicle for proper operation.

Stanza (CA20 Engine)

1. Remove the air cleaner assembly together with all of the hoses.

➥**When unplugging wires and hoses, mark each hose and its connection with a piece of masking tape, then match code the 2 pieces of tape with the numbers 1, 2, 3, etc. When assembling, simply match up the pieces of tape.**

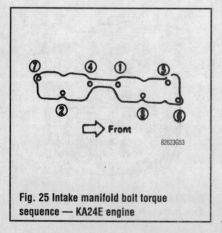

Fig. 25 Intake manifold bolt torque
sequence — KA24E engine

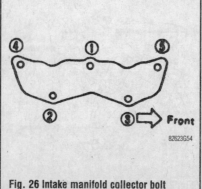

Fig. 26 Intake manifold collector bolt
torque sequence — KA24E engine

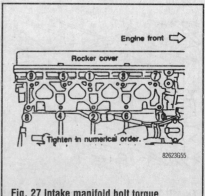

Fig. 27 Intake manifold bolt torque
sequence — KA24DE engine

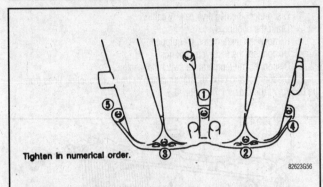

Fig. 28 Intake manifold collector bolt torque sequence — KA24DE engine

2. Disconnect and label the throttle linkage, the fuel and the vacuum lines from the carburetor and the intake manifold components.

➡The carburetor can be removed from the manifold at this point or can be removed as an assembly with the intake manifold.

3. Remove the intake manifold bolts or nuts and the manifold from the engine.

To install:

4. Using a putty knife or equivalent, clean the gasket mounting surfaces.

5. Install the intake manifold and gasket on the engine. Always use a new gasket. Tighten the mounting bolts from the, center working to the end, in two or three stages. Torque the intake manifold bolts to 14–19 ft. lbs. (CA20 engine).

6. Install throttle linkage, fuel and vacuum lines and the air cleaner assembly.

7. Start engine and check for leaks.

Exhaust Manifold

REMOVAL & INSTALLATION

All Models (Except 200SX with VG30 Engine)

▶ See Figure 29

1. Remove the air cleaner assembly, if necessary for access. Remove the heat shield.

2. Disconnect and tag the high tension wires from the spark plugs on the exhaust side of the engine.

3. Disconnect the exhaust pipe from the exhaust manifold. On turbocharged engines remove the exhaust pipe from the turbocharger assembly.

➡Soak the exhaust pipe retaining bolts with penetrating oil if necessary to loosen them.

4. On the carbureted models, remove the air induction and/or the EGR tubes from the exhaust manifold. On the fuel injected models, disconnect the exhaust gas sensor electrical connector.

5. Remove the exhaust manifold mounting nuts and the manifold from the cylinder head.

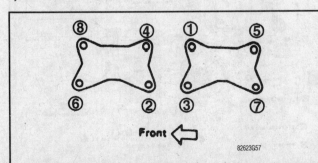

Fig. 29 Exhaust manifold torque sequence — KA24E engine

To install:

6. Using a putty knife or equivalent, clean the gasket mounting surfaces.

7. Install the manifold onto the engine, use new gaskets and from the, center working to the end. Torque the exhaust manifold nuts/bolts EVENLY to 14–22 ft. lbs.

8. Install the air induction and/or the EGR tubes to the exhaust manifold or the exhaust gas sensor electrical connector.

9. Reconnect exhaust pipe. On turbocharged engines reconnect the exhaust pipe to the turbocharger assembly.

10. Connect spark plug wires and air cleaner and any related hoses.

11. Start engine and check for exhaust leaks.

200SX (VG30E Engine)

▶ See Figure 30

1. Remove the exhaust manifold sub-cover and manifold cover. Remove the EGR tube from the right side exhaust manifold. Remove the exhaust manifold stay.

2. Disconnect the left side exhaust manifold at the exhaust pipe by removing retaining nuts and disconnect the right side manifold from the connecting pipe.

➡Soak the exhaust pipe retaining bolts with penetrating oil if necessary to loosen them.

3. Remove bolts for each manifold in the order shown.

To install:

4. Clean all gasket surfaces. Install new gaskets.

5. Install the manifold to the engine, torquing manifold bolts alternately in two stages in the exact reverse order of removal to 13–16 ft. lbs.

6. Reconnect the exhaust pipe and the connecting pipe. Be careful not break these bolts.

7. Install the exhaust manifold stay and the EGR tube to the right side manifold.

8. Install the exhaust manifold covers. Start the engine and check for exhaust leaks.

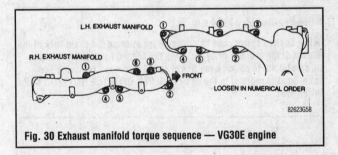

Fig. 30 Exhaust manifold torque sequence — VG30E engine

Turbocharger

REMOVAL & INSTALLATION

200SX (CA18ET Engine)

▶ See Figure 31

1. Drain the engine coolant.

2. Remove the air duct and hoses, and the air intake pipe.

3. Disconnect the front exhaust pipe at the exhaust manifold end (exhaust outlet in the illustration).

4. Remove the heat shield plates.

5. Tag and disconnect the oil delivery tube and return hose.

6. Disconnect the water inlet tube.

7. Unbolt and remove the turbocharger from the exhaust manifold.

➡The turbocharger unit should only be serviced internally by an engine specialist trained in turbocharger repair.

To install:

8. Install the turbocharger to the exhaust manifold torque these bolts evenly and to 22–25 ft. lbs. Torque the turbocharger outlet to housing 16–22 ft. lbs. if the outlet was removed.

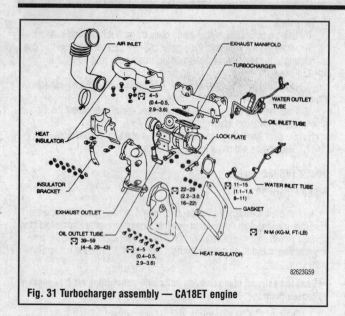

Fig. 31 Turbocharger assembly — CA18ET engine

9. Reconnect the water inlet tube.
10. Connect the oil delivery tube and return hose.
11. Connect the front exhaust pipe at the exhaust manifold end and install the heat shields.
12. Connect the air duct and hoses, and the air intake pipe.
13. Refill the cooling system, start the engine and check for leaks.

Radiator

REMOVAL & INSTALLATION

♦ See Figures 32, 33, 34 and 35

➡The cooling system can be drained from opening the drain cock at the bottom of the radiator or by removing the bottom hose at the radiator. Be careful not to damage the fins or core tubes when removing and installing the radiator to the vehicle. **NEVER OPEN THE RADIATOR CAP WHEN HOT.**

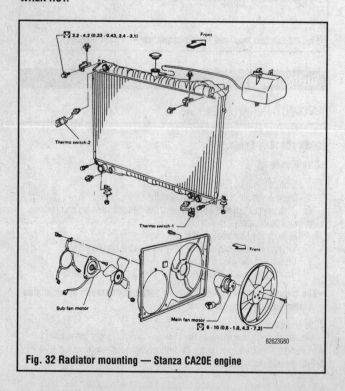

Fig. 32 Radiator mounting — Stanza CA20E engine

1. Disconnect the negative battery cable.
2. Drain the cooling system.
3. Remove the undercover, if equipped.
4. Disconnect the reservoir tank hose.
5. Disconnect all temperature switch connectors.
6. Disconnect and plug the transmission or transaxle cooling lines from the bottom of the radiator, if equipped.

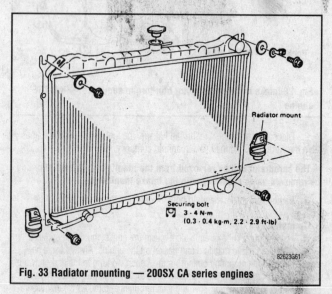

Fig. 33 Radiator mounting — 200SX CA series engines

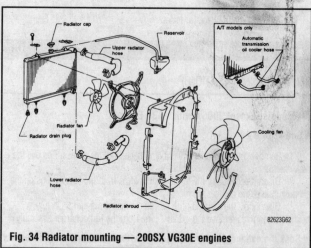

Fig. 34 Radiator mounting — 200SX VG30E engines

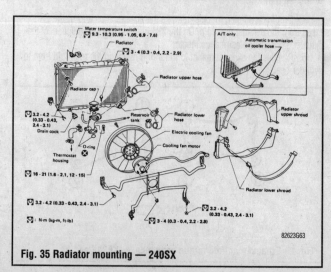

Fig. 35 Radiator mounting — 240SX

7. Remove the fan shroud and position the shroud over the fan and clear of the radiator if so equipped. Remove the condenser and radiator fan assembly from the radiator if so equipped.

8. Disconnect the upper and lower hoses from the radiator.

9. Remove the radiator retaining bolts or the upper supports.

10. Lift the radiator off the mounts and out of the vehicle.

To install:

11. Lower the radiator onto the mounts and bolt in place.

12. Install the lower shroud, if removed.

13. Connect the upper and lower radiator hoses—use NEW water hose clamps.

14. Install the fan shroud assembly as necessary. Install the condenser and radiator fan assembly as necessary.

15. Connect the transaxle or transmission cooling lines, if removed.

16. Reconnect all electrical connectors.

17. Connect the reservoir tank hose.

18. Fill the cooling system to the proper level. Bleed the cooling system—refer to the necessary service procedures.

19. Connect the negative battery cable.

20. Start the engine and check for leaks.

Engine Fan

REMOVAL & INSTALLATION

Belt Drive Type (Engine)

▶ **See Figures 36 and 37**

1. Disconnect the negative battery cable.

2. Remove the fan shroud.

3. Remove the drive belt, fan assembly/pulley retaining bolts.

4. Remove the fan assembly.

5. Installation is the reverse of the removal procedure. Check fan coupling for rough operation before installation. Adjust the drive belt.

➡ **If necessary remove the radiator from the vehicle—refer to the necessary service procedure for additional clearance to remove the fan assembly.**

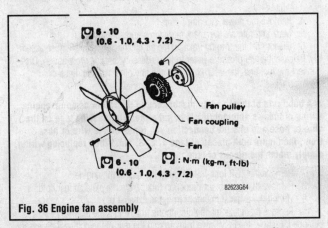

Fig. 36 Engine fan assembly

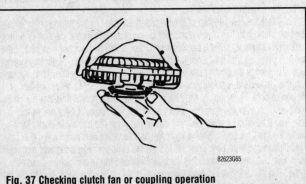

Fig. 37 Checking clutch fan or coupling operation

Electric Type (Radiator Fan)

1. Disconnect the negative battery cable.

2. Unplug the condenser and radiator fan motor wiring harness connectors.

3. Remove the radiator shroud bolts.

4. Separate the shroud and cooling fan assembly from the radiator and remove.

To install:

5. Mount the radiator shroud and cooling fan assembly onto the radiator.

6. Install the radiator shroud bolts.

7. Plug in the radiator and condenser fan motor harness connectors.

8. Connect the negative battery cable.

Water Pump

REMOVAL & INSTALLATION

All Models/Engines (Except 200SX VG30E Engine)

▶ **See Figures 38, 39, 40 and 41**

1. Disconnect the negative battery cable.

2. Drain the coolant from the radiator and cylinder block.

3. Remove all the drive belts.

4. Unbolt the fan assembly/water pump pulley and the water pump attaching bolts.

5. Separate the water pump with the gasket, if installed, from the cylinder block.

6. Remove all gasket material or sealant from the water pump mating surfaces. All sealant must be removed from the groove in the water pump surface also.

To install:

7. Apply a continuous bead of high temperature liquid gasket to the water pump housing mating surface. The housing must be attached to the cylinder block within 5 minutes after the sealant is applied. After the pump housing is bolted to the block, wait at least 30 minutes for the sealant to cure before starting the engine.

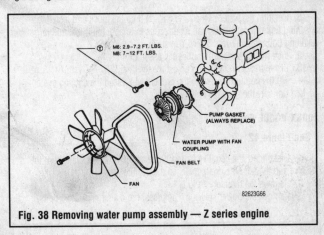

Fig. 38 Removing water pump assembly — Z series engine

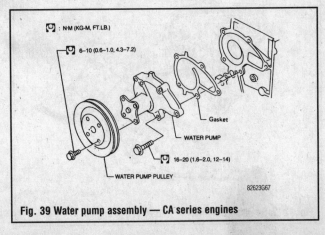

Fig. 39 Water pump assembly — CA series engines

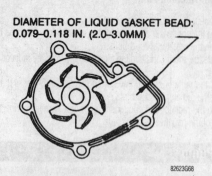

DIAMETER OF LIQUID GASKET BEAD:
0.079–0.118 IN. (2.0–3.0MM)

82623G68

Fig. 40 Apply a continuous bead of high temperature sealant to the water pump housing mating surface

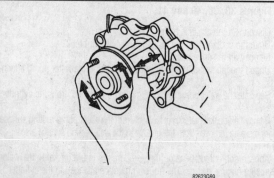

82623G69

Fig. 41 Checking water pump for excessive end play and rough operation

8. Position the water pump (and gasket) onto the block and install the attaching bolts. Torque the small retaining bolts to about 5 ft. lbs. and large retaining bolts 1214 ft. lbs. EVENLY in steps.

9. Install the water pump pulley/fan assembly.

10. Install the drive belts and adjust the tension.

11. Fill the cooling system to the proper level. Bleed the cooling system.

12. Connect the negative battery cable.

200SX VG30E Engine

♦ See Figure 42

1. Disconnect the negative battery cable and drain the coolant from the radiator and the left side drain cocks on the cylinder block.

2. Remove the radiator shroud.

3. Remove the power steering, compressor and alternator drive belts.

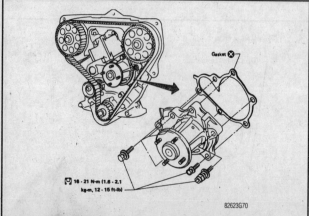

Gasket ⊗

16 - 21 N·m (1.6 - 2.1
kg-m, 12 - 15 ft-lb)

82623G70

Fig. 42 Water pump assembly — 200SX VG30E engine

4. Remove the cooling fan and coupling.

5. Disconnect the water pump hoses.

6. Remove the water pump pulley, then the upper and lower timing covers.

➡ Be careful not to get coolant on the timing belt and to avoid deforming the timing cover, make sure there is enough clearance between the timing cover and the hose clamp.

7. Remove the water pump retaining bolts, note different lengths, and remove the pump.

8. Make sure the gasket sealing surfaces are clean and free of all the old gasket material.

To install:

9. Mount the water pump and gasket onto the cylinder block. Torque the retaining bolts EVENLY in steps to 1215 ft. lbs.

10. Install the upper and lower timing belt covers.

11. Connect the water pump hoses.

12. Install the cooling fan and coupling assembly.

13. Install and tension the drive belts.

14. Install the radiator shroud.

15. Fill and bleed the cooling system and connect the negative battery cable.

Cylinder Head

REMOVAL & INSTALLATION

➡ To prevent distortion or warping of the cylinder head, allow the engine to cool completely before removing the head bolts.

200SX (Z Series Engine)

♦ See Figures 43, 44, 45, 46 and 47

1. Crank the engine until the No. 1 piston is at TDC of the compression stroke, disconnect the battery, and drain the cooling system.

2. Remove the radiator hoses and the heater hoses. Unbolt the alternator mounting bracket and move the alternator to one side, if necessary.

3. If the car is equipped with air conditioning, unbolt the compressor and place it to one side. Do not disconnect the compressor lines. Severe injury could result.

4. Remove the power steering pump.

5. Mark and remove the spark plug wires and spark plugs.

6. Disconnect the throttle linkage, the air cleaner or its intake hose assembly. Release the fuel pressure (refer to the necessary service procedures). Disconnect the fuel line, the return fuel line and any other vacuum lines or electrical leads.

➡ A good rule of thumb when disconnecting the rather complex engine wiring of today's automobiles is to put a piece of masking tape on the wire or hose and one the connection you removed the wire or hose from, then mark both pieces of tape 1, 2, 3, etc. When replacing wiring, simply match the pieces of tape.

7. Remove the EGR tube from around the rear of the engine.

8. Remove the exhaust air induction tubes from the exhaust manifold.

9. Unbolt the exhaust manifold from the exhaust pipe.

10. Remove the intake manifold supports from under the manifold if so equipped. Remove the PCV valve from around the rear of the engine if necessary.

11. Remove the valve cover.

12. Mark the relationship of the camshaft sprocket to the timing chain with paint or chalk. If this is done, it will not be necessary to locate the factory timing marks. Before removing the camshaft sprocket, it will be necessary to wedge the chain in place so that it will not fall down into the front cover. The factory procedure is to wedge the timing chain in place with the wooden wedge. The problem with this procedure is that it may allow the chain tensioner to move out far enough to cock itself against the chain. If this happens, you'll find that the chain won't go back over the sprocket after you've put the sprocket back on. In this case, you'll have to remove the front cover and push the tensioner back. After you've wedged the chain, unbolt the camshaft sprocket and remove it.

13. Working from both ends in, loosen the cylinder head bolts and remove them. Remove the bolts securing the cylinder head to the front cover assembly.

14. Lift the cylinder head off the engine block. It may be necessary to tap the head lightly with a rubber mallet to loosen it.

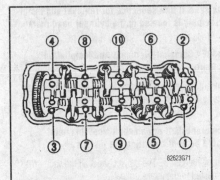

Fig. 43 Cylinder head bolt loosening sequence — 200SX Z series engine

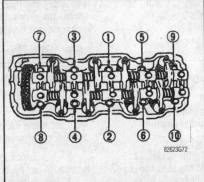

Fig. 44 Cylinder head bolt torque sequence — 200SX Z series engine

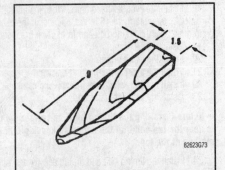

Fig. 45 Wood wedge dimensions — 9 in. (229mm) x 1.5 in. (38mm) — used to hold chain in place

Fig. 46 Wedge the chain with a wooden block (arrow) If you don't you will be fishing for the chain in the engine

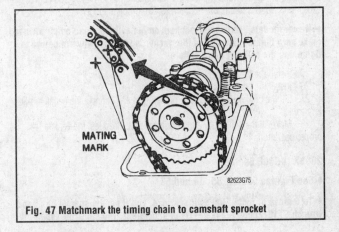

Fig. 47 Matchmark the timing chain to camshaft sprocket

To install:

15. Thoroughly clean the cylinder block and head surfaces and check both for warpage.

16. Fit the new head gasket. Don't use sealant. Make sure that no open valves are in the way of raised pistons, and do not rotate the crankshaft or camshaft separately because of possible damage which might occur to the valves.

17. Temporarily tighten the two center right and left cylinder head bolts to 14 ft. lbs.

18. Install the camshaft sprocket together with the timing chain to the camshaft. Make sure the marks you made earlier line up with each other. If you get into trouble, see Timing Chain Removal and Installation for timing procedures.

19. Install the cylinder head bolts and torque them to 20 ft. lbs., then 40 ft. lbs., then 58 ft. lbs. in the order (sequence) shown in the illustration.

20. Clean and regap the spark plugs then install them in the cylinder head. DO NOT OVERTORQUE THE SPARK PLUGS.

21. Install the valve cover with a new gasket.

22. Install the intake manifold supports to the manifold if so equipped. Install the PCV valve if it was removed.

23. Connect the exhaust pipe to exhaust manifold (use NEW exhaust gasket).

24. Install the exhaust air induction tubes to the exhaust manifold.

25. Install the EGR tube from around the rear of the engine.

26. Connect the throttle linkage, the air cleaner or its intake hose assembly (fuel injection). Reconnect the fuel line, the return fuel line and any other vacuum lines or electrical leads.

27. Install the power steering pump if so equipped and correctly adjust the drive belt.

28. Install the air conditioning compressor and correctly adjust the drive belt.

29. Install the alternator mounting bracket, alternator, electrical connections to the alternator and adjust the drive belt.

30. Reconnect the heater and radiator hoses.

➡It is always wise to drain the crankcase oil after the cylinder head has been installed to avoid coolant contamination.

31. Refill the cooling system. Adjust the valves.

32. Start engine, run engine to normal operating temperature, check for the correct coolant level.

33. Check for leaks and roadtest vehicle for proper operation.

200SX (CA20E and CA18ET Engines), Stanza and Stanza Wagon (CA20E)

◗ See Figures 48, 49, 50, 51 and 52

1. Relieve the fuel system pressure, disconnect the negative battery cable and drain the cooling system.

2. Remove the air intake pipe.

3. Remove the cooling fan and radiator shroud.

4. Remove the alternator drive belt, power steering pump drive belt and the air conditioner compressor drive belt, if equipped.

5. Position the No. 1 cylinder at TDC of the compression stroke and remove the upper and lower timing belt covers.

6. Loosen the timing belt tensioner and return spring, then remove the timing belt.

➡When the timing belt has been removed, do not rotate the crankshaft and the camshaft separately, because the valves will hit the tops of the pistons.

7. Remove the exhaust manifold.

8. Remove the camshaft pulley.

9. Remove the water pump pulley.

10. Remove the crankshaft pulley.

11. Remove the alternator adjusting bracket.

12. Remove the water pump.

13. Remove the oil pump.

14. Loosen the cylinder head bolts in sequence and in several steps.

15. Remove the cylinder head and manifold as an assembly.

To install:

16. Clean the cylinder head gasket surfaces.

17. Lay the cylinder head gasket onto the block and lower the head onto the gasket.

18. Install the cylinder head bolts. When installing the bolts, tighten the two center bolts temporarily to 15 ft. lbs. and install the head bolts loosely. They will be torqued after the timing belt and front cover are installed.

19. Install the oil pump.

20. Install the water pump.

21. Install the alternator adjusting bracket.

22. Install the crankshaft, water pump and camshaft pulleys.

23. Install the exhaust manifold.

➡Before installing the timing belt, be certain the crankshaft pulley key is near the top and that the camshaft knock pin or sprocket aligning mark is at the top.

24. Install the timing belt and timing belt covers. After the timing belt and covers have been installed, torque all the head bolts in the torque sequence provided. Tighten all bolts to 22 ft. lbs. (29 Nm). Re-tighten all bolts to 58 ft. lbs. (78 Nm). Loosen all bolts completely and then re-tighten them once again to 22 ft. lbs. (29 Nm). Tighten all bolts to a final torque of 54–61 ft. lbs. (74–83 Nm) or if using an angle torque wrench, give all bolts a final turn to 75–80 degrees except bolt No. 8 which is 83–88 degrees. No. 8 bolt is longer.

➡Newer models use cupped washers on the cylinder head bolts, always make sure that the flat side of the washer is facing downward before tightening the cylinder head bolts.

25. Install the drive belts.

26. Install the cooling fan and radiator shroud.

27. Fill the cooling system to the proper level and connect the negative battery cable.

28. Make all the necessary engine adjustments. Road test the vehicle for proper operation.

200SX (VG30E Engine)

♦ **See Figures 53, 54, 55, 56 and 57**

➡To remove or install the cylinder head, you'll need a special hex head wrench ST10120000 (J24239–01) or equivalent. The collector assembly and intake manifold have special bolt sequence for removal and installation. The distributor assembly is located in the cylinder head mark and remove it if necessary.

➡See note at 200SX VG30E "Camshaft Removal And Installation" before starting this procedure.

1. Release the fuel pressure. See the procedure in this section for timing belt removal. Set the engine to Top Dead Center and then remove the timing belt.

➡Do not rotate either the crankshaft or camshaft from this point onward, or the valves could be bent by hitting the pistons.

2. Drain the coolant from the engine. Then, disconnect all the vacuum hoses and water hoses connected to the intake collector.

3. Remove the collector cover and the collector. Refer to the section Intake Manifold Removal And Installation for correct bolt removal sequence.

4. Remove the intake manifold and fuel tube assembly.

5. Remove the exhaust collector bracket. Remove the exhaust manifold covers. Disconnect the exhaust manifold when it connects to the exhaust pipe (three bolts).

6. Remove the camshaft pulleys and the rear timing cover securing bolts.

7. Loosen cylinder head bolts a little at a time in numerical order.

8. Remove the cylinder head with the exhaust manifold attached. If you need to remove the exhaust manifold, refer to the procedure in this section.

To install:

9. Check the positions of the timing marks and camshaft sprockets to make sure they have not shifted.

10. Install the head with a new gasket. Apply clean engine oil to the threads and seats of the bolts and install the bolts with washers in the correct position. Note that bolts 4, 5, 12, and 13 are 127mm long. The other bolts are 106mm long.

11. Torque the bolts according to the pattern for the cylinder head on each side in the following stages:
   a. Torque all bolts, in order, to 22 ft. lbs.
   b. Torque all bolts, in order, to 43 ft. lbs.

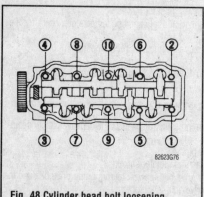

Fig. 48 Cylinder head bolt loosening sequence — 200SX CA series engine

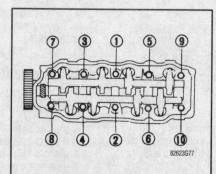

Fig. 49 Cylinder head bolt torque sequence — 200SX CA series engine. Bolt No 8 is the longest

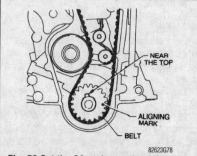

Fig. 50 Set the CA series engines No. 1 cylinder at TDC on the compression stroke The key-way on the crankshaft sprocket will be almost at 12:00 position

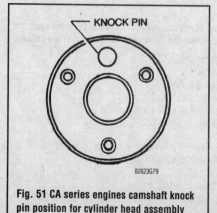

Fig. 51 CA series engines camshaft knock pin position for cylinder head assembly

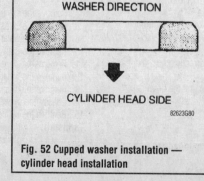

Fig. 52 Cupped washer installation — cylinder head installation

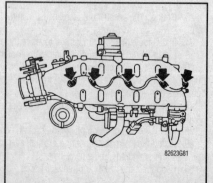

Fig. 53 To remove the collector (VG30E engine), loosen the arrowed bolts

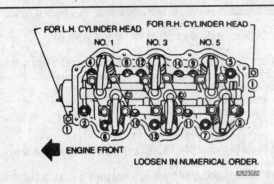

Fig. 54 To remove the cylinder head (VG30E engine), loosen the bolts in numerical order

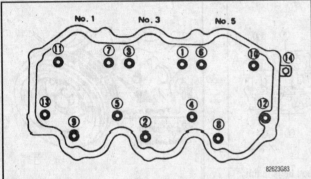

Fig. 55 Torquing pattern for the right side cylinder head — VG30E engine

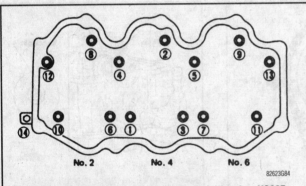

Fig. 56 Torquing pattern for the left side cylinder head — VG30E engine

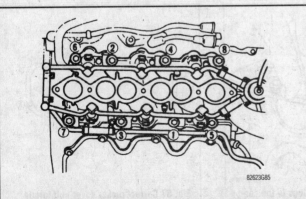

Fig. 57 Torquing pattern for the intake manifold — VG30E engine

  c. Loosen all bolts completely..

  d. Torque all bolts, in order, to 22 ft. lbs.

  e. Torque all bolts, in order, to 40–47 ft. lbs. If you have a special wrench available that torques bolts to a certain angle, torque them 60–65° tighter rather than going to 40–47 ft. lbs.

12. Install the rear timing cover bolts. Install the camshaft pulleys. Make sure the pulley marked R3 goes on the right and that marked L3 goes on the left.

13. Align the timing marks if necessary and then install the timing belt and adjust the belt tension.

14. Install the front upper and lower belt covers.

15. Make sure that the rocker cover bolts, trays and washers are free of oil. Then, install the rocker covers.

16. Install the intake manifold and fuel tube. Torque NUTS as follows:

  a. Torque in numbered order to 26–43 in. lbs.

  b. Torque in numbered order to 17–20 ft. lbs.

17. Torque the BOLTS on the intake manifold as follows:

  a. Torque in numbered order to 26–43 inch lbs.

  b. Torque in numbered order to 12–14 ft. lbs.

18. Install the exhaust manifold if removed from the cylinder head.

19. Connect the exhaust manifold to the exhaust pipe connection (replace the exhaust pipe gasket). Install the exhaust collector bracket.

20. Install the collector and collector cover. Refer to the section for Intake Manifold Removal And Installation for the correct torque pattern.

21. Connect all the vacuum hoses and water hoses to the intake collector.

22. Refill the cooling system. Start the engine check the engine timing. After the engine reaches the normal operating temperature check for the correct coolant level.

23. Roadtest the vehicle for proper operation.

240SX (KA24E Engine) and 1990–92 Stanza (KA24E Engine)

▶ See Figures 58 thru 67

➡After finishing this procedure allow the rocker cover to cylinder head rubber plugs to dry for 30 minutes before starting the engine. This will allow the liquid gasket sealer used to seal these plugs to dry completely.

1. Drain coolant from the radiator and remove drain plug from the cylinder block. Release the fuel pressure.

2. Remove the power steering drive belt, power steering pump, idler pulley and power steering brackets.

3. Mark and disconnect all the vacuum hoses, spark plug wires and electrical connections to gain access to cylinder head. Remove the air induction hose from the collector assembly.

4. Disconnect the accelerator bracket. If necessary mark the position and remove the accelerator cable wire end from the throttle drum.

5. Remove the bolts that hold intake manifold collector to the intake manifold. Remove and position the collector assembly to the side.

6. Remove the bolts that hold intake manifold to the cylinder. Remove the intake manifold. Unplug the exhaust gas sensor and remove the exhaust cover and exhaust pipe at exhaust manifold connection. Remove the exhaust manifold from the cylinder head.

7. Remove the rocker cover. If cover sticks to the cylinder head, tap it with a rubber hammer.

➡After removing the rocker cover matchmark the timing chain with the camshaft sprocket with paint or equivalent. This step is very important for the correct installation of the timing chain to sprocket.

8. Set No. 1 cylinder piston at TDC on its compression stroke. Remove the No.1 spark plug and make sure that the piston is UP.

9. Loosen the camshaft sprocket bolt. Do not turn engine when removing the bolt.

10. Support the timing chain with a block of wood as illustrated.

11. Remove the camshaft sprocket.

12. Remove the front cover to cylinder head retaining bolts.

➡The cylinder head bolts should be loosened in two or three steps in the correct order to prevent head warpage or cracking.

13. Remove the cylinder head bolts in the correct order.

To install:

14. Confirm that the No. 1 is at TDC on its compression stroke as follows:

  a. Align timing mark with 0 mark on the crankshaft pulley.

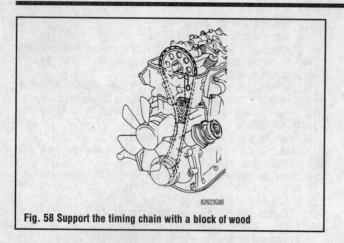
Fig. 58 Support the timing chain with a block of wood

b. Make sure the distributor rotor head is set at No. 1 on the distributor cap.

c. Confirm that the knock pin on the camshaft is set at the top position.

15. Install the cylinder head with a new gasket and torque the head bolts in numerical order in 5 steps (a, b, c, d, e). Do not rotate crankshaft and camshaft separately, or valves will hit the piston heads.

a. Torque all bolts to 22 ft. lbs.

b. Torque all bolts to 58 ft. lbs.

c. Loosen all bolts completely.

d. Torque all bolts to 22 ft. lbs.

e. Torque all bolts to 54–61 ft. lbs., or if you are using an angle wrench, turn all bolts 80–85° clockwise.

16. Remove the block of wood holding timing chain in the correct location. Position the timing chain on the camshaft sprocket by aligning each matchmark. Install the camshaft sprocket to the camshaft.

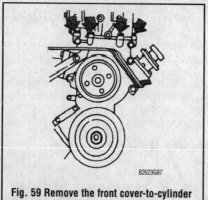
Fig. 59 Remove the front cover-to-cylinder head retaining bolts

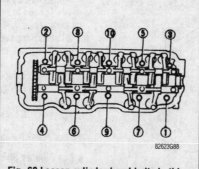
Fig. 60 Loosen cylinder head bolts in this order — KA24E and KA24DE series engines

Fig. 61 Align timing mark with 0 on the timing scale

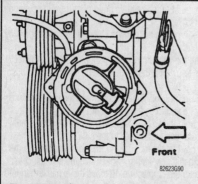
Fig. 62 View of rotor at No. 1 cylinder firing location

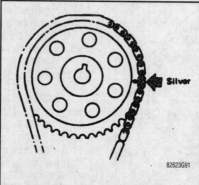
Fig. 63 Matchmark timing chain with camshaft sprocket

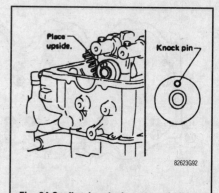
Fig. 64 Confirm knock pin on camshaft is set at the top position

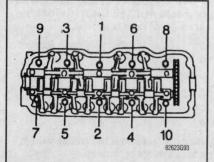
Fig. 65 Torque cylinder head bolts in this order — KA24E and KA24DE series engines

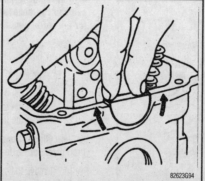
Fig. 66 Installing rubber plugs in the correct manner

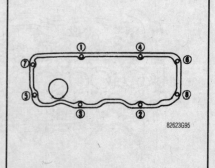
Fig. 67 Correct rocker cover bolt torque sequence

17. Tighten the camshaft sprocket bolt and the front cover to cylinder head retaining bolts.

18. Install the intake manifold and collector assembly with new gaskets. Refer to the Intake Manifold Removal and Installation procedures.

19. Install the exhaust manifold with new gaskets. Refer to the Exhaust Manifold Removal and Installation procedures.

20. Apply liquid gasket to the rubber plugs and install the rubber plugs in the correct location in the cylinder head.

21. Install the rocker cover with new gasket in place. Tighten the retaining bolts in the correct order.

22. Reconnect the accelerator bracket and cable if removed.

23. Connect all the vacuum hoses, and electrical connections that were removed to gain access to cylinder head. Reconnect the air induction hose to collector assembly.

24. Clean and regap the spark plugs if necessary. Install the spark plugs and spark plug wires in the correct location. DO NOT OVERTIGHTEN!

25. Install the power steering brackets, idler pulley, and power steering pump. Install the drive belt and adjust the belt.

26. Install the drain plug in the cylinder block. Refill the cooling system.

27. Start the engine, after the engine reaches the normal operating temperature check for the correct coolant level.

28. Roadtest the vehicle for proper operation.

240SX (KA24DE Engine)

1. Release the fuel system pressure.

2. Disconnect the negative battery cable and drain the cooling system. Drain the engine oil.

3. Remove all vacuum hoses, fuel lines, wires, electrical connections as necessary.

4. Remove the front exhaust pipe and AIV. pipe.

5. Remove the air duct, cooling fan with coupling and radiator shroud.

6. Remove the fuel injector tube assembly with injectors.

7. Disconnect and mark spark plug wires. Remove the spark plugs.

8. Set No. 1 piston at TDC on compression stroke. Remove the rocker cover assembly.

9. Mark and remove the distributor assembly.

10. Remove the cam sprocket, brackets and camshafts. These parts should be reassembled in their original position. Bolts should be loosened in 23 steps—refer to the service procedures and illustrations in this section.

11. Loosen cylinder head bolts in two or three steps in sequence.

12. Remove the cam sprocket cover. Remove the upper chain tensioner and upper chain guides.

13. Remove the upper timing chain and idler sprocket bolt. Lower timing chain will not disengaged from the crankshaft sprocket.

14. Remove the cylinder head with the intake manifold, collector and exhaust manifold assembly.

To install:

15. Check all components for wear. Replace as necessary. Clean all mating surfaces and replace the cylinder head gasket.

16. Install cylinder head. Tighten cylinder head in the following sequence:
   a. Tighten all bolts in sequence to 22 ft. lbs.
   b. Tighten all bolts in sequence to 59 ft. lbs.
   c. Loosen all bolts in sequence completely.
   d. Tighten all bolts in sequence to 18 to 25 ft. lbs.
   e. Tighten all bolts in sequence to 55 to 62 ft. lbs.

17. Install upper timing chain assemble in the correct position. Align all timing marks.

18. Install all other components in the reverse order of the removal procedure. Refill and check all fluid levels. Road test the vehicle for proper operation.

Stanza (CA20 Engine)

♦ See Figures 68 and 69

1. Disconnect the negative battery cable and drain the cooling system.

2. Support vehicle safely, remove the right front wheel.

3. Remove all spark plugs. Tag and disconnect all lines, hoses and wires which may interfere with cylinder removal.

4. Position the No. 1 cylinder at TDC of the compression stroke and remove the dust cover and the under cover.

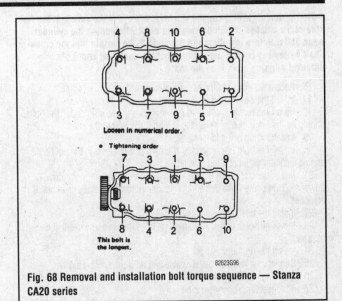

Fig. 68 Removal and installation bolt torque sequence — Stanza CA20 series

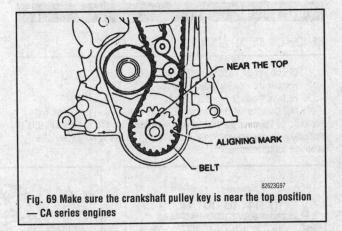

Fig. 69 Make sure the crankshaft pulley key is near the top position — CA series engines

5. Remove the alternator drive belt, power steering pump drive belt and air conditioning compressor drive belt if so equipped.

6. Remove the crankshaft pulley.

7. Support engine and remove right side engine insulator and mounting bracket.

8. Remove front upper and lower timing belt covers.

9. Loosen timing belt tensioner and return spring, then remove the timing belt.

➡When the timing belt has been removed, do not rotate the crankshaft and the camshaft separately, because the valves will hit the piston heads.

10. Remove rocker shafts with rocker arms and securing bolts. The bolts should be loosened in two or three stages.

11. Remove camshaft sprocket.

12. Disconnect exhaust pipe from the exhaust manifold.

13. Remove cylinder head together with manifolds as an assembly. The bolts should be loosened in two or three stages in sequence.

To install:

14. Thoroughly clean both the cylinder block and head mating surfaces. Avoid scratching either.

15. Install a new head gasket on the block and the cylinder head with manifolds attached as an assembly. When installing the bolts tighten the two center bolts temporarily to 15 ft. lbs. and install the head bolts loosely. After the timing belt and front cover have been installed, torque all the head bolts in the torque sequence. Tighten all bolts to 22 ft. lbs. Retighten all bolts to 58 ft. lb. Loosen all bolts completely and then retighten them once again to 22 ft. lbs. Tighten all bolts to a final torque of 54–61 ft. lbs.

➡Newer models utilize cupped washers, always make sure that the flat side of the washer is facing downward before tightening the cylinder head bolts. Before installing the timing belt, be certain that the crankshaft pulley key is near the top and that the camshaft knock pin or sprocket aligning mark is at the top.

16. Reconnect exhaust pipe to exhaust manifold.
17. Install the camshaft sprocket.
18. Install the rocker shafts with rocker arms and securing bolts. The bolts should be tighten in two or three stages from the center to the ends.
19. Install timing belt and tensioner.
20. Install the front upper and lower timing belt covers and the right side engine insulator and mounting bracket.
21. Install the crankshaft pulley. Install and adjust, the alternator drive belt, power steering pump drive belt and air conditioning compressor drive belt if so equipped.
22. Install the dust and under covers.
23. Install all spark plugs. Reconnect all lines, hoses and wires that were removed.
24. Install the right front wheel.
25. Connect the negative battery cable and refill the cooling system.
26. Start engine, check engine timing and for oil or water leaks.
27. Road test for proper operation.

Valve Lifters

REMOVAL & INSTALLATION

1. Disconnect the negative battery cable.
2. Remove the cylinder head, if required.
3. Remove the rocker arms and shafts.
4. Withdraw the lifters from the head or from the bore in the rocker. Tag each lifter to the corresponding cylinder head opening or rocker. If the lifter is installed in the rocker, remove the snapring first. Be careful not to bend the snapring during removal.

➡Do not lay the lifters on their sides because air will be allowed to enter the lifter. When storing lifters, set them straight up. To store lifters on their sides, they must be soaked in a bath of clean engine oil.

To install:

5. Install the lifters in their original locations. Use new lifter snaprings as needed. New lifters should be soaked in a bath of clean engine oil prior to installation to remove the air.
6. Install the rocker arms and shafts.
7. Install the cylinder head and leave the valve cover off.
8. Check the lifters for proper operation by pushing hard on each lifter with fingertip pressure. If the valve lifter moves more than 0.04 in. (1mm), air may be inside it. Make sure the rocker arm is not on the cam lobe when making this check. If there was air in the lifters, bleed the air by running the engine at 1000 rpm for 10 minutes.

Oil Pan

REMOVAL & INSTALLATION

200SX (CA and Z Series Engines)

▶ **See Figures 70, 71, 72, 73 and 74**

1. Disconnect the negative battery cable.
2. Raise the front of the vehicle and support safely.
3. Drain the oil pan.
4. Remove the power steering bracket from the suspension crossmember.
5. Separate the stabilizer bar from the transverse link.
6. Separate the tension rod from the transverse link.
7. Remove the front engine mounting insulator nuts.
8. Lift the engine.
9. Loosen the oil pan bolts in the proper sequence. On Z series engine application follow the CA series pattern.

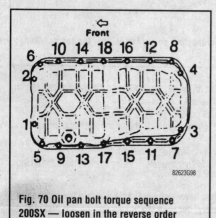

Fig. 70 Oil pan bolt torque sequence 200SX — loosen in the reverse order

Fig. 71 Using a seal cutter on the oil pan gasket

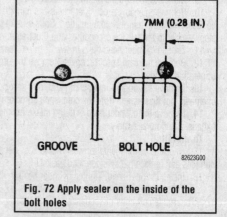

Fig. 72 Apply sealer on the inside of the bolt holes

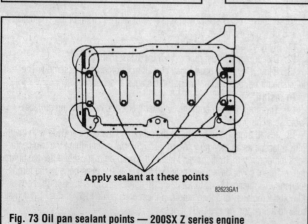

Fig. 73 Oil pan sealant points — 200SX Z series engine

Fig. 74 Apply sealant to the engine oil pan mating surfaces here; also to the corresponding points on the oil pan — CA series engines

10. Remove the suspension crossmember bolts and remove the screws that secure the power steering oil tubes to the crossmember.

11. Lower the suspension crossmember until there is sufficient clearance to remove the oil pan.

12. Insert a seal cutter between the oil pan and the cylinder block.

13. Tapping the seal cutter with a hammer, slide the cutting tool around the entire edge of the oil pan. Do not drive the seal cutter into the oil pump or rear seal retainer portion or the aluminum mating surface will be deformed.

14. Lower the oil pan from the cylinder block and remove it from the front side of the engine.

To install:

15. Carefully scrape the old gasket material away from the pan and cylinder block mounting surfaces.

16. First apply sealant to the oil pump gasket and rear oil seal retainer gasket surfaces. Then, apply a continuous bead (3.5‐4.5mm) of liquid gasket around the oil pan to the 4 corners of the cylinder block mounting surface. Wait 5 minutes and then install the pan. Tighten the oil pan bolts in sequence to 56 ft. lbs. On Z series engine application follow the CA series pattern.

17. Raise the crossmember from the lowered position. Attach the power steering tubes and install the crossmember bolts.

18. Install the front engine mounting insulator nuts.

19. Connect the tension rod and stabilizer bar to the transverse link.

20. Attach the power steering bracket to the crossmember.

21. Lower the vehicle.

22. Fill the crankcase to the proper level.

23. Connect the negative battery cable. Start the engine and check for leaks.

200SX (VG30E Engine)

▶ See Figure 75

1. Remove the front hood if necessary, connect a lifting sling to the engine, and apply upward pressure. Drain the oil pan.

2. Remove the covers from under the engine. Then, remove the engine mount insulator nuts and bolts.

3. Remove the five engine mounting bolts and remove the center crossmember assembly.

4. Remove the exhaust pipe connecting nuts. Unbolt and remove the oil pan.

To install:

5. Clean all the sealing surfaces. Apply sealant to the four joints on the lower surface of the block. Apply sealant to the corresponding areas of the oil pan gasket on both upper and lower surfaces.

6. Install the pan and gasket. Torque the pan bolts EVENLY in the order shown in the illustration to 5–6 ft. lbs and then lower engine assembly.

7. Install the exhaust pipe connection.

8. Install the center crossmember assembly and engine mount bolts.

9. Install the under covers to the engine and refill the oil pan with the specified quantity of clean oil. Operate the engine and check for leaks.

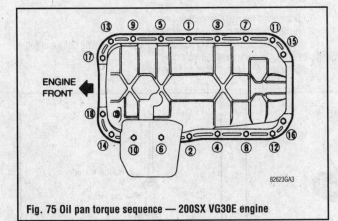

Fig. 75 Oil pan torque sequence — 200SX VG30E engine

240SX

▶ See Figure 76

1. Disconnect the negative battery cable.

2. Raise the front of the vehicle and support safely.

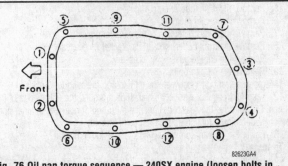

Fig. 76 Oil pan torque sequence — 240SX engine (loosen bolts in the reverse order)

3. Drain the oil pan.

4. Separate the front stabilizer bar from the side member.

5. Position a block of wood between a floor jack and the engine and then raise the engine slightly in its mounts.

6. Remove the oil pan retaining bolts in the proper sequence.

7. Insert a seal cutter between the oil pan and the cylinder block.

8. Tapping the cutter with a hammer, slide it around the entire edge of the oil pan. Do not drive the seal cutter into the oil pump or rear seal retainer portion or the aluminum mating surface will be deformed.

9. Lower the oil pan from the cylinder block and remove it from the front side of the engine.

To install:

10. To install, carefully scrape the old gasket material away from the pan and cylinder block mounting surfaces and then apply a continuous bead (3.5‐4.5mm) of liquid gasket around the oil pan to the 4 corners of the cylinder block mounting surface. Wait 5 minutes and then install the pan.

11. Install the oil pan and tighten the mounting bolts from the inside, out, to 3.6‐5.1 ft. lbs. Wait 30 minutes before refilling the crankcase to allow for the sealant to cure properly.

12. Connect the front stabilizer to the side bar.

13. Lower the vehicle.

14. Fill the crankcase to the proper level.

15. Connect the negative battery cable. Start the engine and check for leaks.

Stanza (CA Series Engine)

1. Disconect the negative battery cable.

2. Drain the oil pan.

3. Raise and support the front of the vehicle safely.

4. Remove the front exhaust pipe section and the center crossmember.

5. Remove the oil pan bolts.

6. Insert a seal cutter between the oil pan and the cylinder block.

7. Tapping the cutter with a hammer, slide it around the entire edge of the oil pan. Do not drive the seal cutter into the oil pump or rear seal retainer portion or the aluminum mating surface will be deformed.

8. Lower the oil pan from the cylinder block and remove it.

To install:

9. Carefully scrape the old gasket material away from the pan and cylinder block mounting surfaces and then apply a thin continuous bead of liquid gasket around the oil pan and to the 4 corners of the cylinder block mounting surface. Do the same to the oil pan gasket; both upper and lower surfaces. Wait 5 minutes and then install the pan. Wait 30 minutes before refilling the crankcase to allow the sealant to cure properly.

10. Install the oil pan and tighten the mounting bolts from the center of the oil pan—to the end of the oil pan to 45 ft. lbs. (57 Nm).

11. Install the center crossmember and front exhaust pipe section.

12. Lower the vehicle.

13. Fill the crankcase to the proper level.

14. Connect the negative battery cable. Start the engine and check for leaks.

Stanza (KA24E Engine)

1. Disconnect the negative battery cable.

2. Raise the vehicle and support safely.

3. Drain the oil pan.

4. Remove the right side splash cover.

5. Remove the right side undercover.
6. Remove the center member.
7. Remove the forward section of the exhaust pipe.
8. Remove the front buffer rod and its bracket if necessary.
9. Remove the engine gussets if necessary.
10. Remove the oil pan bolts.
11. Insert a seal cutter between the oil pan and the cylinder block.
12. Tapping the cutter with a hammer, slide it around the entire edge of the oil pan. Do not drive the seal cutter into the oil pump or rear seal retainer portion or the aluminum mating surface will be deformed.
13. Lower the oil pan from the cylinder block and remove it.

To install:

14. Carefully scrape the old gasket material away from the pan and cylinder block mounting surfaces and then apply a thin continuous bead of liquid gasket around the oil pan and to the 4 corners of the cylinder block mounting surface. Do the same to the oil pan gasket; both upper and lower surfaces. Wait 5 minutes and then install the pan. Wait 30 minutes before refilling the crankcase to allow the sealant to cure properly.
15. Install the oil pan and tighten the mounting bolts from the center of the oil pan to the end of the oil pan to 56 ft. lbs.
16. Install the engine gussets as necessary.
17. Install the front buffer rod and its bracket as necessary.
18. Install the forward section of the exhaust pipe using new gaskets.
19. Install the center member.
20. Install the right side undercover.
21. Install the right side splash cover.
22. Lower the vehicle.
23. Fill the crankcase to the proper level.
24. Connect the negative battery cable. Start the engine and check for leaks.

Oil Pump

REMOVAL & INSTALLATION

200SX (Z Series Engine)

▶ **See Figures 77, 78 and 79**

Before attempting to remove the oil pump, you must perform the following procedures: Drain the oil from the oil pan. Turn the crankshaft so that No. 1 piston is at TDC on its compression stroke. Remove the distributor cap and mark the position of the distributor rotor in relation to the distributor base with a piece of chalk.
1. Remove the front stabilizer bar, if so equipped.
2. Remove the splash shield.
3. Remove the oil pump body with the drive spindle assembly.

To install:

4. Fill the pump housing with engine oil, align the punch mark on the spindle with the hole in the pump. No. 1 piston should be at TDC on its compression stroke.
5. With a new gasket placed over the drive spindle, install the oil pump and drive spindle assembly. Make sure the tip of the drive spindle fits into the dis-

tributor shaft notch securely. The distributor rotor should be pointing to the matchmark you made earlier.

➡**Great care must be taken not to disturb the distributor rotor while installing the oil pump, or the ignition timing will be wrong.**

6. Install the splash shield and front stabilizer bar if it was removed.
7. Install the distributor cap.
8. Refill the engine oil. Start the engine, check ignition timing and check for oil leaks.

All Models (CA Series Engines)

▶ **See Figure 80**

1. Disconnect the negative battery cable.
2. Drain the oil pan.
3. Remove all accessory drive belts.
4. Remove the alternator.
5. Remove the timing belt covers.
6. Remove the timing belt.
7. On 200SX and the Stanza Wagon, unbolt the engine from its mounts and lift or jack the engine up from the body. On the Stanza (except Wagon) remove the center member from the body.
8. Remove the oil pan.
9. Remove the oil pump assembly along with the oil strainer. Remove the O-ring from the oil pump body and replace it.
10. Replace the front seal.

To install:

11. If installing a new or rebuilt oil pump, first pack the pump full of petroleum jelly to prevent the pump from cavitating when the engine is started. Apply RTV sealer to the front oil seal end of the pan prior to installation.
12. Install the pump and torque the oil pump mounting bolts to 8–12 ft. lbs. Make sure the oil pump body O-ring is properly seated.
13. Install the oil pan.
14. On the Stanza (except Wagon), install the center member. On 200SX and the Stanza Wagon, lower and re-mount the engine.
15. Install the timing belt.
16. Install the timing belt covers.
17. Install the alternator.
18. Install and tension the drive belts.
19. Fill the crankcase to the proper level.
20. Connect the negative battery cable. Start the engine and check for leaks.

1990–92 Stanza (KA24E Engine)

▶ **See Figure 81**

The oil pump assembly consists of an inner and outer gear located in the front cover. Removal of the front cover is necessary to gain access to the oil pump.
1. Disconnect the negative battery cable.
2. Remove the front cover with the strainer tube.
3. Loosen the oil pump cover retaining screw and mounting bolts and separate the oil pump cover from the front cover.
4. Remove the oil pump inner and outer gears.

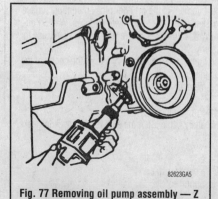

82623GA5

Fig. 77 Removing oil pump assembly — Z series engine

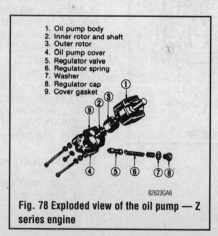

1. Oil pump body
2. Inner rotor and shaft
3. Outer rotor
4. Oil pump cover
5. Regulator valve
6. Regulator spring
7. Washer
8. Regulator cap
9. Cover gasket

82623GA6

Fig. 78 Exploded view of the oil pump — Z series engine

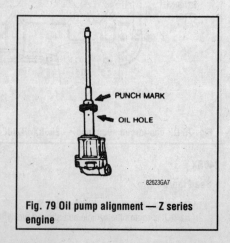

PUNCH MARK

OIL HOLE

82623GA7

Fig. 79 Oil pump alignment — Z series engine

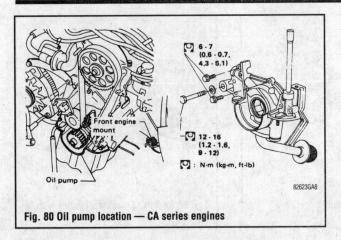

Fig. 80 Oil pump location — CA series engines

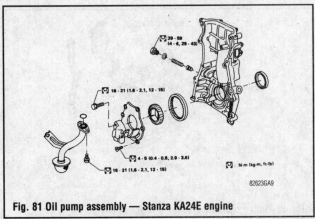

Fig. 81 Oil pump assembly — Stanza KA24E engine

To install:

5. Thoroughly clean the oil pump cover mating surfaces and the gear cavity.

6. Install the outer gear into the cavity.

7. Install the inner gear so the grooved side is facing up (towards the oil pump cover). Make sure the gears mesh properly and pack the pump cavity with petroleum jelly.

8. Install the oil pump cover. On KA24E engine, torque the cover screws to 2.2–3.6 ft. lbs. and the bolts to 12–15 ft. lbs.

9. Install the front cover with a new seal.

10. Connect the negative battery cable. Start the engine and check for leaks.

240SX (KA24DE Engine)

1. Remove the drive belts.

2. Remove the cylinder head and oil pans.

3. Remove the oil strainer and baffle plate.

4. Remove the front cover assembly (oil pump assembly is mounted in the front cover). Remove the oil pump.

To install:

5. Clean the mating surfaces of liquid gasket and apply a fresh bead of ⅛ in. (3mm) thickness.

6. Coat the oil pump gears with oil. Using a new oil seal and O-ring, install the front cover assembly.

7. Install the oil strainer, baffle plate, oil pans, cylinder head and drive belts.

240SX (KA24E Engine)

▶ See Figures 82 and 83

1. Disconnect the negative battery cable.

2. Drain the oil pan.

3. Turn the crankshaft so No. 1 piston is at TDC on its compression stroke.

4. Remove the distributor cap and mark the position of the distributor rotor in relation to the distributor base with a piece of chalk.

5. Remove the splash shield.

6. Remove the oil pump body with the drive spindle assembly.

To install:

7. To install, fill the pump housing with engine oil, align the punch mark on the spindle with the hole in the pump. No. 1 piston should be at TDC on its compression stroke.

8. With a new gasket and seal placed over the drive spindle, install the oil pump and drive spindle assembly. Make sure the tip of the drive spindle fits into the distributor shaft notch securely. The distributor rotor should be pointing to the matchmark made earlier.

9. Install the splash shield.

10. Install the distributor cap.

11. Fill the crankcase to the proper level.

12. Connect the negative battery cable. Start the engine and check for leaks. Check the ignition timing.

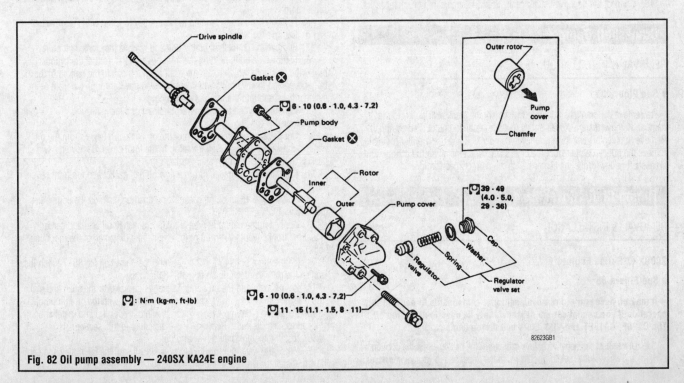

Fig. 82 Oil pump assembly — 240SX KA24E engine

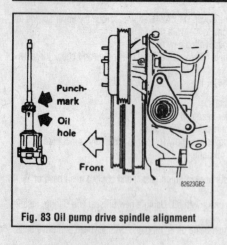

Fig. 83 Oil pump drive spindle alignment

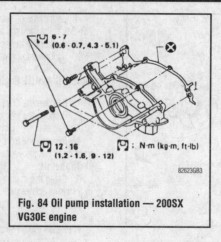

Fig. 84 Oil pump installation — 200SX VG30E engine

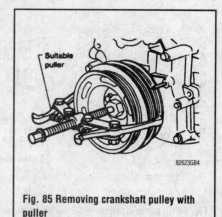

Fig. 85 Removing crankshaft pulley with puller

200SX (VG30 Engine)

♦ **See Figure 84**

1. Disconnect the negative battery cable.
2. Remove the oil pan.
3. Remove the timing belt.
4. Remove the crankshaft timing sprocket using a suitable puller.
5. Remove the timing belt plate.
6. Remove the oil pump strainer and pick-up tube from the oil pump.
7. Remove the mounting bolts and remove the oil pump and gasket.
8. Replace the oil pump seal.

To install:

9. Before installing the oil pump, remove the front cover and pack the pump's cavity with petroleum jelly, then make sure the O-ring is fitted properly. Torque the front cover screws to 34 ft. lbs.
10. Mount the oil pump with a new gasket. Torque the 8mm retaining bolts to 16–22 ft. lbs. and the 6mm bolts to 56 ft. lbs.
11. Install the oil pump strainer and pick-up tube with a new O-ring. Torque the pick-up tube mounting bolts to 12–15 ft. lbs.
12. Install the timing belt plate.
13. Install the crankshaft timing sprocket.
14. Install the timing belt.
15. Install the oil pan.
16. Connect the negative battery cable. Start the engine and check for leaks.

Crankshaft Damper

REMOVAL & INSTALLATION

♦ **See Figure 85**

To remove the crankshaft damper matchmark the crankshaft pulley to the damper. Remove the crankshaft pulley (outside) retaining bolts if so equipped. Remove the (center) crankshaft pulley to damper bolt, the use a puller tool to remove the pulley/damper from the crankshaft. When installing the damper and crankshaft pulley torque the center bolt to the correct specification.

Timing Chain Cover

REMOVAL & INSTALLATION

200SX (Z Series Engine)

♦ **See Figure 86**

➥ **It may be necessary to remove additional components to perform this operation if you cannot cut the gasket cleanly as described in Step 10. The CA20E, CA18ET and VG30E are belt driven engines.**

1. Disconnect the negative battery cable from the battery, drain the cooling system, and remove the radiator together with the upper and lower radiator hoses.

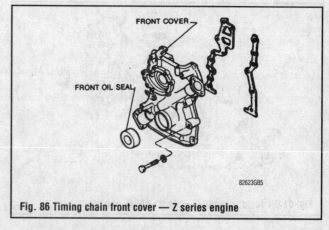

Fig. 86 Timing chain front cover — Z series engine

2. Loosen the alternator drive belt adjusting screw and remove the drive belt. Remove the bolts, which attach the alternator bracket to the engine and set the alternator aside out of the way.
3. Mark and remove the distributor. Refer to Distributor Removal And Installation if necessary.
4. Remove the oil pump attaching screws, and take out the pump and its drive spindle.
5. Remove the cooling fan and the fan pulley together with the drive belt.
6. Remove the water pump.
7. Remove the crankshaft pulley bolt and remove the crankshaft pulley.
8. Remove the bolts holding the front cover to the front of the cylinder block, the four bolts which retain the front of the oil pan to the bottom of the front cover, and the two bolts which are screwed down through the front of the cylinder head and into the top of the front cover.
9. Carefully pry the front cover off the front of the engine.

To install:

10. Cut the exposed front section of the oil pan gasket away from the oil pan. Do the same to the gasket at the top of the front cover. Remove the two side gaskets and clean all of the mating surfaces.
11. Cut the portions needed from a new oil pan gasket and top front cover gasket.
12. Apply sealer to all of the gaskets and position them on the engine in their proper places.
13. Apply a light coating of grease to the crankshaft oil seal and carefully mount the front cover to the front of the engine and install all of the mounting bolts.
Tighten the 8mm bolts to 7–12 ft. lbs. and the 6mm bolts to 36–72 inch lbs. Tighten the oil pan attaching bolts to 48–84 inch lbs.
14. Before installing the oil pump, place the gasket over the shaft and make sure that the mark on the drive spindle faces (aligned) with the oil pump hole.
15. Install the oil pump after priming it with oil. For oil pump installation procedures, see Oil Pump Removal and Installation in this section.
16. Install the crankshaft pulley and bolt.
17. Install the water pump with a new gasket. Install the fan pulley and cooling fan. Install the drive belt and adjust the belt to the correct tension.

18. Install the distributor in the correct position. Reconnect the alternator bracket and alternator if it was removed. Install the drive belt and adjust the belt to the correct tension.

19. Reconnect the upper and lower radiator hoses and refill the cooling system.

20. Reconnect the negative battery cable. Start the engine, check ignition timing and check for leaks.

240SX (KA24DE Engine)

1. Remove the negative battery cable.
2. Drain the engine oil and coolant.
3. Remove the cylinder head assembly.
4. Raise and support the vehicle safely. Remove the oil pan, oil strainer and baffle plate.
5. Remove the crankshaft pulley using a suitable puller. Removal of the radiator may be necessary to gain clearance.
6. Support the engine and remove the front engine mount.
7. Loosen the front cover bolts in two or three steps and remove the front cover.

To install:

8. Clean all mating surfaces of liquid gasket material.
9. Apply a continuos bead of liquid gasket to the mating surface of the timing cover. Install the oil pump drive spacer and front cover. Tighten front cover bolts (in steps) to 56 ft. lbs. (68 Nm). Wipe excess liquid gasket material.

10. Install front engine mount.
11. Install crankshaft pulley and tighten bolt to specifications. Set No. 1 piston at TDC on the compression stroke.
12. Install the oil strainer and baffle. Install the oil pan.
13. Install the cylinder head assembly.
14. Lower the vehicle, connect the negative battery cable, Refill fluid levels, start the engine and check for leaks. Road test the vehicle for proper operation.

240SX (KA24E Engine)

▶ **See Figures 87, 88, 89 and 90**

1. Disconnect the negative battery cable.
2. Drain the cooling system and oil pan. To drain the cooling system, open the radiator drain cock and remove the engine block drain plug. The block plug is located on the left side of the block near the engine freeze plugs.
3. Remove the radiator shroud and the cooling fan.
4. Loosen the alternator drive belt adjusting screw and remove the drive belt.
5. Remove the power steering and air conditioning drive belts.
6. Remove the spark plugs and the distributor cap. Set the No. 1 piston to TDC of the compression stroke. Carefully remove the distributor. Before removal, scribe alignment marks in the timing cover and flat portion of the oil pump/distributor drive spindle. This alignment is critical and if not done properly, it could cause difficulty is aligning the distributor and setting the timing.

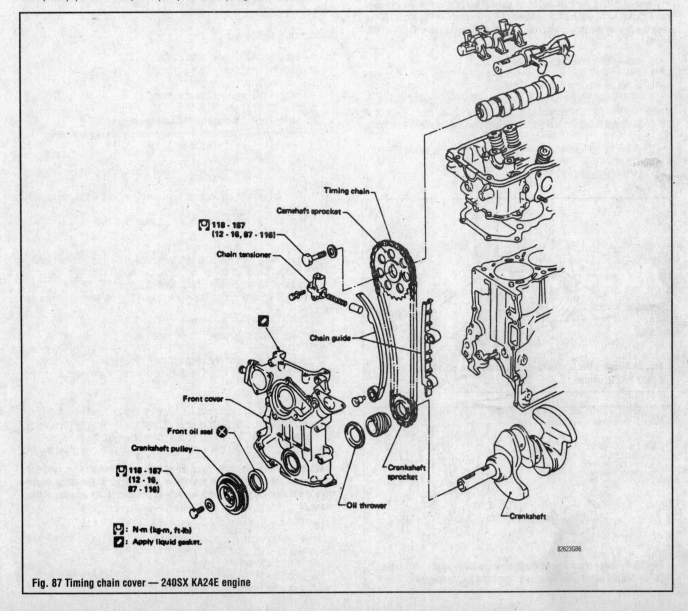

Fig. 87 Timing chain cover — 240SX KA24E engine

7. Remove the power steering pump, idler pulley and the power steering brackets.

8. Remove the air conditioning compressor idler pulley.

9. Remove the crankshaft pulley bolt and remove the crankshaft pulley with a 2 jawed puller.

10. Remove the oil pump attaching screws, and withdraw the pump and its drive spindle.

11. Remove the rocker arm cover.

12. Remove the oil pan.

13. Remove the bolts holding the front cover to the front of the cylinder block, the 4 bolts which retain the front of the oil pan to the bottom of the front cover, and the 4 bolts which are screwed down through the front of the cylinder head and into the top of the front cover. Carefully pry the front cover off the front of the engine. Clean all the old sealant from the surface of the front cover and the cylinder block.

14. Replace the crankshaft oil seal and the 2 timing chain cover oil seals in the block. These two seals should be installed in the block and not in the timing cover.

To install:

15. Verify the No. 1 piston is at TDC of the compression stroke. Apply a very thin bead of high temperature liquid gasket to both sides of the front cover and to where the cover mates with the cylinder head. Apply a light coating of grease to the crankshaft and timing cover oil seals and carefully bolt the front cover to the front of the engine.

➡**When installing the front cover, be careful not to damage the cylinder head gasket or to disturb the position of the oil seals in the block. Make sure the tab on the larger block oil seal is pointing to the exterior of the block.**

16. Install new rubber plugs in the cylinder head.

17. Install the oil pan.

18. Install the rocker arm cover.

19. Before installing the oil pump, place the gasket over the shaft and make sure the mark on the drive spindle faces (aligned) with the oil pump hole. Install the oil pump and distributor driving spindle into the front cover with a new gasket.

20. Install the crankshaft pulley and bolt. Torque the pulley bolt to 87–116 ft. lbs. (118–157 Nm).

21. Install the distributor and the spark plugs.

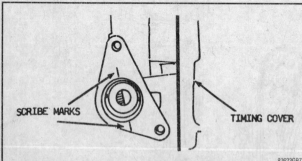

SCRIBE MARKS

TIMING COVER

82623GB7

Fig. 88 Aligning the timing cover and distributor/oil pump drive — 240SX KA24E engine

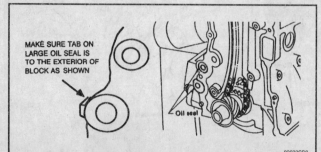

MAKE SURE TAB ON LARGE OIL SEAL IS TO THE EXTERIOR OF BLOCK AS SHOWN

Oil seal

82623GB8

Fig. 89 Cylinder block timing chain cover seals — make sure tab on larger seal is positioned as shown — 240SX KA24E engine

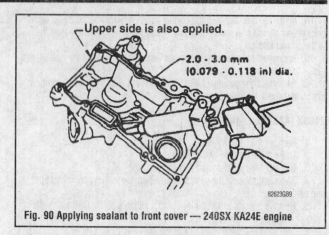

Upper side is also applied.

2.0 - 3.0 mm (0.079 - 0.118 in) dia.

82623GB9

Fig. 90 Applying sealant to front cover — 240SX KA24E engine

22. Install the compressor idler pulley. Install power steering pump brackets, idler pulley and power steering pump. Install the drive belts and adjust the tension.

23. Install the radiator shroud and the cooling fan.

24. Refill the cooling system and crankcase to the proper levels.

25. Connect the negative battery cable.

26. Start the engine, check/set the ignition timing and check for engine leaks. Road test the vehicle for proper operation.

Stanza (KA24E Engine)

1. Disconnect the negative battery cable.

2. Raise the front of the vehicle and support safely.

3. Remove the right front wheel.

4. Remove the dust cover and undercover.

5. Drain the oil pan.

6. Set the No. 1 piston at TDC of the compression stroke.

7. Remove the alternator and air conditioning compressor drive belts.

8. Remove the alternator and adjusting bar.

9. Remove the oil separator.

10. Remove the power steering pump pulley, pump stay and mounting bracket.

11. Discharge the air conditioning system and remove the compressor and mounting bracket.

12. Remove the crankshaft pulley and oil pump drive boss.

13. Remove the oil pan.

14. Remove the oil strainer mounting bolt.

15. Remove the bolts that attach the front cover to the head and the block.

16. Remove the rocker cover.

17. Support the engine with a suitable lifting device.

18. Unbolt the right side engine mount bracket from the block and lower the engine.

19. Remove the front cover.

20. Clean all the old sealant from the surface of the front cover and the cylinder block.

21. Replace the crankshaft oil seal and the 2 timing chain cover oil seals in the block. These two seals should be installed in the block and not in the timing cover.

To install:

22. Verify the No. 1 piston is at TDC. Apply a very thin bead of high temperature liquid gasket to both sides of the front cover and to where the cover mates with the cylinder head. Apply a light coating of grease to the crankshaft and timing cover oil seals and carefully mount the front cover to the front of the engine.

➡**When installing the front cover, be careful not to damage the cylinder head gasket or to disturb the position of the oil seals in the block. Make sure the tab on the larger block oil seal is pointing to the exterior of the block.**

23. Install new rubber plugs in the cylinder head.

24. Raise the engine and install the right engine mount bracket bolts. Torque the bolts to 58–65 ft. lbs. (78–88 Nm).

25. Install the rocker arm cover.

26. Install the front cover bolts.

27. Install the oil strainer mounting bolt.

28. Install the oil pan.

29. Install the oil pump drive boss and the crankshaft pulley. Torque the pulley bolt to 87–116 ft. lbs. (118–157 Nm).

30. Install the air conditioning compressor bracket and mount the compressor.

31. Install the power steering bracket, pump stay and power steering pump.

32. Install the oil separator.

33. Install the dust cover and undercover.

34. Mount the right front wheel and lower the vehicle.

35. Fill the crankcase to the proper level and charge the air conditioning system.

36. Make all the necessary engine adjustments.

Front Cover Oil Seal

REPLACEMENT

▶ **See Figure 91**

1. Install new rubber plugs in the cylinder head.

2. Install the oil pan.

3. Install the rocker arm cover.

4. Before installing the oil pump, place the gasket over the shaft and make sure the mark on the drive spindle faces (aligned) with the oil pump hole. Install the oil pump and distributor driving spindle into the front cover with a new gasket.

5. Install the crankshaft pulley and bolt. Torque the pulley bolt to 87–116 ft. lbs. (118–157 Nm).

6. Install the distributor and the spark plugs.

7. Install the compressor idler pulley. Install power steering pump brackets, idler pulley and power steering pump. Install the drive belts and adjust the tension.

8. Install the radiator shroud and the cooling fan.

9. Refill the cooling system and crankcase to the proper levels.

10. Connect the negative battery cable.

11. Start the engine, check/set the ignition timing and check for engine leaks. Road test the vehicle for proper operation.

12. Disconnect the negative battery cable.

13. Remove the crankshaft pulley.

14. Using a suitable tool, pry the oil seal from the front cover.

➡**When removing the oil seal, be careful not the gouge or scratch the seal bore or crankshaft surfaces.**

15. Wipe the seal bore with a clean rag.

16. Lubricate the lip of the new seal with clean engine oil.

17. Install the seal into the front cover with a suitable seal installer.

18. Install the crankshaft pulley.

19. Connect the negative battery cable.

Timing Chain, Gears and Tensioner

REMOVAL & INSTALLATION

200SX (Z Series)

▶ **See Figures 92, 93, 94, 95 and 96**

1. Before beginning any disassembly procedures, position the No. 1 piston at TDC on the compression stroke.

2. Remove the front cover as previously outlined. Remove the camshaft cover and remove the fuel pump if it runs off a cam lobe in front of the camshaft sprocket.

3. With the No. 1 piston at TDC, the timing marks in the camshaft sprocket and the timing chain should be visible. Mark both of them with paint. Also mark the relationship of the camshaft sprocket to the camshaft. At this point you will notice that there are three sets of timing marks and locating holes in the sprocket. They are for making adjustments to compensate for timing chain stretch. See the following "Timing Chain Adjustment" for more details.

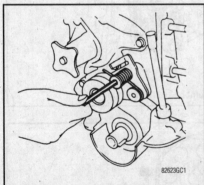

Fig. 91 Timing chain front cover oil seal installation

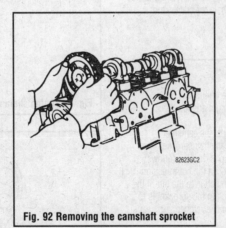

Fig. 92 Removing the camshaft sprocket

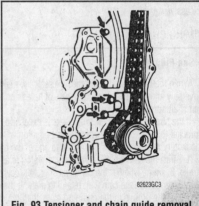

Fig. 93 Tensioner and chain guide removal

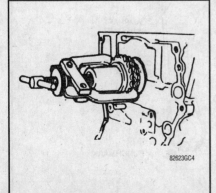

Fig. 94 Crankshaft sprocket removal

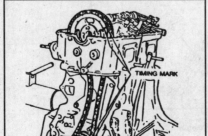

Fig. 95 Timing chain and sprocket alignment — Z series engine

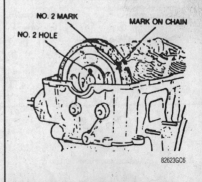

Fig. 96 Use the No. 2 mark and hole to align camshaft — Z series engine

4. With the timing marks on the cam sprocket clearly marked, locate and mark the timing marks on the crankshaft sprocket. Also mark the chain timing mark. Of course, if the chain is not to be re-used, marking it is useless

5. Unbolt the camshaft sprocket and remove the sprocket along with the chain. As you remove the chain, hold it where the chain tensioner contacts it. When the chain is removed, the tensioner is going to come apart. Hold on to it and you won't lose any of the parts. There is no need to remove the chain guide unless it is being replaced.

6. Using a two armed gear puller, remove the crankshaft sprocket assembly.

To install:

7. Install the timing chain and the camshaft sprocket together after first positioning the chain over the crankshaft sprocket. Position the sprocket so that the marks made earlier line up. This is assuming that the engine has not been disturbed. The camshaft and crankshaft keys should both be pointed upward. If a new chain and/or gear is being installed, position the sprocket so that the timing marks on the chain align with the marks on the crankshaft sprocket and the camshaft sprocket (with both keys pointing up). The marks are on the right hand side of the sprockets as you face the engine. The L18 has 42 pins between the mating marks of the chain and sprockets when the chain is installed correctly. The L20B has 44 pins. The 1977–78 L24 engine used in the 810 has 42 pins between timing marks. The L24 (1979–84), Z20E and Z20S engines do not use the pin counting method for finding correct valve timing. Instead, position the key in the crankshaft sprocket so that it is pointing upward and install the camshaft sprocket on the camshaft with its dowel pin at the top using the No. 2 (No. 1 on the L24) mounting hole and timing mark. The painted links of the chain should be on the right hand side of the sprockets as you face the engine. See the illustration.

➡**The factory manual refers to the pins you are to count in the L-series engines as links, but in America, this is not correct. Count the pins. There are two pins per link. This is an important step. If you do not get the exact number of pins between the timing marks, valve timing will be incorrect and the engine will either not run at all, in which case you may stand the chance of bending the valves, or the engine will run very bad.**

8. Install the chain tensioner and the front cover assembly.

If timing chain assembly uses chain guides these guides do not have to be removed to replace the timing chain. Check the timing chain for cracks and excessive wear.

TIMING CHAIN ADJUSTMENT

▶ **See Figure 97**

When the timing chain stretches excessively, the valve timing will be adversely affected. There are three sets of holes and timing marks on the camshaft sprocket.

If the stretch of the chain roller links is excessive, adjust the camshaft sprocket location by transferring the set position of the camshaft sprocket from the factory position of No. 1 or No. 2 to one of the other positions as follows:

1. Turn the crankshaft until the No. 1 piston is at TDC on the compression stroke. Examine whether the camshaft sprocket location notch is to the left of the oblong groove on the camshaft retaining plate. If the notch in the sprocket is to the left of the groove in the retaining plate, then the chain is stretched and needs adjusting.

2. Remove the camshaft sprocket together with the chain and reinstall the sprocket and chain with the locating dowel on the camshaft inserted into either the No. 2 or 3 hole of the sprocket. The timing mark on the timing chain must be aligned with the mark on the sprocket. The amount of modification is 4° of crankshaft rotation for each mark.

3. Recheck the valve timing as outlined in Step 1. The notch in the sprocket should be to the right of the groove in the camshaft retaining plate.

4. If and when the notch cannot be brought to the right of the groove, the timing chain is worn beyond repair and must be replaced.

240SX and 1990–92 Stanza (KA24E Engine)

▶ **See Figures 98 thru 104**

1. Disconnect the negative battery cable.
2. Set the No. 1 piston at TDC of the compression stroke.
3. Remove the front cover.
4. If necessary, define the timing marks with chalk or paint to ensure proper alignment.

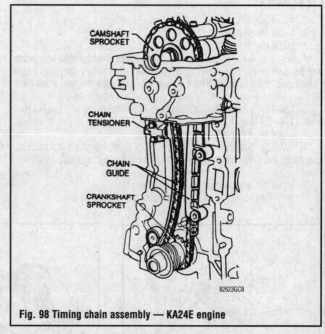

Fig. 98 Timing chain assembly — KA24E engine

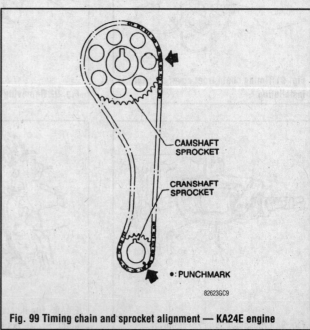

Fig. 99 Timing chain and sprocket alignment — KA24E engine

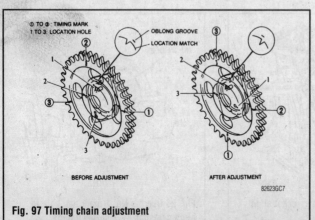

Fig. 97 Timing chain adjustment

5. Hold the camshaft sprocket stationary with a spanner wrench or similar tool and remove the camshaft sprocket bolt.

6. Remove chain tensioner.

7. Remove the chain guides.

8. Remove the timing chain.

9. Remove the sprocket oil slinger, oil pump drive gear and crankshaft gear.

To install:

10. Install the crankshaft sprocket, oil pump drive gear and oil slinger onto the end of the crankshaft. Make sure the crankshaft sprocket timing marks face toward the front.

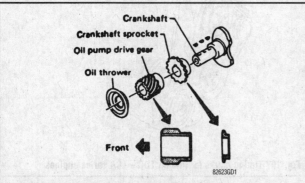

Fig. 100 Correct installation of crankshaft sprocket, oil pump, drive gear, oil thrower — KA24E engine

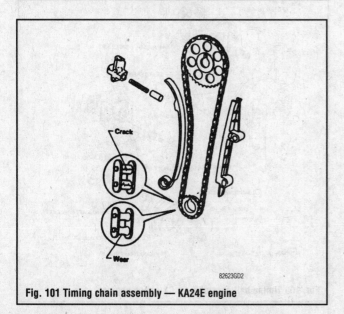

Fig. 101 Timing chain assembly — KA24E engine

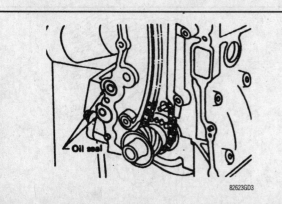

Fig. 102 Oil seals in left side of engine block — KA24E engine

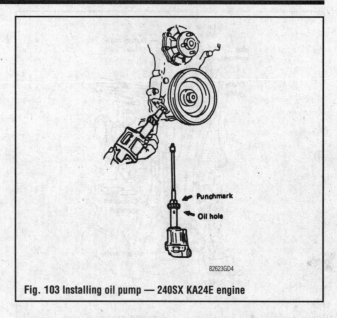

Fig. 103 Installing oil pump — 240SX KA24E engine

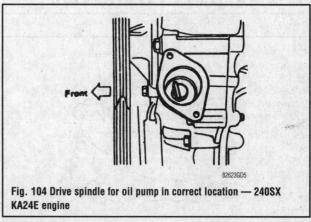

Fig. 104 Drive spindle for oil pump in correct location — 240SX KA24E engine

11. Install the camshaft sprocket, bolt and washer. The alignment mark must face towards the front. Tighten the bolt just enough to hold the sprocket in place.

12. Verify that the No. 1 piston is at TDC of the compression stroke. The crankshaft key-ways should be at the 12 o'clock position.

13. Install the timing chain by aligning the marks on the chain with the marks on the crankshaft and camshaft sprockets. Torque the camshaft sprocket bolt to 87–116 ft. lbs. (118–157 Nm) once the timing chain is in place and aligned.

14. Install the chain tensioner and chain guide.

15. Install the front cover.

16. Connect the negative battery cable.

240SX (KA24DE Engine)

▶ See Figures 105 and 106

1. Release the fuel system pressure.

2. Disconnect the negative battery cable and drain the cooling system. Drain engine oil.

3. Remove the cylinder head assembly.

4. Remove the oil pan.

5. Remove the oil strainer, crankshaft pulley.

6. Remove the front cover assembly.

7. Remove the lower timing chain tensioner, tension arm, lower timing chain guide.

8. Remove the lower timing chain and idler sprocket.

To install:

9. Check all components for wear. Replace as necessary. Clean all mating surfaces and replace the cylinder head gasket.

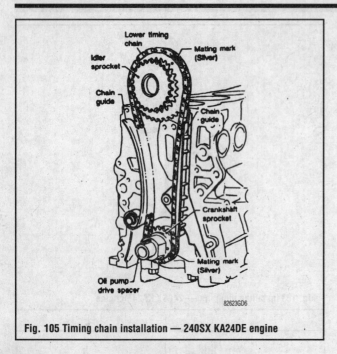

Fig. 105 Timing chain installation — 240SX KA24DE engine

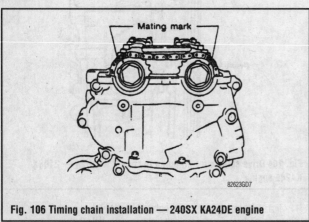

Fig. 106 Timing chain installation — 240SX KA24DE engine

10. Install crankshaft sprocket. Make sure that mating marks of crankshaft sprocket face front of the engine.

11. Rotate crankshaft so that No. 1 piston is set a TDC position.

12. Install idler sprocket and lower timing chain.

13. Install chain tension arm, chain guide and lower timing chain tensioner.

14. Install front cover assembly.

15. Install crankshaft pulley, oil strainer and oil pan.

16. Install the cylinder head assembly.

17. Install all remaining components in reverse order of removal.

18. Connect the negative battery cable. Refill all fluid levels. Road test the vehicle for proper operation.

Timing Belt/Cover

REMOVAL & INSTALLATION

200SX (CA Series Engines)

▶ **See Figures 107 thru 113**

1. Remove the battery ground cable. Release the fuel pressure.

2. On the CA20E engine, remove the air intake ducts.

3. Remove the cooling fan.

4. Remove the power steering, alternator, and air conditioner compressor belts if so equipped.

5. Set the No. 1 cylinder at TDC on the compression stroke. The accompanying illustration shows the timing mark alignment for TDC.

6. Remove the front upper and lower timing belt covers.

7. Loosen the timing belt tensioner and return spring, then remove the timing belt.

To install:

8. Carefully inspect the condition of the timing belt. There should be no breaks or cracks anywhere on the belt. Especially check around the bot-

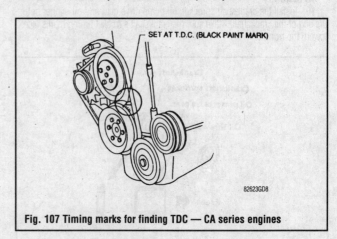

Fig. 107 Timing marks for finding TDC — CA series engines

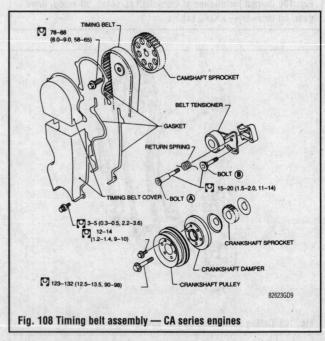

Fig. 108 Timing belt assembly — CA series engines

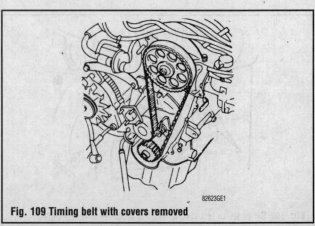

Fig. 109 Timing belt with covers removed

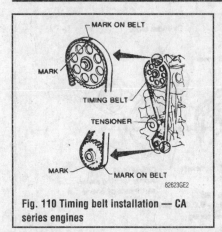

Fig. 110 Timing belt installation — CA series engines

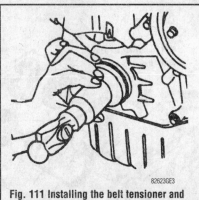

Fig. 111 Installing the belt tensioner and return spring

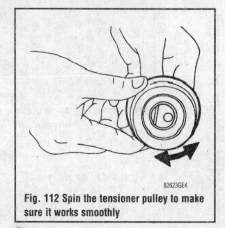

Fig. 112 Spin the tensioner pulley to make sure it works smoothly

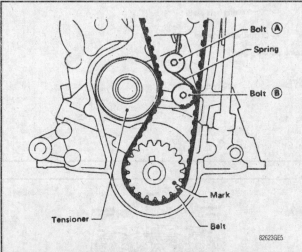

Fig. 113 Set the tensioner spring by first hooking one end to the side of bolt "B", then the other end to the tensioner pawl bracket

toms of the teeth, where they intersect the belt; cracks often show up here. Evidence of any wear or damage on the belt means the belt should be replaced.

9. To install the belt, first make sure that No. 1 cylinder is set at TDC on compression. Install the belt tensioner and return spring.

➡️If the coarse stud has been removed, apply Loctite® or another locking thread sealer to the stud threads before installing.

10. Make sure the tensioner bolts are not securely tightened before the drive belt is installed. Make sure the tensioner pulley can be rotated smoothly.

11. Make sure the timing belt is in good condition and clean. Do not bend it. Place the belt in position, aligning the white lines on the timing belt with the punch mark on the camshaft pulleys and the crankshaft pulley. Make sure the arrow on the belt is pointing toward the front belt covers.

12. Tighten the belt tensioner and assemble the spring. To set the spring, first hook one end on bolt B side, then hook the other end on the tensioner bracket pawl. Rotate the crankshaft two turns clockwise, then tighten bolt B then bolt A. At this point, belt tension will automatically be at the specified value.

13. Install the upper and lower timing belt covers.
14. Install and adjust all the drive belts.
15. Install the cooling fan and reconnect the air intake ducts on the CA20E engine.
16. Connect the battery cable, start engine and check the ignition timing.

200SX (VG30E Engine)—87 Models

▶ See Figures 114 thru 122

➡️After removing timing belt, do not rotate crankshaft and camshaft separately, because valves will hit piston heads. Review the complete procedure before starting this repair.

➡️Timing belt replacement is 60,000 miles—this interval is recommended by Nissan for reliable vehicle operation.

1. Raise vehicle and safely support.
2. Remove the engine under covers and drain engine coolant from the radiator. Be careful not to allow coolant to contact drive belts.
3. Remove the front right side wheel and tire assembly. Remove the engine side cover.
4. Remove the engine coolant reservoir tank and radiator hoses.
5. Remove the A.S.C.D. (speed control device) actuator.
6. Remove all the drive belts from the engine. When removing the power steering drive belt, loosen the idler pulley from the right side wheel housing.
7. Remove the idler bracket of the compressor drive belt and crankshaft pulley.
8. Remove the timing belt covers. Rotate the engine with a socket wrench on the crankshaft pulley bolt to align the two sets of timing marks. The marks are on the camshaft pulleys and rear belt covers.
9. Remove the rocker covers. Loosen the rocker shaft securing bolts so that rockers will no longer bear on the cam lobes. Remove all spark plugs.
10. Use a hexagon wrench to turn the belt tensioner clockwise and tighten the tensioner lock-nut just enough to hold the tensioner in position. This is done to remove tension. Then, remove the old belt.

➡️Be careful not to bend the new belt installing it. Timing belts are designed to flex only the way they turn around the pulleys.

To install:
11. Make sure that all pulleys and the belt are free of oil and water. Install the new belt, aligning the arrow on the timing belt forward. Align the white lines on the timing belt with the punchmarks on all three pulleys.
12. Loosen the tensioner lock-nut to allow spring tension to tension the belt. Then, using the hexagon wrench, turn the tensioner first clockwise, then counterclockwise in three cycles. This will seat the belt. Now, torque the tensioner lock-nut to 32–43 ft. lbs.
13. Tighten rocker shaft bolts alternately in three stages. Before tightening each pair of bolts, turn the engine over so the affected rocker will not touch its cam lobe. Final torque is 13–16 ft. lbs. Install the rocker covers with new gaskets.
14. Install lower and upper timing belt covers.
15. Install crankshaft pulley and idler bracket of the compressor drive belt. Tighten the crankshaft pulley bolt to 90–98 ft. lbs.
16. Install the drive belts. Clean and regap the spark plugs if necessary then install in the cylinder head.

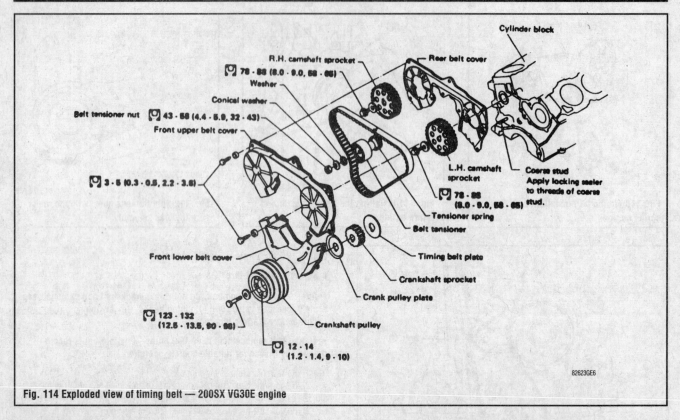

Fig. 114 Exploded view of timing belt — 200SX VG30E engine

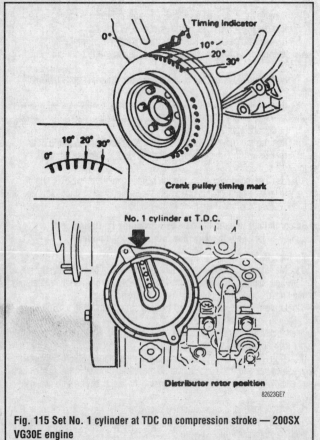

Fig. 115 Set No. 1 cylinder at TDC on compression stroke — 200SX VG30E engine

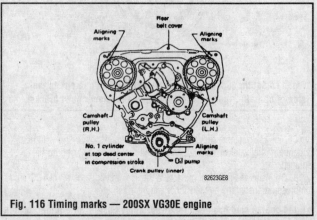

Fig. 116 Timing marks — 200SX VG30E engine

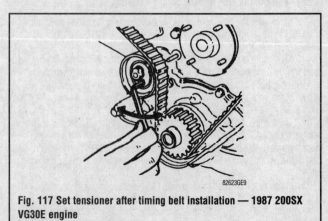

Fig. 117 Set tensioner after timing belt installation — 1987 200SX VG30E engine

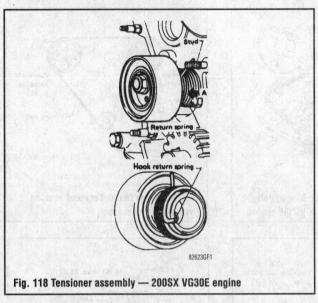

Fig. 118 Tensioner assembly — 200SX VG30E engine

17. Install the coolant reservoir tank, radiator hoses, A.S.C.D. actuator.

18. Install the right front wheel. Install engine under cover and side covers.

19. Refill the cooling system. Check ignition timing and roadtest for proper operation.

200SX (VG30E Engine)—1988 Models

▶ **See Figures 123, 124, 125, 126 and 127**

Timing belt replacement is 60,000 miles—this interval is recommended by Nissan for reliable vehicle operation.

On this model year timing belt removal and installation is the same. Use the above procedure with the exception that the rocker covers and rocker shafts bolts are not removed, but the spark plugs are still removed. The timing belt is installed and adjusted as follows:

1. Confirm that No. 1 cylinder is at TDC on its compression stroke. Install tensioner and tensioner spring. If stud is removed apply locking sealant to threads before installing.

2. Swing tensioner fully clockwise with hexagon wrench and temporarily tighten lock-nut.

3. Set timing belt, align the arrow on the timing belt forward. Align the white lines on the timing belt with the punchmarks on all three pulleys.

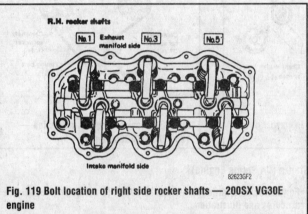

Fig. 119 Bolt location of right side rocker shafts — 200SX VG30E engine

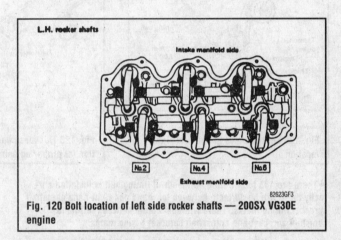

Fig. 120 Bolt location of left side rocker shafts — 200SX VG30E engine

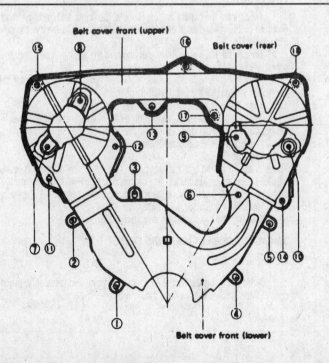

Fig. 121 Timing belt cover bolt locations — 200SX VG30E engine

Tightened parts	Section	Parts tightened with bolts
Bolt A (6 pcs.) Rubber washer Bolt cover front (lower)	①②③④ ⑤⑭	①②③④ Cylinder block ⑤⑭ Compresser bracket
Bolt B (1 pc.) Rubber washer Bolt cover front (lower) Water pump mounting bolt	⑥	Water pump mounting bolt
Bolt C (4 pcs.) Belt cover (rear)	⑦⑧⑨⑩	Cylinder head
Bolt A (7 pcs.) Rubber washer Belt cover front (upper) Belt cover (rear) Welded nut (4 pcs.)	⑮⑯⑰⑱ ⑪⑫ ⑬	⑮⑯⑰⑱: Welded nuts ⑪⑫: Cylinder head ⑬: Water outlet

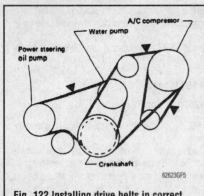

Fig. 122 Installing drive belts in correct position — 200SX VG30E engine

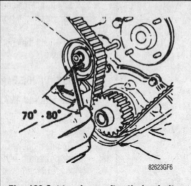

Fig. 123 Set tensioner after timing belt installation — 1988 200SX VG30E engine

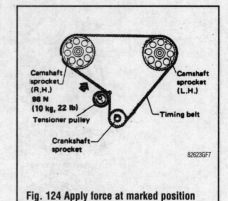

Fig. 124 Apply force at marked position then loosen tensioner

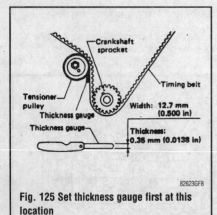

Fig. 125 Set thickness gauge first at this location

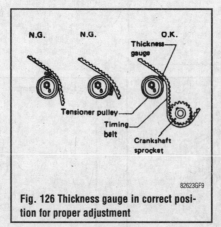

Fig. 126 Thickness gauge in correct position for proper adjustment

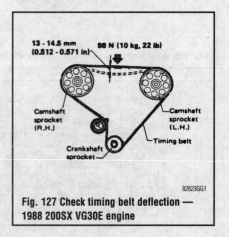

Fig. 127 Check timing belt deflection — 1988 200SX VG30E engine

➡There are 133 total timing belt teeth. If timing belt is installed correctly there will be 40 teeth between left-hand and right-hand camshaft sprocket timing marks. There will be 43 teeth between left-hand camshaft sprocket and crankshaft sprocket timing marks.

4. Loosen tensioner lock-nut, keeping tensioner steady with a hexagon wrench.

5. Swing tensioner 70–80° clockwise with hexagon wrench and temporarily tighten lock-nut.

6. Install all the spark plugs. Turn crankshaft clockwise 2 or 3 times, then slowly set No. 1 cylinder at TDC on its compression stroke.

7. Push middle of timing belt between right-hand camshaft sprocket and tensioner pulley with a force of 22 ft. lbs.

8. Loosen tensioner lock-nut, keeping tensioner steady with a hexagon wrench.

9. Using a feeler gauge or equivalent as shown in the illustration which is 0.35mm thick and 13mm wide, set gauge at the bottom of tensioner pulley and timing belt. Turn crankshaft clockwise and position gauge completely between tensioner pulley and timing belt. The timing belt will move about 2.5 teeth.

10. Tighten tensioner lock-nut, keeping tensioner steady with a hexagon wrench.

11. Turn crankshaft clockwise or counterclockwise and remove the gauge.

12. Rotate the engine 3 times, then set No. 1 at TDC on its compression stroke.

13. Check timing belt deflection on 1988 model year only. Timing belt deflection is 13.0–14.5mm at 22 lbs. of pressure. If it is out of specified range, readjust the timing belt.

Stanza (CA Series Engine)

➡For additional information—Refer to 200SX (C Series Engine) service procedures and illustrations.

FRONT COVER

1. Disconnect the battery cables. Remove the upper and lower alternator securing bolts until the alternator can be moved enough to remove the drive belt from the pulley.

2. Loosen the idler pulley lock-nut and turn the adjusting bolt until the air conditioner compressor belt can be removed.

3. Unbolt and remove the crankshaft pulley, removing the alternator belt along with it. Remove the crankshaft damper.

4. Unbolt and remove the water pump pulley.

5. Remove the upper and lower timing belt covers and their gaskets. If the gaskets are in good condition after removal, they can be reused; if they are in way damaged or broken, replace them.

To install:

6. Install the timing belt covers in place. Torque the front cover bolts evenly to 2.2–3.6 ft. lbs; torque the crank pulley damper bolt to 90–98 ft. lbs.; torque the crank pulley bolt to 9–10 ft. lbs.; torque the water pump pulley bolts to 4.3–7 ft. lbs.

7. Install and adjust all drive belts.

8. Connect the battery cables and start engine.

TIMING BELT/CRANKSHAFT OIL SEAL

▶ **See Figure 128**

1. Refer to the Timing Belt Front Cover, Removal and Installation procedures, in this section and remove the timing cover assembly.

2. If necessary, remove the spark plug, then turn the crankshaft to position the No. 1 piston at TDC of the compression stroke.

➡**Note the position of the timing marks on the camshaft sprocket, the timing belt and the crankshaft sprocket (see illustrations).**

3. Loosen and/or remove the timing belt tensioner. Mark the rotation direction of the timing belt, then remove it from the sprockets.

4. To remove the front oil seal, pull off the crankshaft sprocket, then pry out the oil seal with a small pry bar (be careful not to scratch the crankshaft).

5. Clean the oil seal mounting surface.

6. Install a new oil seal, the timing belt and tensioner. Torque the tensioner pulley bolts to 13–16 ft. lbs., the timing cover bolts to 2.5–4 ft. lbs., the crankshaft pulley bolt to 90–98 ft. lbs.

7. Install the timing belt covers.

8. Start engine and check timing. Road test the vehicle.

BELT INSPECTION

♦ **See Figures 129 thru 136**

The timing belt should be periodically inspected for wear. Removal of the timing cover is necessary to visually check the belt for signs of wear or contamination. The belt should show no signs of wear such as cracked teeth, wear on the belt face, wear on one or both sides of the belt, and there should be no foreign materials on the belt or between the teeth. If there is oil, coolant, lubricant, or any other foreign material on the belt, it is a good idea to replace the belt due to the fact that rapid wear can result from this contamination. Usually sticking to the manufacturer's guide for timing belt replacement interval will ensure little problems but it is still a good idea to periodically inspect your belt. If the belt breaks the engine will shut down and serious engine damage can occur. The proper manufacturer recommended timing belt replacement interval can be found in Section 1.

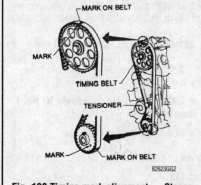

Fig. 128 Timing mark alignment — Stanza CA20 engine

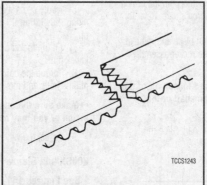

Fig. 129 Check for premature parting of the belt

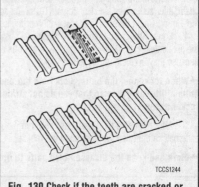

Fig. 130 Check if the teeth are cracked or damaged

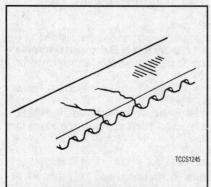

Fig. 131 Look for noticeable cracks or wear on the belt face

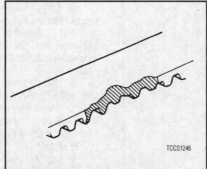

Fig. 132 You may only have damage on one side of the belt; if so, the guide could be the culprit

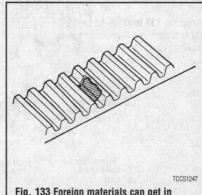

Fig. 133 Foreign materials can get in between the teeth and cause damage

Fig. 134 Inspect the timing belt for cracks, fraying, glazing or damage of any kind

Fig. 135 Damage on only one side of the timing belt may indicate a faulty guide

Fig. 136 ALWAYS replace the timing belt at the interval specified by the manufacturer

Camshaft and Bearings

➡ Since these engines do not use replaceable camshaft bearings, overhaul is performed by replacement of the camshaft or the cylinder head. Check the camshaft bearing surfaces (in the cylinder head) with an internal micrometer and the bearing surfaces (of the camshaft) with a micrometer.

REMOVAL & INSTALLATION

200SX (Z Series Engine)

▶ See Figures 137, 138, 139 and 140

➡ Removal of the cylinder head from the engine is optional. Mark and keep all parts in order for correct installation.

1. Remove the camshaft sprocket from the camshaft together with the timing chain, after setting the No. 1 piston at TDC on its compression stroke. Refer to the Timing Chain Removal and Installation procedures.
2. Loosen the bolts holding the rocker shaft assembly in place and remove the six center bolts. Do not pull the four end bolts out of the rocker assembly because they hold the unit together.

➡ When loosening the bolts, work from the ends in and loosen all of the bolts a little at a time so that you do not strain the camshaft or the rocker assembly.

3. After removing the rocker assembly, remove the camshaft. Slide the camshaft carefully out of the front of the vehicle.

➡ Mark and keep the disassembled parts in order.

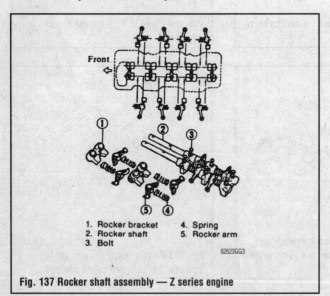

1. Rocker bracket
2. Rocker shaft
3. Bolt
4. Spring
5. Rocker arm

82623GG3

Fig. 137 Rocker shaft assembly — Z series engine

If you disassembled the rocker unit, assemble as follows.

4. Install the mounting brackets, valve rockers and springs observing the following considerations:
   a. The two rocker shafts are different. Both have punch marks in the ends that face the front of the engine. The rocker shaft that goes on the side of the intake manifold has two slits in its end just below the punch mark. The exhaust side rocker shaft does not have slits.
   b. The rocker arms for the intake and exhaust valves are interchangeable between cylinders one and three and are identified by the mark 1. Similarly, the rockers for cylinders two and four are interchangeable and are identified by the mark 2.
   c. The rocker shaft mounting brackets are also coded for correct placement with either an A or a Z plus a number code. See the illustration for proper placement.
5. Check camshaft run-out, end-play wear and journal clearance as described in this section.

To install:

6. Apply sealant to the end camshaft saddles as shown in the accompanying illustration. Place the camshaft on the head with its dowel pin pointing up.
7. Fit the rocker assembly on the head, making sure you mount it on its knock pin.
8. Torque the bolts to 11–18 ft. lbs., in several stages working from the middle bolts and moving outwards on both sides.

➡ Make sure the engine is on TDC of the compression stroke for No. 1 piston or you may damage some valves.

9. Adjust the valves. Refer to the Valve Adjustment procedure.

200SX and Stanza (CA Series Engine)

▶ See Figures 141, 142 and 143

1. Disconnect the negative battery cable and relieve the fuel system pressure if necessary.
2. Set the No. 1 piston to TDC of the compression stroke.
3. Remove the timing belt.
4. Remove the valve rocker cover.
5. Fully loosen all rocker arm adjusting screws (the valve adjusting screws). Loosen the rocker shaft mounting bolts in 23 stages and then remove the rocker shafts as an assembly. Keep all components in the correct order for reassembly.
6. Hold the camshaft pulley and remove the pulley mounting bolt. Remove the pulley. Remove the camshaft thrust plate.
7. Carefully pry the camshaft oil seal out of the front of the cylinder head.
8. Slide the camshaft out the front of the cylinder head, taking extreme care not to score any of the journals.

To install:

9. Coat the camshaft with clean engine oil.
10. Carefully slide the camshaft into the cylinder head, coat the end with oil and install a new oil seal. Install the camshaft thrust plate and wedge the camshaft with a small wooden block inserted between one of the cams and the cylinder head. Torque the thrust plate bolt to 58–65 ft. lbs. (78–88 Nm). Remove the wooden block.

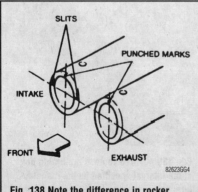

82623GG4

Fig. 138 Note the difference in rocker shafts — Z series engine

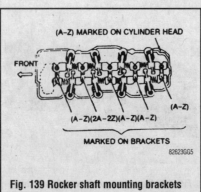

82623GG5

Fig. 139 Rocker shaft mounting brackets are assembled in this order — Z series engine

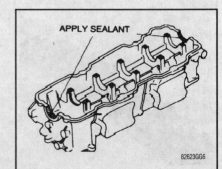

82623GG6

Fig. 140 Apply sealant to these points on the cylinder head just before installing the camshaft — Z series engine

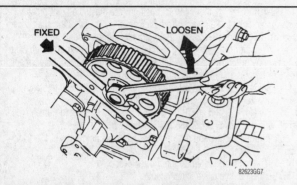

Fig. 141 Use a sprocket holding tool when loosening the cam sprocket — CA series engine

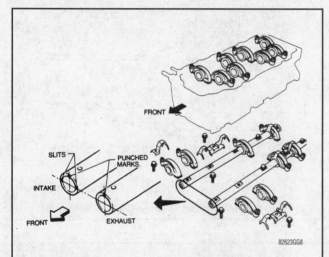

Fig. 142 Note location marks on the end of the shafts, slits on the intake shaft — rocker shaft assembly CA series engine

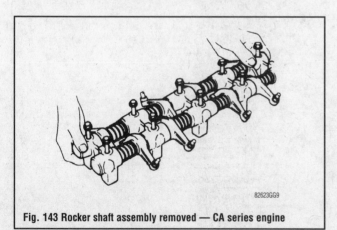

Fig. 143 Rocker shaft assembly removed — CA series engine

11. Lubricate the rocker shafts lightly with clean engine oil and install them, with the rocker arms, into the head. Both shafts have punch marks on their leading edges, while the intake shaft is also marked with 2 slits on its leading edge.

➡**To prevent the rocker shaft springs from slipping out of the shaft, insert the bracket bolts into the shaft prior to installation.**

12. Tighten the rocker shaft bolts gradually, in 23 stages (from the center of the shaft to the end of the shaft assembly) to 13–16 ft. lbs. (18–22 Nm).
13. Install the camshaft pulley and then install the timing belt.
14. Adjust the valves as required and install the cylinder head cover.
15. Connect the negative battery cable.

200SX (VG30E Engine)

♦ **See Figures 144 thru 149**

➡On the 1987 200SX with VG30E engine Nissan recommends that the engine assembly be removed from the vehicle, then the cylinder heads disassembled. On the 1988 200SX with VG30E engine Nissan recommends that the cylinder heads be removed from the engine, with the engine mounted in the vehicle, and then remove the camshafts. This procedure is for removing the camshafts with the engine in the vehicle.

1. Disconnect the negative battery cable.
2. Drain the cooling system.
3. Remove the timing belt.
4. Remove the collector assembly.
5. Remove the intake manifold.
6. Remove the cylinder head.
7. Remove the rocker shafts with rocker arms. Bolts should be loosened in several steps in the proper sequence (from the end to the center of the shaft assembly).
8. Remove hydraulic valve lifters and lifter guide. Hold hydraulic valve lifters with wire so they will not drop from lifter guide.
9. Using a dial gauge measure the camshaft end-play. If the camshaft end-play exceeds the limit — 0.0012–0.0024 in. (0.030–0.060mm), select the thickness of a cam locate plate so the end-play is within specification. For example, if camshaft end play measures 0.0031 in. (0.08mm) with shim 2 used, then change shim 2 to shim 3 so the camshaft end play is 0.0020 in. (0.05mm).
10. Remove the camshaft front oil seal and slide camshaft out the front of the cylinder head assembly.

To install:

11. Install camshaft, locator plates, cylinder head rear cover and front oil seal. Set camshaft knock pin at 12 o'clock position. Install cylinder head with new gasket to engine.
12. Install valve lifter guide assembly. Assemble valve lifters in their original position. After installing them in the correct location remove the wire holding them in lifter guide.

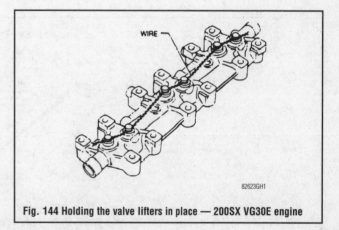

Fig. 144 Holding the valve lifters in place — 200SX VG30E engine

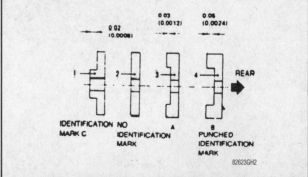

Fig. 145 Select shim thickness so that camshaft thickness is within specifications — 200SX VG30E engine

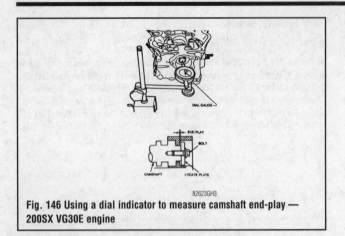

Fig. 146 Using a dial indicator to measure camshaft end-play — 200SX VG30E engine

13. Install rocker shafts in correct position (see illustration) with rocker arms. Tighten bolts in 23 stages (from the center to the end of the shaft assembly) to 13–16 ft. lbs. (18–22 Nm). Before tightening, be sure to set camshaft lobe at the position where lobe is not lifted or the valve closed. Set each cylinder 1 at a time or follow the procedure below. The cylinder head, intake manifold, collector and timing belt must be installed:

a. Set No. 1 piston at TDC of the compression stroke and tighten rocker shaft bolts for No. 2, No. 4 and No. 6 cylinders.

b. Set No. 4 piston at TDC of the compression stroke and tighten rocker shaft bolts for No. 1, No. 3 and No. 5 cylinders.

c. Torque specification for the rocker shaft retaining bolts is 13–16 ft. lbs. (18–22 Nm).

14. Fill the cooling system to the proper level.

15. Connect the negative battery cable.

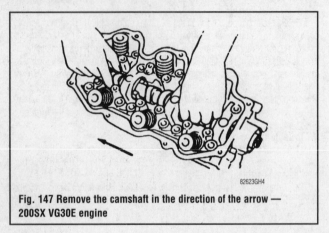

Fig. 147 Remove the camshaft in the direction of the arrow — 200SX VG30E engine

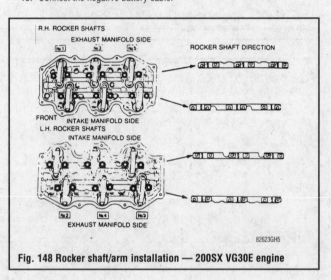

Fig. 148 Rocker shaft/arm installation — 200SX VG30E engine

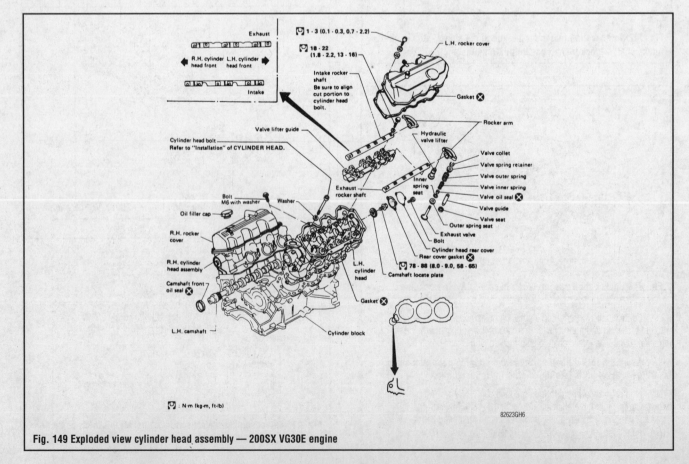

Fig. 149 Exploded view cylinder head assembly — 200SX VG30E engine

240SX and 1990–92 Stanza (KA24E Engine)

▶ **See Figures 150 thru 155**

1. Disconnect the negative battery cable.
2. Remove the timing chain.
3. Remove the cylinder head. Do not remove the camshaft sprocket at this time.
4. Loosen the rocker shaft bolt evenly in proper sequence. Start from the outside and work toward the center.
5. Mount a dial indicator to the cylinder head and set the stylus of the indicator on the head of the camshaft sprocket bolt. Zero the indicator and measure the camshaft end-play by moving the camshaft back and forth. End-play should be within 0.0028–0.0059 in. (0.07–0.15mm).
6. Remove the camshaft brackets and lift the camshaft with sprocket from the cylinder head.

To install:

7. Clean all cylinder head, intake and exhaust manifold gasket surfaces. Lubricate the camshaft and rocker arm/shaft assemblies with a liberal coating of clean engine oil. Lay the camshaft and sprocket into the cylinder head so the knock pin is at the front of the head at the 12 o'clock position. Install the camshaft brackets. The camshaft bracket directional arrows must face the toward the front of the engine.
8. Install the rocker shaft and rocker arms. Both intake and exhaust rocker shafts are stamped with an **F** mark. This mark must face the front of the engine during installation. Install the rocker arm bolts and spring clips so the cut outs are facing as shown. Torque the rocker arm bolts (in several stages) in the proper sequence to 27–30 ft. lbs. (37–41 Nm).
9. Install the timing chain.
10. Install the cylinder head. Use new rubber plugs when installing the cylinder head.
11. Connect the negative battery cable.

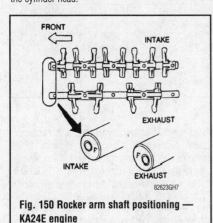

Fig. 150 Rocker arm shaft positioning — KA24E engine

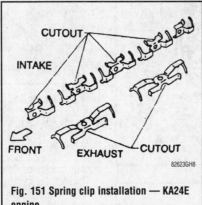

Fig. 151 Spring clip installation — KA24E engine

Fig. 152 Rocker shaft bolt LOOSENING sequence — KA24E engine. TIGHTEN IN REVERSE OF THE LOOSENING SEQUENCE

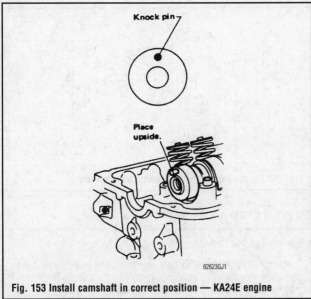

Fig. 153 Install camshaft in correct position — KA24E engine

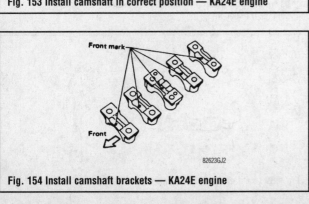

Fig. 154 Install camshaft brackets — KA24E engine

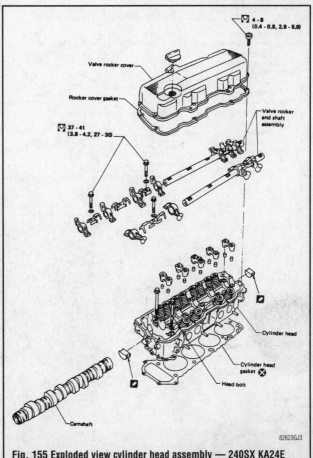

Fig. 155 Exploded view cylinder head assembly — 240SX KA24E engine

240SX (KA24DE Engine)

◗ **See Figures 156 and 157**

➥Modify service steps as necessary. This is a complete disassembly repair procedure. Review the complete procedure before starting this repair.

1. Release the fuel system pressure.
2. Disconnect the negative battery cable and drain the cooling system. Drain the engine oil.
3. Remove all vacuum hoses, fuel lines, wires, electrical connections as necessary.

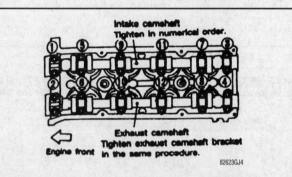

Fig. 156 Camshaft bracket torque sequence — 240SX KA24DE engine

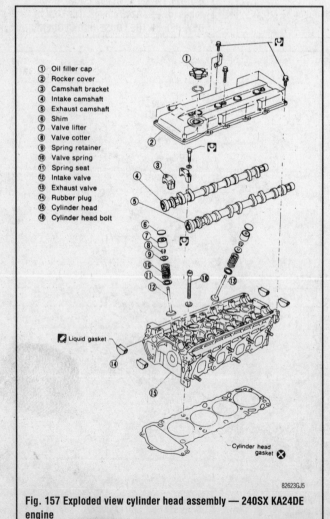

① Oil filler cap
② Rocker cover
③ Camshaft bracket
④ Intake camshaft
⑤ Exhaust camshaft
⑥ Shim
⑦ Valve lifter
⑧ Valve cotter
⑨ Spring retainer
⑩ Valve spring
⑪ Spring seat
⑫ Intake valve
⑬ Exhaust valve
⑭ Rubber plug
⑮ Cylinder head
⑯ Cylinder head bolt

Fig. 157 Exploded view cylinder head assembly — 240SX KA24DE engine

4. Remove the front exhaust pipe and AIV pipe.
5. Remove the air duct, cooling fan with coupling and radiator shroud.
6. Remove the fuel injector tube assembly with injectors.
7. Disconnect and mark spark plug wires. Remove the spark plugs.
8. Set No. 1 piston at TDC on compression stroke. Remove the rocker cover assembly.
9. Mark and remove the distributor assembly.
10. Remove the cam sprocket, brackets and camshafts. These parts should be reassembled in their original position. Bolts should be loosened in 2 or 3 steps (loosen all bolts in the reverse of the tightening order).
To install:
11. Install camshafts and camshafts brackets. Torque camshaft brackets in two or three steps in sequence. After completing assembly check valve clearance.
12. Install camshaft sprockets.
13. Install chain guide between both camshaft sprockets and distributor assembly.
14. Install all remaining components in reverse order of removal.
15. Connect the negative battery cable. Refill all fluid levels. Road test the vehicle for proper operation.

CHECKING CAMSHAFT RUN-OUT

◗ **See Figure 158**

Camshaft run-out should be checked when the camshaft has been removed from the cylinder head. An accurate dial indicator is needed for this procedure; engine specialists and most machine shops have this equipment. If you have access to a dial indicator, or can take your cam to someone who does, measure cam bearing journal run-out. The maximum (limit) run-out on the CA20E, CA18ET and KA24E camshafts is 0.02mm. The run-out limit on the Z20 and Z22 series camshafts is 0.20mm. The maximum (limit) run-out on the VG30E camshaft is 0.01mm. If the run-out exceeds the limit replace the camshaft.

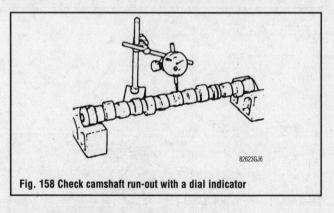

Fig. 158 Check camshaft run-out with a dial indicator

CHECKING CAMSHAFT LOBE HEIGHT

◗ **See Figures 159 and 160**

Use a micrometer to check cam (lobe) height, making sure the anvil and the spindle of the micrometer are positioned directly on the heel and tip of the cam lobe as shown in the accompanying illustration. Use the specifications in the following chart to determine the lobe wear.

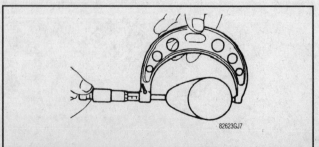

Fig. 159 Use a micrometer to check camshaft cam lobe height

Engine Series	Lobe	Lobe Height (in.)	Wear Limit (in.)
Z20, Z22	Int. and Exh.	1.5148 to 1.5168	0.0098
CA18ET	Intake	1.5055 to 1.5075	0.006
	Exhaust	1.5289 to 1.5309	
CA20E	Int. and Exh.	1.5289 to 1.5309	0.006
KA24E	Int. and Exh.	1.7653–1.7728	0.006
VG30E	Int. and Exh.	1.5566–1.5641	0.0059

82623GJ8

Fig. 160 Camshaft specifications

CHECKING CAMSHAFT JOURNALS & CAMSHAFT BEARING SADDLES

♦ See Figures 161 and 162

While the camshaft is still removed from the cylinder head, the camshaft bearing journals should be measured with a micrometer. Compare the measurements with those listed in the Camshaft Specifications chart in this section. If the measurements are less than the limits listed in the chart, the camshaft will have to be replaced, since the camshafts in all of the engines covered in this guide run directly on the cylinder head surface; no actual bearings or bushings are used, so no oversize bearings or bushings are available.

Using an inside dial gauge or inside micrometer, measure the inside diameter of the camshaft saddles (the camshaft mounts that are either integrally cast as part of the cylinder head, or are a bolted on, one piece unit. The Z-series engines use a saddle-and-cap arrangement. The inside diameter of the saddles on all engines except the CA20E/CA18ET is 48.00–48.01mm. The

CA20E/CA18ET measurement is 46.00–46.01mm. The inside diameter on the KA24E with the camshaft bracket and rocker shaft torque to specifications is 31.5–33.00mm. On the VG30E engine contact a Nissan dealer or local machine shop for that specification. The camshaft journal oil clearances are listed in the Camshaft Specifications chart in this section. If the saddle inside diameters exceed those listed above, the cylinder head must be replaced (again, because oversize bearings or bushings are not available).

CHECKING CAMSHAFT END-PLAY

♦ See Figure 160

After the camshaft has been installed, end-play should be checked. The camshaft sprocket should not be installed on the cam. Use a dial gauge to check the end-play, by moving the camshaft forward and backward in the cylinder head. End-play specifications for the CA20E, CA18ET, Z20/22 series and KA24E engines should not exceed 0.20mm. On the VG30E engine the camshaft end-play should be between 0.03–0.06mm.

Rear Main Bearing Oil Seal

REMOVAL & INSTALLATION

♦ See Figures 163, 164 and 165

1. Remove the transmission or transaxle.
2. Remove the flywheel or drive plate.
3. Remove the rear oil seal retainer from the block. On the early models, the seal retainer is part of the block—using a small pry bar, pry the rear main oil seal from around the crankshaft.
4. Using a suitable prying tool, remove the oil seal from the retainer.

To install:

5. Thoroughly scrape the surface of the retainer to remove any traces of the existing sealant or gasket material.
6. Wipe the seal bore with a clean rag.

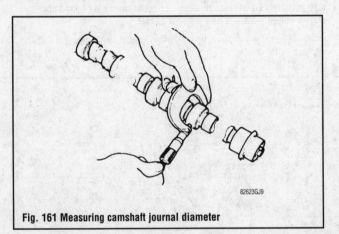

82623GJ9

Fig. 161 Measuring camshaft journal diameter

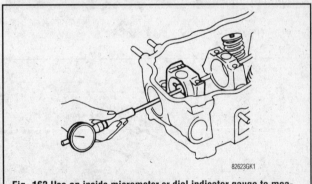

82623GK1

Fig. 162 Use an inside micrometer or dial indicator gauge to measure camshaft bearing saddle diameters

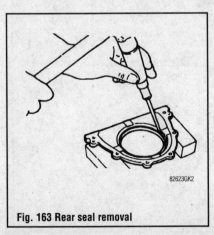

82623GK2

Fig. 163 Rear seal removal

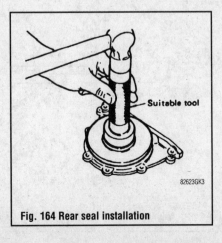

Suitable tool

82623GK3

Fig. 164 Rear seal installation

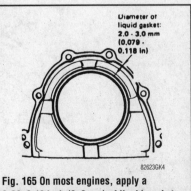

Diameter of liquid gasket: 2.0 - 3.0 mm (0.079 - 0.118 in)

82623GK4

Fig. 165 On most engines, apply a 0.08–0.12 inch (2–3mm) of liquid gasket to the rear oil seal retainer

7. Apply clean engine oil to the new oil seal and carefully install it into the retainer using the proper seal installation tool.

8. Install the rear oil seal retainer into the engine, along with a new gasket. Apply a 0.08–0.12 in. (2–3mm) of liquid gasket to the rear oil seal retainer prior to installation as necessary. Torque the bolts to 36 ft. lbs. (48 Nm).

➡ **On early models apply lithium grease around the sealing lip of the oil seal and install the seal by driving it into the cylinder block using an oil installation tool.**

9. Install the flywheel or driveplate.
10. Install the transmission or transaxle.

Flywheel and Ring Gear

REMOVAL & INSTALLATION

➡ **The clutch cover and the pressure plate are balanced as an assembly; if replacement of either part becomes necessary, replace both parts as an assembly.**

EXHAUST SYSTEM

Safety Precautions

For a number of reasons, exhaust system work can be dangerous. Always observe the following precautions:

1. Support the vehicle securely by using jackstands or equivalent under the frame of the vehicle.

2. Wear safety goggles to protect your eyes from metal chips that may fly free while working on the exhaust system.

3. If you are using a torch be careful not to come close to any fuel lines.

4. Always use the proper tool for the job.

Special Tools

A number of special exhaust tools can be rented or bought from a local auto parts store. It may also be quite helpful to use solvents designed to loosen

➡ **See exploded view of engine assembly for flywheel/drive plate installation and quick torque reference.**

1. On manual transmission/transaxle applications, refer to the "Clutch Removal and Installation" procedures in Section 7 and remove the clutch assembly. On automatic transmission/transaxle applications, remove the automatic transmission/transaxle assembly from the vehicle–refer to the necessary service procedures in Section 7.

2. Remove the flywheel/drive plate-to-crankshaft bolts and the flywheel/driveplate.

➡ **If necessary the clutch disc should be inspected and/or replaced at this time; the clutch lining wear limit is 0.30mm above the rivet heads or equivalent specification.**

3. To install, reverse the removal procedures. Torque the flywheel-to crankshaft bolts to specifications, the clutch cover-to-flywheel bolts and the bearing housing-to-clutch housing bolts to specifications on manual transmission/transaxle applications. On automatic transmission/transaxle applications, torque the driveplate-to crankshaft bolts to specifications, install torque converter then the transmission assembly. Refer to the Torque Specification Chart and Section 7 service procedures.

rusted nuts or bolts. Remember that these products are often flammable, apply only to parts after they are cool.

Front Pipe

REMOVAL & INSTALLATION

◆ **See Figures 166 thru 171**

➡ **Always replace the exhaust gaskets (exhaust pipe gasket to manifold) with new ones when reassembling—clean exhaust pipe flange completely before installing new exhaust gasket.**

1. Support the vehicle securely by using jackstands or equivalent under the frame of the vehicle.

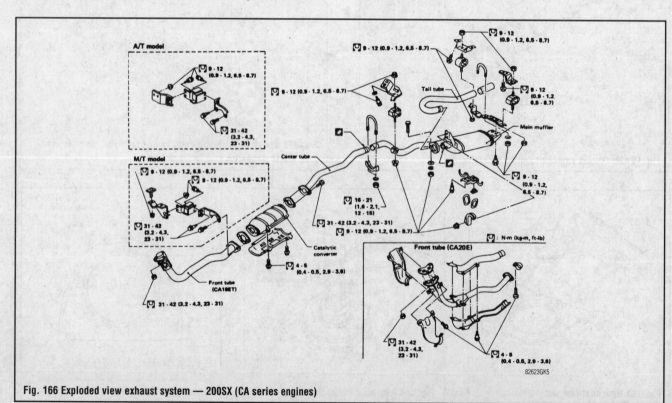

Fig. 166 Exploded view exhaust system — 200SX (CA series engines)

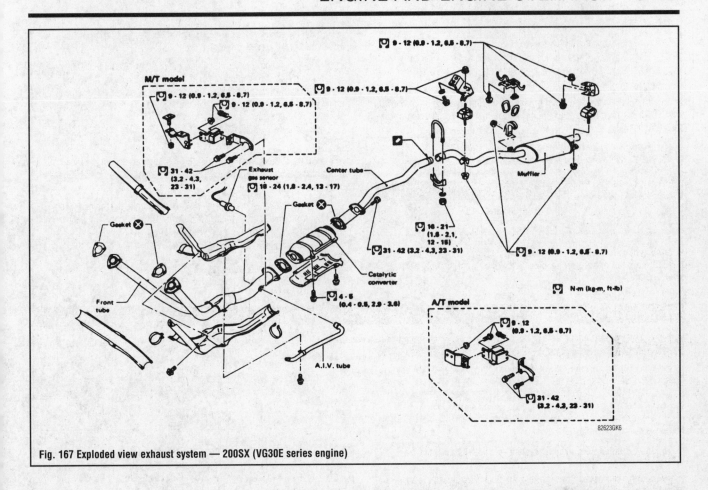

Fig. 167 Exploded view exhaust system — 200SX (VG30E series engine)

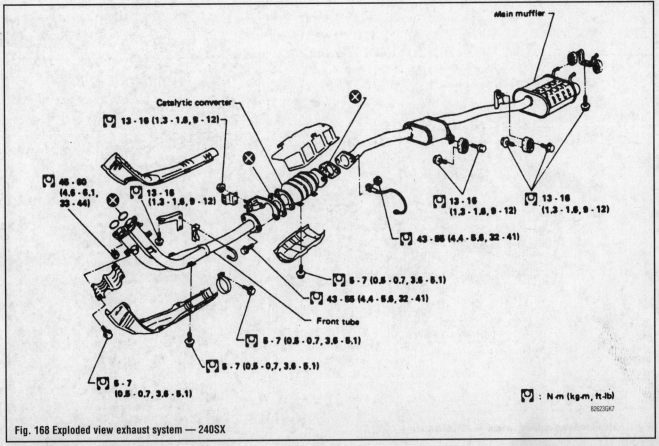

Fig. 168 Exploded view exhaust system — 240SX

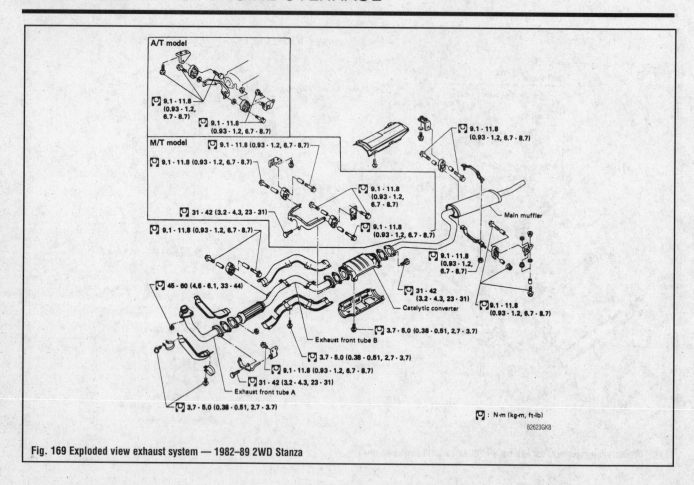

Fig. 169 Exploded view exhaust system — 1982–89 2WD Stanza

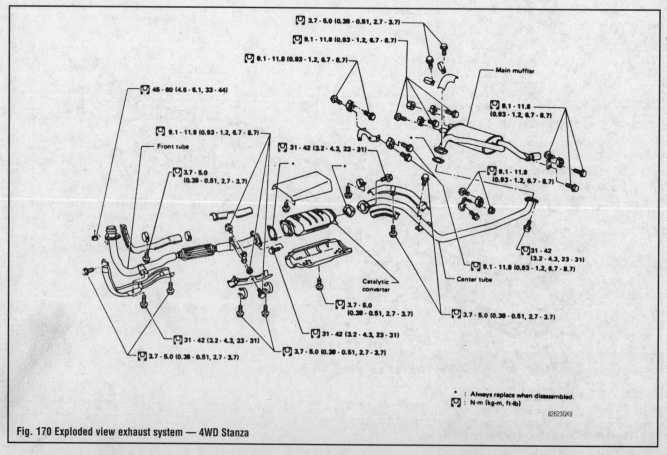

Fig. 170 Exploded view exhaust system — 4WD Stanza

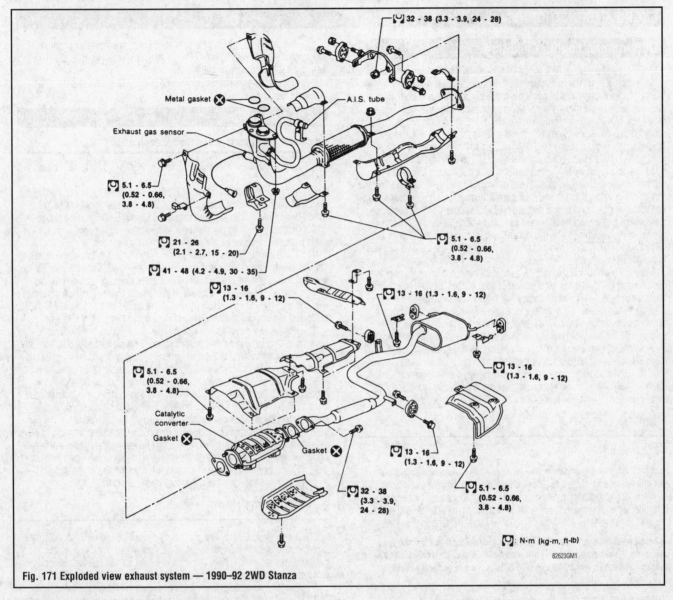

Fig. 171 Exploded view exhaust system — 1990–92 2WD Stanza

2. Remove the exhaust pipe clamps and any front exhaust pipe shield.

3. Soak the exhaust manifold front pipe mounting studs with penetrating oil. Remove attaching nuts and gasket from the manifold.

➡**If these studs snap off, while removing the front pipe the manifold will have to be removed and the stud will have to be drill out and the hole tapped.**

4. Remove any exhaust pipe mounting hanger or bracket.

5. Remove front pipe from the catalytic converter.

To install:

6. Install the front pipe on the manifold with seal if so equipped.

7. Install the pipe on the catalytic converter. Assemble all parts loosely and position pipe to insure proper clearance from body of vehicle.

8. Tighten mounting studs, bracket bolts on exhaust clamps.

9. Install exhaust pipe shield.

10. Start engine and check for exhaust leaks.

Catalytic Converter

REMOVAL & INSTALLATION

1. Remove the converter lower shield.

2. Disconnect converter from front pipe.

3. Disconnect converter from center pipe.

➡**Assemble all parts loosely and position converter before tightening the exhaust clamps.**

4. Remove catalytic converter.

5. To install reverse the removal procedures. Always use new clamps and exhaust seals, start engine and check for leaks.

Tailpipe and Muffler

REMOVAL & INSTALLATION

1. Remove tailpipe connection at center pipe.

2. Remove all brackets and exhaust clamps.

3. Remove tailpipe from muffler. On some models the tailpipe and muffler are one piece.

4. To install reverse the removal procedures. Always use new clamps and exhaust seals, start engine and check for leaks.

ENGINE RECONDITIONING

Determining Engine Condition

Anything that generates heat and/or friction will eventually burn or wear out (for example, a light bulb generates heat, therefore its life span is limited). With this in mind, a running engine generates tremendous amounts of both; friction is encountered by the moving and rotating parts inside the engine and heat is created by friction and combustion of the fuel. However, the engine has systems designed to help reduce the effects of heat and friction and provide added longevity. The oiling system reduces the amount of friction encountered by the moving parts inside the engine, while the cooling system reduces heat created by friction and combustion. If either system is not maintained, a break-down will be inevitable. Therefore, you can see how regular maintenance can affect the service life of your vehicle. If you do not drain, flush and refill your cooling system at the proper intervals, deposits will begin to accumulate in the radiator, thereby reducing the amount of heat it can extract from the coolant. The same applies to your oil and filter; if it is not changed often enough it becomes laden with contaminates and is unable to properly lubricate the engine. This increases friction and wear.

There are a number of methods for evaluating the condition of your engine. A compression test can reveal the condition of your pistons, piston rings, cylinder bores, head gasket(s), valves and valve seats. An oil pressure test can warn you of possible engine bearing, or oil pump failures. Excessive oil consumption, evidence of oil in the engine air intake area and/or bluish smoke from the tailpipe may indicate worn piston rings, worn valve guides and/or valve seals. As a general rule, an engine that uses no more than one quart of oil every 1000 miles is in good condition. Engines that use one quart of oil or more in less than 1000 miles should first be checked for oil leaks. If any oil leaks are present, have them fixed before determining how much oil is consumed by the engine, especially if blue smoke is not visible at the tailpipe.

COMPRESSION TEST

▶ **See Figure 172**

A noticeable lack of engine power, excessive oil consumption and/or poor fuel mileage measured over an extended period are all indicators of internal engine wear. Worn piston rings, scored or worn cylinder bores, blown head gaskets, sticking or burnt valves, and worn valve seats are all possible culprits. A check of each cylinder's compression will help locate the problem.

➡**A screw-in type compression gauge is more accurate than the type you simply hold against the spark plug hole. Although it takes slightly longer to use, it's worth the effort to obtain a more accurate reading.**

1. Make sure that the proper amount and viscosity of engine oil is in the crankcase, then ensure the battery is fully charged.
2. Warm-up the engine to normal operating temperature, then shut the engine **OFF**.
3. Disable the ignition system.
4. Label and disconnect all of the spark plug wires from the plugs.
5. Thoroughly clean the cylinder head area around the spark plug ports, then remove the spark plugs.

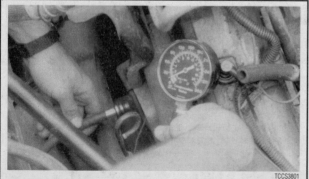

TCCS3801

Fig. 172 A screw-in type compression gauge is more accurate and easier to use without an assistant

6. Set the throttle plate to the fully open (wide-open throttle) position. You can block the accelerator linkage open for this, or you can have an assistant fully depress the accelerator pedal.
7. Install a screw-in type compression gauge into the No. 1 spark plug hole until the fitting is snug.

✳✳ WARNING

Be careful not to crossthread the spark plug hole.

8. According to the tool manufacturer's instructions, connect a remote starting switch to the starting circuit.
9. With the ignition switch in the **OFF** position, use the remote starting switch to crank the engine through at least five compression strokes (approximately 5 seconds of cranking) and record the highest reading on the gauge.
10. Repeat the test on each cylinder, cranking the engine approximately the same number of compression strokes and/or time as the first.
11. Compare the highest readings from each cylinder to that of the others. The indicated compression pressures are considered within specifications if the lowest reading cylinder is within 75 percent of the pressure recorded for the highest reading cylinder. For example, if your highest reading cylinder pressure was 150 psi (1034 kPa), then 75 percent of that would be 113 psi (779 kPa). So the lowest reading cylinder should be no less than 113 psi (779 kPa).
12. If a cylinder exhibits an unusually low compression reading, pour a tablespoon of clean engine oil into the cylinder through the spark plug hole and repeat the compression test. If the compression rises after adding oil, it means that the cylinder's piston rings and/or cylinder bore are damaged or worn. If the pressure remains low, the valves may not be seating properly (a valve job is needed), or the head gasket may be blown near that cylinder. If compression in any two adjacent cylinders is low, and if the addition of oil doesn't help raise compression, there is leakage past the head gasket. Oil and coolant in the combustion chamber, combined with blue or constant white smoke from the tailpipe, are symptoms of this problem. However, don't be alarmed by the normal white smoke emitted from the tailpipe during engine warm-up or from cold weather driving. There may be evidence of water droplets on the engine dipstick and/or oil droplets in the cooling system if a head gasket is blown.

OIL PRESSURE TEST

Check for proper oil pressure at the sending unit passage with an externally mounted mechanical oil pressure gauge (as opposed to relying on a factory installed dash-mounted gauge). A tachometer may also be needed, as some specifications may require running the engine at a specific rpm.

1. With the engine cold, locate and remove the oil pressure sending unit.
2. Following the manufacturer's instructions, connect a mechanical oil pressure gauge and, if necessary, a tachometer to the engine.
3. Start the engine and allow it to idle.
4. Check the oil pressure reading when cold and record the number. You may need to run the engine at a specified rpm, so check the specifications.
5. Run the engine until normal operating temperature is reached (upper radiator hose will feel warm).
6. Check the oil pressure reading again with the engine hot and record the number. Turn the engine **OFF**.
7. Compare your hot oil pressure reading to specification. If the reading is low, check the cold pressure reading against the chart. If the cold pressure is well above the specification, and the hot reading was lower than the specification, you may have the wrong viscosity oil in the engine. Change the oil, making sure to use the proper grade and quantity, then repeat the test.

Low oil pressure readings could be attributed to internal component wear, pump related problems, a low oil level, or oil viscosity that is too low. High oil pressure readings could be caused by an overfilled crankcase, too high of an oil viscosity or a faulty pressure relief valve.

Buy or Rebuild?

Now if you have determined that your engine is worn out, you must make some decisions. The question of whether or not an engine is worth rebuilding is largely a subjective matter and one of personal worth. Is the engine a popular one, or is it an obsolete model? Are parts available? Will it get acceptable gas mileage once it is rebuilt? Is the car it's being put into worth keeping? Would it be less expensive to buy a new engine, have your engine rebuilt by a pro, rebuild it yourself or buy a used engine from a salvage yard? Or would it be simpler and less expensive to buy another car? If you have considered all these matters, and have still decided to rebuild the engine, then it is time to decide how you will rebuild it.

➡The editors at Chilton feel that most engine machining should be performed by a professional machine shop. Think of it as an assurance that the job has been done right the first time. There are many expensive and specialized tools required to perform such tasks as boring and honing an engine block or having a valve job done on a cylinder head. Even inspecting the parts requires expensive micrometers and gauges to properly measure wear and clearances. A machine shop can deliver to you clean, and ready to assemble parts, saving you time and aggravation. Your maximum savings will come from performing the removal, disassembly, assembly and installation of the engine and purchasing or renting only the tools required to perform these tasks.

A complete rebuild or overhaul of an engine involves replacing all of the moving parts (pistons, rods, crankshaft, camshaft, etc.) with new ones and machining the non-moving wearing surfaces of the block and heads. Unfortunately, this may not be cost effective. For instance, your crankshaft may have been damaged or worn, but it can be machined undersize for a minimal fee.

So although you can replace everything inside the engine, it is usually wiser to replace only those parts which are really needed, and, if possible, repair the more expensive ones. Later in this section, we will break the engine down into its two main components: the cylinder head and the engine block. We will discuss each component, and the recommended parts to replace during a rebuild on each.

Engine Overhaul Tips

Most engine overhaul procedures are fairly standard. In addition to specific parts replacement procedures and specifications for your individual engine, this section is also a guide to acceptable rebuilding procedures. Examples of standard rebuilding practice are given and should be used along with specific details concerning your particular engine.

Competent and accurate machine shop services will ensure maximum performance, reliability and engine life. In most instances it is more profitable for the do-it-yourself mechanic to remove, clean and inspect the component, buy the necessary parts and deliver these to a shop for actual machine work.

Much of the assembly work (crankshaft, bearings, piston rods, and other components) is well within the scope of the do-it-yourself mechanic's tools and abilities. You will have to decide for yourself the depth of involvement you desire in an engine repair or rebuild.

TOOLS

The tools required for an engine overhaul or parts replacement will depend on the depth of your involvement. With a few exceptions, they will be the tools found in a mechanic's tool kit (see Section 1 of this manual). More in-depth work will require some or all of the following:
- A dial indicator (reading in thousandths) mounted on a universal base
- Micrometers and telescope gauges
- Jaw and screw-type pullers
- Scraper
- Valve spring compressor
- Ring groove cleaner
- Piston ring expander and compressor
- Ridge reamer
- Cylinder hone or glaze breaker
- Plastigage®
- Engine stand

The use of most of these tools is illustrated in this section. Many can be rented for a one-time use from a local parts jobber or tool supply house specializing in automotive work.

Occasionally, the use of special tools is called for. See the information on Special Tools and the Safety Notice in the front of this book before substituting another tool.

OVERHAUL TIPS

Aluminum has become extremely popular for use in engines, due to its low weight. Observe the following precautions when handling aluminum parts:
- Never hot tank aluminum parts (the caustic hot tank solution will eat the aluminum.)
- Remove all aluminum parts (identification tag, etc.) from engine parts prior to the tanking.
- Always coat threads lightly with engine oil or anti-seize compounds before installation, to prevent seizure.
- Never overtighten bolts or spark plugs especially in aluminum threads.

When assembling the engine, any parts that will be exposed to frictional contact must be prelubed to provide lubrication at initial start-up. Any product specifically formulated for this purpose can be used, but engine oil is not recommended as a prelube in most cases.

When semi-permanent (locked, but removable) installation of bolts or nuts is desired, threads should be cleaned and coated with Loctite® or another similar, commercial non-hardening sealant.

CLEANING

▶ **See Figures 173, 174, 175 and 176**

Before the engine and its components are inspected, they must be thoroughly cleaned. You will need to remove any engine varnish, oil sludge and/or carbon deposits from all of the components to insure an accurate inspection. A crack in the engine block or cylinder head can easily become overlooked if hidden by a layer of sludge or carbon.

Most of the cleaning process can be carried out with common hand tools and readily available solvents or solutions. Carbon deposits can be chipped away using a hammer and a hard wooden chisel. Old gasket material and varnish or sludge can usually be removed using a scraper and/or cleaning solvent. Extremely stubborn deposits may require the use of a power drill with a wire brush. If using a wire brush, use extreme care around any critical machined surfaces (such as the gasket surfaces, bearing saddles, cylinder bores, etc.). USE OF A WIRE BRUSH IS NOT RECOMMENDED ON ANY ALUMINUM COMPONENTS. Always follow any safety recommendations given by the manufacturer of the tool and/or solvent.

✳✳ CAUTION

Always wear eye protection during any cleaning process involving scraping, chipping or spraying of solvents.

An alternative to the mess and hassle of cleaning the parts yourself is to drop them off at a local garage or machine shop. They should have the necessary equipment to properly clean all of the parts for a nominal fee.

Remove any oil galley plugs, freeze plugs and/or pressed-in bearings and carefully wash and degrease all of the engine components including the fasteners and bolts. Small parts such as the valves, springs, etc., should be placed in a metal basket and allowed to soak. Use pipe cleaner type brushes, and clean all passageways in the components.

TCCS3132

Fig. 173 Use a gasket scraper to remove the old gasket material from the mating surfaces

Fig. 174 Before cleaning and inspection, use a ring expander tool to remove the piston rings

Fig. 175 Clean the piston ring grooves using a ring groove cleaner tool, or . . .

Fig. 176 . . . use a piece of an old ring to clean the grooves. Be careful, the ring can be quite sharp

Use a ring expander and remove the rings from the pistons. Clean the piston ring grooves with a special tool or a piece of broken ring. Scrape the carbon off of the top of the piston. You should never use a wire brush on the pistons. After preparing all of the piston assemblies in this manner, wash and degrease them again.

✳✳ WARNING

Use extreme care when cleaning around the cylinder head valve seats. A mistake or slip may cost you a new seat.

When cleaning the cylinder head, remove carbon from the combustion chamber with the valves installed. This will avoid damaging the valve seats.

REPAIRING DAMAGED THREADS

▶ **See Figures 177, 178, 179, 180 and 181**

Several methods of repairing damaged threads are available. Heli-Coil® (shown here), Keenserts® and Microdot® are among the most widely used. All involve basically the same principle—drilling out stripped threads, tapping the hole and installing a prewound insert—making welding, plugging and oversize fasteners unnecessary.

Two types of thread repair inserts are usually supplied: a standard type for most inch coarse, inch fine, metric course and metric fine thread sizes and a spark lug type to fit most spark plug port sizes. Consult the individual tool manufacturer's catalog to determine exact applications. Typical

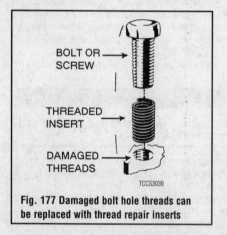

Fig. 177 Damaged bolt hole threads can be replaced with thread repair inserts

Fig. 178 Standard thread repair insert (left), and spark plug thread insert

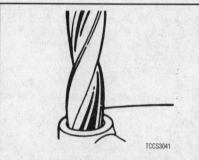

Fig. 179 Drill out the damaged threads with the specified size bit. Be sure to drill completely through the hole or to the bottom of a blind hole

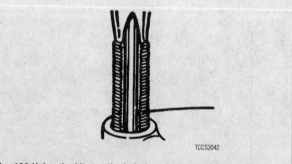

Fig. 180 Using the kit, tap the hole in order to receive the thread insert. Keep the tap well oiled and back it out frequently to avoid clogging the threads

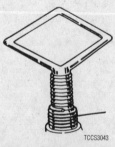

Fig. 181 Screw the insert onto the installer tool until the tang engages the slot. Thread the insert into the hole until it is ¼–½ turn below the top surface, then remove the tool and break off the tang using a punch

thread repair kits will contain a selection of prewound threaded inserts, a tap (corresponding to the outside diameter threads of the insert) and an installation tool. Spark plug inserts usually differ because they require a tap equipped with pilot threads and a combined reamer/tap section. Most manufacturers also supply blister-packed thread repair inserts separately in addition to a master kit containing a variety of taps and inserts plus installation tools.

Before attempting to repair a threaded hole, remove any snapped, broken or damaged bolts or studs. Penetrating oil can be used to free frozen threads. The offending item can usually be removed with locking pliers or using a screw/stud extractor. After the hole is clear, the thread can be repaired as shown in the kit manufacturer's instructions.

Engine Preparation

To properly rebuild an engine, you must first remove it from the vehicle, then disassemble and diagnose it. Ideally you should place your engine on an engine stand. This affords you the best access to the engine components. Remove the flywheel or flexplate before installing the engine to the stand.

Now that you have the engine on a stand, and assuming that you have drained the oil and coolant from the engine, it's time to strip it of all but the necessary components. Before you start disassembling the engine, you may want to take a moment to draw some pictures, or fabricate some labels or containers to mark the locations of various components and the bolts and/or studs which fasten them. Modern day engines use a lot of little brackets and clips which hold wiring harnesses and such, and these holders are often mounted on studs and/or bolts that can be easily mixed up. The manufacturer spent a lot of time and money designing your vehicle, and they wouldn't have wasted any of it by haphazardly placing brackets, clips or fasteners on the vehicle. If it's present when you disassemble it, put it back when you assemble, you will regret not remembering that little bracket which holds a wire harness out of the path of a rotating part.

You should begin by unbolting any accessories still attached to the engine, such as the water pump, power steering pump, alternator, etc. Then, unfasten any manifolds (intake or exhaust) which were not removed during the engine removal procedure. Finally, remove any covers remaining on the engine such as the rocker arm, front or timing cover and oil pan. Some front covers may require the vibration damper and/or crank pulley to be removed beforehand. The idea is to reduce the engine to the bare necessities of cylinder head(s), valve train, engine block, crankshaft, pistons and connecting rods, plus any other `in block' components such as oil pumps, balance shafts and auxiliary shafts.

Finally, remove the cylinder head(s) from the engine block and carefully place on a bench. Disassembly instructions for each component follow later in this section.

Cylinder Head

There are two basic types of cylinder heads used on today's automobiles: the Overhead Valve (OHV) and the Overhead Camshaft (OHC). The latter can also be broken down into two subgroups: the Single Overhead Camshaft (SOHC) and the Dual Overhead Camshaft (DOHC). Generally, if there is only a single camshaft on a head, it is just referred to as an OHC head. Also, an engine with an OHV cylinder head is also known as a pushrod engine.

Most cylinder heads these days are made of an aluminum alloy due to its light weight, durability and heat transfer qualities. However, cast iron was the material of choice in the past, and is still used on many vehicles. Whether made from aluminum or iron, all cylinder heads have valves and seats. Some use two valves per cylinder, while the more hi-tech engines will utilize a multi-valve configuration using 3, 4 and even 5 valves per cylinder. When the valve contacts the seat, it does so on precision machined surfaces, which seals the combustion chamber. All cylinder heads have a valve guide for each valve. The guide centers the valve to the seat and allows it to move up and down within it. The clearance between the valve and guide can be critical. Too much clearance and the engine may consume oil, lose vacuum and/or damage the seat. Too little, and the valve can stick in the guide causing the engine to run poorly if at all, and possibly causing severe damage. The last component all automotive cylinder heads have are valve springs. The spring holds the valve against its seat. It also returns the valve to this position when the valve has been opened by the valve train or camshaft. The spring is fastened to the valve by a retainer and valve locks (sometimes called keepers). Alu-

minum heads will also have a valve spring shim to keep the spring from wearing away the aluminum.

An ideal method of rebuilding the cylinder head would involve replacing all of the valves, guides, seats, springs, etc. with new ones. However, depending on how the engine was maintained, often this is not necessary. A major cause of valve, guide and seat wear is an improperly tuned engine. An engine that is running too rich, will often wash the lubricating oil out of the guide with gasoline, causing it to wear rapidly. Conversely, an engine which is running too lean will place higher combustion temperatures on the valves and seats allowing them to wear or even burn. Springs fall victim to the driving habits of the individual. A driver who often runs the engine rpm to the redline will wear out or break the springs faster then one that stays well below it. Unfortunately, mileage takes it toll on all of the parts. Generally, the valves, guides, springs and seats in a cylinder head can be machined and re-used, saving you money. However, if a valve is burnt, it may be wise to replace all of the valves, since they were all operating in the same environment. The same goes for any other component on the cylinder head. Think of it as an insurance policy against future problems related to that component.

Unfortunately, the only way to find out which components need replacing, is to disassemble and carefully check each piece. After the cylinder head(s) are disassembled, thoroughly clean all of the components.

DISASSEMBLY

▶ See Figures 182 and 183

Whether it is a single or dual overhead camshaft cylinder head, the disassembly procedure is relatively unchanged. One aspect to pay attention to is careful labeling of the parts on the dual camshaft cylinder head. There will be an intake camshaft and followers as well as an exhaust camshaft and followers and they must be labeled as such. In some cases, the components are identical and could easily be installed incorrectly. DO NOT MIX THEM UP! Determining which is which is very simple; the intake camshaft and components are on the same side of the head as was the intake manifold. Conversely, the exhaust camshaft and components are on the same side of the head as was the exhaust manifold.

TCCA3P54

Fig. 182 Exploded view of a valve, seal, spring, retainer and locks from an OHC cylinder head

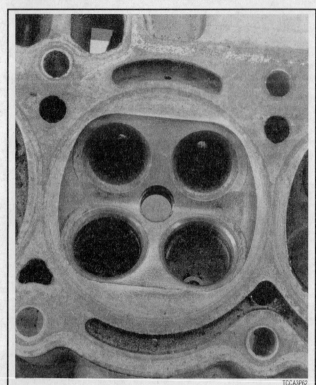

Fig. 183 Example of a multi-valve cylinder head. Note how it has 2 intake and 2 exhaust valve ports

Fig. 185 Most cup type follower cylinder heads retain the camshaft using bolt-on bearing caps

Cup Type Camshaft Followers

▶ See Figures 184, 185 and 186

Most cylinder heads with cup type camshaft followers will have the valve spring, retainer and locks recessed within the follower's bore. You will need a C-clamp style valve spring compressor tool, an OHC spring removal tool (or equivalent) and a small magnet to disassemble the head.

1. If not already removed, remove the camshaft(s) and/or followers. Mark their positions for assembly.

2. Position the cylinder head to allow use of a C-clamp style valve spring compressor tool.

➡It is preferred to position the cylinder head gasket surface facing you with the valve springs facing the opposite direction and the head laying horizontal.

3. With the OHC spring removal adapter tool positioned inside of the follower bore, compress the valve spring using the C-clamp style valve spring compressor.

4. Remove the valve locks. A small magnetic tool or screwdriver will aid in removal.

Fig. 186 Position the OHC spring tool in the follower bore, then compress the spring with a C-clamp type tool

5. Release the compressor tool and remove the spring assembly.
6. Withdraw the valve from the cylinder head.
7. If equipped, remove the valve seal.

➡Special valve seal removal tools are available. Regular or needlenose type pliers, if used with care, will work just as well. If using ordinary pliers, be sure not to damage the follower bore. The follower and its bore are machined to close tolerances and any damage to the bore will effect this relationship.

8. If equipped, remove the valve spring shim. A small magnetic tool or screwdriver will aid in removal.
9. Repeat Steps 3 through 8 until all of the valves have been removed.

Rocker Arm Type Camshaft Followers

▶ See Figures 187 thru 195

Most cylinder heads with rocker arm-type camshaft followers are easily disassembled using a standard valve spring compressor. However, certain models may not have enough open space around the spring for the standard tool and may require you to use a C-clamp style compressor tool instead.

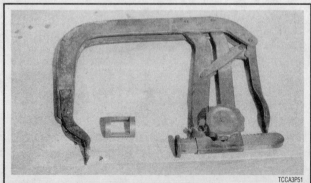

Fig. 184 C-clamp type spring compressor and an OHC spring removal tool (center) for cup type followers

Fig. 187 Example of the shaft mounted rocker arms on some OHC heads

Fig. 188 Another example of the rocker arm type OHC head. This model uses a follower under the camshaft

Fig. 189 Before the camshaft can be removed, all of the followers must first be removed . . .

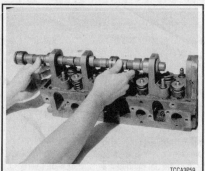

Fig. 190 . . . then the camshaft can be removed by sliding it out (shown), or unbolting a bearing cap (not shown)

Fig. 191 Compress the valve spring . . .

Fig. 192 . . . then remove the valve locks from the valve stem and spring retainer

Fig. 193 Remove the valve spring and retainer from the cylinder head

Fig. 194 Remove the valve seal from the guide. Some gentle prying or pliers may help to remove stubborn ones

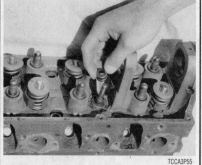

Fig. 195 All aluminum and some cast iron heads will have these valve spring shims. Remove all of them as well

1. If not already removed, remove the rocker arms and/or shafts and the camshaft. If applicable, also remove the hydraulic lash adjusters. Mark their positions for assembly.

2. Position the cylinder head to allow access to the valve spring.

3. Use a valve spring compressor tool to relieve the spring tension from the retainer.

➡️**Due to engine varnish, the retainer may stick to the valve locks. A gentle tap with a hammer may help to break it loose.**

4. Remove the valve locks from the valve tip and/or retainer. A small magnet may help in removing the small locks.

5. Lift the valve spring, tool and all, off of the valve stem.

6. If equipped, remove the valve seal. If the seal is difficult to remove with the valve in place, try removing the valve first, then the seal. Follow the steps below for valve removal.

7. Position the head to allow access for withdrawing the valve.

➡️**Cylinder heads that have seen a lot of miles and/or abuse may have mushroomed the valve lock grove and/or tip, causing difficulty in removal of the valve. If this has happened, use a metal file to carefully remove the high spots around the lock grooves and/or tip. Only file it enough to allow removal.**

8. Remove the valve from the cylinder head.

9. If equipped, remove the valve spring shim. A small magnetic tool or screwdriver will aid in removal.

10. Repeat Steps 3 though 9 until all of the valves have been removed.

INSPECTION

Now that all of the cylinder head components are clean, it's time to inspect them for wear and/or damage. To accurately inspect them, you will need some specialized tools:

- A 0–1 in. micrometer for the valves
- A dial indicator or inside diameter gauge for the valve guides
- A spring pressure test gauge

If you do not have access to the proper tools, you may want to bring the components to a shop that does.

Valves

▶ See Figures 196 and 197

The first thing to inspect are the valve heads. Look closely at the head, margin and face for any cracks, excessive wear or burning. The margin is the best place to look for burning. It should have a squared edge with an even width all around the diameter. When a valve burns, the margin will look melted and the edges rounded. Also inspect the valve head for any signs of tulipping. This will show as a lifting of the edges or dishing in the center of the head and will usually not occur to all of the valves. All of the heads should look the same, any that seem dished more than others are probably bad. Next, inspect the valve lock grooves and valve tips. Check for any burrs around the lock grooves, especially if you had to file them to remove the valve. Valve tips should appear flat, although slight rounding with high mileage engines is normal. Slightly worn valve tips will need to be machined flat. Last, measure the valve stem diameter with the micrometer. Measure the area that rides within the guide, especially towards the tip where most of the wear occurs. Take several measurements along its length and compare them to each other. Wear should be even along the length with little to no taper. If no minimum diameter is given in the specifications, then the stem should not read more than 0.001 in. (0.025mm) below the unworn portion of the stem. Any valves that fail these inspections should be replaced.

Springs, Retainers and Valve Locks

▶ See Figures 198 and 199

The first thing to check is the most obvious, broken springs. Next check the free length and squareness of each spring. If applicable, insure to distinguish between intake and exhaust springs. Use a ruler and/or carpenter's square to measure the length. A carpenter's square should be used to check the springs for squareness. If a spring pressure test gauge is available, check each springs rating and compare to the specifications chart. Check the readings against the specifications given. Any springs that fail these inspections should be replaced.

The spring retainers rarely need replacing, however they should still be checked as a precaution. Inspect the spring mating surface and the valve lock retention area for any signs of excessive wear. Also check for any signs of cracking. Replace any retainers that are questionable.

Valve locks should be inspected for excessive wear on the outside contact area as well as on the inner notched surface. Any locks which appear worn or broken and its respective valve should be replaced.

Cylinder Head

There are several things to check on the cylinder head: valve guides, seats, cylinder head surface flatness, cracks and physical damage.

VALVE GUIDES

▶ See Figure 200

Now that you know the valves are good, you can use them to check the guides, although a new valve, if available, is preferred. Before you measure anything, look at the guides carefully and inspect them for any cracks, chips or breakage. Also if the guide is a removable style (as in most aluminum heads), check them for any looseness or evidence of movement. All of the guides should appear to be at the same height from the spring seat. If any seem lower (or higher) from another, the guide has moved. Mount a dial indicator onto the spring side of the cylinder head. Lightly oil the valve stem and insert it into the cylinder head. Position the dial indicator against the valve stem near the tip and zero the gauge. Grasp the valve stem and wiggle towards and away from the dial indicator and observe the readings. Mount the dial indicator 90 degrees from the initial point and zero the gauge and again take a reading. Compare the two readings for an out of round condition. Check the readings against the specifications given. An Inside Diameter (I.D.) gauge designed for valve guides will

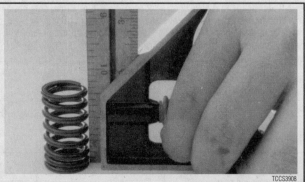

Fig. 196 Valve stems may be rolled on a flat surface to check for bends

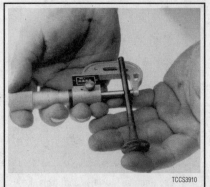

Fig. 197 Use a micrometer to check the valve stem diameter

Fig. 198 Use a caliper to check the valve spring free-length

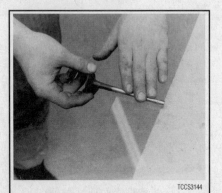

Fig. 199 Check the valve spring for squareness on a flat surface; a carpenter's square can be used

Fig. 200 A dial gauge may be used to check valve stem-to-guide clearance; read the gauge while moving the valve stem

give you an accurate valve guide bore measurement. If the I.D. gauge is used, compare the readings with the specifications given. Any guides that fail these inspections should be replaced or machined.

VALVE SEATS

A visual inspection of the valve seats should show a slightly worn and pitted surface where the valve face contacts the seat. Inspect the seat carefully for severe pitting or cracks. Also, a seat that is badly worn will be recessed into the cylinder head. A severely worn or recessed seat may need to be replaced. All cracked seats must be replaced. A seat concentricity gauge, if available, should be used to check the seat run-out. If run-out exceeds specifications the seat must be machined (if no specification is available given use 0.002 in. or 0.051mm).

CYLINDER HEAD SURFACE FLATNESS

▶ **See Figures 201 and 202**

After you have cleaned the gasket surface of the cylinder head of any old gasket material, check the head for flatness.

Place a straightedge across the gasket surface. Using feeler gauges, determine the clearance at the center of the straightedge and across the cylinder head at several points. Check along the centerline and diagonally on the head surface. If the warpage exceeds 0.003 in. (0.076mm) within a 6.0 in. (15.2cm) span, or 0.006 in. (0.152mm) over the total length of the head, the cylinder head must be resurfaced. After resurfacing the heads of a V-type engine, the intake manifold flange surface should be checked, and if necessary, milled proportionally to allow for the change in its mounting position.

CRACKS AND PHYSICAL DAMAGE

Generally, cracks are limited to the combustion chamber, however, it is not uncommon for the head to crack in a spark plug hole, port, outside of the head or in the valve spring/rocker arm area. The first area to inspect is always the hottest: the exhaust seat/port area.

A visual inspection should be performed, but just because you don't see a crack does not mean it is not there. Some more reliable methods for inspecting

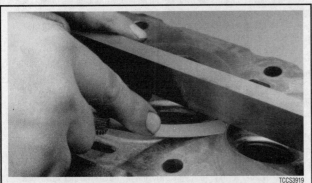

TCCS3919

Fig. 201 Check the head for flatness across the center of the head surface using a straightedge and feeler gauge

TCCS3918

Fig. 202 Checks should also be made along both diagonals of the head surface

for cracks include Magnaflux®, a magnetic process or Zyglo®, a dye penetrant. Magnaflux® is used only on ferrous metal (cast iron) heads. Zyglo® uses a spray on fluorescent mixture along with a black light to reveal the cracks. It is strongly recommended to have your cylinder head checked professionally for cracks, especially if the engine was known to have overheated and/or leaked or consumed coolant. Contact a local shop for availability and pricing of these services.

Physical damage is usually very evident. For example, a broken mounting ear from dropping the head or a bent or broken stud and/or bolt. All of these defects should be fixed or, if unrepairable, the head should be replaced.

Camshaft and Followers

Inspect the camshaft(s) and followers as described earlier in this section.

REFINISHING & REPAIRING

Many of the procedures given for refinishing and repairing the cylinder head components must be performed by a machine shop. Certain steps, if the inspected part is not worn, can be performed yourself inexpensively. However, you spent a lot of time and effort so far, why risk trying to save a couple bucks if you might have to do it all over again?

Valves

Any valves that were not replaced should be refaced and the tips ground flat. Unless you have access to a valve grinding machine, this should be done by a machine shop. If the valves are in extremely good condition, as well as the valve seats and guides, they may be lapped in without performing machine work.

It is a recommended practice to lap the valves even after machine work has been performed and/or new valves have been purchased. This insures a positive seal between the valve and seat.

LAPPING THE VALVES

➡**Before lapping the valves to the seats, read the rest of the cylinder head section to insure that any related parts are in acceptable enough condition to continue. Also, remember that before any valve seat machining and/or lapping can be performed, the guides must be within factory recommended specifications.**

1. Invert the cylinder head.
2. Lightly lubricate the valve stems and insert them into the cylinder head in their numbered order.
3. Raise the valve from the seat and apply a small amount of fine lapping compound to the seat.
4. Moisten the suction head of a hand-lapping tool and attach it to the head of the valve.
5. Rotate the tool between the palms of both hands, changing the position of the valve on the valve seat and lifting the tool often to prevent grooving.
6. Lap the valve until a smooth, polished circle is evident on the valve and seat.
7. Remove the tool and the valve. Wipe away all traces of the grinding compound and store the valve to maintain its lapped location.

✳✳ WARNING

Do not get the valves out of order after they have been lapped. They must be put back with the same valve seat with which they were lapped.

Springs, Retainers and Valve Locks

There is no repair or refinishing possible with the springs, retainers and valve locks. If they are found to be worn or defective, they must be replaced with new (or known good) parts.

Cylinder Head

Most refinishing procedures dealing with the cylinder head must be performed by a machine shop. Read the sections below and review your inspection data to determine whether or not machining is necessary.

VALVE GUIDE

➡️**If any machining or replacements are made to the valve guides, the seats must be machined.**

Unless the valve guides need machining or replacing, the only service to perform is to thoroughly clean them of any dirt or oil residue.

There are only two types of valve guides used on automobile engines: the replaceable-type (all aluminum heads) and the cast-in integral-type (most cast iron heads). There are four recommended methods for repairing worn guides.

- Knurling
- Inserts
- Reaming oversize
- Replacing

Knurling is a process in which metal is displaced and raised, thereby reducing clearance, giving a true center, and providing oil control. It is the least expensive way of repairing the valve guides. However, it is not necessarily the best, and in some cases, a knurled valve guide will not stand up for more than a short time. It requires a special knurlizer and precision reaming tools to obtain proper clearances. It would not be cost effective to purchase these tools, unless you plan on rebuilding several of the same cylinder head.

Installing a guide insert involves machining the guide to accept a bronze insert. One style is the coil-type which is installed into a threaded guide. Another is the thin-walled insert where the guide is reamed oversize to accept a split-sleeve insert. After the insert is installed, a special tool is then run through the guide to expand the insert, locking it to the guide. The insert is then reamed to the standard size for proper valve clearance.

Reaming for oversize valves restores normal clearances and provides a true valve seat. Most cast-in type guides can be reamed to accept an valve with an oversize stem. The cost factor for this can become quite high as you will need to purchase the reamer and new, oversize stem valves for all guides which were reamed. Oversizes are generally 0.003–0.030 in. (0.076–0.762mm), with 0.015 in. (0.381mm) being the most common.

To replace cast-in type valve guides, they must be drilled out, then reamed to accept replacement guides. This must be done on a fixture which will allow centering and leveling off of the original valve seat or guide, otherwise a serious guide-to-seat misalignment may occur making it impossible to properly machine the seat.

Replaceable-type guides are pressed into the cylinder head. A hammer and a stepped drift or punch may be used to install and remove the guides. Before removing the guides, measure the protrusion on the spring side of the head and record it for installation. Use the stepped drift to hammer out the old guide from the combustion chamber side of the head. When installing, determine whether or not the guide also seals a water jacket in the head, and if it does, use the recommended sealing agent. If there is no water jacket, grease the valve guide and its bore. Use the stepped drift, and hammer the new guide into the cylinder head from the spring side of the cylinder head. A stack of washers the same thickness as the measured protrusion may help the installation process.

VALVE SEATS

➡️**Before any valve seat machining can be performed, the guides must be within factory recommended specifications. If any machining occurred or if replacements were made to the valve guides, the seats must be machined.**

If the seats are in good condition, the valves can be lapped to the seats, and the cylinder head assembled. See the valves section for instructions on lapping.

If the valve seats are worn, cracked or damaged, they must be serviced by a machine shop. The valve seat must be perfectly centered to the valve guide, which requires very accurate machining.

CYLINDER HEAD SURFACE

If the cylinder head is warped, it must be machined flat. If the warpage is extremely severe, the head may need to be replaced. In some instances, it may be possible to straighten a warped head enough to allow machining. In either case, contact a professional machine shop for service.

➡️**Any OHC cylinder head that shows excessive warpage should have the camshaft bearing journals align bored after the cylinder head has been resurfaced.**

✳️ WARNING

Failure to align bore the camshaft bearing journals could result in severe engine damage including but not limited to: valve and piston damage, connecting rod damage, camshaft and/or crankshaft breakage.

CRACKS AND PHYSICAL DAMAGE

Certain cracks can be repaired in both cast iron and aluminum heads. For cast iron, a tapered threaded insert is installed along the length of the crack. Aluminum can also use the tapered inserts, however welding is the preferred method. Some physical damage can be repaired through brazing or welding. Contact a machine shop to get expert advice for your particular dilemma.

ASSEMBLY

◆ **See Figure 203**

The first step for any assembly job is to have a clean area in which to work. Next, thoroughly clean all of the parts and components that are to be assembled. Finally, place all of the components onto a suitable work space and, if necessary, arrange the parts to their respective positions.

Cup Type Camshaft Followers

To install the springs, retainers and valve locks on heads which have these components recessed into the camshaft follower's bore, you will need a small screwdriver-type tool, some clean white grease and a lot of patience. You will also need the C-clamp style spring compressor and the OHC tool used to disassemble the head.

1. Lightly lubricate the valve stems and insert all of the valves into the cylinder head. If possible, maintain their original locations.
2. If equipped, install any valve spring shims which were removed.
3. If equipped, install the new valve seals, keeping the following in mind:
- If the valve seal presses over the guide, lightly lubricate the outer guide surfaces.
- If the seal is an O-ring type, it is installed just after compressing the spring but before the valve locks.
4. Place the valve spring and retainer over the stem.
5. Position the spring compressor and the OHC tool, then compress the spring.
6. Using a small screwdriver as a spatula, fill the valve stem side of the lock with white grease. Use the excess grease on the screwdriver to fasten the lock to the driver.
7. Carefully install the valve lock, which is stuck to the end of the screwdriver, to the valve stem then press on it with the screwdriver until the grease squeezes out. The valve lock should now be stuck to the stem.
8. Repeat Steps 6 and 7 for the remaining valve lock.
9. Relieve the spring pressure slowly and insure that neither valve lock becomes dislodged by the retainer.
10. Remove the spring compressor tool.

TCCA3P64

Fig. 203 Once assembled, check the valve clearance and correct as needed

11. Repeat Steps 2 through 10 until all of the springs have been installed.

12. Install the followers, camshaft(s) and any other components that were removed for disassembly.

Rocker Arm Type Camshaft Followers

1. Lightly lubricate the valve stems and insert all of the valves into the cylinder head. If possible, maintain their original locations.

2. If equipped, install any valve spring shims which were removed.

3. If equipped, install the new valve seals, keeping the following in mind:

• If the valve seal presses over the guide, lightly lubricate the outer guide surfaces.

• If the seal is an O-ring type, it is installed just after compressing the spring but before the valve locks.

4. Place the valve spring and retainer over the stem.

5. Position the spring compressor tool and compress the spring.

6. Assemble the valve locks to the stem.

7. Relieve the spring pressure slowly and insure that neither valve lock becomes dislodged by the retainer.

8. Remove the spring compressor tool.

9. Repeat Steps 2 through 8 until all of the springs have been installed.

10. Install the camshaft(s), rockers, shafts and any other components that were removed for disassembly.

Engine Block

GENERAL INFORMATION

A thorough overhaul or rebuild of an engine block would include replacing the pistons, rings, bearings, timing belt/chain assembly and oil pump. For OHV engines also include a new camshaft and lifters. The block would then have the cylinders bored and honed oversize (or if using removable cylinder sleeves, new sleeves installed) and the crankshaft would be cut undersize to provide new wearing surfaces and perfect clearances. However, your particular engine may not have everything worn out. What if only the piston rings have worn out and the clearances on everything else are still within factory specifications? Well, you could just replace the rings and put it back together, but this would be a very rare example. Chances are, if one component in your engine is worn, other components are sure to follow, and soon. At the very least, you should always replace the rings, bearings and oil pump. This is what is commonly called a "freshen up".

Cylinder Ridge Removal

Because the top piston ring does not travel to the very top of the cylinder, a ridge is built up between the end of the travel and the top of the cylinder bore.

Pushing the piston and connecting rod assembly past the ridge can be difficult, and damage to the piston ring lands could occur. If the ridge is not removed before installing a new piston or not removed at all, piston ring breakage and piston damage may occur.

➡**It is always recommended that you remove any cylinder ridges before removing the piston and connecting rod assemblies. If you know that new pistons are going to be installed and the engine block will be bored oversize, you may be able to forego this step. However, some ridges may actually prevent the assemblies from being removed, necessitating its removal.**

There are several different types of ridge reamers on the market, none of which are inexpensive. Unless a great deal of engine rebuilding is anticipated, borrow or rent a reamer.

1. Turn the crankshaft until the piston is at the bottom of its travel.

2. Cover the head of the piston with a rag.

3. Follow the tool manufacturers instructions and cut away the ridge, exercising extreme care to avoid cutting too deeply.

4. Remove the ridge reamer, the rag and as many of the cuttings as possible. Continue until all of the cylinder ridges have been removed.

DISASSEMBLY

▶ **See Figures 204 and 205**

The engine disassembly instructions following assume that you have the engine mounted on an engine stand. If not, it is easiest to disassemble the engine on a bench or the floor with it resting on the bell housing or transmission mounting surface. You must be able to access the connecting rod fasteners and turn the crankshaft during disassembly. Also, all engine covers (timing, front, side, oil pan, whatever) should have already been removed. Engines which are seized or locked up may not be able to be completely disassembled, and a core (salvage yard) engine should be purchased.

If not done during the cylinder head removal, remove the timing chain/belt and/or gear/sprocket assembly. Remove the oil pick-up and pump assembly and, if necessary, the pump drive. If equipped, remove any balance or auxiliary shafts. If necessary, remove the cylinder ridge from the top of the bore. See the cylinder ridge removal procedure earlier in this section.

Fig. 204 Place rubber hose over the connecting rod studs to protect the crankshaft and cylinder bores from damage

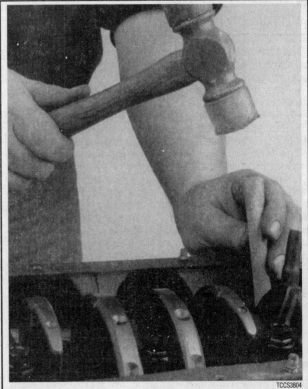

Fig. 205 Carefully tap the piston out of the bore using a wooden dowel

Rotate the engine over so that the crankshaft is exposed. Use a number punch or scribe and mark each connecting rod with its respective cylinder number. The cylinder closest to the front of the engine is always number 1. However, depending on the engine placement, the front of the engine could either be the flywheel or damper/pulley end. Generally the front of the engine faces the front of the vehicle. Use a number punch or scribe and also mark the main bearing caps from front to rear with the front most cap being number 1 (if there are five caps, mark them 1 through 5, front to rear).

** WARNING

Take special care when pushing the connecting rod up from the crankshaft because the sharp threads of the rod bolts/studs will score the crankshaft journal. Insure that special plastic caps are installed over them, or cut two pieces of rubber hose to do the same.

Again, rotate the engine, this time to position the number one cylinder bore (head surface) up. Turn the crankshaft until the number one piston is at the bottom of its travel, this should allow the maximum access to its connecting rod. Remove the number one connecting rods fasteners and cap and place two lengths of rubber hose over the rod bolts/studs to protect the crankshaft from damage. Using a sturdy wooden dowel and a hammer, push the connecting rod up about 1 in. (25mm) from the crankshaft and remove the upper bearing insert. Continue pushing or tapping the connecting rod up until the piston rings are out of the cylinder bore. Remove the piston and rod by hand, put the upper half of the bearing insert back into the rod, install the cap with its bearing insert installed, and hand-tighten the cap fasteners. If the parts are kept in order in this manner, they will not get lost and you will be able to tell which bearings came form what cylinder if any problems are discovered and diagnosis is necessary. Remove all the other piston assemblies in the same manner. On V-style engines, remove all of the pistons from one bank, then reposition the engine with the other cylinder bank head surface up, and remove that banks piston assemblies.

The only remaining component in the engine block should now be the crankshaft. Loosen the main bearing caps evenly until the fasteners can be turned by hand, then remove them and the caps. Remove the crankshaft from the engine block. Thoroughly clean all of the components.

INSPECTION

Now that the engine block and all of its components are clean, it's time to inspect them for wear and/or damage. To accurately inspect them, you will need some specialized tools:

• Two or three separate micrometers to measure the pistons and crankshaft journals
• A dial indicator
• Telescoping gauges for the cylinder bores
• A rod alignment fixture to check for bent connecting rods

If you do not have access to the proper tools, you may want to bring the components to a shop that does.

Generally, you shouldn't expect cracks in the engine block or its components unless it was known to leak, consume or mix engine fluids, it was severely overheated, or there was evidence of bad bearings and/or crankshaft damage. A visual inspection should be performed on all of the components, but just because you don't see a crack does not mean it is not there. Some more reliable methods for inspecting for cracks include Magnaflux®, a magnetic process or Zyglo®, a dye penetrant. Magnaflux® is used only on ferrous metal (cast iron). Zyglo® uses a spray on fluorescent mixture along with a black light to reveal the cracks. It is strongly recommended to have your engine block checked professionally for cracks, especially if the engine was known to have overheated and/or leaked or consumed coolant. Contact a local shop for availability and pricing of these services.

Engine Block

ENGINE BLOCK BEARING ALIGNMENT

Remove the main bearing caps and, if still installed, the main bearing inserts. Inspect all of the main bearing saddles and caps for damage, burrs or high spots. If damage is found, and it is caused from a spun main bearing, the block will need to be align-bored or, if severe enough, replacement. Any burrs or high spots should be carefully removed with a metal file.

Place a straightedge on the bearing saddles, in the engine block, along the centerline of the crankshaft. If any clearance exists between the straightedge and the saddles, the block must be align-bored.

Align-boring consists of machining the main bearing saddles and caps by means of a flycutter that runs through the bearing saddles.

DECK FLATNESS

The top of the engine block where the cylinder head mounts is called the deck. Insure that the deck surface is clean of dirt, carbon deposits and old gasket material. Place a straightedge across the surface of the deck along its centerline and, using feeler gauges, check the clearance along several points. Repeat the checking procedure with the straightedge placed along both diagonals of the deck surface. If the reading exceeds 0.003 in. (0.076mm) within a 6.0 in. (15.2cm) span, or 0.006 in. (0.152mm) over the total length of the deck, it must be machined.

CYLINDER BORES

▶ **See Figure 206**

The cylinder bores house the pistons and are slightly larger than the pistons themselves. A common piston-to-bore clearance is 0.0015–0.0025 in. (0.0381mm–0.0635mm). Inspect and measure the cylinder bores. The bore should be checked for out-of-roundness, taper and size. The results of this inspection will determine whether the cylinder can be used in its existing size and condition, or a rebore to the next oversize is required (or in the case of removable sleeves, have replacements installed).

The amount of cylinder wall wear is always greater at the top of the cylinder than at the bottom. This wear is known as taper. Any cylinder that has a taper of 0.0012 in. (0.305mm) or more, must be rebored. Measurements are taken at a number of positions in each cylinder: at the top, middle and bottom and at two points at each position; that is, at a point 90 degrees from the crankshaft centerline, as well as a point parallel to the crankshaft centerline. The measurements are made with either a special dial indicator or a telescopic gauge and micrometer. If the necessary precision tools to check the bore are not available, take the block to a machine shop and have them mike it. Also if you don't have the tools to check the cylinder bores, chances are you will not have the necessary devices to check the pistons, connecting rods and crankshaft. Take these components with you and save yourself an extra trip.

For our procedures, we will use a telescopic gauge and a micrometer. You will need one of each, with a measuring range which covers your cylinder bore size.

1. Position the telescopic gauge in the cylinder bore, loosen the gauges lock and allow it to expand.

➡ **Your first two readings will be at the top of the cylinder bore, then proceed to the middle and finally the bottom, making a total of six measurements.**

2. Hold the gauge square in the bore, 90 degrees from the crankshaft centerline, and gently tighten the lock. Tilt the gauge back to remove it from the bore.

3. Measure the gauge with the micrometer and record the reading.

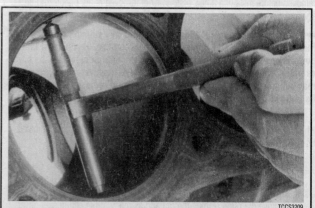

TCCS3209

Fig. 206 Use a telescoping gauge to measure the cylinder bore diameter—take several readings within the same bore

4. Again, hold the gauge square in the bore, this time parallel to the crankshaft centerline, and gently tighten the lock. Again, you will tilt the gauge back to remove it from the bore.

5. Measure the gauge with the micrometer and record this reading. The difference between these two readings is the out-of-round measurement of the cylinder.

6. Repeat steps 1 through 5, each time going to the next lower position, until you reach the bottom of the cylinder. Then go to the next cylinder, and continue until all of the cylinders have been measured.

The difference between these measurements will tell you all about the wear in your cylinders. The measurements which were taken 90 degrees from the crankshaft centerline will always reflect the most wear. That is because at this position is where the engine power presses the piston against the cylinder bore the hardest. This is known as thrust wear. Take your top, 90 degree measurement and compare it to your bottom, 90 degree measurement. The difference between them is the taper. When you measure your pistons, you will compare these readings to your piston sizes and determine piston-to-wall clearance.

Crankshaft

Inspect the crankshaft for visible signs of wear or damage. All of the journals should be perfectly round and smooth. Slight scores are normal for a used crankshaft, but you should hardly feel them with your fingernail. When measuring the crankshaft with a micrometer, you will take readings at the front and rear of each journal, then turn the micrometer 90 degrees and take two more readings, front and rear. The difference between the front-to-rear readings is the journal taper and the first-to-90 degree reading is the out-of-round measurement. Generally, there should be no taper or out-of-roundness found, however, up to 0.0005 in. (0.0127mm) for either can be overlooked. Also, the readings should fall within the factory specifications for journal diameters.

If the crankshaft journals fall within specifications, it is recommended that it be polished before being returned to service. Polishing the crankshaft insures that any minor burrs or high spots are smoothed, thereby reducing the chance of scoring the new bearings.

Pistons and Connecting Rods

PISTONS

◆ See Figure 207

The piston should be visually inspected for any signs of cracking or burning (caused by hot spots or detonation), and scuffing or excessive wear on the skirts. The wrist pin attaches the piston to the connecting rod. The piston should move freely on the wrist pin, both sliding and pivoting. Grasp the connecting rod securely, or mount it in a vise, and try to rock the piston back and forth along the centerline of the wrist pin. There should not be any excessive play evident between the piston and the pin. If there are C-clips retaining the pin in the piston then you have wrist pin bushings in the rods. There should not be any excessive play between the wrist pin and the rod bushing. Normal clearance for the wrist pin is approx. 0.001–0.002 in. (0.025mm–0.051mm).

Fig. 207 Measure the piston's outer diameter, perpendicular to the wrist pin, with a micrometer

TCCS3210

Use a micrometer and measure the diameter of the piston, perpendicular to the wrist pin, on the skirt. Compare the reading to its original cylinder measurement obtained earlier. The difference between the two readings is the piston-to-wall clearance. If the clearance is within specifications, the piston may be used as is. If the piston is out of specification, but the bore is not, you will need a new piston. If the bore is out of specification, you will need the cylinder rebored and oversize pistons installed. Generally if two or more pistons/bores are out of specification, it is best to rebore the entire block and purchase a complete set of oversize pistons.

CONNECTING ROD

You should have the connecting rod checked for straightness at a machine shop. If the connecting rod is bent, it will unevenly wear the bearing and piston, as well as place greater stress on these components. Any bent or twisted connecting rods must be replaced. If the rods are straight and the wrist pin clearance is within specifications, then only the bearing end of the rod need be checked. Place the connecting rod into a vice, with the bearing inserts in place, install the cap to the rod and torque the fasteners to specifications. Use a telescoping gauge and carefully measure the inside diameter of the bearings. Compare this reading to the rods original crankshaft journal diameter measurement. The difference is the oil clearance. If the oil clearance is not within specifications, install new bearings in the rod and take another measurement. If the clearance is still out of specifications, and the crankshaft is not, the rod will need to be reconditioned by a machine shop.

➡ **You can also use Plastigage® to check the bearing clearances. The assembling section has complete instructions on its use.**

Camshaft

Inspect the camshaft and lifters/followers as described earlier in this section.

Bearings

All of the engine bearings should be visually inspected for wear and/or damage. The bearing should look evenly worn all around with no deep scores or pits. If the bearing is severely worn, scored, pitted or heat blued, then the bearing, and the components that use it, should be brought to a machine shop for inspection. Full-circle bearings (used on most camshafts, auxiliary shafts, balance shafts, etc.) require specialized tools for removal and installation, and should be brought to a machine shop for service.

Oil Pump

➡ **The oil pump is responsible for providing constant lubrication to the whole engine and so it is recommended that a new oil pump be installed when rebuilding the engine.**

Completely disassemble the oil pump and thoroughly clean all of the components. Inspect the oil pump gears and housing for wear and/or damage. Insure that the pressure relief valve operates properly and there is no binding or sticking due to varnish or debris. If all of the parts are in proper working condition, lubricate the gears and relief valve, and assemble the pump.

REFINISHING

◆ See Figure 208

Almost all engine block refinishing must be performed by a machine shop. If the cylinders are not to be rebored, then the cylinder glaze can be removed with a ball hone. When removing cylinder glaze with a ball hone, use a light or penetrating type oil to lubricate the hone. Do not allow the hone to run dry as this may cause excessive scoring of the cylinder bores and wear on the hone. If new pistons are required, they will need to be installed to the connecting rods. This should be performed by a machine shop as the pistons must be installed in the correct relationship to the rod or engine damage can occur.

Pistons and Connecting Rods

◆ See Figure 209

Only pistons with the wrist pin retained by C-clips are serviceable by the home-mechanic. Press fit pistons require special presses and/or heaters to remove/install the connecting rod and should only be performed by a machine shop.

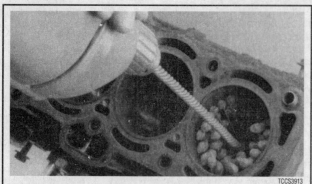

Fig. 208 Use a ball type cylinder hone to remove any glaze and provide a new surface for seating the piston rings

Fig. 209 Most pistons are marked to indicate positioning in the engine (usually a mark means the side facing the front)

All pistons will have a mark indicating the direction to the front of the engine and the must be installed into the engine in that manner. Usually it is a notch or arrow on the top of the piston, or it may be the letter F cast or stamped into the piston.

C-CLIP TYPE PISTONS

1. Note the location of the forward mark on the piston and mark the connecting rod in relation.
2. Remove the C-clips from the piston and withdraw the wrist pin.

➥**Varnish build-up or C-clip groove burrs may increase the difficulty of removing the wrist pin. If necessary, use a punch or drift to carefully tap the wrist pin out.**

3. Insure that the wrist pin bushing in the connecting rod is usable, and lubricate it with assembly lube.
4. Remove the wrist pin from the new piston and lubricate the pin bores on the piston.
5. Align the forward marks on the piston and the connecting rod and install the wrist pin.
6. The new C-clips will have a flat and a rounded side to them. Install both C-clips with the flat side facing out.
7. Repeat all of the steps for each piston being replaced.

ASSEMBLY

Before you begin assembling the engine, first give yourself a clean, dirt free work area. Next, clean every engine component again. The key to a good assembly is cleanliness.

Mount the engine block into the engine stand and wash it one last time using water and detergent (dishwashing detergent works well). While washing it, scrub the cylinder bores with a soft bristle brush and thoroughly clean all of the oil passages. Completely dry the engine and spray the entire assembly down with an anti-rust solution such as WD-40® or similar product. Take a clean lint-free rag and wipe up any excess anti-rust solution from the bores, bearing saddles, etc. Repeat the final cleaning process on the crankshaft. Replace any freeze or oil galley plugs which were removed during disassembly.

Crankshaft

▶ **See Figures 210, 211, 212 and 213**

1. Remove the main bearing inserts from the block and bearing caps.
2. If the crankshaft main bearing journals have been refinished to a definite undersize, install the correct undersize bearing. Be sure that the bearing inserts and bearing bores are clean. Foreign material under inserts will distort bearing and cause failure.
3. Place the upper main bearing inserts in bores with tang in slot.

➥**The oil holes in the bearing inserts must be aligned with the oil holes in the cylinder block.**

4. Install the lower main bearing inserts in bearing caps.
5. Clean the mating surfaces of block and rear main bearing cap.
6. Carefully lower the crankshaft into place. Be careful not to damage bearing surfaces.
7. Check the clearance of each main bearing by using the following procedure:

  a. Place a piece of Plastigage® or its equivalent, on bearing surface across full width of bearing cap and about ¼ in. off center.

  b. Install cap and tighten bolts to specifications. Do not turn crankshaft while Plastigage® is in place.

  c. Remove the cap. Using the supplied Plastigage® scale, check width of Plastigage® at widest point to get maximum clearance. Difference between readings is taper of journal.

  d. If clearance exceeds specified limits, try a 0.001 in. or 0.002 in. undersize bearing in combination with the standard bearing. Bearing clearance must be within specified limits. If standard and 0.002 in. undersize bearing does not bring clearance within desired limits, refinish crankshaft journal, then install undersize bearings.

8. Install the rear main seal.

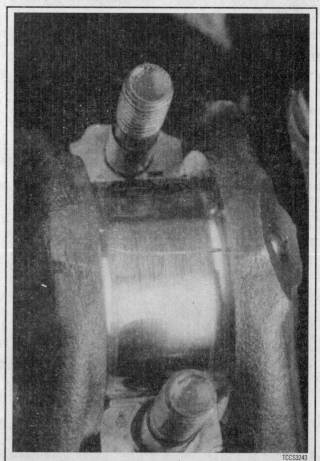

Fig. 210 Apply a strip of gauging material to the bearing journal, then install and torque the

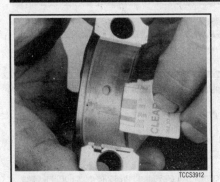

Fig. 211 After the cap is removed again, use the scale supplied with the gauging material to check the clearance

Fig. 212 A dial gauge may be used to check crankshaft end-play

Fig. 213 Carefully pry the crankshaft back and forth while reading the dial gauge for end-play

9. After the bearings have been fitted, apply a light coat of engine oil to the journals and bearings. Install the rear main bearing cap. Install all bearing caps except the thrust bearing cap. Be sure that main bearing caps are installed in original locations. Tighten the bearing cap bolts to specifications.

10. Install the thrust bearing cap with bolts finger-tight.

11. Pry the crankshaft forward against the thrust surface of upper half of bearing.

12. Hold the crankshaft forward and pry the thrust bearing cap to the rear. This aligns the thrust surfaces of both halves of the bearing.

13. Retain the forward pressure on the crankshaft. Tighten the cap bolts to specifications.

14. Measure the crankshaft end-play as follows:

   a. Mount a dial gauge to the engine block and position the tip of the gauge to read from the crankshaft end.

   b. Carefully pry the crankshaft toward the rear of the engine and hold it there while you zero the gauge.

   c. Carefully pry the crankshaft toward the front of the engine and read the gauge.

   d. Confirm that the reading is within specifications. If not, install a new thrust bearing and repeat the procedure. If the reading is still out of specifications with a new bearing, have a machine shop inspect the thrust surfaces of the crankshaft, and if possible, repair it.

15. Rotate the crankshaft so as to position the first rod journal to the bottom of its stroke.

Pistons and Connecting Rods

▶ See Figures 214, 215, 216 and 217

1. Before installing the piston/connecting rod assembly, oil the pistons, piston rings and the cylinder walls with light engine oil. Install connecting rod bolt protectors or rubber hose onto the connecting rod bolts/studs. Also perform the following:

   a. Select the proper ring set for the size cylinder bore.

   b. Position the ring in the bore in which it is going to be used.

   c. Push the ring down into the bore area where normal ring wear is not encountered.

   d. Use the head of the piston to position the ring in the bore so that the ring is square with the cylinder wall. Use caution to avoid damage to the ring or cylinder bore.

   e. Measure the gap between the ends of the ring with a feeler gauge. Ring gap in a worn cylinder is normally greater than specification. If the ring gap is greater than the specified limits, try an oversize ring set.

Fig. 214 Checking the piston ring-to-ring groove side clearance using the ring and a feeler gauge

Fig. 215 The notch on the side of the bearing cap matches the tang on the bearing insert

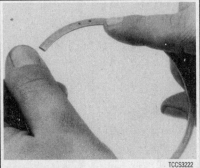

Fig. 216 Most rings are marked to show which side of the ring should face up when installed to the piston

Fig. 217 Install the piston and rod assembly into the block using a ring compressor and the handle of a hammer

f. Check the ring side clearance of the compression rings with a feeler gauge inserted between the ring and its lower land according to specification. The gauge should slide freely around the entire ring circumference without binding. Any wear that occurs will form a step at the inner portion of the lower land. If the lower lands have high steps, the piston should be replaced.

2. Unless new pistons are installed, be sure to install the pistons in the cylinders from which they were removed. The numbers on the connecting rod and bearing cap must be on the same side when installed in the cylinder bore. If a connecting rod is ever transposed from one engine or cylinder to another, new bearings should be fitted and the connecting rod should be numbered to correspond with the new cylinder number. The notch on the piston head goes toward the front of the engine.

3. Install all of the rod bearing inserts into the rods and caps.

4. Install the rings to the pistons. Install the oil control ring first, then the second compression ring and finally the top compression ring. Use a piston ring expander tool to aid in installation and to help reduce the chance of breakage.

5. Make sure the ring gaps are properly spaced around the circumference of the piston. Fit a piston ring compressor around the piston and slide the piston and connecting rod assembly down into the cylinder bore, pushing it in with the wooden hammer handle. Push the piston down until it is only slightly below the top of the cylinder bore. Guide the connecting rod onto the crankshaft bearing journal carefully, to avoid damaging the crankshaft.

6. Check the bearing clearance of all the rod bearings, fitting them to the crankshaft bearing journals. Follow the procedure in the crankshaft installation above.

7. After the bearings have been fitted, apply a light coating of assembly oil to the journals and bearings.

8. Turn the crankshaft until the appropriate bearing journal is at the bottom of its stroke, then push the piston assembly all the way down until the connecting rod bearing seats on the crankshaft journal. Be careful not to allow the bearing cap screws to strike the crankshaft bearing journals and damage them.

9. After the piston and connecting rod assemblies have been installed, check the connecting rod side clearance on each crankshaft journal.

10. Prime and install the oil pump and the oil pump intake tube.

Cylinder Head(s)

1. Install the cylinder head(s) using new gaskets.
2. Install the timing sprockets/gears and the belt/chain assemblies.

Engine Covers and Components

Install the timing cover(s) and oil pan. Refer to your notes and drawings made prior to disassembly and install all of the components that were removed. Install the engine into the vehicle.

Engine Start-up and Break-in

STARTING THE ENGINE

Now that the engine is installed and every wire and hose is properly connected, go back and double check that all coolant and vacuum hoses are connected. Check that your oil drain plug is installed and properly tightened. If not already done, install a new oil filter onto the engine. Fill the crankcase with the proper amount and grade of engine oil. Fill the cooling system with a 50/50 mixture of coolant/water.

1. Connect the vehicle battery.
2. Start the engine. Keep your eye on your oil pressure indicator; if it does not indicate oil pressure within 10 seconds of starting, turn the vehicle OFF.

❊❊ WARNING

Damage to the engine can result if it is allowed to run with no oil pressure. Check the engine oil level to make sure that it is full. Check for any leaks and if found, repair the leaks before continuing. If there is still no indication of oil pressure, you may need to prime the system.

3. Confirm that there are no fluid leaks (oil or other).
4. Allow the engine to reach normal operating temperature (the upper radiator hose will be hot to the touch).
5. At this point any necessary checks or adjustments can be performed, such as ignition timing.
6. Install any remaining components or body panels which were removed.

BREAKING IT IN

Make the first miles on the new engine, easy ones. Vary the speed but do not accelerate hard. Most importantly, do not lug the engine, and avoid sustained high speeds until at least 100 miles. Check the engine oil and coolant levels frequently. Expect the engine to use a little oil until the rings seat. Change the oil and filter at 500 miles, 1500 miles, then every 3000 miles past that.

KEEP IT MAINTAINED

Now that you have just gone through all of that hard work, keep yourself from doing it all over again by thoroughly maintaining it. Not that you may not have maintained it before, heck you could have had one to two hundred thousand miles on it before doing this. However, you may have bought the vehicle used, and the previous owner did not keep up on maintenance. Which is why you just went through all of that hard work. See?

GENERAL ENGINE SPECIFICATIONS

Year	Engine ID/VIN	Engine Displacement liter	Fuel System Type	Net Horsepower @ rpm	Net Torque @ rpm (ft. lbs.)	Bore × Stroke (in.)	Compression Ratio	Oil Pressure @ rpm
1982-83	Z22E	2.2L	EFI	102 @ 5200	129 @ 2800	3.43 × 3.62	8.5:1	50-60
	CA20	2.0L	2 bbl.	88 @ 5200	112 @ 2800	3.33 × 3.46	8.5:1	50-60
1984	CA20E	2.0L	EFI	102 @ 5200	116 @ 3200	3.33 × 3.46	8.5:1	57 @ 4000
	CA18ET	1.8L	EFI	120 @ 5200	134 @ 3200	3.27 × 3.29	8.0:1	71 @ 4000
1985-86	CA20E	2.0L	EFI	102 @ 5200	116 @ 3200	3.33 × 3.46	8.5:1	57 @ 4000
	CA18ET	1.8L	EFI	120 @ 5200	134 @ 3200	3.27 × 3.29	8.0:1	71 @ 4000
1987	CA20E	2.0L	EFI	102 @ 5200	116 @ 3200	3.33 × 3.46	8.5:1	43 @ 2000
	CA18ET	1.8L	EFI	120 @ 5200	134 @ 3200	3.27 × 3.29	8.0:1	43 @ 2000
	VG30E	3.0L	EFI	160 @ 5200	174 @ 4000	3.43 × 3.27	9.0:1	43 @ 2000
1988	CA20E	2.0L	EFI	99 @ 5200	116 @ 2800	3.33 × 3.46	8.5:1	60.5 @ 3200
	VG30E	3.0L	EFI	165 @ 5200	168 @ 3600	3.43 × 3.27	9.0:1	59 @ 3200
	CA18ET	1.8L	EFI	120 @ 5200	134 @ 3200	3.27 × 3.29	8.0:1	43 @ 2000
	KA24E	2.4L	EFI	135 @ 5600	142 @ 4400	3.50 × 3.78	9.0:1	65 @ 3000
1989	CA20E	2.0L	EFI	94 @ 5400	114 @ 2800	3.33 × 3.47	8.5:1	61 @ 3200
	KA24E	2.4L	EFI	140 @ 5600	152 @ 4400	3.50 × 3.78	8.6:1	60-70 @ 3000
1990	KA24E	2.4L	EFI	155 @ 5600	160 @ 4400	3.50 × 3.78	9.5:1	60-70 @ 3000
1991	KA24DE	2.4L	EFI	138 @ 5600	148 @ 4400	3.50 × 3.78	8.6:1	60-70 @ 3000
	KA24E	2.4L	EFI	155 @ 5600	160 @ 4400	3.50 × 3.78	9.5:1	60-70 @ 3000
1992	KA24DE	2.4L	EFI	138 @ 5600	148 @ 4800	3.50 × 3.78	8.6:1	60-70 @ 3000

NOTE: Horsepower and torque are SAE net figures. They are measured at the rear of the transmission with all accessories installed and operating. Since the figures vary when a given engine is installed in different models, some are representative rather than exact.

① Outer Spring-Inner Spring 57 lbs. @ 0.98 inches
② Outer Spring-Inner Spring 24 @ 1.38 inches

VALVE SPECIFICATIONS

Year	Engine ID/VIN	Engine Displacement liter	Seat Angle (deg.)	Face Angle (deg.)	Spring Test Pressure (lbs. @ in.)	Spring Installed Height (in.)	Stem-to-Guide Clearance (in.) Intake	Exhaust	Stem Diameter (in.) Intake	Exhaust
1985	CA20E	2.0L	45	45	118.2 @ 1.00	1.967①	0.0008-0.0021	0.0016-0.0029	0.2742-0.2748	0.2734-0.2740
	CA18ET	1.8L	45	45	118.2 @ 1.00	1.967①	0.0008-0.0021	0.0016-0.0029	0.2742-0.2748	0.2734-0.2740
1986	CA20E	2.0L	45	45	118.2 @ 1.00	1.967①	0.0008-0.0021	0.0016-0.0029	0.2742-0.2748	0.2734-0.2740
	CA18ET	1.8L	45	45	118.2 @ 1.00	1.967①	0.0008-0.0021	0.0016-0.0029	0.2742-0.2748	0.2734-0.2740
1987	CA20E	2.0L	45	45	118.2 @ 1.00	1.967①	0.0008-0.0021	0.0016-0.0029	0.2742-0.2748	0.2734-0.2740
	CA18ET	1.8L	45	45	118.2 @ 1.00	1.967①	0.0008-0.0021	0.0016-0.0029	0.2742-0.2748	0.2734-0.2740
	VG30E	3.0L	45	45	117.7 @ 1.18	2.016①	0.0008-0.0021	0.0016-0.0029	0.2742-0.2748	0.3128-0.3134
1988	CA20E	2.0L	45	45	118.2 @ 1.00	1.967①	0.0008-0.0021	0.0016-0.0029	0.2742-0.2748	0.2734-0.2740
	CA18ET	1.8L	45	45	118.2 @ 1.00	1.967①	0.0008-0.0021	0.0016-0.0029	0.2742-0.2748	0.2734-0.2740
	VG30E	3.0L	45	45	117.7 @ 1.18	2.016①	0.0008-0.0021	0.0016-0.0029	0.2742-0.2748	0.3128-0.3134
1989	KA24E	2.4L	45	45	135.8 @ 1.480	2.261②	0.0008-0.0021	0.0016-0.0028	0.2742-0.2748	0.3129-0.3134
	CA20E	2.0L	45	45	129.9 @ 2.32	1.959①	0.0008-0.0021	0.0016-0.0029	0.2742-0.2748	0.2734-0.2740
1990	KA24E	2.4L	45	45	135.8 @ 1.480	2.261②	0.0008-0.0021	0.0016-0.0028	0.2742-0.2748	0.3129-0.3134
1991	KA24DE	2.4L	45	45	123 @ 1.024	1.756②	0.0008-0.0021	0.0016-0.0028	0.2742-0.2748	0.3129-0.3134
	KA24E	2.4L	45	45	135.8 @ 1.480	2.261②	0.0008-0.0021	0.0016-0.0028	0.2742-0.2748	0.3129-0.3134
1992	KA24DE	2.4L	45	45	123 @ 1.024	1.756②	0.0008-0.0021	0.0016-0.0028	0.2742-0.2748	0.3129-0.3134
	KA24E	2.4L	45	45	135.8 @ 1.480	2.261②	0.0008-0.0021	0.0016-0.0028	0.2742-0.2748	0.3129-0.3134

① Figures are for free height (use spring test pressure as a guide on multi-valve engine applications).

VALVE SPECIFICATIONS

Year	Engine ID/VIN	Engine Displacement liter	Seat Angle (deg.)	Face Angle (deg.)	Spring Test Pressure (lbs. @ in.)	Spring Installed Height (in.)	Stem-to-Guide Clearance (in.) Intake	Exhaust	Stem Diameter (in.) Intake	Exhaust
1982	Z22E	2.2L	45	45	115.3 @ 1.18①	1.575	0.0008-0.0021	0.0016-0.0029	0.3136-0.3142	0.3128-0.3134
	CA20	2.0L	44	—	47 @ 1.58①	1.736	0.0008-0.0021	0.0016-0.0029	0.2742-0.2748	0.2734-0.2740
1983	Z22E	2.2L	45	45	115.3 @ 1.18①	1.575	0.0008-0.0021	0.0016-0.0029	0.3136-0.3142	0.3128-0.3134
	CA20	2.0L	44	—	47 @ 1.58①	1.736	0.0008-0.0021-	0.0016-0.0029	0.2742-0.2748	0.2734-0.2740
1984	CA20E	2.0L	45	45	118.2 @ 1.00	1.967①	0.0008-0.0021	0.0016-0.0029	0.2742-0.2748	0.2734-0.2740
	CA18ET	1.8L	45	45	118.2 @ 1.00	1.967①	0.0008-0.0021	0.0016-0.0029	0.2742-0.2748	0.2734-0.2740

CRANKSHAFT AND CONNECTING ROD SPECIFICATIONS

All measurements are given in inches.

Year	Engine ID/VIN	Engine Displacement liter	Main Brg. Journal Dia.	Crankshaft Main Brg. Oil Clearance	Shaft End-play	Thrust on No.	Connecting Rod Journal Diameter	Oil Clearance	Side Clearance
1982	Z22E	2.2L	2.1631–2.1636	0.0008–0.0024	0.002–0.0071	3	1.967–1.9675	0.001–0.0022	0.008–0.012
	CA20	2.0L	2.0847–2.0852	0.0016–0.0024	0.002–0.007	3	1.7701–1.706	0.0008–0.0024	0.008–0.012
1983	Z22E	2.2L	2.1631–2.1636	0.0008–0.0024	0.002–0.0071	3	1.967–1.9675	0.001–0.0022	0.008–0.012
	CA20	2.0L	2.0847–2.0852	0.0016–0.0024	0.002–0.007	3	1.7701–1.706	0.0008–0.0024	0.008–0.012
1984	CA20E	2.0L	2.0847–2.0852	0.0016–0.0024	0.012	3	1.7701–1.706	0.0008–0.0024	0.008–0.012
	CA18ET	1.8L	2.0847–2.0852	0.0016–0.0024	0.0020–0.0071	3	1.7701–1.706	0.0008–0.0024	0.008–0.012
1985	CA20E	2.0L	2.0847–2.0852	0.0016–0.0024	0.012	3	1.7701–1.706	0.0008–0.0024	0.008–0.012
	CA18ET	1.8L	2.0847–2.0852	0.0016–0.0024	0.0020–0.0071	3	1.7701–1.706	0.0008–0.0024	0.008–0.012
1986	CA20E	2.0L	2.0847–2.0852	0.0008–0.0019	0.0020–0.0071	3	1.7701–1.706	0.0008–0.0024	0.008–0.012
	CA18ET	1.8L	2.0847–2.0852	0.0016–0.0024	0.0020–0.0071	3	1.7701–1.706	0.0008–0.0014	0.008–0.012
1987	CA20E	2.0L	2.0847–2.0852	0.0008–0.0019	0.0020–0.0071	3	1.7701–1.706	0.0008–0.0024	0.008–0.012
	CA18ET	1.8L	2.0847–2.0852	0.0016–0.0024	0.0020–0.0071	3	1.7701–1.706	0.0008–0.0014	0.008–0.012
	VG30E	3.0L	2.4790–2.4793	0.0011–0.0022	0.0020–0.0067	4	1.9667–1.9675	0.0006–0.0021	0.0079–0.0138
1988	CA20E	2.0L	2.0847–2.0852	0.0008–0.0019	0.0020–0.0071	3	1.7701–1.706	0.0004–0.0014	0.008–0.012
	CA18ET	1.8L	2.0847–2.0852	0.0016–0.0024	0.0020–0.0071	3	1.7701–1.706	0.0008–0.0024	0.008–0.012
	VG30E	3.0L	2.4790–2.4793	0.0011–0.0022	0.0020–0.0067	4	1.9667–1.9675	0.0006–0.0021	0.0079–0.0138
1989	KA24E	2.4L	2.3609–2.3612	0.0008–0.0019	2.3609–2.3612	3	1.9672–1.9675	0.0004–0.0014	0.008–0.016
	CA20E	2.0L	2.0847–2.0852	0.0008–0.0019	0.0020–0.0071	3	1.7701–1.706	0.0004–0.0014	0.008–0.012
1990	KA24E	2.4L	2.3609–2.3612	0.0008–0.0019	2.3609–2.3612	3	1.9672–1.9675	0.0004–0.0014	0.008–0.016
1991	KA24DE	2.4L	2.3609–2.3612	0.0008–0.0019	2.3609–2.3612	3	2.3609–2.3612	0.0004–0.0014	0.008–0.016
	KA24E	2.4L	2.3609–2.3612	0.0008–0.0019	2.3609–2.3612	3	1.9672–1.9675	0.0004–0.0014	0.008–0.016
1992	KA24DE	2.4L	2.3609–2.3612	0.0008–0.0019	2.3609–2.3612	3	2.3609–2.3612	0.0004–0.0014	0.008–0.016
	KA24E	2.4L	2.3609–2.3612	0.0008–0.0019	0.0020–0.0071	3	1.7701–1.706	0.0004–0.0014	0.008–0.012

82623C05

CAMSHAFT SPECIFICATIONS

All measurements given in inches.

Year	Engine ID/VIN	Engine Displacement liter	Journal Diameter 1	2	3	4	5	Elevation In.	Ex.	Bearing Clearance	Camshaft End Play
1982	Z22E	2.2L	1.2967–1.2974	1.2967–1.2974	1.2967–1.2974	1.2967–1.2974	1.2967–1.2974	NA	NA	0.0018–0.0035	0.008
	CA20	2.0L	1.8085–1.8092	1.8085–1.8092	1.8085–1.8092	1.8085–1.8092	1.8077–1.8085	NA	0.354	0.0040	0.0028–0.0055
1983	Z22E	2.2L	1.2967–1.2974	1.2967–1.2974	1.2967–1.2974	1.2967–1.2974	1.2967–1.2974	NA	NA	0.0018–0.0035	0.008
	CA20	2.0L	1.8085–1.8092	1.8085–1.8092	1.8085–1.8092	1.8085–1.8092	1.8077–1.8085	NA	0.354	0.0040	0.0028–0.0055
1984	CA20E	2.0L	1.8085–1.8092	1.8085–1.8092	1.8085–1.8092	1.8085–1.8092	1.8077–1.8085	0.354	0.354	0.0040	0.0028–0.0055
	CA18ET	1.8L	1.8085–1.8092	1.8085–1.8092	1.8085–1.8092	1.8085–1.8092	1.8077–1.8055	0.335	0.374	0.0040	0.0028–0.0055
1985	CA20E	2.0L	1.8085–1.8092	1.8085–1.8092	1.8085–1.8092	1.8085–1.8092	1.8077–1.8085	0.354	0.354	0.0040	0.0028–0.0055
	CA18ET	1.8L	1.8085–1.8092	1.8085–1.8092	1.8085–1.8092	1.8085–1.8092	1.8077–1.8055	0.335	0.374	0.0040	0.0028–0.0055
1986	CA20E	2.0L	1.8085–1.8092	1.8085–1.8092	1.8085–1.8092	1.8085–1.8092	1.8077–1.8085	0.354	0.374	0.0040	0.0028–0.0055
	CA18ET	1.8L	1.8085–1.8092	1.8085–1.8092	1.8085–1.8092	1.8085–1.8092	1.8077–1.8055	0.335	0.354	0.0040	0.0028–0.0055
1987	CA20E	2.0L	1.8085–1.8092	1.8085–1.8092	1.8085–1.8092	1.8085–1.8092	1.8077–1.8085	0.335	0.374	0.0040	0.0028–0.0055
	CA18ET	1.8L	1.8085–1.8092	1.8085–1.8092	1.8085–1.8092	1.8085–1.8092	1.8077–1.8055	0.354	0.354	0.0040	0.0028–0.0055
	VG30E	3.0L	1.8866–1.8874①	1.8472–1.8480	1.8085–1.8092	1.8472–1.8480	1.6701–1.6709	NA	NA	0.0018–0.0035	0.0012–0.0024
1988	CA20E	2.0L	1.8085–1.8092	1.8085–1.8092	1.8085–1.8092	1.8085–1.8092	1.8077–1.8055	0.335	0.374	0.0040	0.0028–0.0055
	CA18ET	1.8L	1.8085–1.8092	1.8085–1.8092	1.8085–1.8092	1.8085–1.8092	1.8077–1.8085	0.354	0.354	0.0040	0.0028–0.0055
	VG30E	3.0L	1.8866–1.8874①	1.8472–1.8480	1.8085–1.8092	1.8472–1.8480	1.6701–1.6709	NA	NA	0.0018–0.0035	0.0012–0.0024
1989	KA24E	2.4L	1.2967–1.2974	1.2967–1.2974	1.2967–1.2974	1.2967–1.2974	1.2967–1.2974	0.409	0.409	0.0018–0.0035	0.0028–0.0059
	CA20E	2.0L	1.8085–1.8092	1.8085–1.8092	1.8085–1.8092	1.8085–1.8092	1.8077–1.8055	0.335	0.374	0.0040	0.0028–0.0055
1990	KA24E	2.4L	1.2967–1.2974	1.2967–1.2974	1.2967–1.2974	1.2967–1.2974	1.2967–1.2974	0.409	0.409	0.0018–0.0035	0.0028–0.0059
1991	KA24DE	2.4L	1.0998–1.1006	0.9423–0.9431	0.9423–0.9431	0.9423–0.9431	0.9423–0.9431	NA	NA	0.0018–0.0035	0.0028–0.0059
	KA24E	2.4L	1.2967–1.2974	1.2967–1.2974	1.2967–1.2974	1.2967–1.2974	1.2967–1.2974	0.409	0.409	0.0018–0.0035	0.0028–0.0059
1992	KA24DE	2.4L	1.0998–1.1006	0.9423–0.9431	0.9423–0.9431	0.9423–0.9431	0.9423–0.9431	NA	NA	0.0018–0.0035	0.0028–0.0059
	KA24E	2.4L	1.2967–1.2974	1.2967–1.2974	1.2967–1.2974	1.2967–1.2974	1.2967–1.2974	0.409	0.409	0.0018–0.0035	0.0028–0.0059

① Front of engine—left hand camshaft only

82623C04

TORQUE SPECIFICATIONS
All readings in ft. lbs.

Year	Engine ID/VIN	Engine Displacement liter	Cylinder Head Bolts	Main Bearing Bolts	Rod Bearing Bolts	Crankshaft Damper Bolts	Flywheel Bolts	Intake Manifold	Exhaust Manifold
1982	ZZ22E	2.2L	51-58	33-40	33-40	87-116	101-116	12-15	12-15
	CA20	2.0L	51-58	33-40	22-27	90-98	72-80	13-16	13-17
1983	ZZ22E	2.2L	51-58	33-40	33-40	87-116	101-116	12-15	12-15
	CA20	2.0L	58-65	33-40	22-27	90-98	72-80	13-16	13-17
1984	CA20E	2.0L	①	33-40	24-27	90-98	72-80	14-19	14-22
	CA18ET	1.8L	①	33-40	24-27	90-98	72-80	14-19	14-22
1985	CA20E	2.0L	①	33-40	24-27	90-98	72-80	14-19	14-22
	CA18ET	1.8L	①	33-40	24-27	90-98	72-80	14-19	14-22
1986	CA20E	2.0L	②	33-40	24-27	90-98	72-80	14-19	14-22
	CA18ET	1.8L	②	33-40	24-27	90-98	72-80	14-19	14-22
1987	CA20E	2.0L	②	33-40	24-27	90-98	72-80	14-19	14-22
	CA18ET	1.8L	②	67-74	33-40	90-98	72-80	12-14	13-16
	VG30E	3.0L	⑥	33-40	24-27	90-98	72-80	14-19	14-22
1988	CA20E	2.0L	②	33-40	24-27	90-98	72-80	14-19	14-22
	CA18ET	1.8L	②	67-74	33-40	90-98	72-80	12-14	13-16
	VG30E	3.0L	⑥	34-38	⑦	90-98	72-80	14-19	14-22
1989	KA24E	2.4L	⑧	34-38	⑦	87-116	105-112	12-15	12-15
	CA20E	2.0L	②	33-40	24-27	90-98	72-80	14-19	14-22
1990	KA24E	2.4L	⑧	34-38	⑦	87-116	105-112	12-15	12-15
1991	KA24DE	2.4L	⑧	34-38	⑦	87-116	105-112	12-14	27-35
	KA24E	2.4L	⑧	34-38	⑦	87-116	105-112	12-15	12-15
1992	KA24DE	2.4L	⑧	34-38	⑦	87-116	105-112	12-14	27-35
	KA24E	2.4L	⑧	34-38	⑦	87-116	105-112	12-15	12-15

① A. Torque to 22 ft. lbs. (in sequence)
B. Torque to 58 ft. lbs. (in sequence)
C. Loosen all bolts
D. Torque to 22 ft. lbs. (in sequence)
E. Torque to 54-61 ft. lbs. (in sequence)

② Tighten in two steps: 1st—22 ft. lbs.; 2nd—58 ft. lbs. Then loosen all bolts completely. Final torque is in two steps: 1st—22 ft. lbs.; 2nd—54-61 ft. lbs. If angle torquing, turn all bolts 90-95 degrees clockwise. (All steps in sequence)

③ Torque all bolts in the proper sequence to 22 ft. lbs.

④ Torque all bolts in the proper sequence to 43 ft. lbs. Loosen all bolts completely. Torque all bolts in the proper sequence to 22 ft. lbs.

⑤ Torque all bolts in the proper sequence to 40-47 ft. lbs.

⑥ Tighten in two steps: 1st—22 ft. lbs.; 2nd—58 ft. lbs. Then loosen all bolts completely. Final torque is in 2 steps: 1st—22 ft. lbs.; 2nd—54-61 ft. lbs. (If angle torquing, tighten bolt a to 83-88 degrees and all other bolts to 75-80 degrees clockwise.) NOTE: No. 8 bolt is the longest bolt.

⑦ 1988 model
Tighten in 2 steps:
1st—10-12 ft. lbs.
2nd—28-33 ft. lbs.

⑧ Tighten all bolts in numerical order to 22 ft. lbs. Then tighten all bolts to 58 ft. lbs. Loosen all bolts completely. Tighten all bolts to 22 ft. lbs. Then tighten to 54-61 ft. lbs. Always tighten and loosen bolts in numerical order—see text.

⑨ 2 steps:
Tighten to 10-12 ft. lbs. Then tighten to 28-33 ft. lbs.

⑩ See text for procedure.

82623C07

PISTON AND RING SPECIFICATIONS
All measurements are given in inches.

Year	Engine ID/VIN	Engine Displacement liter	Piston Clearance	Ring Gap Top Compression	Ring Gap Bottom Compression	Ring Gap Oil Control	Ring Side Clearance Top Compression	Ring Side Clearance Bottom Compression	Ring Side Clearance Oil Control
1982	ZZ22E	2.2L	0.001-0.0018	0.0098-0.0157	0.0059-0.0118	0.0118-0.0354	0.0016-0.0029	0.0012-0.0025	—
	CA20	2.0L	0.001-0.0018	0.0096-0.0157	0.0059-0.0118	0.0118-0.0354	0.0016-0.0029	0.0012-0.0025	0.0020-0.0057
1983	ZZ22E	2.2L	0.001-0.0018	0.0098-0.0157	0.0059-0.0118	0.0118-0.0354	0.0016-0.0029	0.0012-0.0025	—
	CA20	2.0L	0.0010-0.0018	0.0098-0.0157	0.0059-0.0118	0.0118-0.0354	0.0016-0.0029	0.0012-0.0025	0.0020-0.0057
1984	CA20E	2.0L	0.0010-0.0018	0.0098-0.0138	0.0059-0.0098	0.0079-0.0236	0.0016-0.0029	0.0012-0.0025	—
	CA18ET	1.8L	0.0010-0.0018	③	0.0059-0.0098	0.0079-0.0236	0.0016-0.0029	0.0012-0.0025	—
1985	CA20E	2.0L	0.0010-0.0018	0.0098-0.0201	0.0059-0.0122	0.0079-0.0299	0.0016-0.0029	0.0012-0.0025	—
	CA18ET	1.8L	0.0010-0.0018	③	0.0059-0.0122	0.0079-0.0299	0.0016-0.0029	0.0012-0.0025	—
1986	CA20E	2.0L	0.0010-0.0018	0.0098-0.0201	0.0059-0.0122	0.0079-0.0299	0.0016-0.0029	0.0012-0.0025	—
	CA18ET	1.8L	0.0010-0.0018	③	0.0059-0.0122	0.0079-0.0299	0.0016-0.0029	0.0012-0.0025	—
1987	CA20E	2.0L	0.0010-0.0018	0.0098-0.0201	0.0059-0.0122	0.0079-0.0299	0.0016-0.0029	0.0012-0.0025	—
	CA18ET	1.8L	0.0010-0.0018	0.0083-0.0173	0.0071-0.0173	0.0079-0.0299	0.0016-0.0029	0.0012-0.0025	—
	VG30E	3.0L	0.0010-0.0018	0.0098-0.0201	0.0059-0.0122	0.0079-0.0299	0.0016-0.0029	0.0012-0.0025	0.0006-0.0075
1988	CA20E	2.0L	0.0010-0.0018	0.0098-0.0201	0.0059-0.0122	0.0079-0.0299	0.0016-0.0029	0.0012-0.0025	—
	CA18ET	1.8L	0.0010-0.0018	0.0083-0.0173	0.0071-0.0173	0.0079-0.0299	0.0016-0.0029	0.0012-0.0025	—
	VG30E	3.0L	0.0010-0.0018	0.0098-0.0201	0.0059-0.0122	0.0079-0.0299	0.0016-0.0029	0.0012-0.0025	0.0006-0.0075
1989	KA24E	2.4L	0.0008-0.0016	0.0110-0.0169	0.0079-0.0236	0.0079-0.0236	0.0016-0.0029	0.0012-0.0028	0.0006-0.0075
	CA20E	2.0L	0.0010-0.0018	0.0098-0.0201	0.0059-0.0129	0.0079-0.0299	0.0016-0.0029	0.0012-0.0028	0.0026-0.0053
1990	KA24E	2.4L	0.0008-0.0016	0.0110-0.0205	0.0177-0.0272	0.0079-0.0236	0.0016-0.0031	0.0012-0.0028	0.0026-0.0053
1991	KA24DE	2.4L	0.0008-0.0016	0.0177-0.0272	0.0177-0.0272	0.0079-0.0272	0.0016-0.0031	0.0012-0.0028	0.0026-0.0053
	KA24E	2.4L	0.0008-0.0016	0.0110-0.0205	0.0177-0.0272	0.0079-0.0272	0.0016-0.0031	0.0012-0.0028	0.0026-0.0053
1992	KA24DE	2.4L	0.0008-0.0016	0.0110-0.0205	0.0177-0.0272	0.0079-0.0272	0.0016-0.0031	0.0012-0.0028	0.0026-0.0053
	KA24E	2.0L	0.0008-0.0016	0.0110-0.0205	0.0177-0.0272	0.0079-0.0272	0.0016-0.0031	0.0012-0.0028	0.0026-0.0053

① Piston grades #1 and #2: 0.0098-0.0126 in. Piston grades #3, 4 and 5: 0.0075-0.0102 in.

② Piston grades #1 and #2: 0.0098-0.0150 Piston grades #3, 4 and 5: 0.0110-0.0165

③ For rings punched with R or T—0.0177-0.0236 For rings punched with N—0.0217-0.0276

82623C06

ENGINE MECHANICAL SPECIFICATIONS
Z22E SERIES ENGINE

Component	English	Metric
Cylinder head surface flatness		
Standard	0.0020 in.	0.05mm
Limit	0.004 in.	0.1mm
Valve head diameter		
Intake	1.654 in.	42mm
Exhaust	1.496 in.	38mm
Valve length		
Intake	4.90-4.91 in.	124.38-124.68mm
Exhaust	4.62-4.63 in.	117.35-117.65mm
Valve stem diameter		
Intake	0.3136-0.3142 in.	7.965-7.980mm
Exhaust	0.3128-0.3134 in.	7.945-7.960mm
Valve face angle	45°	
Valve margin limit	0.020 in.	0.50mm
Valve stem and surface griding limit	0.020 in.	0.50mm
Valve free length	1.9594 in.	49.77mm
Valve stem to guide clearance		
Intake	0.0008-0.0021 in.	0.020-0.053mm
Exhaust	0.0016-0.0029 in.	0.040-0.073mm
Limit	0.004 in.	0.1mm
Rocker arm shaft clearance	0.0003-0.0019 in.	0.007-0.049mm
Camshaft oil clearance		
Standard	0.0018-0.0035 in.	0.045-0.090mm
Limit	0.004 in.	0.1mm
Camshaft endplay	0.008 in.	0.2mm
Cylinder block flatness	0.004 in.	0.1mm
Cylinder out of round	0.0006 in.	0.015mm
Cylinder taper	0.0006 in.	0.015mm
Crankshaft-out of round	0.0012 in.	0.03mm
Crankshaft-taper	0.0012 in.	0.03mm
Crankshaft endplay	0.012 in.	0.3mm
Camshaft runout	0.0039 in.	0.10mm
Flywheel runout	0.0059 in.	0.15mm

82623C08

CA18ET AND CA20E SERIES ENGINES

Component	English	Metric
Cylinder head surface flatness		
Standard	0.0012 in.	0.03mm
Limit	0.004 in.	0.1mm
Valve head diameter		
Intake	1.654 in.	42mm
Exhaust	1.496 in.	38mm
Valve length		
Intake	4.90-4.91 in.	124.38-124.68mm
Exhaust	4.62-4.63 in.	117.35-117.65mm
Valve stem diameter		
Intake	0.2742-0.2748 in.	6.965-6.980mm
Exhaust	0.2734-0.2740 in.	6.945-6.960mm
Valve face angle	45°	
Valve margin limit	0.020 in.	0.50mm
Valve stem and surface griding limit	0.008 in.	0.2mm

82623C09

CA18ET AND CA20E SERIES ENGINES

Component	English	Metric
Outer valve free length		
CA18ET	1.9677 in.	49.98mm
CA20E	1.9594 in.	49.77mm
Inner valve free length		
CA18ET	1.7364 in.	44.1mm
CA20E	1.7364 in.	44.1mm
Valve stem to guide clearance		
Intake	0.0008-0.0021 in.	0.020-0.053mm
Exhaust	0.0016-0.0029 in.	0.040-0.073mm
Limit	0.004 in.	0.1mm
Rocker arm shaft clearance	0.0003-0.0019 in.	0.007-0.049mm
Camshaft oil clearance		
Limit	0.004 in.	0.1mm
Camshaft endplay	0.008 in.	0.2mm
Cylinder block flatness	0.004 in.	0.1mm
Cylinder out of round	0.0008 in.	0.02mm
Cylinder taper	0.0008 in.	0.02mm
Crankshaft-out of round	0.0012 in.	0.03mm
Crankshaft-taper	0.0012 in.	0.03mm
Crankshaft endplay	0.012 in.	0.3mm
Camshaft runout	0.0020 in.	0.05mm
Flywheel runout	0.0059 in.	0.15mm

82623C10

VG30E SERIES ENGINES

Component	English	Metric
Cylinder head surface flatness		
Standard	0.0020 in.	0.05mm
Limit	0.004 in.	0.1mm
Valve head diameter		
Intake	1.654-1.661 in.	42-42.2mm
Exhaust	1.378-1.386 in.	35-35.2mm
Valve length		
Intake	4.933-4.957 in.	125.3-125.9mm
Exhaust	4.890-4.913 in.	124.2-124.8mm
Valve stem diameter		
Intake	0.2742-0.2748 in.	6.965-6.980mm
Exhaust	0.3128-0.3134 in.	7.945-7.960mm
Valve seat angle	45°	
Valve margin limit	0.020 in.	0.50mm
Valve stem and surface griding limit	0.008 in.	0.2mm
Outer valve free length	2.016 in.	51.2mm
Inner valve free length	1.736 in.	44.1mm
Valve stem to guide clearance		
Intake	0.0008-0.0021 in.	0.020-0.053mm
Exhaust	0.0016-0.0029 in.	0.040-0.073mm
Limit	0.004 in.	0.1mm
Rocker arm shaft clearance	0.0003-0.0019 in.	0.007-0.049mm
Camshaft oil clearance		
Limit	0.0059 in.	0.15mm
Camshaft endplay	0.0012-0.0024 in.	0.03-0.06mm
Cylinder block flatness	0.004 in.	0.1mm

82623C11

VG30E SERIES ENGINES

Component	English	Metric
Cylinder out of round	0.0006 in.	0.015mm
Cylinder taper	0.0006 in.	0.015mm
Crankshaft—out of round	0.0002 in.	0.005mm
Crankshaft—taper	0.0002 in.	0.005mm
Crankshaft endplay	0.020–0.0067 in.	0.05–0.17mm
Camshaft runout	0.004 in.	0.01mm
Flywheel runout	0.0059 in.	0.15mm

82623C12

KA24E SERIES ENGINE

Component	English	Metric
Cylinder head surface flatness		
Limit	0.004 in.	0.1mm
Valve head diameter		
Intake	1.339–1.336 in.	34–34.2mm
Exhaust	1.575–1.583 in.	40–40.2mm
Valve length		
Intake	4.720–4.732 in.	119.9–120.2mm
Exhaust	4.7508–4.7626 in.	120.67–120.97mm
Valve stem diameter		
Intake	0.2742–0.2748 in.	6.965–6.980mm
Exhaust	0.3129–0.3134 in.	7.948–7.960mm
Valve face angle	45°	
Valve margin limit	0.020 in.	0.50mm
Spring free height (outer)		
Intake	2.2614	57.44mm
Exhaust	2.0949 in.	53.21
Spring free height (inner)		
Intake	2.1000	53.34mm
Exhaust	1.8878 in.	47.95mm
Valve stem to guide clearance		
Intake	0.0008–0.0021 in.	0.020–0.053mm
Exhaust	0.0016–0.0029 in.	0.040–0.073mm
Limit	0.004 in.	0.1mm
Rocker arm shaft clearance	0.0005–0.0020in.	0.012–0.050mm
Camshaft oil clearance	0.0047 in.	0.12mm
Limit	0.008 in.	0.2mm
Camshaft endplay	0.004 in.	0.1mm
Cylinder block flatness	0.0006 in.	0.015mm
Cylinder out of round	0.0004 in.	0.010mm
Cylinder taper	0.0004 in.	0.01mm
	0.0002 in.	0.005mm
Crankshaft journal—out of round	0.0004 in.	0.01mm
Crankshaft pin—out of round	0.0002 in.	0.005mm
Crankshaft journal—taper	0.0004 in.	0.01mm
Crankshaft pin—taper	0.0002 in.	0.005mm
Crankshaft endplay	0.012 in.	0.3mm
Camshaft runout	0.0008 in.	0.02mm
Flywheel runout	0.004 in.	0.1mm
Driveplate runout	0.004 in.	0.1mm
Camshaft sprocket endplay	0.0047 in.	0.12mm

82623C13

TORQUE SPECIFICATIONS Z SERIES ENGINE

Component	English	Metric
Front cover:		
M8 bolts:	7–12 ft. lbs.	10–16 Nm
M6 bolts:	3–7 ft. lbs.	4–8 Nm
Crank pulley bolt:	101–116 ft. lbs.	137–157 Nm
Intake manifold bolt and nut:	12–15 ft. lbs.	16–21 Nm
Alternator bracket bolt:	33–40 ft. lbs.	44–54 Nm
Alternator mounting:	14–22 ft. lbs.	20–29 Nm
Cylinder head bolts (in sequence):	58–65 ft. lbs.	78–88 Nm
Cylinder head to front cover:	5–8 ft. lbs.	6–10 Nm
Rocker shaft bracket:	11–18 ft. lbs.	15–25 Nm
Camshaft sprocket bolt:	87–116 ft. lbs.	118–157 Nm
Rocker cover bolt:	5–8 ft. lbs.	6–10 Nm
Rocker arm nut:	12–16 ft. lbs.	16–22 Nm
Spark plug:	11–14 ft. lbs.	15–20 Nm
Main bearing cap bolt:	33–40 ft. lbs.	44–54 Nm
Connecting rod assembly:	33–40 ft. lbs.	44–54 Nm
Oil pan:	5–8 ft. lbs.	6–10 Nm
Oil pan drain plug:	14–22 ft. lbs.	20–29 Nm
Oil pump bolt:	8–11 ft. lbs.	11–15 Nm
Flywheel retaining bolts (manual transmission):	101–116 ft. lbs.	137–157 Nm
Driveplate retaining bolts (automatic transmission):	101–116 ft. lbs.	137–157 Nm
Clutch cover bolts:	12–15 ft. lbs.	16–21 Nm
Torque converter bolts (automatic transmission):	29–36 ft. lbs.	39–49 Nm
Transmissions to cylinder block bolt:	32–43 ft. lbs.	43–58 Nm

82623C14

CA20 SERIES ENGINE

Component	English	Metric
Front cover:	2–4 ft. lbs.	3–5 Nm
Crank pulley damper bolt:	90–98 ft. lbs.	123–132 Nm
Crank pulley bolt:	12–14 ft. lbs.	9–10 Nm
Intake manifold bolt and nut:	13–16 ft. lbs.	18–22 Nm
Alternator bracket bolt:	33–40 ft. lbs.	44–54 Nm
Alternator mounting:	14–22 ft. lbs.	20–29 Nm
Distributor hold down bolt:	13–17 ft. lbs.	18–24 Nm
Exhaust manifold nut:	18–24 ft. lbs.	13–17 Nm
Cylinder head bolts (in sequence):	58–65 ft. lbs.	78–88 Nm
Rocker shaft bracket:	13–16 ft. lbs.	18–22 Nm
Camshaft sprocket bolt:	36–43 ft. lbs.	49–59 Nm
Rocker cover retaining bolts:	2–3 ft. lbs.	1–3 Nm
Rocker arm nut:	13–16 ft. lbs.	18–22 Nm
Spark plug:	11–14 ft. lbs.	15–20 Nm
Main bearing cap bolt:	33–40 ft. lbs.	44–54 Nm
Connecting rod assembly:	22–27 ft. lbs.	29–37 Nm
Oil pan:	5–8 ft. lbs.	6–10 Nm
Oil pan drain plug:		
Oil pump bolt:	8–11 ft. lbs.	11–15 Nm
Flywheel retaining bolts (manual transmission):	72–80 ft. lbs.	98–108 Nm

82623C15

CA20 SERIES ENGINE

Component	English	Metric
Driveplate retaining bolts (automatic transmission):	72-80 ft. lbs.	98-108 Nm
Clutch cover bolts:	12-15 ft. lbs.	16-21 Nm
Transmissions to cylinder block bolt:	32-43 ft. lbs.	43-58 Nm
Rear oil seal retainer bolt:	3-5 ft. lbs.	4-6 Nm
Fuel pump cam bolt:	58-65 ft. lbs.	78-88 Nm

82623C16

CA20E AND CA18ET SERIES ENGINES

Component	English	Metric
Alternator adjusting bar:	10-12 ft. lbs.	14-17 Nm
Alternator belt tensioner bolt:	11-14 ft. lbs.	15-20 Nm
Crank pulley damper bolt:	90-98 ft. lbs.	123-132 Nm
Crank pulley to damper bolt:	9-10 ft. lbs.	12-14 Nm
Front cover:	2-4 ft. lbs.	3-5 Nm
Intake manifold bolt and nut:	14-19 ft. lbs.	20-25 Nm
Exhaust manifold:	14-22 ft. lbs.	20-29 Nm
Exhaust outlet to turbo:	16-22 ft. lbs.	20-29 Nm
Exhaust gas sensor:	30-37 ft. lbs.	40-50 Nm
Camshaft sprocket bolt:	58-65 ft. lbs.	78-88 Nm
Cylinder head assembly:	See Text	
Rocker shaft bracket:	13-16 ft. lbs.	18-22 Nm
Rocker arm nut:	13-16 ft. lbs.	18-22 Nm
Rocker cover retaining bolts:	2-3 ft. lbs.	1-3 Nm
Spark plug:	11-14 ft. lbs.	15-20 Nm
Main bearing cap bolt:	33-40 ft. lbs.	44-54 Nm
Connecting rod assembly:	22-27 ft. lbs.	29-37 Nm
Oil pan:	5-8 ft. lbs.	6-10 Nm
Oil pan drain plug:	14-22 ft. lbs.	20-29 Nm
Oil pump retaining bolt:	8-11 ft. lbs.	11-15 Nm
Flywheel retaining bolts (MT):	72-80 ft. lbs.	98-108 Nm
Driveplate retaining bolts (AT):	72-80 ft. lbs.	98-108 Nm
Clutch cover bolts:	12-15 ft. lbs.	16-21 Nm
Rear oil seal retainer bolt:	3-5 ft. lbs.	4-6 Nm
Starter motor:	22-29 ft. lbs.	29-39 Nm
Engine mount to body nut:	50-64 ft. lbs.	68-87 Nm

82623C17

VG30E SERIES ENGINE

Component	English	Metric
Collector cover:	5-7 ft. lbs.	6-8 Nm
Collector assembly:	13-16 ft. lbs.	18-22 Nm
Throttle chamber: See Text		
Intake manifold:	See Text	
Injector mounting:	2-3 ft. lbs.	2-3 Nm
Distributor hold down bolt:	4-7 ft. lbs.	4-6 Nm
Alternator adjusting bar bolt:	10-12 ft. lbs.	14-17 Nm
Rocker cover:	1-3 ft. lbs.	1-3 Nm
Rocker shaft assembly:	13-16 ft. lbs.	18-22 Nm
Camshaft pulley:	58-65 ft. lbs.	78-88 Nm
Cylinder head assembly: See Text		
Water pump:	12-15 ft. lbs.	16-21 Nm
Oil pan:	5-8 ft. lbs.	6-10 Nm
Oil pan drain plug:	22-29 ft. lbs.	29-39 Nm

82623C18

VG30E SERIES ENGINE

Component	English	Metric
Oil pump retaining bolt:	8-11 ft. lbs.	11-15 Nm
	4-6 ft. lbs.	6-7 Nm
Flywheel retaining bolts (manual transmission):	72-80 ft. lbs.	98-108 Nm
Rear oil seal retainer:	4-6 ft. lbs.	6-7 Nm
Connecting rod assembly:	See Text	
Main bearing cap:	67-74 ft. lbs.	90-100 Nm
Spark plug:	14-22 ft. lbs.	20-29 Nm

82623C19

KA24E SERIES ENGINE

Component	English	Metric
Rocker cover bolts:	2.9-5.8 ft. lbs.	4-8 Nm
Crankshaft pulley center bolt:	105-112 ft. lbs.	142-152 Nm
Crank pulley damper bolt:	7-9 ft. lbs.	10-12 Nm
Distributor holddown :	7-9 ft. lbs.	10-13 Nm
Alternator mounitng bolt:	33-44 ft. lbs.	45-60 Nm
Water pump pulley bolts:	5-6 ft. lbs.	7-8 Nm
Exhaust Gas Sensor:	30-37 ft. lbs.	40-50 Nm
Cylinder head assembly: see Text		
Exhaust manifold retaining bolts:	12-15 ft. lbs.	16-21 Nm
Collector assembly:	12-15 ft. lbs.	16-21 Nm
Camshaft sprocket:	87-116 ft. lbs.	118-157 Nm
Flywheel (manual transmission):	105-112 ft. lbs.	142-152 Nm
Driveplate (automatic transmission):	69-76 ft. lbs.	93-103 Nm
Rear oil seal retainer:	4-5 ft. lbs.	7-8 Nm
Connecting rod assembly: See Text		
Water inlet bolt:	5.1-5.8 ft. lbs.	7-8 Nm
Drain plug:	22-29 ft. lbs.	29-39 Nm

81623C20

USING A VACUUM GAUGE

The vacuum gauge is one of the most useful and easy-to-use diagnostic tools. It is inexpensive, easy to hook up, and provides valuable information about the condition of your engine.

White needle = steady needle   Dark needle = drifting needle

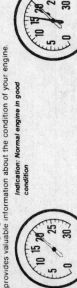

Indication: Normal engine in good condition

Gauge reading: Steady, from 17–22 in./Hg.

Indication: Late ignition or valve timing, low compression, stuck throttle valve, leaking carburetor or manifold gasket.

Gauge reading: Low (15–20 in./Hg.) but steady

Indication: Weak valve springs, worn valve stem guides, or leaky cylinder head gasket (vibrating excessively at all speeds).

NOTE: A plugged catalytic converter may also cause this reading.

Gauge reading: Needle fluctuates as engine speed increases

Indication: Choked muffler or obstruction in system. Speed up the engine. Choked muffler will exhibit a slow drop of vacuum to zero.

Gauge reading: Gradual drop in reading at idle

Indication: Sticking valve or ignition miss

Gauge reading: Needle fluctuates from 15–20 in./Hg. at idle

Indication: Improper carburetor adjustment, or minor intake leak at carburetor or manifold

NOTE: Bad fuel injector O-rings may also cause this reading.

Gauge reading: Drifting needle

Indication: Burnt valve or improper valve clearance. The needle will drop when the defective valve operates.

Gauge reading: Steady needle, but drops regularly

Indication: Worn valve guides

Gauge reading: Needle vibrates excessively at idle, but steadies as engine speed increases

TCCS3C01

Troubleshooting Engine Mechanical Problems

Problem	Cause	Solution
External oil leaks	• Cylinder head cover RTV sealant broken or improperly seated	• Replace sealant; inspect cylinder head cover sealant flange and cylinder head sealant surface for distortion and cracks
	• Oil filler cap leaking or missing	• Replace cap
	• Oil filter gasket broken or improperly seated	• Replace oil filter
	• Oil pan side gasket broken, improperly seated or opening in RTV sealant	• Replace gasket or repair opening in sealant; inspect oil pan gasket flange for distortion
	• Oil pan front oil seal broken or improperly seated	• Replace seal; inspect timing case cover and oil pan seal flange for distortion
	• Oil pan rear oil seal broken or improperly seated	• Replace seal; inspect oil pan rear oil seal flange; inspect rear main bearing cap for cracks, plugged oil return channels, or distortion in seal groove
	• Timing case cover oil seal broken or improperly seated	• Replace seal
	• Excess oil pressure because of restricted PCV valve	• Replace PCV valve
	• Oil pan drain plug loose or has stripped threads	• Repair as necessary and tighten
	• Rear oil gallery plug loose	• Use appropriate sealant on gallery plug and tighten
	• Rear camshaft plug loose or improperly seated	• Seat camshaft plug or replace and seal, as necessary
Excessive oil consumption	• Oil level too high	• Drain oil to specified level
	• Oil with wrong viscosity being used	• Replace with specified oil
	• PCV valve stuck closed	• Replace PCV valve
	• Valve stem oil deflectors (or seals) are damaged, missing, or incorrect type	• Replace valve stem oil deflectors
	• Valve stems or valve guides worn	• Measure stem-to-guide clearance and repair as necessary
	• Poorly fitted or missing valve cover baffles	• Replace valve cover
	• Piston rings broken or missing	• Replace broken or missing rings
	• Scuffed piston	• Replace piston
	• Incorrect piston ring gap	• Measure ring gap, repair as necessary
	• Piston rings sticking or excessively loose in grooves	• Measure ring side clearance, repair as necessary
	• Compression rings installed upside down	• Repair as necessary
	• Cylinder walls worn, scored, or glazed	• Repair as necessary

TCCS3C02

Troubleshooting Engine Mechanical Problems

Problem	Cause	Solution
Excessive oil consumption (cont.)	· Piston ring gaps not properly staggered · Excessive main or connecting rod bearing clearance	· Repair as necessary · Measure bearing clearance, repair as necessary
No oil pressure	· Low oil level · Oil pressure gauge, warning lamp or sending unit inaccurate · Oil pump malfunction · Oil pressure relief valve sticking · Oil passages on pressure side of pump obstructed · Oil pickup screen or tube obstructed · Loose oil inlet tube	· Add oil to correct level · Replace oil pressure gauge or warning lamp · Replace oil pump · Remove and inspect oil pressure relief valve assembly · Inspect oil passages for obstruction · Inspect oil pickup for obstruction · Tighten or seal inlet tube
Low oil pressure	· Low oil level · Inaccurate gauge, warning lamp or sending unit · Oil excessively thin because of dilution, poor quality, or improper grade · Excessive oil temperature · Oil pressure relief spring weak or sticking · Oil inlet tube and screen assembly has restriction or air leak · Excessive oil pump clearance · Excessive main, rod, or camshaft bearing clearance	· Add oil to correct level · Replace oil pressure gauge or warning lamp · Drain and refill crankcase with recommended oil · Correct cause of overheating engine · Remove and inspect oil pressure relief valve assembly · Remove and inspect oil inlet tube and screen assembly. (Fill inlet tube with lacquer thinner to locate leaks.) · Measure clearances · Measure bearing clearances, repair as necessary
High oil pressure	· Improper oil viscosity · Oil pressure gauge or sending unit inaccurate · Oil pressure relief valve sticking closed	· Drain and refill crankcase with correct viscosity oil · Replace oil pressure gauge · Remove and inspect oil pressure relief valve assembly
Main bearing noise	· Insufficient oil supply · Main bearing clearance excessive · Bearing insert missing · Crankshaft end-play excessive · Improperly tightened main bearing cap bolts · Loose flywheel or drive plate · Loose or damaged vibration damper	· Inspect for low oil level and low oil pressure · Measure main bearing clearance, repair as necessary · Replace missing insert · Measure end-play, repair as necessary · Tighten bolts with specified torque · Tighten flywheel or drive plate attaching bolts · Repair as necessary

TCCS3C03

Troubleshooting Engine Mechanical Problems

Problem	Cause	Solution
Connecting rod bearing noise	· Insufficient oil supply · Carbon build-up on piston · Bearing clearance excessive or bearing missing · Crankshaft connecting rod journal out-of-round · Misaligned connecting rod or cap · Connecting rod bolts tightened improperly	· Inspect for low oil level and low oil pressure · Remove carbon from piston crown · Measure clearance, repair as necessary · Measure journal dimensions, repair or replace as necessary · Repair as necessary · Tighten bolts with specified torque
Piston noise	· Piston-to-cylinder wall clearance excessive (scuffed piston) · Cylinder walls excessively tapered or out-of-round · Piston ring broken · Loose or seized piston pin · Connecting rods misaligned · Piston ring side clearance excessively loose or tight · Carbon build-up on piston is excessive	· Measure clearance and examine piston · Measure cylinder wall dimensions, rebore cylinder · Replace all rings on piston · Measure piston-to-pin clearance, repair as necessary · Measure rod alignment, straighten or replace · Measure ring side clearance, repair as necessary · Remove carbon from piston
Valve actuating component noise	· Insufficient oil supply · Rocker arms or pivots worn · Foreign objects or chips in hydraulic tappets · Excessive tappet leak-down · Tappet face worn · Broken or cocked valve springs · Stem-to-guide clearance excessive · Valve bent · Loose rocker arms · Valve seat runout excessive · Missing valve lock · Excessive engine oil	· Check for: (a) Low oil level (b) Low oil pressure (c) Wrong hydraulic tappets (d) Restricted oil gallery (e) Excessive tappet to bore clearance · Replace worn rocker arms or pivots · Clean tappets · Replace valve tappet · Replace tappet; inspect corresponding cam lobe for wear · Properly seat cocked springs; replace broken springs · Measure stem-to-guide clearance, repair as required · Replace valve · Check and repair as necessary · Regrind valve seat/valves · Install valve lock · Correct oil level

TCCS3C04

Troubleshooting Engine Performance

Problem	Cause	Solution
Hard starting (engine cranks normally)	• Faulty engine control system component	• Repair or replace as necessary
	• Faulty fuel pump	• Replace fuel pump
	• Faulty fuel system component	• Repair or replace as necessary
	• Faulty ignition coil	• Test and replace as necessary
	• Improper spark plug gap	• Adjust gap
	• Incorrect ignition timing	• Adjust timing
	• Incorrect valve timing	• Check valve timing; repair as necessary
Rough idle or stalling	• Incorrect curb or fast idle speed	• Adjust curb or fast idle speed (if possible)
	• Incorrect ignition timing	• Adjust timing to specification
	• Improper feedback system operation	• Refer to Chapter 4
	• Faulty EGR valve operation	• Test EGR system and replace as necessary
	• Faulty PCV valve air flow	• Test PCV valve and replace as necessary
	• Faulty TAC vacuum motor or valve	• Repair as necessary
	• Air leak into manifold vacuum	• Inspect manifold vacuum connections and repair as necessary
	• Faulty distributor rotor or cap	• Replace rotor or cap (Distributor systems only)
	• Improperly seated valves	• Test cylinder compression, repair as necessary
	• Incorrect ignition wiring	• Inspect wiring and correct as necessary
	• Faulty ignition coil	• Test coil and replace as necessary
	• Restricted air vent or idle passages	• Clean passages
	• Restricted air cleaner	• Clean or replace air cleaner filter element
Faulty low-speed operation	• Restricted idle air vents and passages	• Clean air vents and passages
	• Restricted air cleaner	• Clean or replace air cleaner filter element
	• Faulty spark plugs	• Clean or replace spark plugs
	• Dirty, corroded, or loose ignition secondary circuit wire connections	• Clean or tighten secondary circuit wire connections
	• Improper feedback system operation	• Refer to Chapter 4
	• Faulty ignition coil high voltage wire	• Replace ignition coil high voltage wire (Distributor systems only)
	• Faulty distributor cap	• Replace cap (Distributor systems only)
Faulty acceleration	• Incorrect ignition timing	• Adjust timing
	• Faulty fuel system component	• Repair or replace as necessary
	• Faulty spark plug(s)	• Clean or replace spark plug(s)
	• Improperly seated valves	• Test cylinder compression, repair as necessary
	• Faulty ignition coil	• Test coil and replace as necessary

TCCS3C05

Troubleshooting Engine Performance

Problem	Cause	Solution
Faulty acceleration (cont.)	• Improper feedback system operation	• Refer to Chapter 4
Faulty high speed operation	• Incorrect ignition timing	• Adjust timing (if possible)
	• Faulty advance mechanism	• Check advance mechanism and repair as necessary (Distributor systems only)
	• Low fuel pump volume	• Replace fuel pump
	• Wrong spark plug air gap or wrong plug	• Adjust air gap or install correct plug
	• Partially restricted exhaust manifold, exhaust pipe, catalytic converter, muffler, or tailpipe	• Eliminate restriction
	• Restricted vacuum passages	• Clean passages
	• Restricted air cleaner	• Cleaner or replace filter element as necessary
	• Faulty distributor rotor or cap.	• Replace rotor or cap (Distributor systems only)
	• Faulty ignition coil	• Test coil and replace as necessary
	• Improperly seated valve(s)	• Test cylinder compression, repair as necessary
	• Faulty valve spring(s)	• Inspect and test valve spring tension, replace as necessary
	• Incorrect valve timing	• Check valve timing and repair as necessary
	• Intake manifold restricted	• Remove restriction or replace manifold
	• Worn distributor shaft	• Replace shaft (Distributor systems only)
	• Improper feedback system operation	• Refer to Chapter 4
Misfire at all speeds	• Faulty spark plug(s)	• Clean or relace spark plug(s)
	• Faulty spark plug wire(s)	• Replace as necessary
	• Faulty distributor cap or rotor	• Replace cap or rotor (Distributor systems only)
	• Faulty ignition coil	• Test coil and replace as necessary
	• Primary ignition circuit shorted or open intermittently	• Troubleshoot primary circuit and repair as necessary
	• Improperly seated valve(s)	• Test cylinder compression, repair as necessary
	• Faulty hydraulic tappet(s)	• Clean or replace tappet(s)
	• Improper feedback system operation	• Refer to Chapter 4
	• Faulty valve spring(s)	• Inspect and test valve spring tension, repair as necessary
	• Worn camshaft lobes	• Replace camshaft
	• Air leak into manifold	• Check manifold vacuum and repair as necessary
	• Fuel pump volume or pressure low	• Replace fuel pump
	• Blown cylinder head gasket	• Replace gasket
	• Intake or exhaust manifold passage(s) restricted	• Pass chain through passage(s) and repair as necessary
Power not up to normal	• Incorrect ignition timing	• Adjust timing
	• Faulty distributor rotor	• Replace rotor (Distributor systems only)

TCCS3C06

Troubleshooting Engine Performance

Problem	Cause	Solution
Power not up to normal (cont.)	• Incorrect spark plug gap	• Adjust gap
	• Faulty fuel pump	• Replace fuel pump
	• Faulty fuel pump	• Replace fuel pump
	• Incorrect valve timing	• Check valve timing and repair as necessary
	• Faulty ignition coil	• Test coil and replace as necessary
	• Faulty ignition wires	• Test wires and replace as necessary
	• Improperly seated valves	• Test cylinder compression and repair as necessary
	• Blown cylinder head gasket	• Replace gasket
	• Leaking piston rings	• Test compression and repair as necessary
	• Improper feedback system operation	• Refer to Chapter 4
Intake backfire	• Improper ignition timing	• Adjust timing
	• Defective EGR component	• Repair as necessary
	• Defective TAC vacuum motor or valve	• Repair as necessary
Exhaust backfire	• Air leak into manifold vacuum	• Check manifold vacuum and repair as necessary
	• Faulty air injection diverter valve	• Test diverter valve and replace as necessary
	• Exhaust leak	• Locate and eliminate leak
Ping or spark knock	• Incorrect ignition timing	• Adjust timing
	• Distributor advance malfunction	• Inspect advance mechanism and repair as necessary (Distributor systems only)
	• Excessive combustion chamber deposits	• Remove with combustion chamber cleaner
	• Air leak into manifold vacuum	• Check manifold vacuum and repair as necessary
	• Excessively high compression	• Test compression and repair as necessary
	• Fuel octane rating excessively low	• Try alternate fuel source
	• Sharp edges in combustion chamber	• Grind smooth
	• EGR valve not functioning properly	• Test EGR system and replace as necessary
Surging (at cruising to top speeds)	• Low fuel pump pressure or volume	• Replace fuel pump
	• Improper PCV valve air flow	• Test PCV valve and replace as necessary
	• Air leak into manifold vacuum	• Check manifold vacuum and repair as necessary
	• Incorrect spark advance	• Test and replace as necessary
	• Restricted fuel filter	• Replace fuel filter
	• Restricted air cleaner	• Clean or replace air cleaner filter element
	• EGR valve not functioning properly	• Test EGR system and replace as necessary
	• Improper feedback system operation	• Refer to Chapter 4

TCCS3C07

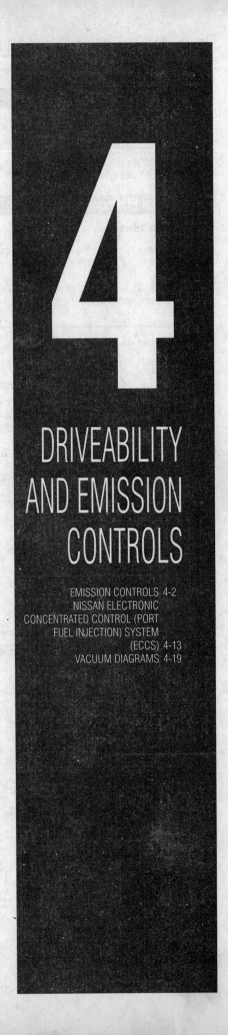

4

DRIVEABILITY AND EMISSION CONTROLS

EMISSION CONTROLS

There are three sources of automotive pollutants: Crankcase fumes, exhaust gases and gasoline evaporation. The pollutants formed from these substances fall into three categories: unburnt hydrocarbons (HC), carbon monoxide (CO) and oxides of nitrogen (NOx). The equipment that is used to limit these pollutants is commonly called emission control equipment.

Crankcase Emission Controls

▶ **See Figures 1 thru 7**

The crankcase emission control equipment consists of a positive crankcase ventilation valve (PCV), a closed or open oil filler cap and hoses to connect this equipment.

When the engine is running, a small portion of the gases which are formed in the combustion chamber during combustion leak by the piston

rings and enter the crankcase. Since these gases are under pressure they tend to escape from the crankcase and enter into the atmosphere. If these gases were allowed to remain in the crankcase for any length of time, they would contaminate the engine oil and cause sludge to build up. If the gases are allowed to escape into the atmosphere, they would pollute the air, as they contain unburned hydrocarbons. The crankcase emission control equipment recycles these gases back into the engine combustion chamber where they are burned.

Crankcase gases are recycled in the following manner: while the engine is running, clean filtered air is drawn into the crankcase through the air filter and then through a hose leading to the rocker cover. As the air passes through the crankcase it picks up the combustion gases and carries them out of the crankcase, up through the PCV valve and into the intake manifold. After they enter the intake manifold they are drawn into the combustion chamber and burned.

The most critical component in the system is the PCV valve. This vacuum controlled valve regulates the amount of gases which are recycled into the combustion changer. At low engine speeds the valve is partially closed, limiting the flow of gases into the intake manifold. As engine speed increases,

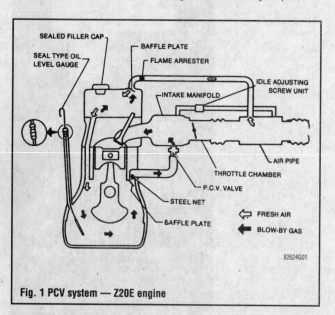

Fig. 1 PCV system — Z20E engine

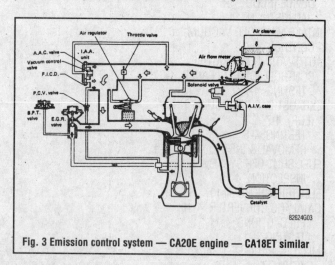

Fig. 3 Emission control system — CA20E engine — CA18ET similar

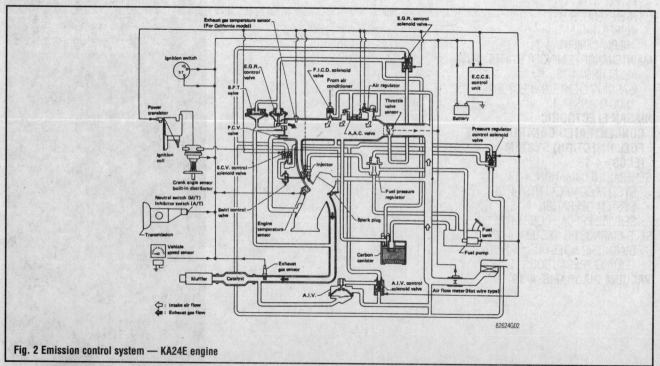

Fig. 2 Emission control system — KA24E engine

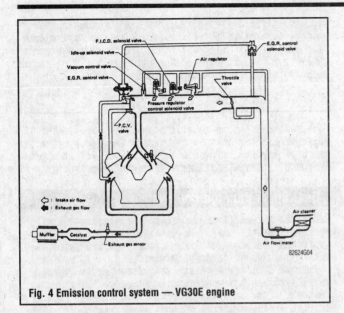

Fig. 4 Emission control system — VG30E engine

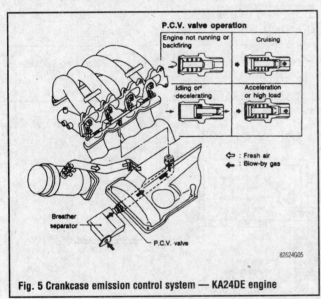

Fig. 5 Crankcase emission control system — KA24DE engine

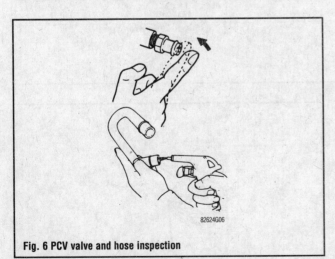

Fig. 6 PCV valve and hose inspection

the valve opens to admit greater quantities of the gases into the intake manifold. If the valve should become blocked or plugged, the gases will be prevented from escaping from the crankcase by the normal route. Since these

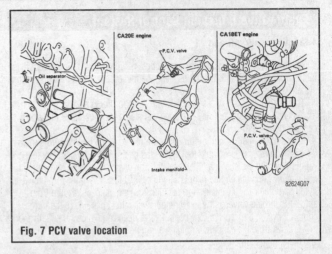

Fig. 7 PCV valve location

gases are under pressure, they will find their own way out of the crankcase. This alternate route is usually a weak oil seal or gasket in the engine. As the gas escapes by the gasket it also creates an oil leak. Besides causing oil leaks, a clogged PCV valve also allows these gases to remain in the crankcase for an extended period of time, promoting the formation of sludge in the engine.

The above explanation and the troubleshooting procedure which follows applies to all engines with PCV systems.

TESTING

♦ See Figure 8

Check the PCV system hoses and connections, to see that there are no vacuum leaks. Then replace or tighten, as necessary.

With the engine running at idle, remove the ventilation hose from the PCV valve. If the valve is working properly, a hissing noise will be heard as air passes through it and a strong vacuum should be felt when a finger is placed over the valve inlet. Refer to the illustrations.

To check the valve, remove it and blow through both of its ends. When blowing from the side which goes toward the intake manifold, very little air should pass through it. When blowing from the crankcase (valve cover) side, air should pass through freely. Replace the valve with a new one, if the valve fails to function as outlined.

REMOVAL & INSTALLATION

To remove the PCV valve, simply loosen the hose clamp and remove the valve from the manifold-to-crankcase hose and intake manifold. Install the PCV valve in the reverse order of removal procedure.

Disconnect all hoses and clean with compressed air. If any hose cannot be freed of obstructions—replace the hose.

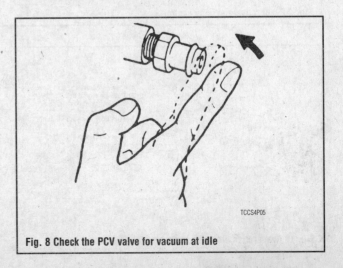

Fig. 8 Check the PCV valve for vacuum at idle

Evaporative Emission Control System

♦ **See Figures 9, 10 and 11**

When raw fuel evaporates, the vapors contain hydrocarbons. To prevent these fumes from escaping into the atmosphere, the fuel evaporative emission control system was developed.

The system consists of a sealed fuel tank, a vapor/liquid separator (certain models only), a vapor vent line, a carbon canister, a vacuum signal line and a canister purge line.

In operation, fuel vapors and/or liquid are routed to the liquid/vapor separator or check valve where liquid fuel is directed back into the fuel tank as fuel vapors flow into the charcoal filled canister. The charcoal absorbs and stores the fuel vapors when the engine is not running or is at idle. When the throttle valves in the carburetor (or air intakes for fuel injection) are opened, vacuum from above the throttle valves is routed through a vacuum signal line to the purge control valve on the canister. The control valve opens and allows the fuel vapors to be drawn from the canister through a purge line and into the intake manifold and the combustion chambers.

INSPECTION AND SERVICE

Check the hoses for proper connections and damage. Replace as necessary. Check the vapor separator tank for fuel leaks, distortion and dents, and replace as necessary.

Carbon Canister and Purge Control Valve

To check the operation of the carbon canister purge control valve, disconnect the rubber hose between the canister control valve and the T-fitting, at the T-fitting.

Apply vacuum to the hose leading to the control valve. The vacuum condition should be maintained indefinitely. If the control valve leaks, remove the top cover of the valve and check for a dislocated or cracked diaphragm. If the diaphragm is damaged, a repair kit containing a new diaphragm, retainer, and spring is available and should be installed or replace the carbon canister assembly.

REMOVAL & INSTALLATION

Removal and installation of the various evaporative emission control system components consists of disconnecting the hoses, loosening retaining screws, and remove the part which is to be replaced or checked. Install in the reverse order. When replacing hose, make sure that it is fuel and vapor resistant type hose.

Dual Spark Plug Ignition System

The 1982–83 Z-series and CA-series engines have two spark plugs per cylinder. This arrangement allows the engine to burn large amounts of recirculated exhaust gases without affecting performance. In fact, the system works so well it improves gas mileage under most circumstances.

Both spark plugs fire simultaneously, which substantially shortens the time required to burn the air/fuel mixture when exhaust gases (EGR) are not being recirculated. When gases are being recirculated, the dual spark plug system brings the ignition level up to that of a single plug system which is not recirculating exhaust gases.

ADJUSTMENT

The only adjustments necessary are the tune-up and maintenance procedures outlined in Sections 1 and 2.

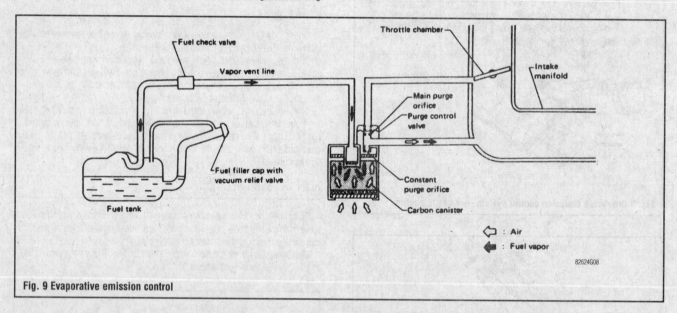

Fig. 9 Evaporative emission control

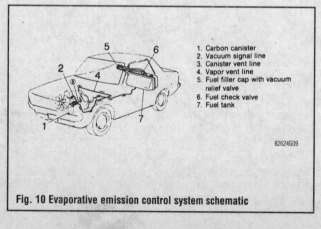

1. Carbon canister
2. Vacuum signal line
3. Canister vent line
4. Vapor vent line
5. Fuel filler cap with vacuum relief valve
6. Fuel check valve
7. Fuel tank

Fig. 10 Evaporative emission control system schematic

Fig. 11 When checking the purge control valve apply vacuum (inhale) to the hose

Spark Timing Control System

▶ **See Figure 12**

The spark timing control system has been used in different forms on Nissan/Datsuns since 1972. The first system, Transmission Controlled Spark System (TCS) was used on most Nissan/Datsuns through 1979. This system consists of a thermal vacuum valve, a vacuum switching valve, a high gear detecting switch, and a number of vacuum hoses. Basically, the system is designed to retard full spark advance except when the car is in high gear and the engine is at normal operating temperature. At all other times, the spark advance is retarded to one degree or another.

The 1980 and later Spark Timing Control System replaces the TCS system. The major difference is that it works solely from engine water temperature changes rather than a transmission mounted switch. The system includes a thermal vacuum valve, a vacuum delay valve, and attendant hoses. It performs the same function as the earlier TCS system. To retard full spark advance at times when high levels of pollutants would otherwise be given off.

INSPECTION AND ADJUSTMENTS

Normally the Spark Timing Control systems should be trouble-free. However, if you suspect a problem in the system, first check to make sure all wiring (if so equipped) and hoses are connected and free from dirt. Also check to make sure the distributor vacuum advance is working properly. If everything appears all right, connect a timing light to the engine and make sure the initial timing is correct.

To test the Spark Timing Control System, connect a timing light and check the ignition timing while the temperature gauge is in the cold position. Write down the reading. Allow the engine to run with the timing light attached until the temperature needle reaches the center of the gauge. As the engine is warming up, check with the timing light to make sure the ignition timing retards. When the temperature needle is in the middle of the gauge, the ignition timing should advance from its previous position. If the ignition timing does not change, replace the thermal vacuum valve.

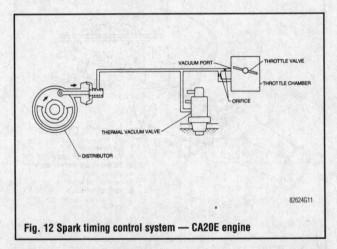

Fig. 12 Spark timing control system — CA20E engine

Early Fuel Evaporation System

▶ **See Figure 13**

The system's purpose is to heat the air/fuel mixture when the engine is below normal operating temperature. The carbureted engines use coolant water heat instead of exhaust gas heat to prewarm the fuel mixture. This system should be trouble-free. Refer to the illustration.

Boost Control Deceleration Device (BCDD)

▶ **See Figures 14 and 15**

The Boost Control Deceleration Device (BCDD) used to reduce hydrocarbon emissions during coasting conditions.

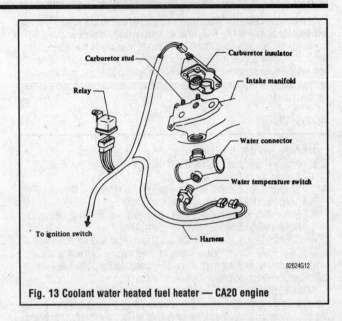

Fig. 13 Coolant water heated fuel heater — CA20 engine

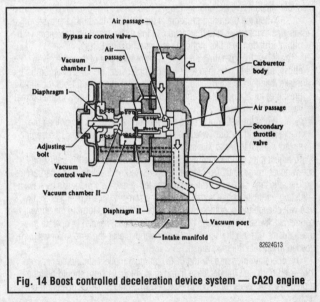

Fig. 14 Boost controlled deceleration device system — CA20 engine

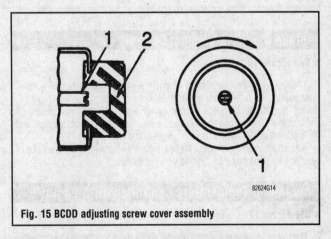

Fig. 15 BCDD adjusting screw cover assembly

High manifold vacuum during coasting prevents the complete combustion of the air/fuel mixture because of the reduced amount of air. This condition will result in a large amount of HC emission. Enriching the air/fuel mixture for a short time (during the high vacuum condition) will reduce the emission of the HC.

However, enriching the air/fuel mixture with only the mixture adjusting screw will cause poor engine idle or invite an increase in the carbon monoxide (CO) content of the exhaust gases. The BCDD consists of an independent system that kicks in when the engine is coasting and enriches the air/fuel mixture, which reduces the hydrocarbon content of the exhaust gases. This is accomplished without adversely affecting engine idle and the carbon monoxide content of the exhaust gases.

ADJUSTMENT

Normally, the BCDD does not need adjustment. However, if the need should arise because of suspected malfunction of the system, proceed as follows:
1. Connect the tachometer to the engine.
2. Connect a quick response vacuum gauge to the intake manifold.
3. Disconnect the solenoid valve electrical leads.
4. Start and warm up the engine until it reaches normal operating temperature.
5. Adjust the idle speed to the proper specification.
6. Raise the engine speed to 3,000–3,500 rpm under no-load (transmission in Neutral or Park), then allow the throttle to close quickly. Take notice as to whether or not the engine rpm returns to idle speed and if it does, how long the fall in rpm is interrupted before it reaches idle speed.

At the moment the throttle is snapped closed at high engine rpm and the vacuum in the intake manifold reaches between 23–27.7 in. Hg and then gradually falls to about 16.5 in. Hg at idle speed. The process of the fall of the intake manifold vacuum and the engine rpm will take one of the following three forms:

a. When the operating pressure of the BCDD is too high, the system remains inoperative, and the vacuum in the intake manifold decreases without interruption just like that of an engine without a BCDD.

b. When the operating pressure is lower than that of the case given above, but still higher than the proper set pressure, the fall of vacuum in the intake manifold is interrupted and kept constant at a certain level (operating pressure) for about one second and then gradually falls down to the normal vacuum at idle speed.

c. When the set of operating pressure of the BCDD is lower than the intake manifold vacuum when the throttle is suddenly released, the engine speed will not lower to idle speed.

To adjust the set operating pressure of the BCDD, remove the adjusting screw cover from the BCDD mechanism mounted on the side of the carburetor.

The adjusting screw is a left hand threaded screw. Late models may have an adjusting nut instead of a screw. Turning the screw 1/8 of a turn in either direction will change the operation pressure about 0.8 in. Hg. Turning the screw counterclockwise will increase the amount of vacuum needed to operate the mechanism. Turning the screw clockwise will decrease the amount of vacuum needed to operate the mechanism.

The operating pressure for the BCDD on most models should be between 19.9–22.05 in. Hg. The decrease in intake manifold vacuum should be interrupted at these levels for about one second when the BCDD is operating correctly.

Don't forget to install the adjusting screw cover after the system is adjusted.

Intake Manifold Vacuum Control

▶ See Figure 16

The vacuum control valve is provided to reduce the engine lubricating oil consumption when the intake manifold vacuum increases to a very high level during deceleration. The vacuum control valve senses the manifold vacuum. As the manifold vacuum increases beyond the specified valve, the valve opens and air is sucked into the intake manifold. Refer to the illustrations.

Aside from a routine check of the hoses and their connections, no service or adjustments should ever be necessary on this system.

Automatic Temperature Controlled Air Cleaner

▶ See Figure 17

The rate at which fuel is drawn into the airstream in a carburetor varies with the temperature of the air that the fuel is being mixed with. The air/fuel ratio cannot be held constant for efficient fuel combustion with a wide range of air temperatures. Cold air being drawn into the engine causes a richer air/fuel mixture, and thus, more hydrocarbons in the exhaust gas. Hot air being drawn into

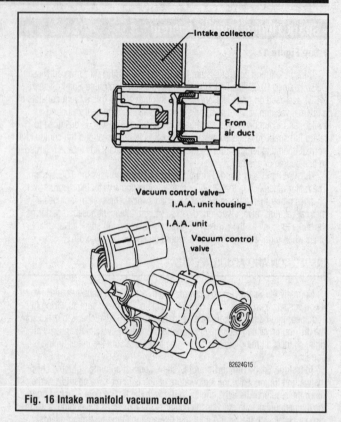

Fig. 16 Intake manifold vacuum control

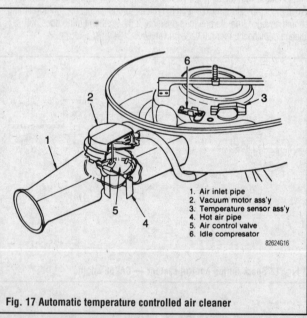

1. Air inlet pipe
2. Vacuum motor ass'y
3. Temperature sensor ass'y
4. Hot air pipe
5. Air control valve
6. Idle compresator

Fig. 17 Automatic temperature controlled air cleaner

the engine causes a leaner air/fuel mixture and more efficient combustion for less hydrocarbons in the exhaust gases.

The automatic temperature controlled air cleaner is designed so that the temperature of the ambient air being drawn into the engine is automatically controlled, to hold the temperature of the air and, consequently, the fuel/air ratio at a constant rate for efficient fuel combustion.

A temperature sensing vacuum switch controls vacuum applied to a vacuum motor operating a valve in the intake snorkel of the air cleaner. When the engine is cold or the air being drawn into the engine is cold, the vacuum motor opens the valve, allowing air heated by the exhaust manifold to be drawn into the engine. As the engine warms up, the temperature sensing unit shuts off the vacuum applied to the vacuum motor which allows the valve to close, shutting off the heated air and allowing cooler, outside (under hood) air to be drawn into the engine.

TESTING

When the air around the temperature sensor of the unit mounted inside the air cleaner housing reaches 100°F (38°C), the sensor should block the flow of vacuum to the air control valve vacuum motor. When the temperature around the temperature sensor is below 100°F (38°C), the sensor should allow vacuum to pass onto the air valve vacuum motor thus blocking off the air cleaner snorkel to under hood (unheated) air.

When the temperature around the sensor is above 118°F (48°C), the air control valve should be completely open to under hood air.

If the air-cleaner fails to operate correctly, check for loose or broken vacuum hoses. If the hoses are not the cause, replace the vacuum motor in the air cleaner.

Exhaust Gas Recirculation (EGR) System

♦ **See Figures 18 thru 26**

· Exhaust gas recirculation is used to reduce combustion temperatures in the engine, thereby reducing the oxides of nitrogen emissions.

An EGR valve is mounted on the center of the intake manifold. The recycled exhaust gas is drawn into the bottom of the intake manifold riser portion through the exhaust manifold heat stove and EGR valve. A vacuum diaphragm is connected to a timed signal port at the carburetor flange.

As the throttle valve is opened, vacuum is applied to the EGR valve vacuum diaphragm. When the vacuum reaches about 2 in. Hg, the diaphragm moves against string pressure and is in a fully up position at 8 in. Hg of vacuum. As the diaphragm moves up, it opens the exhaust gas metering valve which allows exhaust gas to be pulled into the engine intake manifold. The system does not operate when the engine is idling because the exhaust gas recirculation would cause a rough idle.

On some later models, a thermal vacuum valve inserted in the engine thermostat housing controls the application of the vacuum to the EGR valve. When the engine coolant reaches a predetermined temperature, the thermal vacuum valve opens and allows vacuum to be routed to the EGR valve. Below the predetermined temperature, the thermal vacuum valve closes and blocks vacuum to the EGR valve.

Most vehicles have a B.P.T. valve installed between the EGR valve and the thermal vacuum valve. The B.P.T. valve has a diaphragm which is raised or lowered by exhaust back pressure. The diaphragm opens or closes an air bleed, which is connected into the EGR vacuum line. High pressure results in higher levels of EGR, because the diaphragm is raised, closing off the air bleed, which allows more vacuum to reach and open the EGR valve. Thus the amount of recirculated exhaust gas varies with exhaust pressure.

Some early models use a V.V.T. valve (venturi vacuum transducer valve) instead of the B.P.T. valve. The V.V.T. valve monitors exhaust pressure and carburetor vacuum in order to activate the diaphragm which controls the throttle

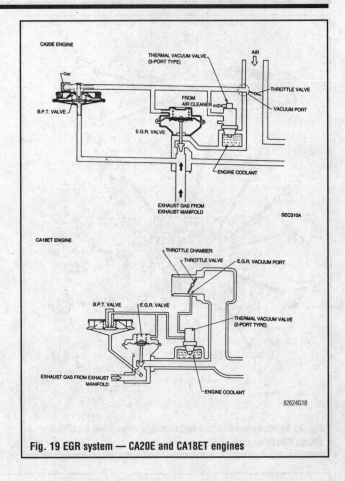

Fig. 19 EGR system — CA20E and CA18ET engines

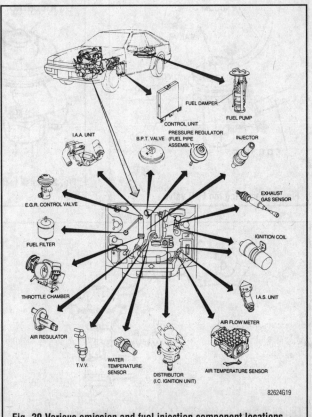

Fig. 20 Various emission and fuel injection component locations — 200SX and 200SX Turbo CA20E and CA18ET engines

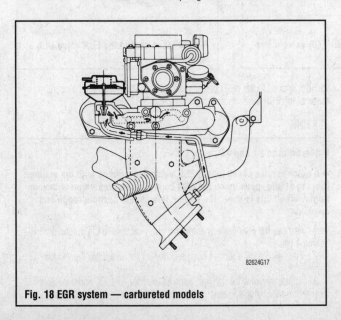

Fig. 18 EGR system — carbureted models

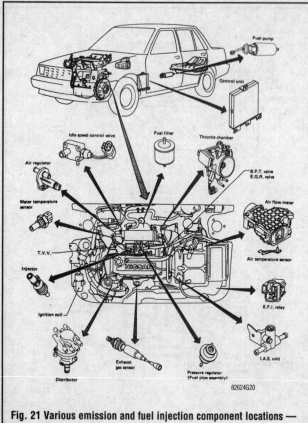

Fig. 21 Various emission and fuel injection component locations — Stanza CA20E engine

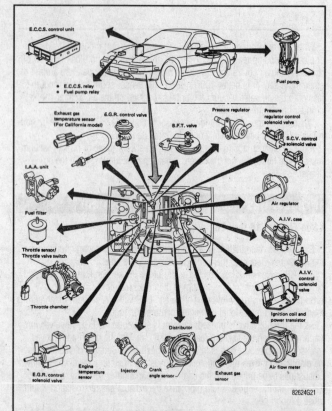

Fig. 22 Various emission and fuel injection component locations — 240SX KA24E engine

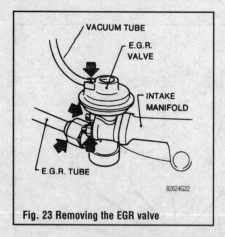

Fig. 23 Removing the EGR valve

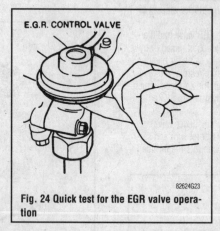

Fig. 24 Quick test for the EGR valve operation

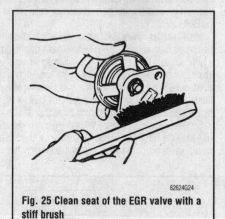

Fig. 25 Clean seat of the EGR valve with a stiff brush

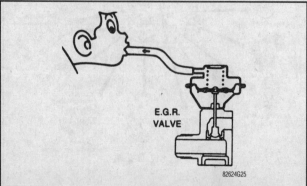

Fig. 26 You can apply vacuum to the EGR valve by sucking on the air tube which is connected to it.

vacuum applied to the EGR control valve. This system expands the operating range of the EGR flow rate as compared to the B.P.T. unit.

TESTING

♦ **See Figures 27 and 28**

➡A quick service check for the EGR valve operation is with the engine running at idle, push up on the EGR control valve diaphragm with your finger. When this is done, the engine idle should become rough and uneven.

1. Remove the EGR valve and apply enough vacuum to the diaphragm to open the valve.
2. The valve should remain open for over 30 seconds after the vacuum is removed.
3. Check the valve for damage, such as warpage, cracks, and excessive wear around the valve and seat.

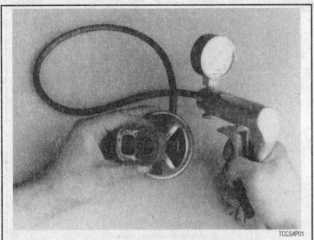

Fig. 27 Some EGR valves may be tested using a vacuum pump by watching for diaphragm movement

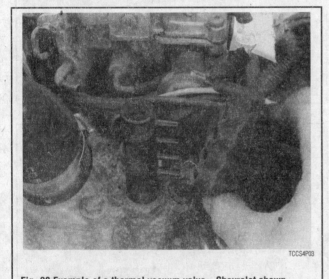

Fig. 28 Example of a thermal vacuum valve—Chevrolet shown

4. Clean the seat with a brush and compressed air and remove any deposits from around the valve and port (seat).

5. To check the operation of the thermal vacuum valve, remove the valve from the engine and apply vacuum to the ports of the valve. The valve should not allow vacuum to pass.

6. Place the valve in a container of water with a thermometer and heat the water. When the temperature of the water reaches 134–145°F (57–63°C), remove the valve and apply vacuum to the ports. The valve should allow vacuum to pass through it.

7. To test the B.P.T. valve, disconnect the two vacuum hoses from the valve. Plug one of the ports. While applying pressure to the bottom of the valve, apply vacuum to the unplugged port and check for leakage. If any exists, replace the valve.

To test the check valve, remove the valve and blow into the side which connects the EGR valve. Air should flow. When air is supplied to the other side, air flow resistance should be greater. If not, replace the valve.

9. To check the V.V.T. valve disconnect the top and bottom center hoses and apply a vacuum to the top hose. Check for leaks. If a leak is present, replace the valve.

REMOVAL & INSTALLATION

EGR Control Valve

1. Remove the nuts which attach the EGR tube and/or the BP tube to the EGR valve (if so equipped).

2. Unscrew the mounting bolts and remove the heat shield plate from the EGR control valve (if so equipped).

3. Tag and disconnect the EGR vacuum hose(s).

4. Unscrew the mounting bolts and remove the EGR control valve.

To install:

5. Install the EGR valve assembly with mounting bolts (torque retaining bolts EVENLY) to intake manifold location.

6. Connect all vacuum hoses and install the heat shield if so equipped.

7. Connect EGR tube or BP tube to the EGR valve if so equipped. If replacing the EGR valve assembly always be sure that the new valve is identical to the old one.

Fuel Shut-Off System

▶ See Figures 29, 30, 31, 32 and 33

This system is designed to reduce HC emissions and also to improve fuel economy during deceleration.

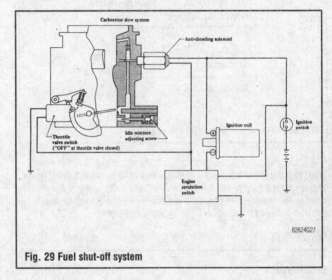

Fig. 29 Fuel shut-off system

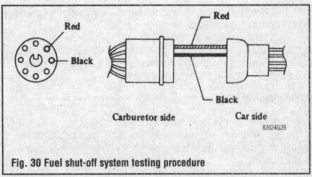

Fig. 30 Fuel shut-off system testing procedure

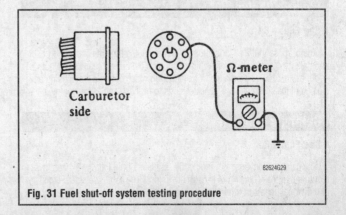

Fig. 31 Fuel shut-off system testing procedure

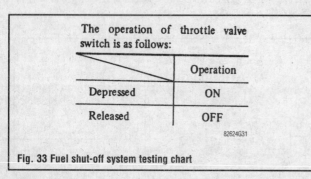

Fig. 32 Fuel shut-off system testing chart

Engine speed	Switch operation			
	Engine revolution switch	Throttle valve switch	Anti-dieseling solenoid	Fuel shut-off system
Higher than 2,200 rpm	OFF	OFF	OFF	Operated
		ON	ON	Not operated
Lower than 1,600 rpm	ON	OFF	ON	Not operated
		ON	ON	Not operated

82624G30

Fig. 32 Fuel shut-off system testing chart

The operation of throttle valve switch is as follows:	
	Operation
Depressed	ON
Released	OFF

82624G31

Fig. 33 Fuel shut-off system testing chart

The fuel shut-off system is operated when the engine runs at higher than 2,200 rpm and the throttle valve is closed. These conditions are detected by the engine revolution switch and the throttle valve switch. As the engine speed goes down to the recovery zone which is lower than 1,600 rpm, the fuel shut-off system does not operate even if the throttle valve is kept closed.

INSPECTION

Entire System

1. Disconnect harness connector on carburetor. Then connect jumper wires between each connector as illustrated.
2. Start the engine and make sure that the engine stops when engine speed increases to about 2,000–2,500 rpm. If not, check the harness connections for engine revolution switch and repair them as necessary. If the harness connections are OK—replace the engine revolution switch.

Throttle Valve Switch

1. Disconnect harness connector on the carburetor.
2. Check the continuity between the terminal of the connector and carburetor body when accelerator pedal is depressed or released—refer to the necessary illustrations.

Electric Choke

♦ See Figure 34

The purpose of the electric choke is to shorten the time the choke is in operation after the engine is started, thus shortening the time of high HC output.

An electric heater warms the bi-metal spring which controls the opening and closing of the choke valve. The heater starts to heat as soon as the engine starts.

Catalytic Converter

♦ See Figure 35

The catalytic converter is a muffler like container built into the exhaust system to aid in the reduction of exhaust emissions. The catalyst element consists of individual pellets or a honeycomb monolithic substrate coated with a noble

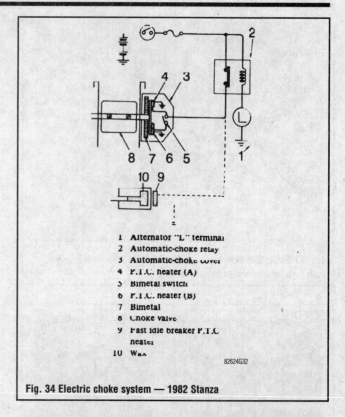

1 Alternator "L" terminal
2 Automatic-choke relay
3 Automatic-choke cover
4 P.T.C. heater (A)
5 Bimetal switch
6 P.T.C. heater (B)
7 Bimetal
8 Choke valve
9 Fast idle breaker P.T.C. heater
10 Wax

82624G32

Fig. 34 Electric choke system — 1982 Stanza

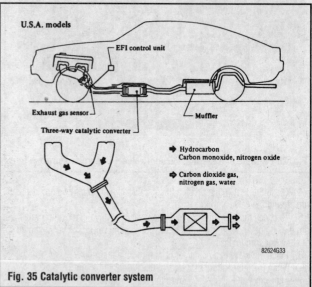

U.S.A. models

EFI control unit

Exhaust gas sensor

Muffler

Three-way catalytic converter

➡ Hydrocarbon Carbon monoxide, nitrogen oxide

➡ Carbon dioxide gas, nitrogen gas, water

82624G33

Fig. 35 Catalytic converter system

metal such as platinum, palladium, rhodium or a combination. When the exhaust gases come into contact with the catalyst, a chemical reaction occurs which will reduce the pollutants into harmless substances like water and carbon dioxide.

There are essentially two types of catalytic converters: an oxidizing type is used on all models before 1980 year. It requires the addition of oxygen to spur the catalyst into reducing the engine's HC and CO emissions into H_2O and CO_2. Because of this need for oxygen, the Air Injection (air pump) system is used with all these models.

The oxidizing catalytic converter, while effectively reducing HC and CO emissions, does little, if anything in the way of reducing NOx emissions. Thus, the three way catalytic converter.

The three way converter, unlike the oxidizing type, is capable of reducing HC, CO and NOx emissions; all at the same time. In theory, it seems impossible to reduce all three pollutants in one system since the reduction of HC and CO requires the addition of oxygen, while the reduction of NOx calls for the removal of oxygen. In actuality, the three way system really can reduce all three pollutants, but only if the amount of oxygen in the exhaust system is precisely controlled. Due to this precise oxygen control requirement, the three way converter system is used only in cars equipped with an oxygen sensor system.

All models with the three way converter have an oxygen sensor warning light on the dashboard, which illuminates at the first 30,000 mile interval, signaling the need for oxygen sensor replacement. The oxygen sensor is part of the Mixture Ratio Feedback System, described in this section. The Feedback System uses the three way converter as one of its major components.

No regular maintenance is required for the catalytic converter system, except for periodic replacement of the Air Induction System filter (if so equipped). The Air Induction System is described earlier in this Section. Filter replacement procedures are in Section 1. The Air Induction System is used to supply the catalytic converter with fresh air. Oxygen present in the air is used in the oxidation process.

PRECAUTIONS

1. Use only unleaded fuel.
2. Avoid prolonged idling. The engine should run on longer than 20 min. at curb idle and no longer than 10 min. at fast idle.
3. Do not disconnect any of the spark plug leads while the engine is running.
4. Make engine compression checks as quickly as possible.

TESTING

At the present time there is no known way to reliably test catalytic converter operation in the field.

An infrared HC/CO tester is not sensitive enough to measure the higher tailpipe emissions from a failing converter. Thus, a bad converter may allow enough emissions to escape so that the car is no longer in compliance with Federal or state levels, but will still not cause the needle on a tester to move off zero.

The chemical reactions which occur inside a catalytic converter generate a great deal of heat. Most converter problems can be traced to fuel or ignition system problems which cause unusually high emissions. As a result of the increased intensity of the chemical reactions, the converter literally burns itself up.

A completely failed converter might cause a tester to show a slight reading. as a result, it is occasionally possible to detect one of these.

As long as you avoid severe overheating and the use of leaded fuels it is reasonably safe to assume that the converter is working properly.

➡ **IF THE CATALYTIC CONVERTER BECOMES BLOCKED, THE ENGINE WILL NOT RUN.**

The converter assembly has a "Emission Warranty" contact your local Datsun/Nissan dealer for more information.

Mixture Ratio Feedback System

The need for better fuel economy coupled to increasingly strict emission control regulations dictates a more exact control of the engine air/fuel mixture. Datsun/Nissan has developed a Mixture Ratio Feedback System in response to these needs. The system is installed on all 200SX, 1984 and later Stanza models and 240SX models.

The principle of the system is to control the air/fuel mixture exactly, so that more complete combustion can occur in the engine, and more thorough oxidation and reduction of the exhaust gases can occur in the catalytic converter. The object is to maintain a stoichiometric air/fuel mixture, which is chemically correct for theoretically complete combustion. The stoichiometric ratio is 14.7:1 (air to fuel). At that point, the converter's efficiency is greatest in oxidizing and reducing HC, CO, and NOx into CO_2, H_2O, O_2, and N_2.

Components used in the system include an oxygen sensor, installed in the exhaust manifold upstream of the converter, a three way oxidation reduction catalytic converter, an electronic control unit, and the fuel injection system itself.

The oxygen sensor reads the oxygen content of the exhaust gases. It generates an electric signal which is sent to the control unit. The control unit then decides how to adjust the mixture to keep it at the correct air/fuel ratio. For example, if the mixture is too lean, the control unit increases the fuel metering

to the injectors. The monitoring process is a continual one, so that fine mixture adjustments are going on at all times.

The system has two modes of operation: open loop and closed loop. Open loop operation takes place when the engine is still cold. In this mode, the control unit ignores signals from the oxygen sensor and provides a fixed signal to the fuel injection unit. Closed loop operation takes place when the engine and catalytic converter have warmed to normal operating temperature. In closed loop operation, the control unit uses the oxygen sensor signals to adjust the mixture. The burned mixture's oxygen content is read by the oxygen sensor, which continues to signal the control unit, and so on. Thus, the closed loop mode is an interdependent system of information feedback.

Mixture is, of course, not readily adjustable in this system. All system adjustments require the use of a CO meter. Thus, they should be entrusted to a qualified technician (ASE certified) with access to the equipment and special training in the system's repair. The only regularly scheduled maintenance is replacement of the oxygen sensor at 30,000 mile intervals. This procedure is covered in the following section.

It should be noted that proper operation of the system is entirely dependent on the oxygen sensor. Thus, if the sensor is not replaced at the correct interval, or if the sensor fails during normal operation, the engine fuel mixture will be incorrect, resulting in poor fuel economy, starting problems, or stumbling and stalling of the engine when warm.

Oxygen Sensor

INSPECTION AND REPLACEMENT

▶ **See Figures 36 and 37**

An exhaust gas sensor warning light will illuminate on the instrument panel when the car has reached 30,000 miles This is a signal that the oxygen sensor must be replaced. It is important to replace the oxygen sensor every 30,000 miles, to ensure proper monitoring and control of the engine air/fuel mixture. Refer to "Maintenance Reminder Lights" section.

The following service procedure is recommend by Nissan Motor Company for all models to 1987 year, after this point complete Engine Self-Diagnosis is necessary. The oxygen sensor can be inspected using the following procedure:

1. Start the engine and allow it to reach normal operating temperature.
2. Run the engine at approximately 2,000 rpm under no load. Block the front wheels and set the parking brake.
3. An inspection lamp has been provided on the bottom of the control unit, which is located in the passenger compartment (refer to the illustrations for location of control unit). If the oxygen sensor is operating correctly, the inspection lamp will go on and off more than 9 times in 10 seconds. The inspection lamp can be more easily seen with the aid of a mirror.
4. If the lamp does not go on and off as specified, the system is not operating correctly. Check the battery, ignition system, engine oil and coolant levels,

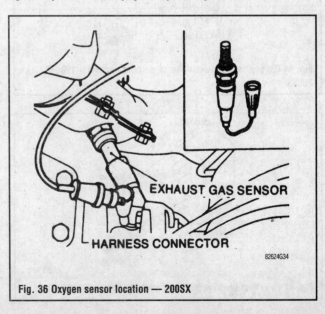

Fig. 36 Oxygen sensor location — 200SX

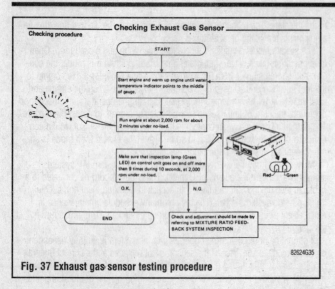

Fig. 37 Exhaust gas sensor testing procedure

all fuses, the fuel injection wiring harness connectors, all vacuum hoses, the oil filler cap and dipstick for proper seating, and the valve clearance and engine compression. If all of these parts are in good order, and the inspection lamp still does not go on and off at least 9 times in 10 seconds the oxygen sensor is probably faulty. However, the possibility exists that the malfunction could be in the fuel injection control unit. The system should be tested by a qualified technician (ASE certified) with specific training in the "Mixture Ratio Feedback System".

To replace the oxygen sensor:

5. Disconnect the negative battery cable and the sensor electrical lead. Unscrew the sensor from the exhaust manifold.

6. Coat the threads of the replacement sensor with a nickel base anti-seize compound. Do not use other types of compounds, since they may electrically insulate the sensor. Do not get compound on sensor housing. Install the sensor into the manifold. On models through 1987, installation torque for the sensor is 18–25 ft. lbs.; on 1988 and later models, torque is 30–37 ft. lbs. (Note, the 1987 200SX model oxygen sensor torque is also 30–37 ft. lbs.) Connect the electrical lead. Be careful handling the electrical lead. It is easily damaged.

7. Reconnect the battery cable.

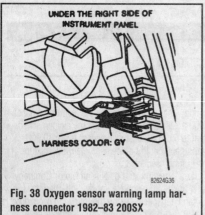

Fig. 38 Oxygen sensor warning lamp harness connector 1982–83 200SX

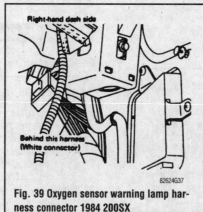

Fig. 39 Oxygen sensor warning lamp harness connector 1984 200SX

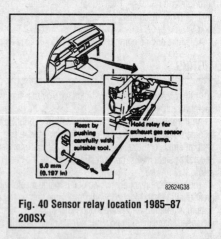

Fig. 40 Sensor relay location 1985–87 200SX

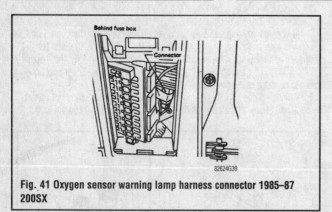

Fig. 41 Oxygen sensor warning lamp harness connector 1985–87 200SX

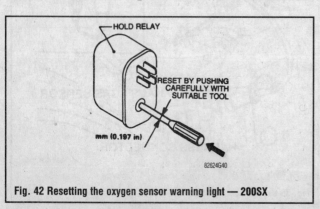

Fig. 42 Resetting the oxygen sensor warning light — 200SX

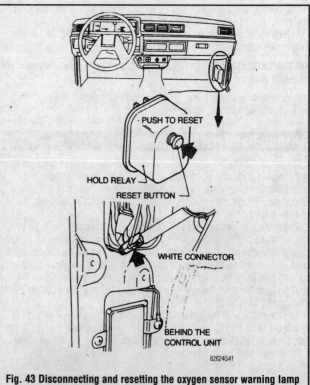

Fig. 43 Disconnecting and resetting the oxygen sensor warning lamp 1984–87 Stanza (except station wagon)

➡The oxygen sensor is installed in the exhaust manifold and is removed in the same manner as a spark plug. Exercise care when handling the sensor do not drop or handle the sensor roughly. Care should be used not to get compound on the sensor itself.

Maintenance Reminder Lights

RESETTING

▶ **See Figures 38 thru 43**

On models with a sensor relay, reset the relay by pushing or inserting a small screwdriver into the reset hole. Reset relay at 30,000 and 60,000 miles. At 90,000 miles, locate and disconnect warning light wire connector.

On models without sensor light relay and Canada models locate and disconnect the warning light harness connector. The reminder light will no longer function. Refer to the illustrations.

WARNING LIGHT CONNECTOR LOCATIONS

After 30,000 miles on Datsun/Nissan (1982–83) 200SX Model disconnect a green/green and white stripe wire under the right side of the instrument panel. On (1984) 200SX models disconnect white connector under the right side of the instrument panel.

On 1985–87 200SX vehicles disconnect the warning lamp harness connector behind the fuse box after 90,000 miles. The sensor relay is located is located to the right of the center console.

On 1984–86 Stanza models disconnect yellow-yellow/green, behind left kick panel. The sensor relay is located on the right side kick panel area.

On 1987 Stanza models disconnect green-brown (with tag), above fuse box. The sensor relay is located on the right side kick panel area.

On 1986–87 Stanza wagon disconnect red-yellow or red/blue, behind instrument panel. On the Stanza wagons the warning lamp relay is located under the passenger seat.

NISSAN ELECTRONIC CONCENTRATED CONTROL (PORT FUEL INJECTION) SYSTEM (ECCS)

General Information

The Nissan Electronic Concentrated Control System (ECCS) is an air flow controlled, port fuel injection and engine control system. The ECCS electronic control unit consists of a microcomputer, inspection lamps, a diagnostic mode selector and connectors for signal input and output and for power supply. The electronic control unit, or ECU, controls the following functions:

- Amount of injected fuel
- Ignition timing
- Mixture ratio feedback
- Pressure regulator control
- Exhaust Gas Recirculation (EGR) operation
- Idle speed control
- Fuel pump operation
- Air regulator control
- Air Injection Valve (AIV) operation
- Self-diagnostics
- Air flow meter self-cleaning control
- Fail safe system

SYSTEM COMPONENTS

Crank Angle Sensor

▶ **See Figure 44**

The crank angle sensor is a basic component of the ECCS system. It monitors engine speed and piston position, as well as sending signals which the ECU uses to control fuel injection, ignition timing and other functions. The crank angle sensor has a rotor plate and a wave forming circuit. On all models, the rotor plate has 360 slits for 1° signals (crank angle). On models equipped with VG30E engine, the rotor plate also consists of 6 slits for 120° signal (engine speed). On models equipped with CA20E, CA18ET, CA18DE and KA24E engines, the rotor plate also consists of 4 slits for 180° signal (engine speed).

The light emitting diodes (LED's) and photo diodes are built into the wave forming circuit. When the rotor plate passes the space between the LED and the photo diode, the slits of the rotor plate continually cut the light which is sent to the photo diode from the LED. This generates rough shaped pulses which are converted into ON/OFF pulses by the wave forming circuit and then sent to the ECU.

Cylinder Head Temperature Sensor

▶ **See Figure 45**

The cylinder head temperature sensor monitors changes in cylinder head temperature and transmits a signal to the ECU. The temperature sensing unit employs a thermistor which is sensitive to the change in temperature, with electrical resistance decreasing as temperature rises.

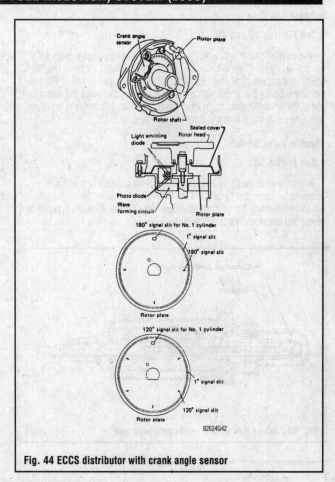

Fig. 44 ECCS distributor with crank angle sensor

Air Flow Meter

▶ **See Figures 46 and 47**

The air flow meter measures the mass flow rate of intake air. The volume of air entering the engine is measured by the use of a hot wire placed in the intake air stream. The control unit sends current to the wire to maintain it at a preset temperature. As the intake air moves past the wire, it removes heat and the control unit must increase the voltage to the wire to maintain it at the preset temperature. By measuring the amount of current necessary to maintain the temperature of the wire in the air stream, the ECU knows exactly how much air is entering the engine. A self-cleaning system briefly heats the hot air wire to

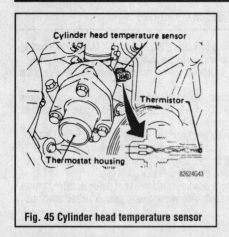

Fig. 45 Cylinder head temperature sensor

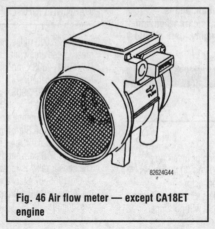

Fig. 46 Air flow meter — except CA18ET engine

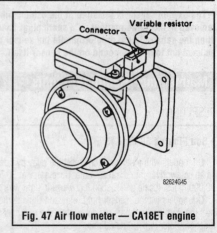

Fig. 47 Air flow meter — CA18ET engine

approximately 1832°F (1000°C) after engine shutdown to burn off any dust or contaminants on the wire.

Exhaust Gas Sensor

♦ See Figures 48 and 49

The exhaust gas sensor, which is placed in the exhaust pipe, monitors the amount of oxygen in the exhaust gas. The sensor is made of ceramic titania which changes electrical resistance at the ideal air/fuel ratio (14.7:1). The control unit supplies the sensor with approximately 1 volt and takes the output voltage of the sensor depending on its resistance. The oxygen sensor is equipped with a heater to bring it to operating temperature quickly.

Throttle Valve Switch

♦ See Figure 50

A throttle valve switch is attached to the throttle chamber and operates in response to accelerator pedal movement. The switch has an idle contact and a full throttle contact. The idle contact closes when the throttle valve is positioned at idle and opens when it is in any other position.

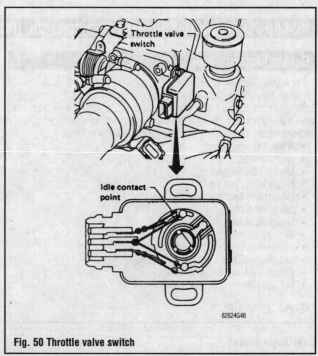

Fig. 50 Throttle valve switch

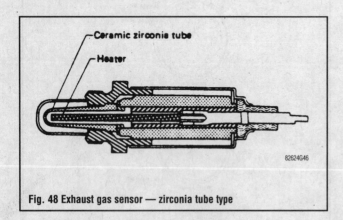

Fig. 48 Exhaust gas sensor — zirconia tube type

Fuel Injector

♦ See Figure 51

The fuel injector is a small, precision solenoid valve. As the ECU sends an injection signal to each injector, the coil built into the injector pulls the needle valve back and fuel is injected through the nozzle and into the intake manifold. The amount of fuel injected is dependent on how long the signal is (pulse duration); the longer the signal, the more fuel delivered.

Detonation Sensor (Turbo Model)

♦ See Figure 52

The detonation sensor is attached to the cylinder block and senses engine knocking conditions. A knocking vibration from the cylinder block is applied as pressure to the piezoelectric element. This vibrational pressure is then converted into a voltage signal which is delivered as output.

Fuel Temperature Sensor

♦ See Figure 53

A fuel temperature sensor is built into the fuel pressure regulator. When the fuel temperature is higher than the preprogrammed level, the ECU will enrich the fuel injected to compensate for temperature expansion. The temperature sensor and pressure regulator should be replaced as an assembly if either malfunc-

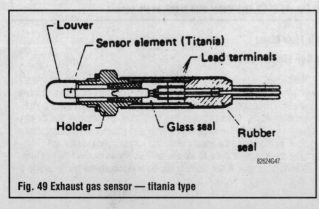

Fig. 49 Exhaust gas sensor — titania type

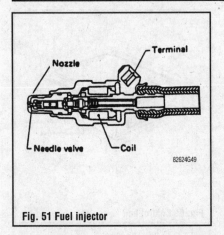

Fig. 51 Fuel injector

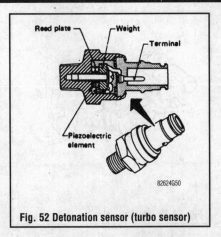

Fig. 52 Detonation sensor (turbo sensor)

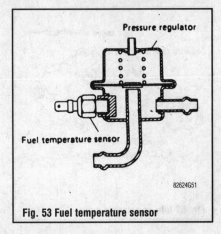

Fig. 53 Fuel temperature sensor

tions. The electric fuel pump with an integral damper is installed in the fuel tank. It is a vane roller type with the electric motor cooled by the fuel itself. The fuel filter is of metal construction in order to withstand the high fuel system pressure. The fuel pump develops 61–71 psi, but the pressure regulator keeps system pressure at 36 psi in operation.

Power Transistor

▶ See Figures 54 and 55

The ignition signal from the ECU is amplified by the power transistor, which turns the ignition coil primary circuit on and off, inducing the necessary high voltage in the secondary circuit to fire the spark plugs. Ignition timing is controlled according to engine operating conditions, with the optimum timing advance for each driving condition preprogrammed into the ECU memory.

Vehicle Speed Sensor

▶ See Figure 56

The vehicle speed sensor provides a vehicle speed signal to the ECU. On conventional speedometers, the speed sensor consists of a reed switch which transforms vehicle speed into a pulse signal. On digital electronic speedometers, the speed sensor consists of an LED, photo diode, shutter and wave forming circuit. It operates on the same principle as the crank angle sensor.

Swirl Control Valve (SCV) Control Solenoid Valve

The SCV control solenoid valve cuts the intake manifold vacuum signal for the swirl control valve. It responds to ON/OFF signal from the ECU. When the solenoid is off, the vacuum signal from the intake manifold is cut. When the control unit sends an ON signal, the coil pulls the plunger and feeds the vacuum signal to the swirl control valve actuator.

Idle-Up Solenoid Valve

▶ See Figure 57

An idle-up solenoid valve is attached to the intake collector to stabilize idle speed when the engine load is heavy because of electrical load, power steering load, etc. An air regulator provides an air bypass when the engine is cold in order to increase idle speed during warm-up (fast idle). A bi-metal, heater and rotary shutter are built into the air regulator. When bi-metal temperature is low, the air bypass port is open. As the engine starts and electric current flows through a heater, the bi-metal begins to rotate the shutter to close off the air bypass port. The air passage remains closed until the engine is stopped and the bi-metal temperature drops.

Air Injection Valve (AIV)

▶ See Figure 58

The Air Injection Valve (AIV) sends secondary air to the exhaust manifold, utilizing a vacuum caused by exhaust pulsation in the exhaust manifold. When the exhaust pressure is below atmospheric pressure (negative pressure), secondary air is sent to the exhaust manifold. When the exhaust pressure is above atmospheric pressure, the reed valves prevent secondary air from being sent to the air cleaner. The AIV control solenoid valve cuts the intake manifold vacuum signal for AIV control. The solenoid valve actuates in response to the ON/OFF signal from the ECU. When the solenoid is off, the vacuum signal from the intake manifold is cut. As the control unit outputs an on signal, the coil pulls the plunger downward and feeds the vacuum signal to the AIV control valve.

Exhaust Gas Recirculation (EGR) Vacuum Cut Solenoid Valve

The EGR vacuum cut solenoid valve is the same type as that of the AIV. The EGR system is controlled by the ECU; at both low and high engine speed (rpm), the solenoid valve turns on and the EGR valve cuts the exhaust gas recirculation

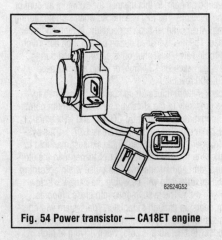

Fig. 54 Power transistor — CA18ET engine

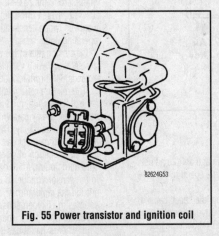

Fig. 55 Power transistor and ignition coil

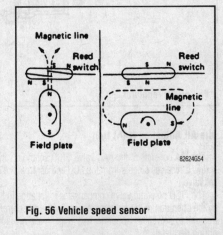

Fig. 56 Vehicle speed sensor

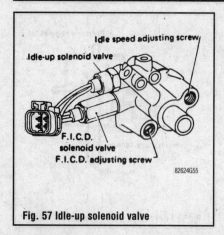

Fig. 57 Idle-up solenoid valve

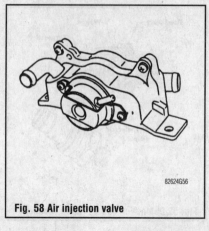

Fig. 58 Air injection valve

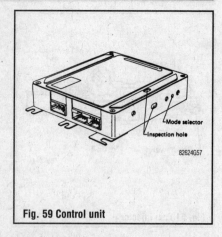

Fig. 59 Control unit

into the intake manifold. The pressure regulator control solenoid valve also actuates in response to the ON/OFF signal from the ECU. When it is off, a vacuum signal from the intake manifold is fed into the pressure regulator. As the control unit outputs an on signal, the coil pulls the plunger downward and cuts the vacuum signal.

Electronic Control Unit (ECU)

▶ See Figure 59

The ECU consists of a microcomputer, inspection lamps, a diagnostic mode selector, and connectors for signal input and output, and for power supply. The unit has control of the engine.

Air Regulator

▶ See Figure 60

The air regulator provides an air bypass when the engine is cold for the purpose of a fast idle during warm-up. A bi-metal, heater and rotary shutter are built into the air regulator. When the bi-metal temperature is low, the air bypass port is open. As the engine starts and electric current flows through a heater, the bi-metal begins to rotate the shutter to close off the bypass port. The air passage remains closed until the engine is stopped and the bi-metal temperature drops.

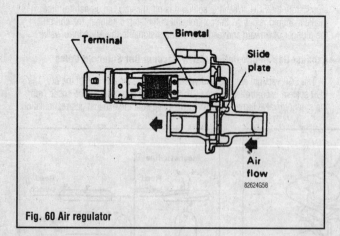

Fig. 60 Air regulator

Idle Air Adjusting (IAA) Unit

The IAA consists of the AAC valve, FICD solenoid valve and an idle adjust screw. It receives signals from the ECU and controls the idle speed to the preset valve.

The FICD solenoid valve compensates for change in the idle speed caused by the operation of the air compressor. A vacuum control valve is installed in this unit to prevent an abnormal rise in the intake manifold vacuum pressure during deceleration.

Auxiliary Air Control (AAC) Valve

▶ See Figure 61

The AAC valve is attached to the intake collector. The ECU actuates the AAC valve by an ON/OFF pulse of approximately 160 Hz. The longer that ON duty is left on, the larger the amount of air that will flow through the AAC valve.

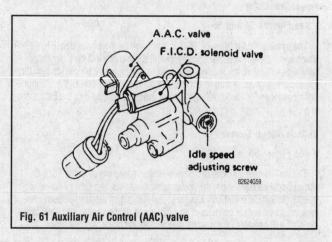

Fig. 61 Auxiliary Air Control (AAC) valve

SYSTEM OPERATION

In operation, the on-board computer (control unit) calculates the basic injection pulse width by processing signals from the crank angle sensor and air flow meter. Receiving signals from each sensor which detects various engine operating conditions, the computer adds various enrichments (which are preprogrammed) to the basic injection amount. In this manner, the optimum amount of fuel is delivered through the injectors. The fuel is enriched when starting, during warm-up, when accelerating, when cylinder head temperature is high and when operating under a heavy load. The fuel is leaned during deceleration according to the closing rate of the throttle valve. Fuel shut-off is accomplished during deceleration, when vehicle speed exceeds 137 mph, or when engine speed exceeds 6400 rpm for about 500 revolutions.

The mixture ratio feedback system (closed loop control) is designed to control the air/fuel mixture precisely to the stoichiometric or optimum point so that the 3-way catalytic converter can minimize CO, HC and NOx emissions simultaneously. The optimum air/fuel fuel mixture is 14.7:1. This system uses an exhaust gas (oxygen) sensor located in the exhaust manifold to give an indication of whether the fuel mixture is richer or leaner than the stoichiometric point. The control unit adjusts the injection pulse width according to the sensor voltage so the mixture ratio will be within the narrow window around the stoichiometric fuel ratio. The system goes into closed loop as soon as the oxygen sensor heats up enough to register. The system will operate under open loop when starting the engine, when the engine temperature is cold, when exhaust gas sensor temperature is cold, when driving at high speeds or under heavy load, at idle (after mixture ratio learning is completed), during deceleration, if the exhaust gas sensor malfunctions, or when the exhaust gas sensor monitors a rich condition for more than 10 seconds and during deceleration.

Ignition timing is controlled in response to engine operating conditions. The optimum ignition timing in each driving condition is preprogrammed in the computer. The signal from the control unit is transmitted to the power transistor and controls ignition timing. The idle speed is also controlled according to engine operating conditions, temperature and gear position. On manual transmission models, if battery voltage is less than 12 volts for a few seconds, a higher idle speed will be maintained by the control unit to improve charging function.

There is a fail-safe system built into the ECCS control unit. If the output voltage of the air flow meter is extremely low, the ECU will substitute a preprogrammed value for the air flow meter signal and allow the vehicle to be driven as long as the engine speed is kept below 2000 rpm. If the cylinder head temperature sensor circuit is open, the control unit clamps the warm-up enrichment at a certain amount. This amount is almost the same as that when the cylinder head temperature is between 68–176°F (20–80°C). If the fuel pump circuit malfunctions, the fuel pump relay comes on until the engine stops. This allows the fuel pump to receive power from the relay.

SERVICE PRECAUTIONS

- Do not operate the fuel pump when the fuel lines are empty.
- Do not reuse fuel hose clamps.
- Do not disconnect the ECCS harness connectors before the battery ground cable has been disconnected.
- Make sure all ECCS connectors are fastened securely. A poor connection can cause an extremely high surge voltage in the coil and condenser and result in damage to integrated circuits.
- Keep the ECCS harness at least 4 in. away from adjacent harnesses to prevent an ECCS system malfunction due to external electronic "noise."
- Keep all parts and harnesses dry during service.
- Before attempting to remove any parts, turn **OFF** the ignition switch and disconnect the battery ground cable.
- Always use a 12 volt battery as a power source.
- Do not attempt to disconnect the battery cables with the engine running.
- Do not depress the accelerator pedal when starting.
- Do not rev up the engine immediately after starting or just prior to shutdown.
- Do not attempt to disassemble the ECCS control unit under any circumstances.
- If a battery cable is disconnected, the memory will return to the ROM (programmed) values. Engine operation may vary slightly, but this is not an indication of a problem. Do not replace parts because of a slight variation.
- If installing a 2-way or CB radio, keep the antenna as far as possible away from the electronic control unit. Keep the antenna feeder line at least 8 in. away from the ECCS harness and do not let the 2 run parallel for a long distance. Be sure to ground the radio to the vehicle body.

Self-Diagnostic System

DIAGNOSIS & TESTING

▶ **See Figures 62, 63, 64, 65 and 66**

The self-diagnostic function is useful for diagnosing malfunctions in major sensors and actuators of the ECCS system. There are 5 modes in self-diagnostics on all models except Stanza. On Stanza, there are 2 modes in self-diagnostics

Mode 1

EXCEPT STANZA

During closed loop operation, the green inspection lamp turns ON when a lean condition is detected and OFF when a rich condition is detected. During open loop operation, the red inspection lamp stays OFF.

STANZA

During this mode, the red LED in the ECU and the CHECK ENGINE LIGHT on the instrument panel stay ON. If either remain OFF, check the bulb in the CHECK ENGINE LIGHT or the red LED.

Mode 2

EXCEPT STANZA

The green inspection lamp function is the same as in Mode 1. During closed loop operation, the red inspection lamp turns ON and OFF simultaneously with the green inspection lamp when the mixture ratio is controlled within the specified value. During open loop operation, the red inspection lamp stays OFF.

STANZA

This models uses Mode 2 for self-diagnostic results and exhaust gas sensor monitor.

When in Mode 2 (self-diagnostic results), a malfunction code is indicated by the number of flashes from the red LED or the CHECK ENGINE LIGHT.

When in Mode 2 (exhaust gas sensor monitor), the CHECK ENGINE LIGHT and red LED display the condition of the fuel mixture (rich/lean) which is monitored by the exhaust gas sensor. If 2 exhaust sensors are used (right side and left side), the left exhaust gas sensor monitor operates first, when selecting this mode.

Mode 3

This mode is the same as the former self-diagnosis mode.

Mode III — Self-Diagnostic System

The E.C.U. constantly monitors the function of these sensors and actuators, regardless of ignition key position. If a malfunction occurs, the information is stored in the E.C.U. and can be retrieved from the memory by turning on the diagnostic mode selector, located on the side of the E.C.U. When activated, the malfunction is indicated by flashing a red and a green L.E.D. (Light Emitting Diode), also located on the E.C.U. Since all the self-diagnostic results are stored in the E.C.U.'s memory even intermittent malfunctions can be diagnosed.

A malfunctioning part's group is indicated by the number of both the red and the green L.E.D.s flashing. First, the red L.E.D. flashes and the green flashes follow. The red L.E.D. refers to the number of tens while the green one refers to the number of units. For example, when the red L.E.D. flashes once and then the green one flashes twice, this means the number "12" showing the air flow meter signal is malfunctioning. In this way, all the problems are classified by the code numbers.

- When engine fails to start, crank engine more than two seconds before starting self-diagnosis.
- Before starting self-diagnosis, do not erase stored memory. If doing so, self-diagnosis function for intermittent malfunctions would be lost.

The stored memory would be lost if:

1. Battery terminal is disconnected.
2. After selecting Mode III, Mode IV is selected.

DISPLAY CODE TABLE

Code No.	Detected items
11	Crank angle sensor circuit
12	Air flow meter circuit
13	Water temperature sensor circuit
21	Ignition signal missing in primary coil
22	Fuel pump circuit
34	Detonation sensor
44	No malfunctioning in the above circuit

82624G60

Fig. 62 Trouble codes—1988 200SX Models with the CA18ET engine

Mode III — Self-Diagnostic System

The E.C.U. constantly monitors the function of these sensors and actuators, regardless of ignition key position. If a malfunction occurs, the information is stored in the E.C.U. and can be retrieved from the memory by turning on the diagnostic mode selector, located on the side of the E.C.U. When activated, the malfunction is indicated by flashing a red and a green L.E.D. (Light Emitting Diode), also located on the E.C.U. Since all the self-diagnostic results are stored in the E.C.U.'s memory even intermittent malfunctions can be diagnosed.

A malfunctioning part's group is indicated by the number of both the red and the green L.E.D.s flashing. First, the red L.E.D. flashes and the green flashes follow. The red L.E.D. refers to the number of tens while the green one refers to the number of units. For example, when the red L.E.D. flashes once and then the green one flashes twice, this means the number "12" showing the air flow meter signal is malfunctioning. In this way, all the problems are classified by the code numbers.

- When engine fails to start, crank engine more than two seconds before starting self-diagnosis.
- Before starting self-diagnosis, do not erase stored memory. If doing so, self-diagnosis function for intermittent malfunctions would be lost.

The stored memory would be lost if:
1. Battery terminal is disconnected.
2. After selecting Mode III, Mode IV is selected.

DISPLAY CODE TABLE

Code No.	Detected items
11	Crank angle sensor circuit
12	Air flow meter circuit
13	Cylinder head temperature sensor circuit
14	Vehicle speed sensor circuit
21	Ignition signal missing in primary coil
22	Fuel pump circuit
23	Idle switch circuit
31	E.C.U. (E.C.C.S. control unit)
33	Exhaust gas sensor circuit
42	Fuel temperature sensor circuit
55	No malfunction in the above circuit

82624G61

Fig. 63 Trouble codes—1988 200SX Models with the VG30E engine

Mode III — Self-Diagnostic System

The E.C.U. constantly monitors the function of these sensors and actuators, regardless of ignition key position. If a malfunction occurs, the information is stored in the E.C.U. and can be retrieved from the memory by turning on the diagnostic mode selector, located on the side of the E.C.U. When activated, the malfunction is indicated by flashing a red and a green L.E.D. (Light Emitting Diode), also located on the E.C.U. Since all the self-diagnostic results are stored in the E.C.U.'s memory even intermittent malfunctions can be diagnosed.

A malfunctioning part's group is indicated by the number of both the red and the green L.E.D.s flashing. First, the red L.E.D. flashes and the green flashes follow. The red L.E.D. refers to the number of tens while the green one refers to the number of units. For example, when the red L.E.D. flashes once and then the green one flashes twice, this means the number "12" showing the air flow meter signal is malfunctioning. In this way, all the problems are classified by the code numbers.

- When engine fails to start, crank engine more than two seconds before starting self-diagnosis.
- Before starting self-diagnosis, do not erase stored memory. If doing so, self-diagnosis function for intermittent malfunctions would be lost.

The stored memory would be lost if:
1. Battery terminal is disconnected.
2. After selecting Mode III, Mode IV is selected.

DISPLAY CODE TABLE

Code No.	Detected items
11	Crank angle sensor circuit
12	Air flow meter circuit
13.	Water temperature sensor circuit
14	Vehicle speed sensor circuit
21	Ignition signal missing in primary coil
22	Fuel pump circuit
23	Idle switch circuit
24	Full switch circuit
31	E.C.U.
33	Exhaust gas sensor circuit
41	Air temperature sensor circuit
55	No malfunctioning in the above circuit

82624G62

Fig. 64 Trouble codes—1988 200SX Models with the CA20E engine

Mode 4

During this mode, the inspection lamps monitor the ON/OFF condition of the idle switch, starter switch and vehicle speed sensor.

In switches ON/OFF diagnosis system, ON/OFF operation of the following switches can be detected continuously:
- Idle switch
- Starter switch
- Vehicle speed sensor

1. Idle switch and starter switch–the switches ON/OFF status at the point when Mode IV is selected is stored in ECU memory. When either switch is turned from ON to OFF or OFF to ON, the red LED on ECU alternately comes on and goes off each time switching is detected.

2. Vehicle speed sensor–The switches ON/OFF status at the point when Mode IV is selected is stored in ECU memory. When vehicle speed is 12 mph (20 km/h) or slower, the green LED on ECU is off. When vehicle speed exceeds 12 mph (20 km/h), the green LED on ECU comes ON.

Mode 5

The moment a malfunction is detected, the display will be presented immediately by flashing the inspection lamps during the driving test.

In real time diagnosis, if any of the following items are judged to be faulty, a malfunction is indicated immediately:
- Crank angle sensor
- Ignition signal
- Air flow meter output signal
- Fuel pump (some models)

Consequently, this diagnosis is a very effective measure to diagnose whether the above systems cause the malfunction or not, during driving test. Compared with self-diagnosis, real time diagnosis is very sensitive, and can detect mal-

functioning conditions in a moment. Further, items regarded to be malfunctions in this diagnosis are not stored in ECU memory.

To switch the modes, turn the ignition switch **ON**, then turn the diagnostic mode selector on the control unit fully clockwise and wait for the inspection lamps to flash. Count the number of flashes until the inspection lamps have flashed the number of the desired mode, then immediately turn the diagnostic mode selector fully counterclockwise.

➡ **When the ignition switch is turned OFF during diagnosis in each mode, and then turned back on again after the power to the control unit has dropped off completely, the diagnosis will automatically return to Mode 1.**

The stored memory will be lost if the battery terminal is disconnected, or Mode 4 is selected after selecting Mode 3. However, if the diagnostic mode selector is kept turned fully clockwise, it will continue to change in the order of Mode 1, 2, 3, etc., and in this case, the stored memory will not be erased.

In Mode 3, the control unit constantly monitors the function of sensors and actuators regardless of ignition key position. If a malfunction occurs, the information is stored in the control unit and can be retrieved from the memory by turning **ON** the diagnostic mode selector on the side of the control unit. When activated, the malfunction is indicated by flashing a red and green LED (also located on the control unit). Since all the self-diagnostic results are stored in the control unit memory, even intermittent malfunctions can be diagnosed. A malfunctioning part's group is indicated by the number of both red and green LED's flashing. First, the red LED flashes and the green flashes follow. The red LED refers to the number of tens, while the green refers to the number of units. If the red LED flashes twice and the green LED flashes once, a Code 21 is being displayed. All malfunctions are classified by their trouble code number.

The diagnostic result is retained in the control unit memory until the starter is operated 50 times after a diagnostic item is judged to be malfunctioning. The

Mode III — Self-Diagnostic System

The E.C.U. constantly monitors the function of these sensors and actuators, regardless of ignition key position. If a malfunction occurs, the information is stored in the E.C.U. and can be retrieved from the memory by turning on the diagnostic mode selector, located on the side of the E.C.U. When activated, the malfunction is indicated by flashing a red and a green L.E.D. (Light Emitting Diode), also located on the E.C.U. Since all the self-diagnostic results are stored in the E.C.U.'s memory even intermittent malfunctions can be diagnosed.

A malfunctioning part's group is indicated by the number of both the red and the green L.E.D.s flashing. First, the red L.E.D. flashes and the green flashes follow. The red L.E.D. refers to the number of tens while the green one refers to the number of units. For example, when the red L.E.D. flashes once and then the green one flashes twice, this means the number "12" showing the air flow meter signal is malfunctioning. In this way, all the problems are classified by the code numbers.

- When engine fails to start, crank engine more than two seconds before starting self-diagnosis.
- Before starting self-diagnosis, do not erase stored memory. If doing so, self-diagnosis function for intermittent malfunctions would be lost.

The stored memory would be lost if:
1. Battery terminal is disconnected.
2. After selecting Mode III, Mode IV is selected.

DISPLAY CODE TABLE

Code No.	Detected items
11	Crank angle sensor circuit
12	Air flow meter circuit
13	Water temperature sensor circuit
14	Vehicle speed sensor circuit
21	Ignition signal missing in primary coil
22	Fuel pump circuit
23	Idle switch circuit
24	Full switch circuit
31	E.C.U.
32*	E.G.R. function
33	Exhaust gas sensor circuit
35*	Exhaust gas temperature sensor circuit
41	Air temperature sensor circuit
45*	Injector leak
55	No malfunctioning in the above circuit

*: For California only

82624G63

Fig. 65 Trouble codes—1988–92 Stanza Models

Self-diagnosis — Mode III (Self-diagnostic system)

The E.C.U. constantly monitors the function of these sensors and actuators, regardless of ignition key position. If a malfunction occurs, the information is stored in the E.C.U. and can be retrieved from the memory by turning on the diagnostic mode selector, located on the side of the E.C.U. When activated, the malfunction is indicated by flashing a red and a green L.E.D. (Light Emitting Diode), also located on the E.C.U. Since all the self-diagnostic results are stored in the E.C.U.'s memory even intermittent malfunctions can be diagnosed.

A malfunction is indicated by the number of both red and green flashing L.E.D.s. First, the red L.E.D. flashes and the green flashes follow. The red L.E.D. corresponds to units of ten and the green L.E.D. corresponds to units of one. For example, when the red L.E.D. flashes once and the green L.E.D. flashes twice, this signifies the number "12", showing that the air flow meter signal is malfunctioning. All problems are classified by code numbers in this way.

- When the engine fails to start, crank it two or more seconds before beginning self-diagnosis.
- Before starting self-diagnosis, do not erase the stored memory before beginning self-diagnosis. If it is erased, the self-diagnosis function for intermittent malfunctions will be lost.

DISPLAY CODE TABLE

Code No.	Detected items	California	Non-California
11	Crank angle sensor circuit	X	X
12	Air flow meter circuit	X	X
13	Engine temperature sensor circuit	X	X
14	Vehicle speed sensor circuit	X	X
21	Ignition signal missing in primary coil	X	X
31	E.C.U. (E.C.C.S. control unit)	X	X
32	E.G.R. function	X	—
33	Exhaust gas sensor circuit	X	X
35	Exhaust gas temperature sensor circuit	X	—
43	Throttle sensor circuit	X	X
45	Injector leak	X	—
55	No malfunction in the above circuit	X	X

X: Available   —: Not available

82624G64

Fig. 66 Trouble codes—1989–92 240SX Models

diagnostic result will then be canceled automatically. If a diagnostic item which has been judged malfunctioning and stored in memory is again judged to be malfunctioning before the starter is operated 50 times, the second result will replace the previous one and stored in the memory until the starter is operated 50 more times.

In Mode 5 (real time diagnosis), if the crank angle sensor, ignition signal or air flow meter output signal are judged to be malfunctioning, the malfunction will be indicated immediately. This diagnosis is very effective for determining whether these systems are causing a malfunction during the driving test. Compared with self-diagnosis, real time diagnosis is very sensitive and can detect malfunctioning conditions immediately. However, malfunctioning items in this diagnosis mode are not stored in memory.

TESTING PRECAUTIONS

❋❋ CAUTION

Before connecting or disconnecting control unit ECU harness connectors, make sure the ignition switch is OFF and the negative bat- tery cable is disconnected to avoid the possibility of damage to the control unit.

- When performing ECU input/output signal diagnosis, remove the pin terminal retainer from the 20 and 16-pin connectors to make it easier to insert tester probes into the connector.
- When connecting or disconnecting pin connectors from the ECU, take care not to bend or break any pin terminals. Check that there are no bends or breaks on ECU pin terminals before attempting any connections.
- Before replacing any ECU, perform the ECU input/output signal diagnosis to make sure the ECU is functioning properly or not.
- After performing the Electronic Control System Inspection, perform the ECCS self-diagnosis and driving test.
- When measuring supply voltage of ECU controlled components with a circuit tester, separate one tester probe from another. If the 2 tester probes accidentally make contact with each other during measurement, a short circuit will result and damage the power transistor in the ECU.

VACUUM DIAGRAMS

Following are vacuum diagrams for most of the engine and emissions package combinations covered by this manual. Because vacuum circuits will vary based on various engine and vehicle options, always refer first to the vehicle emission control information label, if present. Should the label be missing, or should vehicle be equipped with a different engine from the vehicle's original equipment, refer to the diagrams below for the same or similar configuration.

If you wish to obtain a replacement emissions label, most manufacturers make the labels available for purchase. The labels can usually be ordered from a local dealer.

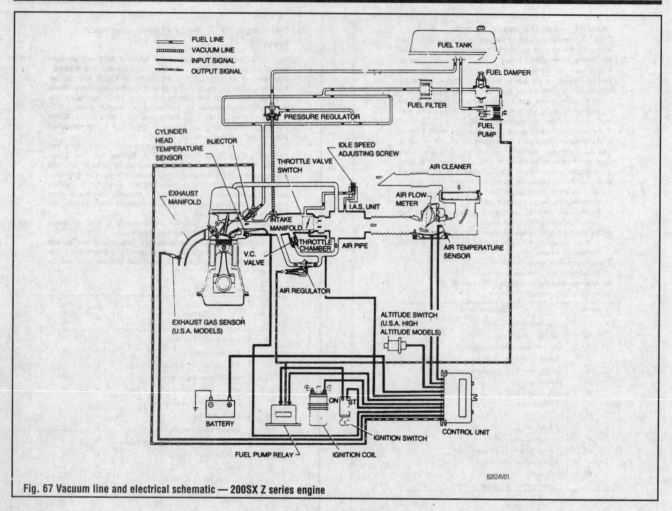

Fig. 67 Vacuum line and electrical schematic — 200SX Z series engine

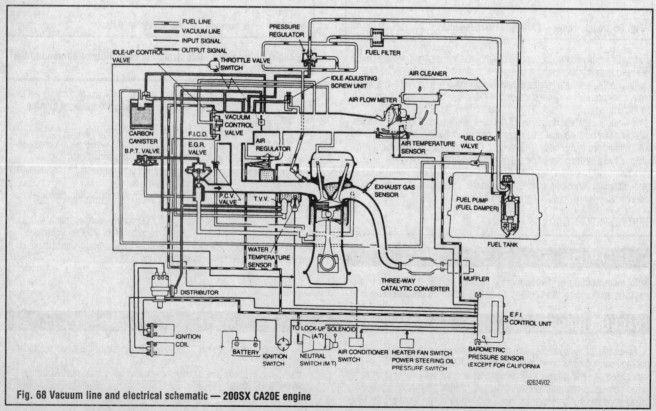

Fig. 68 Vacuum line and electrical schematic — 200SX CA20E engine

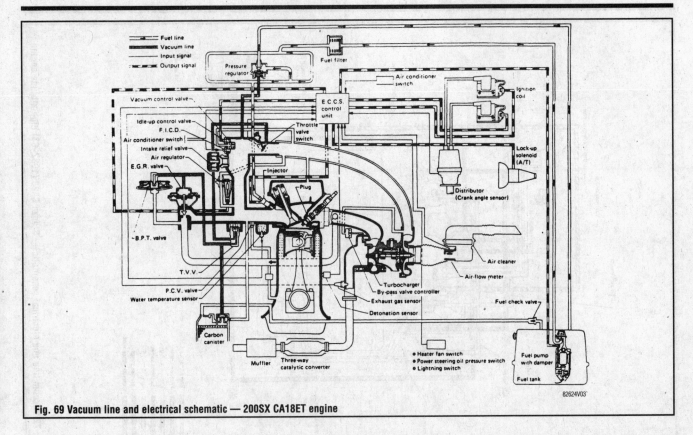

Fig. 69 Vacuum line and electrical schematic — 200SX CA18ET engine

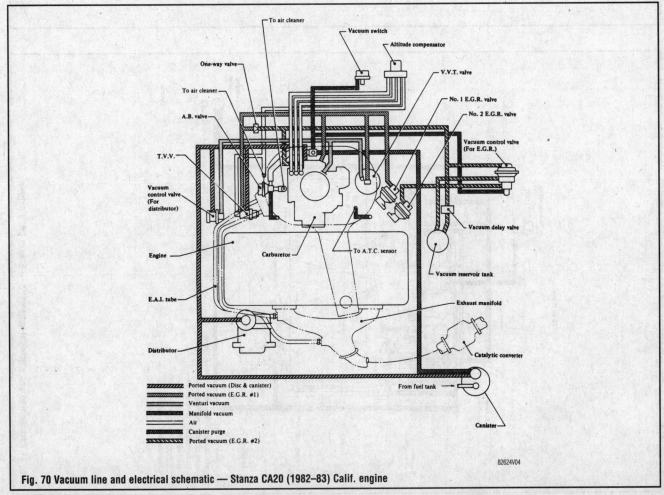

Fig. 70 Vacuum line and electrical schematic — Stanza CA20 (1982–83) Calif. engine

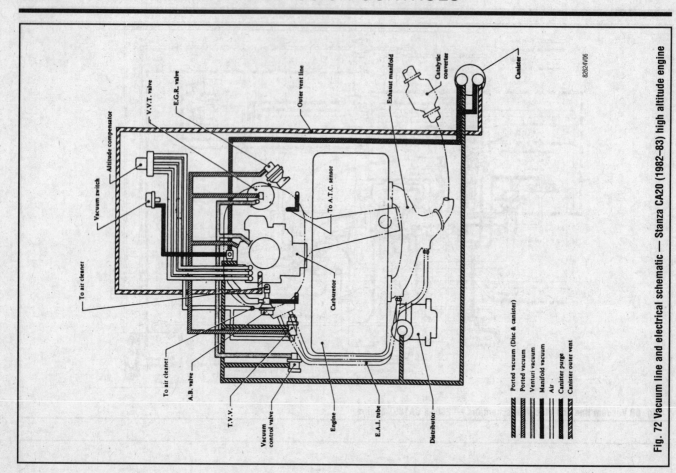

Fig. 72 Vacuum line and electrical schematic — Stanza CA20 (1982-83) high altitude engine

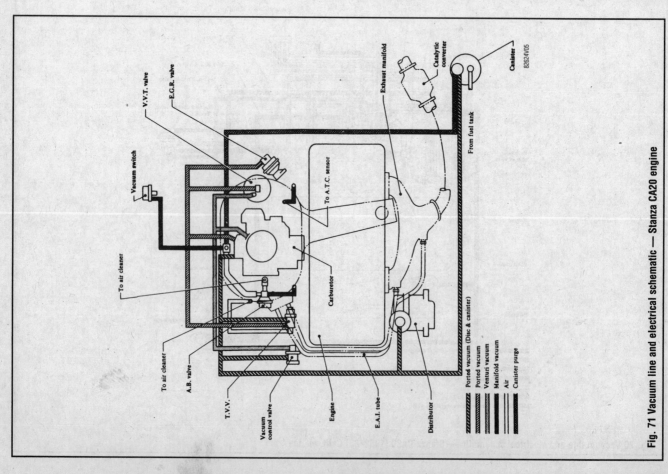

Fig. 71 Vacuum line and electrical schematic — Stanza CA20 engine

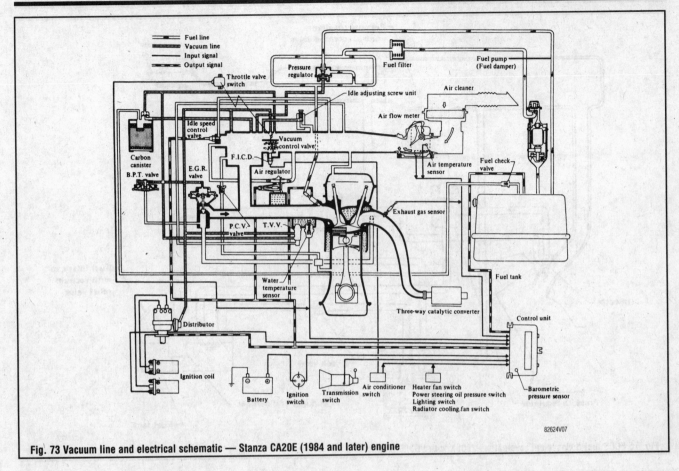

Fig. 73 Vacuum line and electrical schematic — Stanza CA20E (1984 and later) engine

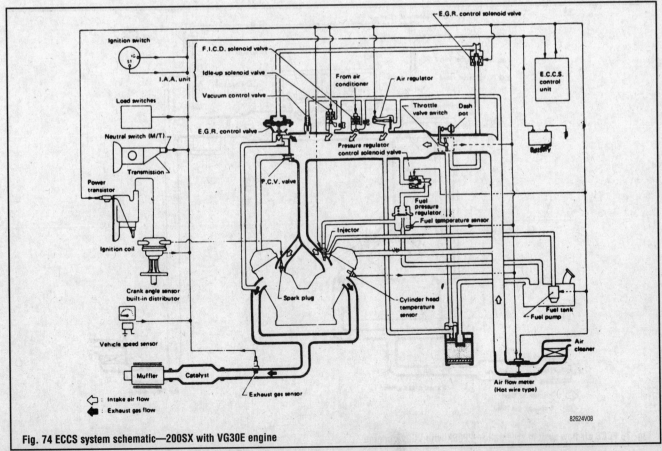

Fig. 74 ECCS system schematic—200SX with VG30E engine

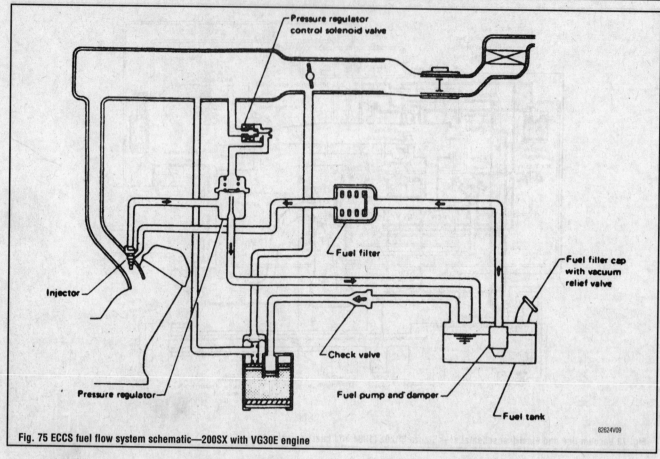

Fig. 75 ECCS fuel flow system schematic—200SX with VG30E engine

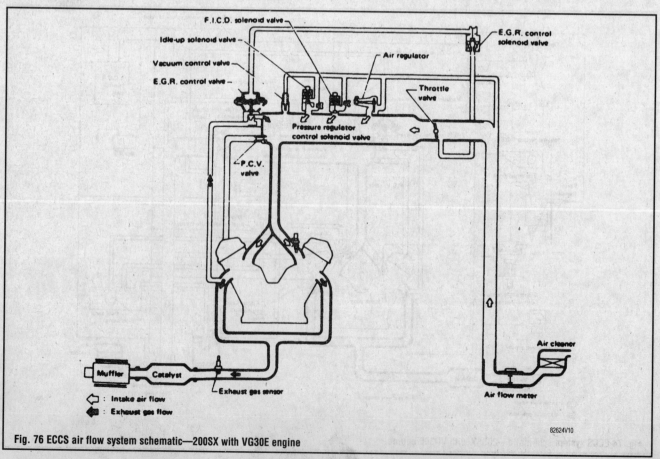

Fig. 76 ECCS air flow system schematic—200SX with VG30E engine

5

FUEL
SYSTEM

CARBURETED FUEL SYSTEM

Mechanical Fuel Pump

♦ See Figures 1 and 2

The fuel pump is a mechanically operated, diaphragm type driven by the fuel pump eccentric on the camshaft. The pump is located on the right rear side of the cylinder head (CA20 engine).

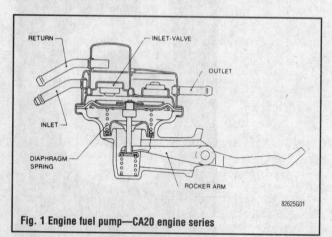

Fig. 1 Engine fuel pump—CA20 engine series

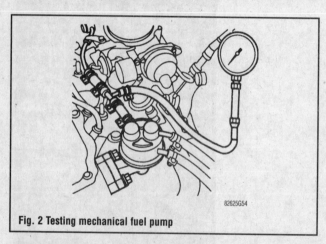

Fig. 2 Testing mechanical fuel pump

REMOVAL & INSTALLATION

❋❋ CAUTION

Never smoke when working around gasoline! Avoid all sources of sparks or ignition. Gasoline vapors are EXTREMELY volatile!

1. Disconnect the fuel lines from the fuel pump. Be sure to keep the line leading from the fuel tank up high to prevent the excess loss of fuel.
2. Remove the two fuel pump mounting nuts and the fuel pump assembly from the right side of the engine.
3. To install, use a new gasket, sealant and reverse the removal procedures. Torque the fuel pump bolts to 79 ft. lbs. Replace the fuel line hose clamps as necessary.

TESTING

Static Pressure

❋❋ CAUTION

Never smoke when working around gasoline! Avoid all sources of sparks or ignition. Gasoline vapors are EXTREMELY volatile!

1. Disconnect the fuel line at the carburetor. Using a T-connector, connect two rubber hoses to the connector, then install it between the fuel line and the carburetor fitting.

➡**When disconnecting the fuel line, be sure to place a container under the line to catch the excess fuel which will be present.**

2. Connect a fuel pump pressure gauge to the T-connector and secure it with a clamp.
3. Start the engine and check the pressure at various speeds. The pressure should be 2.8–3.8 psi (19.3–26.2 kpa). There is usually enough gas in the float bowl to perform this test.
4. If the pressure is OK, perform a capacity test. Remove the gauge and the T-connector assembly, then reinstall the fuel line to the carburetor.

Capacity Test

1. Disconnect the fuel line from the carburetor and place the line in a graduated container.
2. Fill the carburetor float bowl with gas.
3. Start the engine and run it for one minute at about 1,000 rpm. The pump should deliver 1.5 liter of volume per minute.

Carburetor

The carburetor used is a 2-barrel downdraft type with a low speed (primary) side and a high speed (secondary) side.

All models have an electrically operated anti-dieseling solenoid. As the ignition switch is turned off, the valve is energized and shuts off the supply of fuel to the idle circuit of the carburetor.

ADJUSTMENTS

Throttle Linkage

1. Disconnect the negative battery cable.
2. Remove the air cleaner.
3. Open the automatic choke valve by hand, while turning the throttle valve by pulling the throttle lever, then set the choke valve in the open position.

➡**If equipped with a vacuum controlled throttle positioner, use a vacuum hand pump to retract the throttle positioner rod.**

4. Adjust the throttle cable at the carburetor bracket, so that a 1.0–2.0mm of free pedal play exists.

Dashpot

♦ See Figure 3

A dashpot is used on carburetors with automatic transaxles and some manual transaxles. The dashpot slowly closes the throttle on automatic transmissions to prevent stalling and serves as an emission control device on all late model vehicles.

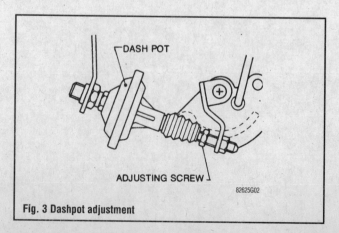

Fig. 3 Dashpot adjustment

The dashpot should be adjusted to contact the throttle lever on deceleration at approximately 1,400–1,600 rpm of engine operation.

➡ **Before attempting to adjust the dashpot, make sure the idle speed, timing and mixture adjustments are correct.**

1. Loosen the lock-nut (turn the dashpot, if necessary) and make sure the engine speed drops smoothly from 2,000 rpm to 1,000 rpm in 3 seconds.

2. If the dashpot has been removed from the carburetor, it must be adjusted when installed. Adjust the gap between the primary throttle valve and the inner carburetor wall, when the dashpot stem comes in contact with the throttle arm. The dashpot gap is 0.66–0.86mm (manual transaxle) or 0.49–0.69mm (automatic transaxle).

Secondary Throttle Linkage

▶ **See Figure 4**

All carburetors discussed in this book are two stage type carburetors. On this type of carburetor, the engine runs on the primary barrel most of the time, with the secondary barrel being used for acceleration purposes. When the throttle valve on the primary side opens to an angle of approximately 50° (from its fully closed position), the secondary throttle valve is pulled open by the connecting linkage. The 50° angle of throttle valve opening works out to a clearance measurement of 7.4–8.4mm (Stanza) between the throttle valve and the carburetor body. The easiest way to measure this is to use a drill bit. Drill bits from sizes H to P (standard letter size drill bits) should fit. Check the appendix in the back of the book for the exact size of the various drill bits. If an adjustment is necessary, bend the connecting link between the two linkage assemblies.

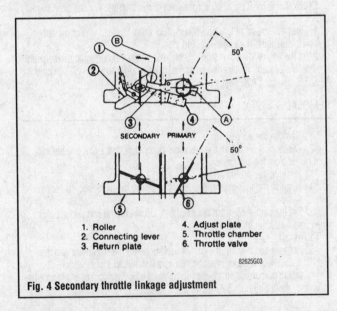

1. Roller
2. Connecting lever
3. Return plate
4. Adjust plate
5. Throttle chamber
6. Throttle valve

82625G03

Fig. 4 Secondary throttle linkage adjustment

Float Level

▶ **See Figure 5**

The fuel level is normal if it is within the lines on the window glass of the float chamber (or the sight glass) when the vehicle is resting on level ground and the engine is off.

If the fuel level is outside the lines, remove the float housing cover. Have an absorbent cloth under the cover to catch the fuel from the fuel bowl. Adjust the float level by bending the needle seat on the float.

The needle valve should have an effective stroke of about 1.5mm. When necessary, the needle valve stroke can be adjusted by bending the float stopper.

➡ **Be careful not to bend the needle valve rod when installing the float and baffle plate, if removed.**

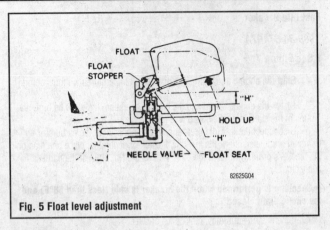

82625G04

Fig. 5 Float level adjustment

Fast Idle

▶ **See Figure 6**

➡ **On the Stanza models, the fast idle cam lever is located next to the fast idle cam screw, so the choke cover does not have to be removed. On the 1985 Stanza, disconnect the Fast Idle Breaker harness at the carburetor.**

1. Remove the carburetor from the vehicle. Refer to the necessary service procedures in this section.

✳✳ CAUTION

Never smoke when working around gasoline! Avoid all sources of sparks or ignition. Gasoline vapors are EXTREMELY volatile!

2. Remove the choke cover, then place the fast idle arm on the 2nd step of the fast idle cam. Using the correct wire gauge, measure the clearance A between the throttle valve and the wall of the throttle valve chamber (at the center of the throttle valve). It should be 0.66–0.80mm (MT) or 0.81–0.95mm (AT).

➡ **The first step of the fast idle adjustment procedure is not absolutely necessary.**

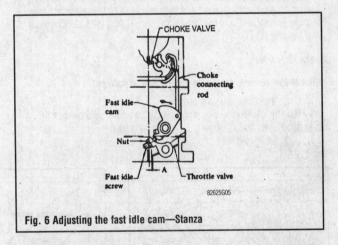

82625G05

Fig. 6 Adjusting the fast idle cam—Stanza

3. Install the carburetor on the engine.
4. Start the engine, warm it to operating temperatures and check the fast idle rpm. The cam should be at the 2nd step. Engine speed should be 2,400–2,700 rpm (MT) or 2,800–3,100 rpm (AT).
5. To adjust the fast idle speed, turn the fast idle adjusting screw counterclockwise to increase the fast idle speed and clockwise to decrease the fast idle speed.

Fast Idle Breaker

1985-86 STANZA

▶ **See Figure 7**

1. Start the engine and warm it to operating temperatures without racing it.
2. Check the engine speed and the breaker operation, it should be high revolution at the start, then idle speed when warm.
3. Disconnect the fast idle breaker harness connector at the carburetor. Using an ohmmeter, check the fast idle breaker for continuity; place one lead on the breaker's ground wire and the other lead on the No. 8 pin of the harness connector.

➡ **Checking is performed when the breaker is cold (less than 68°F) and the choke plate closed.**

4. If there is no continuity, replace the breaker.
5. If an ohmmeter is not available, check the breaker with the engine running (harness connector installed), if the breaker does not warm up, replace it.

Cam Follow Lever

STANZA

▶ **See Figure 8**

Hold the choke plate closed, turn the adjusting screw until there is no clearance between the cam follow lever and the fast idle cam.

Automatic Choke

1. With the engine cold, make sure the choke is fully closed (press the accelerator pedal all the way to the floor and release).
2. Check the choke linkage for binding. The choke plate should be easily opened and closed with your finger. If the choke sticks or binds, it can usually be freed with a liberal application of a carburetor cleaner made for the purpose. A couple of quick squirts normally does the trick; if not, the carburetor will have to be disassembled for repairs.
3. The choke is correctly adjusted when the index mark on the choke housing (notch) aligns with the center mark on the carburetor body. If the setting is incorrect, loosen the three screws clamping the choke body in place and rotate the choke cover left or right until the marks align. Tighten the screws carefully to avoid cracking the housing.

Choke Unloader

➡ **The choke assembly must be cold for this adjustment.**

1. Close the choke valve completely.
2. Hold the choke valve closed by stretching a rubber band between the choke piston lever and a stationary part of the carburetor.
3. Open the throttle lever fully.

➡ On the Stanza, the unloader adjusting lever is connected to the primary throttle plate shaft, an intermediate cam is connected to the choke lever by a choke rod.

4. Adjustment is made by bending the unloader tongue. Gauge the gap between the choke plate and the carburetor body to 2.05-2.85mm.

Vacuum Break

▶ **See Figure 9**

1. With the engine cold, close the choke completely.
2. Pull the vacuum break stem straight up as far as it will go.
3. Check the clearance between the choke plate and the carburetor wall. Clearance should be 3.12–3.72mm above 68°F; 1.65–2.25mm below 41°F.
4. On the Stanza models, adjustment is made by bending the tang at the choke plate lever assembly.

➡ **Remove the choke cover, then connect a rubber band to the choke lever to hold it shut.**

Accelerator Pump

If a smooth constant stream of fuel is not injected into the carburetor bore when the throttle is opened, the accelerator pump needs adjustment.

The Stanza accelerator pump is of a different design and is not adjustable; if it is not operating correctly, replace it.

Anti-Dieseling Solenoid

Check this valve if the engine continues to run after the key has been turned off.

1. Run the engine at idle speed and disconnect the lead wire at the anti-dieseling solenoid. The engine should stop.
2. If the engine does not stop, check the harness for current at the solenoid. If current is present, replace the solenoid. Installation torque for the solenoid is 13–25 ft. lbs. for CA20 engines.

REMOVAL & INSTALLATION

1. Remove the air cleaner.
2. Disconnect and mark the electrical connector(s), the fuel and the vacuum hoses from the carburetor.
3. Remove the throttle lever.
4. Remove the four nuts and washers retaining the carburetor to the manifold.
5. Lift the carburetor from the manifold. Do not tilt the carburetor over when removed from the manifold.
   To install:
6. Remove and discard the gasket used between the carburetor and the manifold. Clean all vacuum passages on intake manifold if necessary.
7. Install carburetor on the manifold, use a new base gasket and torque the carburetor mounting nuts EVENLY to 9–13 ft. lbs.

Fig. 7 Checking the continuity of the fast idle breaker—Stanza 1985 and later models

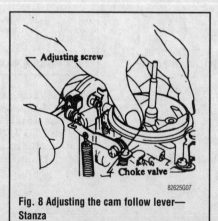

Fig. 8 Adjusting the cam follow lever— Stanza

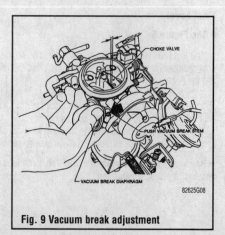

Fig. 9 Vacuum break adjustment

8. Install the throttle lever.

9. Connect the electrical connector(s), the fuel and the vacuum hoses to the carburetor. Replace the fuel line gas clamps as necessary.

10. Install the air cleaner.

11. Start engine, warm engine and adjust as necessary.

OVERHAUL

▶ **See Figures 10, 11 and 12**

✳✳ CAUTION

Never smoke when working around gasoline! Avoid all sources of sparks or ignition. Gasoline vapors are EXTREMELY volatile!

Efficient carburetion depends greatly on careful cleaning and inspection during overhaul, since dirt, gum, water and/or varnish in or on the carburetor parts are often responsible for poor performance.

Overhaul your carburetor in a clean, dust free area. Carefully disassemble the carburetor, referring often to the exploded views. Keep all similar and look-alike parts segregated during disassembly and cleaning to avoid accidental interchange during assembly. Make a note of all jet sizes.

When the carburetor is disassembled, wash all the parts (except diaphragms, electric choke units, pump plunger and any other plastic, leather, fiber or rubber parts) in clean carburetor solvent. Do not leave parts in the solvent any longer than is necessary to sufficiently loosen the deposits. Excessive cleaning may remove the special finish from the float bowl and choke valve bodies, leaving these parts unfit for service. Rinse all parts in clean solvent and blow them dry with compressed air to allow them to air dry. Wipe clean all cork, plastic, leather and fiber parts with a clean, lint-free cloth.

Blow out all passages and jets with compressed air, be sure that there are no restrictions or blockages. Never use wire or similar tools for cleaning purposes; clean the jets and valves separately, to avoid accidental interchange.

Check all the parts for wear or damage. If wear or damage is found, replace the defective parts. Especially check the following:

1. Check the float needle and seat for wear. If wear is found, replace the complete assembly.

2. Check the float hinge pin for wear and the float(s) for dents or distortion. Replace the float if fuel has leaked into it.

3. Check the throttle and choke shaft bores for wear or an out-of-round con-

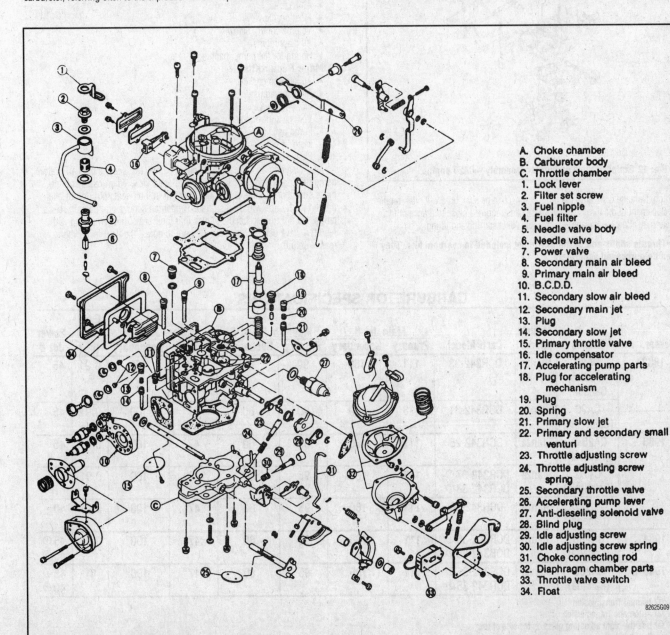

A. Choke chamber
B. Carburetor body
C. Throttle chamber
1. Lock lever
2. Filter set screw
3. Fuel nipple
4. Fuel filter
5. Needle valve body
6. Needle valve
7. Power valve
8. Secondary main air bleed
9. Primary main air bleed
10. B.C.D.D.
11. Secondary slow air bleed
12. Secondary main jet
13. Plug
14. Secondary slow jet
15. Primary throttle valve
16. Idle compensator
17. Accelerating pump parts
18. Plug for accelerating mechanism
19. Plug
20. Spring
21. Primary slow jet
22. Primary and secondary small venturi
23. Throttle adjusting screw
24. Throttle adjusting screw spring
25. Secondary throttle valve
26. Accelerating pump lever
27. Anti-dieseling solenoid valve
28. Blind plug
29. Idle adjusting screw
30. Idle adjusting screw spring
31. Choke connecting rod
32. Diaphragm chamber parts
33. Throttle valve switch
34. Float

82625G09

Fig. 10 Exploded view carburetor assembly—CA20 engine

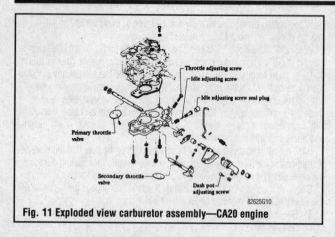

Fig. 11 Exploded view carburetor assembly—CA20 engine

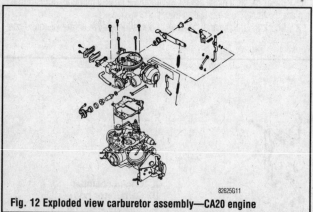

Fig. 12 Exploded view carburetor assembly—CA20 engine

dition. Damage or wear to the throttle arm, shaft or shaft bore will often require replacement of the throttle body. These parts require a close tolerance of fit; wear may allow air leakage, which could affect starting and idling.

➡**Throttle shafts and bushings are not included in overhaul kits. They can be purchased separately.**

4. Inspect the idle mixture adjusting needles for burrs or grooves. Any such condition requires replacement of the needle, since you will not be able to obtain a satisfactory idle.

5. Test the accelerator pump check valves. They should pass air one way but not the other. Test for proper seating by blowing and sucking on the valve. Replace the valve if necessary. If the valve is satisfactory, wash the valve again to remove breath moisture.

6. Check the bowl cover for warped surfaces with a straightedge.

7. Closely inspect the valves and seats for wear and/or damage, replacing as necessary.

8. After the carburetor is assembled, check the choke valve for freedom of operation.

Carburetor overhaul kits are recommended for each overhaul. These kits contain all gaskets and new parts to replace those that deteriorate most rapidly. Failure to replace all parts supplied with the kit (especially gaskets) can result in poor performance later.

Some carburetor manufacturers supply overhaul kits of three basic types: minor repair, major repair and gasket kits. Basically, they contain the following:

Minor Repair Kits:
- All gaskets
- Float needle valve
- Volume control screw
- All diaphragms
- Spring for the pump diaphragm

Major Repair Kits:
- All jets and gaskets
- All diaphragms
- Float needle valve
- Volume control screw
- Pump ball valve
- Main jet carrier
- Float

After cleaning and checking all components, reassemble the carburetor, using new parts and referring to the exploded view. When reassembling, make sure that all screws and jets are tight in their seats but do not overtighten as the tips will be distorted. Tighten all screws gradually in rotation. Do not tighten needle valves into their seats; uneven jetting will result. Always use new gaskets. Be sure to adjust the float level when reassembling.

CARBURETOR SPECIFICATIONS

| Year | Engine | Vehicle Model | Carb Model | Main Jet # | | Main Air Bleed # | | Slow Jet # | | Float Level (in.) | Power Jet # |
				Primary	Secondary	Primary	Secondary	Primary	Secondary		
1982	CA20 (Fed. & Canada)	Stanza	DCR342-33	111	160	90	60	47	100	0.91	45
	CA20 (California)	Stanza	DCR342-31	113	160	90	60	47	100	0.91	45
1983	CA20① (Federal)	Stanza	DCR342-25	111	160	95	60	47	100	0.91	45
	CA20 (California)	Stanza	DCR342-37① DCR342-38②	113	160	95	60	47	100	0.91	45
	CA20② (Canada)	Stanza	DCR342-36	113	160	95	60	47	100	0.91	40
1984	CA20S (Canada)	Stanza	DCR342-35① DCR342-36②	111	155	95	60	47	100	0.91	45① 40②
1985–86	CA20S (Canada)	Stanza	DCR342-35① DCR342-36②	111	155	95	60	47	100	③	45① 40②

① Manual Transmission
② Automatic Transmission
③ Use the sight adjusting glass on the side of the float bowl

82615C01

Troubleshooting Basic Fuel System Problems

Problem	Cause	Solution
Engine cranks, but won't start (or is hard to start) when cold	• Empty fuel tank • Incorrect starting procedure • Defective fuel pump • No fuel in carburetor • Clogged fuel filter • Engine flooded • Defective choke	• Check for fuel in tank • Follow correct procedure • Check pump output • Check for fuel in the carburetor • Replace fuel filter • Wait 15 minutes; try again • Check choke plate
Engine cranks, but is hard to start (or does not start) when hot—(presence of fuel is assumed)	• Defective choke	• Check choke plate
Rough idle or engine runs rough	• Dirt or moisture in fuel • Clogged air filter • Faulty fuel pump	• Replace fuel filter • Replace air filter • Check fuel pump output
Engine stalls or hesitates on acceleration	• Dirt or moisture in the fuel • Dirty carburetor • Defective fuel pump • Incorrect float level, defective accelerator pump	• Replace fuel filter • Clean the carburetor • Check fuel pump output • Check carburetor
Poor gas mileage	• Clogged air filter • Dirty carburetor • Defective choke, faulty carburetor adjustment	• Replace air filter • Clean carburetor • Check carburetor
Engine is flooded (won't start accompanied by smell of raw fuel)	• Improperly adjusted choke or carburetor	• Wait 15 minutes and try again, without pumping gas pedal • If it won't start, check carburetor

TCCA5C01

GASOLINE FUEL INJECTION SYSTEM

General Description

The electronic fuel injection (EFI) system is an electronic type using various types of sensors to convert engine operating conditions into electronic signals. The generated information is fed to a control unit, where it is analyzed, then calculated electrical signals are sent to the various equipment, to control the idle speed, the timing and amount of fuel being injected into the engine.

Relieving Fuel System Pressure

▶ See Figures 13, 14, 15, 16 and 17

The fuel pressure must be released on fuel injected models before removing the any fuel related component. To relieve the fuel pressure remove the gas cap then remove/disconnect the fuel pump fuse, fuel pump relay or electrical fuel pump connection to disable the electrical fuel pump. Refer to the illustrations in this section and in Section 1.

Start the engine and run, after the engine stalls crank the engine a couple times to release pressure. Turn ignition switch OFF and install/connect fuse, relay or electrical connection to fuel pump.

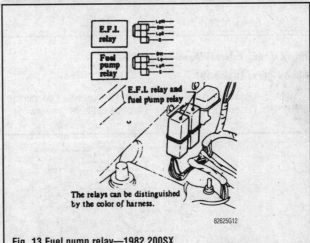

The relays can be distinguished by the color of harness.

82625G12

Fig. 13 Fuel pump relay—1982 200SX

Fig. 14 Access plate and fuel pump electrical connection location—1984–88 200SX

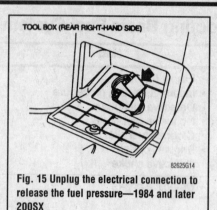

Fig. 15 Unplug the electrical connection to release the fuel pressure—1984 and later 200SX

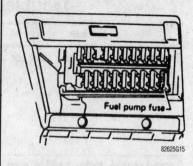

Fig. 16 Removing the fuel pump fuse—1987 Stanza

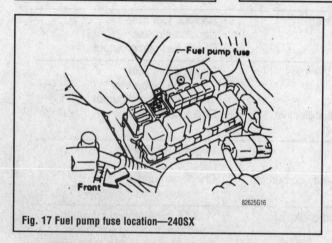

Fig. 17 Fuel pump fuse location—240SX

On some late models the "Check Engine Light" will stay on after installation of the fuel component is completed. The memory code in the control unit must be erased. To erase the code disconnect the battery cable for 1 minute then reconnect after installation of fuel component.

Electric Fuel Pump

REMOVAL & INSTALLATION

200SX Model (External Mount Electric Pump)

♦ See Figures 18 and 19

1. Before disconnecting the fuel lines or any of the fuel system components, refer to "Fuel Pressure Release" procedures and release the fuel pressure.

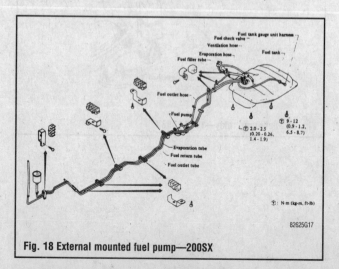

Fig. 18 External mounted fuel pump—200SX

Fig. 19 External mounted fuel pump—200SX

➡Reducing the fuel pressure to zero is a very important step for correct removal of the electric fuel pump. See Fuel Pressure Release procedures in this section. Disconnect the negative battery cable.

2. Disconnect the electrical harness connector at the pump. The 200SX pump is located near the center of the car, except on 1984 200SX, on which the pump is located near the fuel tank assembly. Refer to the illustrations.
3. Clamp the hose between the fuel tank and the pump to prevent gas from spewing out from the tank.
4. Remove the inlet and outlet hoses at the pump. Unclamp the inlet hose and allow the fuel lines to drain into a suitable container.
5. Unbolt and remove the pump. The 200SX pump and fuel damper can be removed at the same time.

To install:

6. Install the fuel pump in the correct position. Reconnect all hoses. Use new clamps and be sure all hoses are properly seated on the fuel pump body.
7. Reconnect the electrical harness connector at the pump. Start enine and check for fuel leaks.

200SX and 240SX (In-Tank Electric Pump)

♦ See Figure 20

1. Before disconnecting the fuel lines or any of the fuel system components, refer to "Fuel Pressure Release" procedures and release the fuel pressure.

➡Reducing the fuel pressure to zero is a very important step for correct removal of the electric fuel pump. See Fuel Pressure Release procedures in this section.

2. Disconnect the negative battery cable. Open the trunk lid, disconnect the fuel gauge electrical connector and remove the fuel tank inspection cover.

➡If vehicle has no fuel tank inspection cover the fuel tank must be lowered or removed to gain access to the in-tank fuel pump. When installing fuel check valve, be careful of its designated direction.

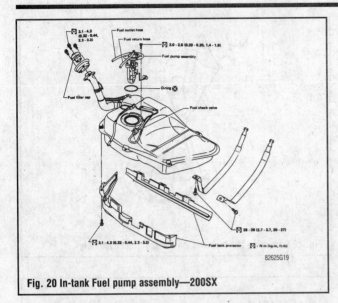

Fig. 20 In-tank Fuel pump assembly—200SX

3. Disconnect the fuel outlet and the return hoses. Remove the fuel tank if necessary. Refer to the Fuel Tank Removal And Installation procedure in this section.

4. Remove the ring retaining bolts and the O-ring, then lift the fuel pump assembly from the fuel tank. Plug the opening with a clean rag to prevent dirt from entering the system.

➡**When removing or installing the fuel pump assembly, be careful not to damage or deform it. Install a new O-ring.**

To install:

5. Install fuel pump assembly in tank with a new O-ring. Install the ring retaining bolts. Install the fuel tank if removed, refer to the Fuel Tank Removal And Installation procedure in this section.

6. Reconnect the fuel lines and the electrical connection.

7. Install the fuel tank inspection cover.

8. Connect battery cable, start engine and check for fuel leaks. On some late models the "Check Engine Light" will stay on after installation is completed. The memory code in the control unit must be erased. To erase the code disconnect the battery cable for 10 seconds then reconnect after installation of fuel pump.

Stanza Model (External Mount Electric Pump)

The Stanza (1984–86) fuel pump is located under the vehicle in front of the fuel tank, the (1987 and later) Stanza vehicles use in-tank fuel pump.

➡**Before disconnecting the fuel lines or any of the fuel system components, refer to "Fuel Pressure Release" procedures, in this section and release the fuel pressure.**

1. Disconnect the negative battery cable.

2. Raise and support the rear of the vehicle on jackstands.

3. Disconnect the electrical connector from the fuel pump.

4. Place fuel container under the fuel lines, then disconnect the fuel lines and drain the excess fuel into the container.

5. Remove the mounting braces and the fuel pump from the vehicle.

To install:

6. Install the vehicle fuel lines to the pump.

7. Install the mounting braces and mount pump to vehicle.

8. Connect fuel pump electrical connector.

9. Reconnect battery cable, start engine and check for leaks.

Stanza Model (In-Tank Electric Pump)

▶ **See Figures 21 thru 29**

1. Disconnect the negative battery cable.

2. Open the trunk lid, disconnect the fuel gauge electrical connector and remove the fuel tank inspection cover.

➡**If vehicle has no fuel tank inspection cover the fuel tank must be removed. When installing fuel check valve, be careful of its designated direction.**

3. Disconnect the fuel outlet and the return hoses.

4. Using a large brass drift pin and a hammer, drive the fuel tank locking ring in the counterclockwise direction.

5. Remove the locking ring and the O-ring, then lift the fuel pump assembly from the fuel tank. Plug the opening with a clean rag to prevent dirt from entering the system. When removing the fuel tank gauge unit, be careful not to damage or deform it. Install a new O-ring.

To install:

6. Install fuel pump assembly in tank. With a new O-ring install the fuel tank locking ring in place.

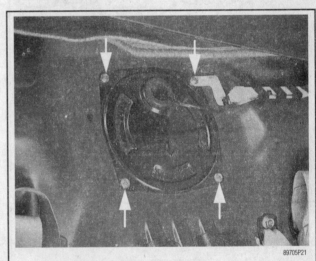

Fig. 21 The fuel pump access cover is located under the rear seat. It is secured by four screws (arrows)

Fig. 22 Fuel pump components include the locking ring (1), fuel pump assembly (2), electrical harness (3), low pressure fuel return line (4), and high pressure fuel feed line (5)

Fig. 23 The locking ring should twist off easily. If it is difficult to remove, it can be tapped around gently with a small hammer and drift

Fig. 24 The fuel pump assembly can then be lifted from the fuel tank

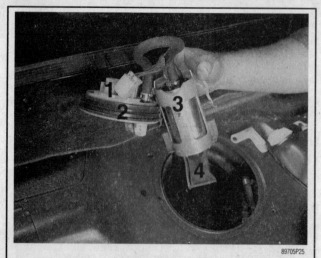

Fig. 25 The fuel pump assembly consists of the pump cover (1), cover gasket (2), electric fuel pump (3), and strainer (4)

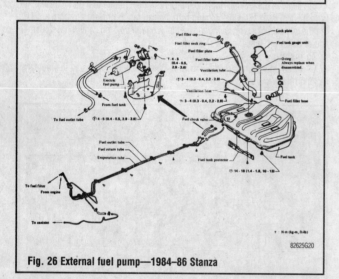

Fig. 26 External fuel pump—1984–86 Stanza

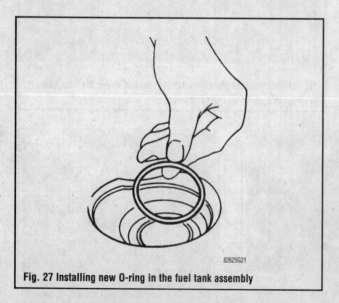

Fig. 27 Installing new O-ring in the fuel tank assembly

7. Reconnect the fuel lines and the electrical connection.
8. Install the fuel tank inspection cover.
9. Connect battery cable, start engine and check for leaks.

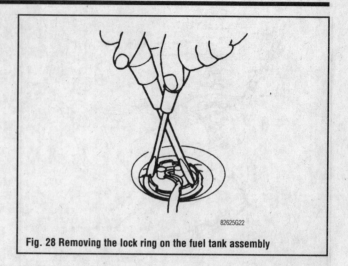

Fig. 28 Removing the lock ring on the fuel tank assembly

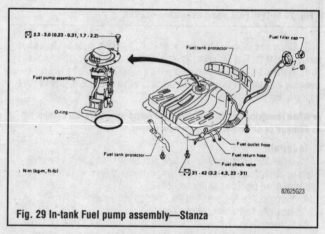

Fig. 29 In-tank Fuel pump assembly—Stanza

TESTING

▶ See Figure 30

1. Release the fuel pressure— refer to the service procedure in this section. Connect a fuel pressure gauge (special tool J2540034 or equivalent) between the fuel filter outlet and fuel feed pipe.

2. Start the engine and read the pressure. All models except the 240SX, it should be 30 psi (207 kpa) at idle, and 37 psi (255 kpa) at the moment the accelerator pedal is fully depressed. On the 240SX model the pressure should be 33 psi (227.5 kpa) at idle.

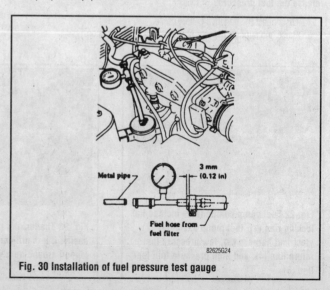

Fig. 30 Installation of fuel pressure test gauge

➡Make sure that the fuel filter is not blocked before replacing any fuel system components.

3. If pressure is not as specified, replace the pressure regulator and repeat the test. If the pressure is still incorrect, check for clogged or deformed fuel lines, then replace the fuel pump or check valve if so equipped.

Throttle Body/Chamber

REMOVAL & INSTALLATION

All Models

◆ See Figure 31

1. Disconnect the negative battery cable and remove the intake duct from the throttle chamber.
2. Disconnect and mark the vacuum hoses and the electrical harness connector from the throttle chamber. Disconnect the accelerator cable from the throttle chamber.
3. Remove the mounting bolts and the throttle chamber from the intake manifold (early years) or intake manifold collector assembly.
4. To install, use a new gasket and reverse the removal procedures. Torque the throttle chamber bolts to 13–16 ft. lbs. in two steps EVENLY. Refer to Throttle Chamber tightening procedure illustration. Adjust the throttle cable if necessary.

Check the throttle for smooth operation and make sure the by-pass port is free from obstacles and is clean. Check to make sure the idle speed adjusting screw moves smoothly. Do not touch the EGR vacuum port screw or, on some later models, the throttle valve stopper screw, as they are factory adjusted.

Because of the sensitivity of the air flow meter, there cannot be any air leaks in the fuel system. Even the smallest leak could unbalance the system and affect the performance of the automobile.

During every check pay attention to VACUUM HOSE connections, dipstick and oil filler cap for evidence of air leaks. Should you encounter any, take steps to correct the problem.

Fuel Injectors/Rail Assembly

REMOVAL & INSTALLATION

200SX (Z-Series Engine)

◆ See Figures 32, 33, 34 and 35

➡Review the entire procedure before starting this repair.

1. Release fuel pressure by following the correct procedure. Refer to Fuel Pressure Release Procedure.
2. Disconnect the negative battery cable and the accelerator cable.
3. Disconnect the injector harness connector.
4. Tag and disconnect the vacuum hose at the fuel pipe connection end. Disconnect the air regulator and its harness connector, and tag and disconnect any other hoses that may hinder removal of the injection assembly.
5. Disconnect the fuel feed hose and fuel return hose from the fuel pipe.

➡Place a rag under the fuel pipe to prevent splashing of the fuel.

6. Remove the vacuum hose connecting the pressure regulator to the intake manifold.
7. Remove the bolts securing the fuel pipe and pressure regulator.
8. Remove the screws securing the fuel injectors. Remove the fuel pipe assembly, by pulling out the fuel pipe, injectors and pressure regulator as an assembly.
9. Unfasten the hose clamp on the injectors and remove the injectors from the fuel pipe.
To install:
10. Install the fuel injectors in the fuel pipe with new hose clamps.

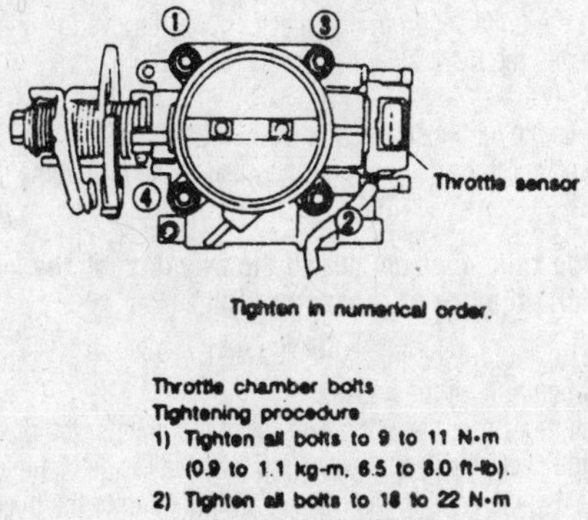

Throttle sensor

Tighten in numerical order.

Throttle chamber bolts
Tightening procedure
1) Tighten all bolts to 9 to 11 N·m
   (0.9 to 1.1 kg-m, 6.5 to 8.0 ft-lb).
2) Tighten all bolts to 18 to 22 N·m
   (1.8 to 2.2 kg-m, 13 to 16 ft-lb).

82625G25

Fig. 31 Throttle chamber tightening procedure

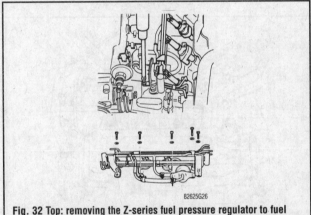

82625G26

Fig. 32 Top: removing the Z-series fuel pressure regulator to fuel pipe screws. Bottom: Fuel pipe assembly retaining screws

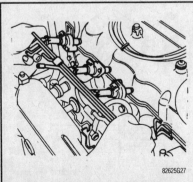

82625G27

Fig. 33 Removing the fuel pipe and injector assembly—Z series engine

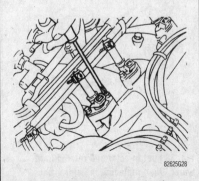

82625G28

Fig. 34 Removing the injector securing screws.

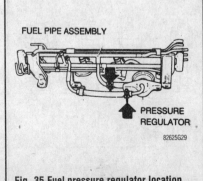

FUEL PIPE ASSEMBLY

PRESSURE REGULATOR

82625G29

Fig. 35 Fuel pressure regulator location and connections

11. Install the fuel pipe assembly, injectors with new O-rings and pressure regulator as an assembly.

12. Connect the fuel feed hose and fuel return hose to the fuel pipe. Use new hose clamps on all connections. Reconnect all vacuum hoses and electrical connections.

13. Reconnect the accelerator cable and battery cable. Note the following:

   a. When installing the injectors, check that there are no scratches or abrasion at the lower rubber insulator, and securely install it, making sure it is air-tight.

   b. When installing the fuel hose, make sure the hose end is inserted onto the metal pipe until the end contacts the unit, as far as it will go. Push the end of the injector rubber hose onto the fuel pipe until it is 25mm from the end of the pipe.

   c. Never reuse hose clamps on the injection system. Always renew the clamps. When tightening clamps, make sure the screw does not come in contact with adjacent parts.

14. Start the engine and check for fuel leaks.

200SX (CA Series Engine)

♦ **See Figures 36, 37, 38 and 39**

➡**On the CA20E engine on late model 200SX vehicles the collector assembly may NOT have to be removed—modify Step 2 of the service procedure below.**

1. Release fuel pressure by following the correct service procedure. Refer to Fuel Pressure Release Procedure. Disconnect the negative battery cable.

2. On the CA20E engine, drain the engine coolant. Disconnect the fuel injection wiring harness, the ignition wires, and remove the collector with the throttle chamber. Tag and disconnect all related hoses.

3. On the CA18ET engine, disconnect the air intake pipe, the fuel injection wiring harness, the ignition wires and accelerator cable. Remove the throttle chamber.

4. On all engines, disconnect the fuel hoses and pressure regulator vacuum hoses.

5. Remove the fuel injectors with the fuel rail assembly.

6. Remove the fuel injector hose-to-fuel rail clamp(s), then pull the injector from the fuel rail.

To install:

7. To remove the fuel hose from the injector, use a hot soldering iron, then cut (melt) a line in the fuel hose (to the braided reinforcement), starting at the injector socket to ¾ in. (19mm) long. Remove the hose from the injector, by hand.

➡**DO NOT allow the soldering iron to cut all the way through the hose, nor touch the injector seat or damage the plastic socket connector.**

8. To install a new fuel hose, clean the injector tail section, wet the inside of the new hose with fuel, push the hose into the fuel injector hose socket (as far as it will go) retain it with a new hose clamp if necessary. Assemble the injector(s) onto the fuel rail.

9. Install the injectors with new O-rings and fuel rail as an assembly.

10. Connect the fuel hoses and pressure regulator vacuum hoses.

11. On the CA18ET engine, connect the air intake pipe, the fuel injection wiring harness, the ignition wires and accelerator cable. Install the throttle chamber.

12. On the CA20E engine, reconnect the fuel injection wiring harness, the ignition wires, and install the collector with the throttle chamber if necessary. Reconnect all related hoses and refill the cooling system if necessary.

13. Reconnect the battery cable. Start the engine and check for fuel leaks.

200SX (VG30 Engine)

♦ **See Figures 40 thru 45**

1. Release fuel pressure by following the correct procedure. Refer to Fuel Pressure Release Procedure. Disconnect the negative battery cable.

2. Disconnect these items at the intake collector: the air intake duct; accelerator linkage; PCV hose; air regulator pressure hose; B.C.D.D. hose; fuel hoses; E.G.R tube; wiring harness clamps; wiring harness connectors; intake collector cover. Then, drain some coolant out of the cooling system and disconnect the coolant hoses connecting into the collector.

3. Remove the intake collector assembly.

4. Remove the bolts securing the fuel tube.

5. Remove the bolts securing the injectors and remove the injectors, fuel tubes, and pressure regulator as an assembly.

To install:

6. To remove the fuel hoses, heat a sharp knife until it is hot. Cut into the braided reinforcement from the mark on the hose to the end of the fuel tube connection.

➡**Make sure the knife does not cut all the way through the hose and nick the injector tail piece or connector fitting.**

7. Pull the hose off of the injectors. DO NOT install the injectors in a vise to hold them as you pull off the hoses.

8. To install new hose, clean the exterior of the injector tail piece and the end of the fuel tube with a safe solvent. Then, wet the inside diameter of the new hose with fuel. Push the ends of the hoses and fittings onto the injector tail piece and the end of the fuel tube as far as they will go by hand, retain it with a new hose clamp if necessary

9. Assemble the injector(s) onto the fuel rail. Install the injectors with new O-rings and fuel rail as an assembly.

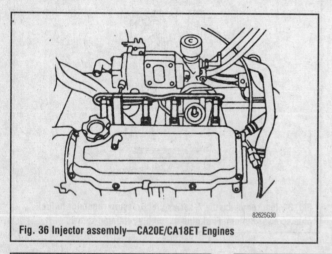

Fig. 36 Injector assembly—CA20E/CA18ET Engines

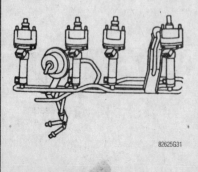

Fig. 37 Injector assembly and fuel pressure regulator—CA20E/CA18ET Engines

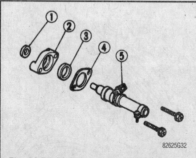

Fig. 38 Fuel injector and related hardware. When replacing injector always replace the lower rubber (1) and upper rubber insulator (3)

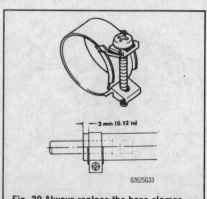

Fig. 39 Always replace the hose clamps. Note proper installation

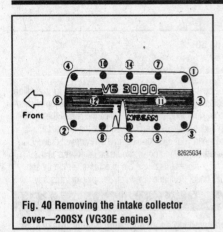

Fig. 40 Removing the intake collector cover—200SX (VG30E engine)

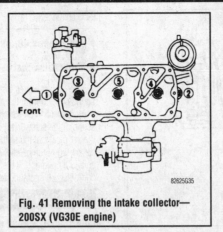

Fig. 41 Removing the intake collector—200SX (VG30E engine)

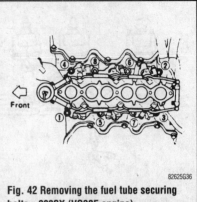

Fig. 42 Removing the fuel tube securing bolts—200SX (VG30E engine)

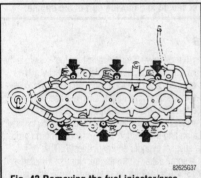

Fig. 43 Removing the fuel injector/pressure regulator assembly—200SX (VG30E engine)

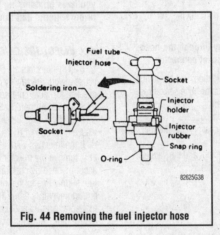

Fig. 44 Removing the fuel injector hose

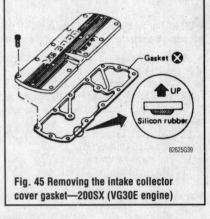

Fig. 45 Removing the intake collector cover gasket—200SX (VG30E engine)

10. Install the intake collector assembly.

11. Connect the air intake duct; accelerator linkage; PCV hose; air regulator pressure hose; B.C.D.D. hose; fuel hoses; E.G.R tube; wiring harness clamps; wiring harness connectors and intake collector cover to the collector assembly.

12. Connect the coolant hoses to the collector and refill the cooling system to the proper level.

13. Reconnect the battery cable. Start the engine and check for fuel leaks.

240SX

▶ See Figure 46

➡On the KA24DE engine on late model 240SX vehicles the BPT valve may NOT have to be removed— modify Step 3 of the service procedure below.

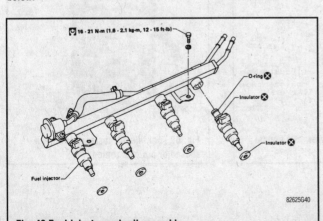

Fig. 46 Fuel injector and rail assembly

1. Relieve the fuel system pressure.
2. Disconnect the negative battery cable.
3. Remove the BPT valve.
4. Remove the fuel tube retaining bolts.
5. Remove the fuel tube and injector assembly from the intake manifold.
6. Withdraw the injectors from the fuel tube.

To install:

7. Clean the injector tail piece and insert the injectors into the fuel tube with new O-rings.

8. Position the injector and fuel tube assembly onto the intake manifold and install the injector tube retaining bolts.

9. Pressurize the fuel system and check for leaks at all fuel connections.

10. Install the BPT valve if necessary.

11. Connect the negative battery cable.

Stanza (CA Series Engine)

▶ See Figure 47

➡On the CA20E engine on late model Stanza vehicles the collector assembly may NOT have to be removed— modify Step 4 of the service procedure below.

1. Refer to the Fuel Pressure Release Procedure in this section and reduce the fuel pressure to zero. Disconnect the negative battery cable.

2. Remove the fuel inlet and outlet hoses from the fuel rail.

3. Disconnect the EFI electrical harness from the fuel injectors and the vacuum hose from the fuel pressure regulator, located at the center of the fuel rail.

4. Remove the fuel rail securing bolts, the collector/throttle chamber (if necessary) and the injector securing bolts.

5. Remove the fuel injectors with the fuel rail assembly.

6. Remove the fuel injector hose-to-fuel rail clamp(s), then pull the injector from the fuel rail.

To install:

7. To remove the fuel hose from the injector, use a hot soldering iron, then cut (melt) a line in the fuel hose (to the braided reinforcement), starting at the

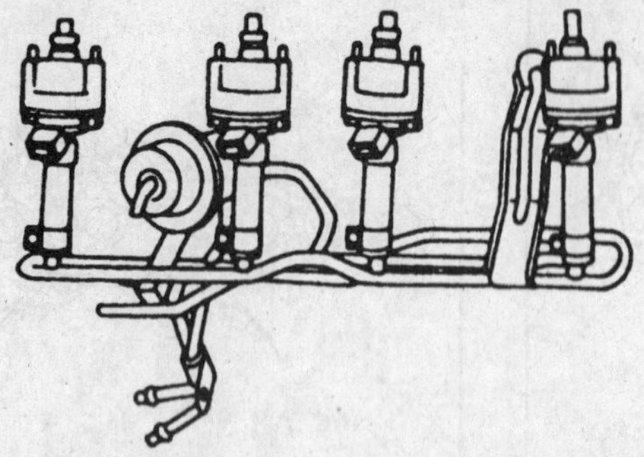

82625G41

Fig. 47 Fuel injector and rail assembly

injector socket to ¾ in. (19mm) long. Remove the hose from the injector, by hand.

➡**DO NOT allow the soldering iron to cut all the way through the hose, nor touch the injector seat or damage the plastic socket connector.**

8. To install a new fuel hose, clean the injector tail section, wet the inside of the new hose with fuel, push the hose into the fuel injector hose socket (as far as it will go). Assemble the injector(s) onto the fuel rail.
9. Install the injectors with new O-rings and securing bolts.
10. Install the collector and the throttle chamber if necessary and the fuel rail securing bolts.
11. Connect the EFI electrical harness to the fuel injectors and the vacuum hose to the fuel pressure regulator.
12. Connect all the fuel lines.
13. Start engine and check for fuel leaks.

Stanza (KA24E Engine)

1. Relieve fuel pressure from system. Disconnect the negative battery cable.
2. Remove or disconnect the following:
   a. Air duct
   b. Fuel hoses
   c. Pressure regulator
   d. Accelerator wire bracket
   e. Injector harness connectors
3. Remove the bolts securing the fuel tube.
4. Remove bolts securing injectors and remove injectors and fuel tube as an assembly.
5. Reverse the service procedure to install.

TESTING

➧ **See Figures 48, 49 and 50**

Audible Click Test

The easiest way to test the operation of the fuel injectors is to listen for a clicking sound coming from the injectors while the engine is running. This is accomplished using a mechanic's stethoscope, or a long screwdriver. Place the end of the stethoscope or the screwdriver (tip end, not handle) onto the body of the injector. Place the ear pieces of the stethoscope in your ears, or if using a screwdriver, place your ear on top of the handle. An audible clicking noise should be heard; this is the solenoid operating. If the injector makes this noise, the injector driver circuit and computer are operating as designed. Continue testing all the injectors this way.

✻✻ CAUTION

Be extremely careful while working on an operating engine, make sure you have no dangling jewelry, extremely loose clothes, power tool cords or other items that might get caught in a moving part of the engine.

ALL INJECTORS CLICKING

If all the injectors are clicking, but you have determined that the fuel system is the cause of your driveability problem, continue diagnostics. Make sure that you have checked fuel pump pressure as outlined earlier in this section. An easy way to determine a weak or unproductive cylinder is a cylinder drop test. This is accomplished by removing one spark plug wire at a time, and seeing which cylinder causes the least difference in the idle. The one that causes the least change is the weak cylinder.

If the injectors were all clicking and the ignition system is functioning properly, remove the injector of the suspect cylinder and bench test it. This is accomplished by checking for a spray pattern from the injector itself. Install a fuel supply line to the injector (or rail if the injector is left attached to the rail) and momentarily apply 12 volts DC and a ground to the injector itself; a visible fuel spray should appear. If no spray is achieved, replace the injector and check the running condition of the engine.

ONE OR MORE INJECTORS ARE NOT CLICKING

If one or more injectors are found to be not operating, testing the injector driver circuit and computer can be accomplished using a "noid" light. First, with the engine not running and the ignition key in the **OFF** position, remove the connector from the injector you plan to test, then plug the "noid" light tool into the injector connector. Start the engine and the "noid" light should flash, signaling that the injector driver circuit is working. If the "noid" light flashes, but the injector does not click when plugged in, replace the injector and retest.

If the "noid" light does not flash, the injector driver circuit is faulty. Disconnect the negative battery cable. Unplug the "noid" light from the injector con-

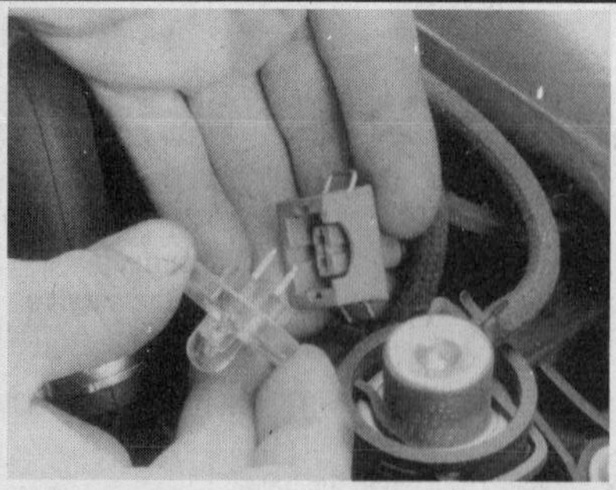

TCCS5P01

Fig. 48 A noid light can be attached to the fuel injector harness in order to test for injector pulse

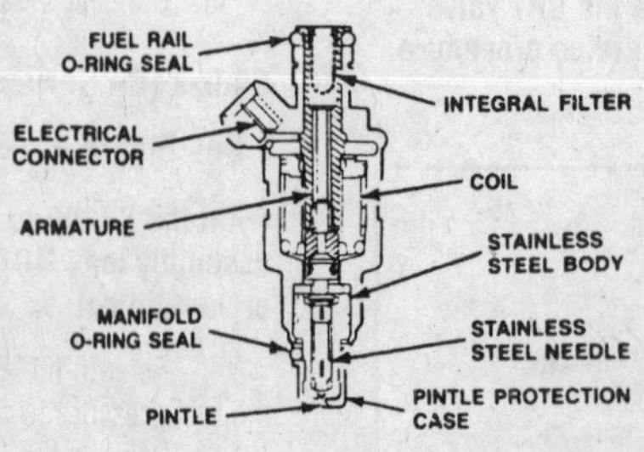
FUEL RAIL
O-RING SEAL
INTEGRAL FILTER
ELECTRICAL
CONNECTOR
COIL
ARMATURE
STAINLESS
STEEL BODY
MANIFOLD
O-RING SEAL
STAINLESS
STEEL NEEDLE
PINTLE
PINTLE PROTECTION
CASE

TCCS5P02

Fig. 49 Cross-sectional view of a typical fuel injector

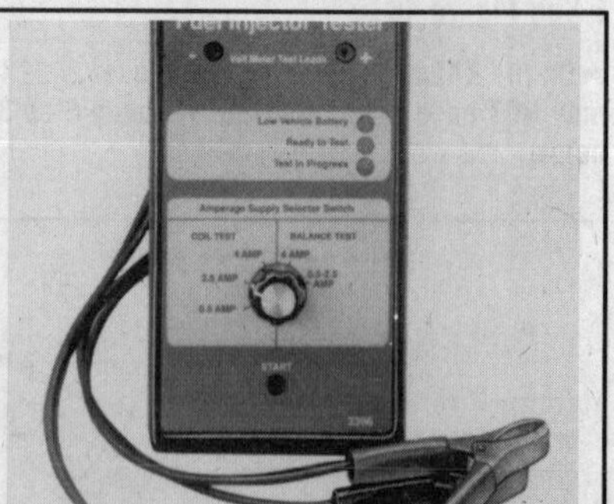
Fuel Injector Tester

TCCS5P03

Fig. 50 Fuel injector testers can be purchased or perhaps rented

nector and also unplug the ECM. Check the harness between the appropriate pins on the harness side of the ECM connector and the injector connector. Resistance should be less than 5.0 ohms; if not, repair the circuit. If resistance is within specifications, the injector driver inside the ECM is faulty and replacement of the ECM will be necessary.

Injector Rubber Hose

REMOVAL & INSTALLATION

▶ **See Figure 51**

1. On injector rubber hose, measure off a point approximately 0.79 in. (20mm) from socket end.
2. Heat soldering iron (150 watt) for 15 minutes. Cut hose into braided reinforcement from mark to socket end.

➡**Do not feed soldering iron until it touches injector tail piece. Be careful not to damage socket, plastic connector, etc. with solder iron. Never place injector in a vise when disconnecting rubber hose.**

3. Pull rubber hose out with hand.
To install:
4. Clean exterior of injector tail piece.
5. Wet inside of new rubber hose with fuel.
6. Push end of rubber hose with hose socket onto injector tail piece by hand as far as it will go. Clamp is not necessary at this connection.

➡**After properly connecting fuel hose to injector, check connection for fuel leakage.**

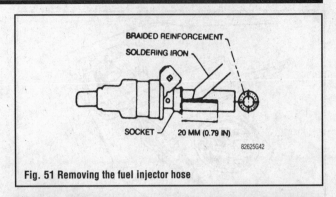

Fig. 51 Removing the fuel injector hose

Fuel Pressure Regulator

REMOVAL & INSTALLATION

1. Relieve fuel pressure from system. Disconnect the negative battery cable.
2. Disengage vacuum tube connecting regulator to intake manifold from pressure regulator.
3. Remove screws securing pressure regulator.
4. Unfasten hose clamps, and disconnect pressure regulator from fuel hose.

➡**Place a rag under fuel pipe to absorb any remaining fuel.**

5. To install, reverse the removal procedure.

FUEL TANK

Tank Assembly

REMOVAL & INSTALLATION

1982–83 200SX Models

▶ **See Figure 52**

➡**Always replace O-rings and gas hose retaining clamps. Do not kink or twist any hose or fuel lines when they are installed. Do not tighten hose clamps excessively to avoid damaging hoses.**

➡**Release the Fuel Pressure— refer to the necessary service procedure.**

➡**When installing fuel check valve, be careful of its designated direction.**

1. Remove the battery ground cable.
2. Drain the fuel from the fuel tank.
3. Remove the protector from the luggage compartment, and then remove the following parts:
   a. Harness connector for the fuel tank gauge unit.
   b. Ventilation hose.
   c. Evaporation hoses
   d. Fuel filler hose (Hatchback)
4. Remove the following parts from beneath the floor:
   a. Fuel outlet hose
   b. Fuel return hose
   c. Evaporation hose
   d. Fuel filler hose (Hardtop)
5. Remove the bolts which secure the fuel tank and remove the tank.
To remove the Reservoir tank from the Hatchback:
6. Remove the battery cable.
7. Remove the protector from the luggage compartment. Also remove the right hand speaker and side lower finisher.
8. Remove the evaporation hoses and then remove the reservoir tank.

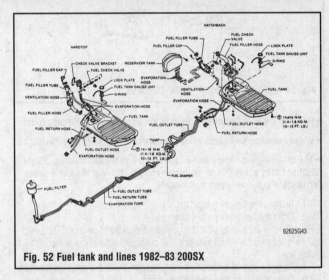

Fig. 52 Fuel tank and lines 1982–83 200SX

To install:
9. Install the reservoir tank in place and fuel tank assembly in the correct position. While supporting the tank in place torque the gas tank strap retaining bolts EVENLY.
10. Reconnect all lines, hoses and the electrical connection.
11. Install the protector in the luggage compartment. Connect the battery ground cable.

1984–88 200SX and 240SX Models

▶ **See Figures 53 and 54**

➡**Always replace O-rings and gas hose retaining clamps. Do not kink or twist any hose or fuel lines when they are installed. Do not tighten hose clamps excessively to avoid damaging hoses.**

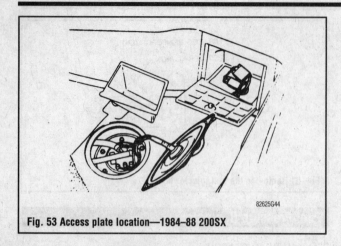

Fig. 53 Access plate location—1984–88 200SX

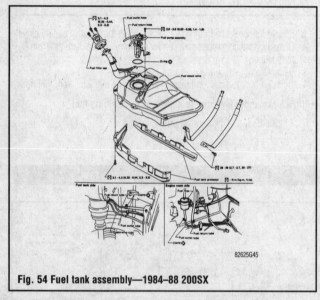

Fig. 54 Fuel tank assembly—1984–88 200SX

➡**Release the Fuel Pressure— refer to the necessary service procedure.**

➡**When installing fuel check valve, be careful of its designated direction.**

➡**The following procedure can be used on all years and models. Slight variations may occur due to extra connections, etc. but the basic procedure should cover all years and models.**

1. Remove the battery ground cable.
2. Drain the fuel from the fuel tank.
3. Remove the access plate if so equipped from the trunk area. Disconnect the hoses, evaporative (vent) tube line if so equipped and fuel pump electrical connection.
4. Raise the rear of vehicle and safely support it with the proper jackstands.
5. Remove the fuel tank protector assembly.
6. Disconnect the fuel filler hose at the gas tank.
7. Remove the gas tank strap retaining bolts and slowly lower the tank assembly down from the vehicle.

To install:

8. Install the tank in the correct position.
9. While supporting the tank in place torque the gas tank strap retaining bolts EVENLY to 20–27 ft. lbs.
10. Reconnect the fuel filler hose at the gas tank using a new clamp.
11. Install the fuel tank protector assembly and connect the evaporative (vent) tube line if so equipped.
12. Lower the vehicle, connect all hoses with new clamps and the electrical connection. Install the access plate if so equipped.
13. Refill the gas tank. Reconnect the battery ground cable.

Stanza and Stanza 2WD/4WD Wagons

♦ **See Figures 55, 56, 57 and 58**

➡**Always replace O-rings and gas hose retaining clamps. Do not kink or twist any hose or fuel lines when they are installed. Do not tighten hose clamps excessively to avoid damaging hoses.**

➡**Release the Fuel Pressure (EFI vehicles)— refer to all necessary service procedures and illustrations.**

➡**When installing fuel check valve, be careful of its designated direction.**

➡**The following procedure can be used on all years and models. Slight variations may occur due to extra connections, etc. but the basic procedure should cover all years and models.**

1. Drain the fuel tank. Disconnect the negative battery cable.
2. Remove the rear seat cushion.
3. Remove the inspection cover.
4. Disconnect the fuel gauge electrical harness connector.
5. Disconnect the fuel filler (if so equipped) and the ventilation hoses. Disconnect the fuel outlet, return and evaporation hoses, at the front of the tank. Plug open fuel lines. Remove the tank protector.
6. Remove the fuel tank mounting bolts and the tank from the vehicle.

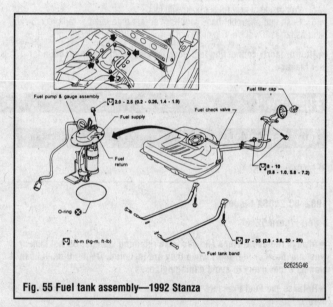

Fig. 55 Fuel tank assembly—1992 Stanza

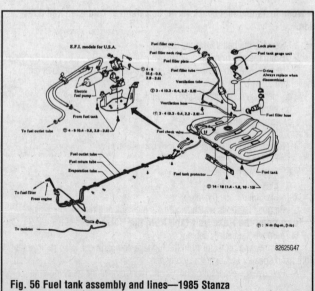

Fig. 56 Fuel tank assembly and lines—1985 Stanza

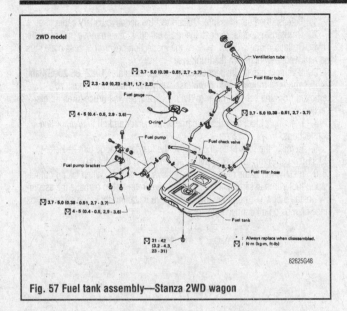

Fig. 57 Fuel tank assembly—Stanza 2WD wagon

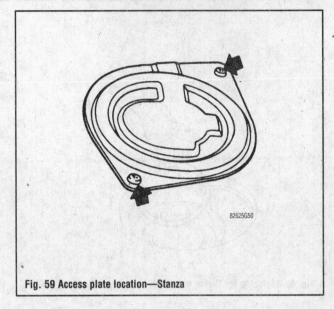

Fig. 59 Access plate location—Stanza

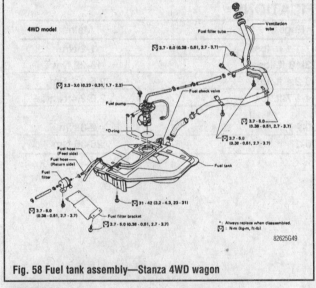

Fig. 58 Fuel tank assembly—Stanza 4WD wagon

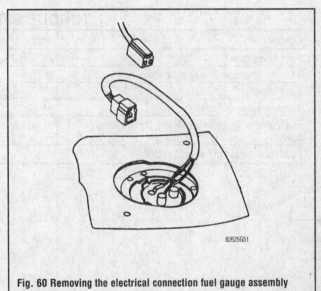

Fig. 60 Removing the electrical connection fuel gauge assembly

To install:

7. Install the fuel tank to vehicle and torque the mounting bolts EVENLY to 2027 ft. lbs.

8. Reconnect all fuel lines, ventilation hoses and the electrical connection.

9. Install the inspection cover and rear seat cushion.

10. Start engine and check for fuel leaks.

SENDING UNIT REPLACEMENT

▶ **See Figures 59, 60, 61 and 62**

➡Always replace O-rings and gas hose retaining clamps. Do not kink or twist any hose or fuel lines when they are installed. Do not tighten hose clamps excessively to avoid damaging hoses.

➡Release the Fuel Pressure (EFI vehicles)— refer to all necessary service procedures and illustrations.

➡When installing fuel check valve, be careful of its designated direction.

➡The following procedure can be used on all years and models. Slight variations may occur due to extra connections, etc. but the basic procedure should cover all years and models.

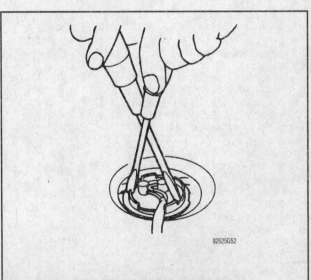

Fig. 61 Removing the lock-ring in the fuel tank assembly

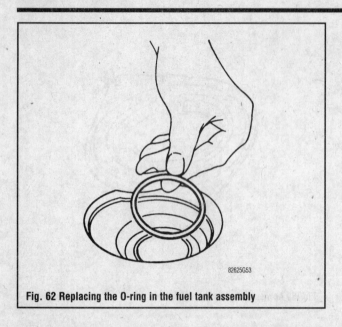

82625G53

Fig. 62 Replacing the O-ring in the fuel tank assembly

1. Release the Fuel Pressure. Disconnect the negative battery cable.

2. On Stanza models, remove the rear seat cushion—remove the inspection cover. On later model 200SX vehicles the inspection cover or access plate must be removed —which is in the trunk area.

3. If vehicle has no inspection cover or access plate (1982–83 200SX and 240SX models) to fuel sending unit assembly the "Fuel Tank" must be removed from the vehicle. Refer to the necessary service procedures in this section.

4. Disconnect fuel tank gauge harness connector and all fuel/vapor line connections.

5. Remove the lock plate and remove the fuel tank gauge unit —Refer to "Electric Fuel Pump In-Tank" service procedures in this section.

6. Installation is the reverse of the removal procedure. When taking out fuel gauge/fuel pump assembly if so equipped be careful not to damage the assembly. Install a new O-ring in the fuel tank before installing lock ring and new gas hose clamps on all connections.

TORQUE SPECIFICATIONS

Component	English	Metric
Fuel hose clamp:	0.7-1.1 ft. lbs.	1-2 Nm
Throttle chamber/body mounting bolts:	13-16 ft. lbs.	18-22 Nm
Fuel injector:	1.8-2.4 ft. lbs.	2.5-3.2 Nm
Throttle valve switch:	1.4-1.7 ft. lbs.	2.0-2.4 Nm
Fuel pump (in-tank assembly) mounting bolts:	2.0-2.7 ft. lbs.	2-3 Nm
Fuel tank retaining strap bolts:	20-27 ft. lbs.	26-36 Nm

82625C02

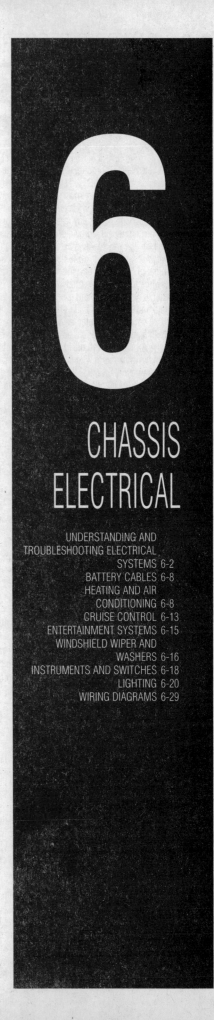

6

CHASSIS ELECTRICAL

UNDERSTANDING AND TROUBLESHOOTING ELECTRICAL SYSTEMS

Basic Electrical Theory

♦ **See Figure 1**

For any 12 volt, negative ground, electrical system to operate, the electricity must travel in a complete circuit. This simply means that current (power) from the positive (+) terminal of the battery must eventually return to the negative (-) terminal of the battery. Along the way, this current will travel through wires, fuses, switches and components. If, for any reason, the flow of current through the circuit is interrupted, the component fed by that circuit will cease to function properly.

Perhaps the easiest way to visualize a circuit is to think of connecting a light bulb (with two wires attached to it) to the battery—one wire attached to the negative (-) terminal of the battery and the other wire to the positive (+) terminal. With the two wires touching the battery terminals, the circuit would be complete and the light bulb would illuminate. Electricity would follow a path from the battery to the bulb and back to the battery. It's easy to see that with longer wires on our light bulb, it could be mounted anywhere. Further, one wire could be fitted with a switch so that the light could be turned on and off.

The normal automotive circuit differs from this simple example in two ways. First, instead of having a return wire from the bulb to the battery, the current travels through the frame of the vehicle. Since the negative (-) battery cable is attached to the frame (made of electrically conductive metal), the frame of the vehicle can serve as a ground wire to complete the circuit. Secondly, most automotive circuits contain multiple components which receive power from a single circuit. This lessens the amount of wire needed to power components on the vehicle.

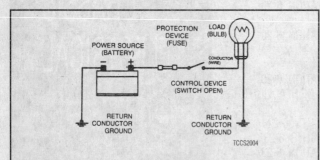

Fig. 1 This example illustrates a simple circuit. When the switch is closed, power from the positive (+) battery terminal flows through the fuse and the switch, and then to the light bulb. The light illuminates and the circuit is completed through the ground wire back to the negative (-) battery terminal. In reality, the two ground points shown in the illustration are attached to the metal frame of the vehicle, which completes the circuit back to the battery

HOW DOES ELECTRICITY WORK: THE WATER ANALOGY

Electricity is the flow of electrons—the subatomic particles that constitute the outer shell of an atom. Electrons spin in an orbit around the center core of an atom. The center core is comprised of protons (positive charge) and neutrons (neutral charge). Electrons have a negative charge and balance out the positive charge of the protons. When an outside force causes the number of electrons to unbalance the charge of the protons, the electrons will split off the atom and look for another atom to balance out. If this imbalance is kept up, electrons will continue to move and an electrical flow will exist.

Many people have been taught electrical theory using an analogy with water. In a comparison with water flowing through a pipe, the electrons would be the water and the wire is the pipe.

The flow of electricity can be measured much like the flow of water through a pipe. The unit of measurement used is amperes, frequently abbreviated as amps (a). You can compare amperage to the volume of water flowing through a pipe. When connected to a circuit, an ammeter will measure the actual amount of current flowing through the circuit. When relatively few electrons flow through a circuit, the amperage is low. When many electrons flow, the amperage is high.

Water pressure is measured in units such as pounds per square inch (psi);

The electrical pressure is measured in units called volts (v). When a voltmeter is connected to a circuit, it is measuring the electrical pressure.

The actual flow of electricity depends not only on voltage and amperage, but also on the resistance of the circuit. The higher the resistance, the higher the force necessary to push the current through the circuit. The standard unit for measuring resistance is an ohm. Resistance in a circuit varies depending on the amount and type of components used in the circuit. The main factors which determine resistance are:

• Material—some materials have more resistance than others. Those with high resistance are said to be insulators. Rubber materials (or rubber-like plastics) are some of the most common insulators used in vehicles as they have a very high resistance to electricity. Very low resistance materials are said to be conductors. Copper wire is among the best conductors. Silver is actually a superior conductor to copper and is used in some relay contacts, but its high cost prohibits its use as common wiring. Most automotive wiring is made of copper.

• Size—the larger the wire size being used, the less resistance the wire will have. This is why components which use large amounts of electricity usually have large wires supplying current to them.

• Length—for a given thickness of wire, the longer the wire, the greater the resistance. The shorter the wire, the less the resistance. When determining the proper wire for a circuit, both size and length must be considered to design a circuit that can handle the current needs of the component.

• Temperature—with many materials, the higher the temperature, the greater the resistance (positive temperature coefficient). Some materials exhibit the opposite trait of lower resistance with higher temperatures (negative temperature coefficient). These principles are used in many of the sensors on the engine.

OHM'S LAW

There is a direct relationship between current, voltage and resistance. The relationship between current, voltage and resistance can be summed up by a statement known as Ohm's law.

Voltage (E) is equal to amperage (I) times resistance (R): $E = I \times R$
Other forms of the formula are $R = E/I$ and $I = E/R$

In each of these formulas, E is the voltage in volts, I is the current in amps and R is the resistance in ohms. The basic point to remember is that as the resistance of a circuit goes up, the amount of current that flows in the circuit will go down, if voltage remains the same.

The amount of work that the electricity can perform is expressed as power. The unit of power is the watt (w). The relationship between power, voltage and current is expressed as:

Power (w) is equal to amperage (I) times voltage (E): $W = I \times E$

This is only true for direct current (DC) circuits; The alternating current formula is a tad different, but since the electrical circuits in most vehicles are DC type, we need not get into AC circuit theory.

Electrical Components

POWER SOURCE

Power is supplied to the vehicle by two devices: The battery and the alternator. The battery supplies electrical power during starting or during periods when the current demand of the vehicle's electrical system exceeds the output capacity of the alternator. The alternator supplies electrical current when the engine is running. Just not does the alternator supply the current needs of the vehicle, but it recharges the battery.

The Battery

In most modern vehicles, the battery is a lead/acid electrochemical device consisting of six 2 volt subsections (cells) connected in series, so that the unit is capable of producing approximately 12 volts of electrical pressure. Each subsection consists of a series of positive and negative plates held a short distance apart in a solution of sulfuric acid and water.

The two types of plates are of dissimilar metals. This sets up a chemical reaction, and it is this reaction which produces current flow from the battery when its positive and negative terminals are connected to an electrical load .

The power removed from the battery is replaced by the alternator, restoring the battery to its original chemical state.

The Alternator

On some vehicles there isn't an alternator, but a generator. The difference is that an alternator supplies alternating current which is then changed to direct current for use on the vehicle, while a generator produces direct current. Alternators tend to be more efficient and that is why they are used.

Alternators and generators are devices that consist of coils of wires wound together making big electromagnets. One group of coils spins within another set and the interaction of the magnetic fields causes a current to flow. This current is then drawn off the coils and fed into the vehicles electrical system.

GROUND

Two types of grounds are used in automotive electric circuits. Direct ground components are grounded to the frame through their mounting points. All other components use some sort of ground wire which is attached to the frame or chassis of the vehicle. The electrical current runs through the chassis of the vehicle and returns to the battery through the ground (-) cable; if you look, you'll see that the battery ground cable connects between the battery and the frame or chassis of the vehicle.

➡**It should be noted that a good percentage of electrical problems can be traced to bad grounds.**

PROTECTIVE DEVICES

▶ **See Figure 2**

It is possible for large surges of current to pass through the electrical system of your vehicle. If this surge of current were to reach the load in the circuit, the

surge could burn it out or severely damage it. It can also overload the wiring, causing the harness to get hot and melt the insulation. To prevent this, fuses, circuit breakers and/or fusible links are connected into the supply wires of the electrical system. These items are nothing more than a built-in weak spot in the system. When an abnormal amount of current flows through the system, these protective devices work as follows to protect the circuit:

• Fuse—when an excessive electrical current passes through a fuse, the fuse "blows" (the conductor melts) and opens the circuit, preventing the passage of current.

• Circuit Breaker—a circuit breaker is basically a self-repairing fuse. It will open the circuit in the same fashion as a fuse, but when the surge subsides, the circuit breaker can be reset and does not need replacement.

• Fusible Link—a fusible link (fuse link or main link) is a short length of special, high temperature insulated wire that acts as a fuse. When an excessive electrical current passes through a fusible link, the thin gauge wire inside the link melts, creating an intentional open to protect the circuit. To repair the circuit, the link must be replaced. Some newer type fusible links are housed in plug-in modules, which are simply replaced like a fuse, while older type fusible links must be cut and spliced if they melt. Since this link is very early in the electrical path, it's the first place to look if nothing on the vehicle works, yet the battery seems to be charged and is properly connected.

⁕⁕⁕ CAUTION

Always replace fuses, circuit breakers and fusible links with identically rated components. Under no circumstances should a component of higher or lower amperage rating be substituted.

SWITCHES & RELAYS

▶ **See Figures 3 and 4**

Switches are used in electrical circuits to control the passage of current. The most common use is to open and close circuits between the battery and the various electric devices in the system. Switches are rated according to the amount of amperage they can handle. If a sufficient amperage rated switch is not used in a circuit, the switch could overload and cause damage.

Some electrical components which require a large amount of current to operate use a special switch called a relay. Since these circuits carry a large amount of current, the thickness of the wire in the circuit is also greater. If this large wire were connected from the load to the control switch, the switch would have to carry the high amperage load and the fairing or dash would be twice as large to accommodate the increased size of the wiring harness. To prevent these problems, a relay is used.

Relays are composed of a coil and a set of contacts. When the coil has a current passed though it, a magnetic field is formed and this field causes the contacts to move together, completing the circuit. Most relays are normally open, prevent-

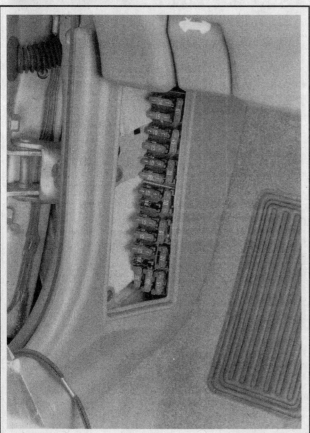

TCCA6P01

Fig. 2 Most vehicles use one or more fuse panels. This one is located on the driver's side kick panel

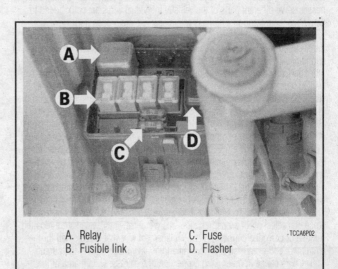

A. Relay   C. Fuse
B. Fusible link   D. Flasher

TCCA6P02

Fig. 3 The underhood fuse and relay panel usually contains fuses, relays, flashers and fusible links

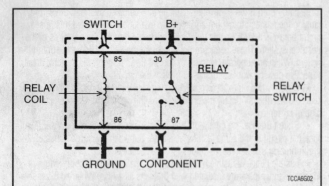

TCCA6G02

Fig. 4 Relays are composed of a coil and a switch. These two components are linked together so that when one operates, the other operates at the same time. The large wires in the circuit are connected from the battery to one side of the relay switch (B+) and from the opposite side of the relay switch to the load (component). Smaller wires are connected from the relay coil to the control switch for the circuit and from the opposite side of the relay coil to ground

ing current from passing through the circuit, but they can take any electrical form depending on the job they are intended to do. Relays can be considered "remote control switches." They allow a smaller current to operate devices that require higher amperages. When a small current operates the coil, a larger current is allowed to pass by the contacts. Some common circuits which may use relays are the horn, headlights, starter, electric fuel pump and other high draw circuits.

LOAD

Every electrical circuit must include a "load" (something to use the electricity coming from the source). Without this load, the battery would attempt to deliver its entire power supply from one pole to another. This is called a "short circuit." All this electricity would take a short cut to ground and cause a great amount of damage to other components in the circuit by developing a tremendous amount of heat. This condition could develop sufficient heat to melt the insulation on all the surrounding wires and reduce a multiple wire cable to a lump of plastic and copper.

WIRING & HARNESSES

The average vehicle contains meters and meters of wiring, with hundreds of individual connections. To protect the many wires from damage and to keep them from becoming a confusing tangle, they are organized into bundles, enclosed in plastic or taped together and called wiring harnesses. Different harnesses serve different parts of the vehicle. Individual wires are color coded to help trace them through a harness where sections are hidden from view.

Automotive wiring or circuit conductors can be either single strand wire, multi-strand wire or printed circuitry. Single strand wire has a solid metal core and is usually used inside such components as alternators, motors, relays and other devices. Multi-strand wire has a core made of many small strands of wire twisted together into a single conductor. Most of the wiring in an automotive electrical system is made up of multi-strand wire, either as a single conductor or grouped together in a harness. All wiring is color coded on the insulator, either as a solid color or as a colored wire with an identification stripe. A printed circuit is a thin film of copper or other conductor that is printed on an insulator backing. Occasionally, a printed circuit is sandwiched between two sheets of plastic for more protection and flexibility. A complete printed circuit, consisting of conductors, insulating material and connectors for lamps or other components is called a printed circuit board. Printed circuitry is used in place of individual wires or harnesses in places where space is limited, such as behind instrument panels.

Since automotive electrical systems are very sensitive to changes in resistance, the selection of properly sized wires is critical when systems are repaired. A loose or corroded connection or a replacement wire that is too small for the circuit will add extra resistance and an additional voltage drop to the circuit.

The wire gauge number is an expression of the cross-section area of the conductor. Vehicles from countries that use the metric system will typically describe the wire size as its cross-sectional area in square millimeters. In this method, the larger the wire, the greater the number. Another common system for

expressing wire size is the American Wire Gauge (AWG) system. As gauge number increases, area decreases and the wire becomes smaller. An 18 gauge wire is smaller than a 4 gauge wire. A wire with a higher gauge number will carry less current than a wire with a lower gauge number. Gauge wire size refers to the size of the strands of the conductor, not the size of the complete wire with insulator. It is possible, therefore, to have two wires of the same gauge with different diameters because one may have thicker insulation than the other.

It is essential to understand how a circuit works before trying to figure out why it doesn't. An electrical schematic shows the electrical current paths when a circuit is operating properly. Schematics break the entire electrical system down into individual circuits. In a schematic, usually no attempt is made to represent wiring and components as they physically appear on the vehicle; switches and other components are shown as simply as possible. Face views of harness connectors show the cavity or terminal locations in all multi-pin connectors to help locate test points.

CONNECTORS

▶ **See Figures 5 and 6**

Three types of connectors are commonly used in automotive applications—weatherproof, molded and hard shell.

- Weatherproof—these connectors are most commonly used where the connector is exposed to the elements. Terminals are protected against moisture and dirt by sealing rings which provide a weathertight seal. All repairs require the use of a special terminal and the tool required to service it. Unlike standard blade type terminals, these weatherproof terminals cannot be straightened once they are bent. Make certain that the connectors are properly seated and all of the sealing rings are in place when connecting leads.

TCCA6P03

Fig. 5 Hard shell (left) and weatherproof (right) connectors have replaceable terminals

TCCA6P04

Fig. 6 Weatherproof connectors are most commonly used in the engine compartment or where the connector is exposed to the elements

• Molded—these connectors require complete replacement of the connector if found to be defective. This means splicing a new connector assembly into the harness. All splices should be soldered to insure proper contact. Use care when probing the connections or replacing terminals in them, as it is possible to create a short circuit between opposite terminals. If this happens to the wrong terminal pair, it is possible to damage certain components. Always use jumper wires between connectors for circuit checking and NEVER probe through weatherproof seals.

• Hard Shell—unlike molded connectors, the terminal contacts in hard-shell connectors can be replaced. Replacement usually involves the use of a special terminal removal tool that depresses the locking tangs (barbs) on the connector terminal and allows the connector to be removed from the rear of the shell. The connector shell should be replaced if it shows any evidence of burning, melting, cracks, or breaks. Replace individual terminals that are burnt, corroded, distorted or loose.

Test Equipment

Pinpointing the exact cause of trouble in an electrical circuit is most times accomplished by the use of special test equipment. The following describes different types of commonly used test equipment and briefly explains how to use them in diagnosis. In addition to the information covered below, the tool manufacturer's instructions booklet (provided with the tester) should be read and clearly understood before attempting any test procedures.

JUMPER WIRES

✳ CAUTION

Never use jumper wires made from a thinner gauge wire than the circuit being tested. If the jumper wire is of too small a gauge, it may overheat and possibly melt. Never use jumpers to bypass high resistance loads in a circuit. Bypassing resistances, in effect, creates a short circuit. This may, in turn, cause damage and fire. Jumper wires should only be used to bypass lengths of wire or to simulate switches.

Jumper wires are simple, yet extremely valuable, pieces of test equipment. They are basically test wires which are used to bypass sections of a circuit. Although jumper wires can be purchased, they are usually fabricated from lengths of standard automotive wire and whatever type of connector (alligator clip, spade connector or pin connector) that is required for the particular application being tested. In cramped, hard-to-reach areas, it is advisable to have insulated boots over the jumper wire terminals in order to prevent accidental grounding. It is also advisable to include a standard automotive fuse in any jumper wire. This is commonly referred to as a "fused jumper". By inserting an in-line fuse holder between a set of test leads, a fused jumper wire can be used for bypassing open circuits. Use a 5 amp fuse to provide protection against voltage spikes.

Jumper wires are used primarily to locate open electrical circuits, on either the ground (-) side of the circuit or on the power (+) side. If an electrical component fails to operate, connect the jumper wire between the component and a good ground. If the component operates only with the jumper installed, the ground circuit is open. If the ground circuit is good, but the component does not operate, the circuit between the power feed and component may be open. By moving the jumper wire successively back from the component toward the power source, you can isolate the area of the circuit where the open is located. When the component stops functioning, or the power is cut off, the open is in the segment of wire between the jumper and the point previously tested.

You can sometimes connect the jumper wire directly from the battery to the "hot" terminal of the component, but first make sure the component uses 12 volts in operation. Some electrical components, such as fuel injectors or sensors, are designed to operate on about 4 to 5 volts, and running 12 volts directly to these components will cause damage.

TEST LIGHTS

◆ **See Figure 7**

The test light is used to check circuits and components while electrical current is flowing through them. It is used for voltage and ground tests. To use a 12 volt test light, connect the ground clip to a good ground and probe wherever

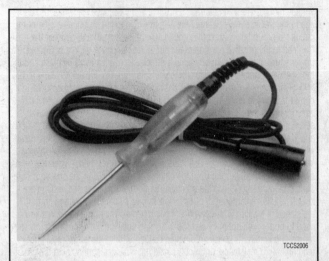

Fig. 7 A 12 volt test light is used to detect the presence of voltage in a circuit

TCCS2006

necessary with the pick. The test light will illuminate when voltage is detected. This does not necessarily mean that 12 volts (or any particular amount of voltage) is present; it only means that some voltage is present. It is advisable before using the test light to touch its ground clip and probe across the battery posts or terminals to make sure the light is operating properly.

✳ WARNING

Do not use a test light to probe electronic ignition, spark plug or coil wires. Never use a pick-type test light to probe wiring on computer controlled systems unless specifically instructed to do so. Any wire insulation that is pierced by the test light probe should be taped and sealed with silicone after testing.

Like the jumper wire, the 12 volt test light is used to isolate opens in circuits. But, whereas the jumper wire is used to bypass the open to operate the load, the 12 volt test light is used to locate the presence of voltage in a circuit. If the test light illuminates, there is power up to that point in the circuit; if the test light does not illuminate, there is an open circuit (no power). Move the test light in successive steps back toward the power source until the light in the handle illuminates. The open is between the probe and a point which was previously probed.

The self-powered test light is similar in design to the 12 volt test light, but contains a 1.5 volt penlight battery in the handle. It is most often used in place of a multimeter to check for open or short circuits when power is isolated from the circuit (continuity test).

The battery in a self-powered test light does not provide much current. A weak battery may not provide enough power to illuminate the test light even when a complete circuit is made (especially if there is high resistance in the circuit). Always make sure that the test battery is strong. To check the battery, briefly touch the ground clip to the probe; if the light glows brightly, the battery is strong enough for testing.

➡**A self-powered test light should not be used on any computer controlled system or component. The small amount of electricity transmitted by the test light is enough to damage many electronic automotive components.**

MULTIMETERS

Multimeters are an extremely useful tool for troubleshooting electrical problems. They can be purchased in either analog or digital form and have a price range to suit any budget. A multimeter is a voltmeter, ammeter and ohmmeter (along with other features) combined into one instrument. It is often used when testing solid state circuits because of its high input impedance (usually 10 megaohms or more). A brief description of the multimeter main test functions follows:

• Voltmeter—the voltmeter is used to measure voltage at any point in a circuit, or to measure the voltage drop across any part of a circuit. Voltmeters usually have various scales and a selector switch to allow the reading of different voltage ranges. The voltmeter has a positive and a negative lead. To avoid damage to the meter, always connect the negative lead to the negative (-) side of the circuit (to ground or nearest the ground side of the circuit) and connect the positive lead to the positive (+) side of the circuit (to the power source or the nearest power source). Note that the negative voltmeter lead will always be black and that the positive voltmeter will always be some color other than black (usually red).

• Ohmmeter—the ohmmeter is designed to read resistance (measured in ohms) in a circuit or component. Most ohmmeters will have a selector switch which permits the measurement of different ranges of resistance (usually the selector switch allows the multiplication of the meter reading by 10, 100, 1,000 and 10,000). Some ohmmeters are "auto-ranging" which means the meter itself will determine which scale to use. Since the meters are powered by an internal battery, the ohmmeter can be used like a self-powered test light. When the ohmmeter is connected, current from the ohmmeter flows through the circuit or component being tested. Since the ohmmeter's internal resistance and voltage are known values, the amount of current flow through the meter depends on the resistance of the circuit or component being tested. The ohmmeter can also be used to perform a continuity test for suspected open circuits. In using the meter for making continuity checks, do not be concerned with the actual resistance readings. Zero resistance, or any ohm reading, indicates continuity in the circuit. Infinite resistance indicates an opening in the circuit. A high resistance reading where there should be none indicates a problem in the circuit. Checks for short circuits are made in the same manner as checks for open circuits, except that the circuit must be isolated from both power and normal ground. Infinite resistance indicates no continuity, while zero resistance indicates a dead short.

✳✳ WARNING

Never use an ohmmeter to check the resistance of a component or wire while there is voltage applied to the circuit.

• Ammeter—an ammeter measures the amount of current flowing through a circuit in units called amperes or amps. At normal operating voltage, most circuits have a characteristic amount of amperes, called "current draw" which can be measured using an ammeter. By referring to a specified current draw rating, then measuring the amperes and comparing the two values, one can determine what is happening within the circuit to aid in diagnosis. An open circuit, for example, will not allow any current to flow, so the ammeter reading will be zero. A damaged component or circuit will have an increased current draw, so the reading will be high. The ammeter is always connected in series with the circuit being tested. All of the current that normally flows through the circuit must also flow through the ammeter; if there is any other path for the current to follow, the ammeter reading will not be accurate. The ammeter itself has very little resistance to current flow and, therefore, will not affect the circuit, but it will measure current draw only when the circuit is closed and electricity is flowing. Excessive current draw can blow fuses and drain the battery, while a reduced current draw can cause motors to run slowly, lights to dim and other components to not operate properly.

Troubleshooting Electrical Systems

When diagnosing a specific problem, organized troubleshooting is a must. The complexity of a modern automotive vehicle demands that you approach any problem in a logical, organized manner. There are certain troubleshooting techniques, however, which are standard:

• Establish when the problem occurs. Does the problem appear only under certain conditions? Were there any noises, odors or other unusual symptoms? Isolate the problem area. To do this, make some simple tests and observations, then eliminate the systems that are working properly. Check for obvious problems, such as broken wires and loose or dirty connections. Always check the obvious before assuming something complicated is the cause.

• Test for problems systematically to determine the cause once the problem area is isolated. Are all the components functioning properly? Is there power going to electrical switches and motors. Performing careful, systematic checks will often turn up most causes on the first inspection, without wasting time checking components that have little or no relationship to the problem.

• Test all repairs after the work is done to make sure that the problem is fixed. Some causes can be traced to more than one component, so a careful verification of repair work is important in order to pick up additional malfunctions that may cause a problem to reappear or a different problem to arise. A blown fuse, for example, is a simple problem that may require more than another fuse to repair. If you don't look for a problem that caused a fuse to blow, a shorted wire (for example) may go undetected.

Experience has shown that most problems tend to be the result of a fairly simple and obvious cause, such as loose or corroded connectors, bad grounds or damaged wire insulation which causes a short. This makes careful visual inspection of components during testing essential to quick and accurate troubleshooting.

Testing

OPEN CIRCUITS

◊ **See Figure 8**

This test already assumes the existence of an open in the circuit and it is used to help locate the open portion.
1. Isolate the circuit from power and ground.
2. Connect the self-powered test light or ohmmeter ground clip to the ground side of the circuit and probe sections of the circuit sequentially.
3. If the light is out or there is infinite resistance, the open is between the probe and the circuit ground.
4. If the light is on or the meter shows continuity, the open is between the probe and the end of the circuit toward the power source.

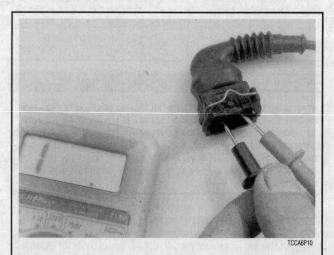

TCCA6P10

Fig. 8 The infinite reading on this multimeter indicates that the circuit is open

SHORT CIRCUITS

➡**Never use a self-powered test light to perform checks for opens or shorts when power is applied to the circuit under test. The test light can be damaged by outside power.**

1. Isolate the circuit from power and ground.
2. Connect the self-powered test light or ohmmeter ground clip to a good ground and probe any easy-to-reach point in the circuit.
3. If the light comes on or there is continuity, there is a short somewhere in the circuit.
4. To isolate the short, probe a test point at either end of the isolated circuit (the light should be on or the meter should indicate continuity).
5. Leave the test light probe engaged and sequentially open connectors or switches, remove parts, etc. until the light goes out or continuity is broken.
6. When the light goes out, the short is between the last two circuit components which were opened.

VOLTAGE

This test determines voltage available from the battery and should be the first step in any electrical troubleshooting procedure after visual inspection. Many electrical problems, especially on computer controlled systems, can be caused by a low state of charge in the battery. Excessive corrosion at the battery cable terminals can cause poor contact that will prevent proper charging and full battery current flow.

1. Set the voltmeter selector switch to the 20V position.
2. Connect the multimeter negative lead to the battery's negative (-) post or terminal and the positive lead to the battery's positive (+) post or terminal.
3. Turn the ignition switch **ON** to provide a load.
4. A well charged battery should register over 12 volts. If the meter reads below 11.5 volts, the battery power may be insufficient to operate the electrical system properly.

VOLTAGE DROP

▶ **See Figure 9**

When current flows through a load, the voltage beyond the load drops. This voltage drop is due to the resistance created by the load and also by small resistances created by corrosion at the connectors and damaged insulation on the wires. The maximum allowable voltage drop under load is critical, especially if there is more than one load in the circuit, since all voltage drops are cumulative.

1. Set the voltmeter selector switch to the 20 volt position.
2. Connect the multimeter negative lead to a good ground.
3. Operate the circuit and check the voltage prior to the first component (load).
4. There should be little or no voltage drop in the circuit prior to the first component. If a voltage drop exists, the wire or connectors in the circuit are suspect.
5. While operating the first component in the circuit, probe the ground side of the component with the positive meter lead and observe the voltage readings. A small voltage drop should be noticed. This voltage drop is caused by the resistance of the component.
6. Repeat the test for each component (load) down the circuit.
7. If a large voltage drop is noticed, the preceding component, wire or connector is suspect.

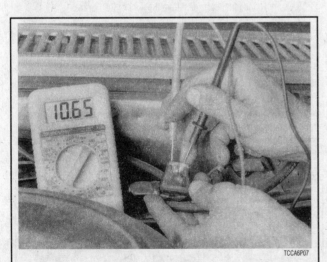

Fig. 9 This voltage drop test revealed high resistance (low voltage) in the circuit

RESISTANCE

▶ **See Figures 10 and 11**

✳✳ WARNING

Never use an ohmmeter with power applied to the circuit. The ohmmeter is designed to operate on its own power supply. The normal 12 volt electrical system voltage could damage the meter!

1. Isolate the circuit from the vehicle's power source.
2. Ensure that the ignition key is **OFF** when disconnecting any components or the battery.

3. Where necessary, also isolate at least one side of the circuit to be checked, in order to avoid reading parallel resistances. Parallel circuit resistances will always give a lower reading than the actual resistance of either of the branches.
4. Connect the meter leads to both sides of the circuit (wire or component) and read the actual measured ohms on the meter scale. Make sure the selector switch is set to the proper ohm scale for the circuit being tested, to avoid misreading the ohmmeter test value.

Fig. 10 Checking the resistance of a coolant temperature sensor with an ohmmeter. Reading is 1.04 kilohms

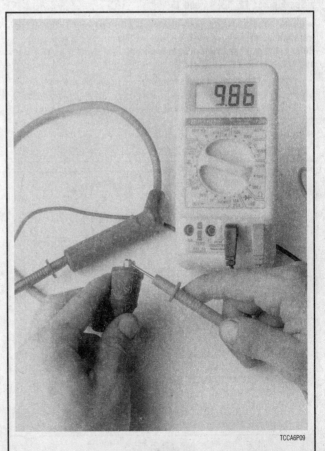

Fig. 11 Spark plug wires can be checked for excessive resistance using an ohmmeter

Wire and Connector Repair

Almost anyone can replace damaged wires, as long as the proper tools and parts are available. Wire and terminals are available to fit almost any need. Even the specialized weatherproof, molded and hard shell connectors are now available from aftermarket suppliers.

Be sure the ends of all the wires are fitted with the proper terminal hardware and connectors. Wrapping a wire around a stud is never a permanent solution and will only cause trouble later. Replace wires one at a time to avoid confusion. Always route wires exactly the same as the factory.

➡ **If connector repair is necessary, only attempt it if you have the proper tools. Weatherproof and hard shell connectors require special tools to release the pins inside the connector. Attempting to repair these connectors with conventional hand tools will damage them.**

BATTERY CABLES

Disconnecting the Cables

When working on any electrical component on the vehicle, it is always a good idea to disconnect the negative (-) battery cable. This will prevent potential damage to many sensitive electrical components such as the Engine Control Module (ECM), radio, alternator, etc.

➡ **Any time you disengage the battery cables, it is recommended that you disconnect the negative (-) battery cable first. This will prevent your accidentally grounding the positive (+) terminal to the body of the vehicle when disconnecting it, thereby preventing damage to the above mentioned components.**

Before you disconnect the cable(s), first turn the ignition to the **OFF** position. This will prevent a draw on the battery which could cause arcing (electricity trying to ground itself to the body of a vehicle, just like a spark plug jumping the gap) and, of course, damaging some components such as the alternator diodes.

When the battery cable(s) are reconnected (negative cable last), be sure to check that your lights, windshield wipers and other electrically operated safety components are all working correctly. If your vehicle contains an Electronically Tuned Radio (ETR), don't forget to also reset your radio stations. Ditto for the clock.

HEATING AND AIR CONDITIONING

Heater Unit Assembly

REMOVAL & INSTALLATION

200SX and 240SX

♦ **See Figures 12, 13, 14 and 15**

➡ **On the 1984–88 200SX and 240SX models, NO factory "Removal and Installation" procedures are given, so use this procedure as a guide. Refer to the exploded view of each heater system—modify service steps as necessary.**

1. Set the TEMP lever to the HOT position and drain the coolant.
2. Disconnect the heater hoses from the driver's side of the heater unit.
3. At this point the manufacturer suggests you remove the front seats. To do this, remove the plastic covers over the ends of the seat runners, both front and back, to expose the seat mounting bolts. Remove the bolts and remove the seats.

4. Remove the console box and the floor carpets.
5. Remove the instrument panel lower covers from both the driver's and passenger's sides of the car. Remove the lower cluster lids.
6. Remove the left hand side ventilator duct.
7. Remove the radio, sound balancer and stereo cassette deck if so equipped.
8. Remove the instrument panel-to-transmission tunnel stay.
9. Remove the rear heater duct from the floor of the vehicle.
10. Remove the center ventilator duct.
11. Remove the left and right hand side air guides from the lower heater outlets.
12. Disconnect the wire harness connections.
13. Remove the two screws at the bottom sides of the heater unit and the one screw and the top of the unit and remove the unit together with the heater control assembly.

➡ **On late models the heater control cables and control assembly may have to be removed before the heater unit is removed. Always mark control cables before removing them to ensure correct adjustment and proper operation.**

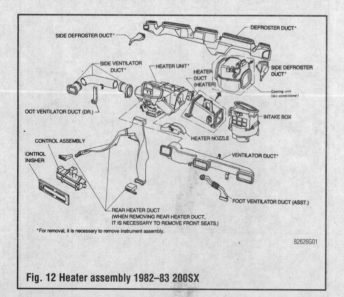

Fig. 12 Heater assembly 1982–83 200SX

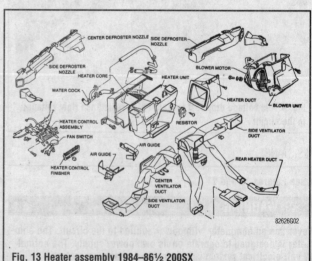

Fig. 13 Heater assembly 1984–86½ 200SX

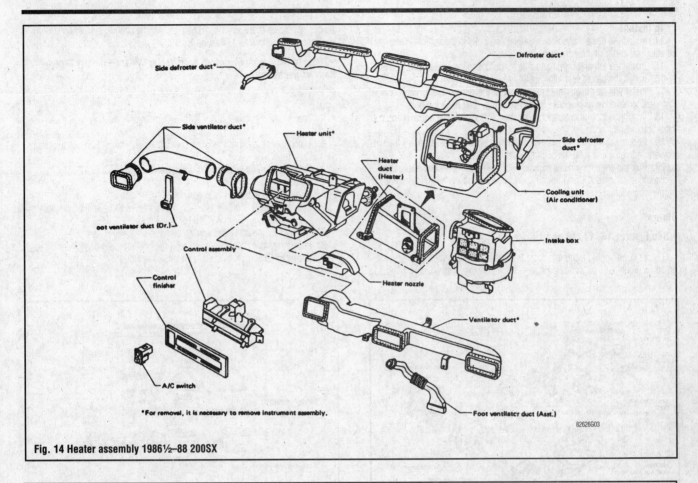

Side defroster duct*

Side ventilator duct*

Heater unit

Heater duct (Heater)

Defroster duct*

Side defroster duct*

Cooling unit (Air conditioner)

oot ventilator duct (Dr.)

Control assembly

Intake box

Control finisher

Heater nozzle

A/C switch

Ventilator duct*

Foot ventilator duct (Asst.)

*For removal, it is necessary to remove instrument assembly.

82626G03

Fig. 14 Heater assembly 1986½–88 200SX

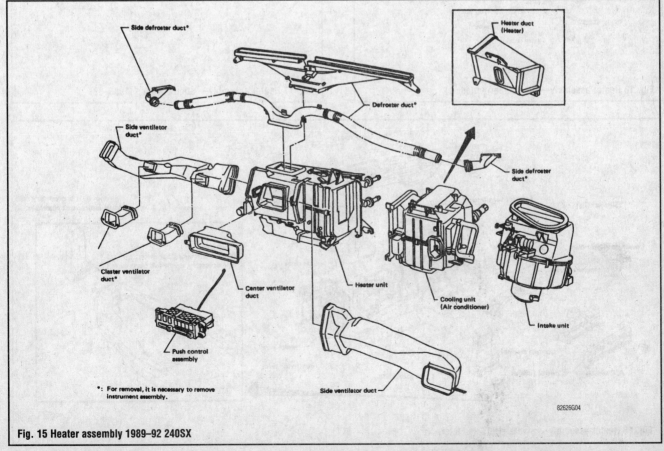

Side defroster duct*

Heater duct (Heater)

Side ventilator duct*

Defroster duct*

Side defroster duct*

Claster ventilator duct*

Center ventilator duct

Heater unit

Cooling unit (Air conditioner)

Intake unit

Push control assembly

Side ventilator duct

*: For removal, it is necessary to remove instrument assembly.

82626G04

Fig. 15 Heater assembly 1989–92 240SX

To install:

14. Install the heater assembly with retaining bolts in the vehicle. Reconnect all electrical and heater control cable connections if removed.

15. Install the left and right hand side air guides to the lower heater outlets.

16. Install the center ventilator duct.

17. Install the rear heater duct to the floor of the vehicle and all components that were removed to gain access to the rear heater duct retaining bolts.

18. Install the instrument panel lower covers, floor carpets, console box and seats if removed.

19. Reconnect the two heater hoses with new hose clamps. Connect the battery ground cable and refill the cooling system.

20. Run the engine for a few minutes with the heater on to make sure the coolant level is correct. Check for any coolant leaks and the heater system for proper operation.

Stanza

▶ **See Figures 16, 17, 18 and 19**

The air conditioning evaporator core is mounted in the engine compartment on some models, no air conditioning interference is experienced when removing the heater core on these vehicles. When refilling the cooling system be sure to bleed the air from it, refer to Section 1.

➡**Refer to the exploded view of each heater system—modify service steps as necessary.**

1. Disconnect the negative battery cable. Remove the instrument panel.

2. Disconnect the heater hoses and vacuum lines in the engine compartment.

3. Disconnect the control lever and electrical connectors. Remove the heater control assembly.

4. Unbolt and remove the heater unit assembly.

To install:

5. Install the heater unit in the vehicle.

6. Install the heater control assembly, control lever and electrical connections.

7. Connect the heater hoses and vacuum tube.

8. Install the instrument panel and refill the cooling system.

9. Start engine and check system for proper operation.

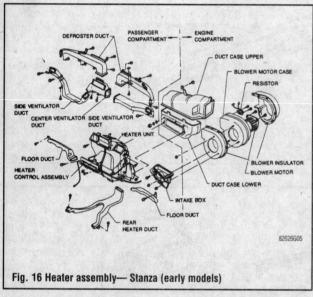

Fig. 16 Heater assembly— Stanza (early models)

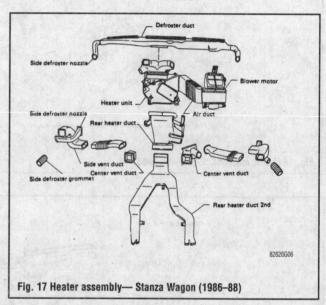

Fig. 17 Heater assembly— Stanza Wagon (1986–88)

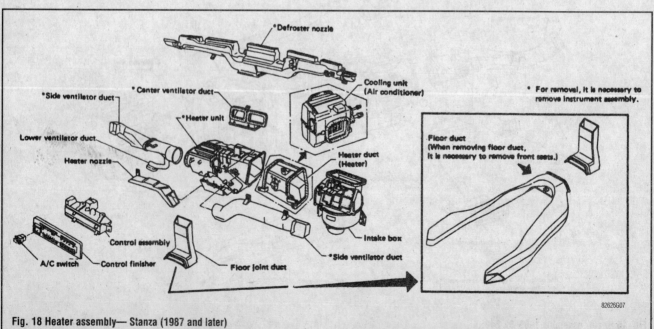

Fig. 18 Heater assembly— Stanza (1987 and later)

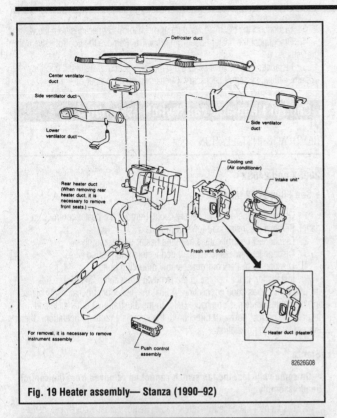

Fig. 19 Heater assembly— Stanza (1990–92)

Blower Motor

REMOVAL & INSTALLATION

200SX and 240SX

➡On all 1984–88 200SX models the blower motor is located behind the glove box, facing the floor in the intake unit of the heater housing.

➡Use this procedure as a guide and refer to the exploded view of the "Heater Assembly".

1. Disconnect the battery ground cable. Remove the instrument panel lower cover and cluster lid on the right hand side.
2. Disconnect the control cable and harness connector from the blower unit.
3. Remove the three bolts and remove the blower unit.
4. Remove the three screws holding the blower motor in the case, unplug the hose running from the rear of the motor into the case and pull the motor together with the fan cage out of the case.
5. Installation is the reverse of removal. With the blower motor assembly removed, check the case for any debris or signs of fan contact. Inspect the fan for wear spots, cracked blades or hub, loose retaining nut or poor alignment. Make sure the electrical connection is installed in the correct position. Check system for proper operation.

Stanza

➡On all 1987 and later Stanza models (except wagons), the blower motor is located behind the glove box, facing the floor in the intake unit of the heater housing. On Stanza wagons, the blower motor is located behind the glove box, facing the floor in the intake unit of the heater housing.

➡Refer to the exploded view of each "Heater Assembly".

EARLY MODELS

1. Disconnect the negative battery cable. Working in the engine compartment, disconnect the blower motor insulator upper fasteners.
2. Remove the blower motor retaining bolts.
3. Push the blower motor insulator down by hand and remove the motor.

4. Installation is the reverse of the removal procedures. With the blower motor assembly removed, check the case for any debris or signs of fan contact. Inspect the fan for wear spots, cracked blades or hub, loose retaining nut or poor alignment. Check system for proper operation.

LATER MODELS

1. Disconnect the negative battery cable. Disconnect the electrical harness from the blower motor.
2. Remove the retaining bolts from the bottom of the blower unit and lower the blower motor from the case.
3. To install, reverse the removal procedures. With the blower motor assembly removed, check the case for any debris or signs of fan contact. Inspect the fan for wear spots, cracked blades or hub, loose retaining nut or poor alignment. Check system for proper operation.

Heater Core

REMOVAL & INSTALLATION

200SX and 240SX

1. Disconnect the negative battery cable.
2. Remove the heater unit assembly (refer to the necessary service procedures and illustrations) and the heater core hoses.
3. Remove the heater core from the heater unit box.
4. Installation is the reverse of removal. Clean heater case of all debris before installation. Check system for proper operation.

Stanza

▶ **See Figures 20 and 21**

➡When refilling the cooling system, be sure to bleed the air from it. Refer to the Draining, Flushing and Refilling procedure in Section 1 and bleed the cooling system. Refer to the exploded view illustration of each Heater Assembly.

1. Remove pedal bracket mounting bolts, the steering column mounting bolts, the brake and the clutch pedal cotter pins.
2. Move the pedal bracket and the steering column to the left.
3. Disconnect the air mix door control cable and the heater valve control lever, then remove the control lever.
4. Remove the core cover and disconnect the hoses at the core. Remove the heater core.
5. Installation is the reverse of the removal procedures. On later models it may be necessary to remove the complete "Heater Assembly" then remove the heater core from the assembly (remove the heater assembly case bolts/clips and

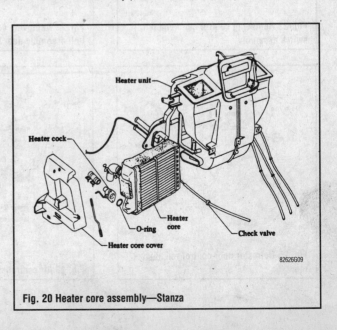

Fig. 20 Heater core assembly—Stanza

Fig. 21 Removing the heater core—Stanza

separate the cases, then pull the heater core from the case) refer to the necessary procedures. Clean heater case of all debris before installation. Check system for proper operation.

Heater Water Control Valve

REMOVAL & INSTALLATION

All Models

1. Disconnect the negative battery cable.
2. Drain the cooling system. Remove all the necessary components in order to gain access to the valve retaining assembly.

3. Disconnect the electrical, vacuum or mechanical connections from the valve.
4. Disconnect the heater hose from the valve. Remove the control valve from the vehicle.
5. Installation is the reverse of the removal procedure. Refill the cooling system—bleed system if necessary. Check system for proper operation.

Control Head and Fan Switch Assembly

REMOVAL & INSTALLATION

200SX and 240SX

♦ **See Figures 22 thru 29**

1. Disconnect the negative battery cable. Remove the heater control trim panel. Remove the instrument lower trim panels.
2. Disconnect control cables from the heater unit assembly.
3. Disconnect harness (electrical) connectors and ground wire.
4. Disconnect heater control assembly mounting bolts.
5. Installation is the reverse of the removal procedures. Make sure the ground wire makes good connection. Adjust the heater control cables by clamping the cables while pushing cable (refer to the illustrations) outer case and lever in the correct (forward) direction to the complete range of operation. Check system for proper operation.

Stanza

➡ **On some vehicles, the fan switch cannot be removed from the control head assembly.**

1. Disconnect the negative battery cable. Remove cluster cover and instrument lower covers.

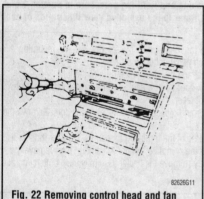

Fig. 22 Removing control head and fan switch assembly

Fig. 23 Removing control cables at heater unit assembly door levers

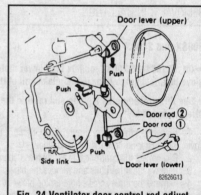

Fig. 24 Ventilator door control rod adjustment

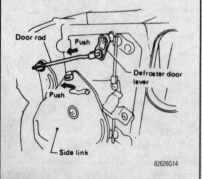

Fig. 25 Defroster door control rod adjustment

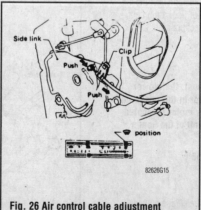

Fig. 26 Air control cable adjustment

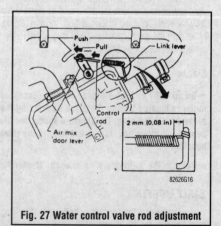

Fig. 27 Water control valve rod adjustment

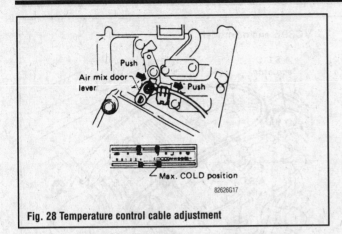

Fig. 28 Temperature control cable adjustment

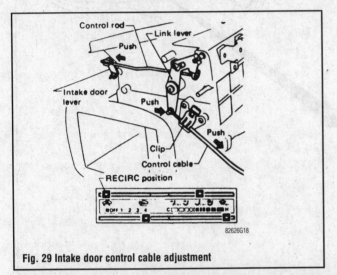

Fig. 29 Intake door control cable adjustment

2. Remove control cables by unfastening clamps at door levers.

3. Disconnect electrical connector and remove heater control head assembly mounting bolts. Remove ground wire from intake box.

4. Remove heater control head assembly.

5. To install reverse the removal procedures. Make sure the ground wire makes good connection. Adjust the heater control cables by clamping the cables while pushing cable (refer to the illustrations) outer case and lever in the correct (forward) direction to the complete range of operation. Check system for proper operation.

Air Conditioning Components

REMOVAL & INSTALLATION

Repair or service of air conditioning components is not covered by this manual, because of the risk of personal injury or death, and because of the legal ramifications of servicing these components without the proper EPA certification and experience. Cost, personal injury or death, environmental damage, and legal considerations (such as the fact that it is a federal crime to vent refrigerant into the atmosphere), dictate that the A/C components on your vehicle should be serviced only by a Motor Vehicle Air Conditioning (MVAC) trained, and EPA certified automotive technician.

➡**If your vehicle's A/C system uses R–12 refrigerant and is in need of recharging, the A/C system can be converted over to R–134a refrigerant (less environmentally harmful and expensive). Refer to Section 1 for additional information on R–12 to R–134a conversions, and for additional considerations dealing with your vehicle's A/C system.**

CRUISE CONTROL

General Description

Datsun/ Nissan refers to their cruise control as the Automatic Speed Control Device (ASCD) system. The ASCD system maintains a desired speed of the vehicle under normal driving conditions. The cruise control system's main parts are the control switches, control unit, actuator, speed sensor, vacuum pump, vacuum pump relay, vacuum switch, vacuum tank, electrical release switches and electrical harness.

➡**The use of the speed control is not recommended when driving conditions do not permit maintaining a constant speed, such as in heavy traffic or on roads that are winding, icy, snow covered or slippery.**

Actuator

REMOVAL & INSTALLATION

◆ **See Figures 30, 31, 32, 33 and 34**

1. Disconnect the negative battery cable.

2. Disconnect the Automatic Speed Control Device (ASCD) cable from the actuator assembly.

3. Disconnect vacuum hose from ASCD release valve.

4. Remove bolts attaching the actuator assembly to the body of the vehicle.

5. Installation is the reverse of the removal procedures. Adjust the ASCD cable as required. Check system for proper operation.

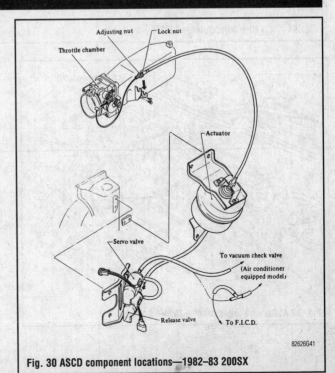

Fig. 30 ASCD component locations—1982–83 200SX

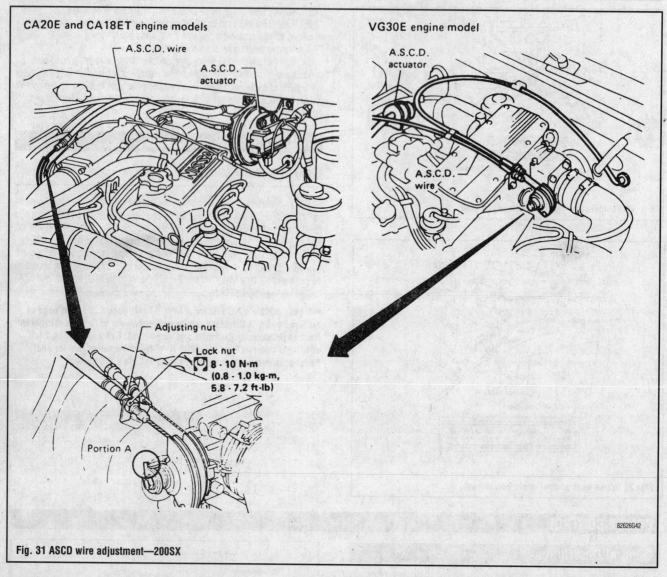

Fig. 31 ASCD wire adjustment—200SX

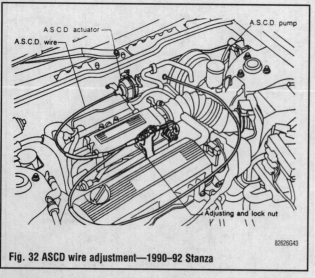

Fig. 32 ASCD wire adjustment—1990–92 Stanza

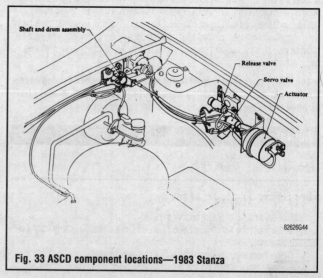

Fig. 33 ASCD component locations—1983 Stanza

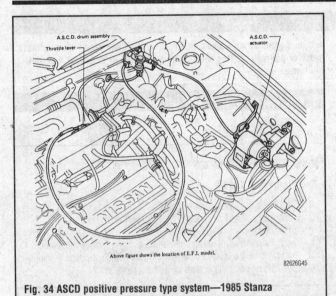

Fig. 34 ASCD positive pressure type system—1985 Stanza

ASCD Cable

REMOVAL & INSTALLATION

1. Disconnect the cable from the actuator assembly—loosen the locknut at actuator assembly and remove the rubber boots.

ENTERTAINMENT SYSTEMS

Radio/Cassette Deck

REMOVAL & INSTALLATION

1982–83 200SX

1. Disconnect the battery. Before removing the radio (audio assembly), you must remove the center instrument cluster which holds the heater controls, etc. Remove the two side screws in the cluster. Remove the heater control and the control panel. Remove the two bolts behind the heater control panel and the two bolts at the case of the cluster. Pull the cluster out of the way after disconnecting the lighter wiring and any other control cables.
2. Remove the radio knobs and fronting panel.
3. Remove the five screws holding the radio assembly in place.
4. Remove the radio after unplugging all connections.
5. Installation is the reverse of removal. Check radio for proper operation.

1984–88 200SX; All 240SX and Stanza Models

♦ See Figure 35

➡On some applications, an auxiliary fuse is located in the rear of the radio. If all other power sources check OK, remove the radio and check the fuse.

1. Disconnect the negative battery cable.
2. Remove all necessary trim panel(s) or ashtray assembly—refer to illustrations.

2. Loosen the locknut at intake manifold bracket. Remove the cable.
3. Installation is the reverse of the removal procedures. Adjust the cable as required. When removing or installing wire end use care not damage. Check system for proper operation.

ADJUSTMENT

1982–83 200SX

Without depressing the accelerator pedal, adjust the adjusting nut until cable free play is within 0.08–0.012 in. (2–3mm) at throttle lever. Tighten the locknut.

1984–88 200SX, 240SX and Stanza (Vacuum Type)

1990–92 Stanza
Without depressing the accelerator pedal, adjust the adjusting nuts until there is no free play or portion A of throttle lever comes in contact with assembly. Then return adjustment (back off) nuts ½–1 turn back to gain free play. Securely tighten locknut to hold adjusting nut in place.

Stanza (Positive Pressure Type)

On the this type system, the actuator cable is operated by compressed air produced in the compressor built into the actuator assembly.
Without depressing the accelerator pedal, adjust the adjusting nuts until there is no free play—tighten locknut.

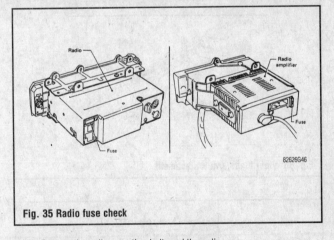

Fig. 35 Radio fuse check

3. Remove the radio mounting bolts and the radio.
4. Disconnect the electrical harness connector and the antenna plug from the radio.
   To install:
5. Connect the electrical harness connector and the antenna plug to the radio.
6. Install the radio and tighten the bolts.
7. Install all necessary trim panel(s) or ashtray assembly.
8. Check radio system for proper operation.

WINDSHIELD WIPER AND WASHERS

Wiper Blade and Arm

REMOVAL & INSTALLATION

Front and Rear

♦ See Figures 36 and 37

➡On some new models a wiper arm lock is used to keep the wiper arm off the glass surface when washing the glass or replacing the blade. On most models the wiper arms are a different length. They have an identifying mark and care must be taken to install them properly.

1. Pull the wiper arm up.
2. Push the lock pin, then remove the wiper blade.
3. Insert the new wiper blade to the wiper arm until a click sounds.
4. Make sure the wiper blade contacts the glass. Otherwise, the arm may be damaged.
5. To remove the arm assembly lift the end of the wiper arm, which is spring loaded, at the base and remove the attaching nut (if a lock type application is used—push lock up). On early models just remove the attaching nut at the base of the wiper arm.

➡Before reinstalling wiper arm, clean up the pivot area with a suitable brush or equivalent. This will reduce possibility of the wiper arm coming loose.

Front Wiper Motor and Linkage

REMOVAL & INSTALLATION

200SX and Stanza (1982–89)

♦ See Figures 38 and 39

1. Disconnect the battery ground cable.
2. Open the hood and disconnect the motor wiring connection.
3. Unbolt the motor from the body.
4. Disconnect the wiper linkage from the motor and remove the motor.
5. Installation is the reverse of removal. Check wiper arm/blade assembly to cowl clearance and complete system for proper operation.

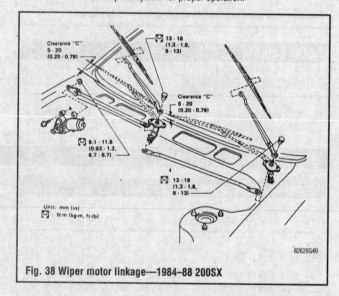

Fig. 38 Wiper motor linkage—1984–88 200SX

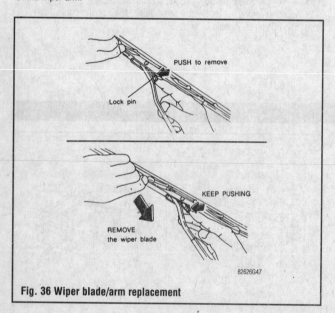

Fig. 36 Wiper blade/arm replacement

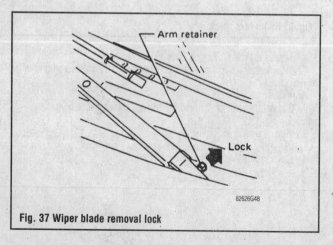

Fig. 37 Wiper blade removal lock

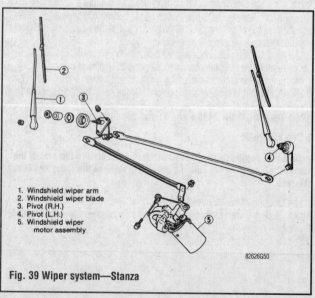

1. Windshield wiper arm
2. Windshield wiper blade
3. Pivot (R.H.)
4. Pivot (L.H.)
5. Windshield wiper motor assembly

Fig. 39 Wiper system—Stanza

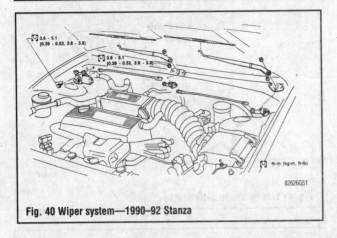

Fig. 40 Wiper system—1990–92 Stanza

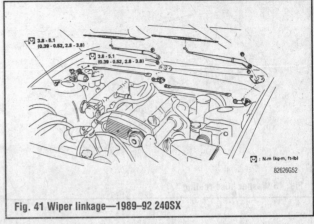

Fig. 41 Wiper linkage—1989–92 240SX

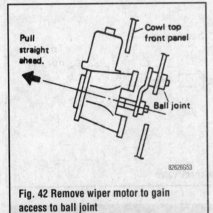

Fig. 42 Remove wiper motor to gain access to ball joint

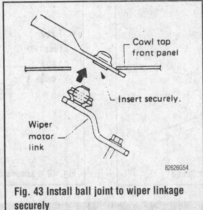

Fig. 43 Install ball joint to wiper linkage securely

Fig. 44 Rear window wiper motor—1983 200SX

240SX and 1990–92 Stanza

▶ See Figures 40, 41, 42 and 43

1. Remove the wiper arm.
2. Remove the cowl cover. Remove the wiper motor so that the wiper motor link comes out of hole in the front cowl top panel.
3. Disconnect the ball joint which connects motor link and wiper link. Remove the wiper motor from the vehicle.
4. Remove wiper link pivot blocks on driver and passenger sides. Remove the wiper link and pivot blocks as an assembly from the oblong hole on the left side of cowl top.
5. To install reverse the removal procedures. Apply a small amount of grease to ball joints before installation. Refer to the illustrations.

Rear Wiper Motor

REMOVAL & INSTALLATION

▶ See Figure 44

1. Disconnect the negative battery cable. Position the wiper arm to raise the wiper blade off the rear window glass. Then, remove the attaching nut and washers; then, work the wiper arm off the motor shaft.
2. Remove the attaching screws and remove the hatchback/liftback area inner finish panel. Carefully peel the plastic water shield off the sealer if so equipped.
3. Disconnect the electrical connector at the motor. Remove the motor mounting bolts and remove the motor.
4. Install the motor in reverse of the removal procedure. Torque the rear window wiper arm-to-motor nut to 9–13 ft. lbs. (13–18 Nm).
5. Before installing the water shield, run a fresh ring of sealer around the outer edge if necessary.

Windshield Washer Fluid Reservoir

REMOVAL & INSTALLATION

Front and Rear

1. Disconnect the negative battery cable and reservoir electrical connector.
2. Disconnect the fluid tube from the washer motor. If the tube is too tight to remove, do not force. Heat the tube with a heat gun if the tube has no extra slack or cut the tube at the motor end.
3. Remove the reservoir retaining bolts and slide out of the bracket.
4. Installation is the reverse of removal. Apply petroleum jelly to the motor nipple before installing the washer tube.

➡A check valve is installed in the washer fluid line. Be careful not to connect check valve to washer tube in the wrong direction.

Windshield Washer Motor

REMOVAL & INSTALLATION

Front and Rear

▶ See Figures 45, 46, 47 and 48

Remove the washer reservoir/motor assembly from the vehicle and drain into a suitable container. Remove all connections. Pull the motor from the rubber grommet. If having difficulty, lubricate the grommet with penetrating oil and try again. Apply petroleum jelly to install the motor. Reconnect all connections.

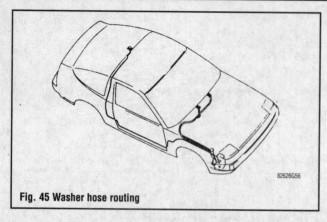

Fig. 45 Washer hose routing

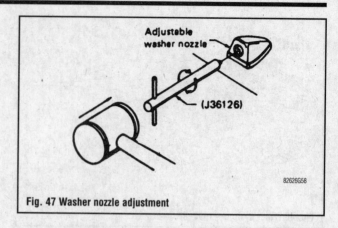

Fig. 47 Washer nozzle adjustment

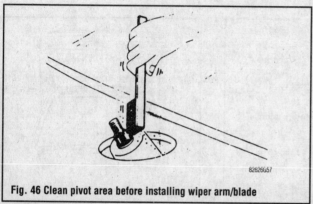

Fig. 46 Clean pivot area before installing wiper arm/blade

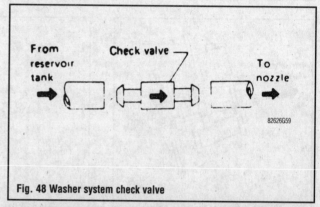

Fig. 48 Washer system check valve

INSTRUMENTS AND SWITCHES

Instrument Cluster/Combination Meter

REMOVAL & INSTALLATION

200SX and 240SX

▶ See Figures 49, 50 and 51

1. Disconnect the negative battery cable. Refer to illustrations.
2. Remove the steering wheel and steering wheel covers, as required.

3. Remove the screws holding the cluster lid in place and remove the lid.
4. On the 200SX, remove the 2 screws and 7 pawls to release the cluster. On the 240SX, the cluster is held with 3 screws.
5. Carefully withdraw the cluster assembly from the instrument panel and disconnect the speedometer cable (analog) and electrical wiring from the rear of the cluster. Make sure the wiring is labeled clearly to avoid confusion during installation.
6. Remove the cluster. Be careful not to damage the printed circuit.
7. Installation is the reverse of the removal procedure.

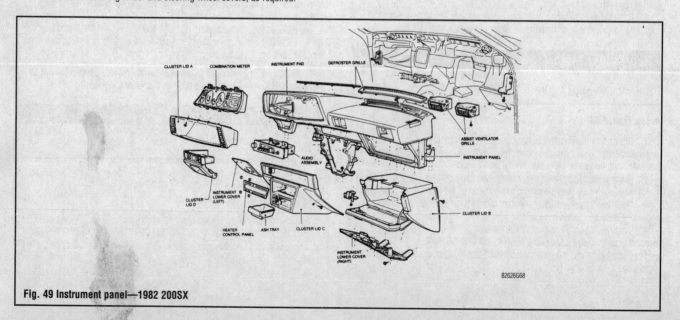

Fig. 49 Instrument panel—1982 200SX

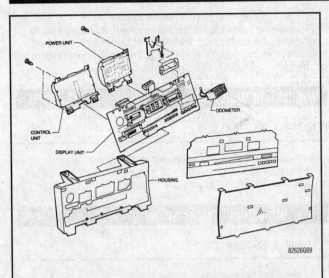

Fig. 50 Electronic digital instrument cluster assembly—1984 200SX

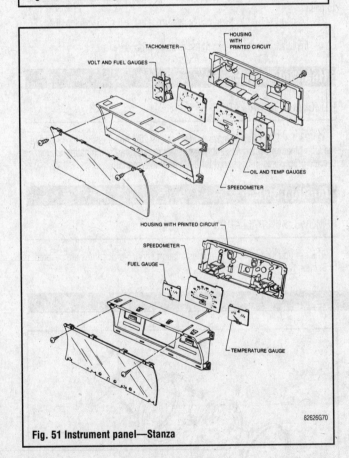

Fig. 51 Instrument panel—Stanza

Stanza

1. Disconnect the negative battery cable. Refer to illustrations.
2. Remove the steering wheel and the steering column covers.
3. Remove the instrument cluster lid by removing its screws.
4. Remove the instrument cluster screws.

5. Gently withdraw the cluster from the instrument pad and disconnect all wiring and speedometer cable. Make sure the wires are marked clearly to avoid confusion during installation. Be careful not to damage the printed circuit.
6. Remove the cluster.
7. Installation is the reverse of removal.

Speedometer

➡️ **If equipped with a digital speedometer, the entire cluster assembly must be replaced if the speedometer is faulty.**

REMOVAL & INSTALLATION

Analog (Needle Type) Speedometers

1. Disconnect the negative battery cable.
2. Remove the cluster.
3. Disconnect the speedometer cable and remove the speedometer fasteners.
4. Carefully remove the speedometer from the cluster. Be careful not to damage the printed circuit board.
5. Installation is the reverse of the removal procedure.

Speedometer Cable

REMOVAL & INSTALLATION

All Models

▸ **See Figures 52, 53 and 54**

➡️ **The speedometer cable connector-to instrument cluster/combination meter has a snap release—simply press on the connector tab to release it.**

1. Loosen the lock nut at the rear extension housing on transmission/transaxle assembly.
2. Disconnect the negative battery cable. Remove the instrument cluster/combination meter—refer to the necessary service procedure.
3. Slide the speedometer cable up to free it.
4. Detach the speedometer cable from all retaining (4) points.
5. Remove the grommet from the upper dash panel by hand.

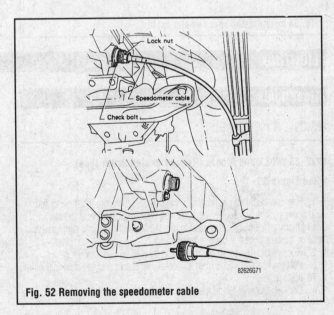

Fig. 52 Removing the speedometer cable

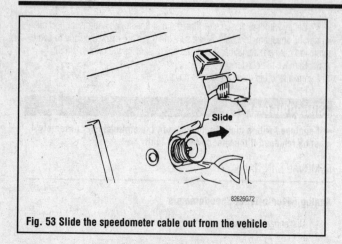

Fig. 53 Slide the speedometer cable out from the vehicle

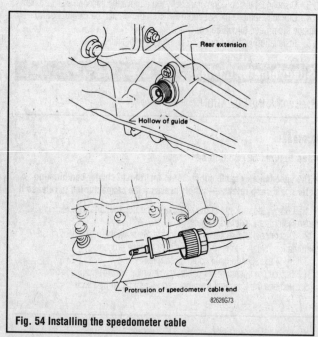

Fig. 54 Installing the speedometer cable

LIGHTING

Headlights

REMOVAL & INSTALLATION

1982–83 200SX and Stanza (Regular Sealed Beam Type)

♦ See Figure 55

1. Remove the headlight retaining ring screws. These are the three or four short screws in the assembly. There are also two longer screws at the top and side of the headlight which are used to aim the headlight. Do not tamper with these or the headlight will have to be reaimed.
2. Remove the ring on round headlights by turning it clockwise.
3. Pull the headlight bulb from its socket and disconnect the electrical plug.
To install:
4. Connect the plug to the new bulb.

6. Pull out the speedometer cable from the vehicle.
7. Installation is the reverse of the removal procedure. Make sure that the speedometer cable assembly is properly lubricated. Install the cable end and hollow portion in the transmission/transaxle rear extension in the correct manner. Torque the lock nut to 7–11 ft. lbs.

Windshield Wiper Switch

REMOVAL & INSTALLATION

On 200SX, 240SX and Stanza model vehicles, the wiper switch is part of the Combination Switch Assembly—refer to Turn Signal/Combination Switch service procedures in Section 8 for additional information.

Rear Windshield Wiper Switch

REMOVAL & INSTALLATION

1. Disconnect the negative battery cable.
2. Remove the rear wiper switch mounting screws/or push in retaining clips to dash.
3. Disconnect the electrical connectors from the rear of the switch, then remove it.
4. Installation is the reverse of the removal procedure.

Headlight Switch

REMOVAL & INSTALLATION

On 200SX, 240SX and Stanza model vehicles, the headlight switch is part of the Combination Switch Assembly—refer to Turn Signal/Combination Switch service procedures in Section 8 for additional information.

Ignition Switch

REMOVAL & INSTALLATION

The ignition switch removal and installation service procedures are covered in Section 8.

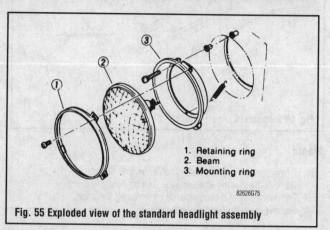

1. Retaining ring
2. Beam
3. Mounting ring

Fig. 55 Exploded view of the standard headlight assembly

5. Position the headlight in the shell. Make sure that the word TOP is, indeed, at the top and that the knobs in the headlight lens engage the slots in the mounting shell.

6. Place the retaining ring over the bulb and install the screws.

7. Check headlight system for proper operation—adjust headlight aim if necessary.

1984–88 200SX and 240SX

♦ See Figures 56, 57 and 58

➡If headlamps do not open on these models, first check the fusible link for the headlight motor. Also check the retract switch. If headlamps do not retract, check the retract control relay. Refer to the "Manual Operation Of Headlight Doors" procedure.

1. Open the headlamp. Disconnect the negative battery cable.
2. Unbolt and remove the finisher.
3. Remove the headlamp lid.
4. Remove the bulb retaining ring. Unplug and remove the headlamp bulb.
5. Reverse the removal procedure to install. Install headlamp rubber cap with electrical connector firmly so that the lip makes contact with the headlamp body. Adjust the headlamp lid so it is flush with the hood and fender, and so the lid joint is as shown in the accompanying illustration. This is done by adjusting the lid mounting screws while open and close the headlamp by operating the manual knob on the headlamp motor. Make sure the lid is not interfering with the protector. Adjust the headlights if necessary.

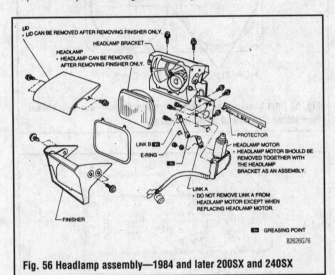
Fig. 56 Headlamp assembly—1984 and later 200SX and 240SX

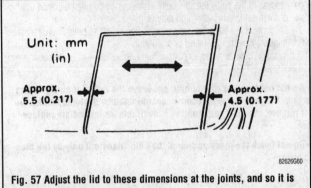
Fig. 57 Adjust the lid to these dimensions at the joints, and so it is flush with the hood and fenders

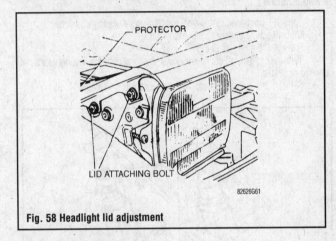
Fig. 58 Headlight lid adjustment

Stanza (Halogen Headlamp Type)

♦ See Figures 59 and 60

The headlight is a semi-sealed beam type which uses a replaceable halogen bulb. A bulb can be replaced from the inside the engine compartment without removing the headlight assembly.

➡Use care and caution when working with this type bulb—high pressure halogen gas is sealed inside the halogen bulb.

1. Disconnect the negative battery cable. On some late model vehicles, remove the Anti-lock brake system electrical connectors and bracket assembly

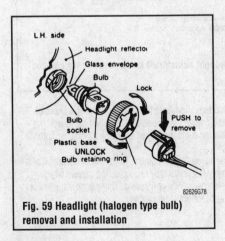
Fig. 59 Headlight (halogen type bulb) removal and installation

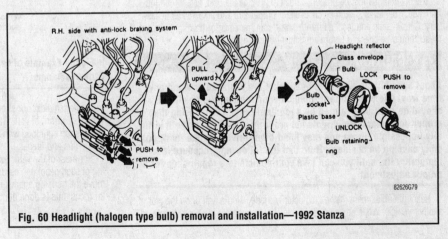
Fig. 60 Headlight (halogen type bulb) removal and installation—1992 Stanza

to gain access to the bulb. Turn the bulb retaining ring counterclockwise until it is free of the headlight reflector, and remove it.

2. Disconnect the electrical connector at the rear of the bulb. Then, remove the bulb carefully without rotating or shaking it.

3. Install in reverse order. Check headlight operation—adjust headlamp aim if necessary.

➡Do not remove a headlight bulb and leave the reflector empty. If you do this, the reflector will become contaminated by dust and smoke. Do not remove one bulb until another is available for immediate replacement.

➡Do not touch the glass portion of the bulb. Handle it only by the plastic base!

MANUAL OPERATION OF HEADLIGHT DOORS

▶ **See Figure 61**

1. Turn OFF both headlight switch and retractable headlight switch.
2. Disconnect the battery negative terminal.
3. Remove the motor shaft cap.
4. Turn the motor shaft counterclockwise by hand until the headlights are opened or closed.
5. Reinstall the motor shaft cap and connect the battery cable.

Fig. 61 Manual operation of power headlight doors

AIMING THE HEADLIGHTS

▶ **See Figures 62, 63, 64, 65 and 66**

The headlights must be properly aimed to provide the best, safest road illumination. The lights should be checked for proper aim and adjusted as necessary. Certain state and local authorities have requirements for headlight aiming; these should be checked before adjustment is made.

※※ CAUTION

About once a year, when the headlights are replaced or when any time front end work is performed on your vehicle, the headlights should be accurately aimed by a reputable repair shop using the proper equipment. Headlights not properly aimed can make it virtually impossible to see and may blind other drivers on the road, possibly causing an accident. Note that the following procedure is a temporary fix, until you can take your vehicle to a repair shop for a proper adjustment.

Headlight adjustment may be temporarily made using a wall or on the rear of another vehicle. When adjusted, the lights should not glare in oncoming car or

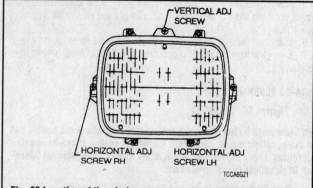

Fig. 62 Location of the aiming screws on most vehicles with sealed beam headlights

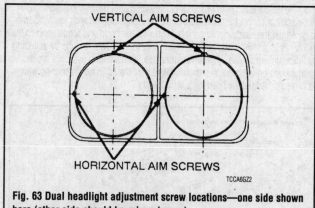

Fig. 63 Dual headlight adjustment screw locations—one side shown here (other side should be mirror image)

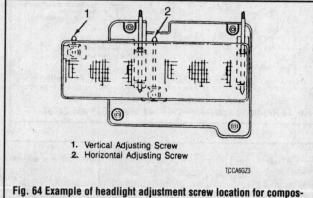

1. Vertical Adjusting Screw
2. Horizontal Adjusting Screw

Fig. 64 Example of headlight adjustment screw location for composite headlamps

truck windshields, nor should they illuminate the passenger compartment of vehicles in front of you. These adjustments should always be fine-tuned by a repair shop equipped with aiming tools. Improper adjustments may be both dangerous and illegal.

For most of the vehicles covered by this manual, horizontal and vertical aiming of each headlamp assembly is provided by two adjusting screws which move the housing against the tension of a coil spring. There is no adjustment for focus; this is done during headlight manufacturing.

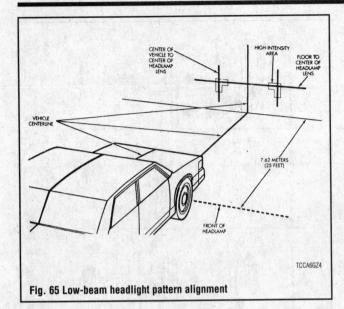

Fig. 65 Low-beam headlight pattern alignment

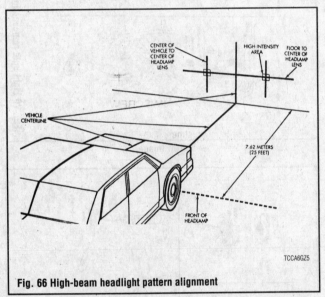

Fig. 66 High-beam headlight pattern alignment

➡**Because the composite headlight assembly is bolted into position, no adjustment should be necessary or possible. Some applications, however, may be bolted to an adjuster plate or may be retained by adjusting screws. If so, follow this procedure when adjusting the lights, BUT always have the adjustment checked by a reputable shop.**

Before removing the headlight bulb or disturbing the headlamp in any way, note the current settings in order to ease headlight adjustment upon reassembly. If the high or low beam setting of the old lamp still works, this can be done using the wall of a garage or a building:

1. Park the vehicle on a level surface, with the fuel tank about ½ full and with the vehicle empty of all extra cargo (unless normally carried). The vehicle should be facing a wall which is no less than 6 feet (1.8m) high and 12 feet (3.7m) wide. The front of the vehicle should be about 25 feet from the wall.

2. If aiming is to be performed outdoors, it is advisable to wait until dusk in order to properly see the headlight beams on the wall. If done in a garage, darken the area around the wall as much as possible by closing shades or hanging cloth over the windows.

3. Turn the headlights **ON** and mark the wall at the center of each light's low beam, then switch on the brights and mark the center of each light's high beam. A short length of masking tape which is visible from the front of the vehicle may be used. Although marking all four positions is advisable, marking one position from each light should be sufficient.

4. If neither beam on one side is working, and if another like-sized vehicle is available, park the second one in the exact spot where the vehicle was and mark the beams using the same-side light. Then switch the vehicles so the one to be aimed is back in the original spot. It must be parked no closer to or farther away from the wall than the second vehicle.

5. Perform any necessary repairs, but make sure the vehicle is not moved, or is returned to the exact spot from which the lights were marked. Turn the headlights **ON** and adjust the beams to match the marks on the wall.

6. Have the headlight adjustment checked as soon as possible by a reputable repair shop.

Signal and Marker Lights

REMOVAL & INSTALLATION

▶ **See Figures 67 thru 78**

Front Turn Signal and Parking Lights

1. Refer to the illustrations. Remove turn signal/parking light lens with retaining screws.
2. Slightly depress the bulb and turn it counterclockwise to release it.
3. To install the bulb carefully push down and turn bulb clockwise at the same time.
4. Install the turn signal/parking light lens with retaining screws.

Side Marker Lights

1. Refer to the illustrations. Remove side marker light lens with retaining screws.
2. Turn the bulb socket counterclockwise to release it from lens.
3. Pull bulb straight out.
4. To install the bulb, carefully push straight in.
5. Turn the bulb socket clockwise to install it in lens.
6. Install side marker light lens with retaining screws.

Rear Turn Signal, Brake and Parking Lights

1. Refer to the illustrations. Remove rear trim panel in rear of vehicle, if necessary, to gain access to the bulb socket.
2. Slightly depress the bulb and turn it counterclockwise to release it.
3. To install the bulb, carefully push down and turn bulb clockwise at the same time.
4. Install trim panel if necessary.

High-Mount Brake Light/Dome Light/Cargo Light/License Plate Light

1. Unfasten any necessary retainers, then remove the lens to access the bulb socket.
2. Identify the type of bulb and remove it using the appropriate technique. Refer to the illustrations.
3. Install the bulb carefully, by reversing the removal steps.
4. Install the lens.

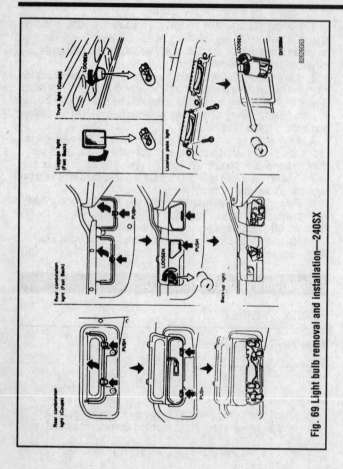

Fig. 69 Light bulb removal and installation—240SX

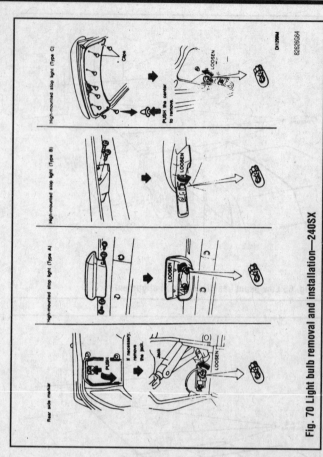

Fig. 70 Light bulb removal and installation—240SX

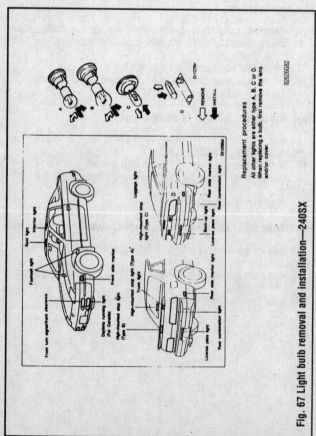

Fig. 67 Light bulb removal and installation—240SX

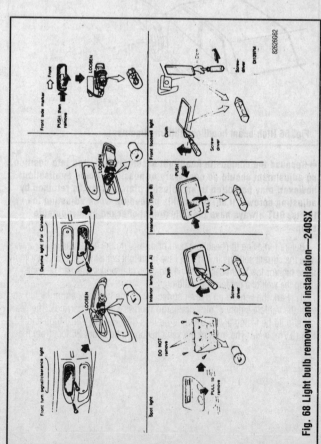

Fig. 68 Light bulb removal and installation—240SX

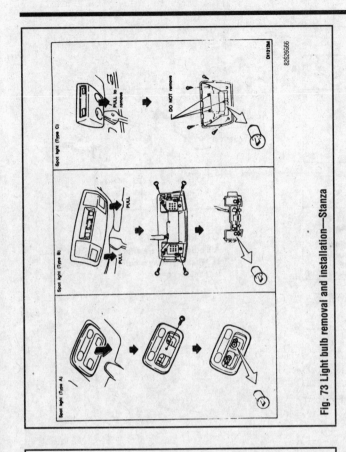

Fig. 73 Light bulb removal and installation—Stanza

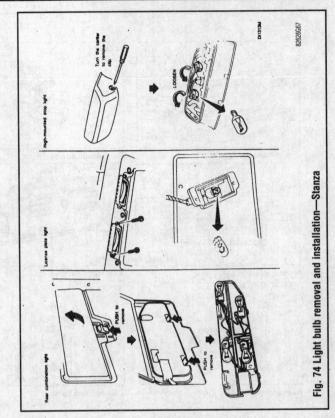

Fig. 74 Light bulb removal and installation—Stanza

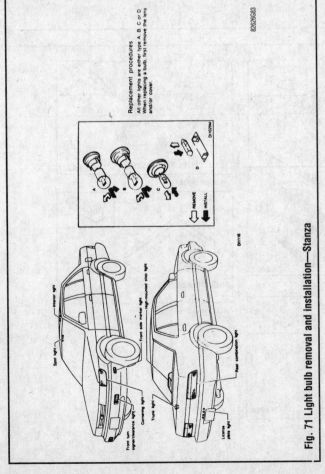

Fig. 71 Light bulb removal and installation—Stanza

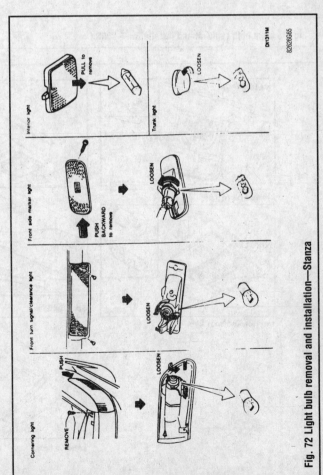

Fig. 72 Light bulb removal and installation—Stanza

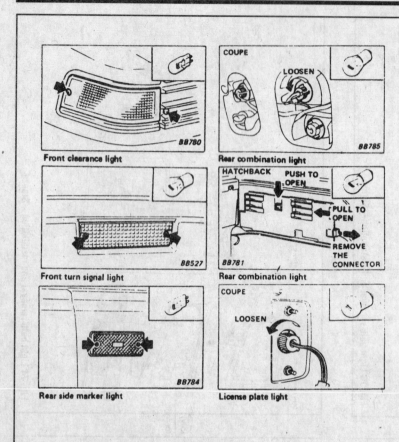

Front clearance light — BB780

Rear combination light (COUPE) — BB785

Front turn signal light — BB527

Rear combination light (HATCHBACK) — BB781 — PUSH TO OPEN / PULL TO OPEN / REMOVE THE CONNECTOR

Rear side marker light — BB784

License plate light (COUPE) — LOOSEN

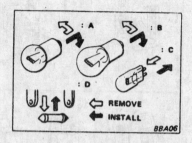

: A : B : C : D

REMOVE
INSTALL

BBA06

OTHER LIGHTS

All other lights are either type A, B, C or D. When replacing a bulb, first remove the lens and/or cover.

82626G84

Fig. 75 Light bulb removal and installation—200SX

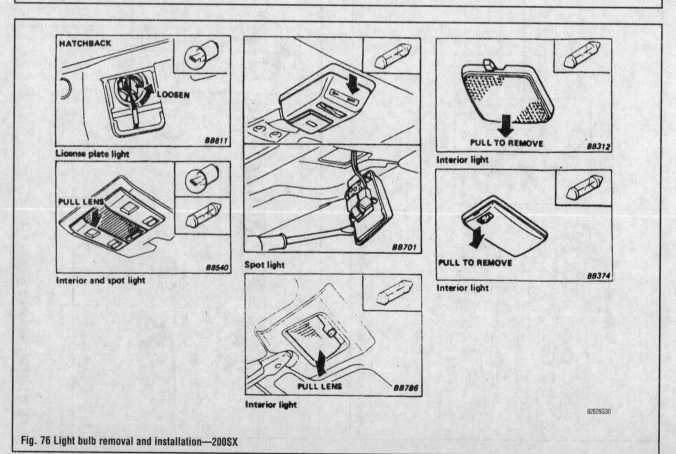

License plate light (HATCHBACK) — LOOSEN — BB811

Interior and spot light — PULL LENS — BB540

Spot light — BB701

Interior light — PULL LENS — BB786

Interior light — PULL TO REMOVE — BB312

Interior light — PULL TO REMOVE — BB374

82626G30

Fig. 76 Light bulb removal and installation—200SX

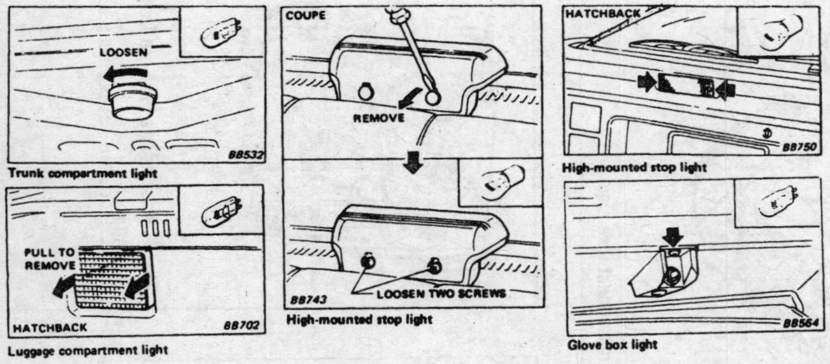

Troubleshooting Basic Lighting Problems

Problem	Cause	Solution
Lights		
One or more lights don't work, but others do	• Defective bulb(s) • Blown fuse(s) • Dirty fuse clips or light sockets • Poor ground circuit	• Replace bulb(s) • Replace fuse(s) • Clean connections • Run ground wire from light socket housing to car frame
Lights burn out quickly	• Incorrect voltage regulator setting or defective regulator • Poor battery/alternator connections	• Replace voltage regulator • Check battery/alternator connections
Lights go dim	• Low/discharged battery • Alternator not charging • Corroded sockets or connections • Low voltage output	• Check battery • Check drive belt tension; repair or replace alternator • Clean bulb and socket contacts and connections • Replace voltage regulator
Lights flicker	• Loose connection • Poor ground • Circuit breaker operating (short circuit)	• Tighten all connections • Run ground wire from light housing to car frame • Check connections and look for bare wires
Lights "flare"—Some flare is normal on acceleration—if excessive, see "Lights Burn Out Quickly"	• High voltage setting	• Replace voltage regulator
Lights glare—approaching drivers are blinded	• Lights adjusted too high • Rear springs or shocks sagging • Rear tires soft	• Have headlights aimed • Check rear springs/shocks • Check/correct rear tire pressure
Turn Signals		
Turn signals don't work in either direction	• Blown fuse • Defective flasher • Loose connection	• Replace fuse • Replace flasher • Check/tighten all connections
Right (or left) turn signal only won't work	• Bulb burned out • Right (or left) indicator bulb burned out • Short circuit	• Replace bulb • Check/replace indicator bulb • Check/repair wiring
Flasher rate too slow or too fast	• Incorrect wattage bulb • Incorrect flasher	• Flasher bulb • Replace flasher (use a variable load flasher if you pull a trailer)
Indicator lights do not flash (burn steadily)	• Burned out bulb • Defective flasher	• Replace bulb • Replace flasher
Indicator lights do not light at all	• Burned out indicator bulb • Defective flasher	• Replace indicator bulb • Replace flasher

TCCA6002A

Fig. 77 Light bulb removal and installation—200SX

Item	Wattage (W)	Bulb No.
Front turn signal/clearance light	27/8	1157
Front side marker light	3.8	194
Rear combination light		
Turn signal	27	1156
Stop/Tail	27/8	1157
Back-up	27	1156
Rear side marker light	3.8	194
License plate light	7.5	89
High-mounted stop light	18	921
Interior light	10	
Spot light	8	
Foot well light	3	
Trunk light (Coupe)	3.4	
Luggage compartment light (Fast Back)	5	
Daytime light (For Canada)	27	1156

Fig. 78 Light Bulb Chart

TRAILER WIRING

Wiring the vehicle for towing is fairly easy. There are a number of good wiring kits available and these should be used, rather than trying to design your own.

All trailers will need brake lights and turn signals as well as tail lights and side marker lights. Most areas require extra marker lights for overwide trailers. Also, most areas have recently required back-up lights for trailers, and most trailer manufacturers have been building trailers with back-up lights for several years.

Additionally, some Class I, most Class II and just about all Class III and IV trailers will have electric brakes. Add to this number an accessories wire, to operate trailer internal equipment or to charge the trailer's battery, and you can have as many as seven wires in the harness.

Determine the equipment on your trailer and buy the wiring kit necessary. The kit will contain all the wires needed, plus a plug adapter set which includes the female plug, mounted on the bumper or hitch, and the male plug, wired into, or plugged into the trailer harness.

When installing the kit, follow the manufacturer's instructions. The color coding of the wires is usually standard throughout the industry. One point to note: some domestic vehicles, and most imported vehicles, have separate turn signals. On most domestic vehicles, the brake lights and rear turn signals operate with the same bulb. For those vehicles without separate turn signals, you can purchase an isolation unit so that the brake lights won't blink whenever the turn signals are operated.

One, final point, the best kits are those with a spring loaded cover on the vehicle mounted socket. This cover prevents dirt and moisture from corroding the terminals. Never let the vehicle socket hang loosely; always mount it securely to the bumper or hitch.

CIRCUIT PROTECTION

Fuses

REMOVAL & INSTALLATION

▶ **See Figures 79 and 80**

The fuses can be easily inspected to see if they are blown. Simply pull the fuse from the block, inspect it and replace it with a new one, if necessary. A vehicle can be equipped with 2 or more fuse block/panels-the engine compartment and passenger compartment are the locations.

➡**When replacing a blown fuse, be certain to replace it with one of the correct amperage.**

Fusible Links

▶ **See Figures 81, 82 and 83**

A fusible link(s) is a protective device used in an electrical circuit. When current increases beyond a certain amperage, the fusible metal wire of the link melts, thus breaking the electrical circuit and preventing further damage to the other components and wiring. Whenever a fusible link is melted because of a short circuit, correct the cause before installing a new link. All fusible links are the plug in kind. To replace them, simply unplug the bad link and insert the new one.

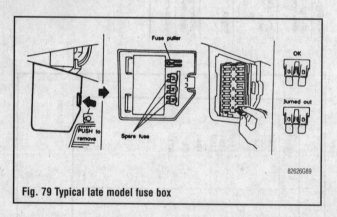

Fig. 79 Typical late model fuse box

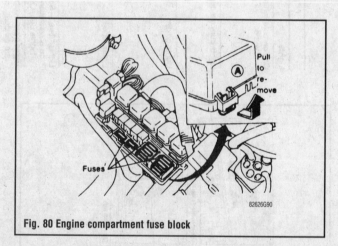

Fig. 80 Engine compartment fuse block

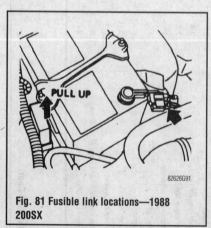

Fig. 81 Fusible link locations—1988 200SX

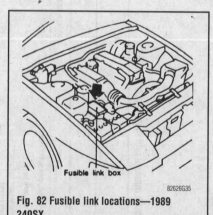

Fig. 82 Fusible link locations—1989 240SX

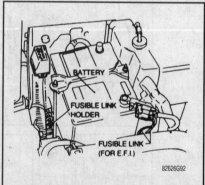

Fig. 83 Most fusible links are found beside the battery

Circuit Breakers

Circuit breakers (can be found anywhere a fuse can be installed) are also located in the fuse block. A circuit breaker is an electrical switch which breaks the circuit during an electrical overload. The circuit breaker will remain open until the short or overload condition in the circuit is corrected.

Flashers

To replace the (turn signal or hazard warning) flasher carefully pull it from the electrical connector. If necessary remove any component/trim panel that restricts removal. On some applications, a combination flasher is used for turn signals and hazard warning lights.

WIRING DIAGRAMS

INDEX OF WIRING DIAGRAMS

82626W01

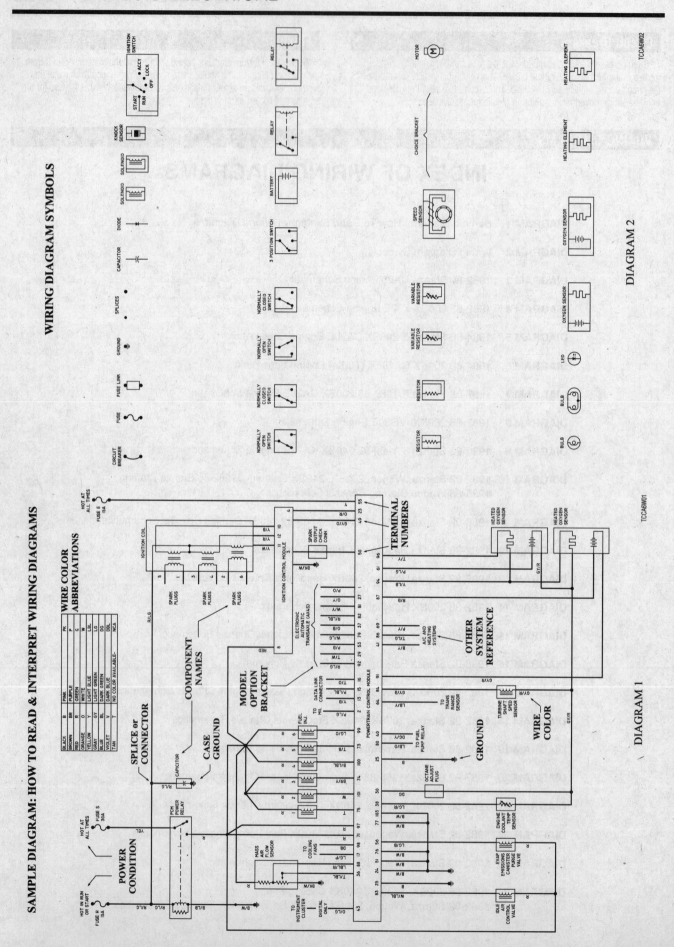

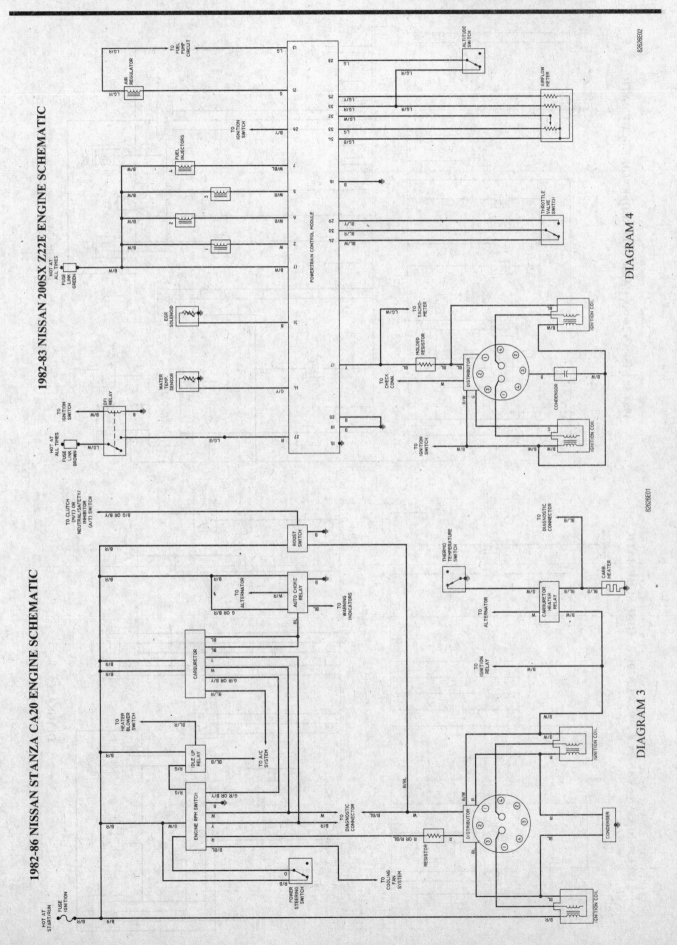

1982-83 NISSAN 200SX Z22E ENGINE SCHEMATIC

DIAGRAM 4

1982-86 NISSAN STANZA CA20 ENGINE SCHEMATIC

DIAGRAM 3

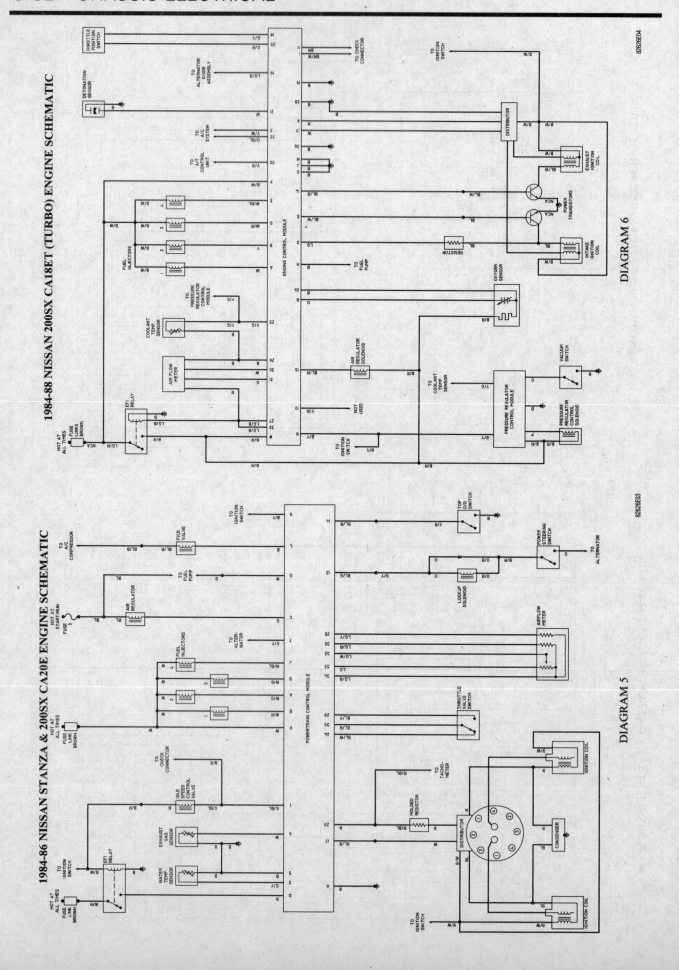

1984-88 NISSAN 200SX CA18ET (TURBO) ENGINE SCHEMATIC

DIAGRAM 6

1984-86 NISSAN STANZA & 200SX CA20E ENGINE SCHEMATIC

DIAGRAM 5

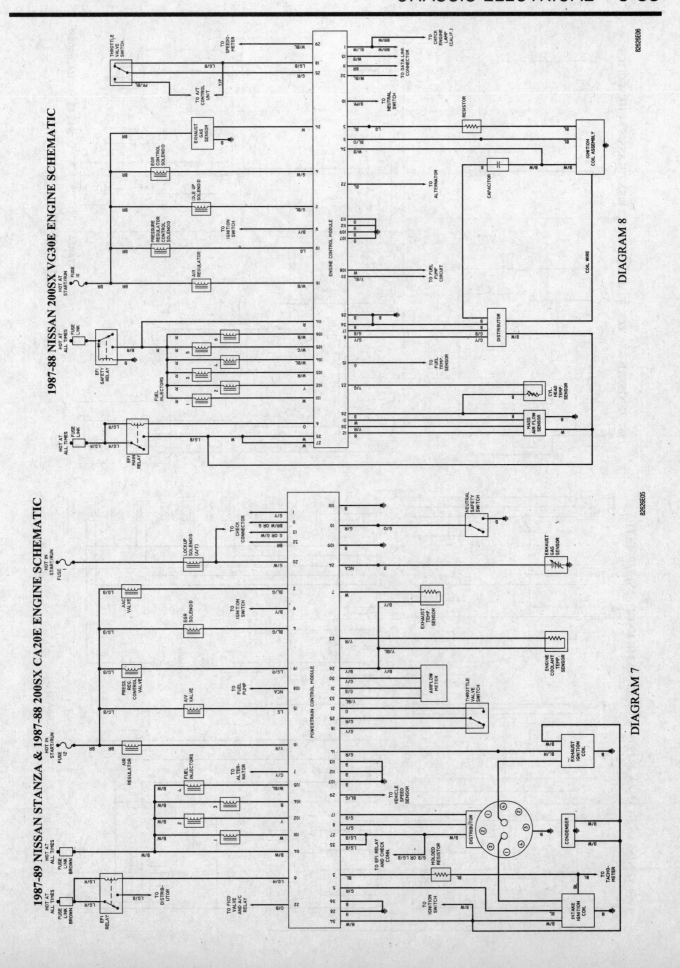

1987-88 NISSAN 200SX VG30E ENGINE SCHEMATIC

DIAGRAM 8

1987-89 NISSAN STANZA & 1987-88 200SX CA20E ENGINE SCHEMATIC

DIAGRAM 7

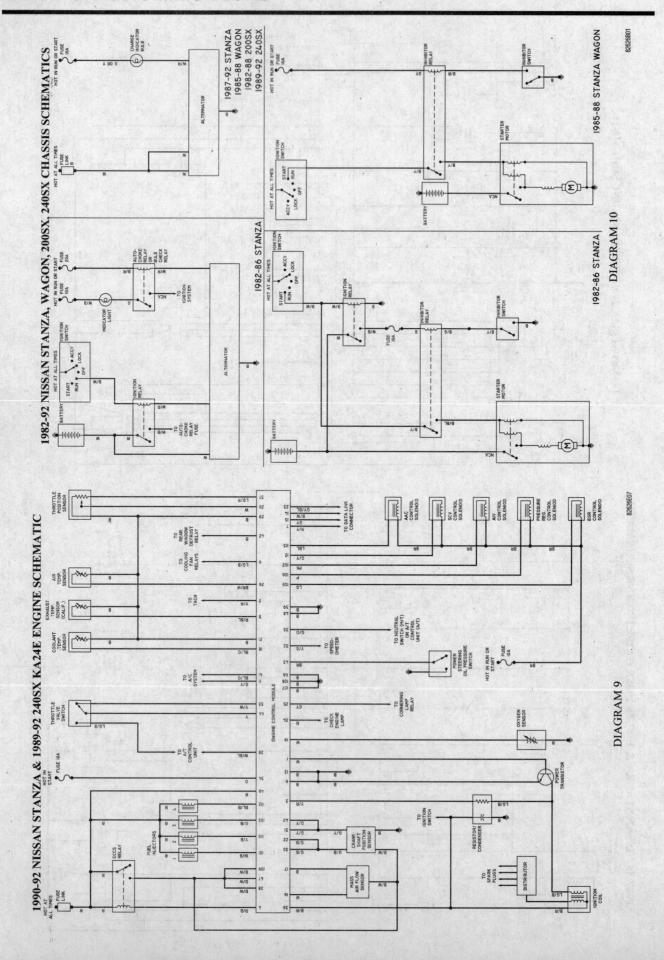

1982-92 NISSAN STANZA, WAGON, 200SX, 240SX CHASSIS SCHEMATICS

1987-92 STANZA
1985-88 WAGON
1982-88 200SX
1989-92 240SX

1985-88 STANZA WAGON

1982-86 STANZA

DIAGRAM 10

1990-92 NISSAN STANZA & 1989-92 240SX KA24E ENGINE SCHEMATIC

DIAGRAM 9

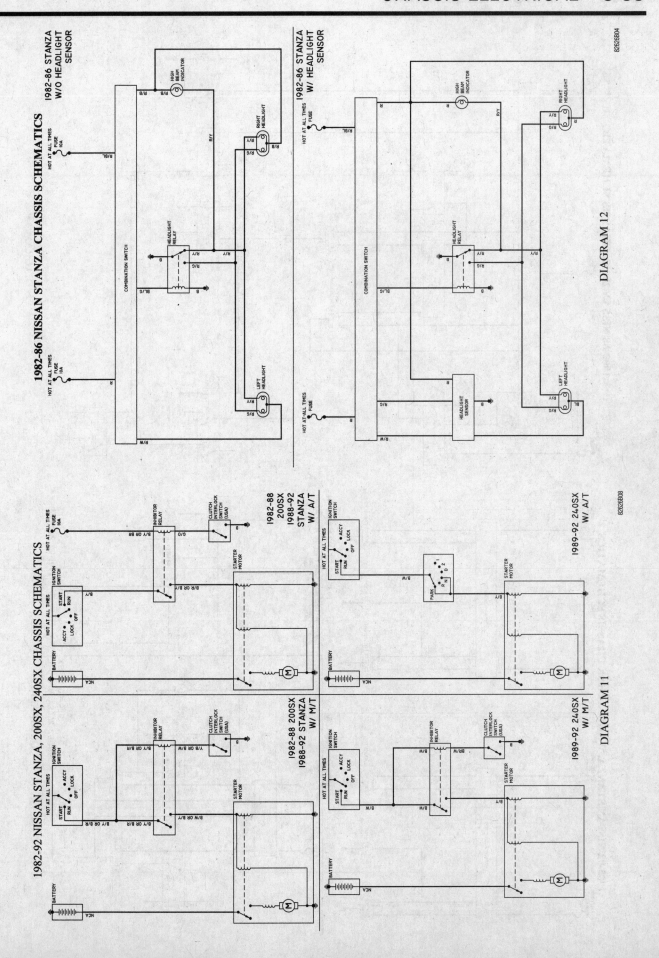

1982-86 NISSAN STANZA CHASSIS SCHEMATICS

1982-86 STANZA W/O HEADLIGHT SENSOR

1982-86 STANZA W/ HEADLIGHT SENSOR

DIAGRAM 12

1982-92 NISSAN STANZA, 200SX, 240SX CHASSIS SCHEMATICS

1982-88 200SX
1988-92 STANZA
W/ A/T

1989-92 240SX
W/ A/T

1982-88 200SX
1988-92 STANZA
W/ M/T

1989-92 240SX
W/ M/T

DIAGRAM 11

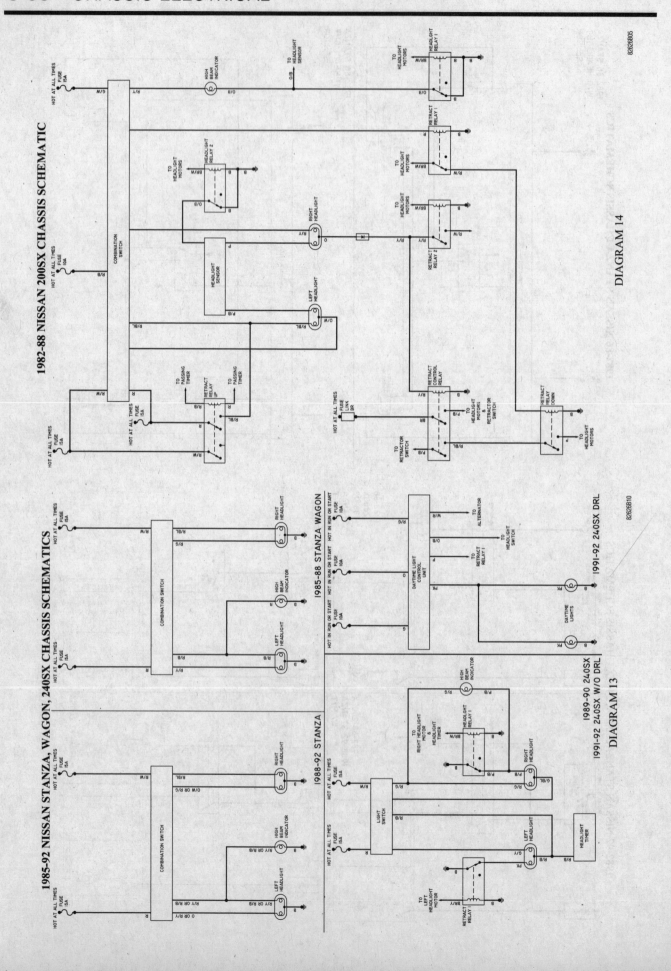

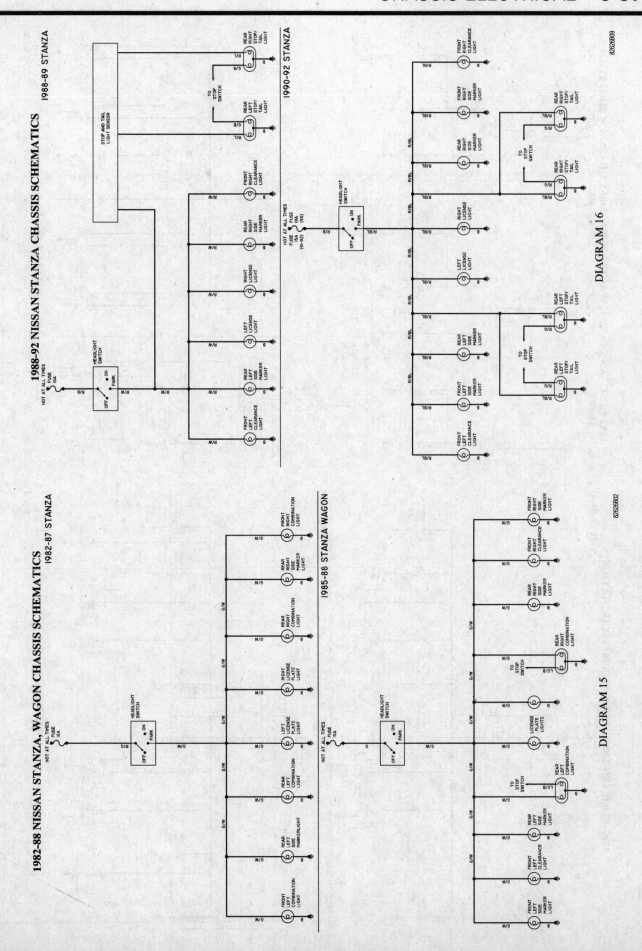

1988-92 NISSAN STANZA CHASSIS SCHEMATICS

1988-89 STANZA

1990-92 STANZA

DIAGRAM 16

1982-88 NISSAN STANZA, WAGON CHASSIS SCHEMATICS

1982-87 STANZA

1985-88 STANZA WAGON

DIAGRAM 15

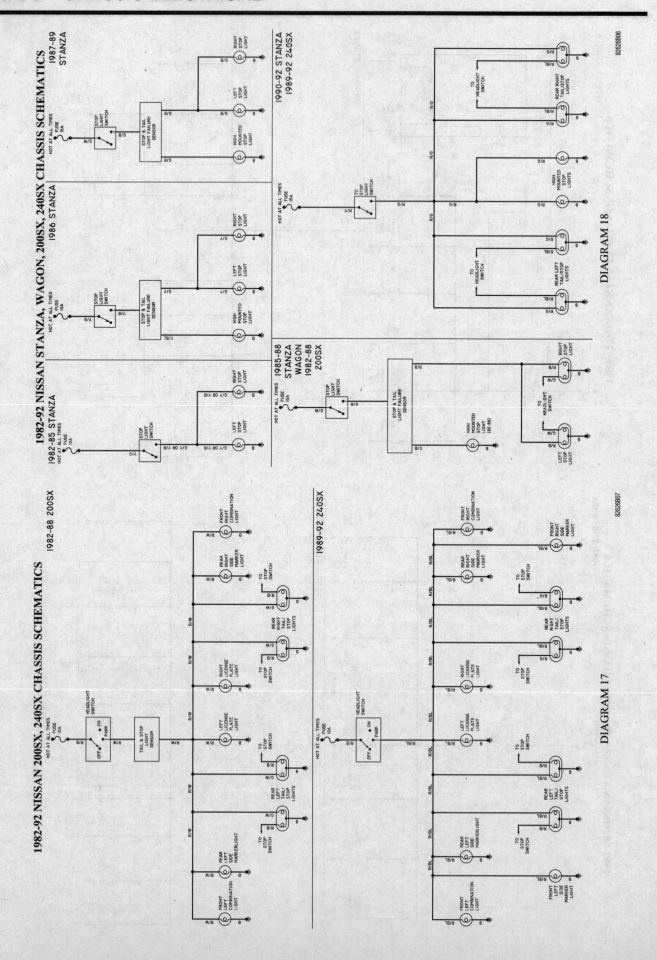

1982-92 NISSAN STANZA, WAGON, 200SX, 240SX CHASSIS SCHEMATICS

1987-89 STANZA

1986 STANZA

1982-85 STANZA

1990-92 STANZA 1989-92 240SX

1985-88 STANZA WAGON 1982-88 200SX

DIAGRAM 18

1982-92 NISSAN 200SX, 240SX CHASSIS SCHEMATICS

1982-88 200SX

1989-92 240SX

DIAGRAM 17

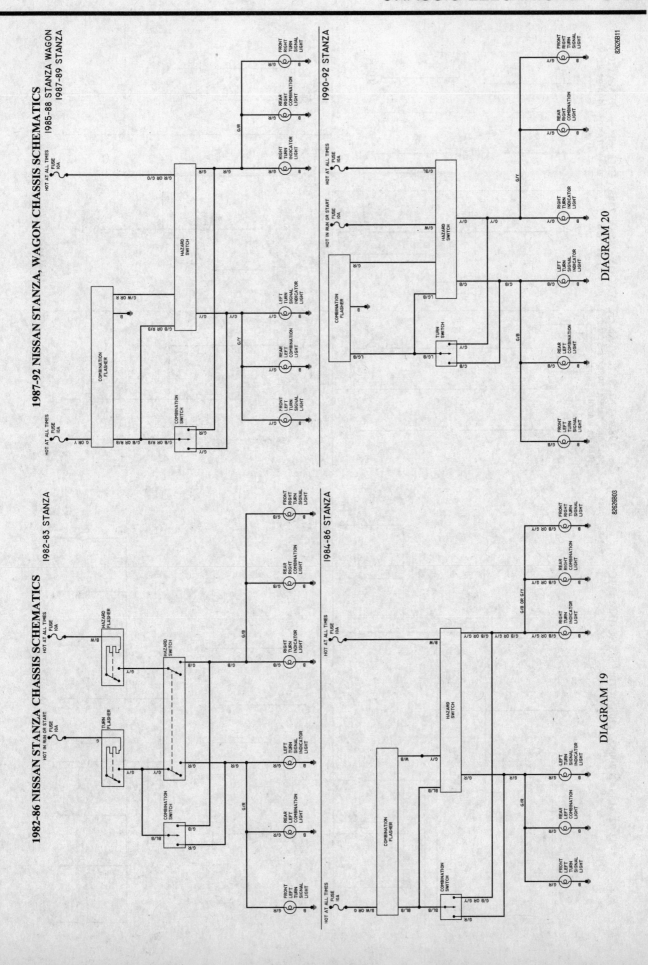

1987-92 NISSAN STANZA, WAGON CHASSIS SCHEMATICS

1985-88 STANZA WAGON
1987-89 STANZA

1990-92 STANZA

DIAGRAM 20

1982-86 NISSAN STANZA CHASSIS SCHEMATICS

1982-83 STANZA

1984-86 STANZA

DIAGRAM 19

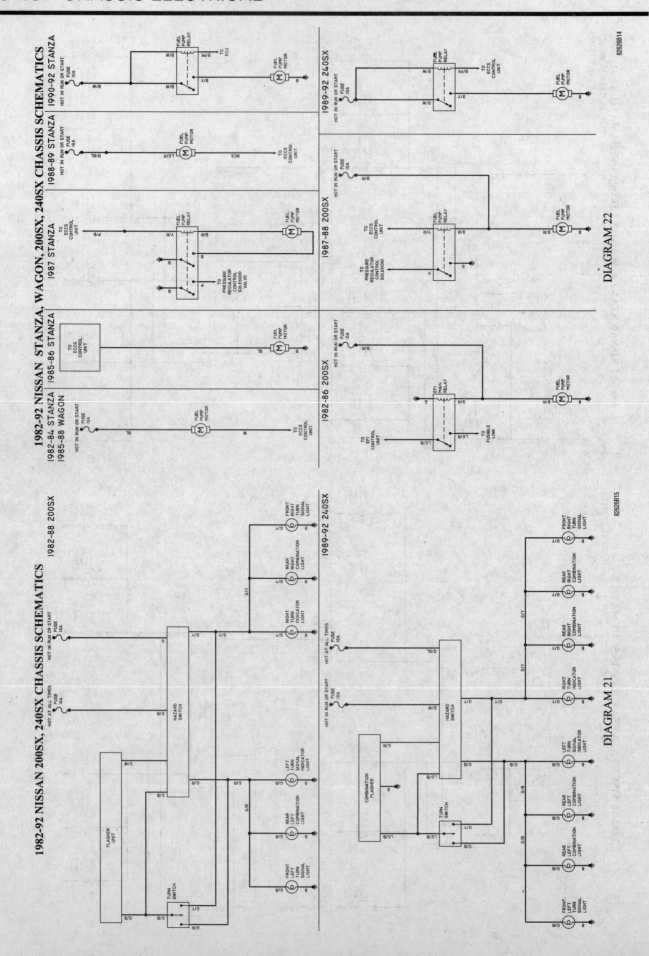

DIAGRAM 22

DIAGRAM 21

1982-92 NISSAN STANZA, WAGON CHASSIS SCHEMATICS

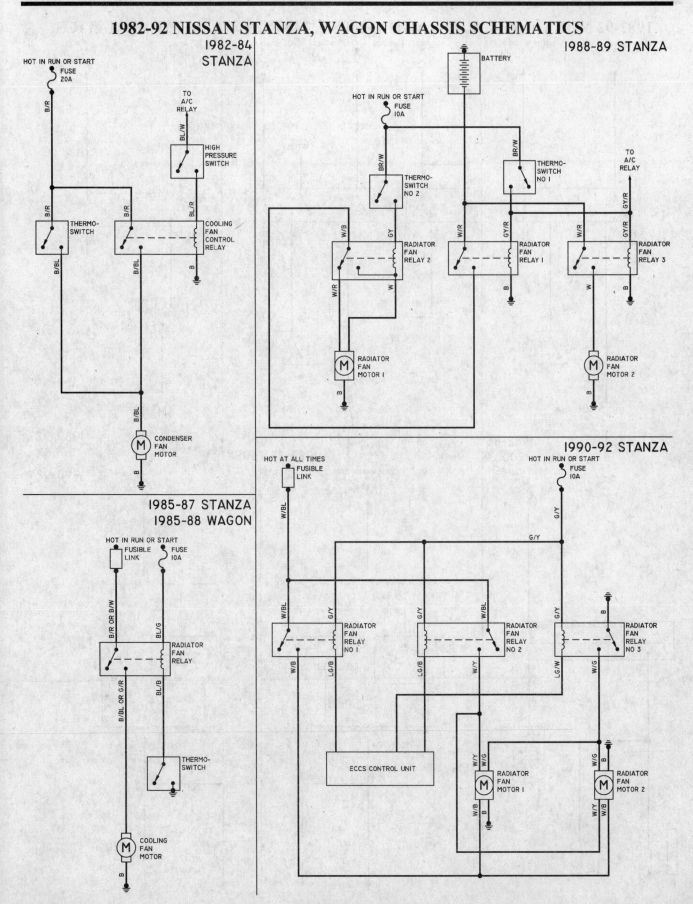

DIAGRAM 23

82626B13

1982-92 NISSAN STANZA, WAGON, 200SX, 240SX, CHASSIS SCHEMATICS

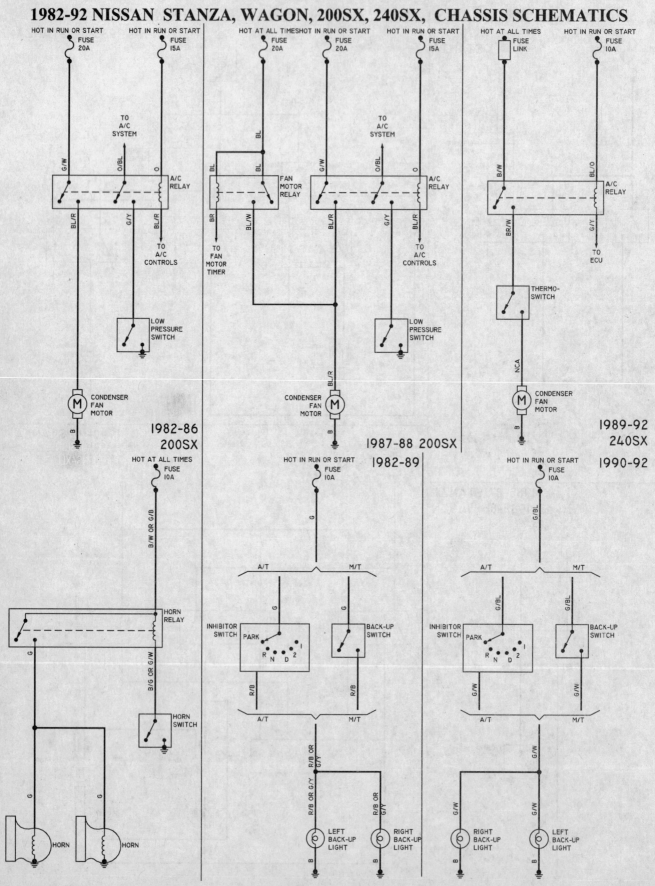

DIAGRAM 24

82626B12

7

DRIVE TRAIN

MANUAL TRANSMISSION

Understanding the Manual Transmission

Because of the way an internal combustion engine breathes, it can produce torque (or twisting force) only within a narrow speed range. Most overhead valve pushrod engines must turn at about 2500 rpm to produce their peak torque. Often by 4500 rpm, they are producing so little torque that continued increases in engine speed produce no power increases.

The torque peak on overhead camshaft engines is, generally, much higher, but much narrower.

The manual transmission and clutch are employed to vary the relationship between engine RPM and the speed of the wheels so that adequate power can be produced under all circumstances. The clutch allows engine torque to be applied to the transmission input shaft gradually, due to mechanical slippage. The vehicle can, consequently, be started smoothly from a full stop.

The transmission changes the ratio between the rotating speeds of the engine and the wheels by the use of gears. 4-speed or 5-speed transmissions are most common. The lower gears allow full engine power to be applied to the rear wheels during acceleration at low speeds.

The clutch driveplate is a thin disc, the center of which is splined to the transmission input shaft. Both sides of the disc are covered with a layer of material which is similar to brake lining and which is capable of allowing slippage without roughness or excessive noise.

The clutch cover is bolted to the engine flywheel and incorporates a diaphragm spring which provides the pressure to engage the clutch. The cover also houses the pressure plate. When the clutch pedal is released, the driven disc is sandwiched between the pressure plate and the smooth surface of the flywheel, thus forcing the disc to turn at the same speed as the engine crankshaft.

The transmission contains a mainshaft which passes all the way through the transmission, from the clutch to the driveshaft. This shaft is separated at one point, so that front and rear portions can turn at different speeds.

Power is transmitted by a countershaft in the lower gears and reverse. The gears of the countershaft mesh with gears on the mainshaft, allowing power to be carried from one to the other. Countershaft gears are often integral with that shaft, while several of the mainshaft gears can either rotate independently of the shaft or be locked to it. Shifting from one gear to the next causes one of the gears to be freed from rotating with the shaft and locks another to it. Gears are locked and unlocked by internal dog clutches which slide between the center of the gear and the shaft. The forward gears usually employ synchronizers; friction members which smoothly bring gear and shaft to the same speed before the toothed dog clutches are engaged.

Identification

▶ **See Figure 1**

On all models covered in this book, the manual transmission serial number is stamped on the front upper face of the transmission case.

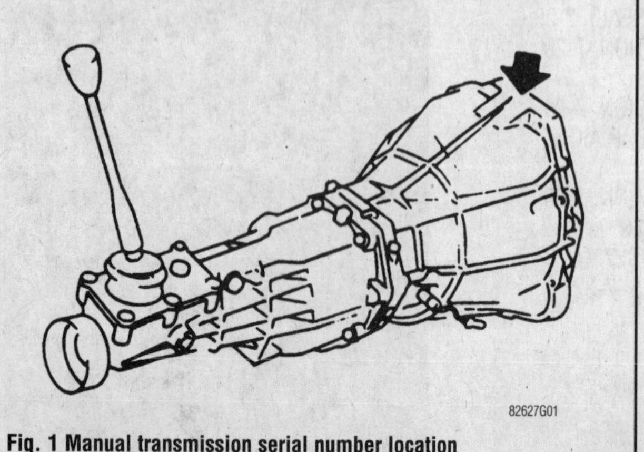

MANUAL TRANSMISSION NUMBER

82627G01

Fig. 1 Manual transmission serial number location

Adjustments

LINKAGE AND SHIFTER

All models are equipped with an integral linkage system. No adjustments are either possible or necessary.

Shifter Lever

REMOVAL & INSTALLATION

The shifter lever is removed by removing the shifter lever trim panel, positioning the rubber boot (remove boot retainer (s), do not damage or rip the boot) on the shifter assembly in a up position then removing the snap-ring that retains the shifter lever in the transmission unit. Refer to the illustrations in this section.

Back-Up Light Switch

REMOVAL & INSTALLATION

1. Raise vehicle and support safely.
2. Disconnect the electrical connections from the switch.
3. Remove switch from transmission housing, when removing place drain pan under transmission to catch fluid.
4. To install reverse removal procedures and check the fluid level. Replace the switch mounting gasket is so equipped.

Extension Housing Seal (in Vehicle)

REMOVAL & INSTALLATION

▶ **See Figures 2 and 3**

1. Raise the vehicle and support safely.
2. Matchmark the driveshaft (if the driveshaft is not installed in the correct position it may cause a vibration) and differential companion flanges. Remove the center bearing and mounting brackets from the crossmember as required.

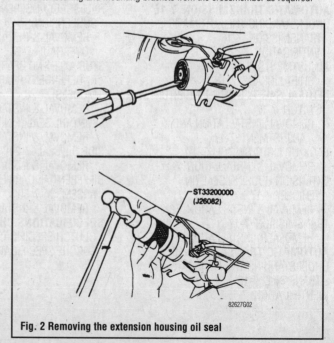

82627G02

Fig. 2 Removing the extension housing oil seal

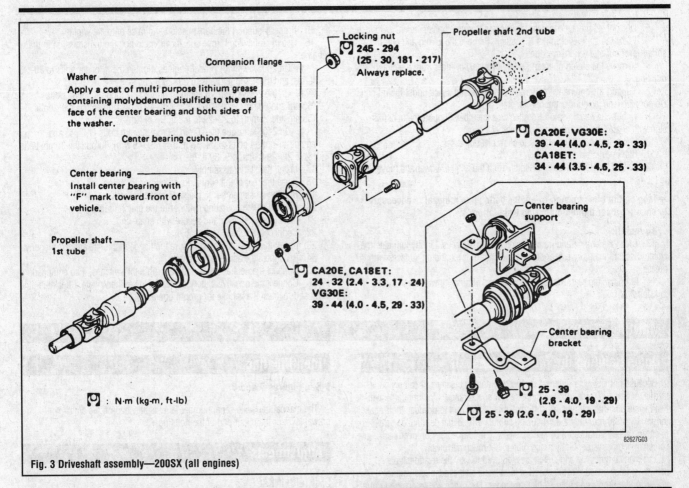

Fig. 3 Driveshaft assembly—200SX (all engines)

3. Loosen the companion flange bolts and lower the driveshaft from the differential.

4. Carefully withdraw the driveshaft from the transmission. Plug the extension opening to prevent leakage.

5. Using the proper tool, remove the oil seal from the extension. Refer to the illustration.

To install:

6. Wipe all seal contact surfaces clean. Coat the lip of the new seal with clean transmission fluid.

7. Using the proper drift tool, drive the new seal into the extension housing.

8. Insert the driveshaft into the extension housing making sure the splines are properly engaged.

9. Raise the driveshaft and align the companion flange marks. Install and EVENLY tighten the flange bolts to 29–33 ft. lbs. Install the center bearing, if removed.

10. Lower the vehicle. Check the fluid level and add as necessary.

Transmission

REMOVAL & INSTALLATION

200SX and 240SX

▶ **See Figures 4, 5 and 6**

1. Raise and support the vehicle safely. Disconnect the negative battery cable.

2. Disconnect the back-up light switch on all units and neutral switch, if equipped.

3. Disconnect the accelerator linkage.

4. Matchmark then unbolt the driveshaft at the rear and remove. If equipped with a center bearing, unbolt it from the crossmember. Plug the end of the transmission extension to prevent leakage.

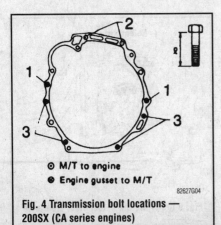

- ⊙ M/T to engine
- ⊛ Engine gusset to M/T

Fig. 4 Transmission bolt locations — 200SX (CA series engines)

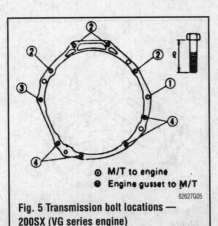

- ⊙ M/T to engine
- ⊛ Engine gusset to M/T

Fig. 5 Transmission bolt locations — 200SX (VG series engine)

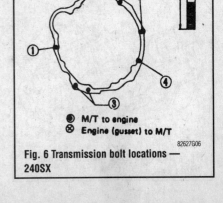

- ⊙ M/T to engine
- ⊛ Engine (gusset) to M/T

Fig. 6 Transmission bolt locations — 240SX

5. Disconnect the speedometer drive cable from the transmission.

6. Place the shift lever in the **N** position. Remove the E-ring and pull the shifter lever out of the transmission.

7. Remove the clutch operating (slave cylinder) cylinder from the clutch housing.

8. Support the engine with a large wood block and a jack under the oil pan. Do not place the jack under the oil pan drain plug.

9. Unbolt the transmission from the crossmember. Support the transmission with a jack and remove the crossmember.

10. Lower the rear of the engine to allow clearance.

11. Remove the starter assembly.

12. Unbolt the transmission assembly from the engine. Lower and move it to the rear.

→ **Tagging the transmission-to-engine bolts upon removal is necessary to ensure proper tightening during installation.**

To install:

13. Clean the engine and transmission mating surfaces. Lightly lubricate the clutch disc and main drive gear splines and control lever sliding surfaces with grease.

14. Lubricate the rear extension oil seal lip and bushing with clean transmission fluid.

15. Properly support the transmission and raise onto the engine.

16. Use the following torque specifications to bolt the transmission to the engine:

   a. On 200SX with 4 cylinder engines, tighten the 4 longer bolts to 29–36 ft. lbs. and the 4 shorter bolts to 22–29 ft. lbs.

   b. On the 200SX with V6 engines, tighten the long mounting bolts (65mm and 60mm) to 29–36 ft. lbs. (39–49 Nm). Tighten the short bolts (55mm and 25mm) to 22–29 ft. lbs. (29–39 Nm).

   c. On 240SX, torque the 70mm, 60mm, 25mm bolts (1, 2, 4) and engine-to-gusset bolts to 29–36 ft. lbs. (39–49 Nm). Torque the 30mm bolts (3) to 22–29 ft. lbs. (29–39 ft. lbs.)

17. Install the starter assembly.

18. Raise the rear of the engine to it's original position.

19. Bolt the crossmember in place. Remove the jack.

20. Bolt the clutch operating cylinder to the clutch housing.

21. Install the shift lever and secure with snap-ring.

22. Connect the speedometer cable.

23. Install the driveshaft making sure the flange marks are aligned properly.

24. Reconnect the accelerator linkage.

25. Connect the neutral safety and back-up light switches, if so equipped.

26. Connect the negative battery cable and lower the vehicle. Check the fluid level and roadtest the vehicle for proper operation.

MANUAL TRANSAXLE

Understanding the Manual Transaxle

Because of the way an internal combustion engine breathes, it can produce torque, or twisting force, only within a narrow speed range. Most modern, overhead valve pushrod engines must turn at about 2500 rpm to produce their peak torque. By 4500 rpm they are producing so little torque that continued increases in engine speed produce no power increases. The torque peak on overhead camshaft engines is generally much higher, but much narrower.

The manual transaxle and clutch are employed to vary the relationship between engine speed and the speed of the wheels so that adequate engine power can be produced under all circumstances. The clutch allows engine torque to be applied to the transaxle input shaft gradually, due to mechanical slippage. Consequently, the vehicle may be started smoothly from a full stop. The transaxle changes the ratio between the rotating speeds of the engine and the wheels by the use of gears. The gear ratios allow full engine power to be applied to the wheels during acceleration at low speeds and at highway/passing speeds.

In a front wheel drive transaxle, power is usually transmitted from the input shaft to a mainshaft or output shaft located slightly beneath and to the side of the input shaft. The gears of the mainshaft mesh with gears on the input shaft, allowing power to be carried from one to the other. All forward gears are in constant mesh and are free from rotating with the shaft unless the synchronizer and clutch is engaged. Shifting from one gear to the next causes one of the gears to be freed from rotating with the shaft and locks another to it. Gears are locked and unlocked by internal dog clutches which slide between the center of the gear and the shaft. The forward gears employ synchronizers; friction members which smoothly bring gear and shaft to the same speed before the toothed dog clutches are engaged.

Identification

♦ **See Figures 7 and 8**

The manual transaxle serial number label is attached on the clutch withdrawal lever or the upper part of the housing.

Adjustments

SHIFTER LINKAGE

♦ **See Figures 9 and 10**

→ **On Stanza models (RS5F31A type transaxle) from 1982–86 adjustment is possible. On Stanza models (RS5F50A type transaxle) from 1987 and later no adjustment is possible. On Stanza wagon (RS5F50A type transaxle) no adjustment is possible.**

1. Raise and support the front of the vehicle on jackstands.

2. Under the vehicle, at the shift control area, loosen the select stopper securing bolts.

3. Shift the gear selector into 1st gear.

4. Adjust the clearance between the control lever and select stopper by sliding the select stopper so that the clearance is 1.00mm.

5. Torque the stopper securing bolts to 5.8–8.0 ft. lbs. Check that the control lever can be shifted without binding or dragging.

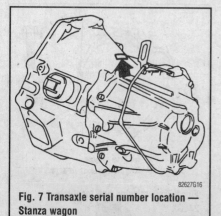
82627G16
Fig. 7 Transaxle serial number location — Stanza wagon

82627G17
Fig. 8 Transaxle serial number location— Stanza

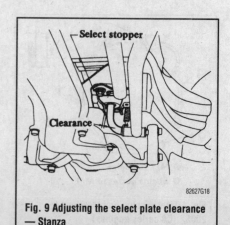
82627G18
Fig. 9 Adjusting the select plate clearance — Stanza

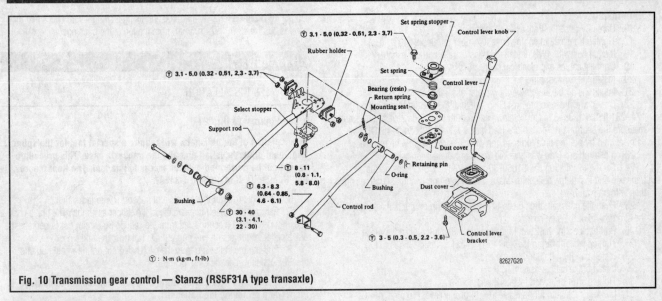

Fig. 10 Transmission gear control — Stanza (RS5F31A type transaxle)

Back-Up Light Switch

REMOVAL & INSTALLATION

1. Raise vehicle and support safely.
2. Disconnect the electrical connections.
3. Remove switch from transaxle housing, when removing place drain pan under transaxle to catch fluid.
4. To install reverse removal procedures.

Transaxle

REMOVAL & INSTALLATION

1982–86 Stanza With RS5F31A Type Transaxle

1. Disconnect the battery. Removing the battery may allow greater ease of access.
2. Raise and safely support the vehicle and drain the gear oil.
3. Remove the wheel bearing lock-nut while depressing the brake pad.
4. Remove the brake caliper assembly. The brake hose does not need to be disconnected from the caliper. Support the caliper.
5. Remove the tie rod and lower ball joint securing nuts.
6. Loosen but do not remove the upper strut mounting nuts.
7. Separate the halfshafts from the knuckle by lightly tapping.
8. Separate the ball joint from steering knuckle and move assembly aside to allow room to remove halfshafts.
9. Remove halfshafts by prying against the reinforcement locations on halfshaft. Do not pull halfshafts, this will damage the sliding boots and oil seals.
10. After removing halfshafts, insert a suitable bar to prevent the side gears from rotating and falling into the differential case.
11. Remove the wheel protector and undercover.
12. Separate the control rod and support rod from the transaxle.
13. Remove the exhaust tube securing nut and bolt.
14. Remove the engine gusset bolt and engine mounting.
15. Remove the clutch control cable from the withdrawal lever.
16. Disconnect the speedometer cable.
17. Disconnect the wire connectors from the backup light and neutral safety switches.
18. Support the engine.
19. Support the transaxle with an suitable transmission jack.
20. Remove the starter.
21. Remove the engine mounting bolts.
22. Remove the transaxle-to-engine bolts.
23. Carefully lower transaxle down and away from engine. Take care not to damage halfshafts or other components in the area.

To install:
24. Clean all mating surfaces.
25. Apply a light coat of lithium based grease to the input shaft splines.
26. Carefully raise the transaxle to the engine.
27. Tighten transaxle to engine bolts to proper torque 22–30 ft. lbs.
28. Install the starter.
29. Connect cables and electrical connectors.
30. Install the exhaust tube securing bolts.
31. Check wheel bearing by installing halfshaft to hub and torqueing nut to 145–203 ft. lbs. (196–275 Nm). Spin wheel in both directions several times and measure the bearing pre-load. If pre-load is not 3.1–10.8 lb. (13.9–48.1 N) pull, as measured by pulling on a lug stud, the wheel bearing should be replaced.
32. If bearing pre-load was checked, remove halfshaft for hub.
33. Set the seal protector KV38105500 on the transaxle and install the half-shafts. Make certain to properly align serrations and then withdraw tool.
34. Push the halfshaft, then press-fit the circular clip on the halfshaft into the clip groove of the side gear.
35. Pull back on the halfshaft to make certain it is fully locked in place.
36. Tighten wheel bearing lock-nut to 145–203 ft. lbs. (196–275 Nm).
37. Install ball joint bolt and tie rod.
38. Install brake caliper assembly.
39. Tighten strut bolts and install wheels.
40. Fill transaxle axle to proper level (5.9 pints API gear oil) with gear lubricant.
41. Install the undercover and wheel house protector.
42. Lower the vehicle.
43. Install and connect the battery.

1987 and Later Stanza; 1986–88 Stanza Wagon 2WD/4WD With RS5F50A Type Transaxle

1. Disconnect the battery. Remove the battery and its bracket.
2. Raise and safely support vehicle. Drain gear oil.
3. Remove the wheel bearing lock-nut while depressing the brake pedal.
4. Remove the brake caliper assembly. The brake hose does not need to be disconnected from the caliper. Support the caliper.
5. Remove the tie rod end and lower ball joint securing nuts.
6. Loosen but do not remove the upper strut mounting nuts.
7. Separate the halfshafts from the knuckle by lightly tapping.
8. Separate the ball joint from steering knuckle and move assembly aside to allow room to remove halfshafts.
9. Remove halfshafts by prying against the reinforcement locations on halfshaft.
10. Remove bolts securing exhaust to front tube.
11. If equipped with 4WD, disconnect (matchmark for correct installation) driveshaft and remove transfer case.
12. Lower vehicle and remove the air cleaner and airflow meter assembly.
13. Disconnect cables and electrical connections from transaxle.
14. Remove transaxle to engine bolts and mount bolts.
15. Carefully lower transaxle from engine.

To install:

16. Carefully raise the transaxle to the engine.

17. Tighten transaxle to engine bolts to proper torque 29–40 ft. lbs.

18. If equipped with 4WD, install the transfer case and driveshaft.

19. Connect cables and electrical connectors.

20. Install the exhaust pipe.

21. Install the air cleaner and airflow meter assemblies.

22. Check wheel bearing by installing halfshaft to hub and torqueing nut to 174–231 ft. lbs. (235–314 Nm). Spin wheel in both directions several times and measure the bearing pre-load. If pre-load is not 1.1–10.1 lb. (4.9–45.1N) pull, as measured by pulling on a lug stud, the wheel bearing should be replaced.

23. If bearing pre-load was checked, remove halfshaft for hub.

24. Set the installation KV381060700 and KV381060800 tools on the transaxle and install the halfshafts. Make certain to properly align serrations and then withdraw tool.

25. Push the halfshaft, then press-fit the circular clip on the halfshaft into the clip groove of the side gear.

26. Pull back on the halfshaft to make certain it is fully locked in place.

27. Tighten wheel bearing lock-nut to 174–231 ft. lbs. (235–314 Nm).

28. Install ball joint bolt and tie rod end.

29. Install brake caliper assembly.

30. Tighten strut bolts and install wheels.

31. Lower vehicle and fill transaxle axle to proper level (10 pints API GL-4 gear oil) with gear lubricant.

32. Install and connect the battery.

CHECKING FLUID LEVEL

▶ **See Figures 11 and 12**

With the vehicle on a level surface, place a drain pan under the vehicle and remove the oil filler plug. The transaxle is correctly filled if the oil just begins to run out of the hole or is level with the bottom of the fill hole.

On vehicles without a filler plug, remove the speedometer cable from the transaxle case. Check that the fluid level is within 0.35 in. of the inside case lip.

On the 4WD Stanza remove filler plug and using a straight wire check that the level is 3.82–4.13 in. (97–105mm) from the top of the housing.

Halfshaft

REMOVAL & INSTALLATION

▶ **See Figures 13 thru 21**

➡**Installation of the halfshafts will require a special tool for the spline alignment of the halfshaft end and the transaxle case. This procedure should not be performed without access to this tool. The Kent Moore tool Number is J-34296 and J-34297.**

1. Raise the front of the vehicle and support it with jackstands.

2. Remove the wheel. Remove the brake caliper assembly. The brake hose does not need to be disconnected from the caliper. Be careful not to depress the brake pedal, or the piston will pop out. Do not twist the brake hose.

3. Pull out the cotter pin from the castellated nut on the wheel hub and then remove the wheel bearing lock nut.

➡**Cover the boots with a shop towel or waste cloth so not to damage them when removing the halfshaft.**

4. Separate the halfshaft from the steering knuckle by tapping it with a block of wood and a mallet. It may be necessary to loosen (do not remove) the strut mounting bolts to gain clearance for steering knuckle removal from the halfshaft.

5. Remove the tie rod ball joint.

➡**Always use a new nut and cotter pin when installing the tie rod ball joint.**

6. On models with a manual transaxle, using a suitable tool, reach through the engine crossmember and carefully tap the right side inner CV-joint out of the transaxle case.

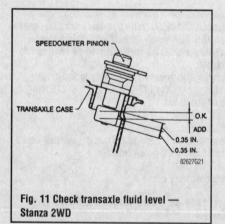

Fig. 11 Check transaxle fluid level — Stanza 2WD

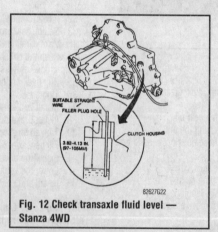

Fig. 12 Check transaxle fluid level — Stanza 4WD

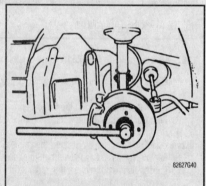

Fig. 13 Removing the wheel bearing lock-nut

Fig. 14 Separating the halfshaft from the steering knuckle

Fig. 15 Loosen (DO NOT REMOVE) strut mounting nuts

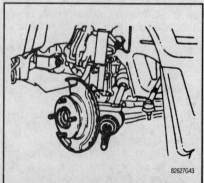

Fig. 16 Removing the halfshaft from the steering knuckle

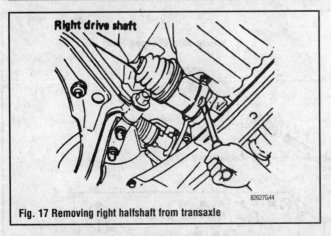

Fig. 17 Removing right halfshaft from transaxle

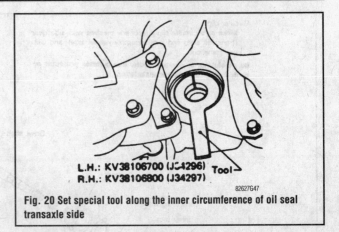

Fig. 20 Set special tool along the inner circumference of oil seal transaxle side

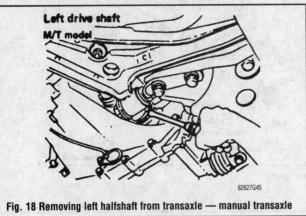

Fig. 18 Removing left halfshaft from transaxle — manual transaxle

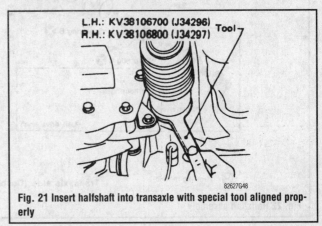

Fig. 21 Insert halfshaft into transaxle with special tool aligned properly

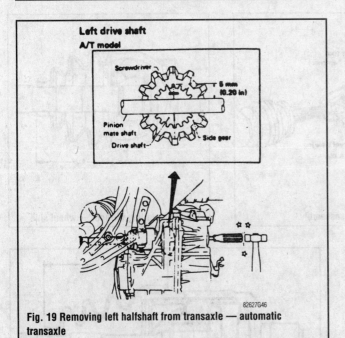

Fig. 19 Removing left halfshaft from transaxle — automatic transaxle

7. If no support bracket is used disregard this step—using a block of wood on an hydraulic floor jack, support the engine under the oil pan if necessary. Remove the support bearing bracket from the engine and then withdraw the right halfshaft if so equipped.

8. On models with manual transaxle, carefully insert a small prybar between the left CV-joint inner flange and the transaxle case mounting surface and pry the halfshaft out of the case. Withdraw the shaft from the steering knuckle and remove it.

9. On models with automatic transaxle, insert a dowel through the right side halfshaft hole (remove the right side halfshaft the same way as on manual transaxle models) and use a small mallet to tap the left halfshaft out of the transaxle case. Withdraw the shaft from the steering knuckle and remove it—refer to the illustrations.

➡**Be careful not to damage the pinion mating shaft and the side gear while tapping the left halfshaft out of the transaxle case.**

10. When installing the shafts into the transaxle, use a new oil seal and then install an alignment tool along the inner circumference of the oil seal.

11. Insert the halfshaft into the transaxle, align the serrations and then remove the alignment tool.

12. Push the halfshaft, then press-fit the circular clip on the shaft into the clip groove on the side gear.

➡**After insertion, attempt to pull the flange out of the side joint to make sure that the circular clip is properly seated in the side gear and will not come out.**

13. Install support bearing bracket retaining bolts and insert the halfshaft in the steering knuckle if so equipped. Tighten the strut mounting bolts if loosen.

14. Connect the tie rod end in the correct position use new nut and cotter pin.

15. Install the caliper assembly and the wheel bearing lock-nut. Tighten the nut to 174–231 ft. lbs.

16. Install a new cotter pin on the wheel hub and install the wheel.

17. Bleed the brake system if necessary. Road test the vehicle for proper operation.

CV-JOINT OVERHAUL

Transaxle Side

▶ **See Figures 22 thru 27**

1. Remove the halfshaft and mount in a protected jaw vise.
2. Remove the boot bands.

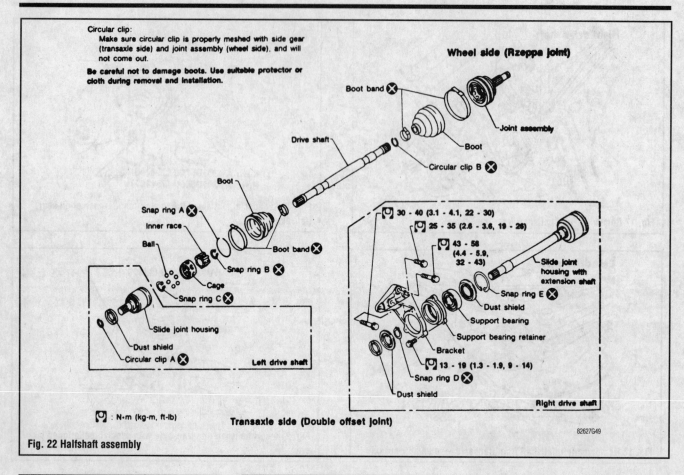

Circular clip:
Make sure circular clip is properly meshed with side gear (transaxle side) and joint assembly (wheel side), and will not come out.

Be careful not to damage boots. Use suitable protector or cloth during removal and installation.

Wheel side (Rzeppa joint)

Boot band ⊗

Joint assembly

Drive shaft

Boot

Circular clip B ⊗

Boot

Snap ring A ⊗

Inner race

Ball

Boot band ⊗

Snap ring B ⊗

Cage

Snap ring C ⊗

Slide joint housing

Dust shield

Circular clip A ⊗

Left drive shaft

⊡ 30 - 40 (3.1 - 4.1, 22 - 30)

⊡ 25 - 35 (2.6 - 3.6, 19 - 26)

⊡ 43 - 58 (4.4 - 5.9, 32 - 43)

Slide joint housing with extension shaft

Snap ring E ⊗

Dust shield

Support bearing

Support bearing retainer

Bracket

⊡ 13 - 19 (1.3 - 1.9, 9 - 14)

Snap ring D ⊗

Dust shield

Right drive shaft

⊡ : N•m (kg-m, ft-lb)

Transaxle side (Double offset joint)

82627G49

Fig. 22 Halfshaft assembly

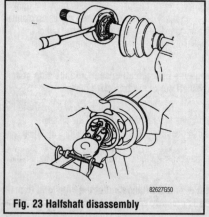

82627G50

Fig. 23 Halfshaft disassembly

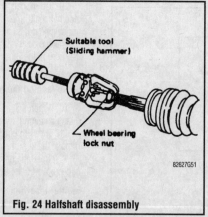

Suitable tool (Sliding hammer)

Wheel bearing lock nut

82627G51

Fig. 24 Halfshaft disassembly

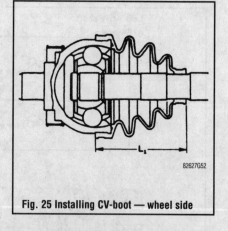

L_1

82627G52

Fig. 25 Installing CV-boot — wheel side

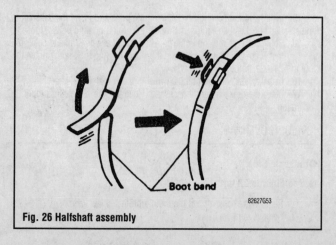

Boot band

82627G53

Fig. 26 Halfshaft assembly

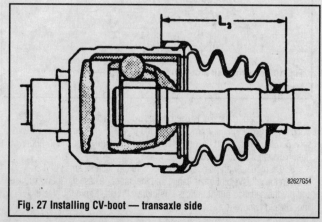

L_3

82627G54

Fig. 27 Installing CV-boot — transaxle side

3. Matchmark the slide joint housing and spider assembly to the half-shaft.

4. Remove the slide joint housing from the halfshaft.

5. Remove the spider snap-ring.

6. Remove the spider assembly from the halfshaft.

7. Cover the driveshaft splined end with tape to protect the CV-boot.

8. Remove the CV-boot.

To install:

9. Install the CV-boot with a new boot band.

10. Install the spider assembly. Make sure the matchmarks are aligned properly.

11. Install a new spider snap-ring. Make sure the snap-ring seats evenly in the groove of the shaft.

12. Pack the CV-boot with grease (holds 5.64–6.35 oz. of proper grease—should be 3.82–3.90 inches or 97–99mm in length after packed with grease, see illustrations).

13. Install the remaining boot bands. Tighten and crimp the bands using the proper tool.

Wheel Side

1. Remove the halfshaft and mount in a protected jaw vise.

2. Matchmark the joint assembly to the shaft.

3. Remove the joint assembly (replace the complete joint assembly if damage or deformed) from the shaft using a suitable puller. Install the axle nut to prevent damage to the threads when removing the joint.

4. Remove the boot bands.

5. Cover the halfshaft splined end with tape to protect the CV-boot.

6. Remove the CV-boot.

To install:

7. Install the CV-boot with a new boot band.

8. Install the joint assembly by tapping lightly. Make sure the axle nut is installed to prevent damage to the threads. Make sure the matchmarks are aligned properly.

9. Pack the CV-boot with the proper grade and amount of grease (holds 7.23–7.94 oz. of proper grease—should be 3.78–3.86 inches or 96–98mm in length after packed with grease, see illustrations).

10. Install the remaining boot bands. Tighten and crimp the bands using the proper tool.

CLUTCH

❋❋ CAUTION

The clutch driven disc may contain asbestos, which has been determined to be a cancer causing agent. Never clean clutch surface with compressed air! Avoid inhaling any dust from any clutch surface! When cleaning clutch surfaces, use a commercially available brake cleaning fluid.

Understanding the Clutch

The purpose of the clutch is to disconnect and connect engine power at the transmission/transaxle. A vehicle at rest requires a lot of engine torque to get all that weight moving. An internal combustion engine does not develop a high starting torque (unlike steam engines) so it must be allowed to operate without any load until it builds up enough torque to move the vehicle. To a point, torque increases with engine rpm. The clutch allows the engine to build up torque by physically disconnecting the engine from the transmission/transaxle, relieving the engine of any load or resistance.

The transfer of engine power to the transmission/transaxle (the load) must be smooth and gradual; if it weren't, drive line components would wear out or break quickly. This gradual power transfer is made possible by gradually releasing the clutch pedal. The clutch disc and pressure plate are the connecting link between the engine and transmission. When the clutch pedal is released, the disc and plate contact each other (the clutch is engaged) physically joining the engine and transmission/transaxle. When the pedal is pushed in, the disc and plate separate (the clutch is disengaged) disconnecting the engine from the transmission/transaxle.

Most clutch assemblies consists of the flywheel, the clutch disc, the clutch pressure plate, the throw out bearing and fork, the actuating linkage and the pedal. The flywheel and clutch pressure plate (driving members) are connected to the engine crankshaft and rotate with it. The clutch disc is located between the flywheel and pressure plate, and is splined to the input shaft of the transmission/transaxle. A driving member is one that is attached to the engine and transfers engine power to a driven member (clutch disc) on the input shaft. A driving member (pressure plate) rotates (drives) a driven member (clutch disc) on contact and, in so doing, turns the input shaft.

There is a circular diaphragm spring within the pressure plate cover (transmission/transaxle side). In a relaxed state (when the clutch pedal is fully released) this spring is convex; that is, it is dished outward toward the transmission/transaxle. Pushing in the clutch pedal actuates the attached linkage. Connected to the other end of this is the throw out fork, which hold the throw out bearing. When the clutch pedal is depressed, the clutch linkage pushes the fork and bearing forward to contact the diaphragm spring of the pressure plate. The outer edges of the spring are secured to the pressure plate and are pivoted on rings so that when the center of the spring is compressed by the throw out bearing, the outer edges bow outward and, by so doing, pull the pressure plate in the same direction – away from the clutch disc. This action separates the disc from the plate, disengaging the clutch and allowing the transmission/transaxle to be shifted into another gear. A coil type clutch return spring attached to the clutch pedal arm permits full release of the pedal. Releasing the pedal pulls the throw out bearing away from the diaphragm spring resulting in a reversal of spring position. As bearing pressure is gradually released from the spring center, the outer edges of the spring bow outward, pushing the pressure plate into closer contact with the clutch disc. As the disc and plate move closer together, friction between the two increases and slippage is reduced until, when full spring pressure is applied (by fully releasing the pedal) the speed of the disc and plate are the same. This stops all slipping, creating a direct connection between the plate and disc which results in the transfer of power from the engine to the transmission/transaxle. The clutch disc is now rotating with the pressure plate at engine speed and, because it is splined to the input shaft, the shaft now turns at the same engine speed.

The clutch is operating properly if:

1. It will stall the engine when released with the vehicle held stationary.

2. The shift lever can be moved freely between 1st and reverse gears when the vehicle is stationary and the clutch disengaged.

Driven Disc and Pressure Plate

REMOVAL & INSTALLATION

♦ See Figures 28 thru 48

➡ **The clutch cover and pressure plate are balanced as an assembly. If replacement of either part becomes necessary—replace both parts (and release bearing) as an assembly.**

The flywheel (check torque on flywheel retaining bolts) should be inspected for wear or scoring and resurfaced or replaced as necessary.

1. Remove the transmission/transaxle from the engine as detailed in this section.

2. Insert a clutch aligning bar or similar tool all the way into the clutch disc hub. This must be done so as to support the weight of the clutch disc during removal. Mark the clutch assembly-to-flywheel relationship with paint or a center punch so that the clutch assembly can be assembled in the same position from which it is removed.

3. Loosen the bolts in sequence, a turn at a time. Remove the bolts.

4. Remove the pressure plate and clutch disc.

5. Remove the release mechanism from the transmission housing. Apply lithium based molybdenum disulfide grease to the bearing sleeve inside groove, the contact point of the withdrawal lever and bearing sleeve, the contact surface of the lever ball pin and lever.

To install:

6. Inspect the release bearing and replace if necessary. Apply a small amount of grease to the transmission splines. Install the disc on the splines and

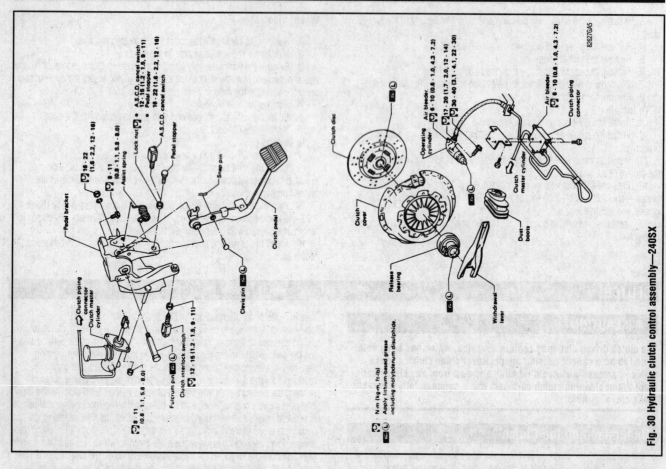

Fig. 30 Hydraulic clutch control assembly—240SX

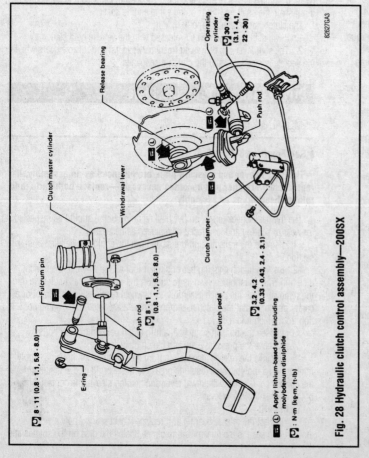

Fig. 28 Hydraulic clutch control assembly—200SX

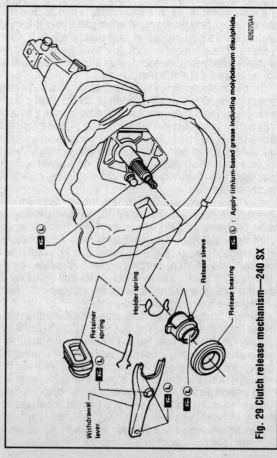

Fig. 29 Clutch release mechanism—240 SX

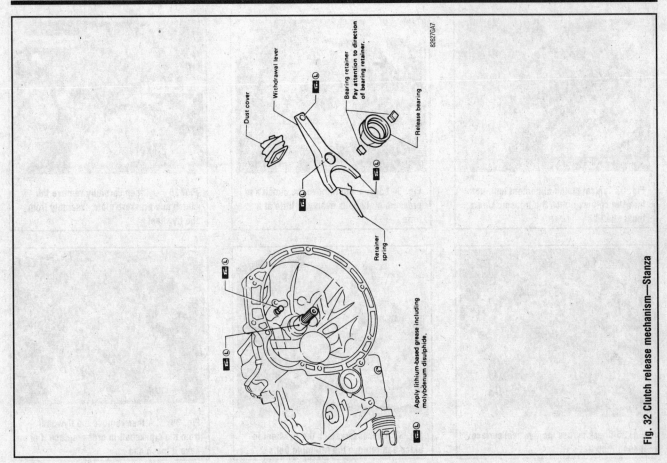

Fig. 32 Clutch release mechanism—Stanza

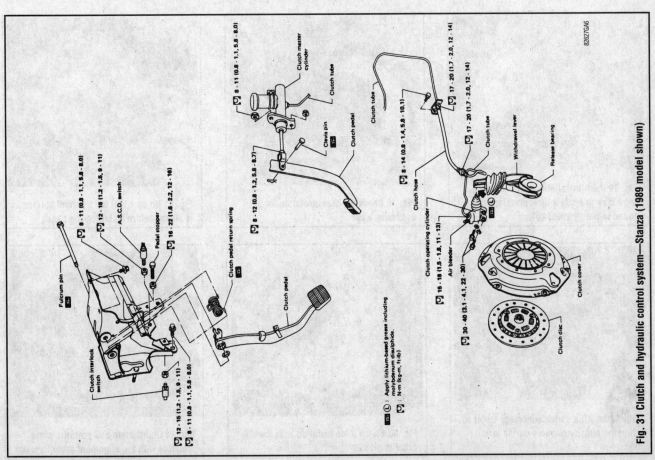

Fig. 31 Clutch and hydraulic control system—Stanza (1989 model shown)

Fig. 33 Typical clutch alignment tool, note how the splines match the transmission's input shaft

Fig. 34 Loosen and remove the clutch and pressure plate bolts evenly, a little at a time . . .

Fig. 35 . . . then carefully remove the clutch and pressure plate assembly from the flywheel

Fig. 36 Check across the flywheel surface, it should be flat

Fig. 37 If necessary, lock the flywheel in place and remove the retaining bolts . . .

Fig. 38 . . . then remove the flywheel from the crankshaft in order replace it or have it machined

Fig. 39 Upon installation, it is usually a good idea to apply a threadlocking compound to the flywheel bolts

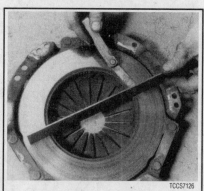

Fig. 40 Check the pressure plate for excessive wear

Fig. 41 Be sure that the flywheel surface is clean, before installing the clutch

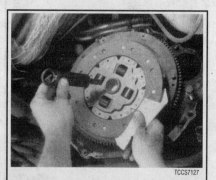

Fig. 42 Install a clutch alignment arbor, to align the clutch assembly during installation

Fig. 43 Clutch plate installed with the arbor in place

Fig. 44 Clutch plate and pressure plate installed with the alignment arbor in place

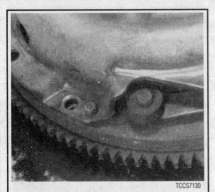

Fig. 45 Pressure plate-to-flywheel bolt holes should align

Fig. 46 You may want to use a threadlocking compound on the clutch assembly bolts

Fig. 47 Install the clutch assembly bolts and tighten in steps, using an X pattern

Fig. 48 Be sure to use a torque wrench to tighten all bolts

slide back and forth a few times. Remove the disc and remove excess grease on hub. Be sure no grease contacts the disc or pressure plate.

7. Install the disc to flywheel, aligning it with a special tool splined dummy shaft.

8. Install the pressure plate and EVENLY IN A CRISSCROSS PATTERN torque the bolts to 16–22 ft. lbs.

9. Remove the dummy shaft.

10. Replace the transmission/transaxle. Check system for proper operation.

Adjustments

PEDAL HEIGHT AND FREE-PLAY

▶ **See Figures 49, 50, 51, 52 and 53**

On all vehicles and clutch type operating systems, refer to the "Clutch Specifications Chart" for clutch pedal height above floor and pedal free play.

On all models with a hydraulically operated clutch system—pedal height is usually adjusted with a stopper limiting the upward travel of the pedal. Pedal free-play is adjusted at the master cylinder pushrod. If the pushrod is non-adjustable, free-play is adjusted by placing shims between the master cylinder and the firewall.

On all models with a mechanical clutch system, follow the service procedure below:

1. Loosen the locknut and adjust the pedal height by means of the pedal stopper. Tighten the locknut.

2. Push the withdrawal lever (refer to the illustration of "B" area) in by hand until resistance is felt. Adjust withdrawal lever play at the lever tip end with the locknuts. Withdrawal lever play should be 0.08–0.12 inch (23mm).

3. Depress and release the clutch pedal several times and then recheck the withdrawal lever play again. Readjust if necessary.

4. Measure the pedal free travel at the center of the pedal pad.

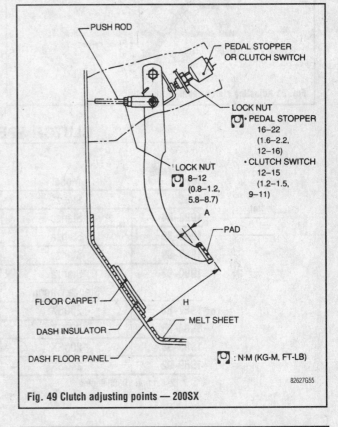

Fig. 49 Clutch adjusting points — 200SX

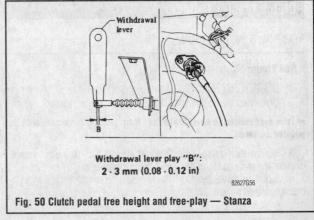

Withdrawal lever play "B":
2 - 3 mm (0.08 - 0.12 in)

Fig. 50 Clutch pedal free height and free-play — Stanza

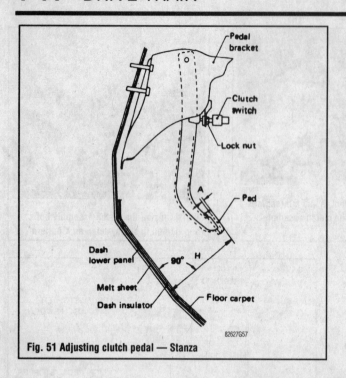

Fig. 51 Adjusting clutch pedal — Stanza

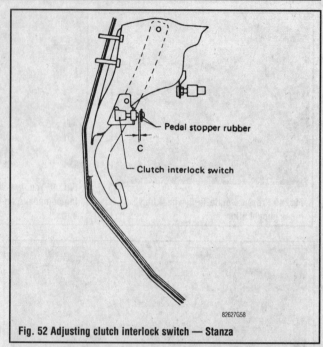

Fig. 52 Adjusting clutch interlock switch — Stanza

CLUTCH SPECIFICATIONS

Year	Model	Pedal Height Above Floor (in.)	Pedal Free-Play (in.)
1982	Stanza	6.00	0.43–0.63
1983–84	Stanza	6.05	0.43–0.63
1985–86	Stanza	6.02	0.47–0.67
1987–89	Stanza	6.73–7.13	0.04–0.12
1990–92	Stanza	6.50–6.89	0.04–0.12
	Stanza Wagon	9.29–9.69	0.04–0.12
1982–83	200SX	6.70	0.04–0.20
1984–85	200SX	7.60–7.99	0.04–0.06
1986–88	200SX	7.44–7.83 ①	0.039–0.118
1989–92	240SX	7.32–7.72	0.039–0.118

① 7.72–8.11 on VG30E engine

82627C01

Clutch Master Cylinder

REMOVAL & INSTALLATION

▶ **See Figure 53**

1. Disconnect the clutch pedal arm from the pushrod.
2. Disconnect the clutch hydraulic line from the master cylinder.

➡**Take precautions to keep brake fluid from coming in contact with any painted surfaces.**

3. Remove the nuts attaching the master cylinder and remove the master cylinder and pushrod toward the engine compartment side.
4. Install the master cylinder in the reverse order of removal and bleed the clutch hydraulic system.

Clutch Slave Cylinder

REMOVAL & INSTALLATION

▶ **See Figure 53**

1. Remove the slave cylinder attaching bolts and the pushrod from the shift fork.
2. Disconnect the flexible fluid hose from the slave cylinder and remove the unit from the vehicle.
3. Install the slave cylinder in the reverse order of removal and bleed the clutch hydraulic system.

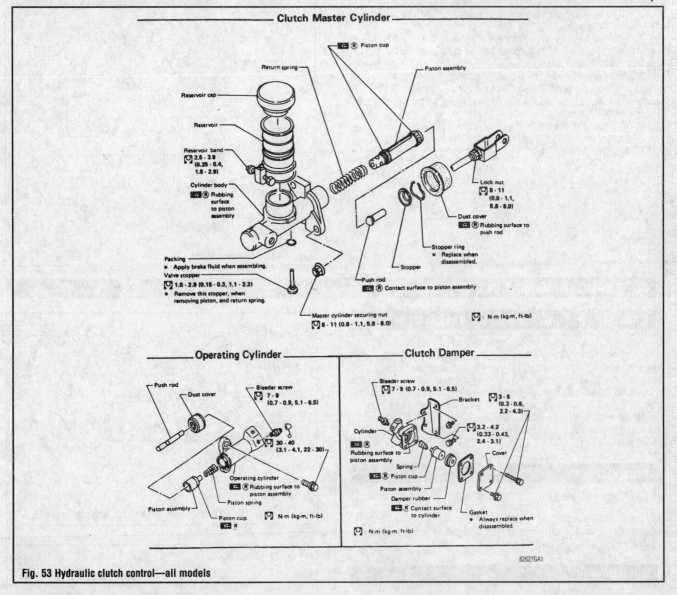

Fig. 53 Hydraulic clutch control—all models

BLEEDING THE CLUTCH HYDRAULIC SYSTEM

♦ See Figures 54, 55 and 56

1. Check and fill the clutch fluid reservoir to the specified level as necessary. During the bleeding process, continue to check and replenish the reservoir to prevent the fluid level from getting lower than ½ the specified level.

2. Remove the dust cap from the bleeder screw on the clutch slave cylinder (and clutch piping connector if so equipped) and connect a tube to the bleeder screw and insert the other end of the tube into a clean glass or metal container.

➡**Take precautionary measures to prevent the brake fluid from getting on any painted surfaces.**

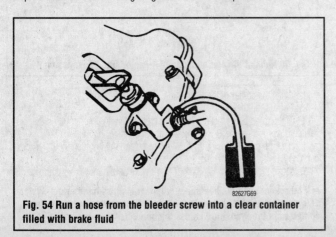

Fig. 54 Run a hose from the bleeder screw into a clear container filled with brake fluid

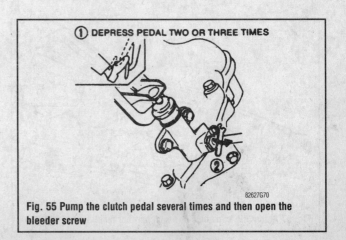

Fig. 55 Pump the clutch pedal several times and then open the bleeder screw

3. Pump the clutch pedal SLOWLY several times, hold it down and loosen the bleeder screw.

4. Tighten the bleeder screw and release the clutch pedal gradually. Repeat this operation until air bubbles disappear from the brake fluid being expelled out through the bleeder screw.

5. Repeat until all evidence of air bubbles completely disappears from the brake fluid being pumped out through the tube.

6. When the air is completely removed, securely tighten the bleeder screw and replace the dust cap.

7. Check and refill the master cylinder reservoir as necessary.

8. Depress the clutch pedal several times to check the operation of the clutch and check for leaks.

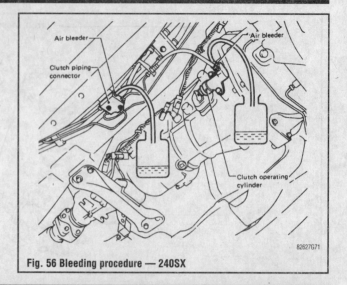

Fig. 56 Bleeding procedure — 240SX

AUTOMATIC TRANSMISSION

Understanding the Automatic Transmission

The automatic transmission allows engine torque and power to be transmitted to the rear wheels within a narrow range of engine operating speeds. It will allow the engine to turn fast enough to produce plenty of power and torque at very low speeds, while keeping it at a sensible rpm at high vehicle speeds (and it does this job without driver assistance). The transmission uses a light fluid as the medium for the transmission of power. This fluid also works in the operation of various hydraulic control circuits and as a lubricant. Because the transmission fluid performs all of these functions, trouble within the unit can easily travel from one part to another.

Identification

♦ **See Figures 57 and 58**

The automatic transmission serial number label is attached to the side of the transmission housing on all models and to the rear tailshaft section on the 240SX model.

Adjustments

SHIFT LINKAGE

♦ **See Figure 59**

If the detents cannot be felt or the pointer indicator is improperly aligned while shifting from the **P** range to range **1**, the linkage should be adjusted.

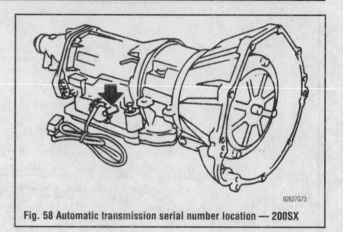

Fig. 58 Automatic transmission serial number location — 200SX

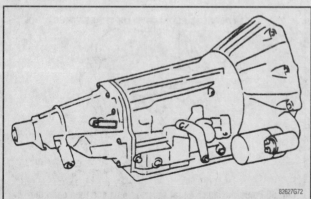

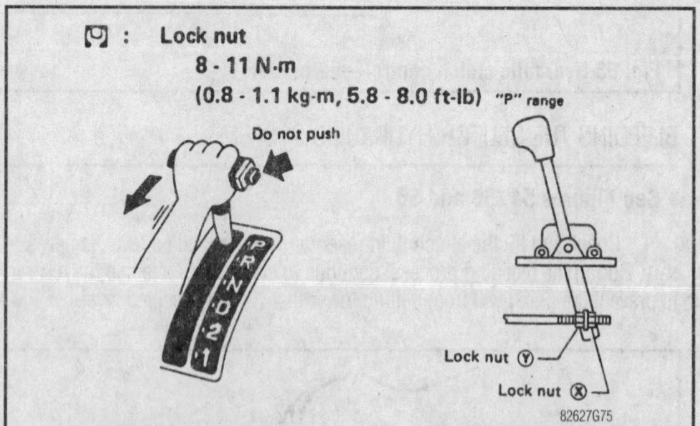

Fig. 59 Manual linkage adjustment — automatic transmission

1. Place the shifter in the **P** position.
2. Loosen the locknuts.
3. Tighten the outer locknut **X** until it touches the trunnion, pulling the selector lever toward the **R** range side without pushing the button.
4. Back off the outer locknut **X** ¼–½ turns and then tighten the inner locknut **Y** to 511 ft. lbs. (815 Nm).
5. Move the selector lever from **P** to **1**. Make sure it moves smoothly.

➡**If late model vehicle has an automatic transmission interlock system. This interlock system prevents the transmission selector from being shifted from the P position unless the brake pedal is depressed.**

Fig. 57 Automatic transmission serial number location — 240SX

Neutral Safety Switch/Inhibitor Switch

REMOVAL, INSTALLATION AND ADJUSTMENT

▶ See Figures 60 and 61

The switch unit is bolted to the transmission case, behind the transmission shift lever. The switch prevents the engine from being started in any transmission position except Park or Neutral. It also controls the backup lights.

1. Place the transmission selector lever in the Neutral range.
2. Remove the screw from the switch (see illustration).
3. Loosen the attaching bolts. With a aligning pin (2.0mm diameter) move the switch until the pin falls into the hole in the rotor.
4. Tighten the attaching bolts equally.
5. Make sure while holding the brakes on, that the engine will start only in Park or Neutral. Check that the backup lights go on only in Reverse.

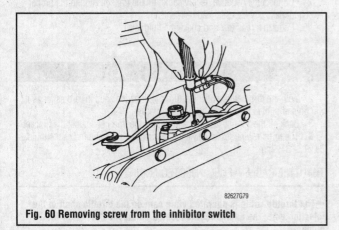

82627G79

Fig. 60 Removing screw from the inhibitor switch

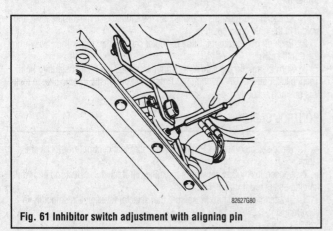

82627G80

Fig. 61 Inhibitor switch adjustment with aligning pin

Back-Up Light Switch

REMOVAL & INSTALLATION

Refer to the "Neutral Safety Switch/Inhibitor Switch" service procedures as this switch also controls the back-up lights.

Extension Housing Seal (in Vehicle)

REMOVAL & INSTALLATION

1. Raise the vehicle and support safely.
2. Matchmark the driveshaft (if the driveshaft is not installed in the correct position it may cause a vibration) and differential companion flanges.
3. Loosen the companion flange bolts and lower the driveshaft from the differential.
4. Carefully withdraw the driveshaft from the transmission. Plug the extension opening to prevent leakage.
5. Using the proper tool, remove the oil seal from the extension.
   To install:
6. Wipe all seal contact surfaces clean. Coat the lip of the new seal with clean transmission fluid.
7. Using the proper drift tool, drive the new seal into the extension housing.
8. Insert the driveshaft into the extension housing making sure the splines are properly engaged.
9. Raise the driveshaft and align the companion flange marks. Install and EVENLY tighten the flange bolts to 29–33 ft. lbs.
10. Lower the vehicle. Check the fluid level and add as necessary.

Transmission

REMOVAL & INSTALLATION

200SX and 240SX

▶ See Figures 62, 63 and 64

1. Disconnect the battery cable.
2. Remove the accelerator linkage.
3. Detach the shift linkage.
4. Disconnect the neutral safety switch and downshift solenoid wiring.
5. Raise and safely support the vehicle. Remove the drain plug and drain the torque converter. If there is no converter drain plug, drain the transmission. If there is no transmission drain plug, remove the pan to drain. Replace the pan to keep out dirt.
6. Remove the front exhaust pipe.
7. Remove the vacuum tube and speedometer cable.
8. Disconnect the fluid cooler tubes. Plug the tube ends to prevent leakage.
9. Remove the driveshaft and remove the starter.

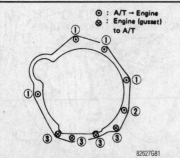

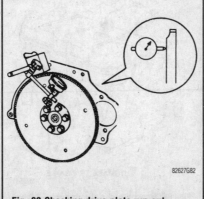

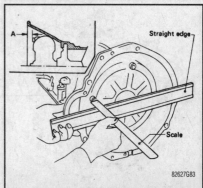

82627G81

Fig. 62 Transmission mounting bolt locations on 240SX; bolt (1) is 40mm, bolt (2) is 50mm, bolt (3) is 25mm and gusset bolts are 20mm

82627G82

Fig. 63 Checking drive plate run-out

82627G83

Fig. 64 Installation of torque converter — refer to text

10. Support the transmission with a jack under the oil pan. Support the engine also.

11. Remove the rear crossmember.

12. Mark the relationship between the torque converter and the driveplate. Remove the bolts holding the torque converter to the driveplate (rotate engine if necessary). Unbolt the transmission from the engine and remove it.

➡ **The transmission bolts are different lengths. Tag each bolt according to location to ensure proper installation. This is particularly important on the 240SX.**

13. Check the driveplate run-out with a dial indicator. Run-out must be no more than 0.020 in. refer to the illustrations.

To install:

14. If the torque converter was removed from the engine for any reason, after it is installed, the distance from the face of the converter to the edge of the converter housing must be checked prior to installing the transmission. This is done to ensure proper installation of the torque converter. On 200SX, the dimension should be 1.38 in. (35mm) or more. On 240SX, the dimension should be 1.02 in. (26mm) or more. Refer to the illustrations.

15. Raise the transmission and bolt the driveplate to the converter and transmission to the engine. Torque the driveplate-to-torque converter and con-verter housing-to-engine bolts to 29–36 ft. lbs. (39–49 Nm) on all except 240SX. On this vehicle, torque the transmission mounting bolts as follows: On 240SX, tighten bolts (1) and (2) to 29–36 ft. lbs. (39–49 Nm); tighten bolt (3) to 22–29 ft. lbs. (29–39 Nm); tighten the gusset-to-engine bolts to 22–29 ft. lbs. (29–39 Nm).

➡ **After the converter is installed, rotate the crankshaft several times to make sure the transmission rotates freely and does not bind.**

16. Install the rear crossmember.

17. Remove the engine and transmission supports.

18. Install the starter and connect the driveshaft. Torque the flange bolts to 29–33 ft. lbs. (34–44 Nm).

19. Unplug, connect and tighten the fluid cooler tubes.

20. Connect the speedometer cable and the vacuum tube.

21. Connect the front exhaust pipe using new gaskets.

22. Connect the switch wiring to the transmission.

23. Connect the shift linkage.

24. Connect the negative battery cable, fill the transmission to the proper level and make any necessary adjustment.

25. Perform a road test and check the fluid level.

AUTOMATIC TRANSAXLE

Understanding the Automatic Transaxle

The automatic transaxle allows engine torque and power to be transmitted to the front wheels within a narrow range of engine operating speeds. It will allow the engine to turn fast enough to produce plenty of power and torque at very low speeds, while keeping it at a sensible rpm at high vehicle speeds (and it does this job without driver assistance). The transaxle uses a light fluid as the medium for the transmission of power. This fluid also works in the operation of various hydraulic control circuits and as a lubricant. Because the transaxle fluid performs all of these functions, trouble within the unit can easily travel from one part to another.

Identification

◆ **See Figures 65 and 66**

The automatic transaxle serial number label is attached to upper portion of the oil pan on all Stanza models.

Adjustments

THROTTLE WIRE—CA20 ENGINE

◆ **See Figure 67**

The throttle wire is adjusted by means of double nuts on the carburetor side.

1. Loosen the adjusting nuts at the carburetor throttle wire bracket.

2. With the throttle fully opened, turn the threaded shaft inward as far as it will go and tighten the 1st nut against the bracket.

3. Back off the 1st nut ½ turns and tighten the 2nd nut against the bracket.

4. The throttle wire stroke between the threaded shaft and the cam should be 27.5–31.5mm.

THROTTLE CABLE—FUEL INJECTED ENGINE

➡ **The throttle cable is operated via a cam on the throttle shaft of the injection unit. The adjustment is located on the side of the air intake plenum.**

1. Loosen the 2 locknuts that position the cable. Open the throttle lever and hold it at the fully open position.

2. Back off both locknuts. Slide the outer cable as far as it will go away from the throttle cam.

3. Turn the nut on the side away from the throttle until it just starts to hold. Then, back it off ¾–1¼ revolutions. Tighten the nut on the throttle side to lock this position securely.

CONTROL CABLE

1. Place selector lever in **P** range. Make sure that control lever locks at **P** range.

2. Loosen locknuts. Screw front locknut until it touches select rod end while holding select rod horizontal.

3. Tighten back locknut. Make sure that selector lever moves smoothly in each range.

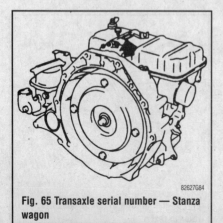

Fig. 65 Transaxle serial number — Stanza wagon

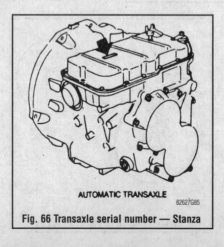

AUTOMATIC TRANSAXLE

Fig. 66 Transaxle serial number — Stanza

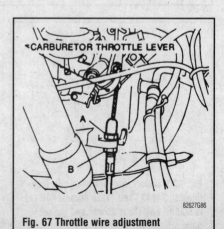

Fig. 67 Throttle wire adjustment

Neutral Safety Switch/Inhibitor Switch

The inhibitor switch allows the back-up lights to work when the transaxle is placed in Reverse range and acts as a Neutral switch, by allowing the current to pass to the starter when the transaxle is placed in Neutral or Park.

REMOVAL & INSTALLATION

1. Raise and support the vehicle on jackstands.
2. Remove the transaxle control cable connection.
3. Disconnect electrical harness, remove switch retaining screws. Remove the switch from the vehicle.
4. Installation is the reverse of the removal procedure. Adjust the inhibitor switch—refer to the service procedure.

ADJUSTMENT

♦ See Figure 68

1. Raise and support the vehicle on jackstands.
2. Loosen the inhibitor switch adjusting screws. Place the select lever in the Neutral position.
3. Using a 2.5mm diameter pin (RL3F01A type transaxle—early model Stanza) or a 4mm diameter pin (RL4F02A type transaxle—late model Stanza) place the pin into the adjustment holes on both the inhibitor switch and the switch lever (the switch lever should be as near vertical position as possible).
4. Tighten the adjusting screws EVENLY to 1.4–1.9 ft. lbs. Check the switch for continuity by making sure the vehicle starts only in P or N.

Back-Up Light Switch

REMOVAL & INSTALLATION

Refer to the Neutral Safety Switch/Inhibitor Switch service procedures.

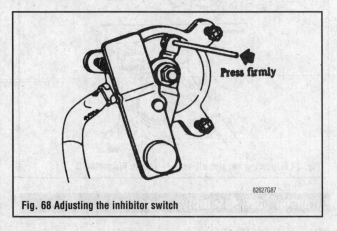

Press firmly

82627G87

Fig. 68 Adjusting the inhibitor switch

Transaxle

REMOVAL & INSTALLATION

♦ See Figures 69, 70 and 71

1. Disconnect the negative battery terminal.
2. Raise and safely support the vehicle.

➡**On Stanza wagon, remove air cleaner, airflow meter and disconnect the front exhaust pipe. On 4WD vehicles remove driveshaft (matchmark for correct installation), support rod, transfer control actuator, all electrical connections and transfer gussets as necessary.**

3. Remove the left front wheel assembly and the left front fender protector. Drain the transaxle fluid.
4. Remove the caliper assembly. Remove the cotter pin and hub nut.
5. Remove the tie rod ball joint. Separate the axle shaft from the knuckle by slightly tapping it with a suitable tool.
6. Disconnect the speedometer cable, the throttle wire from the throttle lever.
7. Remove the control cable from the rear of the transaxle, then the oil level gauge tube.
8. Place a floor jack under the transaxle. Properly support under the engine.
9. Disconnect and plug the oil cooler hoses from the lines. Remove the torque converter to drive plate bolts.

➡**When removing the torque converter to drive plate bolts, turn the crankshaft for access to the bolts and place alignment marks on the converter to drive plate for alignment purposes.**

10. Remove the engine mount securing bolts and the starter motor.
11. Remove the transaxle (note location of bolts as some are different sizes) to engine bolts, pull the transaxle away from the engine and lower it from the vehicle.
To install:
12. Before installing the transaxle check the drive plate for run-out, the maximum allowable run-out is 0.020 in. (0.5mm). Measure the distance between the torque converter and the transaxle housing, on RL3F01A type transaxle (early models) it should be more than 0.831 in. (22mm). On the RL4F02A type transaxle (later models) it should be 0.75 in. (19mm). This measurement is for correct torque converter installation.
13. Install the transaxle assembly in vehicle.
14. On RL3F01A transaxle, torque the converter to drive plate bolts to 36–51 ft. lbs. and converter housing to engine 12–16 ft. lbs. On the RL4F02A type transaxle, torque the converter to drive plate bolts to 29–36 ft. lbs. and converter housing to engine bolts to 29–36 ft. lbs. except 25mm bolts torque to 22–30 ft. lbs.
15. Install the starter motor and all electrical connections.
16. Install the control cable to the rear of the transaxle, then the oil level gauge tube.
17. Install the axle shaft with new circlip. Install the tie rod ball joint with new cotter pin.

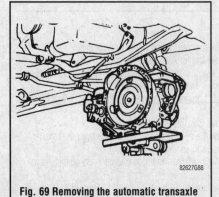

82627G88

Fig. 69 Removing the automatic transaxle — Stanza

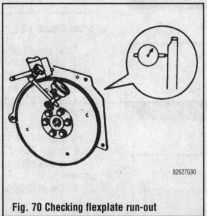

82627G90

Fig. 70 Checking flexplate run-out

82627G89

Fig. 71 Installing the torque converter assembly — automatic transaxle

18. Install the hub nut and torque to 145–203 ft. lbs. for the RL3F01A transaxle or 174–231 ft. lbs. for the RL4F02A transaxle. Install the brake caliper assembly , bleed brakes if necessary.

19. Reconnect the speedometer cable and throttle wire to the throttle lever.

20. Install all securing bolts and brackets. On Stanza wagon, install air cleaner and airflow meter and connect the front exhaust pipe also.

21. On 4WD vehicles install driveshaft, support rod, transfer control actuator, all electrical connections and transfer gussets as necessary.

22. Install the left front wheel assembly and the left front fender protector. Refill the transaxle fluid.

23. Lower the vehicle. Reconnect the negative battery cable and road test for proper operation.

Halfshafts

REMOVAL & INSTALLATION

▶ **See Figure 72**

Refer to the Manual Transaxle procedures with this exception, insert a dowel or equivalent through the right side halfshaft hole and use a small mallet to tap the left halfshaft out of the transaxle case. Withdraw the shaft

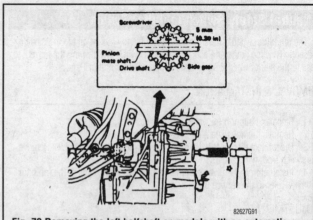

Fig. 72 Removing the left halfshaft on models with an automatic transaxle

from the steering knuckle and remove it. Be careful not to damage the pinion mating shaft and the side gear while tapping the left halfshaft out of the transaxle case.

TRANSFER SYSTEM—STANZA 4WD

Transfer Case

CHECKING TRANSFER OIL

▶ **See Figure 73**

Refer to the illustrations as guide for this service. Remove the plug and place a tool inside the case—fluid level should be to the top of the plug.

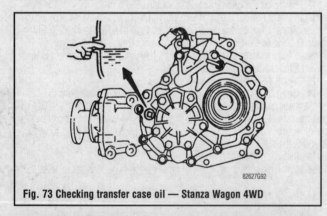

Fig. 73 Checking transfer case oil — Stanza Wagon 4WD

Adapter Oil Seal

REMOVAL & INSTALLATION

▶ **See Figure 74**

Refer to the illustrations as guide for oil seal removal and installation.

Driveshaft Oil Seal

REMOVAL & INSTALLATION

▶ **See Figure 75**

Refer to the illustrations as guide for oil seal removal and installation.

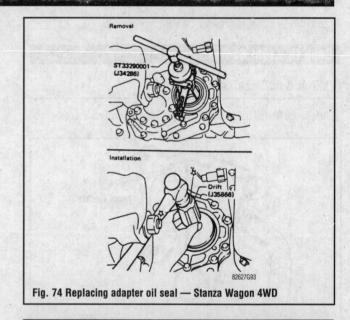

Fig. 74 Replacing adapter oil seal — Stanza Wagon 4WD

Transfer Case Assembly

REMOVAL & INSTALLATION

▶ **See Figure 76**

1. Drain the gear oil from the transaxle and the transfer case.

2. Disconnect and remove the forward exhaust pipe.

3. Using chalk or paint, matchmark the flanges on the driveshaft and then unbolt and remove the driveshaft from the transfer case.

4. Unbolt and remove the transfer control actuator from the side of the transfer case.

5. Disconnect and remove the right side halfshaft.

6. Unscrew and withdraw the speedometer pinion gear from the transfer case. Position it out of the way and secure it with wire.

7. Unbolt and remove the front, rear and side transfer case gussets (support members).

8. Use an hydraulic floor jack and a block of wood to support the transfer

case, remove the transfer case-to-transaxle mounting bolts and then remove the case itself. Be careful when moving it while supported on the jack.

To install:

9. Install the transfer case in the vehicle. Tighten the transfer case-to-transaxle mounting bolts and the transfer case gusset mounting bolts to 22–30 ft. lbs. (30–40 Nm).

10. Be sure to use a multi-purpose grease to lubricate all oil seal surfaces prior to reinstallation.

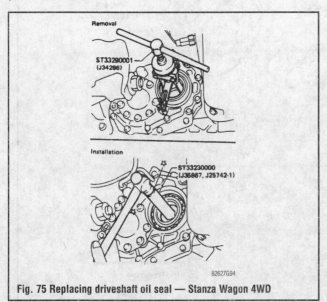

Fig. 75 Replacing driveshaft oil seal — Stanza Wagon 4WD

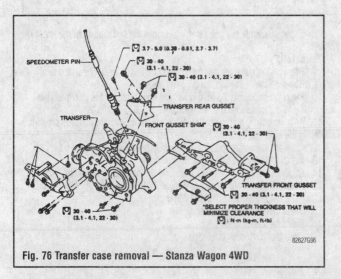

Fig. 76 Transfer case removal — Stanza Wagon 4WD

11. Install the speedometer pinion gear.
12. Install the halfshaft.
13. Connect the transfer control actuator to the side of the transfer case.
14. Install the driveshaft to the transfer case.
15. Install the forward exhaust pipe.
16. Refill all fluid levels, the transfer case and the transaxle use different types and weights of lubricant then road test for proper operation.

Differential Carrier

REMOVAL & INSTALLATION

▶ **See Figures 77, 78, 79, 80 and 81**

1. Jack up the rear of the vehicle and drain the oil from the differential. Support with jackstands. Position the floor jack underneath the differential unit.
2. Disconnect the brake hydraulic lines and the parking brake cable.
3. Disconnect the sway bar from the control arms on either sides.
4. Remove the rear exhaust tube.
5. Disconnect the driveshaft and the rear axle shafts.
6. Remove the rear shock absorbers from the control arms.
7. Unbolt the differential unit from the chassis, at the differential mounting insulator.
8. Lower the rear assembly out of the car using the floor jack. It is best to have at least one other person helping to balance the assembly.

To install:

9. Install the differential unit to the chassis. Torque the rear cover-to-insulator nuts to 72–87 ft. lbs.; the mounting insulator-to-chassis bolts to 22–29 ft. lbs.; the driveshaft-to-flange bolts to 43–51 ft. lbs. Torque the strut nuts to 51–65 ft. lbs.; and the sway bar-to-control arm nuts to 12–15 ft. lbs.

10. Reconnect the rear exhaust tube.
11. Connect the brake hydraulic lines and the parking brake cable.
12. Bleed the brake system.
13. Road test for proper operation.

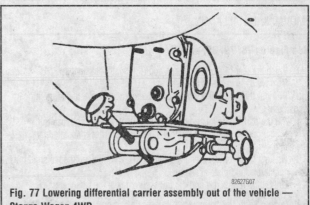

Fig. 77 Lowering differential carrier assembly out of the vehicle — Stanza Wagon 4WD

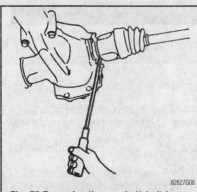

Fig. 78 Removing the rear halfshaft from carrier — Stanza Wagon 4WD

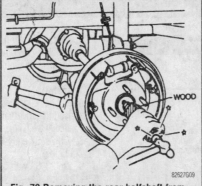

Fig. 79 Removing the rear halfshaft from backing plate — Stanza Wagon 4WD

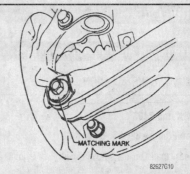

Fig. 80 Matchmark the toe adjustment bolt to the transverse link — Stanza Wagon 4WD

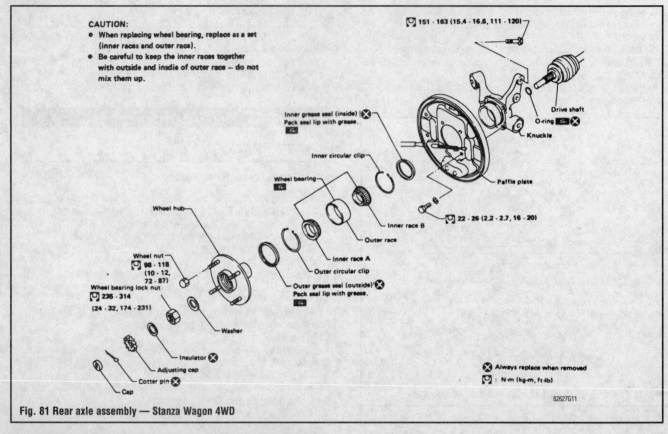

CAUTION:
- When replacing wheel bearing, replace as a set (inner races and outer race).
- Be careful to keep the inner races together with outside and inside of outer race — do not mix them up.

Inner grease seal (inside) ⊗
Pack seal lip with grease.

Inner circular clip

Wheel bearing ⊠

Wheel hub

Wheel nut
⊡ 98 - 118
(10 - 12,
72 - 87)

Wheel bearing lock nut
⊡ 235 - 314
(24 - 32, 174 - 231)

Washer

Insulator ⊗

Adjusting cap

Cotter pin ⊗

Cap

Inner race B

Outer race

Inner race A

Outer circular clip

Outer grease seal (outside) ⊗
Pack seal lip with grease.

⊡ 151 - 163 (15.4 - 16.6, 111 - 120)

Drive shaft

O-ring ⊠

Knuckle

Baffle plate

⊡ 22 - 26 (2.2 - 2.7, 16 - 20)

⊗ Always replace when removed

⊡ : N·m (kg·m, ft·lb)

82627G11

Fig. 81 Rear axle assembly — Stanza Wagon 4WD

Rear Halfshafts

REMOVAL & INSTALLATION

♦ See Figures 78, 79, 80, and 81

1. Raise the rear of the vehicle and support it with jackstands.
2. Remove the wheel and tire assembly.
3. Pull out the wheel bearing cotter pin and then remove the adjusting cap and insulator.
4. Set the parking brake and then remove the wheel bearing lock nut.
5. Disconnect and plug the hydraulic brake lines. Disconnect the parking brake cable.
6. Using a block of wood and a small mallet, carefully tap the halfshaft out of the knuckle/backing plate assembly.
7. Unbolt the radius rod and the transverse link at the wheel end.

➡Before removing the transverse link mounting bolt, matchmark the toe-in adjusting plate to the link.

8. Using a suitable pry bar, carefully remove the halfshaft from the final drive.

To install:

9. Position the halfshaft into the knuckle and then insert it into the final drive; make sure the serrations are properly aligned.
10. Push the shaft into the final drive and then press-fit the circlip on the halfshaft into the groove on the side gear.
11. After insertion, pull the halfshaft by hand to be certain that it is properly seated in the side gear and will not come out.
12. Connect the radius rod and the transverse link at the wheel end.
13. Install the knuckle/backing plate assembly.
14. Connect the hydraulic brake lines and the parking brake cable.
15. Install wheel bearing lock nut (torque 174–231 ft. lbs. refer to the illustrations), insulator, adjusting cap and cotter pin.
16. Install the wheel and tire assembly.
17. Bleed the brake system.
18. Road test for proper operation.

DRIVELINE

Driveshaft and Universal Joints

REMOVAL & INSTALLATION

200SX and 240SX

♦ See Figures 82, 83, 84 and 85

These models use a driveshaft with three U-joints and a center support bearing. The driveshaft is balanced as an assembly.

1. Raise and safely support the vehicle.
2. Matchmark the flanges on the driveshaft and differential so the driveshaft can be reinstalled in its original orientation; this will help maintain driveline balance.

3. Unbolt the rear flange and the center bearing bracket.
4. Withdraw the driveshaft from the transmission and pull the driveshaft down and back to remove.
5. Plug the transmission extension housing to prevent oil leakage.

To install:

6. Lubricate the sleeve yoke splines with clean engine oil prior to installation. Insert the driveshaft into the transmission and align the flange matchmarks.
7. Install the flange and the center bearing bolts.
8. On 200SX and 240SX, torque the center bearing support bracket bolts to 19–29 ft. lbs.
9. On 200SX with CA20E and VG30E engines, torque the flange bolts to 29–33 ft. lbs. (39–44 Nm) and on the 240SX torque to 29–33 ft. lbs. (39–44 Nm).

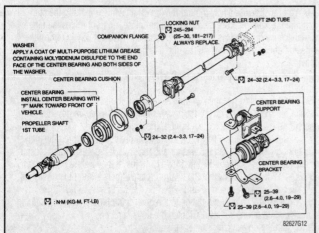

Fig. 82 Exploded view of 2 piece driveshaft assembly

Fig. 83 Matchmark the driveshaft flange to the axle flange before removing

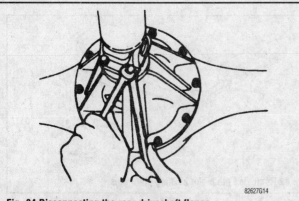

Fig. 84 Disconnecting the rear driveshaft flange

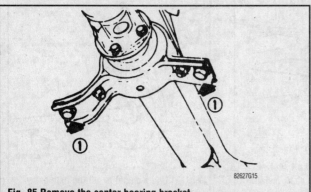

Fig. 85 Remove the center bearing bracket

U-JOINT REPLACEMENT

Disassembly

1. Mark the relationship of all components for reassembly.
2. Remove the snap-rings. On early units, the snap-rings are seated in the yokes. On later units, the snap-rings seat in the needle bearing races.
3. Tap the yoke with brass or rubber mallet to release one bearing cap. Be careful not to lose the needle rollers.
4. Remove the other bearing caps. Remove the U-joint spiders from the yokes.

Inspection

1. Spline backlash should not exceed 0.5mm.
2. Driveshaft run-out should not exceed 0.6mm.
3. On later model with snap-rings seated in the needle bearing races, different thickness of snap-rings are available for U-joint adjustment. Play should not exceed 0.02mm.
4. U-joint spiders must be replaced if their bearing journals are worn more than 0.15mm from their original diameter.

Assembly

1. Place the needle rollers in the races and hold them in place with grease.
2. Put the spider into place in its yokes.
3. Replace all seals.
4. Tap the races into position and secure them with snap-rings.

DRIVESHAFT VIBRATION

To check and correct an unbalanced driveshaft, proceed as follows:
1. Remove the undercoating and other foreign material which could upset shaft balance. Roadtest the vehicle.
2. If vibration is noted, disconnect driveshaft at differential carrier companion flange, rotate companion flange 180° degrees and reconnect the driveshaft.
3. Roadtest the vehicle, if vibration still exists replace driveshaft assembly. Note that driveshaft should be free of dents or cracks and run-out should not exceed 0.6mm.

Center Bearing

REPLACEMENT

▶ See Figures 86 and 87

The center bearing is a sealed unit which must be replaced as an assembly if defective.
1. Remove the driveshaft assembly. Refer to the necessary service procedure.
2. Paint a matchmark across where the flanges behind the center yoke are joined. This is for assembly purposes. If you don't paint or somehow mark the

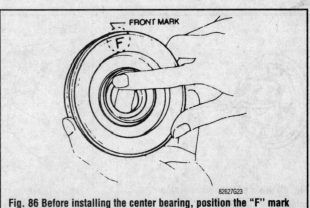

Fig. 86 Before installing the center bearing, position the "F" mark so it is facing the front of the car

Fig. 87 Always use a new nut, and stake it after tightening

relationship between the two shafts, they may be out of balance when you put them back together.

3. Remove the bolts and separate the shafts. Make a matchmark on the front driveshaft half which lines up with the mark you made on the flange half.

REAR AXLE

Identification

There are a few different types of rear axles used on the cars covered in this manual. A solid rear axle is used on 1982–84 200SX (except the 1984 Turbo model). Independent Rear Suspension (IRS) is used on 1984–88 200SX and the 240SX model. In this IRS design, separate axle driveshafts are used to transmit power from the differential to the wheels.

Axle Shaft (Solid Rear Axle)

REMOVAL & INSTALLATION

◗ **See Figures 88 thru 93**

➡**Bearings must be pressed on and off the shaft with an arbor press. Unless you have access to one, it is inadvisable to attempt any repair work on the axle shaft and bearing assemblies.**

1. Remove the hub cap or wheel cover. Loosen the lug nuts.
2. Raise the rear of the car and support it safely on stands.
3. Remove the rear wheel. Remove the four brake backing plate retaining nuts. Detach the parking brake linkage from the brake backing plate.
4. Attach a slide hammer to the axle shaft and remove it. Use a slide hammer and a two pronged puller to remove the oil seal from the housing.

➡**If a slide hammer is not available, the axle can sometimes be pried out using pry bars on opposing sides of the hub.**

If end-play is found to be excessive, the bearing should be replaced. Shimming the bearing is not recommended as this ignores end play of the bearing itself and could result in improper seating of the bearing.

4. You must devise a way to hold the driveshaft while unbolting the companion flange from the front driveshaft. Do not place the front driveshaft tube in a vise, because the chances are it will get crushed. The best way is to grip the flange somehow while loosening the nut. It is going to require some strength to remove.

5. Press the companion flange off the front driveshaft and press the center bearing from its mount.

6. The new bearing is already lubricated. Install it into the mount, making sure that the seals and so on are facing the same way as when removed. Also make sure the F mark is facing the front of the car.

7. Slide the companion flange on to the front driveshaft, aligning the marks made during removal. Install the washer and lock nut. If the washer and locknut are separate pieces, tighten them to 145–175 ft. lbs. If they were a unit. tighten it to 180–217 ft. lbs. Check that the bearing rotates freely around the driveshaft. Stake the nut (always use a new nut).

8. Connect the companion flange to the other half of the driveshaft, aligning the marks made during removal. Tighten the bolts securely.

9. Install the driveshaft.

5. Using a chisel, carefully nick the bearing retainer in three or four places. The retainer does not have to be cut, only collapsed enough to allow the bearing retainer to be slid off the shaft.

6. Pull or press the old bearing off and install the new one by pressing it into position.

7. Install the outer bearing retainer with its raised surface facing the wheel hub, and then install the bearing and the inner bearing retainer in that order on the axle shaft.

8. With the smaller chamfered side of the inner bearing retainer facing the bearing, press on the retainer. The edge of the retainer should fully touch the bearing.

9. Clean the oil seal seat in the rear axle housing. Apply a thin coat of chassis grease.

10. Using a seal installation tool, drive the oil seal into the rear axle housing. Wipe a thin coat of bearing grease on the lips of the seal.

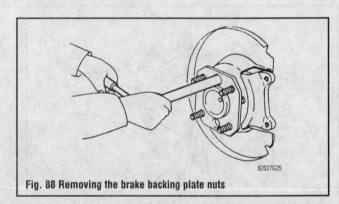

Fig. 88 Removing the brake backing plate nuts

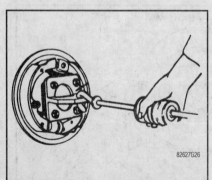

Fig. 89 Use a slide hammer tool to remove the axle shaft — solid rear axle models

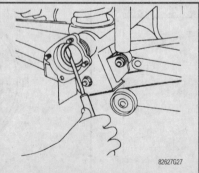

Fig. 90 Carefully remove the oil seal — replace the seal before axle shaft installation

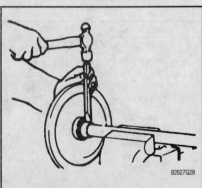

Fig. 91 Use a chisel to cut the axle bearing retainer

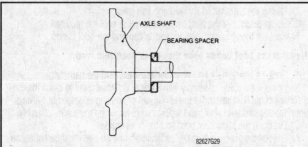

Fig. 92 Install the bearing spacer with the chamfer side facing the axle shaft flange

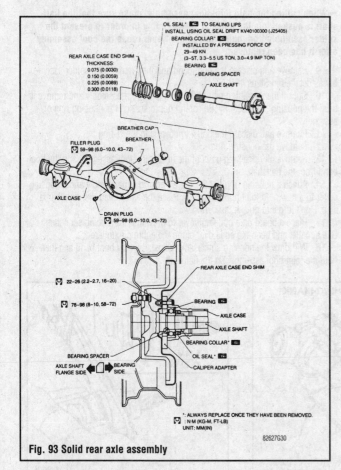

Fig. 93 Solid rear axle assembly

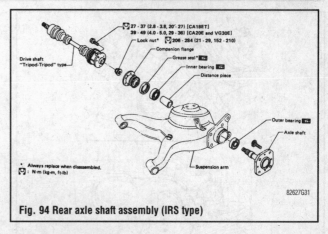

Fig. 94 Rear axle shaft assembly (IRS type)

1. Raise and support the rear of the car.
2. Remove the spring stay.
3. Disconnect the halfshaft on the wheel side by removing the four flange bolts.
4. Grasp the halfshaft at the center and extract it from the differential carrier by prying it with a suitable pry bar.
5. Installation is in the reverse order of removal. Install the differential end first and then the wheel end. Tighten the four flange bolts to 20–27 ft. lbs. on CA18ET engine and 29–36 ft. lbs. on the CA20E and VG30E engines.

240SX

◆ **See Figures 95 and 96**

➡When removing the rear halfshafts, cover the CV-boots with cloth to prevent damage.

1. Raise and support the rear of the vehicle safely.
2. Remove the rear wheel and tire assembly.
3. Remove the adjusting cap and cotter pin from the wheel bearing locknut.
4. Apply the parking brake and remove the rear wheel locknut.
5. Disconnect the halfshaft from the differential side by removing the side flange bolts.
6. Grasp the halfshaft at the center and extract if from the wheel hub by prying it with a suitable prybar or with the use of a wood block and mallet.

➡To protect the threads of the shaft, temporarily install the locknut when loosening the shaft from the wheel hub.

To install:
7. Insert the shaft into the wheel hub and temporarily install the locknut.

➡Take care not to damage the oil seal or either end of the halfshaft during installation.

8. Connect the halfshaft to the differential and install the flange bolts and torque the flange bolts to 25–33 ft. lbs.
9. Apply the parking brake and tighten the locknut. Torque the locknut to 174–231 ft. lbs. (1989–90) 152–203 ft. lbs. (1991–92).

11. Determine the number of retainer gaskets which will give the correct bearing-to-outer retainer clearance of 0.25mm.
12. Insert the axle shaft assembly into the axle housing, being careful not to damage the seal. Ensure that the shaft splines engage those of the differential pinion. Align the vent holes of the gasket and the outer bearing retainer. Install the retaining bolts.
13. Install the nuts on the bolts and tighten them evenly, and in a criss-cross pattern, to 20 ft. lbs.

Halfshaft (Independent Rear Suspension)

REMOVAL & INSTALLATION

200SX

◆ **See Figure 94**

➡When removing the halfshaft be careful not damage oil seal of differential carrier. Do not damage the CV-boot.

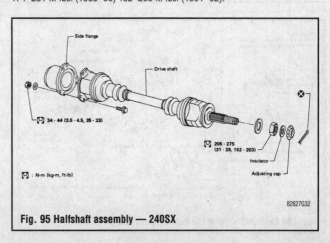

Fig. 95 Halfshaft assembly — 240SX

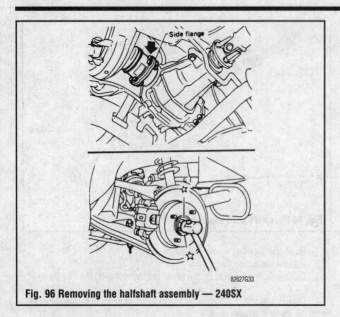

Fig. 96 Removing the halfshaft assembly — 240SX

10. Install a new locknut cotter pin and install the adjusting cap.
11. Mount the rear wheel and tire assembly.
12. Lower the vehicle.

OVERHAUL

200SX (Halfshaft Assembly)

▶ **See Figures 97 thru 107**

➡ **When overhauling the halfshaft assembly on the 240SX use this procedure as a service guide. Review the complete procedure before starting.**

1. Clamp the halfshaft in a vise using soft jaws.
2. Using pliers, pry the plug from the wheel side of the halfshaft.
3. Remove the plug seal, spring, spring cap and the boot bands.

➡ **Never reuse boot bands once they have been removed.**

4. Scribe a matchmark on the spider assembly and the halfshaft.
5. Remove the spider assembly with a press. Do not attempt to touch the contact surface of the halfshaft end at the spring cap or housing subassembly. Always support the halfshaft with your hand while you are removing the spider assembly.
6. Draw out the slide joint boot and the boot bands.
7. Loosen the vise and turn the halfshaft around so that the differential end is up.
8. Using a hacksaw, cut off the hold joint boot assembly and then remove the housing subassembly.

➡ **When cutting the hold joint boot assembly, make sure that the halfshaft is pushed into the housing subassembly in order to prevent the spider assembly from being scratched. Never reuse the boot assembly after it has been removed.**

9. Remove and discard the boot band and then remove the spider assembly as detailed in Steps 4–5.
10. Cut off the remaining part of the hold joint boot assembly and remove it from the housing subassembly. Be careful not to scratch the housing ring or assembly.
11. Remove and discard the housing cover and the O-ring.
12. Remove the housing ring.
13. Remove all remaining parts of the hold joint boot assembly and the boot band from the halfshaft.
14. Attach a housing ring, an O-ring, a housing subassembly and a housing cover to a new hold joint boot assembly. Place the assembled unit flange in a vise. Don't forget to grease the O-ring.
15. Place a board on a housing cover to prevent it from being scratched. Use a mallet and bend the edge over along the entire circumference.
16. Withdraw the housing subassembly, install a new boot band and then hold the joint boot assembly on the halfshaft.

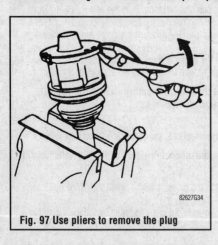

Fig. 97 Use pliers to remove the plug

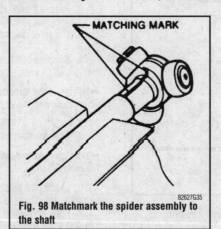

Fig. 98 Matchmark the spider assembly to the shaft

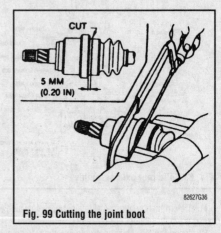

Fig. 99 Cutting the joint boot

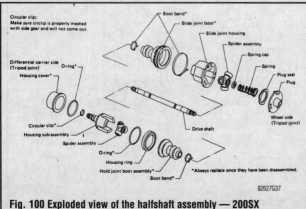

Fig. 100 Exploded view of the halfshaft assembly — 200SX

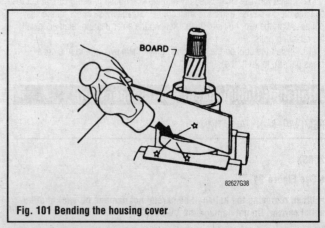

Fig. 101 Bending the housing cover

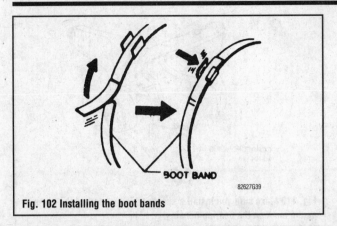

Fig. 102 Installing the boot bands

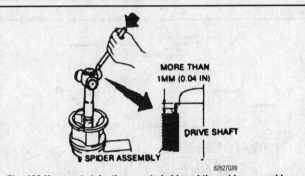

Fig. 103 You must stake the serrated sides of the spider assembly upon installation

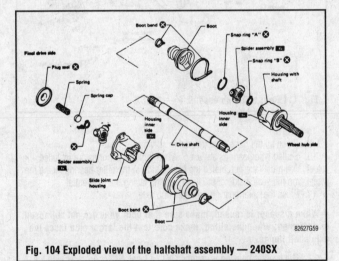

Fig. 104 Exploded view of the halfshaft assembly — 240SX

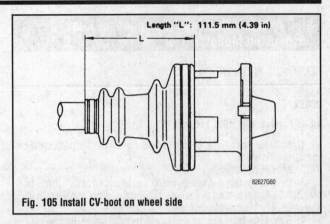

Length "L": 111.5 mm (4.39 in)

Fig. 105 Install CV-boot on wheel side

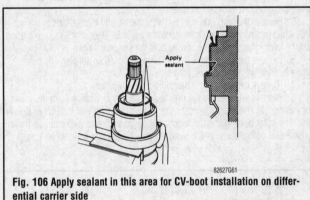

Apply sealant

Fig. 106 Apply sealant in this area for CV-boot installation on differential carrier side

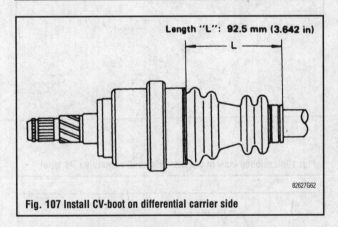

Length "L": 92.5 mm (3.642 in)

Fig. 107 Install CV-boot on differential carrier side

17. Install the spider assembly securely, making sure that the matchmarks are aligned. Make sure that when press fitting the assembly, the serration chamfer faces the shaft.

18. Stake the serration sides evenly at three places, avoiding areas that have been previously staked. Always stake two or three teeth in an area where the staked gap is more than 0.1mm.

19. Pack with grease.

20. Install the greased O-ring to the housing assembly and then place the hold joint boot assembly so that its flange is in the vise. Be sure that no other part of the assembly is in the vise.

21. Insert the housing subassembly into place and then bend the edge as detailed in Step 2 for the housing cover.

22. Apply sealant. Set the boot and install the boot bands.

23. Turn the halfshaft in the vise so that the wheel side is up.

24. Install the new boot bands, slide joint boot and slide joint housing on the halfshaft. Be careful not to scratch the boot with the end of the shaft.

25. Install the spider assembly as previously detailed.

26. Install the large diameter boot band and then pack with grease.

27. Install the spring cap, spring and plug seal. Install the plug and secure with dummy bolts. Lock the plug by bending it and then remove the dummy bolts.

28. Install the small diameter boot band and replace the halfshaft.

29. The specific amount of grease for the wheel side boot is 6.52–6.8 oz. of suitable grease. The specific amount of grease for the differential side boot is 5.47–5.82 oz. of suitable grease. Refer to the illustrations.

Stub Axle and Bearings (Independent Rear Suspension Models)

REMOVAL & INSTALLATION

200SX

♦ **See Figures 108, 109, 110 and 111**

1. Block the front wheels. Loosen the wheel nuts, raise and support the car, and remove the wheel.
2. Remove the halfshaft.
3. On cars with rear disc brakes, unbolt the caliper and move it aside. Do not allow the caliper to hang by the hose. Support the caliper with a length of wire or rest it on a suspension member.
4. Remove the brake disc on models with rear disc brakes. Remove the brake drum on cars with drum brakes.
5. Remove the stub axle nut. You will have to hold the sub axle at the outside while removing the nut from the axle shaft side. The nut will require a good deal of force to remove, so be sure to hold the stub axle firmly.
6. Remove the stub axle with a slide hammer and an adapter. The outer wheel bearing will come off with the stub axle.
7. Remove the companion flange from the lower arm.
8. Remove and discard the grease seal and inner bearing from the lower arm using a drift made for the purpose or a length of pipe of the proper diameter. The outer bearing can be removed from the stub axle with a puller. If the grease seal or the bearings are removed, new parts must be used on assembly.

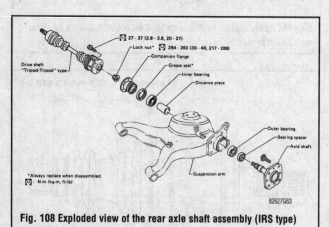

Fig. 108 Exploded view of the rear axle shaft assembly (IRS type)

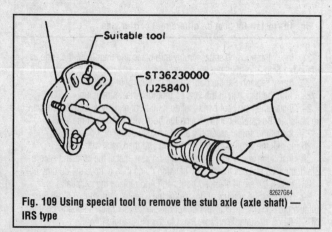

Fig. 109 Using special tool to remove the stub axle (axle shaft) — IRS type

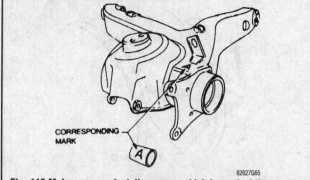

Fig. 110 Make sure you install a spacer which is marked the same as the mark on the bearing housing

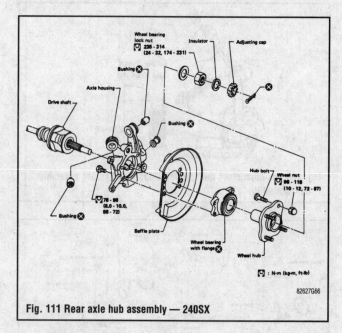

Fig. 111 Rear axle hub assembly — 240SX

To install:

9. Clean all the parts to be reused in solvent.
10. Sealed type bearings are used. When the new bearings are installed, the sealed side must face out. Install the sealed side of the outer bearing facing the wheel, and the sealed side of the inner bearing facing the differential.
11. Press the outer bearing onto the stub axle.

➡**When a spacer is reused, make sure that both ends are not collapsed or deformed. When installing, make sure that the larger side faces the axle shaft flange.**

12. The bearing housing is stamped with a letter. Select a spacer with the same marking. Install the spacer on the stub axle.
13. Install the stub axle into the lower arm.
14. Install the new inner bearing into the lower arm with the stub axle in place. Install a new grease seal.
15. Install the companion flange onto the stub axle.
16. Install the stub axle nut. On 1984–87 200SX models the torque specification is 217–289 ft. lbs. for the axle stub nut. On the 1988 200SX model the torque specification is 152–210 ft. lbs. for the axle stub nut.
17. Install the brake disc or drum, and the caliper if removed.
18. Install the halfshaft. Install the wheel and lower the car.

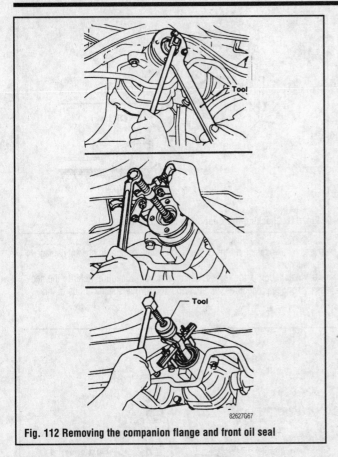

Fig. 112 Removing the companion flange and front oil seal

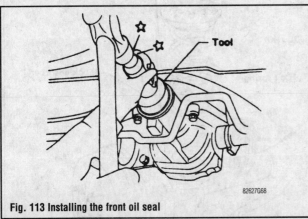

Fig. 113 Installing the front oil seal

Front Oil Seal (Pinion Seal)

REMOVAL & INSTALLATION

▶ **See Figures 112 and 113**

1. Remove the driveshaft—refer to the necessary service procedures.
2. Loosen drive pinion nut a special tool J34311 is required to hold companion flange.
3. Remove companion flange (matchmark for correct installation) using suitable puller.
4. Remove the front oil seal from differential carrier.

To install:

5. Apply multi-purpose grease to sealing lips of oil seal. Press front oil seal into carrier.
6. Install companion flange and drive pinion nut. Torque drive pinion nut to specification.

7. Install the driveshaft. Check fluid level. Refer to the specifications below:
• The drive pinion nut torque specification for model H190-ML (200SX solid rear axle type) is total pre-load 10–19 in. lbs. is obtained (94–217 ft. lbs.)
• The drive pinion nut torque specification for (1984–85 200SX) model R200 (IRS type) is 137–159 ft. lbs.
• The drive pinion nut torque specification for (1986–88 200SX and 240SX) model R200 (IRS type) is 137–217 ft. lbs.
• The drive pinion nut torque specification for (1985–88 200SX) model R180 (IRS type) is 123–145 ft. lbs.
• The drive pinion nut torque specification for (1986–88 Stanza Wagon) model R180 is 123–145 ft. lbs.

Side Oil Seal

REMOVAL & INSTALLATION

▶ **See Figures 114, 115 and 116**

1. Remove the halfshaft—refer to the necessary service procedures.
2. Remove side flange if so equipped (matchmark for correct installation) using suitable puller.
3. Remove the oil seal.

To install:

4. Apply multi-purpose grease to sealing lips of oil seal. Press oil seal into carrier.
5. Install side flange if so equipped with special tool J39352 or equivalent.
6. Install the halfshaft. Check fluid level.

Fig. 114 Removing side oil seal

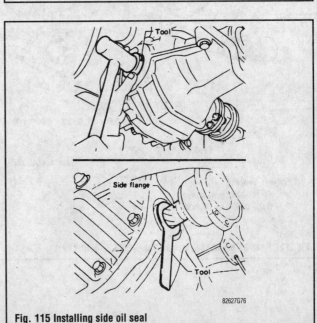

Fig. 115 Installing side oil seal

Differential Carrier/Rear Axle Assembly

REMOVAL & INSTALLATION

♦ **See Figures 117, 118, 119 and 120**

➡ **This is a complete rear axle housing and rear suspension service procedure—modify the steps as necessary. Refer to the illustrations.**

1. Raise the rear of the vehicle and support safely. Drain the oil from the differential. Position a floor jack underneath the differential unit.
2. Disconnect the brake hydraulic lines and the parking brake cable. Remove the brake caliper leaving the brake line connected. Plug the brake lines to prevent leakage.
3. Disconnect the sway bar from the control arms on either side.
4. Remove the rear exhaust pipe.
5. Disconnect the driveshaft and the rear axle shafts.
6. Remove the rear shock absorbers from the control arms.
7. Unbolt the differential unit from the chassis at the differential mounting insulator. Remove the mounting member from the front of the final drive unit if so equipped.
8. Lower the rear assembly out of the vehicle using the floor jack. It is best to have at least one other person helping to balance the assembly. After the final

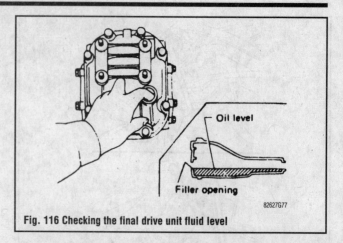

Fig. 116 Checking the final drive unit fluid level

drive is removed, support the center suspension member to prevent damage to the insulators.

9. Installation is the reverse of the removal procedure. Refer to the necessary service procedures, illustrations and torque specifications in this manual.

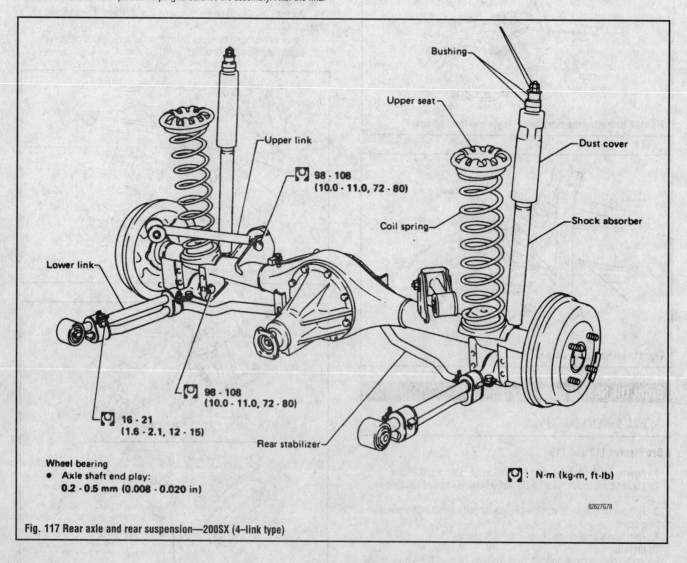

98 - 108
(10.0 - 11.0, 72 - 80)

98 - 108
(10.0 - 11.0, 72 - 80)

16 - 21
(1.6 - 2.1, 12 - 15)

Wheel bearing
● Axle shaft end play:
  0.2 - 0.5 mm (0.008 - 0.020 in)

🔲 : N·m (kg-m, ft-lb)

Fig. 117 Rear axle and rear suspension—200SX (4–link type)

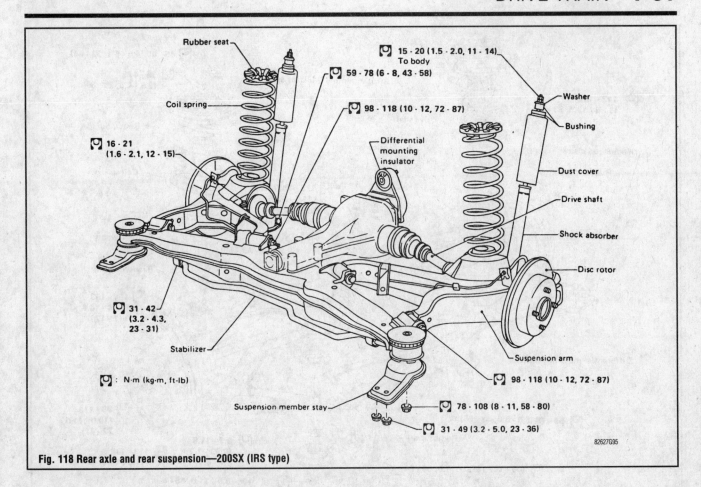

Rubber seat

Coil spring

15 - 20 (1.5 - 2.0, 11 - 14)
To body

59 - 78 (6 - 8, 43 - 58)

Washer

98 - 118 (10 - 12, 72 - 87)

Bushing

16 - 21
(1.6 - 2.1, 12 - 15)

Differential
mounting
insulator

Dust cover

Drive shaft

Shock absorber

Disc rotor

31 - 42
(3.2 - 4.3,
23 - 31)

Suspension arm

Stabilizer

98 - 118 (10 - 12, 72 - 87)

: N·m (kg·m, ft-lb)

78 - 108 (8 - 11, 58 - 80)

Suspension member stay

31 - 49 (3.2 - 5.0, 23 - 36)

82627G95

Fig. 118 Rear axle and rear suspension—200SX (IRS type)

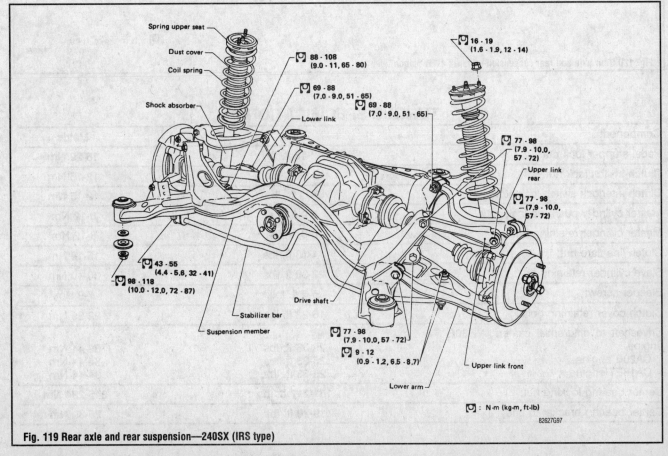

Spring upper seat

Dust cover

Coil spring

88 - 108
(9.0 - 11, 65 - 80)

16 - 19
(1.6 - 1.9, 12 - 14)

Shock absorber

69 - 88
(7.0 - 9.0, 51 - 65)

69 - 88
(7.0 - 9.0, 51 - 65)

Lower link

77 - 98
(7.9 - 10.0,
57 - 72)

Upper link
rear

77 - 98
— (7.9 - 10.0,
57 - 72)

43 - 55
(4.4 - 5.6, 32 - 41)

98 - 118
(10.0 - 12.0, 72 - 87)

Stabilizer bar

Suspension member

Drive shaft

77 - 98
(7.9 - 10.0, 57 - 72)

9 - 12
(0.9 - 1.2, 6.5 - 8.7)

Upper link front

Lower arm

: N·m (kg·m, ft-lb)

82627G97

Fig. 119 Rear axle and rear suspension—240SX (IRS type)

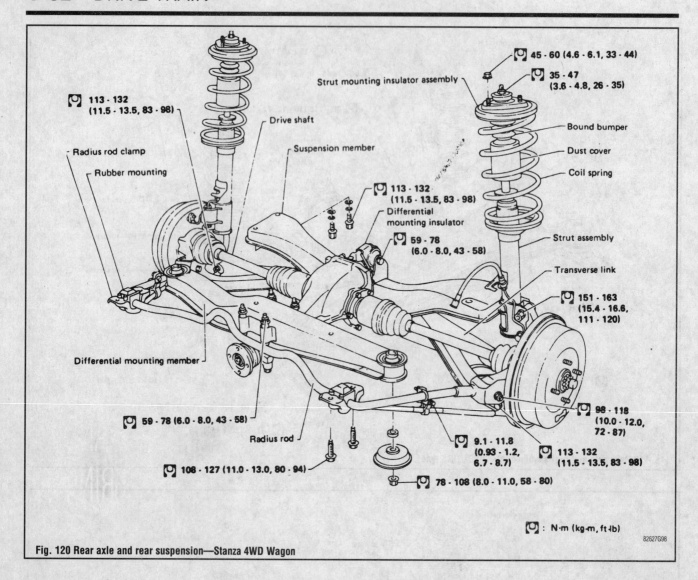

Fig. 120 Rear axle and rear suspension—Stanza 4WD Wagon

TORQUE SPECIFICATIONS

Component	English	Metric
Pedal stopper lock nut:	12-16 ft. lbs.	16-22 Nm
Clutch switch lock nut:	9-11 ft. lbs.	12-15 Nm
Clutch interlock switch lock nut:	9-11 ft. lbs.	12-15 Nm
Master cylinder push rod lock nut:	6-9 ft. lbs.	8-12 Nm
Master cylinder retaining nut:	6-9 ft. lbs.	8-12 Nm
Clutch line flare nut:	11-13 ft. lbs.	15-18 Nm
Slave cylinder retaining bolt:	22-30 ft. lbs.	30-40 Nm
Bleeder screw:	5-6 ft. lbs.	7-9 Nm
Clutch cover retaining bolts:	16-22 ft. lbs.	22-29 Nm
Driveshaft to differential carrier: VG30E engine	29-33 ft. lbs.	39-44 Nm
CA20E engine	25-33 ft. lbs.	34-44 Nm
CA18ET engine	25-33 ft. lbs.	34-44 Nm
Center bearing locking nut:	181-217 ft. lbs.	245-294 Nm
Center bearing bracket to body:	19-29 ft. lbs.	25-39 Nm

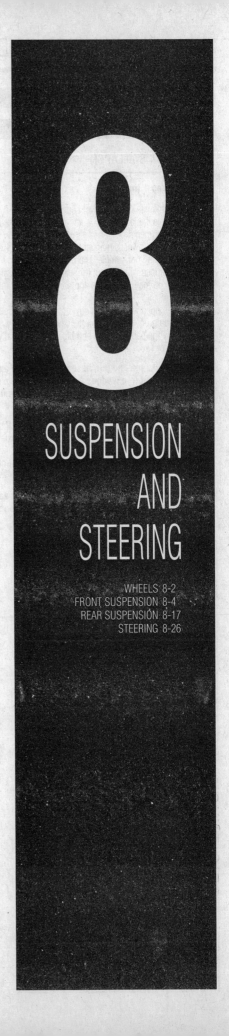

8

SUSPENSION
AND
STEERING

WHEELS

Wheels

REMOVAL & INSTALLATION

▶ **See Figures 1 thru 7**

1. Park the vehicle on a level surface.
2. Remove the jack, tire iron and, if necessary, the spare tire from their storage compartments.
3. Check the owner's manual or refer to Section 1 of this manual for the jacking points on your vehicle. Then, place the jack in the proper position.
4. If equipped with lug nut trim caps, remove them by either unscrewing or pulling them off the lug nuts, as appropriate. Consult the owner's manual, if necessary.
5. If equipped with a wheel cover or hub cap, insert the tapered end of the tire iron in the groove and pry off the cover.
6. Apply the parking brake and block the diagonally opposite wheel with a wheel chock or two.

➡ **Wheel chocks may be purchased at your local auto parts store, or a block of wood cut into wedges may be used. If possible, keep one or two of the chocks in your tire storage compartment, in case any of the tires has to be removed on the side of the road.**

7. If equipped with an automatic transmission/transaxle, place the selector lever in **P** or Park; with a manual transmission/transaxle, place the shifter in Reverse.
8. With the tires still on the ground, use the tire iron/wrench to break the lug nuts loose.

➡ **If a nut is stuck, never use heat to loosen it or damage to the wheel and bearings may occur. If the nuts are seized, one or two heavy ham-mer blows directly on the end of the bolt usually loosens the rust. Be careful, as continued pounding will likely damage the brake drum or rotor.**

9. Using the jack, raise the vehicle until the tire is clear of the ground. Support the vehicle safely using jackstands.
10. Remove the lug nuts, then remove the tire and wheel assembly.

To install:

11. Make sure the wheel and hub mating surfaces, as well as the wheel lug studs, are clean and free of all foreign material. Always remove rust from the wheel mounting surface and the brake rotor or drum. Failure to do so may cause the lug nuts to loosen in service.
12. Install the tire and wheel assembly and hand-tighten the lug nuts.
13. Using the tire wrench, tighten all the lug nuts, in a crisscross pattern, until they are snug.
14. Raise the vehicle and withdraw the jackstand, then lower the vehicle.
15. Using a torque wrench, tighten the lug nuts in a crisscross pattern to the appropriate torque:
   - 1982–86 200SX: 58–72 ft. lbs. (79–98 Nm)
   - 1987–88 200SX: 87–108 ft. lbs. (118–146 Nm)
   - 1989–92 240SX: 72–87 ft. lbs. (98–118 Nm)
   - 1982–86 Stanza and 1986 Stanza Wagon: 58–72 ft. lbs. (79–98 Nm)
   - 1987–92 Stanza and 1987–88 Stanza Wagon: 72–87 ft. lbs. (98–118 Nm)

✳✳ WARNING

Do not overtighten the lug nuts, as this may cause the wheel studs to stretch or the brake disc (rotor) to warp.

16. If so equipped, install the wheel cover or hub cap. Make sure the valve stem protrudes through the proper opening before tapping the wheel cover into position.

TCCA8P00

Fig. 1 Place the jack at the proper lifting point on your vehicle

TCCA8P01

Fig. 2 Before jacking the vehicle, block the diagonally opposite wheel with one or, preferably, two chocks

TCCA8P02

Fig. 3 With the vehicle still on the ground, break the lug nuts loose using the wrench end of the tire iron

TCCA8P03

Fig. 4 After the lug nuts have been loos-ened, raise the vehicle using the jack until the tire is clear of the ground

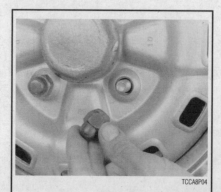

TCCA8P04

Fig. 5 Remove the lug nuts from the studs

TCCA8P05

Fig. 6 Remove the wheel and tire assem-bly from the vehicle

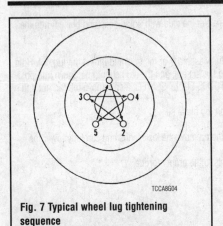

Fig. 7 Typical wheel lug tightening sequence

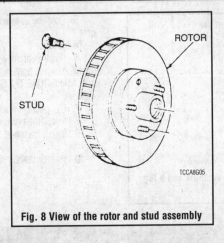

Fig. 8 View of the rotor and stud assembly

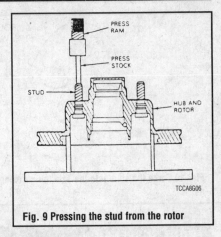

Fig. 9 Pressing the stud from the rotor

17. If equipped, install the lug nut trim caps by pushing them or screwing them on, as applicable.

18. Remove the jack from under the vehicle, and place the jack and tire iron/wrench in their storage compartments. Remove the wheel chock(s).

19. If you have removed a flat or damaged tire, place it in the storage compartment of the vehicle and take it to your local repair station to have it fixed or replaced as soon as possible.

INSPECTION

Inspect the tires for lacerations, puncture marks, nails and other sharp objects. Repair or replace as necessary. Also check the tires for treadwear and air pressure as outlined in Section 1 of this manual.

Check the wheel assemblies for dents, cracks, rust and metal fatigue. Repair or replace as necessary.

Wheel Lug Studs

REMOVAL & INSTALLATION

With Disc Brakes

▶ See Figures 8, 9 and 10

1. Raise and support the appropriate end of the vehicle safely using jackstands, then remove the wheel.

2. Remove the brake pads and caliper. Support the caliper aside using wire or a coat hanger. For details, please refer to Section 9 of this manual.

3. Remove the outer wheel bearing and lift off the rotor. For details on wheel bearing removal, installation and adjustment, please refer to Section 1 of this manual.

4. Properly support the rotor using press bars, then drive the stud out using an arbor press.

➡If a press is not available, CAREFULLY drive the old stud out using a blunt drift. MAKE SURE the rotor is properly and evenly supported or it may be damaged.

To install:

5. Clean the stud hole with a wire brush and start the new stud with a hammer and drift pin. Do not use any lubricant or thread sealer.

6. Finish installing the stud with the press.

➡If a press is not available, start the lug stud through the bore in the hub, then position about 4 flat washers over the stud and thread the lug nut. Hold the hub/rotor while tightening the lug nut, and the stud should be drawn into position. MAKE SURE THE STUD IS FULLY SEATED, then remove the lug nut and washers.

7. Install the rotor and adjust the wheel bearings.

8. Install the brake caliper and pads.

9. Install the wheel, then remove the jackstands and carefully lower the vehicle.

10. Tighten the lug nuts to the proper torque.

With Drum Brakes

▶ See Figures 11, 12 and 13

1. Raise the vehicle and safely support it with jackstands, then remove the wheel.

2. Remove the brake drum.

3. If necessary to provide clearance, remove the brake shoes, as outlined in Section 9 of this manual.

4. Using a large C-clamp and socket, press the stud from the axle flange.

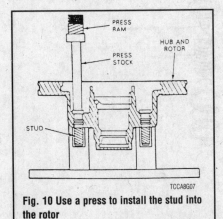

Fig. 10 Use a press to install the stud into the rotor

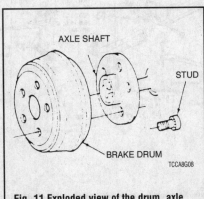

Fig. 11 Exploded view of the drum, axle flange and stud

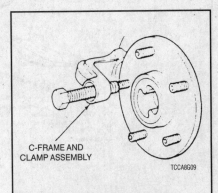

Fig. 12 Use a C-clamp and socket to press out the stud

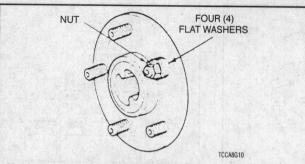

NUT

FOUR (4)
FLAT WASHERS

TCCA8G10

Fig. 13 Force the stud onto the axle flange using washers and a lug nut

5. Coat the serrated part of the stud with liquid soap and place it into the hole.

To install:

6. Position about 4 flat washers over the stud and thread the lug nut. Hold the flange while tightening the lug nut, and the stud should be drawn into position. MAKE SURE THE STUD IS FULLY SEATED, then remove the lug nut and washers.

7. If applicable, install the brake shoes.

8. Install the brake drum.

9. Install the wheel, then remove the jackstands and carefully lower the vehicle.

10. Tighten the lug nuts to the proper torque.

FRONT SUSPENSION

MacPherson Strut

REMOVAL & INSTALLATION

200SX

▶ See Figure 14

1. Jack up the car and support it safely. Remove the wheel/tire assembly.

2. Remove the brake caliper. Remove the disc and hub assembly—refer to the necessary service procedures.

3. Remove the tension rod arm and knuckle arm to lower strut assembly retaining bolts.

4. Pry the lower assembly down to detach it from the strut.

5. Support strut assembly with a suitable stand or jack.

6. Open the hood, and remove the nuts holding the top of the strut to the tower (hoodledge).

7. Lower the jack/stand slowly and cautiously until the strut assembly can be removed.

To install:

8. Install the strut assembly on the vehicle and torque the strut-to-knuckle arm to 53–72 ft. lbs. Torque the tension rod to transverse link to 33–40 ft. lbs. and the strut to tower (hoodledge) bolts to 23–31 ft. lbs.

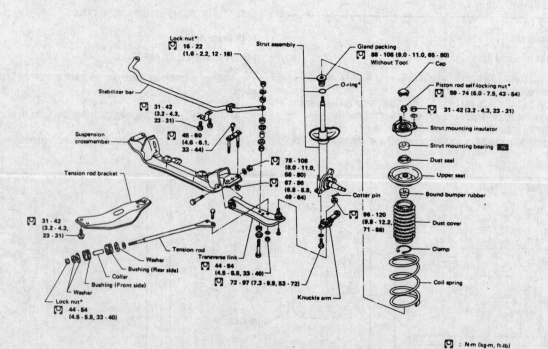

When installing a bushing, do not allow it to project beyond the surface area of the washer.
Do not allow the bushings and washers to come in contact with grease, oil, soapy water, etc.

* : Always replace whenever disassembled.

• Final tightening should be carried out under unladen condition**
  with tires on ground when installing each bushing.
  **Fuel, radiator coolant and engine oil are filled up.
  Spare tire, jack, hand tools and mats are in designed position.

82628G01

Fig. 14 Front suspension — 200SX

➡The self-locking nuts holding the top of the strut must always be replaced when removed.

9. Bleed the brakes.
10. Install the wheel.

240SX/Stanza/Stanza Wagon 2WD and 4WD

▸ **See Figures 15, 16, 17, 18 and 19**

1. Raise and safely support the vehicle.
2. Remove the wheel. Mark the position of the strut-to-steering knuckle location.
3. Detach the brake tube from the strut.
4. Support the control arm.
5. Remove the strut-to-steering knuckle bolts.
6. Support the strut assembly and remove the 3 upper strut to hoodledge nuts. Remove the strut assembly from the vehicle.

To install:

7. Install the strut assembly onto the vehicle and torque the following:
- 240SX model—Strut-to-body (hoodledge) nuts: 29–40 ft. lbs.
- 240SX model—Strut-to-knuckle bolts: 114–133 ft. lbs.
- 1982–86 Stanza—Strut-to-body (hoodledge) nuts: 23–31 ft. lbs.
- 1982–86 Stanza—Strut-to-knuckle bolts: 56–80 ft. lbs.
- 1987–89 Stanza—Strut-to-body (hoodledge) nuts: 23–31 ft. lbs.
- 1987–89 Stanza—Strut-to-knuckle bolts: 82–91 ft. lbs.
- 1990–92 Stanza—Strut-to-body (hoodledge) nuts: 29–40 ft. lbs.
- 1990–92 Stanza—Strut-to-knuckle bolts: 116–123 ft. lbs.
- Stanza Wagon 2WD—Strut-to-body (hoodledge) nuts: 23–31 ft. lbs.
- Stanza Wagon 2WD—Strut-to-knuckle bolts: 72–87 ft. lbs.
- Stanza Wagon 4WD—Strut-to-body (hoodledge) nuts: 11–17 ft. lbs.
- Stanza Wagon 4WD—Strut-to-knuckle bolts: 72–87 ft. lbs.

8. If brake hose was disconnected from the brake caliper, bleed brakes and install the wheel.

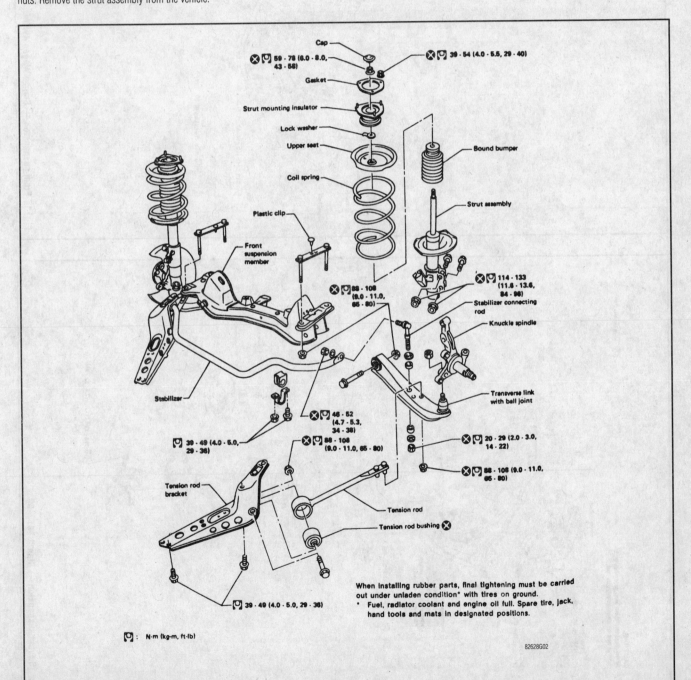

Fig. 15 Front suspension — 240SX

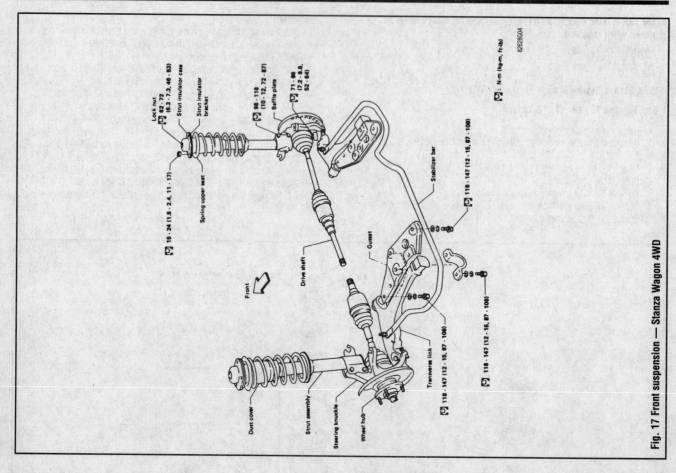

Fig. 17 Front suspension — Stanza Wagon 4WD

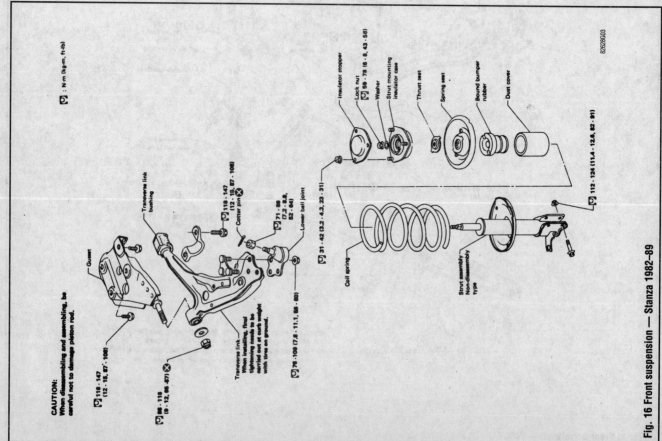

Fig. 16 Front suspension — Stanza 1982–89

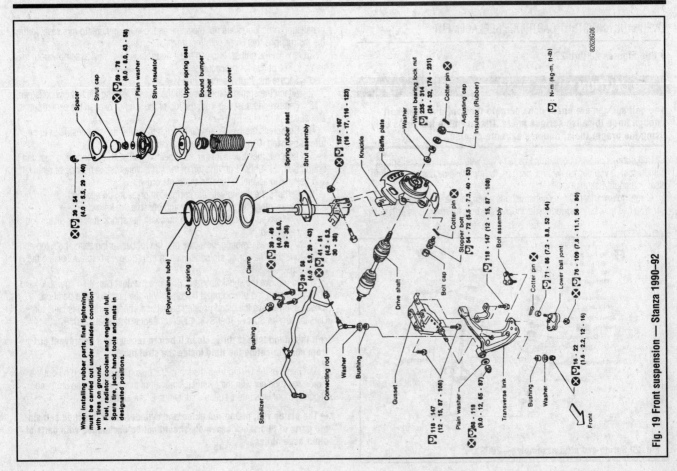

When installing rubber parts, final tightening must be carried out under unladen condition* with tires on ground.
* Fuel, radiator coolant and engine oil full. Spare tire, jack, hand tools and mats in designated positions.

Fig. 19 Front suspension — Stanza 1990-92

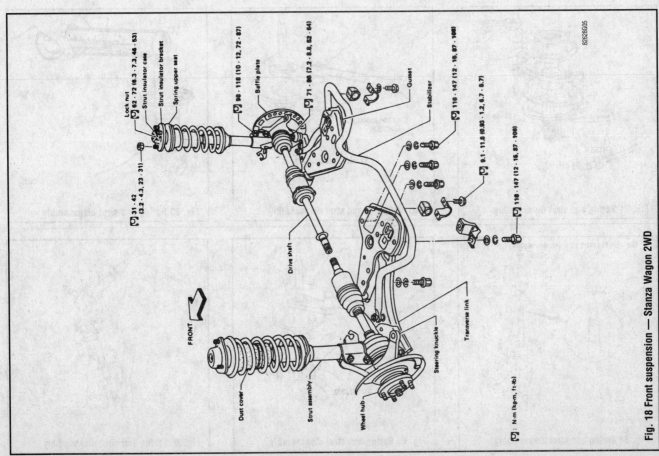

Fig. 18 Front suspension — Stanza Wagon 2WD

OVERHAUL AND STRUT CARTRIDGE REPLACEMENT

◆ **See Figures 20 thru 27**

❊❊ CAUTION

The coil springs are under considerable tension, and can exert enough force to cause serious injury. Disassemble the struts only using the proper tools, and use extreme caution.

Coil springs on all models must be removed with the aid of a coil spring compressor. If you don't have one, don't try to improvise by using something else: you could risk injury.

Always follow manufacturer's instructions when operating a spring compressor. You can now buy cartridge type shock absorbers for many Datsun/Nissan:

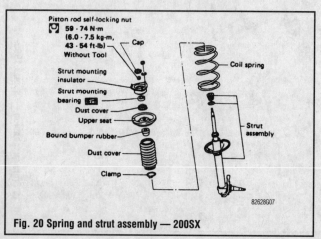

Fig. 20 Spring and strut assembly — 200SX

installation procedures are not the same as those given here. In this case, follow the instructions that come with the shock absorbers.

To remove the coil spring, you must first remove the strut assembly from the vehicle. See above for procedures.

1. Secure the strut assembly in a vise.
2. Attach the spring compressor to the spring, leaving the top few coils free.
3. Remove the dust cap from the top of the strut to expose the center nut, if a dust cap is provided.
4. Compress the spring just far enough to permit the strut insulator to be turned by hand. Remove the self locking center nut.
5. Take out the strut insulator, strut bearing, oil seal, upper spring seat and bound bumper rubber from the top of the strut. Note their sequence of removal and be sure to assemble them in the same order.
6. Remove the spring with the spring compressor still attached.
7. Reassembly the strut assembly and observe the following:
   a. Make sure you assemble the unit with the shock absorber piston rod fully extended.
   b. When assembling, take care that the rubber spring seats, both top and bottom, and the spring are positioned in their grooves before releasing the spring.
8. To remove the shock absorber: Remove the dust cap, if so equipped, and push the piston rod down until it bottoms. With the piston in this position, loosen and remove the gland packing shock absorber retainer. This calls for Datsun/ Nissan Special Tool ST35490000 or equivalent tool J26083.

➠**If the gland tube is dirty, clean it before removing it to prevent dirt from contaminating the fluid inside the strut tube.**

9. Remove the O-ring from the top of the piston rod guide and lift out the piston rod together with the cylinder. Drain all of the fluid from the strut and shock components into a suitable container. Clean all parts.

➠**The piston rod, piston rod guide and cylinder are a matched set: single parts of this shock assembly should not be exchanged with parts of other assemblies.**

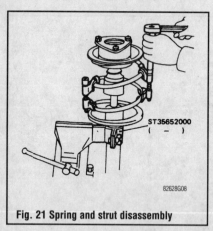

Fig. 21 Spring and strut disassembly

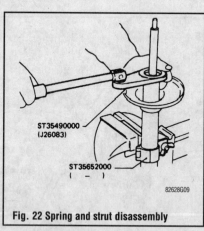

Fig. 22 Spring and strut disassembly

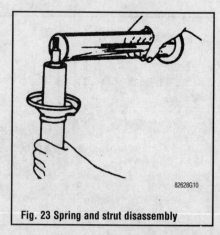

Fig. 23 Spring and strut disassembly

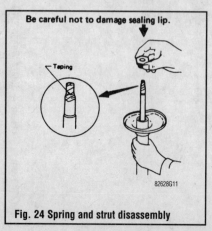

Fig. 24 Spring and strut disassembly

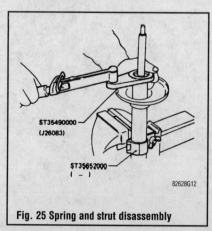

Fig. 25 Spring and strut disassembly

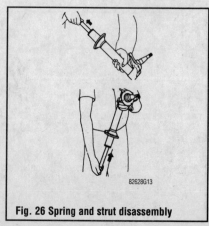

Fig. 26 Spring and strut disassembly

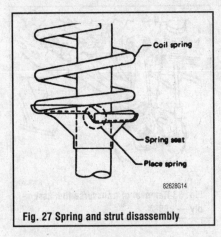

Fig. 27 Spring and strut disassembly

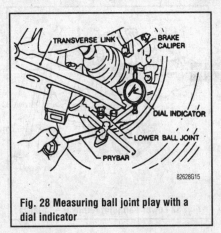

Fig. 28 Measuring ball joint play with a dial indicator

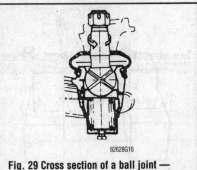

Fig. 29 Cross section of a ball joint — note the plug (remove the plug) at the bottom for a grease fitting — make sure the rubber boot is in good condition

10. Assembly the shock absorber into the assembly with the following notes:

a. After installing the cylinder and piston rod assembly (the shock absorber kit) in the outer casing, remove the piston rod guide, if so equipped, from the cylinder and pour the correct amount of new fluid into the cylinder and strut outer casing. To find this amount consult the instructions with your shock absorber kit. The amount of oil should be listed. Use only Nissan Genuine Strut Oil or its equivalent.

➡ **It is important that the correct amount of fluid be poured into the strut to assure correct shock absorber damping force.**

b. Install the O-ring, fluid and any other cylinder components. Fit the gland packing and tighten it after greasing the gland packing-to-piston rod mating surfaces.

➡ **When tightening the gland packing, extend the piston rod about 3–5 in. (76–127mm) from the end of the outer casing to expel most of the air from the strut.**

c. After the kit is installed, bleed the air from the system in the following manner: hold the strut with its bottom end facing down. Pull the piston rod out as far as it will go. Turn the strut upside down and push the piston in as far as it will go. Repeat this procedure several times until an equal pressure is felt on both the pull out and the push in strokes of the piston rods. The remaining assembly is the reverse of disassembly.

Lower Ball Joints

INSPECTION

Dial Indicator Method

▶ **See Figure 28**

1. Raise and support the vehicle safely.
2. Clamp a dial indicator to the transverse link and place the tip of the dial on the lower edge of the brake caliper.
3. Zero the indicator.
4. Make sure the front wheels are straight ahead and the brake pedal is fully depressed.
5. Insert a long prybar between the transverse link and the inner rim of the wheel.
6. Push down and release the prybar and observe the reading (deflection) on the dial indicator. Take several readings and use the maximum dial indicator deflection as the ball joint vertical end-play. Make sure to **0** the indicator after each reading. If the reading is not within specifications, replace the transverse link or the ball joint. Ball joint vertical end-play specifications are as follows:

- 200SX and 240SX— 0 in. (0mm)
- 1982–89 Stanza — 0.0040.–039 in. (0.1–1.0mm)
- 1990–92 Stanza — 0 in. (0mm)
- Stanza Wagon—0.098 in. (2.5mm) or less

Visual Approximation Method

The lower ball joint should be replaced when play becomes excessive. An effective way to visually approximate ball joint vertical end-play without the use of a dial indicator is to perform the following:

1. Raise and safely support the vehicle until the wheel is clear of the ground. Do not place the jack under the ball joint; it must be unloaded.
2. Place a long prybar under the tire and move the wheel up and down. Keep one hand on top of the tire while doing this.
3. If ¼ in. (6mm) or more of play exists at the top of the tire, the ball joint should be replaced. Be sure the wheel bearings are properly adjusted before making this measurement. A double check can be made; while the tire is being moved up and down, observe the ball joint. If play is seen, replace the ball joint.

REMOVAL & INSTALLATION

Rear Wheel Drive

▶ **See Figures 29, 30 and 31**

If there is a plugged hole in the bottom of the joint for installation of a grease fitting, install a fitting. The ball joint should be greased every 15,000 miles or 1 year.

➡ **The transverse link (lower control arm) must be removed and then the ball joint must be pressed out.**

1. Raise and support the vehicle safely.
2. Remove the front wheels.

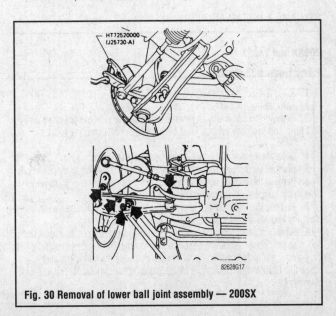

Fig. 30 Removal of lower ball joint assembly — 200SX

Fig. 31 Separate ball joint from the knuckle arm with press — 200SX

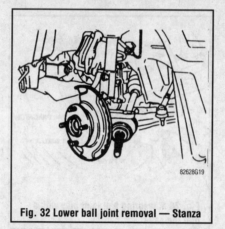

Fig. 32 Lower ball joint removal — Stanza

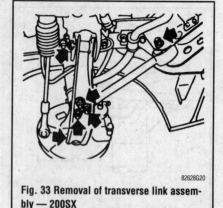

Fig. 33 Removal of transverse link assembly — 200SX

3. Remove the stabilizer bar and tension rod.
4. Remove the transverse link and knuckle arm.
5. Separate the knuckle arm from the ball joint with a suitable press.
6. Replace the transverse link/ball joint assembly.
7. Installation is the reverse of the removal procedure. Refer to the illustrations. Final tightening needs to be carried out under Unladen conditions with tires on ground. All fluid levels and fuel full and all components installed in the correct position.

Front Wheel Drive

♦ See Figure 32

1. Raise and support the vehicle safely.
2. Remove the front wheel.
3. Remove the wheel bearing lock-nut.
4. Separate the tie rod end ball joint from the steering knuckle with a ball joint remover, being careful not to damage the ball joint dust cover if the ball joint is to be used again.
5. Loosen, but do not remove the strut retaining upper nuts.
6. Remove the nut that attaches the ball joint to the transverse link.
7. Separate the halfshaft from the knuckle by lightly taping the end of the shaft.
8. Separate the ball joint from the knuckle using the proper tool.
9. Installation is the reverse of the removal procedure. Always replace the ball joint retaining bolts and cotter pins after each disassembly. Refer to the illustrations as guide for additional specifications.

Lower Control Arm (Transverse Link)

REMOVAL & INSTALLATION

200SX and 240SX

♦ See Figures 33 and 34

1. Raise and support the vehicle safely.
2. Remove the front wheel.
3. Remove the cotter pin and castle nut from the side rod (steering arm) ball joint and separate the ball joint from the side rod using the proper tool.
4. Separate the steering knuckle arm from the MacPherson strut.
5. Remove the tension rod and stabilizer bar from the lower arm.
6. Remove the nuts or bolts connecting the lower control arm (transverse link) to the suspension crossmember.
7. Remove the lower control arm (transverse link) with the suspension ball joint and knuckle arm still attached.
8. When installing the control arm, temporarily tighten the nuts and/or bolts securing the control arm to the suspension crossmember. Tighten them fully only after the vehicle is sitting on its wheels. Lubricate the ball joints after assembly. Refer to the illustrations for additional specifications. Check wheel alignment.

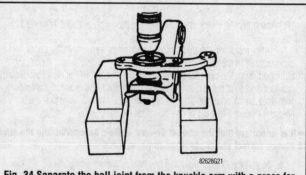

Fig. 34 Separate the ball joint from the knuckle arm with a press for transverse link removal — 200SX

1982–89 Stanza 2WD and 4WD Wagon

♦ See Figure 35

➡Always use new nuts when installing the ball joint assembly to the control arm.

1. Raise the vehicle and support it safely.
2. Remove the front wheels.
3. Remove the lower ball joint bolts from the control arm.

➡If equipped with a stabilizer bar, disconnect it at the control arm. Refer to the necessary service procedures.

4. Remove the control arm-to-body bolts.
5. Remove the gusset.
6. Remove the control arm.
7. Installation is the reverse of the removal procedure. Always replace the ball joint retaining bolts and cotter pins after each disassembly. Refer to the illustrations as guide for additional specifications.

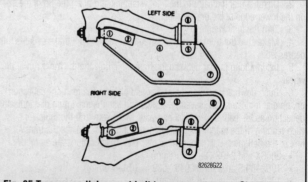

Fig. 35 Transverse link gusset bolt torque sequence — Stanza Wagon 4WD

➥ Final tightening should be made with the weight of the vehicle on the wheels.

➥ On the Stanza Wagon, make sure to torque the gusset bolts in the proper sequence.

1990–92 Stanza

♦ See Figure 36

1. Raise the vehicle and support it safely.
2. Unbolt and remove the stabilizer bar. The bar is removed by unfastening the clamp bolts and the bolts that hold the bar to the transverse link gusset plate. When removing the clamps, note the relationship between the clamp and paint mark on the bar.
3. Unbolt and remove the transverse link and gusset.
4. Inspect the transverse link, gusset and bushings for cracks, damage and deformation.
5. To install, bolt the transverse link and gusset into place. Lower the vehicle and torque the bolts and nuts in the proper sequence as illustrated. Torque the nuts to 30–35 ft. lbs. and the bolts to 87–108 ft. lbs. The vehicle must at curb weight and the tires must be on the ground. After installation is complete, check the front end alignment.

Tension Rod and Stabilizer Bar

REMOVAL & INSTALLATION

200SX and 240SX

♦ See Figures 37, 38 and 39

1. Raise and support the vehicle safely.
2. Remove the tension rod-to-frame lock nuts.
3. Remove the 2 mounting bolts at the transverse link, lower control arm, and then slide out the tension rod.

4. On 240SX, to remove the tension rod, remove the bolt and nut that holds the rod to the tension rod bracket (through the bushing), then swing the rod upward and remove the transverse link bolts, nuts, bushings and washers. If the bushings are worn replace them.
5. Unbolt the stabilizer bar at each transverse link or connecting rod. On 240SX, engage the flats of stabilizer bar connecting rod with a wrench to keep the rod from moving when removing the nuts.
6. Remove the 4 stabilizer bar bracket bolts, and remove the stabilizer bar.
7. During installation observe the following:
   a. Tighten the stabilizer bar-to-transverse link bolts to 12–16 ft. lbs. and 34–38 ft. lbs. on 240SX.
   b. Tighten the stabilizer bar bracket bolts to 22–29 ft. lbs. and 29–36 ft. lbs. on 240SX.
   c. Tighten the tension rod-to-transverse link nuts to 31–43 ft. lbs. On 240SX, torque the plain nuts to 65–80 ft. lbs. and the nuts with bushings and washers to 14–22 ft. lbs. Make sure to hold the connecting rod stationary.
   d. Tighten the tension rod-to-frame nut (bushing end) to 33–40 ft. lbs. Always use a new lock-nut when reconnecting the tension rod to the frame.
   e. Be certain the tension rod bushings are installed properly. Make sure the stabilizer bar ball joint socket is properly positioned.

➥ Never tighten any bolts or nuts to their final torque unless the vehicle is resting, unsupported, on the wheels (Unladen condition).

Stanza/Stanza Wagon 2WD and 4WD

♦ See Figures 40 and 41

➥ On this service procedure—modify the steps to the correct application—perform only the necessary service steps.

1. Raise and support the vehicle safely. Disconnect the parking brake cable at the equalizer on the Stanza Wagon (2WD).
2. On the Stanza Wagon (4WD), remove the mounting nuts for the transaxle support rod and the transaxle control rod.
3. Disconnect the front exhaust pipe at the manifold and position it aside (not required on Stanza car).

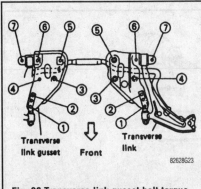

Fig. 36 Transverse link gusset bolt torque sequence — Stanza 1990–92

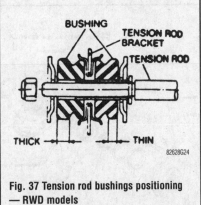

Fig. 37 Tension rod bushings positioning — RWD models

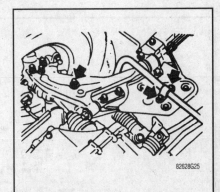

Fig. 38 Tension rod and bar attaching points — 240SX

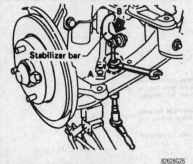

Fig. 39 Hold the stabilizer connecting rod with a wrench when removing and installing the mounting nuts

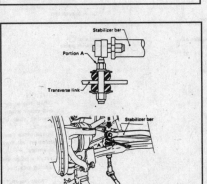

Fig. 40 Stabilizer bar removal and installation — Stanza

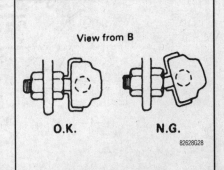

Fig. 41 Install stabilizer bar and joint socket in the correct position

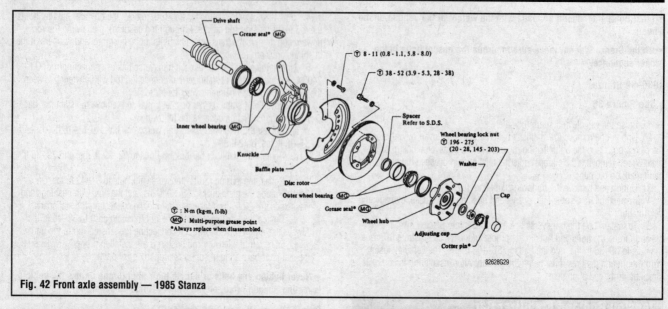

Fig. 42 Front axle assembly — 1985 Stanza

4. On the Stanza Wagon (4WD), matchmark the flanges and then separate the driveshaft from the transfer case.

5. Remove the stabilizer bar-to-transverse link (lower, control arm) mounting bolts. Engage the flats of stabilizer bar connecting rod with a wrench to keep the rod from moving when removing (and installing) the bolts.

6. Matchmark the stabilizer bar to the mounting clamps.

7. Remove the stabilizer bar mounting clamp bolts and then pull the bar out, around the link and exhaust pipe.

8. Installation is the reverse of the removal procedure. Never tighten the mounting bolts unless the vehicle is resting on the ground with normal weight upon the wheels. Be sure the stabilizer bar ball joint socket is properly positioned. Refer to the illustrations.

Front Axle, Knuckle and Bearing

REMOVAL & INSTALLATION

Stanza

▶ **See Figures 42 and 43**

1. Raise and support the front of the vehicle safely and remove the wheels.
2. Remove wheel bearing lock nut.

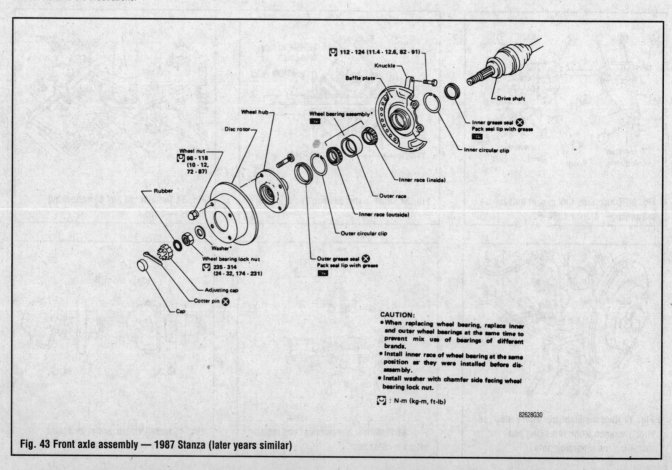

Fig. 43 Front axle assembly — 1987 Stanza (later years similar)

3. Remove brake caliper assembly. Make sure not to twist the brake hose.
4. Remove tie rod ball joint.

➡ Cover axle boots with waste cloth or equivalent so as not to damage them when removing driveshaft. Make a matching mark on strut housing and adjusting pin before removing them.

5. Separate halfshaft from the knuckle by slightly tapping it.
6. Mark and remove the strut mounting bolts.
7. Remove lower ball joint from knuckle.
8. Remove knuckle from lower control arm.

To install:

➡ To replace the wheel bearings and races they must be pressed in and out of the knuckle assembly. To pack the wheel bearings they will have to be removed from the knuckle assembly. Refer to the illustrations.

9. Install the knuckle to the lower control arm and connect the ball joint, use a NEW retaining nut and cotter pin on ball joint assembly.
10. Connect the knuckle to the strut and to the halfshaft.
11. Install the tie rod ball joint, use a NEW cotter pin.
12. Install the brake caliper assembly.
13. Install the wheel bearing lock nut torque hub nut to 145–203 ft. lbs. (1982–87 Stanza with plain rotor assembly—see illustrations) and all other applications to 174–231 ft. lbs.—see the illustrations.
14. Install the front wheels. Check front end alignment.

Front Wheel Bearings

REMOVAL & INSTALLATION

Rear Wheel Drive

▶ **See Figures 44 thru 51**

➡ After the wheel bearings have been removed or replaced or the front axle has been reassembled be sure to adjust wheel bearing preload. Refer to the Adjustment service procedure below. On the 1989–92 240SX there is just one wheel bearing, pressed into the hub and no adjusting cap. Refer to the exploded views of the Front Axle Hub Assembly. Review the complete service procedure.

1. Raise and support the vehicle safely.
2. Remove the front wheels and the brake caliper assemblies.

➡ Brake hoses do not need to be disconnected from the brake caliper assemblies. Make sure the brake hoses are secure and do not let caliper assemblies hang unsupported from the vehicle.

3. Work off center hub cap by using thin tool. If necessary tap around it with a soft hammer while removing.
4. Pry off cotter pin and take out adjusting cap and wheel bearing lock nut.
5. Remove wheel hub with disc brake rotor from spindle with bearings installed. Remove the outer bearing from the hub.
6. Remove inner bearing and grease seal from hub using long brass drift pin or equivalent.
7. If it is necessary to replace the bearing outer races, drive them out of the hub with a brass drift pin and mallet.
8. Install the outer bearing race with a tool (KV401021S0 special tool number) until it seats in the hub flush.

➡ Place a large glob of grease into the palm of one hand and push the bearing through it with a sliding motion. The grease must be forced through the side of the bearing and in between each roller. Continue until the grease begins to ooze out the other side through the gaps between the rollers. The bearing must be completely packed with grease.

9. Pack each wheel bearing with high temperature wheel bearing grease. Pack hub and hub cap with the recommended wheel bearing grease up to shaded portions. Refer to the illustration.
10. Install the inner bearing and grease seal in the proper position in the hub.
11. Install the wheel hub with disc brake rotor to the spindle.
12. Install the outer wheel bearing, lock washer, wheel bearing lock nut, adjusting cap, cotter pin (always use a new cotter pin and O-ring for installation after adjustment), spread cotter pin then install the O-ring and dust cap.
13. Install the brake caliper assemblies and bleed brakes if necessary. Install the front wheels.

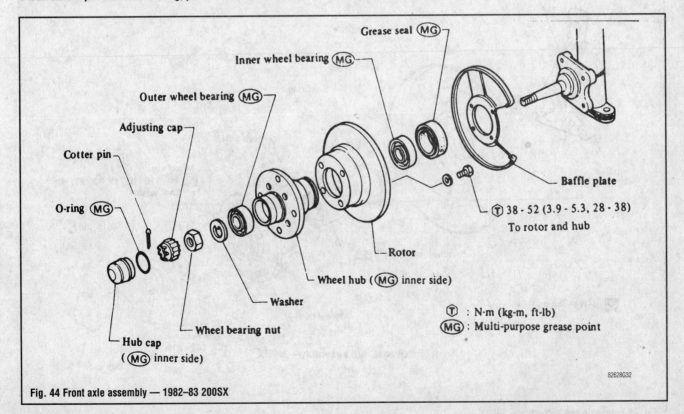

Fig. 44 Front axle assembly — 1982–83 200SX

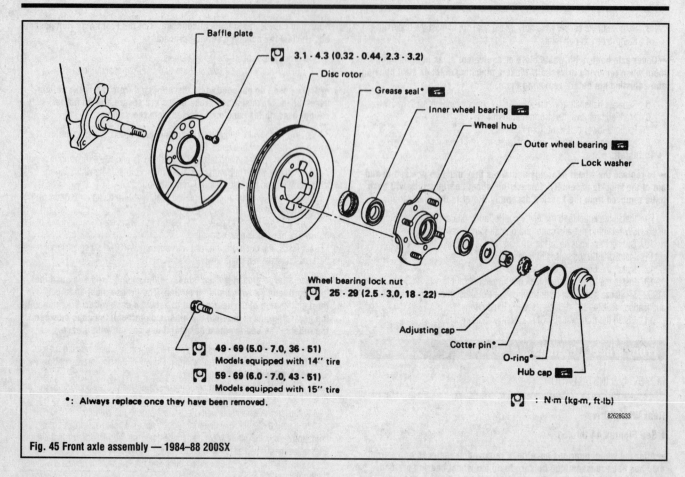

Fig. 45 Front axle assembly — 1984–88 200SX

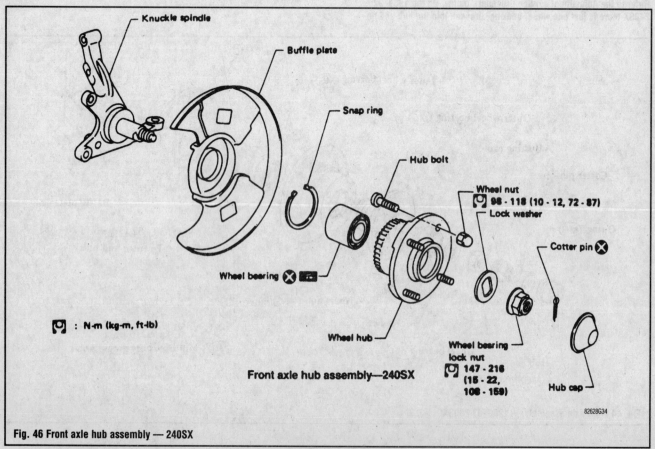

Fig. 46 Front axle hub assembly — 240SX

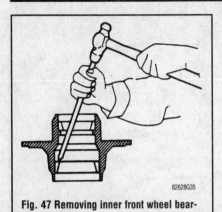

Fig. 47 Removing inner front wheel bearing — RWD model

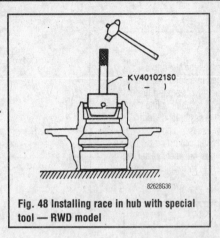

Fig. 48 Installing race in hub with special tool — RWD model

Fig. 49 Packing front wheel bearings — RWD model

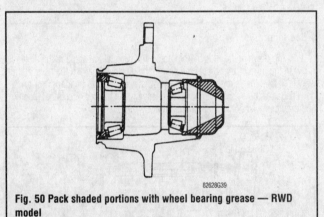

Fig. 50 Pack shaded portions with wheel bearing grease — RWD model

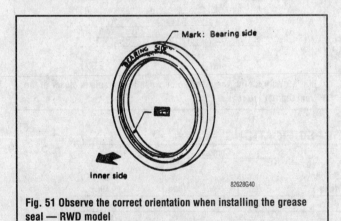

Fig. 51 Observe the correct orientation when installing the grease seal — RWD model

one wheel bearing and no adjusting cap on this model, just use a new cotter pin after the torque specification is reached.

3. Turn the wheel hub several times in both directions to seat wheel bearing correctly.

4. Again tighten wheel bearing nut to specification 18–22 ft. lbs.

5. Loosen lock nut approximately 60°. Install adjusting cap and align groove of nut with hole in spindle. If alignment cannot be obtained, change position of adjusting cap. Also, if alignment cannot be obtained, loosen lock nut slightly but not more than 15°.

➡️If possible measure the wheel bearing preload and axial play. Repeat above procedures until correct starting torque is obtained. Refer to the illustration.

6. Spread the cotter pin and install hub cap with a new O-ring.

7. Install caliper assemblies and front wheels.

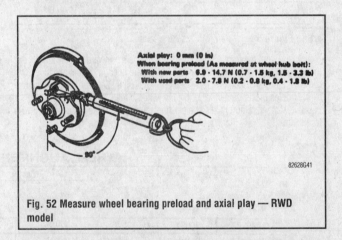

Fig. 52 Measure wheel bearing preload and axial play — RWD model

ADJUSTMENT

Rear Wheel Drive

▶ See Figure 52

➡️Before adjustment clean all parts. Apply wheel bearing grease sparingly to the threaded portion of spindle and contact surface between lock washer and outer wheel bearing.

1. Raise and support the vehicle safely, remove the front wheels and the brake caliper assemblies.

2. Torque wheel bearing lock nut to 18–22 ft. lbs.

➡️On the 1989–92 240SX model, the wheel bearing lock nut torque is 108–159 ft. lbs. On this model make sure that the wheel bearing is properly seated and then just torque it to the specification. There is just

Wheel Alignment

If the tires are worn unevenly, if the vehicle is not stable on the highway or if the handling seems uneven in spirited driving, the wheel alignment should be checked. If an alignment problem is suspected, first check for improper tire inflation and other possible causes. These can be worn suspension or steering components, accident damage or even unmatched tires. If any worn or damaged components are found, they must be replaced before the wheels can be properly aligned. Wheel alignment requires very expensive equipment and involves minute adjustments which must be accurate; it should only be performed by a trained technician. Take your vehicle to a properly equipped shop.

Following is a description of the alignment angles which are adjustable on most vehicles and how they affect vehicle handling. Although these angles can apply to both the front and rear wheels, usually only the front suspension is adjustable.

CASTER

▶ **See Figure 53**

Looking at a vehicle from the side, caster angle describes the steering axis rather than a wheel angle. The steering knuckle is attached to a control arm or strut at the top and a control arm at the bottom. The wheel pivots around the line between these points to steer the vehicle. When the upper point is tilted back, this is described as positive caster. Having a positive caster tends to make the wheels self-centering, increasing directional stability. Excessive positive caster makes the wheels hard to steer, while an uneven caster will cause a pull to one side. Overloading the vehicle or sagging rear springs will affect caster, as will raising the rear of the vehicle. If the rear of the vehicle is lower than normal, the caster becomes more positive.

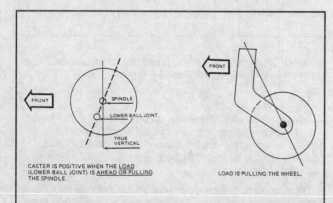

Fig. 53 Caster affects straight-line stability. Caster wheels used on shopping carts, for example, employ positive caster

CAMBER

▶ **See Figure 54**

Looking from the front of the vehicle, camber is the inward or outward tilt of the top of wheels. When the tops of the wheels are tilted in, this is negative camber; if they are tilted out, it is positive. In a turn, a slight amount of negative camber helps maximize contact of the tire with the road. However, too much negative camber compromises straight-line stability, increases bump steer and torque steer.

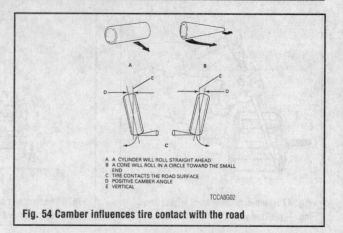

A A CYLINDER WILL ROLL STRAIGHT AHEAD
B A CONE WILL ROLL IN A CIRCLE TOWARD THE SMALL END
C TIRE CONTACTS THE ROAD SURFACE
D POSITIVE CAMBER ANGLE
E VERTICAL

Fig. 54 Camber influences tire contact with the road

TOE

▶ **See Figure 55**

Looking down at the wheels from above the vehicle, toe angle is the distance between the front of the wheels, relative to the distance between the back of the wheels. If the wheels are closer at the front, they are said to be toed-in or to have negative toe. A small amount of negative toe enhances directional stability and provides a smoother ride on the highway.

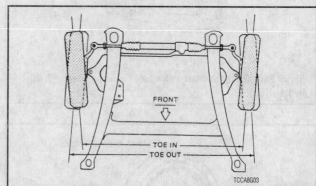

Fig. 55 With toe-in, the distance between the wheels is closer at the front than at the rear

WHEEL ALIGNMENT SPECIFICATIONS

Year	Model		Caster Range (deg.)	Caster Preferred Setting (deg.)	Camber Range (deg.)	Camber Preferred Setting (deg.)	Toe-In (in.)
1982–83	200SX		$1^3/_4$–$3^1/_4$	$2^1/_2$	$-^{11}/_{16}$–$^{13}/_{16}$	$^1/_{16}$	$^3/_{64}$
1982–84	Stanza	(Front)	$^{11}/_{16}$–$2^3/_{16}$	—	$-^3/_4$–$^3/_4$	—	0–$^5/_{64}$
		(Rear)	—	—	0–$1^1/_2$	—	$^{13}/_{64}$–$^5/_{16}$
1984	200SX		$2^3/_4$–$4^1/_4$	$3^1/_2$	$-^3/_8$–$1^1/_{16}$	$1^7/_8$	$^3/_{64}$
1985–86	200SX		$2^3/_4$–$4^1/_4$	$3^1/_2$	$-^1/_4$–$1^1/_{20}$	$^1/_3$	$^3/_8$
	Stanza	(Front)	$^{11}/_{16}$–$2^3/_{16}$	—	$-^7/_{16}$–$1^1/_{16}$	—	0–$^1/_{16}$
		(Rear)	—	—	0–$1^1/_2$	—	$^9/_{32}$–$^1/_4$
1987–88	200SX	(Front)	$2^3/_4$–$4^1/_4$	$3^1/_2$P	$^7/_{16}$N–$1^1/_{16}$P	$^1/_4$P	$^1/_{32}$N–$^1/_{32}$P
		(Rear)	—	—	$1^1/_4$N–$1^1/_4$P	$^1/_2$N	$^5/_{64}$N–0
	Stanza	(Front)	$1^1/_4$–$2^3/_4$	—	$-^7/_{16}$–$1/_{16}$	—	$^1/_{32}$–$^1/_8$
		(Rear)	—	—	$-1^3/_{16}$–$^5/_{16}$	—	$^5/_{16}$–$^3/_{32}$
1989–92	240SX	(Front)	6P–7P	$6^1/_2$P	1N–0	$^1/_2$N	0
		(Rear)	—	—	1N–0	$^1/_2$N	0
	Stanza	(Front)	$^5/_8$–$2^1/_{16}$	—	$-^1/_2$–1	—	$^1/_{16}$–$^1/_8$
		(Rear)	—	—	$-1^5/_{16}$–$^3/_{16}$	—	0

NOTE: The minimum and maximum settings that are specified are a guide to use when checking alignment specifications.

82628C01

REAR SUSPENSION

Coil Springs

REMOVAL & INSTALLATION

200SX With 4-Link Type Suspension

♦ **See Figure 56**

1. Raise the car and support it with jackstands.
2. Support the center of the differential with a jack or other suitable tool.
3. Remove the rear wheels.
4. Remove the bolts securing the lower ends of the shock absorbers.
5. Lower the jack under the differential slowly and carefully and remove the coil springs (note location of spring seat—for correct installation) after they are fully extended.

6. Installation is in the reverse order of removal. Refer to the illustration for additional specifications.

200SX With Independent Rear Suspension (IRS)

♦ **See Figures 57 and 58**

1. Set a suitable spring compressor on the coil spring.
2. Jack up the rear end of the car.
3. Compress the coil spring until it is of sufficient length to be removed. Remove the spring.
4. When installing the spring, be sure the upper and lower spring seat rubbers are not twisted and have not slipped off when installing the coil spring. Refer to the illustrations for additional specifications.

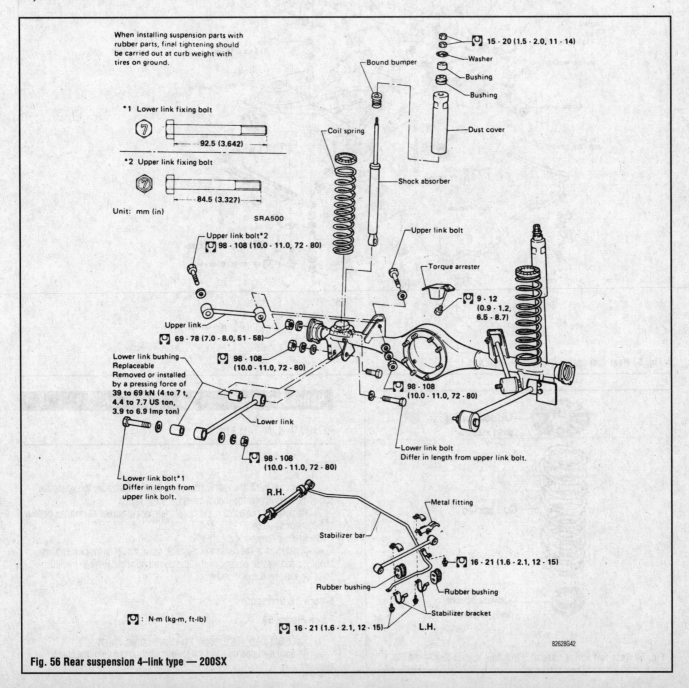

Fig. 56 Rear suspension 4–link type — 200SX

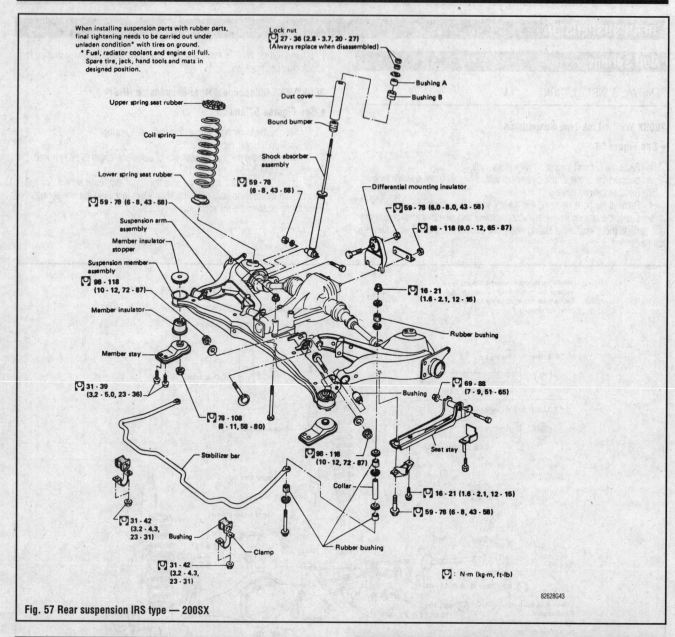

When installing suspension parts with rubber parts, final tightening needs to be carried out under unladen condition* with tires on ground.
* Fuel, radiator coolant and engine oil full. Spare tire, jack, hand tools and mats in designed position.

Lock nut
27 - 36 (2.8 - 3.7, 20 - 27)
(Always replace when disassembled)

Bushing A
Bushing B
Dust cover
Bound bumper
Shock absorber assembly
Differential mounting insulator
59 - 78 (6 - 8, 43 - 58)
59 - 78 (6.0 - 8.0, 43 - 58)
98 - 118 (9.0 - 12, 65 - 87)
Upper spring seat rubber
Coil spring
Lower spring seat rubber
59 - 78 (6 - 8, 43 - 58)
Suspension arm assembly
Member insulator stopper
Suspension member assembly
98 - 118 (10 - 12, 72 - 87)
Member insulator
16 - 21 (1.6 - 2.1, 12 - 15)
Rubber bushing
Member stay
31 - 39 (3.2 - 5.0, 23 - 36)
69 - 88 (7 - 9, 51 - 65)
78 - 108 (8 - 11, 58 - 80)
Bushing
Seat stay
Stabilizer bar
98 - 118 (10 - 12, 72 - 87)
Collar
16 - 21 (1.6 - 2.1, 12 - 15)
31 - 42 (3.2 - 4.3, 23 - 31)
Bushing
Clamp
Rubber bushing
59 - 78 (6 - 8, 43 - 58)
31 - 42 (3.2 - 4.3, 23 - 31)
: N·m (kg·m, ft-lb)

82628G43

Fig. 57 Rear suspension IRS type — 200SX

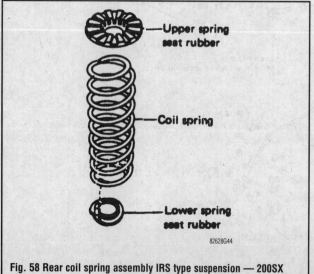

Upper spring seat rubber

Coil spring

Lower spring seat rubber

82628G44

Fig. 58 Rear coil spring assembly IRS type suspension — 200SX

Shock Absorber

REMOVAL & INSTALLATION

200SX

1. Open the trunk and remove the cover panel if necessary to expose the shock mounts. Pry off the mount covers, if so equipped.
2. Remove the nut holding the top of the shock absorber. Unbolt the bottom of the shock absorber.
3. Remove the shock absorber.
4. Installation is the reverse of removal. Make sure rear shock retaining bushings and washer are installed in the correct position. Refer to the illustrations for additional specifications.

Stanza 2WD Wagon

▶ **See Figure 59**

1. Raise and support the rear of the vehicle on jackstands.
2. Remove the upper nut and the lower mounting bolt form the shock absorber.

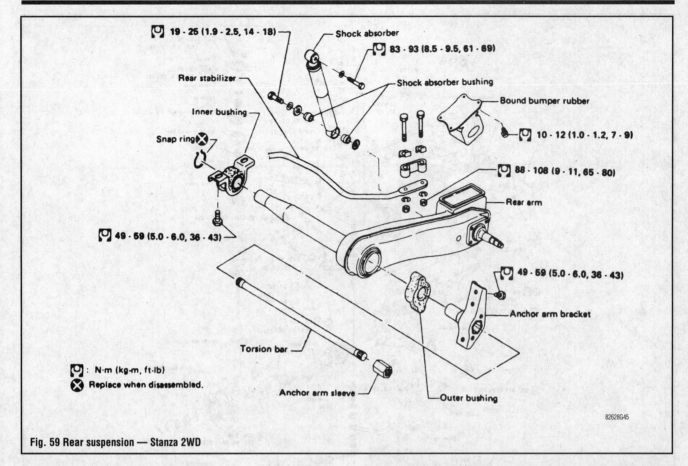

Fig. 59 Rear suspension — Stanza 2WD

3. Remove the shock absorber from the vehicle.
4. To install, reverse the removal procedures. Make sure rear shock retaining bushings and washer are installed in the correct position. Refer to the illustrations for additional specifications.

TESTING

▶ **See Figure 60**

The purpose of the shock absorber is simply to limit the motion of the spring during compression and rebound cycles. If the vehicle is not equipped with these motion dampers, the up and down motion would multiply until the vehicle was alternately trying to leap off the ground and to pound itself into the pavement.

Contrary to popular rumor, the shocks do not affect the ride height of the vehicle. This is controlled by other suspension components such as springs and tires. Worn shock absorbers can affect handling; if the front of the vehicle is rising or falling excessively, the "footprint" of the tires changes on the pavement and steering is affected.

The simplest test of the shock absorber is simply push down on one corner of the unladen vehicle and release it. Observe the motion of the body as it is released. In most cases, it will come up beyond it original rest position, dip back below it and settle quickly to rest. This shows that the damper is controlling the spring action. Any tendency to excessive pitch (up-and-down) motion or failure to return to rest within 2–3 cycles is a sign of poor function within the shock absorber. Oil-filled shocks may have a light film of oil around the seal, resulting from normal breathing and air exchange. This should NOT be taken as a sign of failure, but any sign of thick or running oil definitely indicates failure. Gas filled shocks may also show some film at the shaft; if the gas has leaked out, the shock will have almost no resistance to motion.

While each shock absorber can be replaced individually, it is recommended that they be changed as a pair (both front or both rear) to maintain equal response on both sides of the vehicle. Chances are quite good that if one has failed, its mate is weak also.

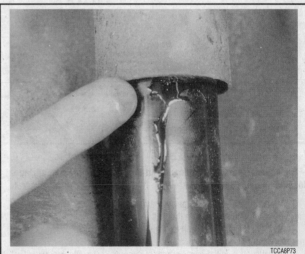

Fig. 60 When fluid is seeping out of the shock absorber, it's time to replace it

MacPherson Strut

REMOVAL & INSTALLATION

240SX

▶ **See Figure 61**

1. Block the front wheels.
2. Raise and support the vehicle safely.

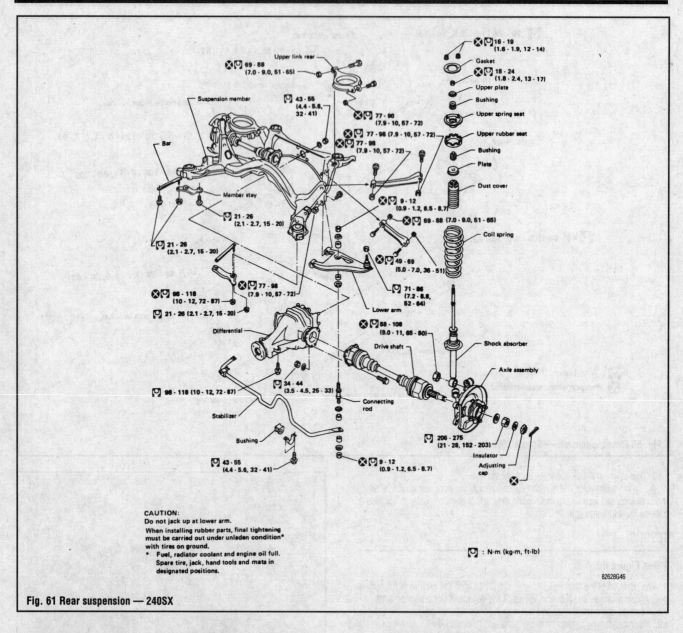

CAUTION:
Do not jack up at lower arm.
When installing rubber parts, final tightening must be carried out under unladen condition* with tires on ground.
* Fuel, radiator coolant and engine oil full. Spare tire, jack, hand tools and mats in designated positions.

🔧 : N·m (kg-m, ft-lb)

82628G46

Fig. 61 Rear suspension — 240SX

➡The vehicle should be far enough off the ground so the rear spring does not support any weight.

3. Working inside the luggage compartment, turn and remove the caps above the strut mounts. Remove the strut mounting nuts.
4. Remove the mounting bolt for the strut at the lower arm (transverse link) and then lift out the strut.
5. Installation is in the reverse order of removal. Install the upper end first and secure with the nuts snugged down but not fully tightened. Attach the lower end of the strut to the transverse link and the tighten the upper nuts to 12–14 ft. lbs. Tighten the lower mounting bolt to 65–80 ft. lbs.

1982–86 Stanza

▸ See Figure 62

1. Raise and support the rear of the vehicle on jackstands.
2. Remove the wheel.
3. Disconnect the brake tube and parking brake cable.
4. If necessary, remove the brake assembly and wheel bearing.
5. Disconnect the parallel links and radius rod assembly from the strut or knuckle.
6. Support the strut with a jackstand.

7. Remove the strut upper end nuts and then remove the strut from the vehicle.
8. Install the strut assembly to the vehicle and tighten the strut-to-parallel link nuts to 65–87 ft. lbs., the strut-to-radius rod nuts to 54–69 ft. lbs. and the strut-to-body nuts to 23–31 ft. lbs. Refer to the illustrations.
9. Reconnect the brake tube and parking brake cable.
10. Install the wheel.

1987–92 Stanza

▸ See Figure 63

1. Remove wheel and unclip the rear brake line at the strut. Unbolt and remove the brake assembly, wheel bearings and backing plate. Position the brake caliper out of the way and suspend it so as not to stress the brake line.
2. Remove the radius rod mounting bolt, radius rod mounting bracket.
3. Remove the 2 parallel link mounting bolts.
4. Remove the rear seat and parcel shelf.
5. Position a floor jack under the strut and raise it just enough to support the strut.
6. Remove the 3 upper strut mounting nuts and then lift out the strut.
7. Install the strut assembly in the vehicle. Tighten all bolts sufficiently to safely support the vehicle and then lower the car to the ground so it rests on its

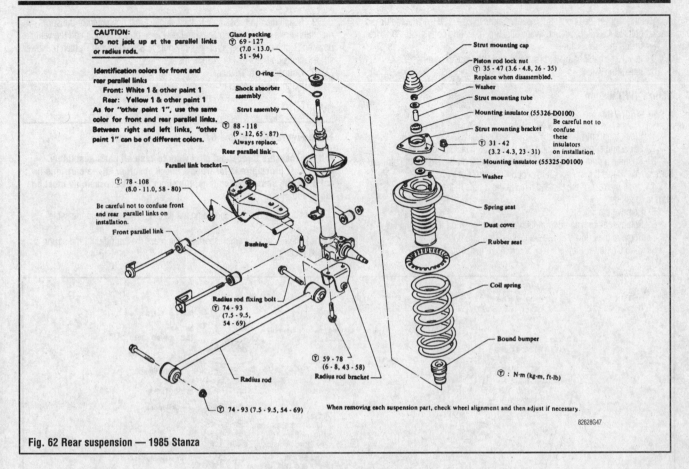

CAUTION:
Do not jack up at the parallel links or radius rods.

Identification colors for front and rear parallel links
Front: White 1 & other paint 1
Rear: Yellow 1 & other paint 1
As for "other paint 1", use the same color for front and rear parallel links. Between right and left links, "other paint 1" can be of different colors.

Gland packing
(T) 69 - 127
(7.0 - 13.0, 51 - 94)

O-ring

Shock absorber assembly

Strut assembly
(T) 88 - 118
(9 - 12, 65 - 87)
Always replace.

Rear parallel link

Parallel link bracket

(T) 78 - 108
(8.0 - 11.0, 58 - 80)

Be careful not to confuse front and rear parallel links on installation.

Front parallel link

Bushing

Radius rod fixing bolt
(T) 74 - 93
(7.5 - 9.5, 54 - 69)

(T) 59 - 78
(6 - 8, 43 - 58)
Radius rod bracket

Radius rod

(T) 74 - 93 (7.5 - 9.5, 54 - 69)

Strut mounting cap

Piston rod lock nut
(T) 35 - 47 (3.6 - 4.8, 26 - 35)
Replace when disassembled.

Washer

Strut mounting tube

Mounting insulator (55326-D0100)

Strut mounting bracket

(T) 31 - 42
(3.2 - 4.3, 23 - 31)

Be careful not to confuse these insulators on installation.

Mounting insulator (55325-D0100)

Washer

Spring seat

Dust cover

Rubber seat

Coil spring

Bound bumper

(T) : N·m (kg-m, ft-lb)

When removing each suspension part, check wheel alignment and then adjust if necessary.

82628G47

Fig. 62 Rear suspension — 1985 Stanza

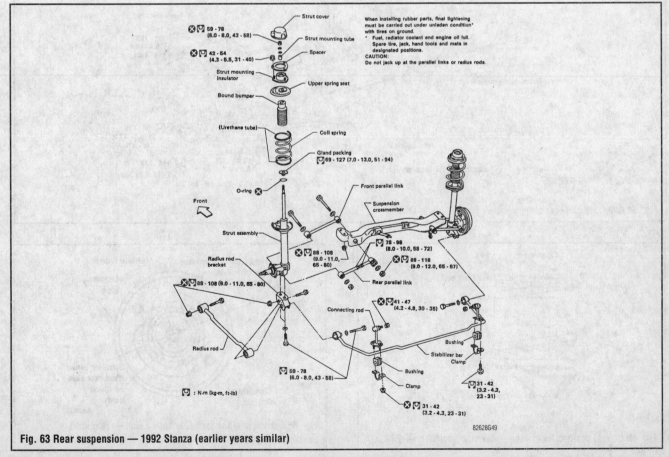

(X) 59 - 78
(8.0 - 8.0, 43 - 58)

(X) 42 - 54
(4.3 - 5.5, 31 - 40)

Strut cover

Strut mounting tube

Spacer

Strut mounting insulator

Upper spring seat

Bound bumper

(Urethane tube)

Coil spring

Gland packing
69 - 127 (7.0 - 13.0, 51 - 94)

O-ring (X)

Front

Strut assembly

Radius rod bracket

(X) 88 - 108 (9.0 - 11.0, 65 - 80)

Radius rod

(X) 88 - 108 (9.0 - 11.0, 65 - 80)

When installing rubber parts, final tightening must be carried out under unladen condition* with tires on ground.
* Fuel, radiator coolant and engine oil full. Spare tire, jack, hand tools and mats in designated positions.
CAUTION:
Do not jack up at the parallel links or radius rods.

Front parallel link

Suspension crossmember

78 - 96
(8.0 - 10.0, 58 - 72)

(X) 88 - 118
(9.0 - 12.0, 65 - 87)

Rear parallel link

(X) 41 - 47
(4.2 - 4.8, 30 - 35)

Connecting rod

Bushing

Stabilizer bar
Clamp

(X) 31 - 42
(3.2 - 4.3, 23 - 31)

Bushing

Clamp

(X) 31 - 42
(3.2 - 4.3, 23 - 31)

59 - 78
(6.0 - 8.0, 43 - 58)

: N·m (kg-m, ft-lb)

82628G49

Fig. 63 Rear suspension — 1992 Stanza (earlier years similar)

own weight. Tighten the upper strut mounting nuts to 23–31 ft. lbs., the radius rod bracket bolts to 43–58 ft. lbs. and the parallel link mounting bolts to 65–87 ft. lbs.

8. Install the brake caliper.
9. Install the backing plate, brake assembly and wheel bearings.
10. Install the wheel.

Stanza 4WD Wagon

♦ **See Figure 64**

1. Block the front wheels.
2. Raise and support the rear of the vehicle with jackstands.
3. Position a floor jack under the transverse link on the side of the strut to be removed. Raise it just enough to support the strut.
4. Open the rear of the car and remove the 3 nuts that attach the top of the strut to the body.
5. Remove the wheel.
6. Remove the brake line from its bracket and position it out of the way.
7. Remove the 2 lower strut-to-knuckle mounting bolts.
8. Carefully lower the floor jack and remove the strut.

9. Install the strut assembly in the vehicle. Final tightening of the strut mounting bolts should take place with the wheels on the ground and the vehicle unladen. Tighten the upper strut-to-body nuts to 33–40 ft. lbs. Tighten the lower strut-to-knuckle bolts to 111–120 ft. lbs.

10. Connect the brake line.
11. Install the wheel.

OVERHAUL

♦ **See Figures 65, 66 and 67**

➡ **It is necessary throughout strut work to keep all parts absolutely clean. This procedure is for when a shock absorber kit—a cartridge is not used. On some applications, the shock absorber assembly must be replaced.**

1. Matchmark the strut mounting insulator for reassembly at the same angle.
2. Install a spring compressor and compress the spring until the spring insulator can be turned by hand.

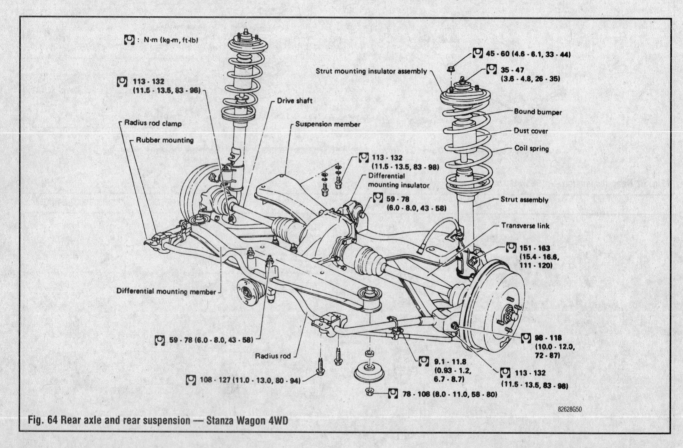

Fig. 64 Rear axle and rear suspension — Stanza Wagon 4WD

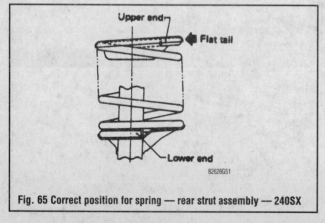

Fig. 65 Correct position for spring — rear strut assembly — 240SX

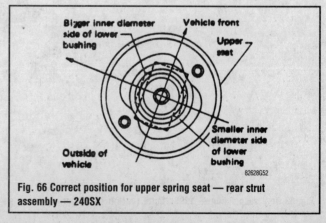

Fig. 66 Correct position for upper spring seat — rear strut assembly — 240SX

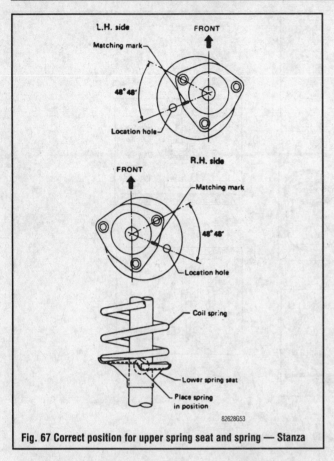

Fig. 67 Correct position for upper spring seat and spring — Stanza

3. Remove the rebound stop lock-nut so the threads on the piston rod will not be damaged. Use a tool such as ST35490000 (J26083) or equivalent to remove the packing. Then, force the piston rod downward until it bottoms.

4. Withdraw the piston rod and guide from the strut cylinder.

5. Pour the correct amount of an approved strut fluid into the strut. Use 11.2 fl. oz. for non-adjustable struts and 11.0 fl. oz. for adjustable struts.

6. Then, lubricate the sealing lip of the gland packing. Tape over the strut rod threads and then install the gland packing. Tighten it with the special wrench. Torque to 65–80 ft. lbs.

7. Pump the strut rod up and down several times with it in its normal vertical position and upside down to remove air bubbles.

8. Install the upper spring seat and mounting insulator. Make sure the matchmark on the insulator corresponds with the location hole on the upper spring seat.

9. Position the spring so its end rests against the stop on the lower seat. Install the remaining spring retaining parts including the piston rod self locking nut (torque to 43–58 ft. lbs.) and the upper nut that retains the flexible washer (torque to 26–35 ft. lbs.).

Transverse Link

REMOVAL & INSTALLATION

Stanza Wagon 4WD

▶ See Figure 68

1. Raise and support the rear of the vehicle on jackstands.

2. Before removing transverse link retaining bolts, matchmark the toe-in adjustment. Refer to the illustrations.

3. Remove the link retaining bolts.

4. Installation is the reverse of the removal procedure. Final tightening of the transverse link mounting bolts should take place with the wheels on the ground and the vehicle unladen. Check rear alignment.

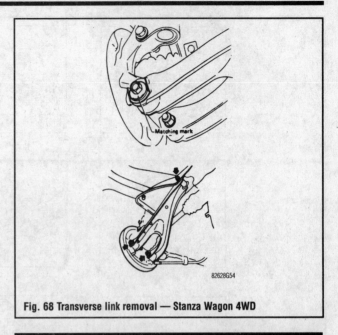

Fig. 68 Transverse link removal — Stanza Wagon 4WD

Stabilizer Bar

REMOVAL & INSTALLATION

Stanza Wagon 4WD

▶ See Figure 69

1. Raise and support the rear of the vehicle on jackstands.

2. Before removing stabilizer retaining bolts, matchmark the brackets. Refer to the illustrations.

3. Remove the bracket retaining bolts. Remove the stabilizer bar.

4. Installation is the reverse of the removal procedure. Make sure the stabilizer retaining brackets are even spaced when installed.

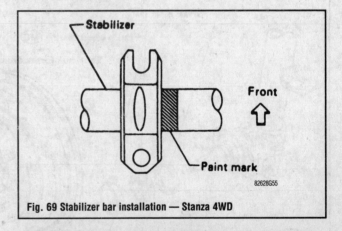

Fig. 69 Stabilizer bar installation — Stanza 4WD

Rear Wheel Bearings

REMOVAL & INSTALLATION

1982–89 Stanza Wagon 2WD

▶ See Figures 70, 71 and 72

1. Raise and support the vehicle safely.

2. Remove the rear wheel. Release the parking brake.

3. Work off center hub cap by using thin tool. If necessary tap around it with a soft hammer while removing.

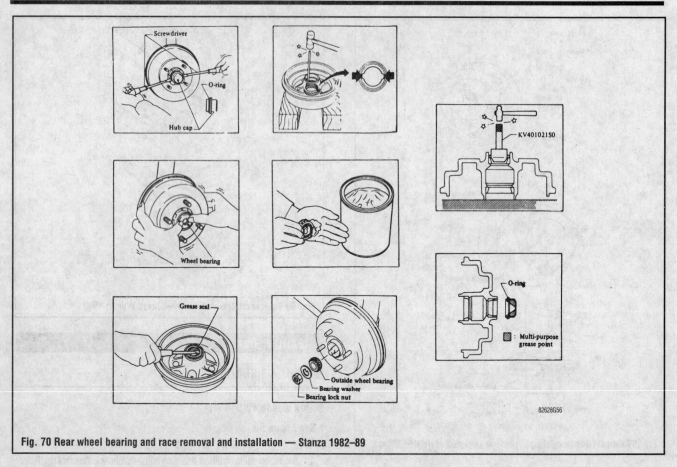

Fig. 70 Rear wheel bearing and race removal and installation — Stanza 1982–89

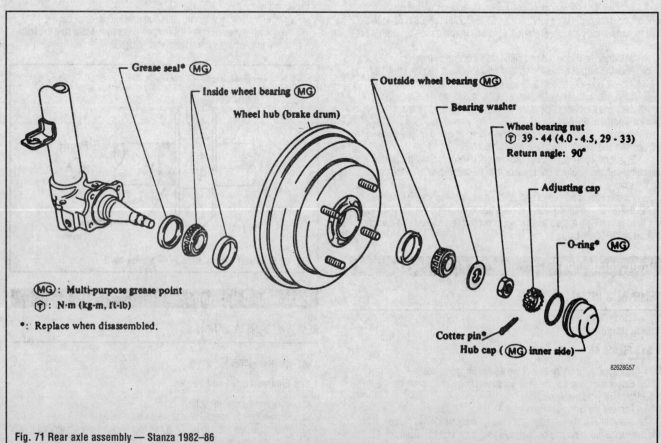

Fig. 71 Rear axle assembly — Stanza 1982–86

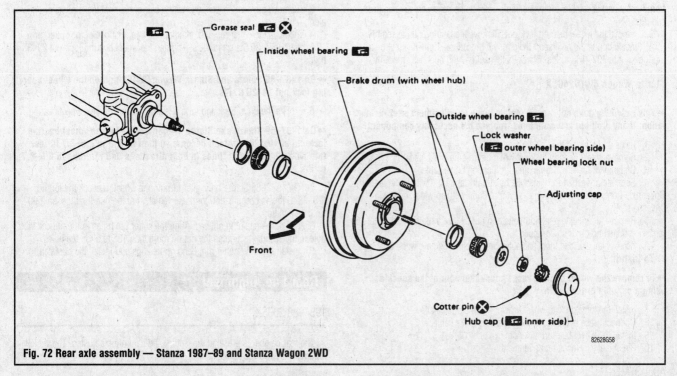

Fig. 72 Rear axle assembly — Stanza 1987–89 and Stanza Wagon 2WD

4. Pry off cotter pin and take out adjusting cap and wheel bearing lock nut.

➡ **During removal, be careful to avoid damaging O ring in dust cap if so equipped.**

5. Remove rear drum with outer bearing and washer and inner bearing and seal inside the drum.

6. Remove inner bearing and seal from drum using long brass drift pin or equivalent.

To install:

7. Install the inner bearing (and seal in the correct position) assembly in the brake drum and install the drum on the vehicle.

➡ **The rear wheel bearings must be adjusted after installation, if one piece bearing is used just the torque wheel bearing lock nut.**

8. Install the outer bearing assembly, wheel bearing lock nut, adjusting cap and NEW cotter pin. Adjust the wheel bearings—refer to the necessary procedure.

9. Install the center cap and the wheel assembly. To remove the wheel bearing races knock them out of the brake drum using a suitable brass punch.

1990–92 Stanza

▶ See Figure 73

➡ **On these vehicles a one-piece bearing hub assembly is used. This assembly does not require maintenance or adjustment after installation. If any problem (noise, excessive drag, etc.) replace the wheel hub assembly.**

1. Raise and support the vehicle safely. Remove the rear wheel.
2. Remove the brake caliper (brake hose does not have to be disconnect

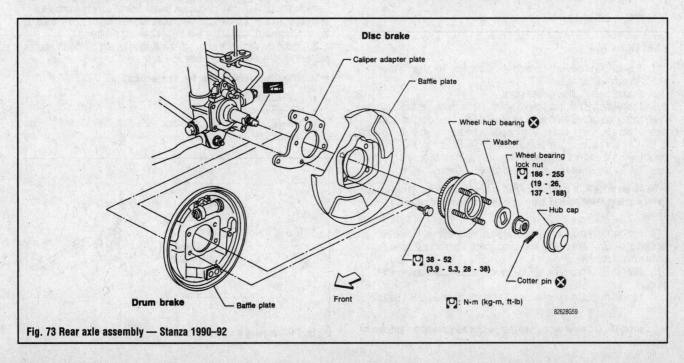

Fig. 73 Rear axle assembly — Stanza 1990–92

from the caliper) assembly and reposition—refer to the necessary service procedures.

3. Remove the wheel bearing lock-nut. Remove the bearing hub assembly.

4. Installation is the reverse of the removal procedure. Tighten wheel bearing lock-nut to 137–188 ft. lbs. Check that wheel bearing operates smoothly.

Stanza Wagon 4WD/240SX

➡**This assembly does not require maintenance or adjustment after installation. If any problem is encountered, replace the necessary component.**

1. Raise and support the vehicle safely.
2. Remove wheel bearing lock nut while depressing brake pedal.
3. Disconnect brake hydraulic line and parking brake cable.
4. Separate driveshaft from knuckle by slightly tapping it with suitable tool. Cover axle boots with waste cloth so as not to damage them when removing driveshaft.
5. Remove all knuckle retaining bolts and nuts. Make a match mark before removing adjusting pin if so equipped.
6. Remove knuckle and inner and outer circular clips. Remove wheel bearings.

To install:

➡**To remove the wheel bearing races knock them out of the knuckle using a suitable brass punch.**

7. Install the knuckle with wheel bearings to the driveshaft.
8. Connect brake hydraulic line and parking brake cable.
9. Install the wheel bearing lock nut.
10. Bleed brakes. Check rear alignment.

ADJUSTMENT

➡**No adjustment is necessary on Stanza Wagon 4WD, 240SX and 1990–92 Stanza (one-piece bearing hub assembly).**

➡**Make sure all parts are cleaned, apply multi-purpose grease sparingly to rubbing surface of the spindle, between surface of lock washer and outer wheel bearing, grease seal and dust cap in the proper areas.**

1. Raise the rear of the vehicle and support it on jackstands.
2. Remove the wheel.

3. Remove the bearing dust cap with a pair of channel locks pliers or equivalent.

4. Remove the cotter pin and retaining nut cap, dispose of the cotter pin.

5. On 1982–86 Stanza models—tighten the wheel bearing lock-nut 29–33 ft. lbs.

➡**On 1987–89 Stanza and Stanza Wagon 2WD—tighten the wheel bearing lock-nut 18–25 ft. lbs.**

6. Rotate the drum back and forth a few revolutions to seat wheel bearing.

➡**On 1987–89 Stanza and Stanza Wagon 2WD—loosen wheel bearing lock-nut so that the preload becomes 0 then torque to 6.5–8.7 ft. lbs. turn wheel hub several times in both directions and retorque to 6.5–8.7 ft. lbs.**

7. On 1982–86 Stanza only, after turning the wheel, recheck the torque (29–33 ft. lbs. is specification for these vehicles) of the nut, then loosen it 90° from its position.

8. Install the retaining nut cap. Align the cotter pin holes in the nut cap with hole in the spindle by tighten the nut no more than 15° to align the holes.

9. Install the NEW cotter pin, bend up its ends and install the dust cap.

Rear End Alignment

1984–88 200SX

The rear camber is preset at the factory and cannot be adjusted. The vehicle requires only rear toe adjustment.

1989–92 240SX

The rear camber and rear toe can be adjusted on this model.

STANZA

The camber is preset at the factory and cannot be adjusted; if the camber alignment is not within specifications, check the associated parts, then repair or replace them. The only adjustment that can be performed is toe adjustment.

STEERING

Steering Wheel

REMOVAL & INSTALLATION

▶ **See Figure 74**

1. Position the wheels in the straight ahead direction. The steering wheel should be right side up and level.

2. Disconnect the battery ground cable.

3. Look at the back of your steering wheel. If there are countersunk screws in the back of the spokes, remove the screws and pull of the horn pad. Some models have a horn wire running from the pad to the steering wheel. Disconnect it. There are other types of horn buttons or rings. The first simply pulls off. The second, which is usually a large, semi-triangular pad, must be pushed up, then pulled off. The third must be pushed in and turned clockwise.

➡**On newer models, if it is hard to pull out horn pad, temporarily loosen fixing screw (behind back of steering wheel) of horn pad retaining spring.**

4. Remove the rest of the horn switching mechanism, noting the relative location of the parts. Remove the mechanism only if it hinders subsequent wheel removal procedures.

5. Matchmark the top of the steering column shaft and the steering wheel flange.

6. Remove the attaching nut and remove the steering wheel with a suitable puller.

➡**Do not strike the shaft with a hammer, which may cause the column to collapse.**

7. Install the steering wheel in the reverse order of removal, aligning the punch marks. Coat the entire surface of the turn signal canceling pin and the horn contact slip ring with multipurpose grease. Do not drive or hammer the wheel into place, or you may cause the collapsible steering column to collapse, in which case you'll have to buy a whole new steering column unit.

8. Torque the steering wheel nut to specifications. Reinstall the horn button, pad, or ring. Check system for proper operation.

➡**Steering wheel retaining nut torque specification:**

- 1982–83 200SX—28–36 ft. lbs.
- 1982–86 Stanza—27–38 ft. lbs.
- 1984–88 200SX and 1987–92 Stanza—22–29 ft. lbs.
- 1989–92 240SX—22–29 ft. lbs.

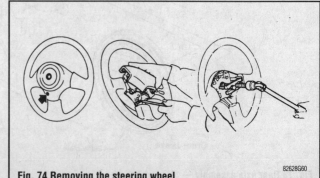

Fig. 74 Removing the steering wheel

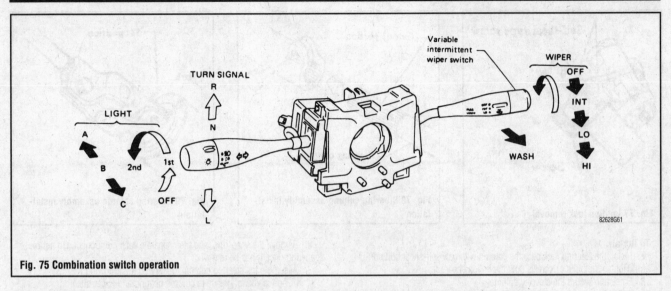

Fig. 75 Combination switch operation

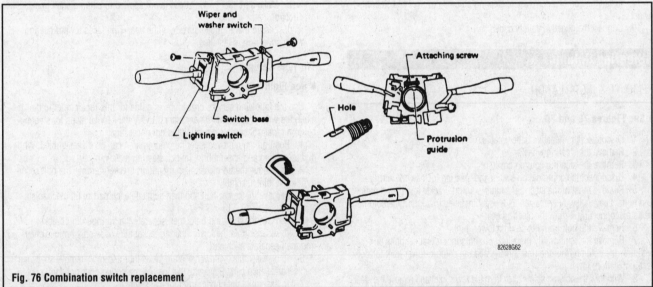

Fig. 76 Combination switch replacement

Turn Signal/Combination Switch

REMOVAL & INSTALLATION

▶ **See Figures 75 and 76**

1. Disconnect the battery ground cable.
2. Remove the steering wheel as previously outlined. Observe the caution on the collapsible steering column.
3. Remove the steering column cover(s).
4. Disconnect the electrical connections from the combination switch assembly.

➡**On most model vehicles, the control (lighting, wiper and washer, hazard and cruise control set) switches can be replaced without removing the combination base. Refer to the illustration of Combination Switch.**

5. To remove the combination switch base—remove the base attaching screw and turn after pushing on it—refer to the illustration.
6. Install the switch/combination base in the proper position. The switch base has a tab which must fit into a hole in the steering shaft in order for the system to return the switch to the neutral position after the turn has been made. Be sure to align the tab and the hole when installing.
7. Install the steering wheel and steering column cover(s)—observe steering wheel retaining nut torque upon installation.

8. Reconnect the battery cable. Turn key to the ON position and check system for proper operation. Make sure that the turn signals will cancel after the vehicle has made a turn.

Ignition Lock/Switch

REMOVAL & INSTALLATION

▶ **See Figure 77**

The steering lock/ignition switch/warning buzzer switch assembly is attached to the steering column by special screws or bolts whose heads shear off on installation. The screws must be drilled out to remove the assembly or removed with an appropriate tool.

The ignition switch or warning switch can be replaced without removing the assembly. The ignition switch is on the back of the assembly, and the warning switch on the side.

1. Disconnect the negative battery cable.
2. Remove the steering wheel, steering column cover(s) and combination switch.
3. Disconnect the switch wiring.
4. Lower the steering column, as required.
5. Break the self-shear screws with a drill or other appropriate tool.
6. Remove the steering lock from the column.

Fig. 77 Ignition lock removal

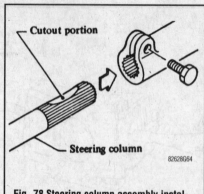

Fig. 78 Steering column assembly installation

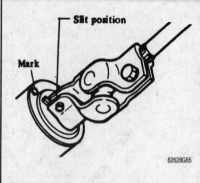

Fig. 79 Steering column assembly installation

To install:

7. Install the steering lock onto the column with new self-shear bolts or screws. Tighten the bolts or screws until the heads shear off.

8. Raise and secure the steering column.

9. Install the combination switch, steering column cover(s) and steering wheel.

10. Connect the negative battery cable.

Steering Column

REMOVAL & INSTALLATION

♦ **See Figures 78 and 79**

1. Disconnect the negative battery cable.
2. Remove the steering wheel.
3. Remove the steering column covers.
4. Disconnect the combination switch and steering lock switch wiring.
5. Remove most of the steering column support bracket and clamp nuts and bolts. Leave a few of the fasteners loosely installed to support the column while disconnecting it from the steering gear.
6. Remove the bolt from the column lower joint.
7. Remove the temporarily installed column support bracket bolts and withdraw the column from the (matchmark steering column-lower joint for correct installation) lower joint.
8. Withdraw the column spline shaft from the lower joint and remove the steering column. Be careful not to tear the column tube jacket insulator during removal.

To install:

9. Insert the column spline shaft into the lower joint and install all column fasteners finger-tight.

10. Install the lower joint bolt. The cutout portion of the spline shaft must perfectly aligned with the bolt. Torque the bolt to 23–31 ft. lbs. (17–22 ft. lbs. on later models) Tighten the steering bracket and clamp fasteners gradually. While tightening, make sure no stress is placed on the column.

11. Connect the combination switch and steering lock switch wiring.
12. Install the steering column covers.
13. Install the steering wheel.
14. Connect the negative battery cable.
15. After the installation is complete, turn the steering wheel from stop to stop and make sure it turns smoothly. The number of turns to the left and right stops must be equal.

OVERHAUL

Non-Tilt Type Column

♦ **See Figure 80**

Use the following service procedure as guide for this repair, refer to the exploded view illustrations if necessary. Modify the service steps for steering column repairs if complete overhaul is not necessary.

1. Position the removed steering column so it can be disassembled. While disassembling and assembling, unlock steering lock with key.

2. Remove the snap-ring, and then separate each component. Do not reuse snap-ring once it has be removed.

3. Assemble the steering column, observing the following:

a. Aply a coat of grease to column bearing and lower bushing.

b. Make sure that undue stress is not applied to column shaft in axial direction.

c. Ensure that rounded surface of the snap-ring faces toward bearing when snap-ring is installed.

Tilt Type Column

♦ **See Figure 81**

Use the following service procedure as guide for this repair, refer to the exploded view illustrations if necessary. Modify the service steps for steering column repairs if complete overhaul is not necessary.

1. Position the removed steering column so it can be disassembled. While disassembling and assembling, unlock steering lock with key.

2. To remove the tilt mechanism mounting bracket, remove the bolt securing the tilt joint assembly.

3. Remove the center bolt and then separate each part of tilt mechanism assembly.

4. Remove the retaining bolts then separate the tilt mounting bracket.

5. To disassemble the lower steering jacket tube assembly remove snap-ring then separate each part.

6. To disassemble the lower steering jacket tube assembly remove snap-ring then separate each part.. Be careful that the column spring does not spring out.

7. To assemble the upper jacket tube assembly:

a. Place the spring washer and spring seat to upper column shaft and then insert upper column shaft to upper jacket tube. Apply a coat of grease to the bearings.

b. Set spring seat and washer and then install snap-ring.

8. To assemble the lower jacket tube assembly:

a. Fit lower bushing to lower jacket tube perfectly.

b. Apply a coat of grease to column bearing and lower bushing.

c. Insert lower column shaft into lower jacket tube, then install wave washer, washer and snap-ring. Ensure that the snap-ring is positioned with its round surface facing toward the bearing. Make sure that undue stress is not applied to column shaft in axial direction.

9. Install tilt mechanism component parts, and then adjust tilt mechanism. Move the tilt lever from lock to release position several times to ensure that the upper jacket tube is tight when lever is at lock and upper jacket moves smoothly when lever is at release. If necessary, adjust tilt mechanism.

Tie Rod Ends (Steering Side Rods)

REMOVAL & INSTALLATION

♦ **See Figure 82**

1. Raise the front of the vehicle and support it on jackstands. Remove the wheel.

2. Locate the faulty tie rod end. It will have a lot of play in it and the dust cover will probably be ripped.

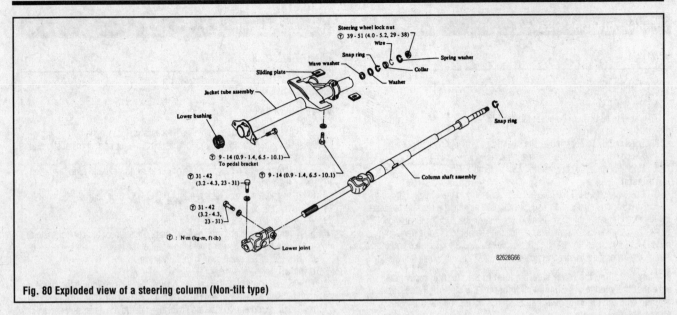

Fig. 80 Exploded view of a steering column (Non-tilt type)

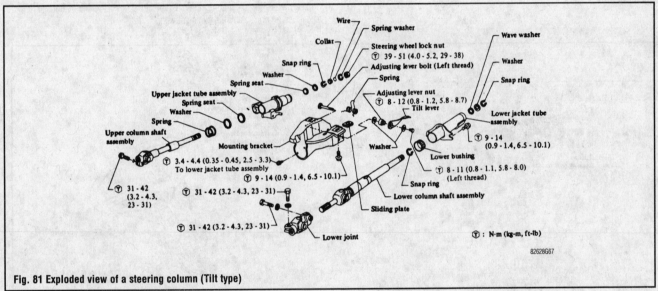

Fig. 81 Exploded view of a steering column (Tilt type)

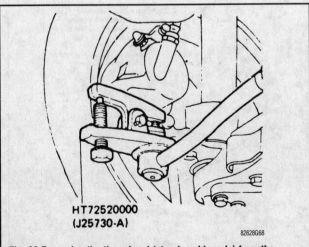

Fig. 82 Removing the tie rod end (steering side rods) from the steering knuckle using special tool

3. Remove the cotter pin and the tie rod ball joint stud nut. Note the position of the steering linkage.

4. Loosen the tie rod-to-steering gear lock-nut.

5. Using the Ball Joint Remover tool HT72520000 or equivalent, remove the tie rod ball joint from the steering knuckle.

6. Loosen the lock-nut and remove the tie rod end from the tie rod, counting the number of complete turns it takes to completely free it.

To install:

7. Install the new tie rod end, turning it in exactly as far as you screwed out the old one. Make sure it is correctly positioned in relationship to the steering linkage.

8. Fit the ball joint and nut, tighten them and install a NEW cotter pin. Torque the ball joint stud nut to specifications. Check front end alignment.

• The outer tie rod end-to-steering knuckle torque specification is 40–72 ft. lbs. on the 200SX model.

• The outer tie rod end-to-steering knuckle torque specification is 22–36 ft. lbs. on the 240SX model.

• The outer tie rod end-to-steering knuckle torque specification is 22–29 ft. lbs. on all Stanza models.

• Use these specifications as guide always replace the cotter pins and if necessary replace the retaining nut.

Manual Steering Gear

REMOVAL & INSTALLATION

▶ **See Figure 83**

1. Raise and support the car on jackstands.
2. Using the Ball Joint Remover tool HT72520000 or equivalent, remove tie rod end from the steering knuckle.
3. Loosen, but do not remove, the steering gear mounting bolts.
4. Matchmark and remove the steering column lower joint.
5. Unbolt and remove the steering gear assembly.

To install:

6. Position and install the steering gear assembly to the vehicle. Torque the tie rod-to-steering knuckle nut to specifications. The outer tie rod end-to-steering knuckle torque specification is 40–72 ft. lbs. on the 200SX model and 22–29 ft. lbs. on all Stanza models. Torque the steering gear-to-frame clamp bolts EVENLY in steps, to 43–58 ft. lbs. on Stanza and 33–44 ft. lbs. on 200SX. Torque the lower joint-to-steering gear bolt to 23–31 ft. lbs. on all models.

➥ **When installing the lower steering joint to the steering gear, make sure that the wheels are aligned straight and the steering joint slot is aligned with the steering gear cap or spacer mark. Check front end alignment if necessary.**

Power Steering Gear

REMOVAL & ADJUSTMENT

200SX

▶ **See Figure 84**

1. Raise and support the vehicle as necessary. Remove the bolt securing the lower shaft (matchmark shaft to joint assembly—for correct installation) to power steering gear assembly.
2. Disconnect the hoses from the power steering gear and plug the hoses to prevent leakage.
3. Using the Ball Joint Remover tool HT72520000 or equivalent, remove tie rod ends from the steering knuckle.
4. Remove the power steering gear mounting bolts.
5. Remove the exhaust pipe mounting nut. Disconnect the control cable or linkage for the transmission and position it out of the way.
6. Remove the steering gear from the vehicle.

To install:

7. Position and install the steering gear to the vehicle. Torque the clamp retaining bolts to EVENLY in steps to 29–36 ft. lbs. Refer to the illustration.
8. Install tie rod end to steering knuckle—refer to the necessary service procedures for torque specifications. Connect the control cable or linkage to the transmission and install the exhaust system.

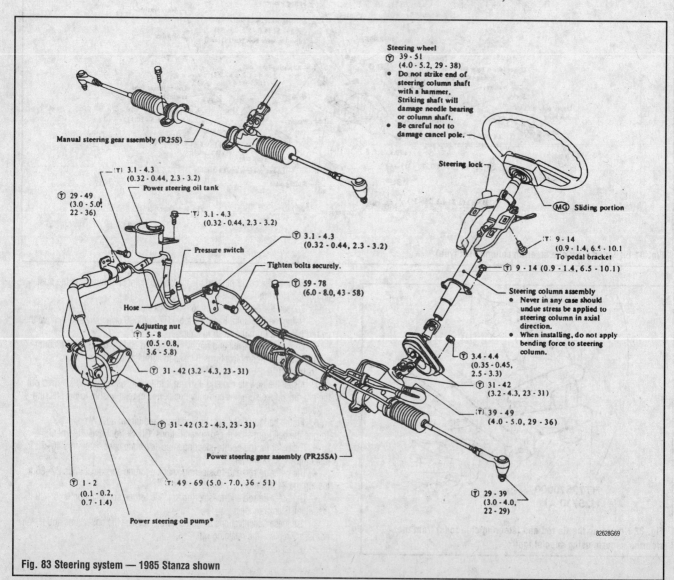

Fig. 83 Steering system — 1985 Stanza shown

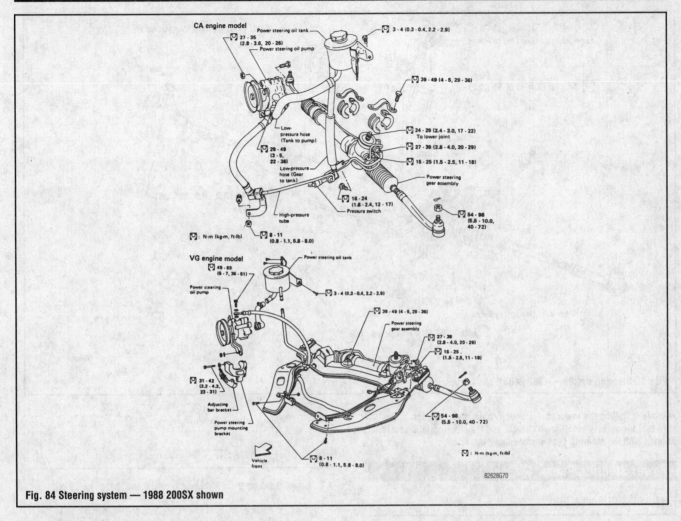

Fig. 84 Steering system — 1988 200SX shown

9. Reconnect the hoses to the power steering gear. Install the bolt securing the lower shaft to power steering gear assembly torque to 17–22 ft. lbs. (26–31 ft. lbs. on older applications).

10. Check the fluid level. Bleed system as necessary. Start the engine check for leaks and for proper operation of the system. Check front end alignment if necessary.

➡**When installing the lower steering joint to the steering gear, make sure that the wheels are aligned straight and the steering joint slot is aligned.**

240SX

▶ **See Figure 85**

1. Raise and support the front of the vehicle safely and remove the wheels.
2. Disconnect the power steering hose from the power steering gear and plug all hoses to prevent leakage.
3. Disconnect the tie rod ends from the steering knuckle using a suitable tools.
4. Remove the lower joint assembly (matchmark for correct installation) from the steering gear pinion.
5. Remove the steering gear and linkage assembly from the vehicle.
6. Installation is the reverse order of the removal procedure. Bleed system as necessary. Torque the lower joint to steering assembly 17–22 ft. lbs. and gear housing mounting brackets EVENLY in steps to 65–80 ft. lbs. Refer to the illustrations and necessary service procedures for torque specifications. Check front end alignment if necessary.

➡**Observe tightening torque when installing high and low pressure pipes. The O-ring in the low pressure is larger than in the high pressure side. Take care to install the proper O-ring.**

- Low pressure pipe torque—20–29 ft. lbs.
- High pressure pipe torque—11–18 ft. lbs.

➡**When installing the lower steering joint to the steering gear, make sure that the wheels are aligned straight and the steering joint slot is aligned.**

Stanza

1. Raise and support the car on jackstands.
2. Disconnect the hose clamp and hose at the steering gear. Disconnect the flare nut and the tube at the steering gear, then drain the fluid from the gear.
3. Using the Ball Joint Remover tool HT72520000 or equivalent, remove the tie rod from the knuckle.
4. Loosen, but do not remove, the steering gear mounting bolts.
5. Remove the steering column lower joint (matchmark shaft to joint assembly—for correct installation).
6. Unbolt and remove the steering gear.

To install:

7. Position and install the power steering gear assembly to the vehicle. Torque the tie rod-to-steering knuckle nut to 22–29 ft. lbs., the steering gear-to-frame clamp bolts to EVENLY in steps to 43–58 ft. lbs., the lower joint-to-steering column bolt to 23–31 ft. lbs.
8. Torque the low pressure hose clip bolt to 9–17 inch lbs. and the high pressure hose-to-gear to 29–36 ft. lbs.
9. On most later models, observe tightening torque when installing high and low pressure pipes. The O-ring in the low pressure is larger than in the high pressure side. Take care to install the proper O-ring.

- Low pressure pipe torque—20–29 ft. lbs.
- High pressure pipe torque—11–18 ft. lbs.

10. Bleed the power steering system and check the wheel alignment.

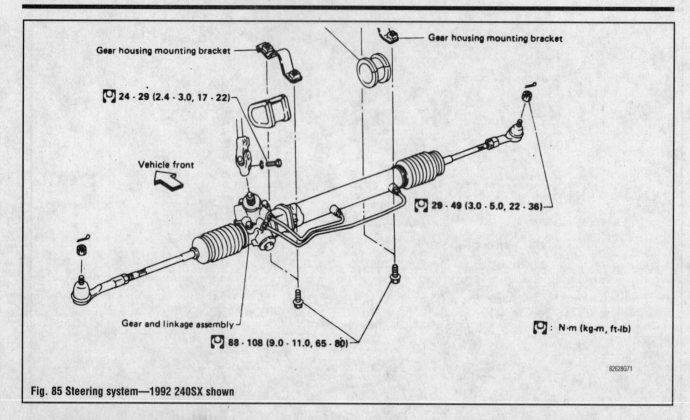

Fig. 85 Steering system—1992 240SX shown

➡When installing the lower steering joint to the steering gear, make sure that the wheels are aligned straight and the steering joint slot is aligned with the steering gear cap or spacer mark.

Power Steering Pump

REMOVAL & INSTALLATION

1. Remove the hoses at the pump and plug the openings shut to prevent contamination. Position the disconnected lines in a raised attitude to prevent leakage.
2. Remove the pump belt.
3. Loosen the retaining bolts and any braces, and remove the pump.
4. Installation is the reverse of removal procedure. Use the following torque specifications as a guide pulley lock-nut 23–31 ft. lbs. and pump bracket to engine 20–26 ft. lbs. Adjust the belt—refer to Section 1. Bleed the system.

BLEEDING THE POWER STEERING SYSTEM

1. Fill the pump reservoir and allow to remain undisturbed for a few minutes.
2. Raise the car until the front wheels are clear of the ground.
3. With the engine off, quickly turn the wheels right and left several times, lightly contacting the stops.
4. Add fluid if necessary.
5. Start the engine and let it idle.
6. Repeat Steps 3 and 4 with the engine idling.
7. Stop the engine, lower the car until the wheels just touch the ground. Start the engine, allow it to idle, and turn the wheels back and forth several times. Check the fluid level and refill if necessary.

TORQUE SPECIFICATIONS

Component	English	Metric
Steering wheel nut:	22-29 ft. lbs.	29-39 Nm
Lower joint to column (later models):	17-22 ft. lbs.	24-29 Nm
Lower joint to gear (later models):	17-22 ft. lbs.	24-29 Nm
Steering column clamp to mounting bracket:	7-11 ft. lbs.	9-14 Nm
Tie-rod to steering knuckle (Stanza):	22-29 ft. lbs.	29-39 Nm
Tie-rod to steering knuckle (200SX):	40-72 ft. lbs.	54-98 Nm
Tie-rod locknut (200SX):	58-72 ft. lbs.	78-98 Nm .
Tie-rod locknut (Stanza):	27-34 ft. lbs.	37-46 Nm
Tie-rod to steering gear:	58-72 ft. lbs.	78-98 Nm
Steering gear housing clamp (200SX):	29-36 ft. lbs.	39-49 Nm
Steering gear housing clamp (Stanza):	54-72 ft. lbs.	73-97 Nm
Power steering pump pulley locknut:	40-50 ft. lbs.	54-68 Nm

Power steering pump to bracket:
  M8 type bolts:
  M10 type bolts:
	
	12-15 ft. lbs.
	23-31 ft.lbs.
		
		16-21 Nm
		31-42 Nm

Power steering tank bracket:	3-4 ft. lbs.	5-6 Nm

82628C02

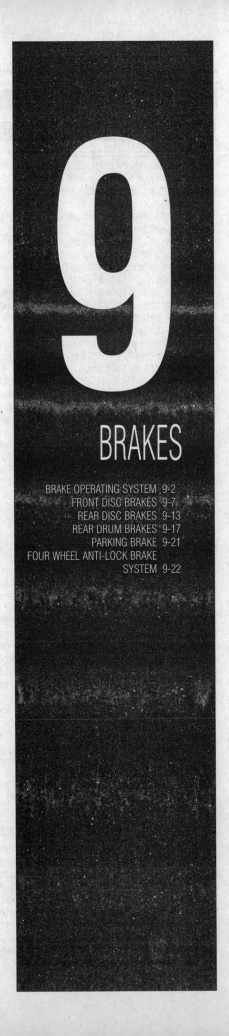

9

BRAKES

BRAKE OPERATING SYSTEM

Basic Operating Principles

Hydraulic systems are used to actuate the brakes of all modern automobiles. The system transports the power required to force the frictional surfaces of the braking system together from the pedal to the individual brake units at each wheel. A hydraulic system is used for two reasons.

First, fluid under pressure can be carried to all parts of an automobile by small pipes and flexible hoses without taking up a significant amount of room or posing routing problems.

Second, a great mechanical advantage can be given to the brake pedal end of the system, and the foot pressure required to actuate the brakes can be reduced by making the surface area of the master cylinder pistons smaller than that of any of the pistons in the wheel cylinders or calipers.

The master cylinder consists of a fluid reservoir along with a double cylinder and piston assembly. Double type master cylinders are designed to separate the front and rear braking systems hydraulically in case of a leak. The master cylinder coverts mechanical motion from the pedal into hydraulic pressure within the lines. This pressure is translated back into mechanical motion at the wheels by either the wheel cylinder (drum brakes) or the caliper (disc brakes).

Steel lines carry the brake fluid to a point on the vehicle's frame near each of the vehicle's wheels. The fluid is then carried to the calipers and wheel cylinders by flexible tubes in order to allow for suspension and steering movements.

In drum brake systems, each wheel cylinder contains two pistons, one at either end, which push outward in opposite directions and force the brake shoe into contact with the drum.

In disc brake systems, the cylinders are part of the calipers. At least one cylinder in each caliper is used to force the brake pads against the disc.

All pistons employ some type of seal, usually made of rubber, to minimize fluid leakage. A rubber dust boot seals the outer end of the cylinder against dust and dirt. The boot fits around the outer end of the piston on disc brake calipers, and around the brake actuating rod on wheel cylinders.

The hydraulic system operates as follows: When at rest, the entire system, from the piston(s) in the master cylinder to those in the wheel cylinders or calipers, is full of brake fluid. Upon application of the brake pedal, fluid trapped in front of the master cylinder piston(s) is forced through the lines to the wheel cylinders. Here, it forces the pistons outward, in the case of drum brakes, and inward toward the disc, in the case of disc brakes. The motion of the pistons is opposed by return springs mounted outside the cylinders in drum brakes, and by spring seals, in disc brakes.

Upon release of the brake pedal, a spring located inside the master cylinder immediately returns the master cylinder pistons to the normal position. The pistons contain check valves and the master cylinder has compensating ports drilled in it. These are uncovered as the pistons reach their normal position. The piston check valves allow fluid to flow toward the wheel cylinders or calipers as the pistons withdraw. Then, as the return springs force the brake pads or shoes into the released position, the excess fluid reservoir through the compensating ports. It is during the time the pedal is in the released position that any fluid that has leaked out of the system will be replaced through the compensating ports.

Dual circuit master cylinders employ two pistons, located one behind the other, in the same cylinder. The primary piston is actuated directly by mechanical linkage from the brake pedal through the power booster. The secondary piston is actuated by fluid trapped between the two pistons. If a leak develops in front of the secondary piston, it moves forward until it bottoms against the front of the master cylinder, and the fluid trapped between the pistons will operate the rear brakes. If the rear brakes develop a leak, the primary piston will move forward until direct contact with the secondary piston takes place, and it will force the secondary piston to actuate the front brakes. In either case, the brake pedal moves farther when the brakes are applied, and less braking power is available.

All dual circuit systems use a switch to warn the driver when only half of the brake system is operational. This switch is usually located in a valve body which is mounted on the firewall or the frame below the master cylinder. A hydraulic piston receives pressure from both circuits, each circuit's pressure being applied to one end of the piston. When the pressures are in balance, the piston remains stationary. When one circuit has a leak, however, the greater pressure in that circuit during application of the brakes will push the piston to one side, closing the switch and activating the brake warning light.

In disc brake systems, this valve body also contains a metering valve and, in some cases, a proportioning valve. The metering valve keeps pressure from traveling to the disc brakes on the front wheels until the brake shoes on the rear wheels have contacted the drums, ensuring that the front brakes will never be used alone. The proportioning valve controls the pressure to the rear brakes to lessen the chance of rear wheel lock-up during very hard braking.

Warning lights may be tested by depressing the brake pedal and holding it while opening one of the wheel cylinder bleeder screws. If this does not cause the light to go on, substitute a new lamp, make continuity checks, and, finally, replace the switch as necessary.

The hydraulic system may be checked for leaks by applying pressure to the pedal gradually and steadily. If the pedal sinks very slowly to the floor, the system has a leak. This is not to be confused with a springy or spongy feel due to the compression of air within the lines. If the system leaks, there will be a gradual change in the position of the pedal with a constant pressure.

Check for leaks along all lines and at wheel cylinders. If no external leaks are apparent, the problem is inside the master cylinder.

DISC BRAKES

Instead of the traditional expanding brakes that press outward against a circular drum, disc brake systems utilize a disc (rotor) with brake pads positioned on either side of it. An easily-seen analogy is the hand brake arrangement on a bicycle. The pads squeeze onto the rim of the bike wheel, slowing its motion. Automobile disc brakes use the identical principle but apply the braking effort to a separate disc instead of the wheel.

The disc (rotor) is a casting, usually equipped with cooling fins between the two braking surfaces. This enables air to circulate between the braking surfaces making them less sensitive to heat buildup and more resistant to fade. Dirt and water do not drastically affect braking action since contaminants are thrown off by the centrifugal action of the rotor or scraped off the by the pads. Also, the equal clamping action of the two brake pads tends to ensure uniform, straight line stops. Disc brakes are inherently self-adjusting. There are three general types of disc brake:

- A fixed caliper.
- A floating caliper.
- A sliding caliper.

The fixed caliper design uses two pistons mounted on either side of the rotor (in each side of the caliper). The caliper is mounted rigidly and does not move.

The sliding and floating designs are quite similar. In fact, these two types are often lumped together. In both designs, the pad on the inside of the rotor is moved into contact with the rotor by hydraulic force. The caliper, which is not held in a fixed position, moves slightly, bringing the outside pad into contact with the rotor. There are various methods of attaching floating calipers. Some pivot at the bottom or top, and some slide on mounting bolts. In any event, the end result is the same.

DRUM BRAKES

Drum brakes employ two brake shoes mounted on a stationary backing plate. These shoes are positioned inside a circular drum which rotates with the wheel assembly. The shoes are held in place by springs. This allows them to slide toward the drums (when they are applied) while keeping the linings and drums in alignment. The shoes are actuated by a wheel cylinder which is mounted at the top of the backing plate. When the brakes are applied, hydraulic pressure forces the wheel cylinder's actuating links outward. Since these links bear directly against the top of the brake shoes, the tops of the shoes are then forced against the inner side of the drum. This action forces the bottoms of the two shoes to contact the brake drum by rotating the entire assembly slightly (known as servo action). When pressure within the wheel cylinder is relaxed, return springs pull the shoes back away from the drum.

Most modern drum brakes are designed to self-adjust themselves during application when the vehicle is moving in reverse. This motion causes both shoes to rotate very slightly with the drum, rocking an adjusting lever, thereby causing rotation of the adjusting screw. Some drum brake systems are designed to self-adjust during application whenever the brakes are applied. This on-board adjustment system reduces the need for maintenance adjustments and keeps both the brake function and pedal feel satisfactory.

POWER BOOSTERS

Virtually all modern vehicles use a vacuum assisted power brake system to multiply the braking force and reduce pedal effort. Since vacuum is always available when the engine is operating, the system is simple and efficient. A vacuum diaphragm is located on the front of the master cylinder and assists the driver in applying the brakes, reducing both the effort and travel he must put into moving the brake pedal.

The vacuum diaphragm housing is normally connected to the intake manifold by a vacuum hose. A check valve is placed at the point where the hose enters the diaphragm housing, so that during periods of low manifold vacuum brakes assist will not be lost.

Depressing the brake pedal closes off the vacuum source and allows atmospheric pressure to enter on one side of the diaphragm. This causes the master cylinder pistons to move and apply the brakes. When the brake pedal is released, vacuum is applied to both sides of the diaphragm and springs return the diaphragm and master cylinder pistons to the released position.

If the vacuum supply fails, the brake pedal rod will contact the end of the master cylinder actuator rod and the system will apply the brakes without any power assistance. The driver will notice that much higher pedal effort is needed to stop the car and that the pedal feels harder than usual.

Vacuum Leak Test

1. Operate the engine at idle without touching the brake pedal for at least one minute.
2. Turn off the engine and wait one minute.
3. Test for the presence of assist vacuum by depressing the brake pedal and releasing it several times. If vacuum is present in the system, light application will produce less and less pedal travel. If there is no vacuum, air is leaking into the system.

System Operation Test

1. With the engine **OFF**, pump the brake pedal until the supply vacuum is entirely gone.
2. Put light, steady pressure on the brake pedal.
3. Start the engine and let it idle. If the system is operating correctly, the brake pedal should fall toward the floor if the constant pressure is maintained.

Power brake systems may be tested for hydraulic leaks just as ordinary systems are tested.

✳✳ WARNING

Clean, high quality brake fluid is essential to the safe and proper operation of the brake system. You should always buy the highest quality brake fluid that is available. If the brake fluid becomes contaminated, drain and flush the system, then refill the master cylinder with new fluid. Never reuse any brake fluid. Any brake fluid that is removed from the system should be discarded.

Adjustments

DRUM TYPE BRAKES

1. Raise and support the rear of the vehicle on jackstands.
2. Remove the rubber cover from the backing plate.
3. Insert a brake adjusting tool through the hole in the brake backing plate. Turn the toothed adjusting nut to spread the brake shoes, making contact with the brake drum.

➡**When adjusting the brake shoes, turn the wheel until considerable drag is felt.**

4. When considerable drag is felt, back off the adjusting nut a few notches, so that the correct clearance is maintained between the brake drum and the brake shoes. Make sure that the wheel rotates freely.

BRAKE PEDAL

Pedal Free-Play

▶ **See Figure 1**

Before adjusting the pedal, make sure that the brakes are correctly adjusted. Adjust the pedal free-play by means of the adjustable pushrod or by replacing shims between the master cylinder and the brake booster or firewall. Free-play should be approximately 15mm on all models through 1984. On all models from 1985–92, the pedal free-play should be 13mm. Refer to the illustration.

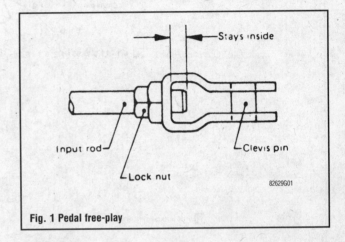

Fig. 1 Pedal free-play

Pedal Height

▶ **See Figure 2**

Adjust the pedal height by means of the adjustable pedal arm stop pad in the driver's compartment on models through 1984. On later models, adjust the brake booster input rod by loosening the lock-nut and turning the rod.

The pedal height (floorboard-to-pedal pad) should be approximately 178mm for 1982–83 200SX model.

On the 1984–86½ 200SX, it should be 189–199mm on cars with a manual transmission and 191–201mm on cars with automatic transmission.

On the 1986½–88 200SX, it should be 185–195mm on cars with a manual transmission and 187–197mm on cars with automatic transmission.

The brake pedal free height for the 1989–92 240SX model is 177–187mm for manual transmission and 186–196mm for automatic transmission.

The brake pedal free height for the Stanza models is 159–169mm for manual transaxle and 169–179mm for automatic transaxle. The early Stanza models pedal height (floorboard to pedal pad) is 152mm. Refer to the illustration.

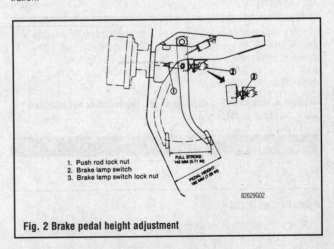

Fig. 2 Brake pedal height adjustment

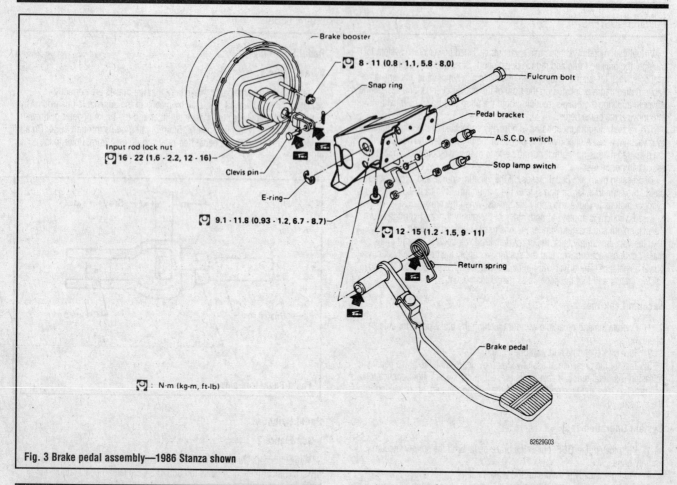

Fig. 3 Brake pedal assembly—1986 Stanza shown

Brake Light Switch

REMOVAL & INSTALLATION

1. Disconnect the negative battery cable.
2. Disconnect the wiring connector at the switch.
3. Remove the switch lock nut.
4. Remove the switch.
5. Install the switch and adjust it so the brake lights are not on unless the brake pedal is depressed.

ADJUSTMENT

Adjust the clearance between the brake pedal and the stop lamp switch or the ASCD switch, by loosening the lock-nut and adjusting the switch. The clearance should be approximately 1.0mm for 1982–84 Stanza or 0.30–1.00mm for 1985–92 Stanza and all other models. Use this service procedure as a guide if necessary.

➡The stop light switch is adjusted so that the switch is not activated when the brake pedal is relaxed.

Brake Pedal

REMOVAL & INSTALLATION

♦ See Figures 3 and 4

Refer to the exploded view illustration as a guide for the necessary service removal and installation information.

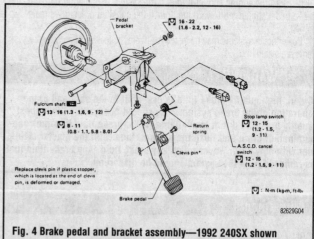

Fig. 4 Brake pedal and bracket assembly—1992 240SX shown

Master Cylinder

REMOVAL & INSTALLATION

♦ See Figures 5 and 6

1. Disconnect the negative battery cable. Clean the outside of the master cylinder thoroughly, particularly around the cap and fluid lines. Disconnect the fluid lines and cap them to exclude dirt.
2. If equipped with a fluid level sensor, disconnect the wiring harness from the master cylinder.

3. Disconnect the brake fluid tubes, then plug the openings to prevent dirt from entering the system.

4. Remove the mounting bolts at the firewall or the brake booster (if equipped) and remove the master cylinder from the vehicle.

To install:

5. Bench bleed the master cylinder assembly before installation—refer to the service procedure below. Install the master cylinder to the vehicle. Connect all brake lines and fluid level sensor wiring is so equipped. Refill the reservoir with brake fluid and bleed the system. Adjust the brake system if necessary.

➡Ordinary brake fluid will boil and cause brake failure under the high temperatures developed in disc brake systems; use DOT 3 brake fluid in the brake systems. The adjustable pushrod is used to adjust brake pedal free-play. If the pushrod is not adjustable, there will be shims between the cylinder and the mount. These shims, or the adjustable pushrod, are used to adjust brake pedal free play.

MASTER CYLINDER BLEEDING

1. Place the master cylinder in a vise.
2. Connect two lines to the fluid outlet orifices, and into the reservoir.
3. Fill the reservoir with brake fluid.
4. Using a wooden dowel, depress the pushrod slowly, allowing the pistons to return. Do this several times until the air bubbles are all expelled.

5. Remove the bleeding tubes from the master cylinder, plug the outlets and install the caps.

Power Brake Booster

REMOVAL & INSTALLATION

♦ **See Figures 7, 8 and 9**

➡Make sure all vacuum lines and connectors are in good condition. A small vacuum leak will cause a big problem in the power brake system.

1. Disconnect the negative battery cable. Remove the master cylinder mounting nuts and pull the master cylinder assembly (brake lines connected) away from the power booster.
2. Detach the vacuum lines from the booster.
3. Detach the booster pushrod at the pedal clevis.
4. Unbolt the booster from under the dash and lift it out of the engine compartment.

To install:

5. Install the brake booster assembly to the vehicle. Install the master cylinder assembly to brake booster assembly.
6. Connect the booster pushrod to the pedal clevis. Connect the vacuum lines to brake booster.

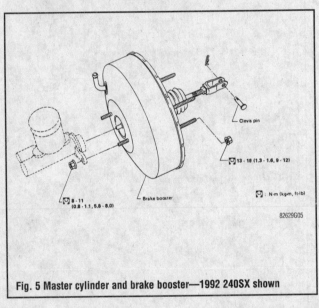

Fig. 5 Master cylinder and brake booster—1992 240SX shown

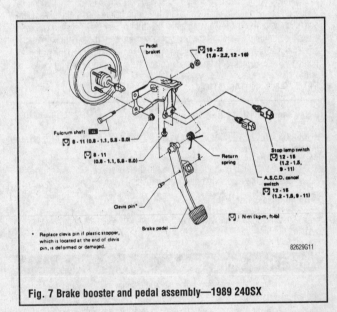

Fig. 7 Brake booster and pedal assembly—1989 240SX

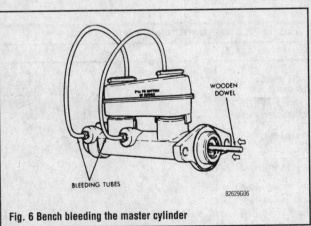

Fig. 6 Bench bleeding the master cylinder

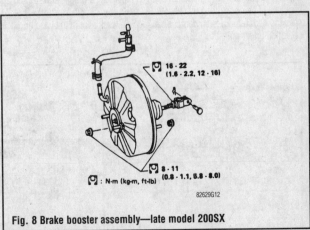

Fig. 8 Brake booster assembly—late model 200SX

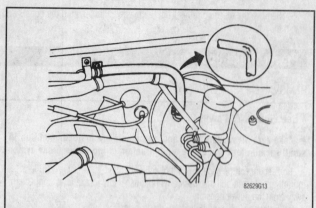

Fig. 9 Check condition of the vacuum hose on power brake booster

7. Connect the battery. Start the engine and check brake operation.

Brake Proportioning Valve

All Datsun/Nissans covered in this manual are equipped with brake proportioning valves of several different types. The valves all do the same job, which is to separate the front and rear brake lines, allowing them to function independently, and preventing the rear brakes from locking before the front brakes. Damage, such as brake line leakage, in either the front or rear brake system will not affect the normal operation of the unaffected system. If, in the event of a panic stop, the rear brakes lock up before the front brakes, it could mean the proportioning valve is defective. In that case, replace the entire proportioning valve.

REMOVAL & INSTALLATION

▶ See Figures 10, 11 and 12

➡ **Models built in 1985 and later years do not use a separate proportioning valve.**

1. Disconnect and plug the brake lines at the valve.
2. Unscrew the mounting bolt(s) and remove the valve.

➡ **Do not disassemble the valve.**

3. Installation is in the reverse order of removal. Bleed the complete brake system.

Brake Hoses and Lines

Metal lines and rubber brake hoses should be checked frequently for leaks and external damage. Metal lines are particularly prone to crushing and kinking under the vehicle. Any such deformation can restrict the proper flow of fluid and therefore impair braking at the wheels. Rubber hoses should be checked for cracking or scraping; such damage can create a weak spot in the hose and it could fail under pressure.

Any time the lines are removed or disconnected, extreme cleanliness must be observed. Clean all joints and connections before disassembly (use a stiff bristle brush and clean brake fluid); be sure to plug the lines and ports as soon as they are opened. New lines and hoses should be flushed clean with brake fluid before installation to remove any contamination.

REMOVAL & INSTALLATION

▶ See Figures 13, 14, 15 and 16

1. Disconnect the negative battery cable.
2. Raise and safely support the vehicle on jackstands.
3. Remove any wheel and tire assemblies necessary for access to the particular line you are removing.
4. Thoroughly clean the surrounding area at the joints to be disconnected.
5. Place a suitable catch pan under the joint to be disconnected.

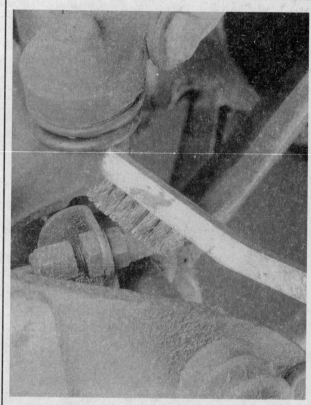

Fig. 13 Use a brush to clean the fittings of any debris

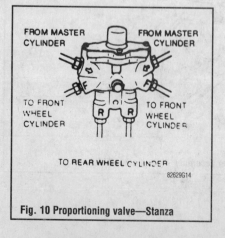

Fig. 10 Proportioning valve—Stanza

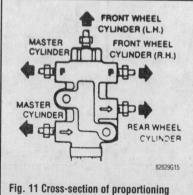

Fig. 11 Cross-section of proportioning valve—most models similar

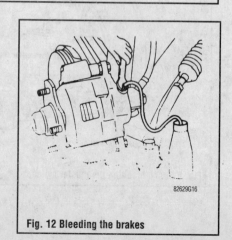

Fig. 12 Bleeding the brakes

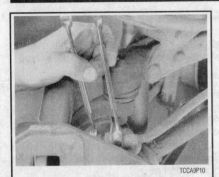

Fig. 14 Use two wrenches to loosen the fitting. If available, use flare nut type wrenches

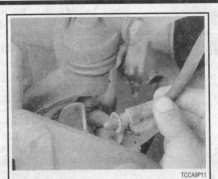

Fig. 15 Any gaskets/crush washers should be replaced with new ones during installation

Fig. 16 Tape or plug the line to prevent contamination

6. Using two wrenches (one to hold the joint and one to turn the fitting), disconnect the hose or line to be replaced.

7. Disconnect the other end of the line or hose, moving the drain pan if necessary. Always use a back-up wrench to avoid damaging the fitting.

8. Disconnect any retaining clips or brackets holding the line and remove the line from the vehicle.

➡ If the brake system is to remain open for more time than it takes to swap lines, tape or plug each remaining clip and port to keep contaminants out and fluid in.

To install:

9. Install the new line or hose, starting with the end farthest from the master cylinder. Connect the other end, then confirm that both fittings are correctly threaded and turn smoothly using finger pressure. Make sure the new line will not rub against any other part. Brake lines must be at least 1/2 in. (13mm) from the steering column and other moving parts. Any protective shielding or insulators must be reinstalled in the original location.

❋❋ WARNING

Make sure the hose is NOT kinked or touching any part of the frame or suspension after installation. These conditions may cause the hose to fail prematurely.

10. Using two wrenches as before, tighten each fitting.
11. Install any retaining clips or brackets on the lines.
12. If removed, install the wheel and tire assemblies, then carefully lower the vehicle to the ground.
13. Refill the brake master cylinder reservoir with clean, fresh brake fluid, meeting DOT 3 specifications. Properly bleed the brake system.
14. Connect the negative battery cable.

Brake System Bleeding

➡ If vehicle is equipped with a Anti-Lock Brake System (ABS) refer to the service procedure later this section.

The purpose of bleeding the brakes is to expel air trapped in the hydraulic system. The system must be bled whenever the pedal feels spongy, indicating that air, which is compressible, has entered the system. It must also be bled whenever the system has been opened or repaired. You will need a helper for this job.

Never reuse brake fluid which has been bled from the system.

The usual sequence for bleeding is right rear (RR), left rear (LR), right front (RF), left front (LF). The service procedure is to bleed at the points farthest from the master cylinder assembly first. Follow this order when bleeding the brake system on your vehicle:

• 1982–88 200SX bleed in this order RR, LR, RF, LF wheels
• 1989–92 240SX bleed in this order LR, RR, LF, RF wheels
• 1982–85 Stanza bleed in this order RR, LF, LR, RF wheels
• 1986–92 Stanza, Stanza Wagon bleed in this order LR, RF, RR, LF wheels

BLEEDING PROCEDURE

1. Clean all dirt from around the master cylinder reservoir caps. Remove the caps and fill the master cylinder to the proper level with clean, fresh brake fluid meeting DOT 3 specifications.

➡ Brake fluid picks up moisture from the air, which reduces its effectiveness and causes brake line corrosion. Don't leave the master cylinder or the fluid container open any longer than necessary. Be careful not to spill brake fluid on painted surfaces. Wipe up any spilled fluid immediately and rinse the area with clear water.

2. Clean all the bleeder screws. You may want to give each one a shot of penetrating solvent to loosen it up. Seizure is a common problem with bleeder screws, which then break off, sometimes requiring replacement of the part to which they are attached.

3. Attach a length of clear vinyl tubing to the bleeder screw on the wheel cylinder. Insert the other end of the tube into a clear, clean jar half filled with brake fluid.

4. Have your helper SLOWLY depress the brake pedal. As this is done, open the bleeder (follow the correct bleeding order) screw 1/2–1/3 of a turn, and allow the fluid to run through the tube. Close the bleeder screw before the pedal reaches the end of its travel. Have your assistant slowly release the pedal. Repeat this process until no air bubbles appear in the expelled fluid.

5. Repeat the procedure on the other three brakes, checking the fluid level in the master cylinder reservoirs often. Do not allow the reservoirs to run dry, or the bleeding process will have to be repeated.

FRONT DISC BRAKES

❋❋ CAUTION

Brake shoes may contain asbestos, which has been determined to be a cancer causing agent. Never clean the brake surfaces with compressed air! Avoid inhaling any dust from any brake surface! When cleaning brake surfaces, use a commercially available brake cleaning fluid.

Brake Pads

INSPECTION

You should be able to check the pad lining thickness without removing the pads. Check the Brake Specifications chart at the end of this section to find the manufacturer's pad wear limit. However, this measurement may disagree with your state inspection laws. When replacing pads, always check the surface of the rotors for scoring or wear. The rotors should be removed for resurfacing if badly scored.

REMOVAL & INSTALLATION

➡ **All 4 front brake pads MUST ALWAYS be replaced as a complete set. Bleed the brake system only if necessary. Refer to the necessary illustrations as guide for this repair.**

Type N22 Series Disc Brake Assembly

▸ **See Figures 17, 18 and 19**

1. Raise and support the front of the vehicle. Remove the wheels.
2. Remove the retaining clip from the outboard pad.
3. Remove the pad pins retaining the anti-squeal springs.
4. Remove the pads.

To install:

5. To install, open the bleeder screw slightly and push the outer piston into the cylinder until the dust seal groove aligns with the end of the seal retaining ring, then close the bleed screw. Be careful because the piston can be pushed too far, requiring disassembly of the caliper to repair. Install the inner pad.
6. Pull the yoke to push the inner piston into place. Install the outer pad.
7. Lightly coat the areas where the pins touch the pads, and where the pads touch the caliper (at the top) with grease. Do not allow grease to get on the pad friction surfaces.
8. Install the anti-squeal springs and pad pins. Install the clip.
9. Apply the brakes a few times to seat the pads. Check the master cylinder level. Add fluid if necessary. Bleed and adjust the brakes if necessary.

Type CL22V Series Disc Brake Assembly

▸ **See Figures 20, 21 and 22**

1. Raise the front of the car and support it with safety stands.

2. Unscrew and remove the lower pin bolt (sub pin).
3. Swing the cylinder body upward and then remove the pad retainer, the inner and outer shims and the pads themselves. Do not depress the brake pedal when the cylinder body is in the raised position or the piston will pop out.

To install:

4. Clean the piston end of the cylinder body and the pin bolt holes. Be careful not to get oil on the rotor.
5. Pull the cylinder body to the outer side and install the inner pad.
6. Install the outer pad, the shim and the pad retainer.
7. Reposition the cylinder body and then tighten the pin bolt to 12–15 ft. lbs.
8. Apply the brakes a few times to seat the new pads. Check the fluid level and bleed and adjust the brakes if required.

Type AD22V Series Disc Brake Assembly

▸ **See Figures 23, 24 and 25**

1. Remove the road wheel.
2. Remove the lower caliper guide pin. See the accompanying illustration.
3. Rotate the brake caliper body upward.
4. Remove the brake pad retainer and the inner and outer pad shims.
5. Remove the brake pads. Do not depress the brake pedal when the caliper body is raised. The brake piston will be forced out of the caliper.

To install:

6. Clean the piston end of the caliper body and the pin bolt holes. Be careful not to get oil on the brake rotor.
7. Pull the caliper body to the outer side and install the inner brake pad. Make sure both new pads are kept clean!
8. Install the outer pad, shim and pad retainer.
9. Reposition the caliper body and then tighten the guide pin bolt to 23–30 ft. lbs.
10. Apply the brakes a few times to seat the pads (bleed and adjust brakes if necessary) before driving out on the road.

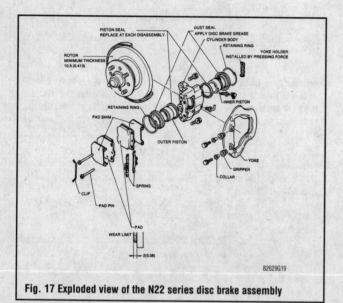

Fig. 17 Exploded view of the N22 series disc brake assembly

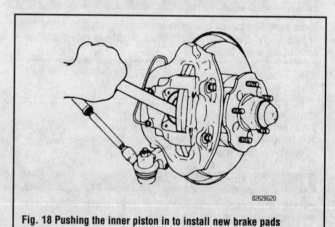

Fig. 18 Pushing the inner piston in to install new brake pads

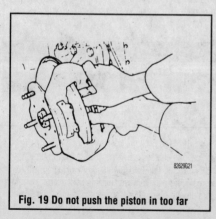

Fig. 19 Do not push the piston in too far

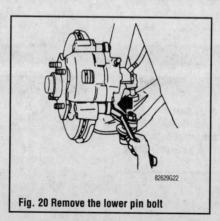

Fig. 20 Remove the lower pin bolt

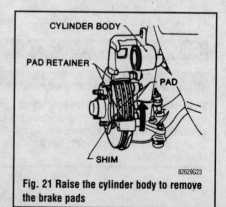

Fig. 21 Raise the cylinder body to remove the brake pads

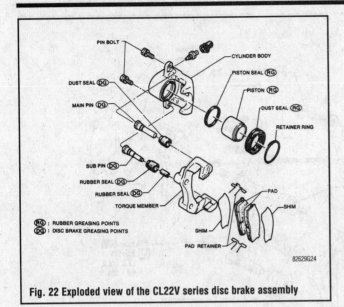

Fig. 22 Exploded view of the CL22V series disc brake assembly

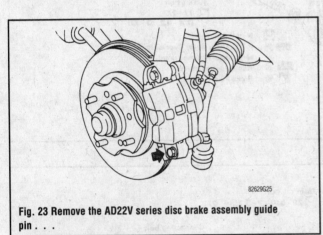

Fig. 23 Remove the AD22V series disc brake assembly guide pin . . .

Types CL28VB, CL22VB and CL25VB Series Disc Brake Assembly

♦ See Figures 26, 27 and 28

➡Use this service procedure and illustrations as a guide for all other CL type Series Disc Brake Systems.

1. Raise the vehicle and support it securely. Remove the front wheel. Remove the pin (lower) bolt from the caliper.

2. Swing the caliper body upward on the upper bolt. Remove the pad retainers and inner and outer shims. Do not depress the brake pedal when the cylinder body is in the raised position or the piston will pop out. Avoid damaging the piston seal when removing/installing the pads and retainers.

To install:

3. Check the level of fluid in the master cylinder. If the fluid is near the maximum level, use a clean syringe to remove fluid until the level is down well below the lip of the reservoir. Then, use a large C-clamp to press the caliper piston back into the caliper, to allow room for the installation of the thicker new pads.

4. Install the new pads, utilizing new shims, in reverse order. Torque the lower retaining bolt to 16–23 ft. lbs. Bleed and adjust the brakes if necessary. Make sure you pump the brakes and get a hard pedal before driving the car!

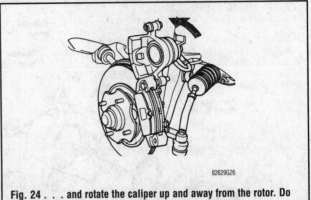

Fig. 24 . . . and rotate the caliper up and away from the rotor. Do not apply the brakes with the caliper in this position!

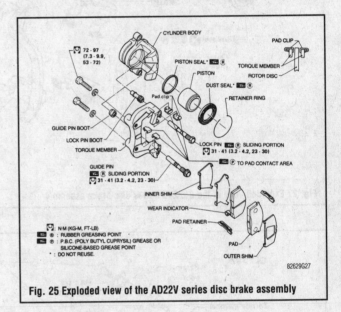

Fig. 25 Exploded view of the AD22V series disc brake assembly

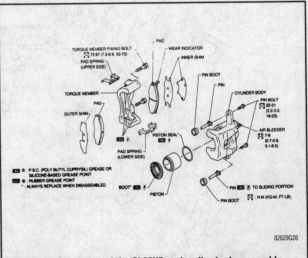

Fig. 26 Exploded view of the CL28VB series disc brake assembly

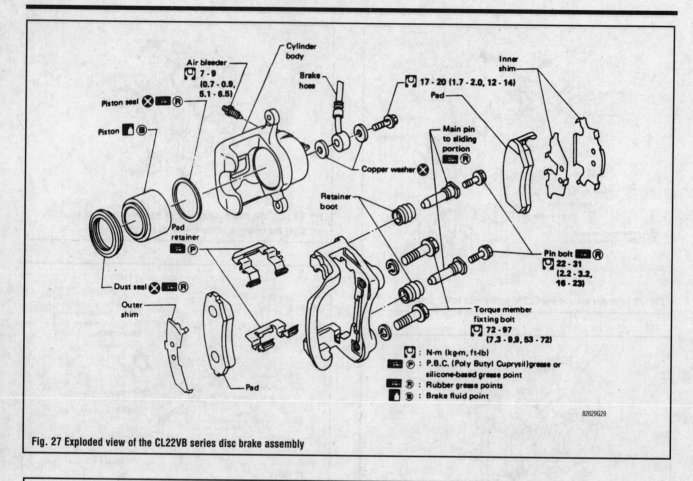

Fig. 27 Exploded view of the CL22VB series disc brake assembly

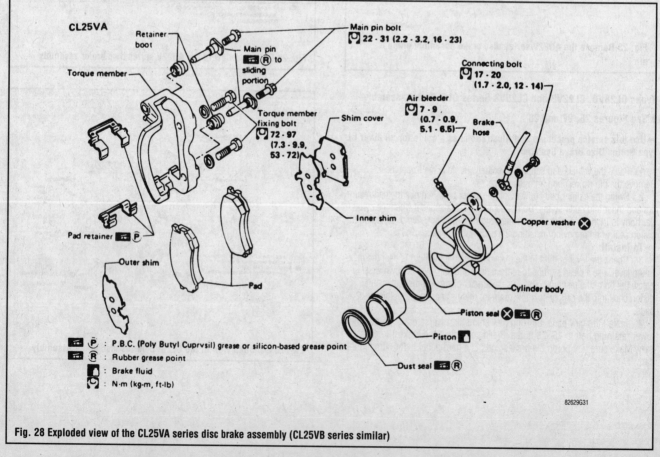

Fig. 28 Exploded view of the CL25VA series disc brake assembly (CL25VB series similar)

Brake Caliper

REMOVAL & INSTALLATION

Refer to "Brake Pads Removal and Installation" procedure in this section. Remove the brake pads. Remove both guide pins, torque member fixing bolts and brake hose connector. Remove the caliper assembly from the vehicle. The brake system must be bled after this repair—refer to the necessary procedure.

OVERHAUL

▶ **See Figures 17, 22, and 25 thru 36**

➡**Some vehicles may be equipped dual piston calipers. The procedure to overhaul the caliper is essentially the same with the exception of multiple pistons, O-rings and dust boots.**

1. Remove the caliper from the vehicle and place on a clean workbench.

✳✳ CAUTION

NEVER place your fingers in front of the pistons in an attempt to catch or protect the pistons when applying compressed air. This could result in personal injury!

➡**Depending upon the vehicle, there are two different ways to remove the piston from the caliper. Refer to the brake pad replacement procedure to make sure you have the correct procedure for your vehicle.**

2. The first method is as follows:
   a. Stuff a shop towel or a block of wood into the caliper to catch the piston.
   b. Remove the caliper piston using compressed air applied into the caliper inlet hole. Inspect the piston for scoring, nicks, corrosion and/or worn or damaged chrome plating. The piston must be replaced if any of these conditions are found.

3. For the second method, you must rotate the piston to retract it from the caliper.
4. If equipped, remove the anti-rattle clip.
5. Use a prytool to remove the caliper boot, being careful not to scratch the housing bore.
6. Remove the piston seals from the groove in the caliper bore.
7. Carefully loosen the brake bleeder valve cap and valve from the caliper housing.
8. Inspect the caliper bores, pistons and mounting threads for scoring or excessive wear.
9. Use crocus cloth to polish out light corrosion from the piston and bore.
10. Clean all parts with denatured alcohol and dry with compressed air.

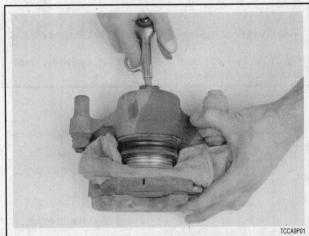

Fig. 29 For some types of calipers, use compressed air to drive the piston out of the caliper, but make sure to keep your fingers clear

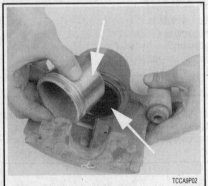

Fig. 30 Withdraw the piston from the caliper bore

Fig. 31 On some vehicles, you must remove the anti-rattle clip

Fig. 32 Use a prytool to carefully pry around the edge of the boot . . .

Fig. 33 . . . then remove the boot from the caliper housing, taking care not to score or damage the bore

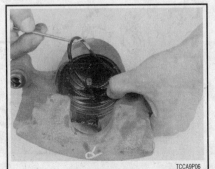

Fig. 34 Use extreme caution when removing the piston seal; DO NOT scratch the caliper bore

Fig. 35 Use the proper size driving tool and a mallet to properly seal the boots in the caliper housing

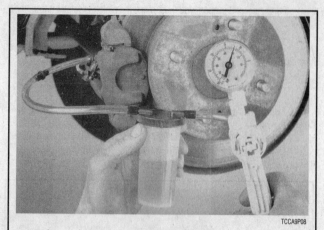

Fig. 36 There are tools, such as this Mighty-Vac, available to assist in proper brake system bleeding

To assemble:

11. Lubricate and install the bleeder valve and cap.

12. Install the new seals into the caliper bore grooves, making sure they are not twisted.

13. Lubricate the piston bore.

14. Install the pistons and boots into the bores of the calipers and push to the bottom of the bores.

15. Use a suitable driving tool to seat the boots in the housing.

16. Install the caliper in the vehicle.

17. Install the wheel and tire assembly, then carefully lower the vehicle.

18. Properly bleed the brake system.

Brake Disc (Rotor)

REMOVAL & INSTALLATION

200SX and 240SX Models—Rear Wheel Drive

1. Raise and support the front of the vehicle safely and remove the wheels.

2. Remove brake caliper assembly and wheel hub and bearing assembly if necessary. Refer to the necessary procedures in Section 8. Make sure not to twist the brake hose.

3. Remove the brake disc/wheel hub from the vehicle.

4. Installation is the reverse of removal. Adjust the wheel bearings if necessary.

INSPECTION

Check the brake rotor for roughness, cracks or chips. The rotor can be machined on a brake lathe most auto parts stores have complete machine shop service. The rotors should be machined or replaced during every front disc brake pad replacement.

Stanza and Stanza Wagon Models—Front Wheel Drive

▶ See Figures 37 and 38

※※ CAUTION

Brake shoes may contain asbestos, which has been determined to be a cancer causing agent. Never clean the brake surfaces with compressed air! Avoid inhaling any dust from any brake surface! When cleaning brake surfaces, use a commercially available brake cleaning fluid.

EARLY TYPE ROTOR/DISC ASSEMBLY

1. Refer to the Caliper, Removal and Installation procedures, in this section and remove the caliper and the cylinder body and the torque member from the steering knuckle. Do not disconnect the brake tube (if possible), support the assembly on a wire.

2. Remove the grease cap, the cotter pin, the adjusting cap, the wheel bearing lock-nut and the thrust washer from the drive shaft.

3. Using Wheel Hub Remover tools KV40101000 and ST36230000 press the wheel hub/disc assembly from the steering knuckle.

4. Remove the disc-to-wheel hub bolts and separate the disc from the wheel hub.

5. Install wheel hub/disc assembly to the vehicle. Refer to Section 8 for the necessary torque specifications and service procedures.

6. Install the caliper assembly and any other components to the vehicle.

7. Bleed brake system if necessary.

LATER TYPE ROTOR/DISC ASSEMBLY

1. Raise and safely support the vehicle.

2. Remove the caliper assembly as outlined.

3. Remove the rotor/disc assembly from the vehicle.

4. Installation is the reverse of removal procedure.

INSPECTION

Check the brake rotor for roughness, cracks or chips. The rotor can be machined on a brake lathe most auto parts stores have complete machine shop service. The rotors should be machined or replaced during every front disc brake pad replacement.

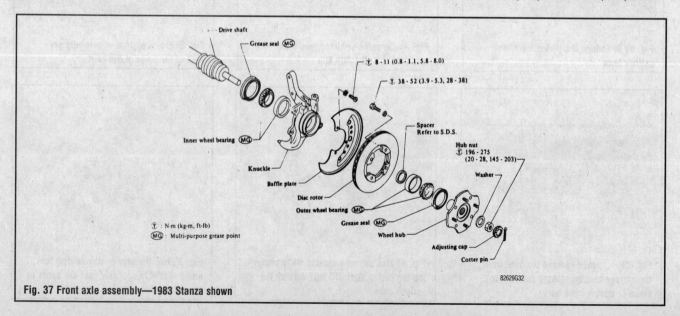

Fig. 37 Front axle assembly—1983 Stanza shown

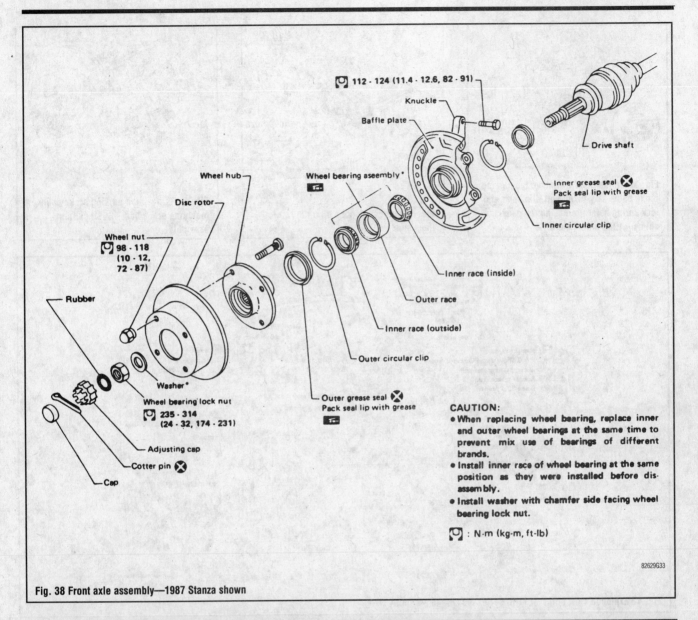

Fig. 38 Front axle assembly—1987 Stanza shown

REAR DISC BRAKES

✳✳ CAUTION

Brake shoes may contain asbestos, which has been determined to be a cancer causing agent. Never clean the brake surfaces with compressed air! Avoid inhaling any dust from any brake surface! When cleaning brake surfaces, use a commercially available brake cleaning fluid.

Brake Pads

INSPECTION

You should be able to check the pad lining thickness without removing the pads. Check the Brake Specifications chart at the end of this section to find the manufacturer's pad wear limit. However, this measurement may disagree with your state inspection laws. When replacing pads, always check the surface of the rotors for scoring or wear. The rotors should be removed for resurfacing if badly scored.

REMOVAL & INSTALLATION

➡All 4 rear brake pads MUST ALWAYS be replaced as a complete set. Bleed the brake system only if necessary. Refer to the necessary illustrations as a guide for this repair.

Types CL11H and CL9H Series Disc Brake Assembly

▶ **See Figures 39 thru 44**

1. Raise the rear of the car and support it with safety stands. Remove the brake pads.
2. Remove the pin bolts and lift off the caliper body.
3. Pull out the pad springs and then remove the pads and their shims.
To install:
4. Clean the piston end of the caliper body and the area around the pin holes. Be careful not to get oil on the rotor.
5. Using a pair of needle nosed pliers, carefully turn the piston clockwise back into the caliper body (remove some brake fluid from the master cylinder if necessary). Take care not to damage the piston boot.

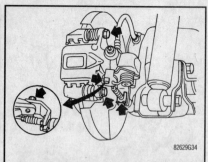

Fig. 39 On the 200SX, remove the parking brake cable stay fixing bolt, pin bolts and lock spring before removing the pads and shims—1984 model shown

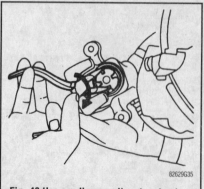

Fig. 40 Use needlenose pliers to retract the piston

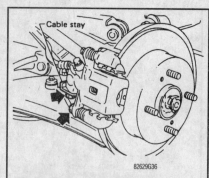

Fig. 41 Remove the parking brake cable mounting brace bolt—CL9H caliper assembly

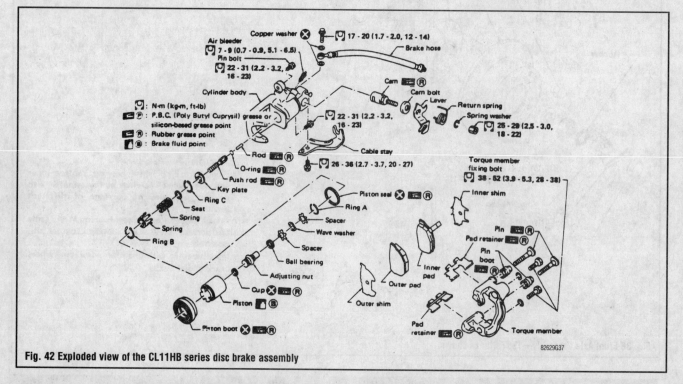

Fig. 42 Exploded view of the CL11HB series disc brake assembly

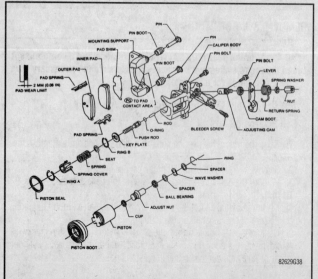

Fig. 43 Exploded view of the CL11H series disc brake assembly

6. Coat the pad contact area on the mounting support with a silicone based grease.

7. Install the pads, shims and the pad springs.

➡**Always use new shims.**

8. Position the caliper body in the mounting support and tighten the pin bolts to 16–23 ft. lbs.

9. Replace the wheel, lower the car and bleed the system if necessary.

Types CL11HB and CL14B Series Disc Brake Assembly

1. Raise the vehicle and support it securely. Remove the rear wheel.

2. Remove the two pin bolts and the lock spring. Remove the caliper, suspending it above the disc so as to avoid putting any strain on the hose.

3. Remove the pad retainers, pads, and shims.

➡**Do not depress the brake pedal when the cylinder body is in the raised position or the piston will pop out. Avoid damaging the piston seal when removing/installing the pads and retainers.**

4. Check the level of fluid in the master cylinder. If the fluid is near the maximum level, use a clean syringe to remove fluid until the level is down well below the lip of the reservoir. Then, press the caliper piston back into the caliper by turning it clockwise (it has a helical groove on the outer diameter). This will allow room for the installation of the thicker new pads.

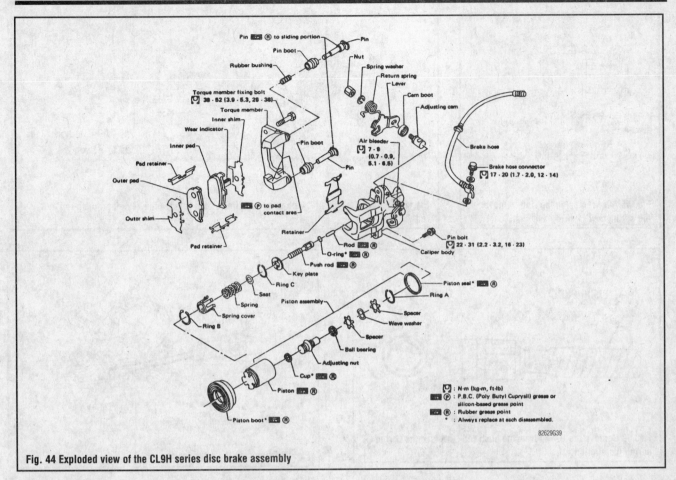

Fig. 44 Exploded view of the CL9H series disc brake assembly

5. Install the new pads using new shims in reverse order of the removal procedure. Torque the caliper pin bolts to 16–23 ft. lbs. Bleed the brakes if necessary. Make sure you pump the brakes and get a hard pedal before driving the car.

Brake Caliper

REMOVAL & INSTALLATION

Types CL11H, CL11HB, CL14B and CL9H Series Disc Brake Assembly

▶ **See Figures 45 thru 52**

1. See the appropriate procedure and remove the brake pads.
2. Disconnect the parking brake cable and brake hose. Unscrew the mounting bolts and remove the caliper assembly.

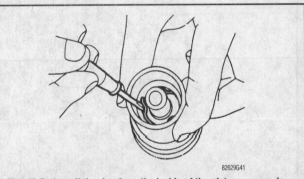

Fig. 46 Prying off the ring from the inside of the piston—some rings may be the snapring type

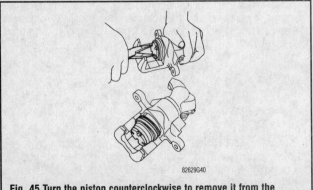

Fig. 45 Turn the piston counterclockwise to remove it from the caliper body

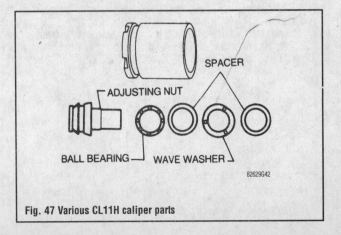

Fig. 47 Various CL11H caliper parts

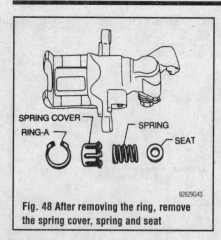

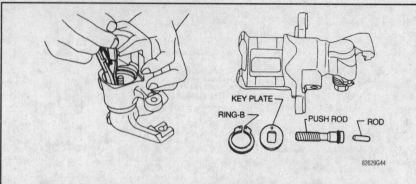

Fig. 48 After removing the ring, remove the spring cover, spring and seat

Fig. 49 Remove the ring "B" with snapring pliers, then remove the key plate, push rod and rod

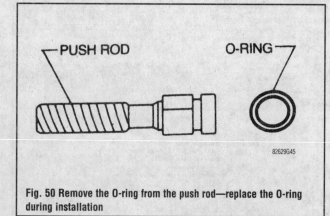

Fig. 50 Remove the O-ring from the push rod—replace the O-ring during installation

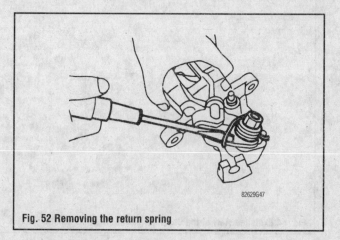

Fig. 52 Removing the return spring

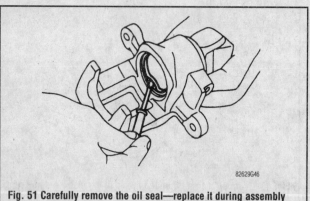

Fig. 51 Carefully remove the oil seal—replace it during assembly

3. Remove the pin bolts and separate the caliper body from the mounting support.

4. Using needlenosed pliers, turn the piston counterclockwise and remove it.

5. Pry out the ring from inside the piston. You can now remove the adjusting nut, the ball bearing, the wave washer and the spacers.

6. Installation is in the reverse order of removal. Replace all seals and O-rings. Tighten the caliper mounting bolts to 2838 ft. lbs.

Brake Disc (Rotor)

REMOVAL & INSTALLATION

1. Raise and support the rear of the vehicle safely and remove the wheels.

2. Remove brake caliper assembly. Refer to the necessary procedure. Make sure not to twist the brake hose.

3. Remove the brake disc from the vehicle.

4. Installation is the reverse of removal procedure.

INSPECTION

Check the brake rotor for roughness, cracks or chips. The rotor can be machined on a brake lathe most auto parts stores have complete machine shop service. The rotors should be machined or replaced during every rear disc brake pad replacement.

REAR DRUM BRAKES

✳✳ CAUTION

Brake shoes may contain asbestos, which has been determined to be a cancer causing agent. Never clean the brake surfaces with compressed air! Avoid inhaling any dust from any brake surface! When cleaning brake surfaces, use a commercially available brake cleaning fluid.

Brake Drums

REMOVAL & INSTALLATION

200SX and 1990–92 Stanza Models

▶ **See Figures 53 and 54**

1. Raises the rear of the vehicle and support it on jack stands.
2. Remove the wheels.
3. Release the parking brake.
4. Pull off the brake drums. On some models there are two threaded service holes in each brake drum. If the drum will not come off, fit two correct size bolts in the service holes and screw them in: this will force the drum away from the axle.
5. If the drum cannot be easily removed, back off the brake adjustment.

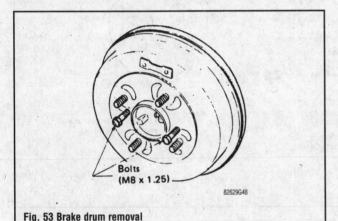

Fig. 53 Brake drum removal

➡**Never depress the brake pedal while the brake drum is removed.**

6. Installation is the reverse of removal procedure.

1982–89 Stanza and Stanza Wagon Models

➡**For rear wheel bearing service procedures refer to Section 8.**

1. Raise the rear of the vehicle and support it on jackstands.
2. Remove the wheels.
3. Release the parking brake.
4. Remove the grease cap, the cotter pin and the adjusting cap and the wheel bearing nut.
5. Pull off the drum, taking care not to drop the tapered bearing assembly.
6. Install the drum assembly to the vehicle. Adjust the wheel bearing—refer to the necessary service procedures.
7. Install the wheels.

INSPECTION

After removing the brake drum, wipe out the accumulated dust with a damp cloth.

✳✳ CAUTION

Do not blow the brake dust out of the drums with compressed air or lung power. Brake linings may contain asbestos, a known cancer causing substance. Dispose of the cloth after use.

Inspect the drum for cracks, deep grooves, roughness, scoring, or out-of-roundness. Replace any brake drum which is cracked.

Smooth any slight scores by polishing the friction surface with the fine emery cloth or have the drum machined (trued) at a machine shop. Heavy or extensive scoring will cause excessive brake lining wear and should be removed from the brake drum through resurfacing.

Brake Shoes

INSPECTION

You should be able to check the brake shoe lining thickness after removing the brake drum. Check the Brake Specifications chart at the end of this section to find the manufacturer's wear limits. However, this measurement may disagree with your state inspection laws. When replacing brake shoes, always check the

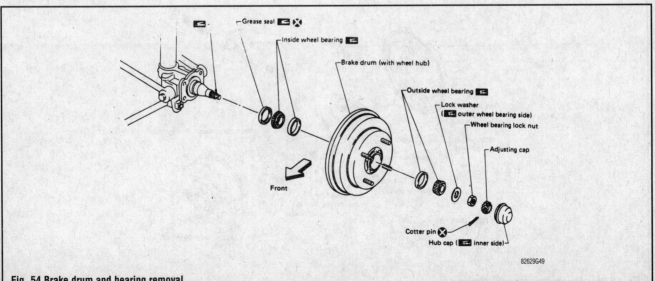

Fig. 54 Brake drum and bearing removal

surface of the brake drums for scoring or wear. The brake drums should resurfaced or machined if badly scored.

REMOVAL & INSTALLATION

▶ **See Figures 55, 56 and 57**

➡**If you are not thoroughly familiar with the procedures involved in brake replacement, disassemble and assemble one side at a time, leaving the other wheel intact, as a reference. This will reduce the risk of assembling brakes incorrectly. Special brake tools are available to make this repair easier. Refer to the illustrations and modify service steps for removal and installation.**

1. Raise the vehicle and remove the wheels.
2. Release the parking brake. Disconnect the cross rod from the lever of the brake cylinder if so equipped. Remove the brake drum. Place a heavy rubber band or clamp around the wheel cylinder to prevent the piston from coming out.
3. Remove the return springs, adjuster assembly, hold-down springs and brake shoes.

To install:
4. Clean the backing plate and check the wheel cylinder for leaks.
5. The brake drums must be machined if scored or out of round.
6. Hook the return springs into the new shoes. The return spring ends should be between the shoes and the backing plate. The longer return spring must be adjacent to the wheel cylinder. A very thin film of grease may be

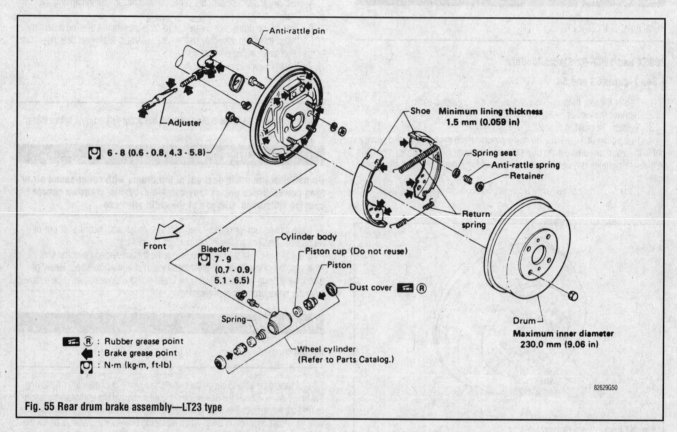

Fig. 55 Rear drum brake assembly—LT23 type

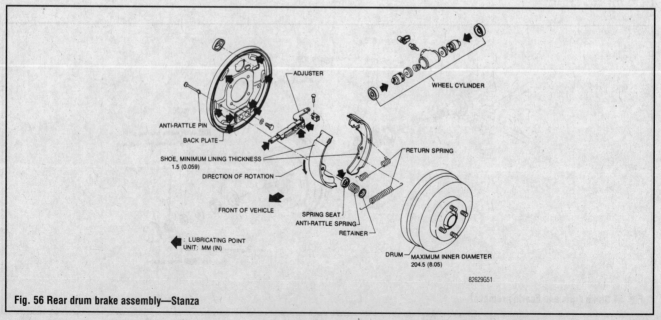

Fig. 56 Rear drum brake assembly—Stanza

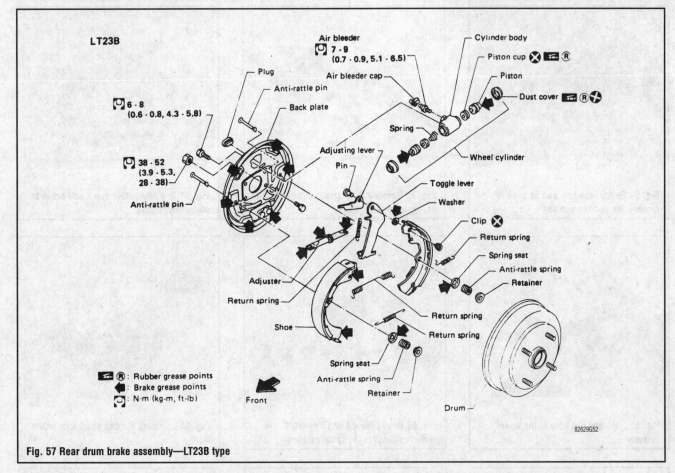

LT23B

Air bleeder
7 - 9
(0.7 - 0.9, 5.1 - 6.5)

Cylinder body
Piston cup
Piston
Dust cover
Air bleeder cap
Plug
Anti-rattle pin
Back plate
6 - 8
(0.6 - 0.8, 4.3 - 5.8)
38 - 52
(3.9 - 5.3, 28 - 38)
Anti-rattle pin
Adjusting lever
Pin
Spring
Wheel cylinder
Toggle lever
Washer
Clip
Return spring
Spring seat
Anti-rattle spring
Retainer
Adjuster
Return spring
Shoe
Return spring
Return spring
Spring seat
Anti-rattle spring
Retainer
Front
Drum

: Rubber grease points
: Brake grease points
: N·m (kg·m, ft-lb)

82629G52

Fig. 57 Rear drum brake assembly—LT23B type

applied to the pivot points at the ends of the brake shoes. Grease the shoe locating buttons on the backing plate, also. Be careful not to get grease on the linings or drums.

7. Install the adjuster assembly (rotate nut until adjuster rod is at its shortest point) between brake shoes. Place one shoe in the adjuster and piston slots, and pry the other shoe into position. Install hold down springs.

8. Replace the drums (adjust wheel bearings if necessary) and wheels. Adjust the brakes. Bleed the hydraulic system if necessary.

9. Reconnect the handbrake, making sure that it does not cause the shoes to drag when it is released.

Wheel Cylinder

REMOVAL & INSTALLATION

❊❊ CAUTION

Brake shoes may contain asbestos, which has been determined to be a cancer causing agent. Never clean the brake surfaces with compressed air! Avoid inhaling any dust from any brake surface! When cleaning brake surfaces, use a commercially available brake cleaning fluid.

1. Refer to the Brake Drum, Removal and Installation procedures, in this section and remove the brake drum.
2. Disconnect the flare nut and the brake tube from the wheel cylinder, then plug the line to prevent dirt from entering the system.
3. Remove the brake shoes from the backing plate.
4. Remove the wheel cylinder-to-backing plate bolts and the wheel cylinders.

➡**If the wheel cylinder is difficult to remove, bump it with a soft hammer to release it from the backing plate.**

5. Install the wheel cylinder assembly to the backing plate.
6. Connect all brake lines and install the brake drum.
7. Bleed the brake system.

OVERHAUL

◆ **See Figures 58 thru 67**

Wheel cylinder overhaul kits may be available, but often at little or no savings over a reconditioned wheel cylinder. It often makes sense with these components to substitute a new or reconditioned part instead of attempting an overhaul.

TCCA9P13

Fig. 58 Remove the outer boots from the wheel cylinder

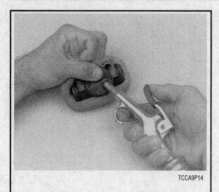

Fig. 59 Compressed air can be used to remove the pistons and seals

Fig. 60 Remove the pistons, cup seals and spring from the cylinder

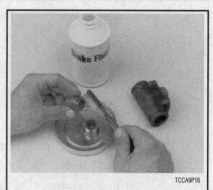

Fig. 61 Use brake fluid and a soft brush to clean the pistons . . .

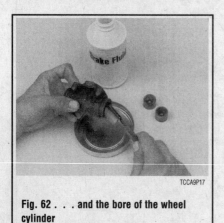

Fig. 62 . . . and the bore of the wheel cylinder

Fig. 63 Once cleaned and inspected, the wheel cylinder is ready for assembly

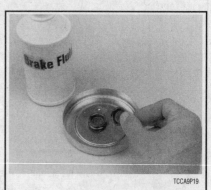

Fig. 64 Lubricate the cup seals with brake fluid

Fig. 65 Install the spring, then the cup seals in the bore

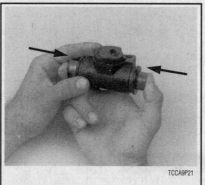

Fig. 66 Lightly lubricate the pistons, then install them

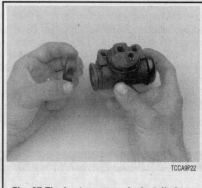

Fig. 67 The boots can now be installed over the wheel cylinder ends

If no replacement is available, or you would prefer to overhaul your wheel cylinders, the following procedure may be used. When rebuilding and installing wheel cylinders, avoid getting any contaminants into the system. Always use clean, new, high quality brake fluid. If dirty or improper fluid has been used, it will be necessary to drain the entire system, flush the system with proper brake fluid, replace all rubber components, then refill and bleed the system.

1. Remove the wheel cylinder from the vehicle and place on a clean workbench.

2. First remove and discard the old rubber boots, then withdraw the pistons. Piston cylinders are equipped with seals and a spring assembly, all located behind the pistons in the cylinder bore.

3. Remove the remaining inner components, seals and spring assembly. Compressed air may be useful in removing these components. If no compressed air is available, be VERY careful not to score the wheel cylinder bore when removing parts from it. Discard all components for which replacements were supplied in the rebuild kit.

4. Wash the cylinder and metal parts in denatured alcohol or clean brake fluid.

⁂ WARNING

Never use a mineral-based solvent such as gasoline, kerosene or paint thinner for cleaning purposes. These solvents will swell rubber components and quickly deteriorate them.

5. Allow the parts to air dry or use compressed air. Do not use rags for cleaning, since lint will remain in the cylinder bore.

6. Inspect the piston and replace it if it shows scratches.

7. Lubricate the cylinder bore and seals using clean brake fluid.

8. Position the spring assembly.

9. Install the inner seals, then the pistons.

10. Insert the new boots into the counterbores by hand. Do not lubricate the boots.

11. Install the wheel cylinder.

PARKING BRAKE

Cables

ADJUSTMENT

1. Pull up the hand brake lever, counting the number of notches for full engagement. Full engagement should be:

To install:
- 200SX: 7–8 notches
- 240SX: 6–8 notches
- 1982–88 Stanza sedan: 9–11 notches
- 1989–92 Stanza sedan: 11–13 notches
- 2WD Stanza Wagon: 11–17 notches
- 4WD Stanza Wagon: 8–9 notches

2. Release the parking brake.

3. Except on 200SX, adjust the lever stroke by loosening the lock-nut and tightening the adjusting nut to reduce the number of notches necessary for full engagement. Tighten the lock-nut. The lock-nut and adjuster can be found inside the handbrake assembly, in the passenger compartment. Some vehicles just have an adjusting nut. Access to the lock-nut is gained by removing the parking brake console or through an access hole in the console itself. On 200SX, the lever stroke is adjusted by turning the equalizer under the vehicle.

4. Check the adjustment and repeat as necessary.

5. After adjustment, check to see that the rear brake levers, at the calipers, return to their full off positions when the lever is released, and that the rear cables are not slack when the lever is released.

REMOVAL & INSTALLATION

▶ **See Figures 68, 69 and 70**

Front Cable

1. Remove the parking brake console box.
2. Remove the heat insulator, if equipped.
3. Remove the front passenger seat, if required.
4. Disconnect the warning lamp switch plate connector.
5. Unbolt the lever from the floor.
6. Working from under the vehicle, remove the lock-nut, adjusting nut and equalizer.
7. Pull the front cable out through the compartment and remove it from the vehicle.

➡ **On some vehicles it may be necessary to separate the front cable from the lever by breaking the pin.**

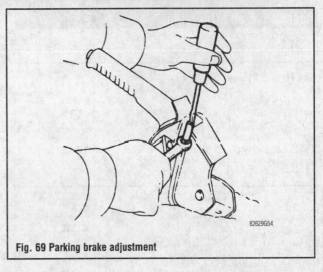

Fig. 69 Parking brake adjustment

8. Installation is the reverse of the removal procedure. Adjust the lever stroke.

Rear Cable

1. Back off on the adjusting nut or equalizer to loosen the cable tension.
2. Working from underneath the vehicle, disconnect the cable at the equalizer.
3. Remove the cable lock plate from the rear suspension member.
4. Disconnect the cable from the rear brakes.
5. Disconnect the cable from the suspension arm.
6. Remove the cable.
7. Installation is the reverse of the removal procedure. Adjust the lever stroke.

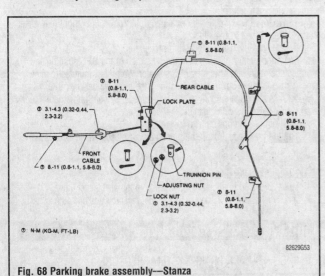

Fig. 68 Parking brake assembly—Stanza

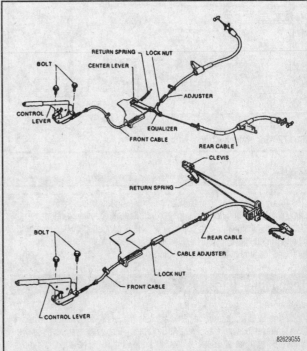

Fig. 70 Two common types of parking brake cables—most vehicles are similar

FOUR WHEEL ANTI-LOCK BRAKE SYSTEM

Description and Operation

STANZA

♦ **See Figures 71 and 72**

The Anti-lock Brake System (ABS) system employs a speed sensor at each wheel sending signals to the ECU. The control unit can trigger any or all of 4 solenoids within the hydraulic actuator. This system allows optimal control of the braking effort at each wheel. This model use a Dual Proportioning Valve (DPV) to further control distribution to the rear wheels. On this model the primary circuit is the right front and left rear wheels.

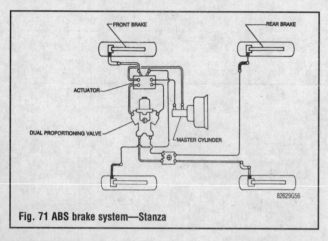

Fig. 71 ABS brake system—Stanza

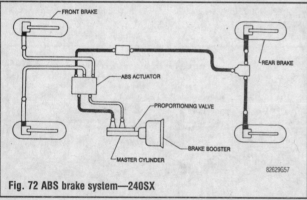

Fig. 72 ABS brake system—240SX

240SX

The Anti-lock Brake System (ABS) system uses a 3-solenoid system within the actuator. Brake fluid line pressure is controlled separately to each of the wheels, while the signal line to both rear wheels is controlled by the remaining solenoid. This model uses only 3 sensors, one at each front wheel and one mounted in the side of the differential housing.

Troubleshooting

When the ECU detects a fault, the ANTI-LOCK warning lamp on the dash will be light. The ECU will perform a self-diagnosis to identify the problem. When a vehicle is presented with a apparent ABS problem, it must be test driven above 19 mph (30 km/h) for at least 1 minute; this allows the ECU time to test the system and store a diagnostic code if possible.

The stored code will be displayed by the flashing of the LED on the electronic control unit. The display begins when the vehicle comes to a full stop after the self-diagnosis process. The engine must be running for the code to display. The stored code will repeat after a 5–10 second pause.

➥**Both the ANTI-LOCK warning lamp and the LED will remain light after repairs are made. The vehicle must be driven above 19 mph for at least 1 minute. If the ECU performs the self-diagnosis and finds no fault, the lamps will extinguish.**

After the visual checks of the complete brake system, (normal brake system problems corrected) and detailed description is obtained of the problem, proceed as follows:
1. Refer to the Symptom Chart to determine diagnostic path.
2. Perform preliminary and visual checks.
3. Put the vehicle through the self-diagnosis cycle and record any fault code. Refer to the proper Diagnostic Chart for the code.
4. If no code is stored, refer to other diagnostic procedures listed in the Symptom Chart.
5. The diagnostic Charts direct the testing of components, connectors and ground circuits. Once the problem is identified, repair or replace items as needed.
6. Put the vehicle through another self-diagnosis cycle, checking for both stored codes and proper ABS performance.

➥**Certain driver induced faults, such as not releasing the parking brake fully, excessive wheel spin on low traction surfaces, high speed acceleration or riding the brake pedal may set fault codes and trigger a warning lamp. These induced faults are not system failures but examples of vehicle performance outside the parameters of the control unit.**

Brake System Bleeding

PRECAUTIONS

- Carefully monitor the brake fluid level in the master cylinder at all times during the bleeding procedure. Keep the reservoir full at all times.
- Only use brake fluid that meets or exceeds DOT 3 specifications.
- Place a suitable container under the master cylinder to avoid spillage of brake fluid.
- Do not allow brake fluid to come in contact with any painted surface. Brake fluid makes excellent paint remover.
- Make sure to use the proper bleeding sequence.

BLEEDING PROCEDURE

The brake bleeding sequence varies from vehicle to vehicle and whether the vehicle is equipped with ABS or not. Bleeding sequences are as follows:
- **240SX (with ABS)**—left rear caliper, right rear caliper, right front caliper, left front caliper, front side air bleeder on ABS actuator, rear side air bleeder on ABS actuator
- **Stanza**—left wheel cylinder or caliper, right front caliper, right rear wheel cylinder or caliper, left front caliper

To bleed the brakes, use the following procedure:
1. If equipped with ABS, turn the ignition switch to the **OFF** position and disconnect the connectors from the ABS actuator. Wait a few minutes to allow for the system to bleed down, then disconnect the negative battery cable.
2. Connect a transparent vinyl tube to the bleeder valve. Submerge the tube in a container half filled with clean brake fluid.
3. Fully depress the brake pedal several times.
4. With the brake pedal depressed, open the air bleeder valve to release the air.
5. Close the air bleeder valve.
6. Release the brake pedal slowly.
7. Repeat Steps 36 until clear fluid flows from the air bleeder valve.
8. Check the fluid level in the master cylinder reservoir and add as necessary.

Anti-Lock Brake System Service

RELIEVING ANTI-LOCK BRAKE SYSTEM PRESSURE

To relieve the pressure from the ABS system, turn the ignition switch to the **OFF** position. Disconnect the connectors from the ABS actuator. Wait a few minutes to allow for the system to bleed down, then disconnect the negative battery cable.

Actuator

REMOVAL & INSTALLATION

1. Relieve the pressure from the ABS system.
2. Disconnect the negative battery cable.
3. Disconnect the electrical harness connectors from the actuator.
4. Disconnect the fluid lines from the actuator. Plug the ends of the lines to prevent leakage.
5. On 240SX, remove the relay bracket.
6. Remove the actuator mounting bolts and nuts.
7. Remove the actuator from the mounting bracket.

To install:
8. Position the actuator onto the mounting bracket.
9. Install the actuator mounting fasteners.
10. On 240SX, install the relay bracket.
11. Connect the fluid lines and the harness connectors.
12. Connect the negative battery cable.
13. Bleed the brake system.

Front Wheel Sensor

REMOVAL & INSTALLATION

▶ **See Figures 73, 74 and 75**

1. Raise and support the vehicle safely.
2. Remove the front wheels.
3. Disconnect the sensor harness connector.
4. Detach the sensor mounting brackets.
5. Unbolt the sensor from the rear of the steering knuckle.
6. Withdraw the sensor from the sensor rotor. Remove the sensor mounting brackets from the sensor wiring.

➥During removal and installation, take care not to damage the sensor or the teeth of the rotor.

To install:
7. Transfer the mounting brackets to the new sensor. Insert the sensor through the opening in the rear of the knuckle and engage the sensor with the rotor teeth.
8. Install the sensor mounting bolts. Check and adjust the sensor-to-rotor clearance as described below. Once the clearance is set, tighten the sensor mounting bolt(s) to 8–12 ft. lbs. on the 240SX and 13–17 ft. lbs. on the Stanza.
9. Position and install the sensor mounting brackets. Make the sure the sensor wiring is routed properly.
10. Connect the sensor harness connector.
11. Mount the front wheels and lower the vehicle.

Rear Wheel Sensor

REMOVAL & INSTALLATION

▶ **See Figures 76 and 77**

1. Raise and support the vehicle safely.
2. Remove the rear wheels.
3. Disconnect the sensor harness connector.
4. Detach the sensor mounting brackets.
5. Remove the sensor mounting bolts.
6. On Stanza, withdraw the sensor from the rear gusset. On 240SX, the sensor is located on the side of the differential carrier near the driveshaft companion flange.
7. Remove the sensor mounting brackets from the sensor wiring.

To install:
8. Transfer the mounting brackets to the new sensor.
9. Install the sensor. Check and adjust the sensor-to-rotor clearance as described below. Once the clearance is set, tighten the sensor mounting bolt(s) to 13–20 ft. lbs.
10. Install the sensor mounting brackets. Make the sure the sensor wiring is routed properly.
11. Connect the sensor harness connector.
12. Mount the rear wheels and lower the vehicle.

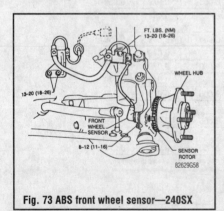

Fig. 73 ABS front wheel sensor—240SX

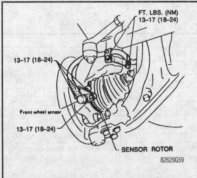

Fig. 74 ABS front wheel sensor—Stanza

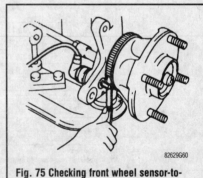

Fig. 75 Checking front wheel sensor-to-rotor clearance

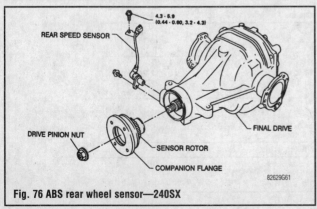

Fig. 76 ABS rear wheel sensor—240SX

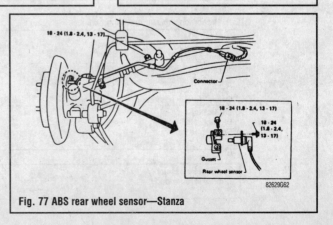

Fig. 77 ABS rear wheel sensor—Stanza

WHEEL SENSOR CLEARANCE ADJUSTMENT

▶ **See Figure 78**

1. Install the rear wheel sensor.
2. Check the clearance between the edge of the sensor and rotor teeth using a feeler gauge. Clearances should be as follows:

    a. On 240SX, rear wheel sensor clearance should 0.0138–0.0246 in. (0.035–0.625mm).

    b. On Stanza, the clearance should be 0.008–0.039 in. (0.2–1.0mm).

3. To adjust the clearance, loosen the sensor mounting bolt(s) and move the sensor back and forth until the clearance is as specified.

4. Once the clearance is set, tighten the sensor mounting bolt(s) to 13–20 ft. lbs.

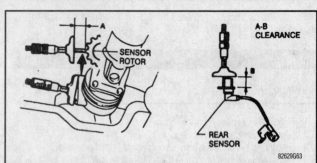

82629G63

Fig. 78 Checking rear wheel sensor-to-rotor clearance—240SX model

BRAKE SPECIFICATIONS

All measurements in inches unless noted

Year	Model	Master Cylinder Bore	Brake Disc Minimum Thickness	Brake Disc Maximum Runout	Brake Drum Diameter Original Inside Diameter	Brake Drum Diameter Max. Wear Limit	Brake Drum Diameter Maximum Machine Diameter	Minimum Lining Thickness Front	Minimum Lining Thickness Rear
1982	200SX	0.875	0.413/0.339	0.0047/0.0059	—	—	—	0.079	0.079
	Stanza	0.812	0.630	0.0059	8.000	8.090	8.060	0.080	0.059
1983	200SX	0.875	0.413/0.339	0.0047/0.0059	—	—	—	0.079	0.079
	Stanza	0.812	0.630	0.0028	8.000	8.090	8.060	0.079	0.059
1984	200SX	0.938	0.630/0.354	0.0028/0.0028	9.000	9.090	9.060	—	—
	Stanza	0.812	0.63	0.0028	8.000	8.090	8.060	0.079	0.059
1985	200SX	0.937	0.630/0.354	0.0028	—	—	—	0.08	0.08
	Stanza	0.812	0.630	0.0028	8.000	8.090	8.060	0.079	0.059
1986	200SX	0.937	0.630/0.354	0.0028	—	—	—	0.08	0.08
	Stanza	0.812	0.630	0.0028	8.000	8.090	8.060	0.079	0.059
1987	200SX	0.937	0.630/0.354	0.0028	—	—	—	0.08	0.08
	Stanza	0.812	0.630	0.0028	8.000	8.090	8.060	0.079	0.059
1988	200SX	0.937	0.630/0.354	0.0028	—	—	—	0.08	0.08
	Stanza	0.812	0.630	0.0028	8.000	8.090	8.060	0.079	0.059
1989	240SX	0.875	0.709	0.0028	—	—	—	0.079	0.079
	Stanza	1.000	0.787	0.0028	9.000	9.090	9.060	0.079	0.079
1990	240SX	0.937	0.709	0.0028	—	—	—	0.079	0.079
	Stanza	1.000	0.787	0.0028	9.000	9.090	9.060	0.079	0.079
1991	240SX	0.937	0.709	0.0028	—	—	—	0.079	0.079
	Stanza	1.000	0.787	0.0028	9.000	9.090	9.060	0.079	0.079
1992	240SX	0.937	0.709	0.0028	—	—	—	0.079	0.079
	Stanza	1.000	0.787	0.0028	9.000	9.090	9.060	0.079	0.079

NOTE: Minimum lining thickness is as recommended by the manufacturer. Due to variation in state inspection regulations, the minimum allowable thickness may be different than recommended by the manufacturer.

82629C01

TORQUE SPECIFICATIONS

Component	English	Metric
Dual Proportioning valve mounting bolt:	3-4 ft. lbs.	4-5 Nm
Power Booster		
Booster mounting nuts:	9-12 ft. lbs.	13-16 Nm
Master cylinder-to-booster nuts:	6-8 ft. lbs.	8-11 Nm
Disc Brakes		
Brake hose-to-caliper:	12-14 ft. lbs.	17-20 Nm
Caliper retaining bolts:	16-23 ft. lbs.	22-31 Nm
Caliper torque member:	53-72 ft. lbs.	72-97 Nm
Drum Brakes		
Backing plate nut:	18-25 ft. lbs.	25-33 Nm
Brake tube flare nut:	11-13 ft. lbs.	15-18 Nm
Wheel cylinder attaching nuts:	4-7 ft. lbs.	6-8 Nm
Air bleeder valve:	5-7 ft. lbs.	7-9 Nm
Parking brake assembly		
Control lever to body:	8-11 ft. lbs.	5-8 Nm
Clamp to body:	2-3 ft. lbs.	3-4 Nm

82629C07

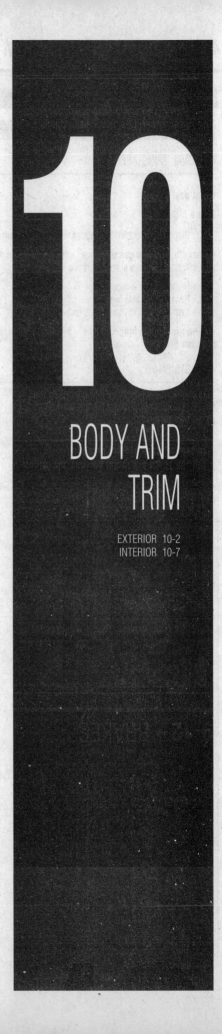

10

BODY AND TRIM

EXTERIOR

Doors

REMOVAL & INSTALLATION

Front and Rear

▶ **See Figure 1**

1. Place a jack or stand beneath the door to support its weight.

➡ **Place a rag between the lower edge of the door and jack or stand to prevent damage to painted surface.**

2. Remove door without hinge.
3. Remove the door hinge.
4. Installation is in the reverse order of removal.

➡ **When installing hinge, coat the hinge link with recommended multi-purpose grease.**

ADJUSTMENT

Front and Rear

▶ **See Figures 2 and 3**

Proper door alignment can be obtained by adjusting the door hinge and door lock striker. The door hinge and striker can be moved up and down fore and aft in enlarged holes by loosening the attaching bolts.

➡ **The door should be adjusted for an even and parallel fit for the door opening and surrounding body panels.**

Hood

REMOVAL & INSTALLATION

1. Open the hood and protect the body with covers to protect the painted surfaces.
2. Mark the hood hinge locations on the hood for proper reinstallation.
3. Holding both sides of the hood, unscrew the bolts securing the hinge to the hood. This operation requires a helper.
4. Installation is the reverse of removal.

ALIGNMENT

▶ **See Figures 4, 5 and 6**

The hood can be adjusted with bolts attaching the hood to the hood hinges, hood lock mechanism and hood bumpers. Adjust the hood for an even fit between the front fenders.

1. Adjust the hood fore and aft by loosening the bolts attaching the hood to the hinge and repositioning hood.
2. Loosen the hood bumper lock nuts and lower bumpers until they do not contact the front of the hood when the hood is closed.
3. Set the striker at the center of the hood lock, and tighten the hood lock securing bolts temporarily.
4. Raise the two hood bumpers until the hood is flush with the fenders.
5. Tighten the hood lock securing bolts after the proper adjustment has been obtained.

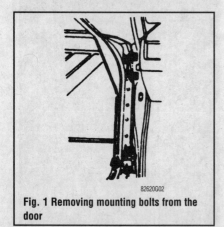

Fig. 1 Removing mounting bolts from the door

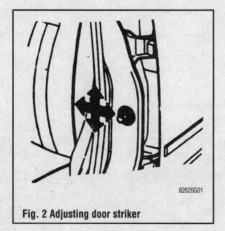

Fig. 2 Adjusting door striker

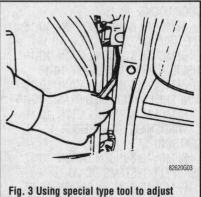

Fig. 3 Using special type tool to adjust hinge

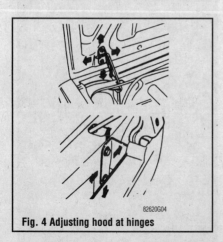

Fig. 4 Adjusting hood at hinges

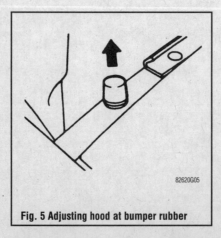

Fig. 5 Adjusting hood at bumper rubber

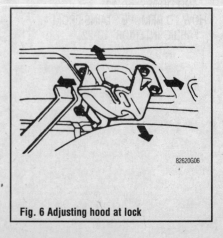

Fig. 6 Adjusting hood at lock

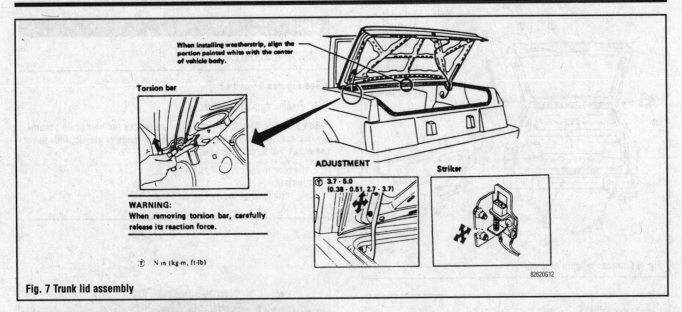

Fig. 7 Trunk lid assembly

Trunk Lid

REMOVAL & INSTALLATION

▶ **See Figure 7**

1. Open the trunk lid and position a cloth or cushion to protect the painted areas.
2. Mark the trunk lid hinge locations or trunk lid for proper reinstallation.
3. Support the trunk lid by hand and remove the bolts attaching the trunk lid to the hinge. Then remove the trunk lid.
4. Installation is the reverse of removal.

ALIGNMENT

▶ **See Figure 7**

1. Loosen the trunk lid hinge attaching bolts until they are just loose enough to move the trunk lid.
2. Move the trunk lid for and aft to obtain a flush fit between the trunk lid and the rear fender.
3. To obtain a snug fit between the trunk lid and weather-strip, loosen the trunk lid lock striker attaching bolts enough to move the lid, working the striker up and down and from side to side as required.
4. After the adjustment is made tighten the striker bolts securely.

Hatchback or Tailgate Lid

REMOVAL & INSTALLATION

▶ **See Figures 8, 9 and 10**

1. Open the lid and disconnect the rear defogger harness if so equipped.
2. Mark the hinge locations on the lid for proper relocation.
3. Support the lid by hand and remove the bolts attaching it to the hinge. Remove the lid.
4. Installation is the reverse of removal.

ALIGNMENT

▶ **See Figures 8, 9 and 10**

1. Open the hatchback lid.
2. Loosen the lid hinge to body attaching bolts until they are just loose enough to move the lid.
3. Move the lid up and down to obtain a flush fit between the lid and the roof.
4. After adjustment is completed tighten the hinge attaching bolts securely.

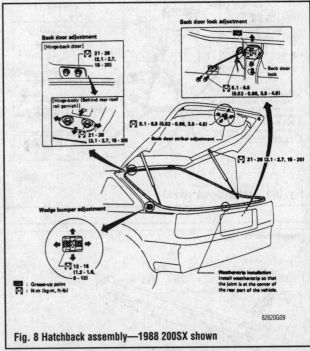

Fig. 8 Hatchback assembly—1988 200SX shown

Bumpers

REMOVAL & INSTALLATION

Front and Rear

▶ **See Figure 11**

1. Disconnect all electrical connectors at bumper assembly if so equipped.
2. Remove bumper mounting bolts and bumper assembly.
3. Remove shock absorbers from bumper.

✳✳ CAUTION

The shock absorber is filled with a high pressure gas and should not be disassembled, drilled or exposed to an open flame.

4. Install shock absorbers and bumper in reverse order of removal.

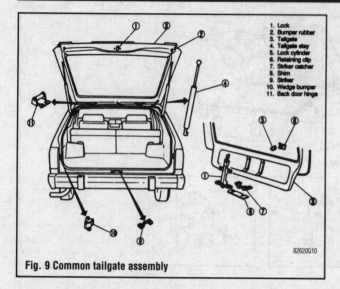

1.	Lock
2.	Bumper rubber
3.	Tailgate
4.	Tailgate stay
5.	Lock cylinder
6.	Retaining clips
7.	Striker catcher
8.	Shim
9.	Striker
10.	Wedge bumper
11.	Back door hinge

82620G10

Fig. 9 Common tailgate assembly

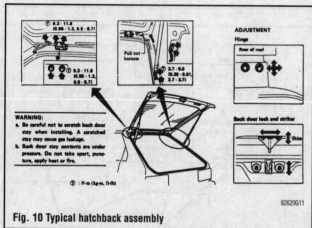

WARNING:
a. Be careful not to scratch back door stay when installing. A scratched stay may cause gas leakage.
b. Back door stay contents are under pressure. Do not take apart, puncture, apply heat or fire.

ⓣ : N·m (kg-m, ft-lb)

82620G11

Fig. 10 Typical hatchback assembly

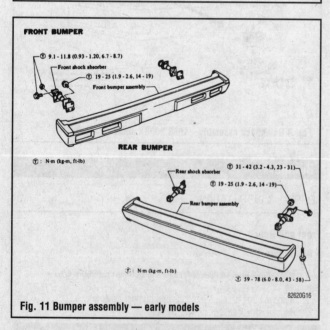

FRONT BUMPER

ⓣ 9.1 - 11.8 (0.93 - 1.20, 6.7 - 8.7)
Front shock absorber
ⓣ 19 - 25 (1.9 - 2.6, 14 - 19)
Front bumper assembly

REAR BUMPER

ⓣ : N·m (kg-m, ft-lb)

Rear shock absorber
ⓣ 31 - 42 (3.2 - 4.3, 23 - 31)
ⓣ 19 - 25 (1.9 - 2.6, 14 - 19)
Rear bumper assembly

ⓣ : N·m (kg-m, ft-lb)

ⓣ 59 - 78 (6.0 - 8.0, 43 - 58)

82620G16

Fig. 11 Bumper assembly — early models

Grille

REMOVAL & INSTALLATION

▶ **See Figures 12 and 13**

1. Remove radiator grille bracket bolts.

➡ Some early vehicles may use clips to hold the radiator grille assembly in place. The radiator grille assembly is made of plastic, thus never use excessive force to remove it.

2. Remove radiator grille from the vehicle.

To install:

3. To install reverse the removal procedures.

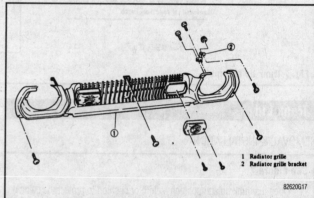

1 Radiator grille
2 Radiator grille bracket

82620G17

Fig. 12 Removing radiator grille retaining screws

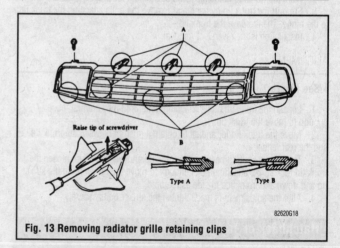

Raise tip of screwdriver

Type A   Type B

82620G18

Fig. 13 Removing radiator grille retaining clips

Outside Mirrors

REMOVAL & INSTALLATION

Manual Type

▶ **See Figures 14, 15 and 16**

1. Remove control knob handle.
2. Remove door corner finisher panel.

82620G22

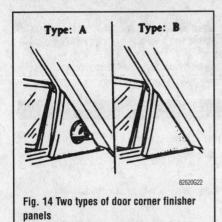

Fig. 14 Two types of door corner finisher panels

82620G23

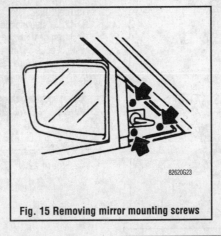

Fig. 15 Removing mirror mounting screws

82620G24

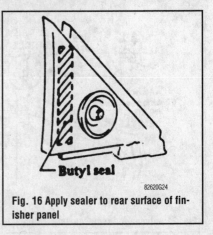

Fig. 16 Apply sealer to rear surface of finisher panel

3. Remove mirror body attaching screws, and then remove mirror body
4. Installation is in the reverse order of removal.

➡Apply sealer to the rear surface of door corner finisher panel during installation to prevent water leak.

Power Type

➧ See Figure 17

1. Remove door corner finisher panel.
2. Remove mirror body attaching screws, and then remove mirror body
3. Disconnect the electrical connection.

➡It may be necessary to remove the door trim panel to gain access to the electrical connection.

4. Installation is in the reverse order of removal.

82620G25

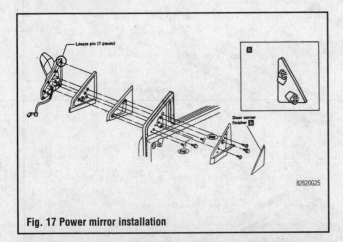

Fig. 17 Power mirror installation

Antenna

REMOVAL & INSTALLATION

Fender Mounted (Fixed)

1. Remove antenna mounting nut.
2. Disconnect the antenna lead at the radio.
3. Remove antenna from vehicle.
4. Installation is in the reverse order of removal.

Power Antenna

➧ See Figures 18, 19, 20 and 21

1. Remove the antenna nut and antenna base.
2. Remove the antenna rod while raising it by operating antenna motor. Turn radio switch from OFF to ON to operate antenna motor.

82620G26

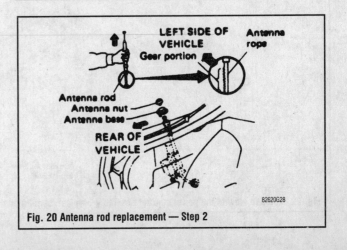

Fig. 18 Antenna location — 240SX model

82620G27

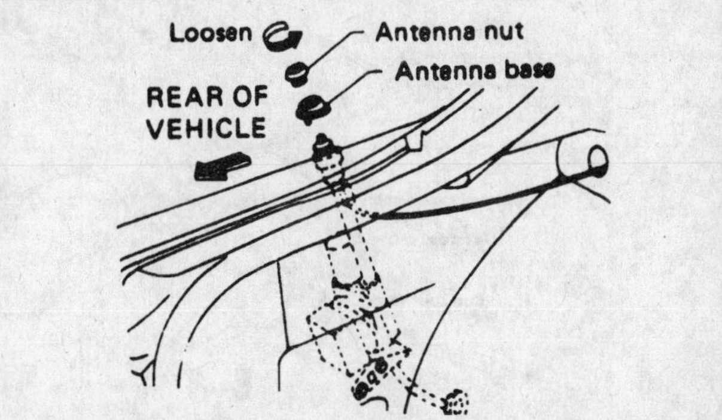

Fig. 19 Antenna rod replacement — Step 1

82620G28

Fig. 20 Antenna rod replacement — Step 2

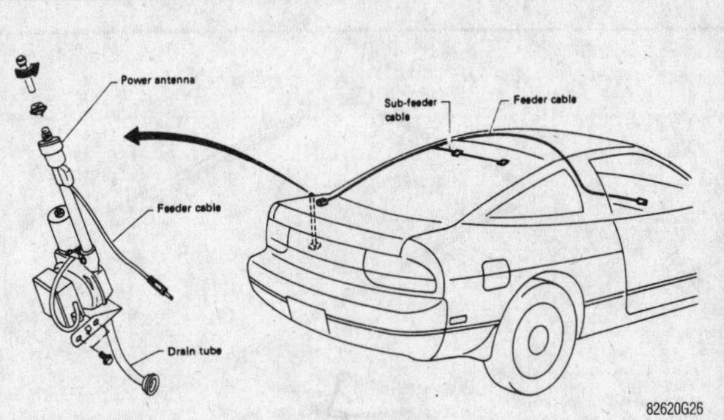

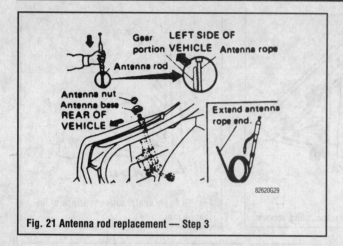

Fig. 21 Antenna rod replacement — Step 3

To install:
3. Lower antenna rod by operating antenna motor.
4. Insert gear section of antenna into place with it facing (see illustration) in the correct position for proper operation.
5. Retract antenna rod completely-attach antenna rod into housing.
6. Install antenna nut and base, check for proper operation.

Power Sunroof

REMOVAL & INSTALLATION

◆ **See Figure 22**

Refer to the exploded view illustration for the necessary information.

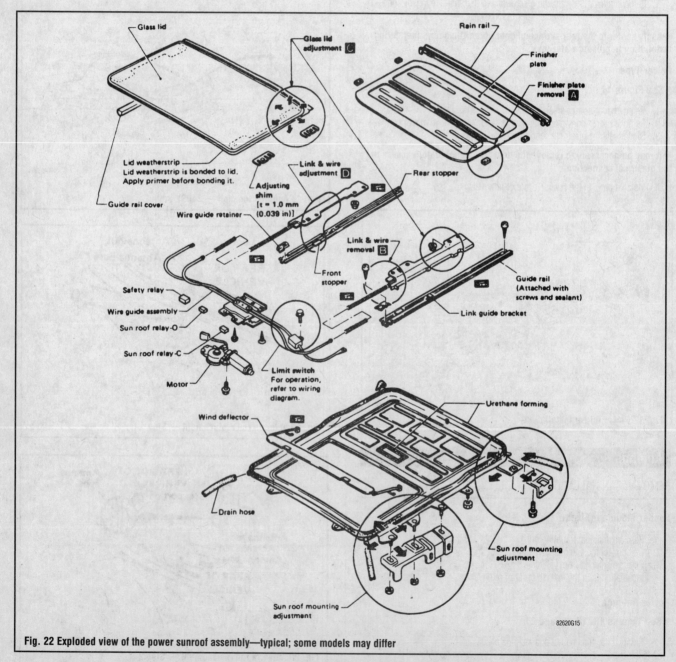

Fig. 22 Exploded view of the power sunroof assembly—typical; some models may differ

INTERIOR

▶ **See Figures 23, 24 and 25**

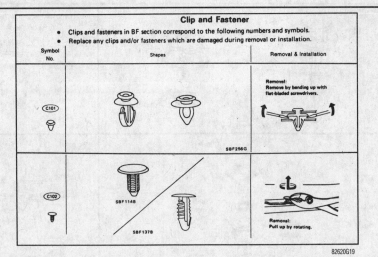

Fig. 23 Various clips and fasteners

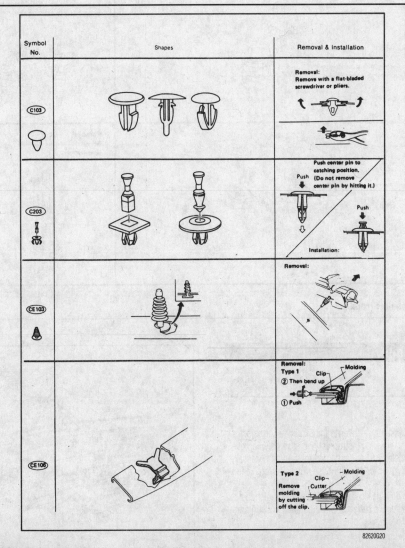

Fig. 24 Various clips and fasteners (continued)

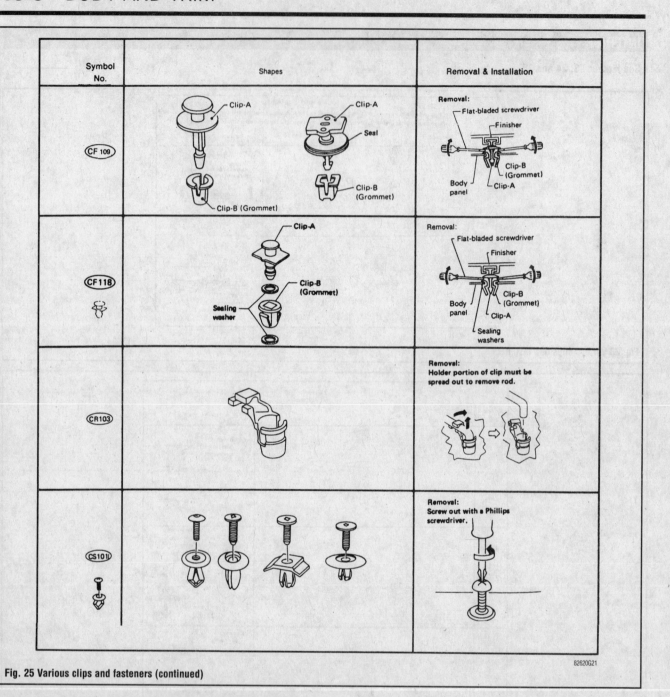

Fig. 25 Various clips and fasteners (continued)

82620G21

Instrument Pad Assembly

REMOVAL & INSTALLATION

♦ **See Figures 26 thru 33**

To remove the instrument pad assembly—refer to the Exploded Views of "Instrument Pad Assembly". When removing instrument pad assembly, remove the defroster grille, combination meter, A/C or heater control, and all necessary trim panels. These parts are mostly plastic, so do not use excessive force and be careful not to damage them.

On 240SX models, when removing the Head-Up Display (HUD) finisher, be careful not to scratch the HUD's reflective surface. To prevent this, cover the finisher and reflective surface with a protective covering.

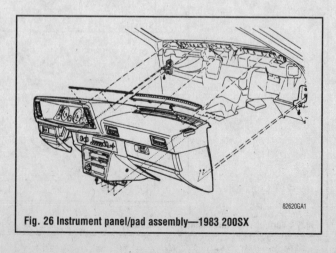

Fig. 26 Instrument panel/pad assembly—1983 200SX

82620GA1

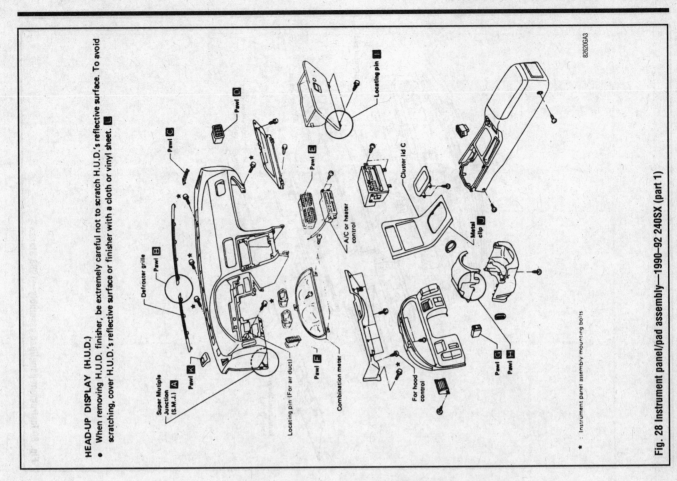

HEAD-UP DISPLAY (H.U.D.)

- When removing H.U.D. finisher, be extremely careful not to scratch H.U.D.'s reflective surface. To avoid scratching, cover H.U.D.'s reflective surface or finisher with a cloth or vinyl sheet. **L**

Fig. 28 Instrument panel/pad assembly—1990–92 240SX (part 1)

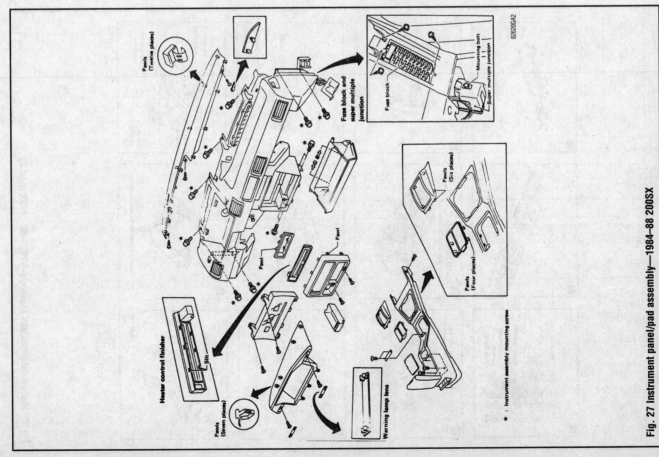

Fig. 27 Instrument panel/pad assembly—1984–88 200SX

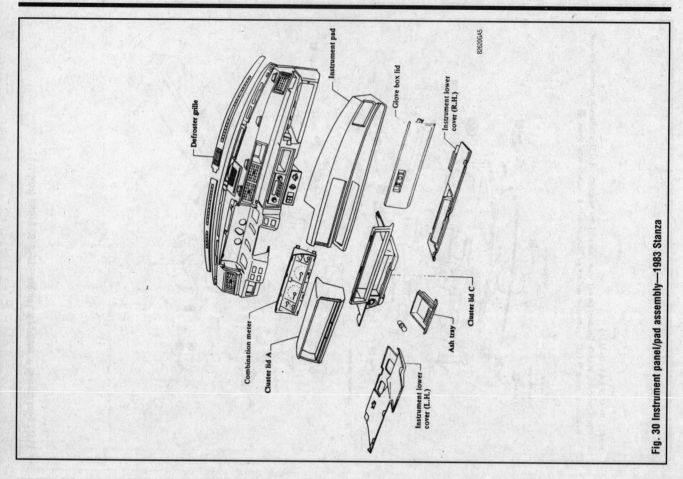

Fig. 30 Instrument panel/pad assembly—1983 Stanza

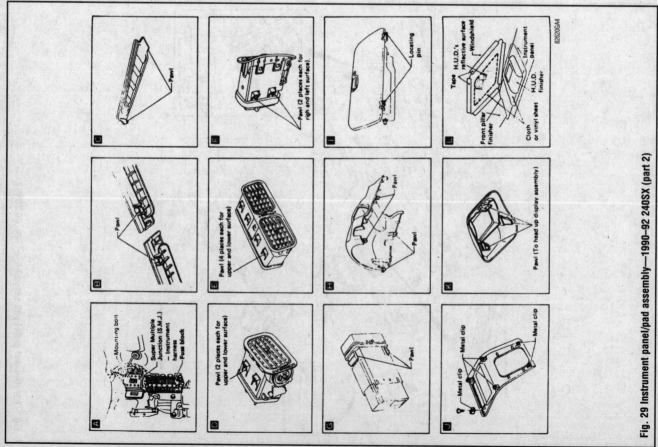

Fig. 29 Instrument panel/pad assembly—1990–92 240SX (part 2)

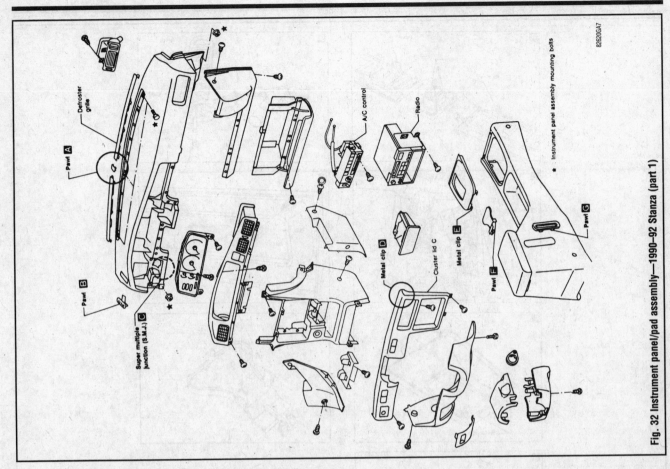

Fig. 32 Instrument panel/pad assembly—1990–92 Stanza (part 1)

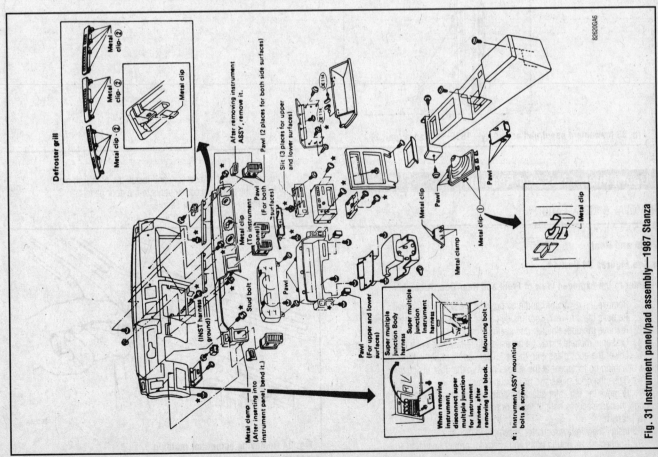

Fig. 31 Instrument panel/pad assembly—1987 Stanza

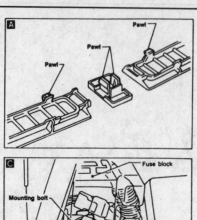

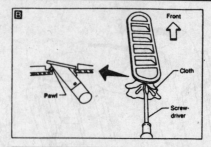

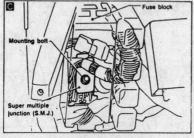

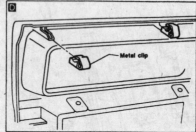

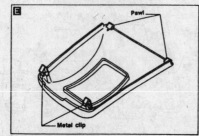

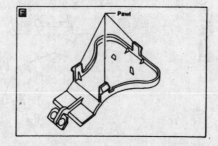

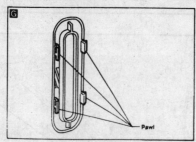

82620GA8

Fig. 33 Instrument panel/pad assembly—1990–92 Stanza (part 2)

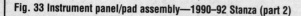

Door Panel, Glass and Regulator

REMOVAL & INSTALLATION

Front and Rear

▶ See Figures 34 thru 44

➡Refer to the exploded view of Front and Rear Door Assembly.

1. Remove the regulator handle by pushing the set pin spring off.
2. Remove the arm rest, door inside handle escutcheon and door lock.
3. Remove the door finisher and sealing screen.
4. On some models it may be necessary to remove the outer door molding.
5. Lower the door glass with the regulator handle until the regulator-to-glass attaching bolts appear at the access holes in the door inside panel.
6. Raise the door glass and draw it upwards.
7. Remove the regulator attaching bolts and remove the regulator assembly through the large access hole in the door panel.

To install:

8. Install the window regulator assembly in the door.
9. Connect all mounting bolts and check for proper operation.
10. Adjust the window if necessary and install the door trim panel.
11. Install all the attaching components to the door panel.
12. Install the window regulator handle.

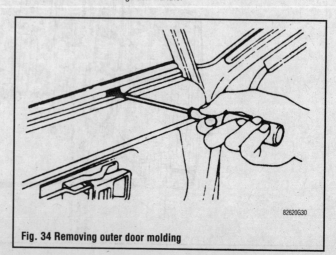

82620G30

Fig. 34 Removing outer door molding

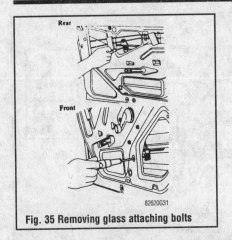

Fig. 35 Removing glass attaching bolts

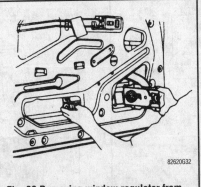

Fig. 36 Removing window regulator from the door

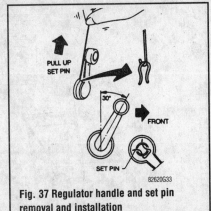

Fig. 37 Regulator handle and set pin removal and installation

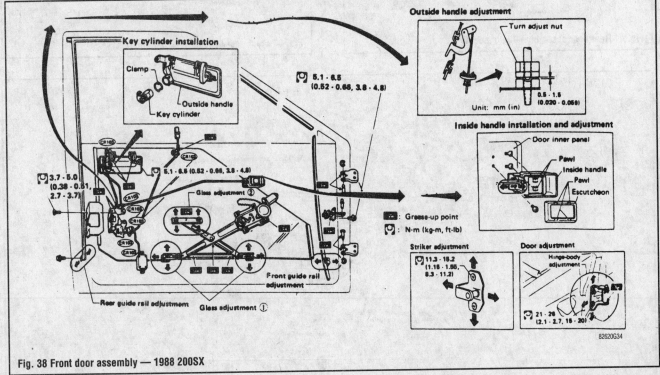

Fig. 38 Front door assembly — 1988 200SX

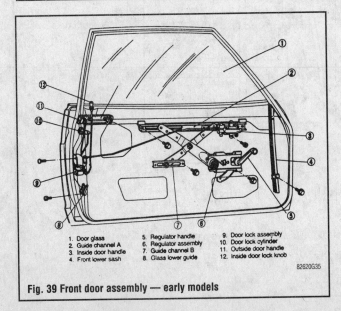

1. Door glass
2. Guide channel A
3. Inside door handle
4. Front lower sash
5. Regulator handle
6. Regulator assembly
7. Guide channel B
8. Glass lower guide
9. Door lock assembly
10. Door lock cylinder
11. Outside door handle
12. Inside door lock knob

Fig. 39 Front door assembly — early models

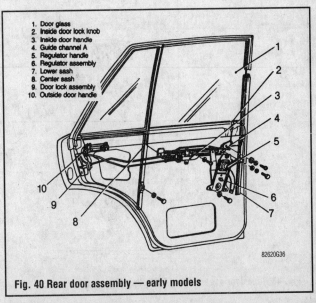

1. Door glass
2. Inside door lock knob
3. Inside door handle
4. Guide channel A
5. Regulator handle
6. Regulator assembly
7. Lower sash
8. Center sash
9. Door lock assembly
10. Outside door handle

Fig. 40 Rear door assembly — early models

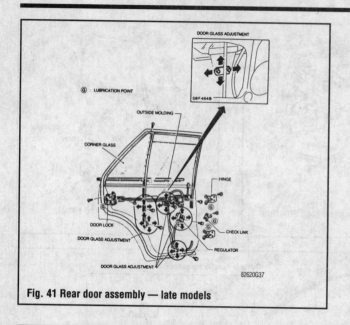

Fig. 41 Rear door assembly — late models

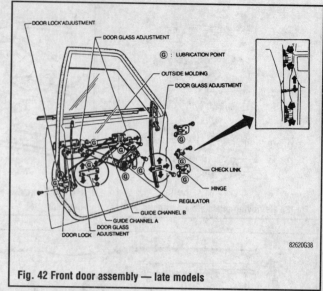

Fig. 42 Front door assembly — late models

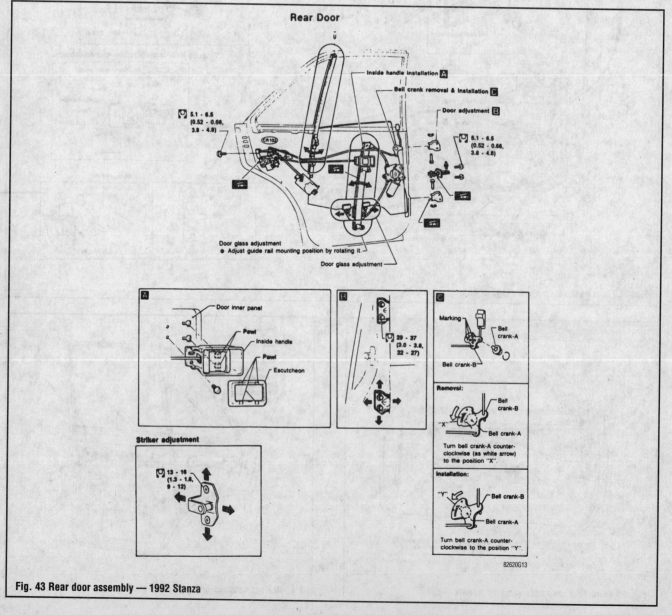

Fig. 43 Rear door assembly — 1992 Stanza

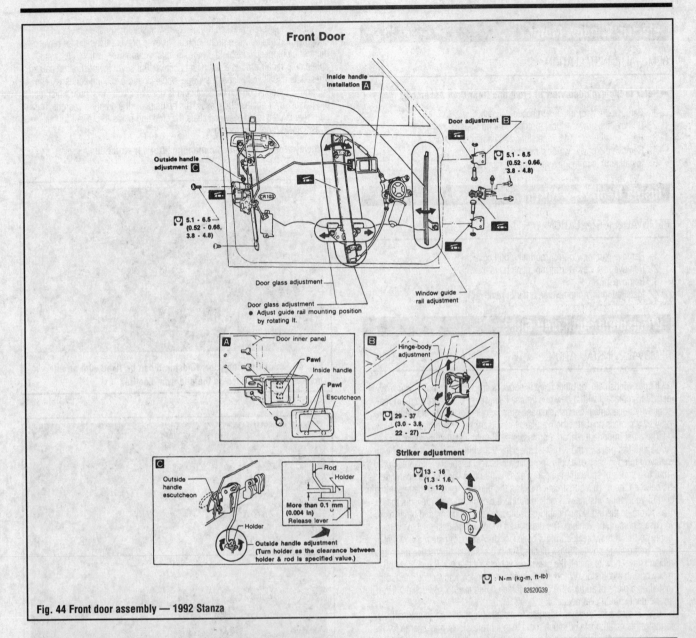

Fig. 44 Front door assembly — 1992 Stanza

Door Locks

REMOVAL & INSTALLATION

▶ **See Figure 45**

➡️ **Refer to the exploded view of Front and Rear Door Assembly.**

1. Remove the door panel and sealing screen.
2. Remove the lock cylinder from the rod by turning the resin clip.
3. Loosen the nuts attaching the outside door handle and remove the outside door handle.
4. Remove the screws retaining the inside door handle and door lock, and remove the door lock assembly from the hole in the inside of the door.
5. Remove the lock cylinder by removing the retaining clip.

To install:

6. Install the lock cylinder and clip to the door.
7. Install the door lock assembly and handles.
8. Install door panel and all attaching parts.

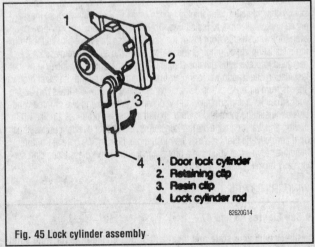

1. Door lock cylinder
2. Retaining clip
3. Resin clip
4. Lock cylinder rod

Fig. 45 Lock cylinder assembly

Electric Window Motor

REMOVAL & INSTALLATION

➡ **Refer to the exploded view of Front and Rear Door Assembly.**

1. Remove the door panel and sealing screen.
2. Remove the power widow motor mounting bolts
3. Remove all electrical connections and cable connection.
4. Remove the power window motor from the vehicle
5. Installation is in the reverse order of removal.

Inside Rear View Mirror

REMOVAL & INSTALLATION

1. Remove rear view mirror mounting bolt cover.
2. Remove rear view mirror mounting bolts.
3. Remove mirror.
4. Installation is in the reverse order of removal.

Windshield and Fixed Glass

REMOVAL & INSTALLATION

If your windshield, or other fixed window, is cracked or chipped, you may decide to replace it with a new one yourself. However, there are two main reasons why replacement windshields and other window glass should be installed only by a professional automotive glass technician: safety and cost.

The most important reason a professional should install automotive glass is for safety. The glass in the vehicle, especially the windshield, is designed with safety in mind in case of a collision. The windshield is specially manufactured from two panes of specially-tempered glass with a thin layer of transparent plastic between them. This construction allows the glass to "give" in the event that a part of your body hits the windshield during the collision, and prevents the glass from shattering, which could cause lacerations, blinding and other harm to passengers of the vehicle. The other fixed windows are designed to be tempered so that if they break during a collision, they shatter in such a way that there are no large pointed glass pieces. The professional automotive glass technician knows how to install the glass in a vehicle so that it will function optimally during a collision. Without the proper experience, knowledge and tools, installing a piece of automotive glass yourself could lead to additional harm if an accident should ever occur.

Cost is also a factor when deciding to install automotive glass yourself. Performing this could cost you much more than a professional may charge for the same job. Since the windshield is designed to break under stress, an often life saving characteristic, windshields tend to break VERY easily when an inexperienced person attempts to install one. Do-it-yourselfers buying two, three or even four windshields from a salvage yard because they have broken them during installation are common stories. Also, since the automotive glass is designed to prevent the outside elements from entering your vehicle, improper installation can lead to water and air leaks. Annoying whining noises at highway speeds from air leaks or inside body panel rusting from water leaks can add to your stress level and subtract from your wallet. After buying two or three windshields, installing them and ending up with a leak that produces a noise while driving and water damage during rainstorms, the cost of having a professional do it correctly the first time may be much more alluring. We here at Chilton, therefore, advise that you have a professional automotive glass technician service any broken glass on your vehicle.

WINDSHIELD CHIP REPAIR

▶ **See Figures 46 and 47**

➡ **Check with your state and local authorities on the laws for state safety inspection. Some states or municipalities may not allow chip repair as a viable option for correcting stone damage to your windshield.**

Although severely cracked or damaged windshields must be replaced, there is something that you can do to prolong or even prevent the need for replacement of a chipped windshield. There are many companies which offer windshield chip repair products, such as Loctite's® Bullseye™ windshield repair kit. These kits usually consist of a syringe, pedestal and a sealing adhesive. The syringe is mounted on the pedestal and is used to create a vacuum which pulls the plastic layer against the glass. This helps make the chip transparent. The adhesive is then injected which seals the chip and helps to prevent further stress cracks from developing

➡ **Always follow the specific manufacturer's instructions.**

TCCA0P00

Fig. 46 Small chips on your windshield can be fixed with an aftermarket repair kit, such as the one from Loctite®

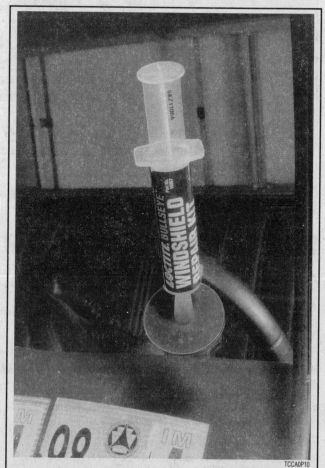

TCCA0P10

Fig. 47 Most kits use a self-stick applicator and syringe to inject the adhesive into the chip or crack

Seats

REMOVAL & INSTALLATION

Front Assembly

▶ **See Figures 48, 49 and 50**

➡On power seat models remove the seat then remove the power seat motor assembly and drive cable. Refer to the exploded view of Front Seat Assembly.

1. Remove front seat mounting bolts.
2. Remove front seat assembly.
3. Installation is in the reverse order of removal.

Rear Assembly

▶ **See Figures 51, 52 and 53**

1. Remove rear seat cushion mounting bolts.
2. Remove screw attaching luggage floor carpet.
3. Remove rear seat back by tilting forward and pulling straight up.

➡On hatchback models the rear seat back is remove similar as above.

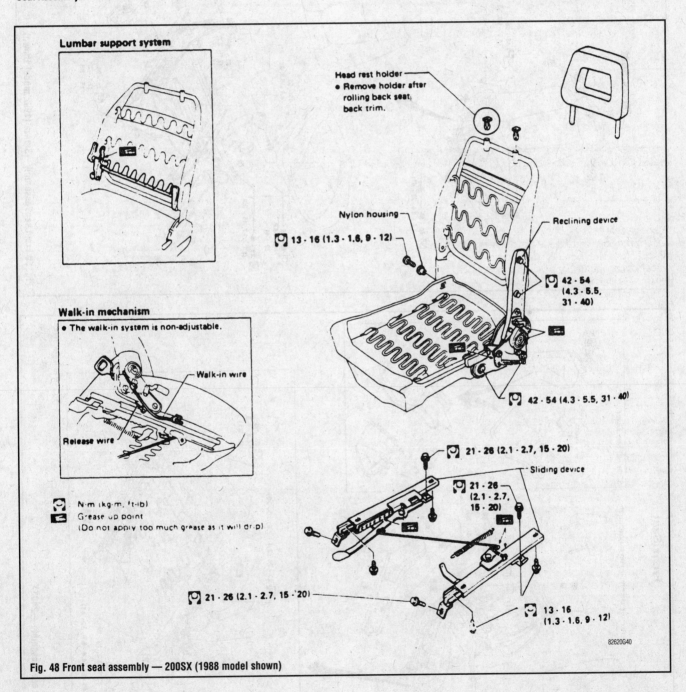

Fig. 48 Front seat assembly — 200SX (1988 model shown)

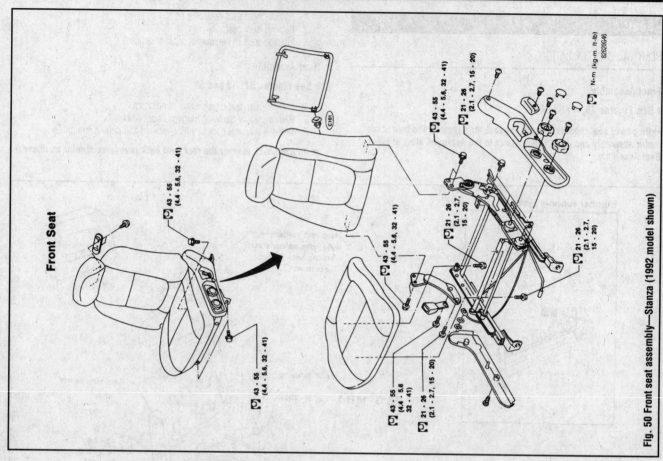

Fig. 50 Front seat assembly—Stanza (1992 model shown)

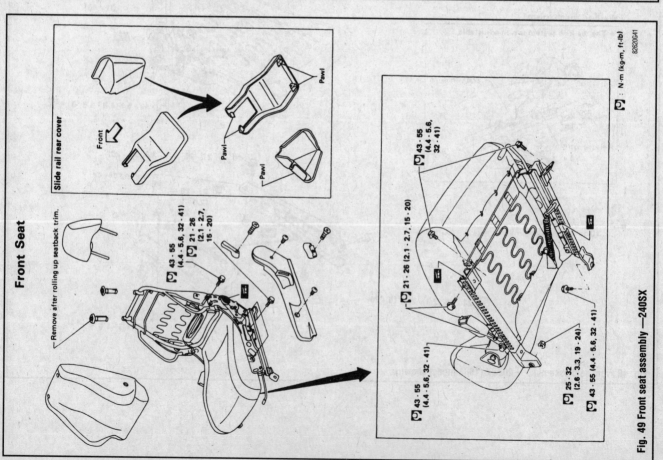

Fig. 49 Front seat assembly —240SX

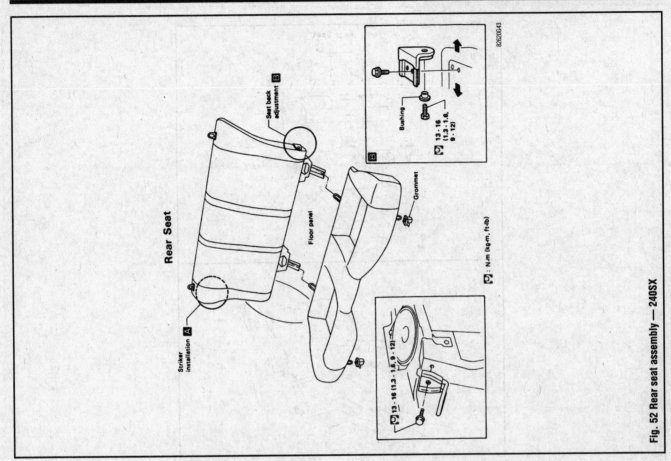

Fig. 52 Rear seat assembly — 240SX

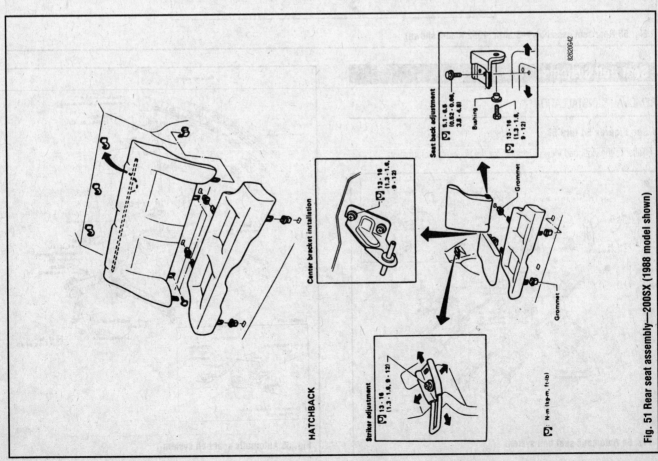

Fig. 51 Rear seat assembly—200SX (1988 model shown)

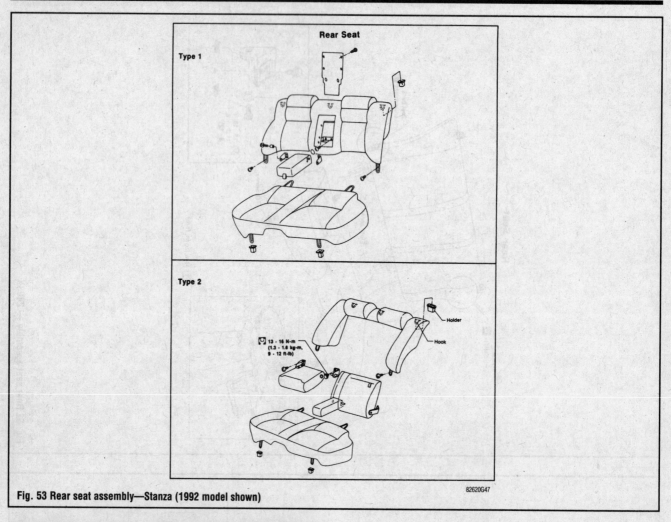

Fig. 53 Rear seat assembly—Stanza (1992 model shown)

82620G47

Seat Belt Systems

REMOVAL & INSTALLATION

▶ See Figures 54 thru 57

Refer to the exploded view illustration for the necessary information.

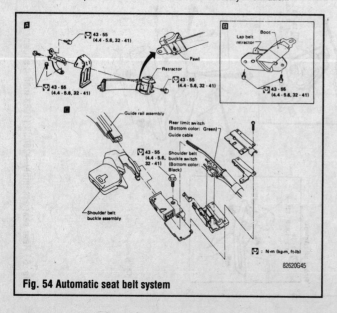

Fig. 54 Automatic seat belt system

82620G45

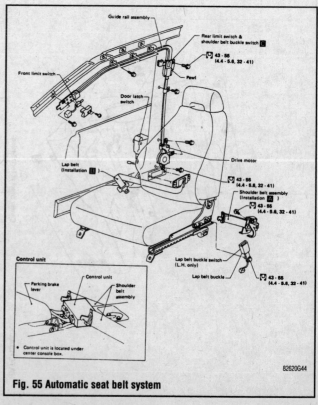

Fig. 55 Automatic seat belt system

82620G44

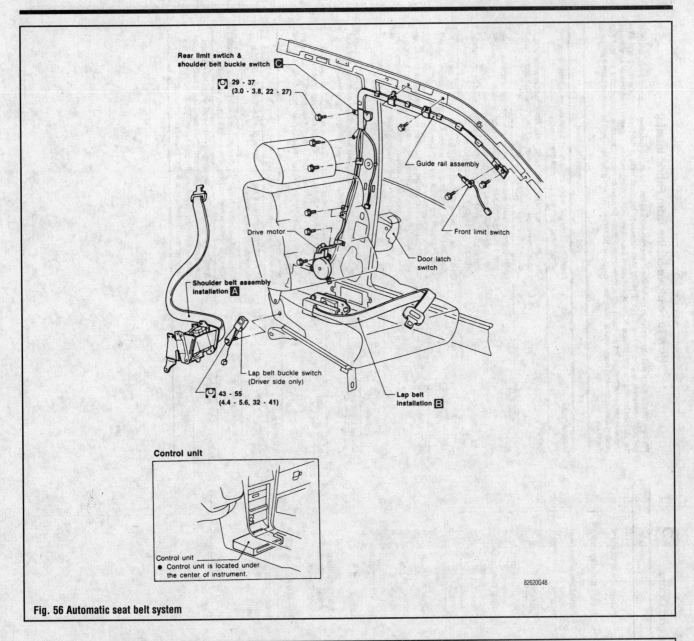

Rear limit swtich &
shoulder belt buckle switch **C**

⊡ 29 - 37
(3.0 - 3.8, 22 - 27)

Guide rail assembly

Front limit switch

Drive motor

Door latch
switch

Shoulder belt assembly
installation **A**

Lap belt buckle switch
(Driver side only)

Lap belt
installation **B**

⊡ 43 - 55
(4.4 - 5.6, 32 - 41)

Control unit

Control unit
● Control unit is located under
the center of instrument.

82620G48

Fig. 56 Automatic seat belt system

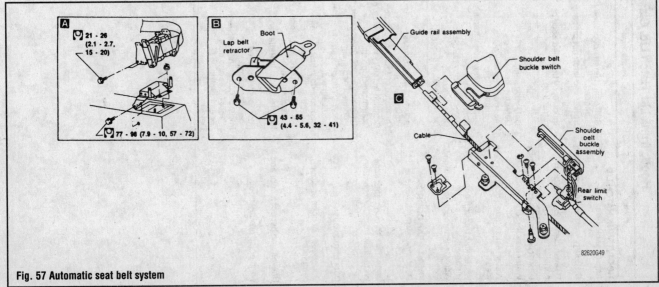

A

⊡ 21 - 26
(2.1 - 2.7,
15 - 20)

⊡ 77 - 96 (7.9 - 10, 57 - 72)

B

Boot

Lap belt
retractor

⊡ 43 - 55
(4.4 - 5.6, 32 - 41)

Guide rail assembly

Shoulder belt
buckle switch

C

Cable

Shoulder
belt
buckle
assembly

Rear limit
switch

82620G49

Fig. 57 Automatic seat belt system

Hood, Trunk Lid, Hatch Lid, Glass and Doors

Problem	Possible Cause	Correction
HOOD/TRUNK/HATCH LID		
Improper closure.	• Striker and latch not properly aligned.	• Adjust the alignment.
Difficulty locking and unlocking.	• Striker and latch not properly aligned.	• Adjust the alignment.
Uneven clearance with body panels.	• Incorrectly installed hood or trunk lid.	• Adjust the alignment.
WINDOW/WINDSHIELD GLASS		
Water leak through windshield	• Defective seal. • Defective body flange.	• Fill sealant • Correct.
Water leak through door window glass.	• Incorrect window glass installation. • Gap at upper window frame.	• Adjust position. • Adjust position.
Water leak through quarter window.	• Defective seal. • Defective body flange.	• Replace seal. • Correct.
Water leak through rear window.	• Defective seal. • Defective body flange.	• Replace seal. • Correct.
FRONT/REAR DOORS		
Door window malfunction.	• Incorrect window glass installation. • Damaged or faulty regulator.	• Adjust position.
Water leak through door edge.	• Cracked or faulty weatherstrip.	• Correct or replace.
Water leak from door center.	• Drain hole clogged. • Inadequate waterproof skeet contact or damage.	• Replace. • Remove foreign objects. • Correct or replace.
Door hard to open.	• Incorrect latch or striker adjustment.	• Adjust.
Door does not open or close completely.	• Incorrect door installation. • Defective door check strap. • Door check strap and hinge require grease.	• Adjust position. • Correct or replace. • Apply grease.
Uneven gap between door and body.	• Incorrect door installation.	• Adjust position.
Wind noise around door.	• Improperly installed weatherstrip. • Improper clearance between door glass and door weatherstrip. • Deformed door.	• Repair or replace. • Adjust. • Repair or replace.

82620C01

How to Remove Stains from Fabric Interior

For best results, spots and stains should be removed as soon as possible. Never use gasoline, lacquer thinner, acetone, nail polish remover or bleach. Use a 3' x 3' piece of cheesecloth. Squeeze most of the liquid from the fabric and wipe the stained fabric from the outside of the stain toward the center with a lifting motion. Turn the cheesecloth as soon as one side becomes soiled. When using water to remove a stain, be sure to wash the entire section after the spot has been removed to avoid water stains. Encrusted spots can be broken up with a dull knife and vacuumed before removing the stain.

Type of Stain	How to Remove It
Surface spots	Brush the spots out with a small hand brush or use a commercial preparation such as K2R to lift the stain.
Mildew	Clean around the mildew with warm suds. Rinse in cold water and soak the mildew area in a solution of 1 part table salt and 2 parts water. Wash with upholstery cleaner.
Water stains	Water stains in fabric materials can be removed with a solution made from 1 cup of table salt dissolved in 1 quart of water. Vigorously scrub the solution into the stain and rinse with clear water. Water stains in nylon or other synthetic fabrics should be removed with a commercial type spot remover.
Chewing gum, tar, crayons, shoe polish (greasy stains)	Do not use a cleaner that will soften gum or tar. Harden the deposit with an ice cube and scrape away as much as possible with a dull knife. Moisten the remainder with cleaning fluid and scrub clean.
Ice cream, candy	Most candy has a sugar base and can be removed with a cloth wrung out in warm water. Oily candy, after cleaning with warm water, should be cleaned with upholstery cleaner. Rinse with warm water and clean the remainder with cleaning fluid.
Wine, alcohol, egg, milk, soft drink (non-greasy stains)	Do not use soap. Scrub the stain with a cloth wrung out in warm water. Remove the remainder with cleaning fluid.
Grease, oil, lipstick, butter and related stains	Use a spot remover to avoid leaving a ring. Work from the outside of the stain to the center and dry with a clean cloth when the spot is gone.
Headliners (cloth)	Mix a solution of warm water and foam upholstery cleaner to give thick suds. Use only foam—liquid may streak or spot. Clean the entire headliner in one operation using a circular motion with a natural sponge.
Headliner (vinyl)	Use a vinyl cleaner with a sponge and wipe clean with a dry cloth.
Seats and door panels	Mix 1 pint upholstery cleaner in 1 gallon of water. Do not soak the fabric around the buttons.
Leather or vinyl fabric	Use a multi-purpose cleaner full strength and a stiff brush. Let stand 2 minutes and scrub thoroughly. Wipe with a clean, soft rag.
Nylon or synthetic fabrics	For normal stains, use the same procedures you would for washing cloth upholstery. If the fabric is extremely dirty, use a multi-purpose cleaner full strength with a stiff scrub brush. Scrub thoroughly in all directions and wipe with a cotton towel or soft rag.

82620C02

GLOSSARY

AIR/FUEL RATIO: The ratio of air-to-gasoline by weight in the fuel mixture drawn into the engine.

AIR INJECTION: One method of reducing harmful exhaust emissions by injecting air into each of the exhaust ports of an engine. The fresh air entering the hot exhaust manifold causes any remaining fuel to be burned before it can exit the tailpipe.

ALTERNATOR: A device used for converting mechanical energy into electrical energy.

AMMETER: An instrument, calibrated in amperes, used to measure the flow of an electrical current in a circuit. Ammeters are always connected in series with the circuit being tested.

AMPERE: The rate of flow of electrical current present when one volt of electrical pressure is applied against one ohm of electrical resistance.

ANALOG COMPUTER: Any microprocessor that uses similar (analogous) electrical signals to make its calculations.

ARMATURE: A laminated, soft iron core wrapped by a wire that converts electrical energy to mechanical energy as in a motor or relay. When rotated in a magnetic field, it changes mechanical energy into electrical energy as in a generator.

ATMOSPHERIC PRESSURE: The pressure on the Earth's surface caused by the weight of the air in the atmosphere. At sea level, this pressure is 14.7 psi at 32°F (101 kPa at 0°C).

ATOMIZATION: The breaking down of a liquid into a fine mist that can be suspended in air.

AXIAL PLAY: Movement parallel to a shaft or bearing bore.

BACKFIRE: The sudden combustion of gases in the intake or exhaust system that results in a loud explosion.

BACKLASH: The clearance or play between two parts, such as meshed gears.

BACKPRESSURE: Restrictions in the exhaust system that slow the exit of exhaust gases from the combustion chamber.

BAKELITE: A heat resistant, plastic insulator material commonly used in printed circuit boards and transistorized components.

BALL BEARING: A bearing made up of hardened inner and outer races between which hardened steel balls roll.

BALLAST RESISTOR: A resistor in the primary ignition circuit that lowers voltage after the engine is started to reduce wear on ignition components.

BEARING: A friction reducing, supportive device usually located between a stationary part and a moving part.

BIMETAL TEMPERATURE SENSOR: Any sensor or switch made of two dissimilar types of metal that bend when heated or cooled due to the different expansion rates of the alloys. These types of sensors usually function as an on/off switch.

BLOWBY: Combustion gases, composed of water vapor and unburned fuel, that leak past the piston rings into the crankcase during normal engine operation. These gases are removed by the PCV system to prevent the buildup of harmful acids in the crankcase.

BRAKE PAD: A brake shoe and lining assembly used with disc brakes.

BRAKE SHOE: The backing for the brake lining. The term is, however, usually applied to the assembly of the brake backing and lining.

BUSHING: A liner, usually removable, for a bearing; an anti-friction liner used in place of a bearing.

CALIPER: A hydraulically activated device in a disc brake system, which is mounted straddling the brake rotor (disc). The caliper contains at least one piston and two brake pads. Hydraulic pressure on the piston(s) forces the pads against the rotor.

CAMSHAFT: A shaft in the engine on which are the lobes (cams) which operate the valves. The camshaft is driven by the crankshaft, via a belt, chain or gears, at one half the crankshaft speed.

CAPACITOR: A device which stores an electrical charge.

CARBON MONOXIDE (CO): A colorless, odorless gas given off as a normal byproduct of combustion. It is poisonous and extremely dangerous in confined areas, building up slowly to toxic levels without warning if adequate ventilation is not available.

CARBURETOR: A device, usually mounted on the intake manifold of an engine, which mixes the air and fuel in the proper proportion to allow even combustion.

CATALYTIC CONVERTER: A device installed in the exhaust system, like a muffler, that converts harmful byproducts of combustion into carbon dioxide and water vapor by means of a heat-producing chemical reaction.

CENTRIFUGAL ADVANCE: A mechanical method of advancing the spark timing by using flyweights in the distributor that react to centrifugal force generated by the distributor shaft rotation.

CHECK VALVE: Any one-way valve installed to permit the flow of air, fuel or vacuum in one direction only.

CHOKE: A device, usually a moveable valve, placed in the intake path of a carburetor to restrict the flow of air.

CIRCUIT: Any unbroken path through which an electrical current can flow. Also used to describe fuel flow in some instances.

CIRCUIT BREAKER: A switch which protects an electrical circuit from overload by opening the circuit when the current flow exceeds a predetermined level. Some circuit breakers must be reset manually, while most reset automatically.

COIL (IGNITION): A transformer in the ignition circuit which steps up the voltage provided to the spark plugs.

COMBINATION MANIFOLD: An assembly which includes both the intake and exhaust manifolds in one casting.

COMBINATION VALVE: A device used in some fuel systems that routes fuel vapors to a charcoal storage canister instead of venting them into the atmosphere. The valve relieves fuel tank pressure and allows fresh air into the tank as the fuel level drops to prevent a vapor lock situation.

COMPRESSION RATIO: The comparison of the total volume of the cylinder and combustion chamber with the piston at BDC and the piston at TDC.

CONDENSER: 1. An electrical device which acts to store an electrical charge, preventing voltage surges. 2. A radiator-like device in the air conditioning system in which refrigerant gas condenses into a liquid, giving off heat.

CONDUCTOR: Any material through which an electrical current can be transmitted easily.

CONTINUITY: Continuous or complete circuit. Can be checked with an ohmmeter.

COUNTERSHAFT: An intermediate shaft which is rotated by a mainshaft and transmits, in turn, that rotation to a working part.

CRANKCASE: The lower part of an engine in which the crankshaft and related parts operate.

CRANKSHAFT: The main driving shaft of an engine which receives reciprocating motion from the pistons and converts it to rotary motion.

CYLINDER: In an engine, the round hole in the engine block in which the piston(s) ride.

CYLINDER BLOCK: The main structural member of an engine in which is found the cylinders, crankshaft and other principal parts.

CYLINDER HEAD: The detachable portion of the engine, usually fastened to the top of the cylinder block and containing all or most of the combustion chambers. On overhead valve engines, it contains the valves and their operating parts. On overhead cam engines, it contains the camshaft as well.

DEAD CENTER: The extreme top or bottom of the piston stroke.

DETONATION: An unwanted explosion of the air/fuel mixture in the combustion chamber caused by excess heat and compression, advanced timing, or an overly lean mixture. Also referred to as "ping".

DIAPHRAGM: A thin, flexible wall separating two cavities, such as in a vacuum advance unit.

DIESELING: A condition in which hot spots in the combustion chamber cause the engine to run on after the key is turned off.

DIFFERENTIAL: A geared assembly which allows the transmission of motion between drive axles, giving one axle the ability to turn faster than the other.

DIODE: An electrical device that will allow current to flow in one direction only.

DISC BRAKE: A hydraulic braking assembly consisting of a brake disc, or rotor, mounted on an axle, and a caliper assembly containing, usually two brake pads which are activated by hydraulic pressure. The pads are forced against the sides of the disc, creating friction which slows the vehicle.

DISTRIBUTOR: A mechanically driven device on an engine which is responsible for electrically firing the spark plug at a predetermined point of the piston stroke.

DOWEL PIN: A pin, inserted in mating holes in two different parts allowing those parts to maintain a fixed relationship.

DRUM BRAKE: A braking system which consists of two brake shoes and one or two wheel cylinders, mounted on a fixed backing plate, and a brake drum, mounted on an axle, which revolves around the assembly.

DWELL: The rate, measured in degrees of shaft rotation, at which an electrical circuit cycles on and off.

ELECTRONIC CONTROL UNIT (ECU): Ignition module, module, amplifier or igniter. See Module for definition.

ELECTRONIC IGNITION: A system in which the timing and firing of the spark plugs is controlled by an electronic control unit, usually called a module. These systems have no points or condenser.

END-PLAY: The measured amount of axial movement in a shaft.

ENGINE: A device that converts heat into mechanical energy.

EXHAUST MANIFOLD: A set of cast passages or pipes which conduct exhaust gases from the engine.

FEELER GAUGE: A blade, usually metal, or precisely predetermined thickness, used to measure the clearance between two parts.

FIRING ORDER: The order in which combustion occurs in the cylinders of an engine. Also the order in which spark is distributed to the plugs by the distributor.

FLOODING: The presence of too much fuel in the intake manifold and combustion chamber which prevents the air/fuel mixture from firing, thereby causing a no-start situation.

FLYWHEEL: A disc shaped part bolted to the rear end of the crankshaft. Around the outer perimeter is affixed the ring gear. The starter drive engages the ring gear, turning the flywheel, which rotates the crankshaft, imparting the initial starting motion to the engine.

FOOT POUND (ft. lbs. or sometimes, ft.lb.): The amount of energy or work needed to raise an item weighing one pound, a distance of one foot.

FUSE: A protective device in a circuit which prevents circuit overload by breaking the circuit when a specific amperage is present. The device is constructed around a strip or wire of a lower amperage rating than the circuit it is designed to protect. When an amperage higher than that stamped on the fuse is present in the circuit, the strip or wire melts, opening the circuit.

GEAR RATIO: The ratio between the number of teeth on meshing gears.

GENERATOR: A device which converts mechanical energy into electrical energy.

HEAT RANGE: The measure of a spark plug's ability to dissipate heat from its firing end. The higher the heat range, the hotter the plug fires.

HUB: The center part of a wheel or gear.

HYDROCARBON (HC): Any chemical compound made up of hydrogen and carbon. A major pollutant formed by the engine as a byproduct of combustion.

HYDROMETER: An instrument used to measure the specific gravity of a solution.

INCH POUND (inch lbs.; sometimes in.lb. or in. lbs.): One twelfth of a foot pound.

INDUCTION: A means of transferring electrical energy in the form of a magnetic field. Principle used in the ignition coil to increase voltage.

INJECTOR: A device which receives metered fuel under relatively low pressure and is activated to inject the fuel into the engine under relatively high pressure at a predetermined time.

INPUT SHAFT: The shaft to which torque is applied, usually carrying the driving gear or gears.

INTAKE MANIFOLD: A casting of passages or pipes used to conduct air or a fuel/air mixture to the cylinders.

JOURNAL: The bearing surface within which a shaft operates.

KEY: A small block usually fitted in a notch between a shaft and a hub to prevent slippage of the two parts.

MANIFOLD: A casting of passages or set of pipes which connect the cylinders to an inlet or outlet source.

MANIFOLD VACUUM: Low pressure in an engine intake manifold formed just below the throttle plates. Manifold vacuum is highest at idle and drops under acceleration.

MASTER CYLINDER: The primary fluid pressurizing device in a hydraulic system. In automotive use, it is found in brake and hydraulic clutch systems and is pedal activated, either directly or, in a power brake system, through the power booster.

MODULE: Electronic control unit, amplifier or igniter of solid state or integrated design which controls the current flow in the ignition primary circuit based on input from the pick-up coil. When the module opens the primary circuit, high secondary voltage is induced in the coil.

NEEDLE BEARING: A bearing which consists of a number (usually a large number) of long, thin rollers.

OHM: (Ω) The unit used to measure the resistance of conductor-to-electrical flow. One ohm is the amount of resistance that limits current flow to one ampere in a circuit with one volt of pressure.

OHMMETER: An instrument used for measuring the resistance, in ohms, in an electrical circuit.

OUTPUT SHAFT: The shaft which transmits torque from a device, such as a transmission.

OVERDRIVE: A gear assembly which produces more shaft revolutions than that transmitted to it.

OVERHEAD CAMSHAFT (OHC): An engine configuration in which the camshaft is mounted on top of the cylinder head and operates the valve either directly or by means of rocker arms.

OVERHEAD VALVE (OHV): An engine configuration in which all of the valves are located in the cylinder head and the camshaft is located in the cylinder block. The camshaft operates the valves via lifters and pushrods.

OXIDES OF NITROGEN (NOx): Chemical compounds of nitrogen produced as a byproduct of combustion. They combine with hydrocarbons to produce smog.

OXYGEN SENSOR: Use with the feedback system to sense the presence of oxygen in the exhaust gas and signal the computer which can reference the voltage signal to an air/fuel ratio.

PINION: The smaller of two meshing gears.

PISTON RING: An open-ended ring with fits into a groove on the outer diameter of the piston. Its chief function is to form a seal between the piston and cylinder wall. Most automotive pistons have three rings: two for compression sealing; one for oil sealing.

PRELOAD: A predetermined load placed on a bearing during assembly or by adjustment.

PRIMARY CIRCUIT: the low voltage side of the ignition system which consists of the ignition switch, ballast resistor or resistance wire, bypass, coil, electronic control unit and pick-up coil as well as the connecting wires and harnesses.

PRESS FIT: The mating of two parts under pressure, due to the inner diameter of one being smaller than the outer diameter of the other, or vice versa; an interference fit.

RACE: The surface on the inner or outer ring of a bearing on which the balls, needles or rollers move.

REGULATOR: A device which maintains the amperage and/or voltage levels of a circuit at predetermined values.

RELAY: A switch which automatically opens and/or closes a circuit.

RESISTANCE: The opposition to the flow of current through a circuit or electrical device, and is measured in ohms. Resistance is equal to the voltage divided by the amperage.

RESISTOR: A device, usually made of wire, which offers a preset amount of resistance in an electrical circuit.

RING GEAR: The name given to a ring-shaped gear attached to a differential case, or affixed to a flywheel or as part of a planetary gear set.

ROLLER BEARING: A bearing made up of hardened inner and outer races between which hardened steel rollers move.

ROTOR: 1. The disc-shaped part of a disc brake assembly, upon which the brake pads bear; also called, brake disc. 2. The device mounted atop the distributor shaft, which passes current to the distributor cap tower contacts.

SECONDARY CIRCUIT: The high voltage side of the ignition system, usually above 20,000 volts. The secondary includes the ignition coil, coil wire, distributor cap and rotor, spark plug wires and spark plugs.

SENDING UNIT: A mechanical, electrical, hydraulic or electro-magnetic device which transmits information to a gauge.

SENSOR: Any device designed to measure engine operating conditions or ambient pressures and temperatures. Usually electronic in nature and designed to send a voltage signal to an on-board computer, some sensors may operate as a simple on/off switch or they may provide a variable voltage signal (like a potentiometer) as conditions or measured parameters change.

SHIM: Spacers of precise, predetermined thickness used between parts to establish a proper working relationship.

SLAVE CYLINDER: In automotive use, a device in the hydraulic clutch system which is activated by hydraulic force, disengaging the clutch.

SOLENOID: A coil used to produce a magnetic field, the effect of which is to produce work.

SPARK PLUG: A device screwed into the combustion chamber of a spark ignition engine. The basic construction is a conductive core inside of a ceramic insulator, mounted in an outer conductive base. An electrical charge from the spark plug wire travels along the conductive core and jumps a preset air gap to a grounding point or points at the end of the conductive base. The resultant spark ignites the fuel/air mixture in the combustion chamber.

SPLINES: Ridges machined or cast onto the outer diameter of a shaft or inner diameter of a bore to enable parts to mate without rotation.

TACHOMETER: A device used to measure the rotary speed of an engine, shaft, gear, etc., usually in rotations per minute.

THERMOSTAT: A valve, located in the cooling system of an engine, which is closed when cold and opens gradually in response to engine heating, controlling the temperature of the coolant and rate of coolant flow.

TOP DEAD CENTER (TDC): The point at which the piston reaches the top of its travel on the compression stroke.

TORQUE: The twisting force applied to an object.

TORQUE CONVERTER: A turbine used to transmit power from a driving member to a driven member via hydraulic action, providing changes in drive ratio and torque. In automotive use, it links the driveplate at the rear of the engine to the automatic transmission.

TRANSDUCER: A device used to change a force into an electrical signal.

TRANSISTOR: A semi-conductor component which can be actuated by a small voltage to perform an electrical switching function.

TUNE-UP: A regular maintenance function, usually associated with the replacement and adjustment of parts and components in the electrical and fuel systems of a vehicle for the purpose of attaining optimum performance.

TURBOCHARGER: An exhaust driven pump which compresses intake air and forces it into the combustion chambers at higher than atmospheric pressures. The increased air pressure allows more fuel to be burned and results in increased horsepower being produced.

VACUUM ADVANCE: A device which advances the ignition timing in response to increased engine vacuum.

VACUUM GAUGE: An instrument used to measure the presence of vacuum in a chamber.

VALVE: A device which control the pressure, direction of flow or rate of flow of a liquid or gas.

VALVE CLEARANCE: The measured gap between the end of the valve stem and the rocker arm, cam lobe or follower that activates the valve.

VISCOSITY: The rating of a liquid's internal resistance to flow.

VOLTMETER: An instrument used for measuring electrical force in units called volts. Voltmeters are always connected parallel with the circuit being tested.

WHEEL CYLINDER: Found in the automotive drum brake assembly, it is a device, actuated by hydraulic pressure, which, through internal pistons, pushes the brake shoes outward against the drums.

MASTER INDEX